The
Yorkshire County
Cricket Club Limited

Registered Number 28929R

YEARBOOK
2009

111th EDITION

Sponsors of

THE YORKSHIRE COUNTY CRICKET CLUB

Editor:
DAVID WARNER

Records and Statistics:
First-Class Cricket
ROY D. WILKINSON

Limited-Overs Matches
PAUL E. DYSON

Production Editor:
JAMES M. GREENFIELD

Published by
THE YORKSHIRE COUNTY CRICKET CLUB LTD
HEADINGLEY CARNEGIE STADIUM
LEEDS LS6 3BU
Tel: 0870 4296774 Fax: 0113 278 4099
Internet: http://www.yorkshireccc.com
e-mail: cricket@yorkshireccc.com

Solicitors:
DLA PIPER RUDNICK GRAY CARY

Auditors:
KPMG Audit plc

Medical Officer: Dr JAMES W.D. MOXON, MRCGP

The opinions expressed by contributors are not necessarily those of the Board.

TELEPHONE AND FAX NUMBERS

HEADINGLEY CARNEGIE STADIUM	**Tel: 0870 429 6774** Fax: 0113 278 4099
NORTH MARINE ROAD, SCARBOROUGH	**Tel: 01723 365625** Fax: 01723 364287
BURNLEY ROAD, TODMORDEN	**Tel: 01706 813140**
SHIPTON ROAD, YORK	**Tel: 01904 623602**
BRADFORD & BINGLEY	**Tel: 01274 775441**
STAMFORD BRIDGE	**Tel: 01759 371545**

Produced by:

Great Northern Books
PO Box 213, Ilkley LS29 9WS
www.greatnorthernbooks.co.uk

ISBN: 978-1-905080-57-1

Printed in India

CONTENTS

3

Officers for 2009

**Changes announced after February 1 will be recorded in the
2010 edition of the Yorkshire County Cricket Club Yearbook**

'Bearders' Frindall dies

Cricket followers around the world were saddened by the death
in January from Legionnaires' Disease of BBC Radio's *Test
Match Special* scorer, Bill Frindall, at the age of 69. The
"Bearded Wonder", as he was known, had a particular interest
in Yorkshire cricket, and The Yearbook's statistician, Roy
Wilkinson, regularly asked him to run his eye over facts and
figures which were intended for the publication. It is particularly sad that Bill will not be with us to pass an opinion on the
new £21m pavilion and media centre when it is completed in
2010 — and from which he would have been working.

SPEED UP THE OVER RATE
AND ASK THE QUESTIONS

By Brian Close CBE

It was very good news that Yorkshire staged such a magnificent fightback against Sussex in the final Championship match of the season that we were able to preserve our First Division status.

In addition, promotion in the *NatWest Pro40* League meant that we go into the 2009 season in the top flight of both competitions — which is exactly where a county of Yorkshire's status should be.

Nevertheless, we must not lose sight of the fact that overall it was still a disappointing season for Yorkshire, because we would have been relegated in the Championship had not **Adil Rashid** and **David Wainwright** both hit centuries to rescue us from 80-6 and take us to maximum batting-bonus points and a draw. Even then, we would have gone down had Kent not collapsed to Durham.

So where did Yorkshire go wrong, and what can we do to avoid a similar situation in future?

If you study the final Championship table you will see that Yorkshire collected more batting-bonus points than anyone else in the First Division and only one team, Hampshire, gained more bowling-bonus points.

That is commendable, but the problem for Yorkshire was that we could not finish our opponents off quickly enough on several occasions and were, therefore, unable to go on and win these matches.

Even taking into account the very wet weather, Yorkshire should have been able to win more than two first class matches all season. We are going to have to become more proficient at bowling sides out.

I remain convinced that one of the main reasons why teams do not learn to bowl sides out is because all leagues these days play limited-overs matches rather than time cricket — where you had to bowl sides out if you were to obtain wins. In first-class cricket it is the bowling side who ask the questions and the batting side who have to find the answers, but in limited-overs cricket the roles are reversed. Bowlers generally are concentrating on "where can I bowl where he cannot score?" instead of bowling positively.

In the 1960s when limited-overs cricket first came in for the counties we at Yorkshire were accused of not being particularly good at it, primarily because in first-class cricket our bowlers attacked the batsman.

We gave the ball to the bat to encourage strokes in the hope that we would create mistakes. This we did exceptionally well with all the variety of bowling we had, but

BRIAN CLOSE
Give ball to bat

in limited-overs cricket this gave our opponents more opportunities of scoring runs.

In order to correct the situation, I had to force our bowlers to be more negative. We had to learn to achieve the different types of play that were needed in both formats — and we won two Gillette Cup finals as well as six Championship titles in the 60s!

If our local leagues played time cricket — and I would like to see them go back to it — then our young bowling talent would have to develop their skills of pace, swing, seam, spin and flight to help their sides to win matches. When I played for Rawdon, Guiseley and Yeadon as a youngster there was a time to start the matches and a time to finish, and either side could claim an extra four overs at the end if they felt they could go on and win. It you wanted to win the game you had to bowl your opponents out. It was that simple.

As a result Yorkshire produced in the leagues a lot of young bowling talent, players of the calibre of Bob Appleyard, Johnny Wardle, Freddie Trueman and Raymond Illingworth.

I am delighted that **Anthony McGrath** has been chosen to replace Darren Gough as captain, and I wish him every success in his second spell at the helm. When he was in charge in 2003 he also had his England career to think about, but now he has matured both as a player and a batsman, and he can concentrate fully on the job in hand.

I would love to see Championship cricket going back to three days and being played on uncovered pitches, but the reality is that this will not happen, so Anthony is going to have to do the very best he can for the team in the circumstances which prevail.

And if I can offer him one piece of advice it is to make sure that his bowlers get through their overs far more quickly than they do at present. If they can do this they will advance the game more quickly, and they will not allow the batsman time to sit on his bat handle between deliveries and gather his thoughts.

"Bomber" Wells, for instance, the Gloucestershire and Nottinghamshire slow bowler between 1951 and 1965, got through an over in a minute-and-a-half, and the batsman had hardly the time to put his bat down before "Bomber" was coming at him again. He was rushing the batsman all the time, thereby unsettling him.

Anthony must try to improve the over rate, because only bowling 96 overs in a day is quite ridiculous and is defaulting on the cricket-watching public. When I started out in 1949 I bowled as fast as Fred Trueman off a 12-yard run, but now they go back 20 yards or more, and there is absolutely no need for it.

I know you cannot turn the clock back, but I would like to see the Yorkshire players talking about their cricket in the same way that we did in my day. We learned about the mistakes and the right things to do by talking and discussing the day's cricket with the senior players, and following each day's play the lads got together with their opponents and chatted.

The same "Bomber" Wells used to say that his side loved playing against Yorkshire, because at the end of the day they would go into the bar and talk to Fred and Raymond and the others. He said they learned more about cricket in that half hour or so than at any other time.

I learned a lot about the right way to play cricket from such as Johnny Wardle, Len Hutton and Norman Yardley, and I would say to Anthony McGrath that as a captain you have to learn to do the right things at the right times. You are in charge of your own actions, and you have to show your team how to win as well as how to bat and bowl.

Our Yorkshire team of the 1960s were magnificent because we played with great honour and skill, and these are still the priorities, despite all pressures which money has brought to the game these days.

YEARBOOK, YORKSHIRE
AND CRICKET MOVE ON

By David Warner

The authoritative Yorkshire County Cricket Club Yearbook sees its first major change this year since it first appeared in 1893.

It has been tastefully cloaked in a colour jacket, which we hope will give the reader some indication of the excitement and the action which is contained within its pages.

We would also like to think that the new-look Yearbook will prove particularly attractive to the younger generation of Yorkshire cricket followers without offending the eye of our more traditionalist readers, who will be relieved to know that the hardback cover remains exactly as it always has done — green this year, followed by red in 2010 and then blue before the sequence is repeated.

Should any collector of the Yearbook — and there are many — feel that the colour jacket disturbs the symmetry of his or her collection it can always be removed, but most readers will doubtless be happy to keep this quality product under wraps.

It is a fitting time to adjust the appearance of the Yearbook because cricket, too, is undergoing change, and this is reflected in our pages. *Twenty20* is now just as much a part of the county season as the LV Championship, and each must live in harmony with the other.

The more "mature" Yorkshire followers will still see the Championship as being the competition they most wish their side to win, but success in every sphere has to be the goal towards which the Club and the players work.

It may not unduly concern some as to how well Yorkshire do in *Twenty20* or other limited-overs games, but it has to be admitted that these are the contests which swell the crowd, particularly when the home team is on a winning run. And big one-day crowds — whether they be in Yorkshire or elsewhere — boost cricket's finances, and help to keep the Championship afloat.

It is also appropriate that the change in some of the style of the Yearbook should come at a time when Yorkshire have a new captain in **Anthony McGrath**, who replaces that old warhorse, Darren Gough, and when McGrath's charges are in the top flight of both the LV Championship and the NatWest Pro40 League, which enters its final season in 2009.

DAVID WARNER
Succeeds Derek Hodgson

How satisfying it would be if Yorkshire's should be the last name to be engraved on that Trophy. Only the most blinkered Yorkshire fans, however, would argue that because their team have double First Division status it proves that they are a big success.

The truth is that Yorkshire only stayed in the First Division of the Championship as a consequence of the second set of extraordinary circumstances in three years working in their favour — who says that lightning does not strike twice? — and their elevation in the *NatWest Pro40* also came only when all had appeared lost.

The reason why Yorkshire struggled generally was because they under-achieved, rather than because they were simply too weak. This under-achievement and a tendency to run out of steam after starting the season at full throttle has afflicted them for too long, and it is to be hoped that Director of Professional Cricket Martyn Moxon and his dedicated backup staff can quickly put an end to it.

Martyn places strong emphasis on talented young players serving a sound apprenticeship with the Academy before filtering into the Second XI, and then being given their chance at senior level when the moment is right. The signs last season were that this policy is working; perhaps it should even be applied more vigorously.

Despite feeling strengthened and comforted when **Michael Vaughan** was able to turn out for them or when Darren Gough or Rana Naved-ul-Hasan were fit to take their places in the side, the fact remains that two of Yorkshire's most remarkable Championship per-formances of the season were achieved by 11 players who would not all have been in the team together had everyone on the staff been available.

The magnificent 40-run victory over Somerset at Taunton was achieved with the uncapped **Adam Lyth**, **Stephen Patterson**, **Richard Pyrah** and **David Wainwright** in the side — plus the newly capped **Adil Rashid** and **Andrew Gale** — and the same team were responsible for gathering maximum bonus points and salvaging a draw against Sussex at Hove in the final match, when they had seemed down and out and doomed to the Second Division.

Of course we want to see our top players performing, but the young guns showed last summer that they are good enough to step forward and enjoy a slice of the action whenever required.

What a summer of action we are going to see at Headingley Carnegie, not all of it from Yorkshire by any means. The *NatWest* One-Day Series clash between England and the West Indies takes place on the newly levelled and redrained ground on May 21 — and the showpiece of the season begins on August 7 when England battle it out with Australia in the Fourth Npower Ashes Test.

It would be remiss of me not to make special mention of Derek Hodgson, whom I have succeeded as editor of the Yearbook. Derek has put away his pen (and, I would like to think, his green eye-shade) after loyal service which dates back to 1989, the first two years jointly with the County Club's former secretary, the late Joe Lister.

It was Derek who was largely responsible for making the Yearbook much more than a book of record — and he did so with a charm and a style that is all his own and a love for Yorkshire cricket which comes direct from the heart.

Also, I would have been completely lost in taking over from Derek without having Yearbook Statistician Roy Wilkinson and Production Editor James Greenfield guiding me firmly in the right direction. Few are aware how much time and energy they put into their work or how dedicated they are in maintaining the highest standards.

All contributors, particularly Nigel Pullan, have earned my heartfelt thanks, and I am indebted to Yorkshire CCC's Chief Executive, Stewart Regan, for his swift and skilful negotiations which ensured that the idea of a Yearbook jacket quickly became fact.

The new BlackBerry®
Storm™ purpose-built
for Vodafone
Make the most of now

Officials of the Yorkshire County Cricket Club

President	Treasurer	Captain	Captain (Contd)
T R Barker 1863	M J Ellison 1863-1893	R Iddison 1863-1872	D L Bairstow 1984-1986
M J Ellison 1864-97	M Ellison, jun 1894-1898	J Rowbotham 1873	P Carrick 1987-1989
Lord Hawke 1898-1938	Chas Stokes 1899-1912	L Greenwood 1874	M D Moxon 1990-1995
Rt Hon Sir F S Jackson 1939-1947	R T Heselton 1913-1931	J Rowbotham 1875	D Byas 1996-2001
T L Taylor 1948-1960	A Wyndham Heselton 1932-1962	E Lockwood 1876-1877	D S Lehmann 2002
Sir W A Worsley Bart 1961-1973	M G Crawford 1963-1979	T Emmett 1878-1882	A McGrath 2003
Sir K Parkinson 1974-1981	J D Welch 1980-1984	Hon M B (Lord) Hawke 1883-1910	C White 2004-6
N W D Yardley 1981-1983	P W Townend 1984-2002	E J R H Radcliffe 1911	D Gough 2007-8
The Viscount Mountgarret 1984-1989	*Chairman*	Sir A W White 1912-1918	A McGrath 2009-
Sir Leonard Hutton 1990	A H Connell, DL 1971-1979	D C F Burton 1919-1921	*Secretary*
Sir Lawrence Byford QPM, LLD, DL 1991-1999	M G Crawford 1980-1984	Geoff Wilson 1922-1924	Geo Padley 1863
R A Smith TD, LLB, DL 2000-4	H R Kirk 1984-1985	A W Lupton 1925-1927	J B Wostinholm 1864-1902
Sir David Jones 2004-6	B Walsh, QC 1986-1991	W A Worsley 1928-1929	F C (Sir Fredk.) Toone 1903-1930
Robert Appleyard 2006-8	Sir Lawrence Byford CBE, QPM, LLD, DL 1991-1998	A T Barber 1930	J H Nash 1931-1971
Brian Close CBE 2008-9	K H Moss 1998-2002	F E Greenwood 1931-1932	J Lister 1972-1991
	G A Cope 2002	A B Sellers 1933-1947	D M Ryder 1991-2002
	R A Smith TD, LLB, DL 2002-5	N W D Yardley 1948-1955	*Company Secretary*
	Colin J Graves 2005-	W H H Sutcliffe 1956-1957	B Bouttell 2002-5
		J R Burnet 1958-1959	*Chief Executive*
		J V Wilson 1960-1962	C D Hassell 1991-2002
		D B Close 1963-1970	Colin J Graves 2002-5
		G Boycott 1971-1978	Stewart Regan 2006-
		J H Hampshire 1979-1980	
		C M Old 1981-1982	
		R Illingworth 1982-1983	

COUNTY FIXTURES — 2009

LV COUNTY CHAMPIONSHIP — Division 1
(All four-day matches)

Date			*Opponents*	*Venue*
Wed	22-25	April	Durham	Chester-le-Street
TUE	**28-1**	**APRIL/MAY**	**WORCESTERSHIRE**	**HEADINGLEY CARNEGIE**
Wed	6-9	May	Warwickshire	Edgbaston
SAT	**6-9**	**TUE**	**SUSSEX**	**HEADINGLEY CARNEGIE**
THU	**11-14**	**JUNE**	**SOMERSET**	**HEADINGLEY CARNEGIE**
Tue	16-19	June	Worcestershire	New Road
Tue	30-3	June/July	Somerset	Taunton
FRI	**10-13**	**JULY**	**DURHAM**	**HEADINGLEY CARNEGIE**
TUE	**21-24**	**JULY**	**NOTTINGHAMSHIRE**	**SCARBOROUGH**
Fri	31-3	July/August	Lancashire	Old Trafford
Tue	11-14	August	Hampshire	Rose Bowl
WED	**19-22**	**AUGUST**	**LANCASHIRE**	**HEADINGLEY CARNEGIE**
WED	**26-29**	**AUGUST**	**WARWICKSHIRE**	**SCARBOROUGH**
Thu	3-6	September	Nottinghamshire	Trent Bridge
Wed	16-19	September	Sussex	Hove
WED	**23-26**	**SEPTEMBER**	**HAMPSHIRE**	**HEADINGLEY CARNEGIE**

FRIENDS PROVIDENT TROPHY

Sun	19	April	Durham	Chester-le-Street
SUN	**26**	**APRIL**	**SUSSEX**	**HEADINGLEY CARNEGIE**
SUN	**3**	**MAY**	**GLOUCESTERSHIRE**	**HEADINGLEY CARNEGIE**
MON	**4**	**MAY**	**SURREY**	**HEADINGLEY CARNEGIE**
Mon	11	May	Gloucestershire	Bristol
WED	**13**	**MAY**	**DURHAM**	**HEADINGLEY CARNEGIE**
Mon	18	May	Sussex	Hove
Wed	20	May	Surrey	The Oval
Sat	23	May	Quarter-Finals	
Sun	5	July	Semi-Finals	
Sat	25	July	Final	Lord's

NATWEST PRO40 OVERS LEAGUE — DIVISION 1

Wed	15	July	Worcestershire (Floodlit)	Worcester
SUN	**19**	**JULY**	**DURHAM**	**SCARBOROUGH**
Wed	5	August	Hampshire (Floodlit)	Southampton
Sun	9	August	Somerset	Taunton
SUN	**30**	**AUGUST**	**SUSSEX**	**SCARBOROUGH**
Wed	2	September	Nottinghamshire (Floodlit)	Trent Bridge
THU	**10**	**SEPTEMBER**	**GLOUCESTERSHIRE (FLOODLIT)**	**HEADINGLEY CARNEGIE**
SUN	**27**	**SEPTEMBER**	**ESSEX**	**HEADINGLEY CARNEGIE**
Sun	21	September	Play-off	

TWENTY20 CUP

MON	**25**	**MAY**	**LEICESTERSHIRE**	**HEADINGLEY CARNEGIE**
Tue	26	May	Lancashire	Old Trafford
FRI	**29**	**MAY**	**LANCASHIRE**	**HEADINGLEY CARNEGIE**
Sun	31	May	Derbyshire	Chesterfield
TUE	**2**	**JUNE**	**DURHAM**	**HEADINGLEY CARNEGIE**
THU	**4**	**JUNE**	**NOTTINGHAMSHIRE**	**HEADINGLEY CARNEGIE**
Mon	22	June	Nottinghamshire	Trent Bridge
Wed	24	June	Durham	Riverside
Fri	26	June	Leicestershire	Grace Road
SUN	**28**	**JUNE**	**DERBYSHIRE**	**HEADINGLEY CARNEGIE**
Mon	27	July	Quarter Finals	
Tue	28	July	Quarter Finals	
Wed	29	July	Quarter Finals	
Sat	15	August	Finals Day	Edgbaston

OTHER MATCHES

Sat   11-13   April   Cambridge UCCE . . . . .Fenners

NPOWER TEST MATCHES
(All five-day matches)

ENGLAND v. WEST INDIES

Wed 6 May . . . . .Lord's   Thu 14 May . . . . Chester-le-Street

ENGLAND v. AUSTRALIA

Wed 8 July . . . . .Cardiff   Thu 16 July . . . . Lord's
Thu 30 July . . . . .Edgbaston   Fri 7 August . . **HEADINGLEY CARNEGIE**
Thu 20 August . . . . The Oval

NATWEST INTERNATIONAL TWENTY20

| Sun | 30 | August | England v Australia | . . . . Old Trafford |
| Tue | 1 | September | England v Australia (Floodlit) | . . . . Old Trafford |

NATWEST SERIES

THU	**21**	**MAY**	**ENGLAND V WEST INDIES**	. **HEADINGLEY CARNEGIE**
Sun	24	May	England v West Indies	. . . . Bristol
Tue	26	May	England v West Indies	. . . . Edgbaston
Fri	4	September	England v Australia (Floodlit)	. . . . The Oval
Sun	6	September	England v Australia	. . . . Lord's
Wed	9	September	England v Australia (Floodlit)	. . . . Rose Bowl
Sat	12	September	England v Australia	. . . . Lord's
Tue	15	September	England v Australia (Floodlit)	. . . . Trent Bridge
Thu	17	September	England v Australia (Floodlit)	. . . . Trent Bridge
Sun	20	September	England v Australia	. . . . Chester-le-Street

SECOND ELEVEN CHAMPIONSHIP

Wed	22-24	April	Worcester	. . . . .Away
Wed	29-1	May	Warwickshire	. . . . .King's Heath
Tue	2-4	June	Leicestershire	. . . . .Away
WED	**24-26**	**JUNE**	**MCC YC**	. . . .**STAMFORD BRIDGE**
WED	**1-3**	**JULY**	**NOTTINGHAMSHIRE**	. .**HEADINGLEY CARNEGIE**
WED	**15-17**	**JULY**	**GLAMORGAN**	. . . .**BARNSLEY**
TUE	**28-30**	**JULY**	**DERBYSHIRE**	. . . .**YORK**
Tue	25-27	August	Durham	. . . . .Middlesbrough
TUE	**1-3**	**SEPTEMBER**	**LANCASHIRE**	. . . . . .**HEADINGLEY CARNEGIE**
Wed	16-18	September	Final	. . . . .TBC

SECOND ELEVEN TROPHY

Tue	21	April	Worcester	. . . . .Away
Tue	28	April	Warwickshire	. . . . .Edgbaston
TUE	**19**	**MAY**	**LANCASHIRE**	. . . .**BINGLEY**
Mon	1	June	Leicestershire	. . . . .Grace Road
TUE	**23**	**JUNE**	**MCC YC**	. . . .**STAMFORD BRIDGE**
TUE	**30**	**JUNE**	**NOTTINGHAMSHIRE**	. .**HEADINGLEY CARNEGIE**
TUE	**14**	**JULY**	**GLAMORGAN**	. . . .**BARNSLEY**
MON	**27**	**JULY**	**DERBYSHIRE**	. . . .**YORK**
Mon	24	August	Durham	. . . . .Middlesbrough
Mon	7	September	Semi-Finals	. . . . .TBC
Mon	21	Sept	Final	. . . . .TBC

SECOND ELEVEN FRIENDLIES

TUES	**5-7**	**MAY**	**MIDDLESEX**	. . . .**TODMORDEN**
Tue	12-15	May	Lancashire	. . . . .Crosby
Mon	18	May	Lancashire (Twenty20)	. . . . .Bingley
Fri	22	May	Lancashire (Twenty20)	. . . . .Heywood
Mon	8-11	June	Kent/Northants	. . . . .Beckenham

SECOND ELEVEN FRIENDLIES (Continued)

TUE	16-18	JUNE	SCOTLAND	WEETWOOD
THU	9	JULY	PCA	ABBEYDALE PARK/TBC
Tue	11-14	August	Surrey	Guildford
Wed	9-11	September	Somerset	Taunton Vale

YORKSHIRE ACADEMY IN THE YORKSHIRE LEAGUE

SAT	25	APRIL	BARNSLEY	WEETWOOD
Mon	4	May	Rotherham	Away
Sat	9	May	Sheffield Collegiate	Away
Sun	10	May	Driffield	Venue TBC
Sat	16	May	Doncaster	Away
SAT	23	MAY	CLEETHORPES	WEETWOOD
Mon	25	May	Sheffield United	Away
Sat	30	May	Harrogate	Away
SAT	6	JUNE	CASTLEFORD	WEETWOOD
Sat	13	June	Scarborough	Away
SAT	20	JUNE	APPLEBY FRODINGHAM	WEETWOOD
Sat	27	June	Hull	Away
SAT	4	JULY	YORK	WEETWOOD
Sat	11	July	Barnsley	Away
SUN	12	JULY	ROTHERHAM	WEETWOOD
Sat	18	July	Driffield	Away
SUN	19	JULY	ROTHERHAM	WEETWOOD
SAT	25	JULY	SHEFFIELD COLLEGIATE	WEETWOOD
SAT	1	AUGUST	DONCASTER	WEETWOOD
Sat	8	August	Cleethorpes	Away
SUN	9	AUGUST	SHEFFIELD UNITED	WEETWOOD
SAT	15	AUGUST	HARROGATE	WEETWOOD
Sat	22	August	Castleford	Away
SAT	29	AUGUST	SCARBOROUGH	WEETWOOD
Mon	31	August	Appleby Frodingham	Away
Sat	5	September	York	Away
SAT	12	SEPTEMBER	HULL	WEETWOOD

YORKSHIRE ACADEMY FRIENDLIES

THU	16	APRIL	DURHAM ACADEMY	HEADINGLEY CARNEGIE
Thu	7	May	British Universities	Bawtry Road
Sun	17	May	Barnsley LKO	Away
Tue	19	May	Derbyshire Academy	Staveley
Tue	26-28	May	Durham Academy	Longhurst
Sun	7	June	LKO Round 2	
TUE	16-17	JUNE	CHESHIRE	BARNSLEY
TUE	23-25	JUNE	IRELAND	HOME
Mon	29-30	June	Lancashire	Away
Mon	13	July	YSSCA	St Peter's, York
Sun	19	July	LKO Semi-Finals	
Sun	16	August	LKO Final	

YORKSHIRE IN UNDER-17s' CUP

THU	2	JULY	DURHAM	NEW ROVER
Tue	7	July	Lancashire	Away
Tue	28	July	Derby	Away
TUE	4	AUGUST	CHESHIRE	HOME
Wed	12-13		Possible Play-off	
Sun	16	August	Quarter-Final	
Sun	30	August	Semi-Final	
Sun	13	September	Final	

YORKSHIRE UNDER-17s' TWO-DAY NATIONAL CHAMPIONSHIP

Wed	8-9	July	Lancashire	Away
WED	15-16	JULY	DURHAM	HOME
Wed	29-30	July	Derbyshire	Away
WED	5-6	AUGUST	CHESHIRE	BARNSLEY
Wed	2-3	September	Final	Venue TBC

Fixtures listed on this page are subject to confirmation, and should be regarded as provisional only.

NEW COACHING SET-UP
WILL IDENTIFY TALENT

I have been talking with Martyn Moxon, Director of Professional cricket, in his office in the Cricket Centre with a view over to the East Stand at Headingley Carnegie. We discussed the season that had just ended and his plans for the future. He thought that it had been something of a "split season".

On the one hand Yorkshire had been successful in all the one-day competitions. They reached the semi-finals of the *Friends Provident Trophy*; they won promotion in the *Pro40 League*, and they were within one win of Finals day in the *Twenty20 Cup* when the **Azeem Rafiq** debacle occurred.

The Championship was the closest ever between the top and bottom teams, so that Yorkshire were in contention to win it at one stage, and yet in the end only escaped relegation in the final match at Hove. Martyn acknowledged that Yorkshire had been inconsistent, but said they had played some very good cricket at times, and had obtained 95 bonus points. There were occasions, however, when the bowlers had put them in a strong position but then failed to bowl a side out, and at other times the batting had let them down.

Martyn pointed out that of the five games Yorkshire lost they had been in a strong position in three of them, and should have won or, at any rate, not lost. In the home match with Durham the visitors were 161-7, but Mustard and Plunkett added 143 for the eighth wicket. Down at Canterbury Yorkshire were 352-2, but managed only 410.

Kent were reduced to 305-7, but eventually reached 457, and even at the end with Kent on 108-7 Yorkshire could have won. At The Rose Bowl a disastrous second innings meant defeat by 10 wickets. In the match with Kent at Scarborough Yorkshire had a lead of 230, but allowed their opponents to recover and nearly win.

There were, of course, many good days. Martyn argued that Yorkshire had remained competitive until the end of the season and sustained their form better than they had in 2007. The problem was that they missed opportunities to press home their advantage when they were on top, and this is what they have been discussing and are hoping to rectify this summer. Some of the good days were right at the end at Hove, when one of the most remarkable recoveries in Yorkshire's history was achieved. I asked Martyn about this.

"It was going to be a tough day to bat first. Conditions were really difficult for batting, but it was a good pitch and the forecast was for sunny weather later. At the end of the first day we were 84-6.

"We sat down to discuss it, and we realised we were in a big hole. We needed something special to get out of it. You can't give enough praise to the later batsmen for their skill, concentration and determination.

MARTYN MOXON
Backs county's own

"When Sussex batted our brilliant performance in the field was equally creditworthy — we bowled with great discipline, and Adil was outstanding."

Martyn expressed his appreciation of Darren Gough's work as captain over two years. He thought that Darren's injuries early in the 2008 season had denied him the chance to bowl himself to full fitness, but he had made a significant contribution to the team's success. I asked him about the captaincy for this summer"

"We decided to appoint **Anthony McGrath** captain and **Jacques Rudolph** vice-captain. Mags is looking forward to taking on the role and all that goes with being captain of Yorkshire. He is steeped in Yorkshire cricket history, and will maintain our traditions.

"Jacques has made a great contribution, both on and off the field, so together they will make a good team. **Matthew Hoggard** got better as the season went on, and he will have a big part to play in the management of the team as a senior professional. If **Michael Vaughan** is not selected for England he will play for us."

As Director of Professional Cricket in Yorkshire, Martyn wants to give as many opportunities as possible to players who have been developed by the Club. If they do not have the opportunity to play regularly the Club will never know which of their many talented young cricketers have the ability to make the grade.

There may not be an official overseas player — we shall know by the time you read this — and Rudolph, **Gerard Brophy** and **Deon Kruis** learned their cricket in South Africa. But Martyn pointed out that the teams that did so well at Taunton and Hove were developed predominantly through Yorkshire's own coaching system. He talked about some of these young players:

"**Tim Bresnan's** injuries in 2007 meant that he had more time to recharge his batteries last winter. He is a member of the England Development Squad, and they get less time off than the England players! We want Tim to bowl fast, and not see himself as a stock bowler. He could bat as high as No. 6, as he is a very good all round cricketer.

"**Adil Rashid** continued to progress, and took 62 first-class wickets at the age of 20. At the beginning of the season, I think, he was striving too hard, putting too much pressure on himself. His five wickets at Canterbury settled him down. He is bowling his leg-spin more accurately, and from this secure base he will be able to introduce more variety as he gains experience. He is a very good batsman as well, as he showed at Hove.

"I have been very pleased with **Andy Gale**, who was awarded his county cap. He batted very well at No. 5, and has acquired the skill and discipline to make hundreds. He has grown into the difficult role of opening in one-day cricket, and he had to open occasionally in the Championship.

"**Adam Lyth** is an exciting batsman, and his next step is to convert 50s into 100s. He did really well in his first season. I was disappointed that **David Wainwright** did not have more opportunities. He had an excellent match at Hove, and maybe if we get dry weather we can play two spinners more often.

"We have a number of promising young fast bowlers, and there should be more opportunities now that Darren has retired. **Ajmal Shahzad** and **Steven Patterson** have considerable first-team experience, and **Ben Sanderson**, **James Lee** and **Oliver Hannon-Dalby** will be in contention. We need to find out about their abilities at top level. **Richard Pyrah** had a good year in the one-day competitions.

"**Joe Sayers** had a disappointing run, but we have been working on one or two technical problems, and he has been getting runs in the Second XI and the leagues. He would probably have played if he had not broken a finger, and I am confident that he will come back. We hope that **Chris Taylor's** hamstring problems have been sorted out, and he will be another contender.

"**Gerard Brophy** remains our first-choice wicket-keeper. He does not make many mistakes, and scores valuable runs, but he does need someone to put pressure on him. **Simon Guy** has played well in the Second XI, and **Jonathan Bairstow** has now made the step up from the Academy, so they will be keeping the pressure on him to perform."

This season Martyn has organised the structure of team management

Yorkshire Young Player of 2008: Adam Lyth receives his award from Chief Executive Stewart Regan.

and coaching into a pattern. He and Anthony McGrath will manage the First XI; Kevin Sharp and **Craig White** as captain will be the Second XI management team; Steve Oldham will be responsible for the Academy, and Steve, Kevin, Ian Dews and John Blain — the new assistant bowling coach — will be flexible, so that they can be involved wherever there is a need for their services. Andy Rowsell has been appointed to oversee age-group cricket from 11 to 15. He is the emerging-players coach, and each age group has its own management and coaching staff.

What is most encouraging is that there is another generation waiting in the wings. Bairstow, **Gary Ballance** and Hannon-Dalby are all at Leeds Met University benefiting from the link with Yorkshire CCC. Other young players like Azeem Rafiq, now accepted as an England-qualified player by the ECB, **Joe Root**, **Charlie Roebuck** and many others will be ambitious to do well.

Martyn hopes that this coaching structure will enable the Club to identify talent at an early stage, so that the choice of those entering the Academy can be as accurate as possible and the best youngsters can gain experience with the YCA side in the Yorkshire League, then play in the Second XI, and eventually become established Yorkshire cricketers.

RAFIQ AFFAIR CAUSED TEAM FORM TO SLUMP

By Chris Waters

Yorkshire's embarrassing failure to register 17-year-old **Azeem Rafiq** properly led to their exit from the *Twenty20 Cup* at the Quarter-Final stage, but more serious than any financial consequences or the lost opportunity of a first appearance at a *Twenty20* finals day was the damage caused to the remainder of the season. When the *Twenty20 Cup* began Yorkshire were top of the Championship and had high hopes of ending a six-year search for silverware.

But they went into their final game against Sussex occupying the last relegation place — four points behind Sussex and Kent — and they avoided the drop by only a whisker.

Towards the end of a rain-hit first day at Hove, Yorkshire were 80-6, and seemingly destined for Division Two. The next day desperation turned to disbelief as Yorkshire masterminded one of the most extraordinary recoveries of this or any other season — rising to the improbable heights of 400-9 before acting captain **Anthony McGrath** declared on the acquirement of a fifth and final batting point.

The heroes were the spin bowlers, **Adil Rashid** and **David Wainwright**, who scored 111 and 104 not out respectively, Wainwright recording a maiden first-class century. Wainwright was jubilant, and not a little overcome: "My dad sent me a text the previous night saying I would score a century," he revealed afterwards. "I just humoured him. This was a day I will remember for the rest of my life."

Rashid's also was a career-best score, and sprinkled some glitter on an otherwise less than sparkling season with the willow; prior to that fixture he had mustered only 405 runs in 15 Championship games at 19.28, with two half-centuries. Suitably inspired, the leg-spinner twirled his way to match figures of 9-177 as Yorkshire enjoyed the better of a hard-fought draw — which also ensured Sussex's survival.

Yorkshire finished seventh on 159 points — five above Kent, who lost heavily at home to champions Durham, and were relegated along with winless Surrey. Following the mayhem of midsummer, Yorkshire's survival felt like a great achievement for a side that had seemed in inexorable decline.

Viewed in isolation it was, indeed, a great achievement, but when analysed as a whole Yorkshire's season flattered to deceive.

With sixth place in 2006 and 2007, the Club were technically worse off, and ended the year with an unenviable record of three victories in 28 Championship games dating back to May 2007.

Potential problems seemed obvious long before the 2008 cam-

AZEEM RAFIQ
Now on county's books

paign got under way — principally, who was going to score the top-order runs? Yorkshire undoubtedly had proven quality in **Jacques Rudolph** and McGrath.

Supporters' fears were justified as **Joe Sayers** lost form, **Michael Vaughan** never looked like rediscovering his touch, and injuries restricted **Chris Taylor** to four Championship appearances. Rudolph was the only player to pass 1,000 runs, while McGrath was steady rather than spectacular by his own lofty standards with 728 Championship runs at 34.66.

There was no more damning indictment of Yorkshire's batting problems than that their 10th-wicket partnership averaged more than their first-wicket partnership, surely some sort of record.

There were encouraging displays by **Andrew Gale** and **Adam Lyth** — Adam achieving his maiden century against Nottinghamshire at Trent Bridge, but that game highlighted one of Yorkshire's fundamental Achilles heels throughout 2008: a maddening tendency to lose wickets in clusters. So often did this occur that Martyn Moxon, the county's Director of Professional Cricket, spent much of his time walking around with a sore head caused by repeatedly banging it against brick walls.

Indeed, the season could have had no more fitting conclusion had the loss of those six wickets on the opening day at Hove resulted in Championship demotion, the last three falling in the final three overs as batsmen switched off.

On the bowling front Rashid failed to pull up trees during the first half of the year — but ripped them out like a lumberjack towards the end of the campaign, managing 50 wickets in his last nine matches. Only Hampshire's James Tomlinson (67) claimed more first-class victims than Rashid, who ended up with 65 to finish streets ahead of any other English spinner.

Tim Bresnan (45) and **Matthew Hoggard** (42) claimed useful wickets, without Matthew ever really suggesting that he was going to force his way back into the England fold, but by far the highlight of Yorkshire's year was their one-day form.

Darren Gough had harped on about the need for improvement in limited-overs cricket since returning to Yorkshire in the spring of 2007 and, in his final year as a professional cricketer, that improvement was forthcoming. Yorkshire won *Pro40* promotion, reached the semi-finals of the *Friends Provident Trophy*, and progressed to the last eight of the *Twenty20 Cup* before calamity struck.

Gough led by example on his way to 21 List A wickets at 24.28 — only Bresnan (24 at 20.20) and the excellent **Richard Pyrah** (24 at 24.37) captured more — and the former England fast bowler will be difficult to replace in the one-day arena.

Not so in the Championship, perhaps, where he managed only eight games and nine wickets at 58.66 as advancing years finally caught up with him. Gough turned 38 in September. He struggled to cope with the physical demands of four-day competition, although there was a memorable last hurrah on his final day in first-class cricket, against Somerset at Scarborough, when he signed off with the scalp of Justin Langer.

Rana Naved-ul-Hasan, the Pakistan pace bowler, was a predictable disappointment following the shoulder injury he suffered towards the end of the 2007 season, while his decision to join the rebel Indian Cricket League without Yorkshire's knowledge made one query his commitment to the cause — and also reflect on the way professional sport is heading.

Chris Waters is Cricket Correspondent
of the Yorkshire Post

THIRD OF GAMES WASHED OUT
— AND ONE REQUISITIONED

By Michael Snook

A year ago, it was surmised that the 2007 season would be remembered for being wet...that memory lasted one season — for what had been one of the wettest seasons on record was eclipsed by the monsoon summer of 2008!

SIMON GUY
Topped the batting

It rained and rained...and rained...to such an extent that more than 2,000 overs in the Second XI's season were lost — the equivalent of more than 20 full days of cricket, a third of the fixtures planned.

Two Championship matches were abandoned without a ball bowled. Indeed, the match against Durham — the last of the season — was called off two days before the scheduled date because the Seaton Carew ground was waterlogged. Surely unprecedented?

Of the remaining 12 Championship fixtures four were won, four lost and four drawn. Leicestershire were bowled out for 49 before lunch on the first day and beaten in two days at Grace Road, and Nottinghamshire were beaten by an innings before lunch on the third day. These two impressive victories to start the season, separated by a washout in Glamorgan, were followed by defeats to Lancashire at Headingley — the Red Rosebuds won by 252 runs — and Somerset at Todmorden after three declarations.

Two rain-affected draws followed, the second of which saw Scotland's last man survive a hat-trick ball delivered by leg-spinner

Mark Lawson — the last ball of the last over. Warwickshire won the next match, reaching the victory target after an hour or so of play on the fourth day. Their neighbours, Worcestershire, avoided an innings defeat at Headingley: with 10 overs remaining and two wickets to be taken Nos. 9 and 10 survived until to stumps.

A forfeited innings and declaration bowling saw Surrey set Yorkshire a target of 351 in a four-day match, the first and third days lost to the weather. The White Rose went down by 85 runs. The most satisfying win of the season came at Horsham. Sussex had not lost a Championship match for three years, but after the visitors had scored 337 the home side were bowled out for 181 and, following on, 181 again to leave Yorkshire 26 to score for victory.

The opportunity to reverse the result of the Lancashire match was washed out at Tordmorden.

The last home match was scheduled for Headingley Carnegie, but the ground-levelling and drainage works saw it moved to Elland, and then to Barnsley — the first fixture there for more than 20 years. Derbyshire were beaten by an innings at mid-afternoon on the third day. The two impressive victories, mirroring the start to the season, resulted in fifth position in the Championship, an improvement of five places on the previous season.

Simon Guy topped Yorkshire's Championship run-makers with 632 and a couple of centuries to his name. **Adam Lyth** also scored a couple of centuries in the four matches he played before becoming a permanent fixture in the Firsts: he was second with 354 runs, eight ahead of captain **Craig White**, who missed several matches in the middle of the season through injury. Craig has been confirmed as captain again for 2009, and with his experience he will surely prove an ideal mentor.

Oliver Hannon-Dalby, with 26 wickets, was the leading bowler, closely followed by **Ben Sanderson**, **Steven Patterson** and **Ajmal Shahzad**. Sanderson's 4-51 in the first innings against Nottinghamshire, followed by 6-30 in the second, the best innings return of the season, was the only 10-wicket match haul of 2008.

If there were some golden moments to be savoured in the Championship season, the Trophy was a damp squib. Two matches were abandoned without a ball bowled, and a third was abandoned after five overs when the umpires decided that the pitch was unfit to allow play to continue. Only one match was won, at Denby against Derbyshire, when the home side failed by 16 runs, despite a Frederick Klokker century scored off **Rana Naved-ul Hasan's** and **Deon Kruis's** bowling.

The two experienced bowlers turned out at a dry Seaton Carew, when Durham easily overhauled Yorkshire's 154, winning with 22 overs to spare. The pair also played at Hinckley, where the result was decided by the *Duckworth-Lewis* method. Leicestershire accumulated 293 in their full innings, but Yorkshire were interrupted for 17 overs by the inevitable rain, and the revised target of 221 was too much for them.

Leicestershire also won on their visit to Bingley — their innings of 283 being interrupted four times by rain. A whirlwind 91 from **Ajmal Shahzad**, easily beating his previous best of 12 not out, helped Yorkshire almost to achieve a victory that had seemed most unlikely at 83-5. It was to no avail: his side were out 18 runs short.

Chris Taylor was the leading batsman with 200 runs, ahead of Shahzad with 148, and **Jonathan Bairstow** was the only other batsman to pass 100 runs in the Trophy. **Richard Pyrah** and **Azeem Rafiq** led the bowlers with five wickets each.

Yorkshire had arranged a couple of one-day games against Durham to get the season going...but both were washed out — as was a further match, hastily arranged when the forecast suggested that play might be possible on the next day.

The most bizarre abandonment of the season came when Yorkshire travelled to Beckenham to play a Kent-Northamptonshire side. Rain interrupted play on the first of four scheduled days, and the match was called off at lunchtime on the second when the ground was requisitioned for the Kent v. Somerset *Friends' Provident* Quarter-Final which had to be moved from a waterlogged Canterbury. Yorkshire had lost nine wickets — all to Kent's Martin Saggers, who was left so near and yet so far from his first 10-for.

Three weeks later Saggers was to take the 10th when he dismissed Rafiq, one of the last wicket pair at Beckenham, as he turned out for the PCA Masters in a charity match at Abbeydale Park against a Yorkshire XI!

**Michael Snook is Yorkshire
Second XI Scorer**

BALLANCE SUPERB — BUT WHAT'S IN THE MIDDLE?

By Harold Galley

Yorkshire Academy got away to a splendid start in the ECB Oxbridge Yorkshire Premier League. An undefeated opening stand of 49 against Cleethorpes by **Callum Geldart** and **Charlie Roebuck** — helped by **Oliver Hannon-Dalby's** excellent 5-10 — gained the eight points. An eight-wicket victory and maximum points followed against Harrogate, when Roebuck (104) and **Joe Root** (54) had an opening stand of 144. Roebuck's fine knock earned him early promotion to the Seconds.

Sadly, poor middle-order batting then brought three defeats, but Geldart's 93 at Sheffield Collegiate and **Gary Ballance's** 73 were indications of improvements to follow. Our inexperienced opening attack failed to make initial breakthroughs, so May was a barren month, the only success being a winning draw against Rotherham out of seven matches played.

Fortunately, as has happened in previous seasons, success came in the League Cup. A two-wicket win against Scarborough was followed by the 163-run defeat of Cleethorpes.

The Academy were much improved against bogey-team Castleford: **Azeem Rafiq** — a fine captain — returned 5-12 and 5-25 with his off-spin in two outright wins. Azeem was leading wicket-taker with 42 League and Cup wickets, and was second to former Academy spinner **James Finch** in the League's Junior Bowling Awards.

Root took the Junior Batting Award with an average of 45.90, and third was **Jonathan Bairstow** (35). Both played a number of Second XI matches for Yorkshire.

The Academy finished in grand style — winning seven of their last eight league matches. The first of these at Weetwood saw Sheffield United defeated by 91 runs: a superb 176 by opener

Ballance after the Academy had been 35-3 led to a total of 290-5 — and Gary followed this with 112 against Barnsley, 64 against Sheffield Collegiate and 64 against Rotherham.

Unfortunately, he did not play enough games to qualify for League honours, but averaged 65.57 for the season.

Our Cup run finished at the Semi-Final stage. Needing 196, the Academy were 193-7 with one over left after Ballance had scored a fine 105 to put victory in sight.

In the last over Castleford's David Wainwright conceded a leg-bye, took a wicket, conceded one run, and there was

GARY BALLANCE
Burst on the scene

a run-out. Thus we failed to progress to the Final, having lost more wickets with the totals tied.

A good season in all and an excellent finish. But for our middle-order batting weaknesses and injuries to strike bowlers it could have been so much better.

Harold Galley is Yorkshire
Academy Scorer

Top Test batsmen

Test batsmen to score over 1,000 runs in 2008 were: G C Smith (South Africa, 1,656), V Sehwag (India, 1,462), R T Ponting (Australia, 1,182), H M Amla (South Africa, 1,161), G Gambhir (India, 1,134), V V S Laxman (India, 1,065), N D McKenzie (South Africa, 1,073), M J Clarke (Australia 1,063), S R Tendulkar (India, 1,063), A B. de Villiers (South Africa, 1,061).

WHITE ROSE BLOOMS
IN OASIS OF GREEN

By James Buttler

Pre-season in Abu Dhabi, guaranteed weather, excellent practice facilities and a top-notch stadium in which to play cricket. What more could you want? A Yorkshire Carnegie win was the icing on the cake.

Darren Gough led a squad of 22 to the United Arab Emirates for two weeks of season-shaping practice, team-bonding and the Pro-ARCH Trophy competition. Six sides, each playing matches against four of the other five teams, with the team finishing top of the league the victors.

Yorkshire's competitors were Lancashire, Somerset, Sussex and the UAE, with Essex being the team Yorkshire did not play. A slightly confusing format, a problem the organisers have resolved for 2009. It was a tour of firsts. The players ran out as Yorkshire Carnegie for the first time, the gold one-day kit made its debut, and the first competitive overseas *Roses* match kicked off Yorkshire's tournament in style.

The Sheikh Zayed Stadium, where all of Carnegie's matches were played, was stunning. Completely surrounded by desert, it was an oasis of green amidst miles of sand and dust. The large arched stand resembled something out of a sci-fi movie at one end of the ground, which was transformed into a bowl of shining light as the floodlights came on. The crowds were sparse but passionate. The locals played cricket deep into the evening on the surrounding concrete strips and sand-based outfields, seeing the ball through the dark, helped only by the light of the stadium.

March 21: Yorkshire Carnegie beat Lancashire Lightning by 41 runs. All of the batsmen chipped in after Carnegie won the toss and a credible 237 was posted — **Anthony McGrath** top-scoring with 41. Lancashire stuttered in reply — but with Andrew Flintoff and Glen Chapple well set they appeared favourites. **David Wainwright** was the leading wicket-taker and sealed the win, while two wickets for **Steven Patterson** included a maiden over in the heat of the run chase.

March 25: Yorkshire Carnegie beat Somerset Sabres by 51 runs. A Yorkshire total of 264 was enough to secure a second victory. **Andrew Gale** cracked 63 from 61 balls, and McGrath weighed in with a half cen-

HEROES OF HOVE...but not just yet. Adil Rashid and David Wainwright warm up in Abu Dhabi.

tury. Somerset were all out for 213 after a fine Carnegie bowling display.

March 26: Yorkshire Carnegie lost to Sussex Sharks by nine runs. Sussex amassed 209 on a slow wicket, and Carnegie fell just short as **Craig White** top-scored with 40.

March 28: Yorkshire Carnegie beat UAE by four wickets. Yorkshire Carnegie entered this match needing something special to take the Pro ARCH Trophy. The UAE were all out for 190 after **Mark Lawson** (3-36) and Wainwright (1-19) strangled the home side's progress. Carnegie had to score 191 within 25 overs to boost their run rate and top the table. **Greg Wood** (50) and Gale flew out of the blocks with the rest of the side chipping in. **Adam Lyth** hit the winning boundary with only 24.1 overs gone, and the celebrations began.

**James Buttler is Yorkshire County Cricket Club
PR and Communications Manager**

TURNING THE CORNER
TO PROMISED LAND

By Sarah Pickford

It was acknowledged after a disappointing 2007 that 2008 would be a challenging season for Yorkshire Women at all age groups — but there was a clear belief that with the level of potential in the county the future should be bright, backed up by a determination to work hard to ensure that this potential was realised.

Work started during the winter with a realignment of the Yorkshire Cricket Board (YCB) Pathways programme to link more closely with the women's county structure, a process closely supported by Yorkshire County Cricket Club's Head of Operations, Ian Dews. An "Elite Centre" was also instigated outside the Pathways scheme to allow senior players to train together to best prepare them for the season.

The benefits of this forward thinking and flexibility by the board — specifically Howard Clayton — the county club and Yorkshire Women's Cricket Association are clear from the results.

The Under-13s showed everyone what they could do by beating all teams in front of them to win through — first to the semi-final against much-fancied Kent, and then to the final against Devon, who eventually won by 22 runs. Highlights of that final for Yorkshire were Ellyn Clarkes's stoic 25 to keep her side in the game and Millie Wallis's 6-1-10-4, including a hat-trick. Millie is only 11, so not only is this a great achievement but it bodes well for the future. Coaches Wendy Brown and Jo Ward have done well to take a relatively inexperienced team to the national finals and, most importantly, all the girls clearly enjoyed it.

The Under-15s under the guidance of Graham Tipping and Rebecca Vernon and managed by Jane Pratt were unlucky not to reach the semi-finals. They won five of their six games in the ECB LV Women's North League — the only loss being against red-rose

MAJESTY AND POWER: Anthony McGrath shows the full range of his batting skills during his sparkling 128 against Somerset in the LV Championship clash at Scarborough last summer. Despite some other fine innings Anthony was unable to complete 1,000 first-class runs, but he hopes to rectify that omission this summer when he takes over the Yorkshire captaincy from Darren Gough.

(Photo: VAUGHN RIDLEY.)

YORKSHIRE — 2008

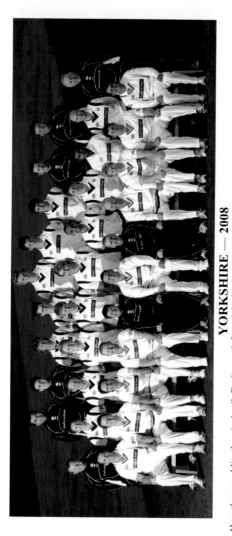

How the squad lined up in April. Back row, left to right: Mohammed Seraj (2nd XI Physiotherapist), Tom Summers (Head of Strength and Conditioning), Mark Lawson, David Wainwright, Oliver Hannon-Dalby, James Finch, Ben Sanderson, Scott McAllister (1st XI Physiotherapist) and Richard Wilkinson (Academy Coach). Middle row: Kevin Sharp (Batting Coach), Simon Guy, Gerard Brophy, Andrew Gale, Steve Patterson, Chris Taylor, Ajmal Shahzad, Richard Pyrah, Adil Rashid, Adam Lyth and Steve Oldham (Bowling Coach). Front row: Deon Kruis, Joe Sayers, Michael Vaughan, Anthony McGrath (Vice-Captain), Martyn Moxon (Director of Professional Cricket), Darren Gough (Captain), Ian Dews (Director of Cricket Operations), Craig White, Matthew Hoggard, Tim Bresnan and Jacques Rudolph. *(Photo: BEN DUFFY).*

HOT OFF THE PRESS: Yorkshire's Adil Rashid on the 2009 tour of the West Indies. Things just keep getting better for Adil — and he is still only 21! In 2007 he scooped two major Young Cricketer of the Year Awards; last year he was Yorkshire's leading wicket-taker with 62 Championship dismissals...and in January he was in the England Test squad for the Caribbean. Will an Ashes baptism follow this summer? *(Photo: GETTY IMAGES.)*

YORKSHIRE — 1959

Golden Anniversary Champions: Back row, left to right: Arthur Mitchell (Coach), Jackie Birkenshaw, Harold "Dickie" Bird, Don Wilson, David Pickles, Mel Ryan, Brian Bolus, Jimmy Binks, Philip Sharpe and Maurice Leyland (Coach). Centre row: Fred Trueman, Vic Wilson, Ronnie Burnet (Captain), Brian Close and Ray Illingworth. Front row: Ken Taylor, Doug Padgett and Bryan Stott. *(Photo: RON DEATON Archive.)*

PROUD CENTURIONS:
Adil Rashid, above left, and David Wainwright, in a historic picture taken at Hove by Southern Group member DAVID HIRST. Their magnificent centuries rescued Yorkshire from the depths of 80-6 and took them to 400-9 declared — so ensuring survival in the First Division of the LV Championship for 2009. David the bowler, right, and Adil then turned their attentions to the ball to work their way through 14 Sussex wickets between them, Adil claiming 7-136 in the second innings. Rarely, if ever, have two young players made such an impact on a game.

GETTING THEIR EYES IN: Allan Beaumont, left, Conservation Manager for West Yorkshire Archive Service, and Yorkshire County Cricket Club Archives Committee chairman David Hall inspect progress on the restoration of the scorebook which records Yorkshire's first-ever match against Surrey at The Oval on June 5 and 6, 1863.

HOUSE OF CARDS: Immediate Past President of Yorkshire County Cricket Club Bob Appleyard, second left, and Ron Deaton, of the Archives Committee, extreme right, receive the Cyril Wright Memorial Cigarette Card Collection from Cyril's widow, Dorothy, and son Steven. Sections from this vast library will be displayed in glass cases on a rotational basis.

IN THE FRAME:
This splendid portrait of Sir Leonard Hutton, which belongs to his sons, Richard and John, was moved from Lord's to Headingley Carnegie last April to mark the 70th anniversary of Sir Leonard's 364 for England v. Australia at The Oval in 1938.

TOP PICTURE: John is on the left with his son, Robert, and Richard is second right with son Olly.

LEFT: The book containing the list of subscribers when the portrait was commissioned in 1951.

LAST HURRAH!
Darren Gough marks his retirement from first-class cricket with an explosive spell of bowling after leading Yorkshire out for the last time against Somerset at Scarborough.

rivals Lancashire — but the failure of one county to rearrange two postponed games meant that they missed the opportunity to progress. This squad was hit also by the fact that a number of players were good enough for the Under-17s.

Previous county champions, the Under-17s made it to the national semi-finals, taking on a strong Somerset side.

No one would dispute that this squad's potential was not fully realised this season, and the players did not do themselves justice on the day. Yorkshire's 121- 9, including a

**KATHERINE BRUNT:
Triumphant return**

50 from Charlotte Boulton, was simply not enough to prevent Somerset winning by 10 wickets.

Financial shortages brought about by ECB changes to the age-group structure which were not backed up by additional funding meant that the Development Squad managed only one game, against Cheshire: it showed the benefits of running such a squad, giving a number of junior players the chance to play with and against more experienced players. Yorkshire won with 16 overs to spare, Sarah Riggs's 59 and Robyn Stills's 44 forming the bedrock of their innings.

At Senior level the memory of 2007 — when the squad were unable to win any of their five county-championship games — only spurred on the players and staff to work hard to turn the tide. The first team ended 2008 unbeaten with double victories against Middlesex, Cheshire and Derbyshire. The closest game was against Cheshire, where despite a batting collapse Yorkshire showed deter-mination and strength in depth to win through, which bodes well for the future. Credit must go to the coaching and management team of Richard Damms, Barry Petty, Paul Farmer and Melissa Reynard, who with the players turned things around.

A number of players achieved representative honours, including: England: Katherine Brunt; England Academy: Rochelle Petty

(YCCC Academy Member), Salliann Briggs, Danielle Hazell and Kathryn Doherty; Senior Super 4s: Katherine Brunt, Salliann Briggs, Kathryn Doherty, Rochelle Petty Laura Spragg and Danielle Hazell; Junior Super 4s: Katie Levick, Lauren Winfield and Charlotte Boulton

Special mention must go to Katherine Brunt, back from serious injury after nearly two years away from county cricket. Her return has been greatly welcomed by both the Yorkshire squad and by England. Katherine contributed greatly to series wins over West Indies, South Africa and India, and the highlight of her tour was 5-25 in the drubbing of South Africa by 255 runs — the best bowling figures by an England player, male or female, in a one-day international at Lord's.

Katherine was named Player of the Series against India — an emotional moment for someone who thought she may never play cricket again. Katherine has done herself and Yorkshire proud.

As ever women's cricket has been supported by a large number of volunteers from Yorkshire Women's Cricket Association, local clubs and the District Women and Girls' Cricket Development Groups/Associations who strive to give as many females as possible the opportunity to try and enjoy being involved.

With the continued support of all these people Yorkshire women are looking forward to raising the bar in 2009 — an exciting year with the ICC Women's World Cup in Australia in March, followed by the Women's *Twenty20* World Cup in June running alongside the men's World Cup in England.

The association is working closely with YCB and YCCC to use these events as a catalyst to encourage as many women and girls as possible to get involved in cricket, supporting ECB's "One Game" philosophy.

We do believe that a corner has been turned. Hopefully, with the continued support of YCCC, YCB, development groups, players, parents and a clear focus on getting our clubs in a position to welcome openly women and girls to the game, Yorkshire Women will move back to where they aspire to be — at the top!

Sarah Pickford is Vice-Chair of Yorkshire Women's Cricket Association.

LEANING IS TOWER OF STRENGTH FOR NORTH

By Chris Hassell

With the Under-15s suffering serious injuries to three frontline bowlers, it was a considerable achievement to end with W-12, L-2, D-4, A-3. The main failure was with the bat in two crucial matches.

Yorkshire finished only one point behind Lancashire at the head of the northern section in the ECB time championship with wins against Durham, Shropshire and, notably, Cheshire, in a real thriller to qualify for the finals as best runners-up. At Oundle, the weather was a factor as usual, and the first match, against Wales, was abandoned. An excellent start in the second match against Kent of 129-3 turned into the disaster of 144 all out, but the bowlers made a good effort, and had seven Kent wickets down before their target was reached.

The third match, the first *Roses* encounter on foreign soil, saw **James Wainman** (Leeds Grammar School) reduce the enemy to 0-2 in the first over, and they never recovered. The Yorkshire boys were at their best, bowling Lancashire out for 78 to win by eight wickets and finish as runners-up to Kent.

The boys enjoyed easy victories in the North Division of the ECB Cup (50 overs), but slipped up badly against Derbyshire in the Quarter-Final, losing by nine wickets. A full programme of 21 matches was played through the season, including a couple of two-day fixtures. The first resulted in a comprehensive win against Wales, when the whole team made good individual contributions. The second, against Lancashire, was rain-affected, but it was a moral victory, and confirmed our superiority over our northern rivals.

The South West Tour, based at Exeter, saw victories against Devon, Somerset, Dorset and Warwickshire, with the Cornwall match abandoned after heavy rain. All in all, a most satisfactory season with the side supporting each other throughout. **Alex Lees** (Holy Trinity) won the batting award, **Ryan McKendry** (Thirsk) the fielding award and Wainman the bowling award. Alex, Ryan and **David Girling** (King James) represented the North of England.

A change in the Yorkshire County Cricket Club structure sees Andy Rowsell appointed as head coach for emerging players, which gives him a wider role with responsibility for co-ordinating an even stronger link between schools and the Yorkshire Academy, although he will continue his usual hands-on role with the Under-15s.

The Under 15s B side had an extensive 15-match programme (W-6, L-4, D-2, P-3) which included the Ampleforth Festival and used 19 players with **Jack Price** (Bradfield School) as captain. Seven of the boys progressed to the A team. **Peter Barnes** (King James) took the batting award, and **Jack Hughes** (Airedale High School) the bowling.

The Under-14s were in the South West tour, but also travelled to Taunton for their Festival: both are five-day events which are good for the development of young players. **Henry Chadwick** (Stokesley School) captained the side, and his knowledge of the game was always of the highest standard. **Johnny Booth** (Airedale HS), **Jack Leaning** (Archbishop Holgate), **James Lines** (Lawrence Jackson) and **George Ross** (Ilkley Grammar School) all represented the North. One highlight was Leaning's 164 not out against Cheshire (50 overs) to establish a new record at all levels of Yorkshire Schools' Association cricket.

The season generally was a mixture of success and disappointment, with a record of P-24, W-11, L-6, D-2, T-1, Ab-1, C-3. The team won their group section of the ECB Cup (45 overs) and overcame Lancashire in the Quarter-Final with a really professional performance. They then lost to a better Essex side in the Semi-Final at Oundle.

The B team had a mixed season with P-12, W-6, L-4, C-2), but provided plenty of opportunities for boys to shine as **Rishi Patel** (Leeds Grammar School and Mahir Yousuff (Hymers College) both scored centuries. **Tom Kohler-Cadmore** (Hornsea School) was leading run-scorer, and captained the side when Rishi was absent. Both boys demonstrated tactical knowledge and skill in reading the game.

The Under-13s enjoyed a highly successful year with P-16, W-10, Lost-2, A-1, C-3, although it ended in disappointment. Defeat by Surrey in the ECB County Cup Semi-Final (40 overs) was hard to take after the boys had dominated each and every team they had faced. Too much should not be read into one match, as cricket at this level is as much about development as about one-off performances.

It was a strong side, and the top four batsmen each scored over 350 runs, with **Will Rhodes** (Cottingham High School) averaging 96.75 and taking 5-24 in one match. The others were captain **Josh Inglis** (St Marys) 386, **Jordan Bethel** (Birkdale School) 380, and **Kris Ward** (Brigshaw High School) 353. The captain did exceptionally well, and the wicket-keeping by four different boys was excellent throughout. The bowling and most-promising-newcomer awards went to **Curtis Free** (Hallcross School) with 15 wickets, including 5-11. The outfielding and catching were sound, but there was no really outstanding close fielder.

The highlight was the victory over a strong Nottinghamshire side in the Quarter-Final at New Rover, where the team excelled in all departments. The one earlier defeat against Nottinghamshire came when 11 boys were missing, nine of them at the North of England trials.

The Under-13s B team in only its second year enjoyed an entertaining and successful season. More time for preparation resulted in a more talented and better balanced squad. The fixture list was enlarged to include matches against Lincolnshire, Warwickshire, Northumberland and Durham, all planned as annual encounters. The batting became more consistent as the season progressed — and on occasions quite explosive.

Top scorer was **Keegan Moodley** (St Mary's) with 90 against South Yorkshire, followed by **Harry Edwards** (Spen Valley Sports College) with 78, **Jack Seddon** (Whitcliffe Mount) 78, **Johnny Tattersall** (King James) 73 not out, and **Alex Mellor** (Hipperholme and Lightcliffe) 57 not out. The fielding was good, and improved throughout the season. Captain **Damon Reeve** (Guiseley) created a good team spirit, which manifested itself into a well organised and talented unit. Conduct on the field were a credit to all concerned (P-11, W-8, L-1, Ab-2).

The Under-12s enjoyed a good season (P-14, W-9, L-3, A-2) and won the Ampleforth Festival. **Josh Shaw** (Crofton High School) was star performer with 219 runs and 16 wickets, and had strong support from **Barney Gibson** (Crawshaw High School), an outstanding wicket-keeper who represented the North at Under-13A level. **Ryan Gibson** (Fyling Hall) with 140 runs and 15 wickets, **Alex Leyshon** (Ossett School) 15 wickets and **Tim Taylor** (King James, Huddersfield) 12 wickets all made their mark. **Charlie Elliot** (St Olave's) with 160 runs led very well, and scored an excellent 71 in a good victory over Lancashire.

Jack Harrison (Westville House), **Felix Adams** (Cundall Manor) and **Mack Collinson** (Bradfield School) all contributed with the bat, but the bowlers gained the honours, **Jordan Thompson** (Yeadon Westfield), **Matthew Waite** (Brigshaw High School) and **Aidan Hall** (Macaulay Catholic High School) all performing very effectively.

Manager Dick Whaley assembled a team at a late hour to fill a gap in the Ampleforth Festival, where they overcame Wales, Essex and London to reach the final against Yorkshire A: they acquitted themselves very well, scoring 101-8 and reducing the A side to 66-5 before eventual defeat. **Callum Goldthorp** (Benton Park) was the highest run scorer with 204, ably assisted by **Dylan Budge** (Woodhouse Grove) with 150 and Will Simpson (Queen Elizabeth Grammar School, Wakefield) 137. Spinners **Stuart Ward** (Benton Park) with 8-63 and **George Robson** (Morley High School) 7-67 were the pick of the bowlers. Budge also captained the side (P-6, W-4, L-1, D-1) and captured 10 victims behind the stumps.

HELLO, ALONZO — AND END GAME FOR A GREAT HUNTER

By Derek Hodgson

If 1908 was the summer of the "surprise" Championship, then the following year saw Yorkshire in a much more realistic light, finishing third to eventual champions Kent.

Batsmen **Charlie Hardisty** and **Billy Bates** jun. struggled to find form, while **Jack Newstead**, the Middlesbrough fast bowler who was a sensation in 1908 with 131 wickets at an average of 15 and 885 runs lost his edge. The mighty **George Hirst** was 38, and **Wilfred Rhodes** had been asked to fulfil a dual role as an opening batsman.

More trials brought more new names: **Benny Wilson**, a stubborn batsman who became an outstanding coach, and a player first registered as a left-hand batsman — the exotically named **Alonzo Drake**. "Lonza" had a rough upbringing, and when his wife sent him a telegram to congratulate him on his first big score his team-mates, unsure of whether he could read, opened it for him and read the message.

Drake asked to see the telegram, and then exclaimed: "You're kidding me. That's not my wife's writing."

It was the last playing season for **David Hunter**, possibly Yorkshire's best ever wicket-keeper, and it saw the death of Joe Wostinholm, the Club's Honorary Secretary from 1864 to 1902. Joe also was secretary of Sheffield United for 40 years, and saw that club advance into the top ranks of the Football League.

It was a summer of poor weather, but a Test series against Australia kept the treasurers happy, and Yorkshire's imperial old guard of Hirst, **Schofield Haigh**, Rhodes and **David Denton** ensured that even if the Championship was beyond reach status was retained.

Yorkshire were still the team to beat. Haigh took his benefit that year, his chosen match being the second against Lancashire, the August Bank Holiday fixture at Bradford Park Avenue. The scene had been set with a mighty Whitsuntide encounter at Old Trafford, when Walter Brearley had broken the Yorkshire first innings with 9-80 in 35 overs for a dismissal of 133. The sun broke through next day, leaving Lancashire to bat on a drying surface: Haigh took two wickets with successive balls, and followed with a hat-trick. Lancashire were all out for 89, Haigh 7-25.

Yorkshire were 44-4 and 88 ahead at the start of the last day, but at the final reckoning Lancashire needed 123. Hirst took the new ball; five batsmen were dismissed for six runs, and three stunning catches helped to shoot out Lancashire for 57 (Hirst 6-23).

So to Bradford. The weather again was poor, and in the hour possible on the first day Yorkshire, hitting out, reached 111-4. A collapse followed next morning, and Yorkshire were dismissed for 159.

This time Rhodes was the destroyer, his 7-68 leaving

DAVID HUNTER: Yorkshire's greatest wicket-keeper?

Lancashire 39 behind. Left 186 to make to win, Lancashire again were Wilfred's victims: his 6-40 saw Yorkshire home by the extraordinary margin of 100. Lancashire still had the last laugh: they finished second.

If Rhodes was turning his analytical mind more and more to the science of batting — eventually becoming **Jack Hobbs's** regular opening partner for England — his reading and dissection of every opposing batsman continued. He was to tell Sidney Rogerson some 40 years later: "All my life I bowled to make a batsman play forward to me. When he plays forward with his right foot anchored he is half-way on the stretch, and when he's on the stretch he's half-way to being out."

In 1909 Bleriot became the first man to fly across the Channel. Edward VII, a good friend to cricket, opened the Victoria and Albert Museum. Gustav Mahler became conductor of the New York Philharmonic. In January, old-age pensions were paid for the first time, and Flora Thomson, in Candleford, recalled seeing old folk in tears as they drew their four shillings allowance (20p) a week at the Post Office, crying "Bless that Lloyd George". They would bring apples and flowers from their gardens as gifts to the girls who handed out the money.

100 YEARS AGO

HIGHLIGHTS OF 1909

Wins by an innings (3)

Yorkshire (381) beat Derbyshire (112 and 142) by an innings and 127 runs at Derby
Yorkshire (292) beat Essex (90 and 114) by an innings and 88 runs at Leeds
Yorkshire (410) beat Leicestershire (235 and 154) by an innings and 21 runs at Dewsbury

Totals of 400 and over (3)

500	versus Warwickshire at Birmingham
489	versus Sussex at Sheffield
410	versus Leicestershire at Dewsbury

Opponents dismissed for under 100 (6)

57	Lancashire at Manchester (2nd inns)	85	Lancashire at Bradford
62	Surrey at Sheffield	89	Lancashire at Manchester (1st inns)
62	Surrey at The Oval	90	Essex at Leeds

Century Partnerships (10)

For the 1st wicket (1)

128   B B Wilson and J W Rothery versus Sussex at Sheffield

For the 2nd wicket (3)

175	B B Wilson and D Denton versus Warwickshire at Birmingham
170	B B Wilson and D Denton versus Leicestershire at Dewsbury
122	W Rhodes and D Denton versus Nottinghamshire at Nottingham

For the 3rd wicket (2)

147	W Rhodes and J W Rothery versus Sussex at Hove
134	B B Wilson and W H Wilkinson versus Sussex at Sheffield

For the 4th wicket (3)

226	W H Wilkinson and G H Hirst versus Northamptonshire at Hull
149	W Rhodes and G H Hirst versus Kent at Huddersfield
136	D Denton and G H Hirst versus Derbyshire at Derby

For the 6th wicket (1)

137   D Denton and H Myers versus Australians at Bradford

Centuries (15)

D Denton (5)

184 versus Nottinghamshire at Nottingham
140 versus Warwickshire at Birmingham
130 versus Derbyshire at Sheffield
129 versus Leicestershire at Dewsbury
106 versus Australians at Bradford

W Rhodes (5)

199 versus Sussex at Hove
114 versus Essex at Leeds
108 versus Australians at Sheffield
101 versus Kent at Huddersfield
101 versus MCC at Scarborough

B B Wilson (3)

116 versus Sussex at Sheffield
109 versus Leicestershire at Dewsbury
102 versus Warwickshire at Birmingham

G H Hirst (1)

140 versus Northamptonshire at Hull

W H Wilkinson (1)

103 versus Sussex at Sheffield

Hat-trick (1)

S Haigh (1)

versus Lancashire at Manchester

5 wickets in an innings (29)

W Rhodes (11)

7 for 68 versus Lancashire at Bradford (1st innings)
7 for 83 versus Warwickshire at Birmingham
7 for 87 versus Nottinghamshire at Bradford
6 for 29 versus Essex at Leyton
6 for 36 versus Middlesex at Lord's
6 for 40 versus Lancashire at Bradford (2nd innings)
6 for 47 versus Leicestershire at Dewsbury (2nd innings)
6 for 57 versus Leicestershire at Leicester
6 for 59 versus Warwickshire at Leeds
6 for 68 versus Leicestershire at Dewsbury (2nd innings)
6 for109 versus Somerset at Bath

S Haigh (8)

7 for 25 versus Lancashire at Manchester
7 for 32 versus Essex at Leeds
7 for 43 versus Leicestershire at Leicester
7 for 46 versus Worcestershire at Harrogate
7 for 65 versus Surrey at The Oval
6 for 33 versus Nottinghamshire at Bradford
6 for 35 versus Surrey at Sheffield
6 for 56 versus Essex at Leyton

G H Hirst (7)

7 for 95 versus Middlesex at Leeds
6 for 20 versus Surrey at Sheffield
6 for 23 versus Lancashire at Manchester
6 for 27 versus Surrey at The Oval
6 for 43 versus Essex at Leeds
5 for 49 versus Warwickshire at Leeds
5 for 57 versus Nottinghamshire at Nottingham

J T Newstead (2)

7 for 77 versus Sussex at Hove
5 for 93 versus Australians at Sheffield

A Drake (1)

6 for 34 versus Middlesex at Leeds

10 wickets in a match (8)

S Haigh (3)

11 for	91 (4 for 48 and 7 for 43)	versus Leicestershire at Leicester
10 for	46 (4 for 11 and 6 for 35)	versus Surrey at Sheffield
10 for	81 (6 for 56 and 4 for 25)	versus Essex at Leyton

W Rhodes (2)

13 for	108 (7 for 68 and 6 for 40)	versus Lancashire at Bradford
12 for	115 (6 for 68 and 6 for 47)	versus Leicestershire at Dewsbury

The Double (all First-Class matches) (2)

G H Hirst	1256 runs @ 27.30	115 wickets @ 20.05
W Rhodes	2094 runs @ 40.26	141 wickets @ 15.89

3 catches in an innings (9)

D Hunter (5)

6	versus Middlesex at Leeds
4	versus Australians at Sheffield
3	versus Cambridge University at Cambridge
3	versus Kent at Huddersfield
3	versus Leicestershire at Dewsbury

S Haigh (2)

3	versus Kent at Huddersfield
3	versus Essex at Leyton

J T Newstead (1)

3	versus Australians at Sheffield

W Rhodes (1)

3	versus Derbyshire at Sheffield

5 catches in a match (2)

D Hunter (1)

6 (6 + 0)	versus Middlesex at Leeds

S Haigh (1)

5 (2 + 3)	versus Essex at Leyton

3 dismissals in an innings (3)

D Hunter (3)

3 (2ct, 1st)	versus Derbyshire at Derby
3 (2ct, 1st)	versus Warwickshire at Birmingham
3 (2 ct, 1st)	versus Leicestershire at Leicester

Debuts (4)

A Broadbent, A Drake, L Linaker, E J R H Radcliffe

Last Appearances (4)

C H Hardisty, D Hunter, L Linaker, C Oyston

R D W

100 YEARS AGO

YORKSHIRE AVERAGES 1909

ALL FIRST-CLASS MATCHES

Played 30   Won 12   Lost 5   Drawn 13

(County Championship: Played 26   Won 12   Lost 4   Drawn 10)

BATTING AND FIELDING

Player	M.	I.	N.O.	Runs	H.S.	Avge	100s	50s	ct/st
W Rhodes	27	45	2	1663	199	38.67	5	5	19
D Denton	30	49	1	1765	184	36.77	5	7	13
G H Hirst	27	42	6	1151	140	31.97	1	9	33
A Drake	7	11	3	192	54	24.00	0	1	5
B B Wilson	28	48	3	1054	116	23.42	3	0	12
H Myers	20	28	6	482	91	21.90	0	3	5
J W Rothery	26	42	3	832	83	21.33	0	3	12
W E Bates	22	33	4	565	81	19.48	0	2	10
W H Wilkinson	15	23	1	409	103	18.59	1	1	7
S Haigh	29	38	14	376	46*	15.66	0	0	28
J T Newstead	30	41	6	509	51	14.54	0	1	28
C H Hardisty	9	14	0	193	72	13.78	0	1	5
E J R H Radcliffe	17	24	3	265	54	12.61	0	1	4
Lord Hawke	8	9	1	71	22*	8.87	0	0	0
D Hunter	26	33	14	157	14*	8.26	0	0	38/8

Also batted: H Watson (4 matches) 9*, 12, 3, 6, 0* (3 ct/1st); A Broadbent (2 matches) 29, 12, 1 (1ct); D C F Burton (1 match) 15, 5; L Linaker (1 match) 0, 0; C Oyston (1 match) 2.

BOWLING

Player	Overs	Mdns	Runs	Wkts	Avge	Best	5wI	10wM
S Haigh	799.2	196	1601	120	13.34	7-25	8	3
W Rhodes	725.5	187	1793	115	15.59	7-68	11	2
C Oyston	48.2	19	72	4	18.00	3-54	0	0
G H Hirst	718.3	151	1807	89	20.30	7-95	7	0
A Drake	88	23	249	12	20.75	6-34	1	0
J T Newstead	780.2	216	1730	80	21.62	7-77	2	0
H Myers	189.2	43	543	24	22.62	3-23	0	0

Also bowled: D Denton 13.1-2-48-2 (best 2-35); A Broadbent 46-6-133-1 (best 1-74); L Linaker 8-3-28-1 (best 1-28); E J R H Radcliffe 9-2-32-1 (best 1-23); W H Wilkinson 17-6-45-1 (best 1-7); B B Wilson 8-0-24-1 (best 1-16).

R D W

THE CHAMPIONSHIP
OF 1959

By Anthony Bradbury

When Yorkshire finished the 1958 season their cricket-followers had good reason to feel dispirited. **Bob Appleyard**, **Frank Lowson** and **Johnny Wardle** had not been retained; the appointment of another amateur as captain with limited experience of first-class cricket — **J R Burnet** — seemingly was not working, and the team had finished 11th in the Championship table. No one anticipated the wonders of 1959 when Yorkshire after a roller-coaster a season were again crowned the Champion County.

Yorkshire did have one early-season advantage over some of their rivals in 1959. They began with a largely young and enthusiastic squad who, when mixed with the more mature players, produced an appropriate blend of quality, knowledge and determination with which to challenge for a Championship. Only 19 men were used, many of whom had known one another since their days of school and youth cricket.

The towns in which they were born were all in Yorkshire — Barnsley, Bradford, Halifax, Holmfirth, Huddersfield, Hull, Leeds, Pudsey, Rawdon, Saltaire, Scampton, Settle, Shipley, Stainton and Yeadon. Many years were still to elapse before the county would need to abandon its home-grown policy.

The 28 Championship games spanned a period of just 115 days between May 9 and September 1, 1959. They were preceded by the then traditional match against MCC at Lord's, and there were brief interludes for less competitive games against Oxford University and a friendly against Lancashire, and then two keenly contested matches against the Indian Tourists. Otherwise, the team moved on from week to week in a well ordered way, playing two three-day games between each Saturday and the following Friday, with Sunday as the rest day.

At one stage to ease the travelling Yorkshire played six consecutive matches at the home grounds of Bradford, Harrogate, Leeds, Middlesbrough, Sheffield and Hull. That indulgence did mean that the season from mid-August would have to end far away from Yorkshire —

at Lord's, immediately followed by Bath, Bristol, Worcester and Hove.

Yorkshire were given a kindly start with a home game against Nottinghamshire — kindly because Nottinghamshire had finished bottom in 1958, as they were to do in 1959, so an easy win did not excite particular attention. Still, **Ken Taylor** scored a century as a prelude to the year in which he was to make his Test debut.

Fred Trueman in fine form took seven Nottinghamshire wickets in one innings, and **Don Wilson** took the only hat-trick by anyone that season — and the first of the three that he was to capture in his career.

A loss to Lancashire in the next game was followed by three draws and one win, and Yorkshire were

RONNIE BURNET
Earned years of thanks
(Photo: Hawke to Hutton
Publishing.)

looking comfortable, but not yet Championship material. Even so **Doug Padgett**, who with the admirable wicket-keeper, **Jimmy Binks**, played in every match, was showing good form with early centuries against Lancashire and Somerset, preceded by 161 not out against Oxford — to be the highest score of his career. He had scored more than 600 runs by the end of May, and would increase that to over 2,000 by September.

Then 26-year-old **H D Bird**, brought into the side because Taylor was playing in the Gentlemen v. Players fixture, put the cat amidst the selectors' pigeons by scoring the only century of his first-class career — a monumental 181 not out against Glamorgan. With everyone else playing their proper part in the side "Dicky" lost his place for the next game when Taylor returned. The following year Bird was playing for Leicestershire, but he never lost affection for the county of his birth.

Early June saw **Bryan Stott** and **Bob Platt** enhance their early-season form. In a low-scoring match against Hampshire, where each team innings was in the range of 200-215, Bryan stroked his way to 94 and 130 not out as Yorkshire won by four wickets. Later that year at Worcester he made 144 not out in a completed innings of 262 to become only the ninth Yorkshire batsman to carry his bat through a completed innings. He has been joined in the following 50 years by Padgett, **Geoffrey Boycott**, **Matthew Wood** and **Joe Sayers**. Stott went on to complete 2,000 runs in the season. Meantime Platt in three mid-season fixtures took six wickets in an innings against Derbyshire, 10 in the game against Surrey at The Oval, and nine more in the first game against Sussex. His Championship return in 1959 was 85 wickets.

Yorkshire bowled out Surrey for 87 in their second innings at The Oval in mid-June, but still lost. Surrey had been Champions for the previous seven seasons, and were in no mood to relinquish their title: their bowlers twice had Yorkshire out for less than 150. A high-scoring draw against Nottinghamshire in the return match with Padgett scoring 139 not out and **Brian Close** making 154 did not add greatly to their tally. Whereas a win brought 12 points, a draw gave no points, although there were two for a first-innings lead with a "further two bonus points awarded to the team gaining first-innings points if, at the moment of doing so, they have scored faster than their opponents." Yorkshire needed wins, not high-score draws.

Those wins duly came in the last 10 days of June — three in succession against Sussex, Warwickshire and Essex that took Yorkshire to the top. The Sussex game was won by an innings, but the Warwickshire match was affected badly by rain. Warwickshire were bowled out a second time on a nail-biting third day, **Ray Illingworth** taking 4-15 in 15 overs, and Yorkshire scrambled to a win at 5.53pm. Illingworth had a wonderful season, achieving the double of 100 wickets and 1,000 runs, playing for England and being top of the Yorkshire batting averages. Close had 5-12 in 10 overs in Warwickshire's first innings. The third consecutive win was against Essex at Colchester, where Illingworth scored 150.

Now the chase was on. Warwickshire, Derbyshire and Glamorgan were close at hand by early July, with Surrey not far behind. An unexpected loss to Hampshire was a setback for Yorkshire — who had had the confidence to declare behind on first innings. Then Derbyshire were defeated in a magnificent run chase that saw Yorkshire hit 304-4 in 57 overs to win on the last afternoon, Taylor scoring 144. This was before any limited-overs cricket had become a feature in England at a senior level. Another match going to the wire saw Yorkshire bowl out Essex at Scarborough during the extra half hour to win a thriller by 69 runs.

By mid-July the Surrey bowlers were plying their trade only too well. The return fixture at Bradford seemed crucial, and on July 21 Surrey were to win and leapfrog Yorkshire to the top. Surrey made 153 and 159 in a low-scoring game, and Yorkshire 91 and 173. **Peter Loader**, who played so much in the shadow of other great Surrey bowlers, took six Yorkshire wickets in each innings — 12 in the match for 99 runs, one of the performances of the season.

Yorkshire went off to Ireland for a gentle friendly, and must have lost their concentration. They were crushed by Northamptonshire on their return by an innings and 144 runs. Yorkshire's 64 remains their lowest score against the Midlands county — for whom **Frank Tyson** and **Albert Lightfoot** bowled rather well! Little did Yorkshire know that an even worse score was looming that season.

Yorkshire fought back very well, and other teams faltered. Yorkshire went to Leicester for the last three days of July with nine Championship matches to play: Leicester were overcome, again after 5pm on the third day, and there was stalemate against Lancashire. Another trio of wins, two against Middlesex, saw Yorkshire back on top, although Surrey had games in hand. The first Middlesex win came after Yorkshire had been bowled out for 84 at Scarborough. Illingworth, with nine wickets in the game, and Close with eight turned the tables.

A brave victory against Kent followed — Yorkshire's last home Championship game: Burnet declared 134 behind, and on the last day Close — with his best bowling figures of 8-41 — bundled out Kent for 109. Yorkshire, having to make 244 to win in under three hours, did so with two wickets and two minutes to spare.

Now came the final five matches. Middlesex at Lord's lost by six wickets — but again the margin of time was close, 10 minutes on this occasion. A hard-fought match at Bath resulted in a loss to Somerset by 16 runs, despite Close excelling with 128. That was as nothing to the next event: Yorkshire lost to Gloucestershire on August 25 by an innings and 77 runs, the game irrevocably lost when Yorkshire were bowled out for 35 in their first innings — the lowest score by any team that season, and Yorkshire's lowest ever against Gloucestershire. The last six all made ducks, and **Tony Brown** took 7-11. Gloucester on a roll found themselves top with Warwickshire — who only had one match to play — second, and Yorkshire third. Surrey, with a game in hand over Yorkshire, were two points behind them.

The cause may have seemed lost, but not to the Yorkshire players.

Events and good cricket conspired to turn the tables in the last week. As Yorkshire were beating Worcestershire, Surrey were disposing of Gloucestershire, and Warwickshire were not playing. Yorkshire just had their noses ahead of Surrey, and went to Hove knowing that they must win to have a chance of the title. If Surrey were to win their last two games then they would retain the Championship — and Surrey were playing the first of those games against Middlesex at the same time as

Yorkshire were playing Sussex. Middlesex gave no licence to Surrey, and nearly won a match that ended in a draw. Surrey now needed Yorkshire to draw or lose. That did not happen, and Yorkshire secured their triumph after bowling out an obstinate Sussex on the last afternoon, and then majestically scoring 216 runs for victory in 28.3 overs — just like Twenty20 cricket.

Journalists present were in praise of this wonderful batting. *The Times* Special Correspondent — maybe John Woodcock, but in those days they were unnamed — wrote: "With a joyous level of hitting unequalled in this lovely summer, Yorkshire regained the County Championship when, with seven minutes to spare, Bolus glanced Dexter for four, and ended a dramatic dash for victory. Against the clock and contrary to all expectations they had scored the 216 they needed in 96 minutes. Stott (96) and Padgett (79) let forth a torrent of strokes, many of them of a daring and power that had the crowd on their feet. [They] made the partnership of their lives. The 100 was hoisted in 13 overs; the 150 in 61 minutes. The more commanding innings was Stott's, the more rugged Padgett's. But some inspiration touched them both..."

E W Swanton in the *Daily Telegraph* was not initially so generous, and perhaps a little churlish: "There was a strange notion during the interval between innings that Yorkshire had only the slimmest chance. They would try, of course, because they had nothing to lose. But 215 in one-and-three quarter hours — well! In fact, of course, a much higher rate has been gone for and achieved hundreds of times. And what better circumstances than a combination of the Sussex bowling and a brick-hard field."

"Then his mood changed: "All possible praise to Stott and Padgett...The stroke play was unforgettable. It was not in any sense blind hitting. They made ground to almost everything, so dictating the length, and in turn showed every stroke...Their driving, especially, was magnificent. They ran very fast between the wickets, and though with five men as a rule on the boundary there were not many fours, the number of twos was unusually large...The difficulty that Illingworth and Bolus had in squeezing the last runs only emphasised the excellence of the batting that had gone before."

J M Kilburn, always objective, in his brief *History of Yorkshire Cricket* (1970) did not spare the Sussex bowling: "They bowled wide, they bowled short, they scattered fieldsmen to leave broad pathways to the boundary and ample scope for running singles and twos. The batting was superbly enterprising without being recklessly uninhibited. The out-cricket was pathetically unsophisticated. Yorkshire won the championship romantically, and literally 'off their own bats'."

That night Yorkshire journeyed home to Scarborough, and next morning appeared before and between a rapturous crowd as a prelude to defeating the MCC. Bryan Stott has spoken of Yorkshire fielding first and of the Yorkshire team walking on to that Scarborough field in an inverted V, as if themselves off the ground in their pride and delight. Eleven days later, as Champion County, they defeated the Rest of England after the little problem of having to follow on. **Vic Wilson** was a centurion on that occasion, and late in 1959 he was appointed the first professional captain of Yorkshire since **Tom Emmett** in the previous century. Ronnie Burnet had done his job, and retired to years of grateful thanks.

Cat among the pigeons: 'Dickie' Bird on the sweep during his 181 not out at Bradford Park Avenue.
(Photo: Dickie Bird Archive.)

The cricketers who participated in this wonderful season, and the number of Championship matches in which they played were: J G Binks and D E V Padgett 28, W B Stott 26, J R Burnet and D B Close 25, R K Platt 24, K Taylor and D Wilson 23, R Illingworth 21, F S Trueman 18, P J Sharpe and J V Wilson 15, J Birkenshaw 9, J B Bolus 7, H D Bird and D Pickles 6, M Ryan 5, C H Wood 3 and B Stead 1.

50 YEARS AGO

HIGHLIGHTS OF 1959

Wins by an innings (3)

Yorkshire (304) beat Sussex (161 and 103) by an innings and 40 runs at Bradford
Yorkshire (405 for 8 wkts dec) beat Glamorgan (137 and 233) by an innings and 35 runs at Bradford
Yorkshire (348) beat Lancashire (180 and 151) by an innings and 17 runs at Midlesbrough (non-Championship)

Win after following on (1)

Yorkshire (160 and 425) beat Rest of England (384 for 8 wkts dec and 135) by 66 runs at The Oval

Totals of 400 and over (4)

425	versus Rest of England at The Oval
418 for 3 wkts dec	versus Nottinghamshire at Nottingham
405 for 8 wkts dec	versus Glamorgan at Bradford
400 for 3 wkts dec	versus Oxford University at Oxford

Opponents dismissed for under 100 (3)

77	MCC at Lord's
77	Warwickshire at Sheffield
87	Surrey at The Oval

Century Partnerships (20)

For the 1st wicket (3)

161	W B Stott and K Taylor versus Nottinghamshire at Middlesbrough
148	W B Stott and P J Sharpe versus Derbyshire at Sheffield
146	W B Stott and H D Bird versus MCC at Scarborough

For the 2nd wicket (4)

127	P J Sharpe and D E V Padgett versus Essex at Scarborough
113	K Taylor and D E V Padgett versus Derbyshire at Chesterfield
109	W B Stott and D E V Padgett versus MCC at Scarborough
107	W B Stott and D E V Padgett versus Worcestershire at Worcester

For the 3rd wicket (7)

252	D E V Padgett and D B Close versus Nottinghamshire at Nottingham
244	D E V Padgett and D B Close versus Oxford University at Oxford
205	D E V Padgett and D B Close versus Somerset at Bath
141	W B Stott and D E V Padgett versus Sussex at Hove
126	D E V Padgett and D B Close versus Somerset at Harrogate
117	W B Stott and D B Close versus Lancashire at Middlesbrough (non-Championship)
100*	D E V Padgett and D B Close versus Derbyshire at Sheffield

For the 4th wicket (2)

124	D B Close and J V Wilson versus Rest of England at The Oval
119*	D E V Padgett and R Illingworth versus Leicestershire at Leicester

For the 5th wicket (2)

159	D B Close and R Illingworth versus Lancashire at Sheffield
107	R Illingworth and J B Bolus versus MCC at Scarborough

For the 6th wicket (2)

169	R Illingworth and J Birkenshaw versus Indians at Sheffield
112	R Illingworth and J Birkenshaw versus Sussex at Hove

Centuries (19)

D B Close (4)

154	versus Nottinghamshire at Nottingham
144	versus Oxford University at Oxford
128	versus Lancashire at Sheffield
128	versus Somerset at Bath

R Illingworth (4)

162	versus Indians at Sheffield
150	versus Essex at Colchester (Castle Park)
122	versus Sussex at Hove
105*	versus MCC at Scarborough

D E V Padgett (4)

161*	versus Oxford University at Oxford
139*	versus Nottinghamshire at Nottingham
122	versus Somerset at Harrogate
100	versus Lancashire at Manchester

W B Stott (3)

144*	versus Worcestershire at Worcester
130*	versus Hampshire at Hull
110	versus Lancashire at Middlesbrough (non-Championship)

K Taylor (2)

144	versus Derbyshire at Chesterfield
103	versus Nottinghamshire at Middlesbrough

H D Bird (1)

181*	versus Glamorgan at Bradford

J V Wilson (1)

105	versus Rest of England at The Oval

Carried bat through completed innings (1)

W B Stott (1)

144* out of 262 versus Worcestershire at Worcester

5 wickets in an innings (24)

F S Trueman (6)

7 for 57	versus Nottinghamshire at Middlesbrough
5 for 51	versus Surrey at The Oval
5 for 56	versus Glamorgan at Bradford
5 for 65	versus Essex at Colchester (Castle Park)
5 for 72	versus Warwickshire at Birmingham
5 for 77	versus Hampshire at Hull

D B Close (5)

8 for 41	versus Kent at Leeds
6 for 87	versus Somerset at Bath
5 for 12	versus Warwickshire at Sheffield
5 for 47	versus Rest of England at The Oval
5 for 75	versus Middlesex at Scarborough

R K Platt (4)

    6 for 72 versus Derbyshire at Chesterfield
    5 for 26 versus Sussex at Bradford
    5 for 31 versus Surrey at The Oval (2nd innings)
    5 for 56 versus Surrey at The Oval (1st innings)

D Wilson (3)

    5 for 57 versus Somerset at Bath
    5 for 67 versus Kent at Leeds
    5 for 129 versus Nottinghamshire at Nottingham

J Birkenshaw (2)

    5 for 39 versus Lancashire at Middlesbrough (non-Championship)
    5 for 54 versus Glamorgan at Bradford

R Illingworth (2)

    5 for 35 versus Middlesex at Scarborough
    5 for 38 versus Surrey at Bradford

M Ryan (1)

    5 for 45 versus Nottinghamshire at Nottingham

B Stead (1)

    7 for 76 versus Indians at Bradford

10 wickets in a match (1)

R K Platt (1)

    10 for 87 (5 for 56 and 5 for 31)   versus Surrey at The Oval

Century and 5 wickets in an innings (1)

D B Close (1)

    128 and 6 for 87 versus Somerset at Bath

The Double (all First-Class matches) (1)

R Illingworth 1726 runs @ 46.64   110 wickets @ 21.46

3 catches in an innings (7)

J G Binks (1)

    4   versus Nottinghamshire at Nottingham

J Birkenshaw (1)

    4   versus Sussex at Hove

P J Sharpe (2)

    3   versus Warwickshire at Sheffield (1st innings)
    3   versus Warwickshire at Sheffield (2nd innings)

J B Bolus (1)

    3   versus Somerset at Bath

D B Close (1)

    3   versus Northamptonshire at Leeds

D E V Padgett (1)

    3   versus Rest of England at The Oval

3 dismissals in an innings (5)

J G Binks (5)

    5 (4ct, 1st) versus Essex at Colchester (Castle Park)
    4 (1ct, 3st) versus Indians at Sheffield
    3 (2ct, 1st) versus Glamorgan at Bradford
    3 (2ct, 1st) versus Surrey at Bradford
    3 (2ct, 1st) versus Worcestershire at Worcester

5 catches in a match (1)

P J Sharpe (1)

    6 (3 + 3)   versus Warwickshire at Sheffield

5 dismissals in a match(1)

J G Binks (1)

    5 (4ct, 1st) versus Essex at Colchester (Castle Park)

Cap Awarded (1)

R K Platt

Debuts (2)

B Stead, C H Wood

Last Appearances (4)

H D Bird, J R Burnet, B Stead, C H Wood

R D W

Vaughan's Test record

When Yorkshire's **Michael Vaughan** relinquished the England captaincy after the Edgbaston Test last summer — and said goodbye to his Test place — he had played in 82 Test matches, scoring 5,719 runs. In 51 Tests as captain he had scored 3,170 runs at 36.02, and as non-captain he had racked up 2,549 runs in 31 matches at 50.98. Although he had yet to regain his Test place at the start of the 2009 season,m his appetite for international cricket was just as sharp as ever.

50 YEARS AGO

YORKSHIRE AVERAGES 1959

ALL FIRST-CLASS MATCHES

Played 35　　　　Won 18　　　　Lost 8　　　　Drawn 9

(County Championship: Played 28　　Won 14　　Lost 7　　Drawn 7)

COUNTY CHAMPIONS

BATTING AND FIELDING

Player	M.	I.	N.O.	Runs	H.S.	Avge	100s	50s	ct/st
R Illingworth	27	44	12	1490	162	46.56	4	4	24
D E V Padgett	35	60	8	2158	161*	41.50	4	11	21
W B Stott	32	56	2	2034	144*	37.66	3	13	23
H D Bird	7	12	2	374	181*	37.40	1	2	1
J B Bolus	10	17	5	431	91	35.91	0	2	12
D B Close	31	54	3	1740	154	34.11	4	8	32
K Taylor	27	49	1	1306	144	27.20	2	8	14
P J Sharpe	17	27	1	642	73	24.69	0	5	24
J V Wilson	20	31	5	608	105	23.38	1	2	25
F S Trueman	22	30	6	464	54	19.33	0	1	18
J Birkenshaw	15	21	3	326	40	18.11	0	0	12
D Wilson	29	35	7	432	55	15.42	0	1	21
J R Burnet	30	40	4	413	47	11.47	0	0	6
J G Binks	35	40	6	325	37	9.55	0	0	46/22
R K Platt	27	31	14	131	57*	7.70	0	1	7

Also batted: D Pickles (8 matches) 5, 0*, 1*, 9, 0 (3ct); M Ryan (7 matches) 0, 4*, 4*, 12*, 5*, 17 (3 ct); C H Wood (4 matches) 4*, 8, 10, 0 (1ct); B Stead (2 matches) 8, 0, 0.

BOWLING

Player	Overs	Mdns	Runs	Wkts	Avge	Best	5wI	10wM
B Stead	41.2	7	115	7	16.42	7-76	1	0
F S Trueman	808.4	200	2051	104	19.72	7-57	6	0
R Illingworth	830.5	267	1931	92	20.98	5-35	2	0
M Ryan	261.4	77	640	30	21.33	5-45	1	0
K Taylor	282.3	90	633	27	23.44	4-25	0	0
R K Platt	906.2	282	2090	89	23.48	6-72	4	1
D B Close	726.2	206	2031	81	25.07	8-41	5	0
J Birkenshaw	398	114	1006	38	26.47	5-39	2	0
C H Wood	125.2	31	319	11	29.00	4-39	0	0
D Wilson	744.2	217	2055	62	33.14	5-57	3	0
D Pickles	162.1	29	538	13	41.38	4-35	0	0

Also bowled: J B Bolus 12-2-44-1 (best 1-25); J R Burnet 2-0-21-1 (best 1-8); D E V Padgett 29.1-10-80-1 (best 1-13); W B Stott 6-2-17-1 (best 1-5); J G Binks 2-1-8-0; P J Sharpe 4-1-22-0; J V Wilson 8-1-31-0.

R D W

BURNET'S YOUNG LIONS
ROAR TO SUCCESS

BRYAN STOTT
Suicide escapes
(Photo: Hawke
to Hutton Publishing.)

The inevitable consequence of the traumatic changes that had taken place during the 1958 season naturally resulted in **Ronnie Burnet's** "Young Pretenders" being considered the most inexperienced team in the county's history.

A period of near misses and disappointing Championship results, followed in 1957 by the resignations of **Willie Watson**, who had been my mentor in the team, and **Billy Sutcliffe**, and in 1958 the health-related retirements of **Frank Lowson** and **Bob Appleyard**, plus the sacking of **Johnny Wardle**, all presented a formidable challenge to the skipper and the team as we assembled for outdoor practice in April 1959.

Our most senior professional was **Vic Wilson**, who went on to experience a wretched run of bad form, and ultimately played in the Second XI for most of the season. Then came **Brian Close** and **Fred Trueman** who, in a happy and encouraging team environment, were both to benefit considerably from the new responsibilities that their outstanding talents obliged them to accept. Indeed, those of us who were fielding away from the wicket were expected to keep one eye on the skipper and the other on Brian as he continually made fine adjustments to the field to suit changing circumstances. This was with the skipper's permission — a situation which radically changed when the new captain, Vic, took control in 1960.

Then there was **Raymond Illingworth**, whose rapidly accepted status as a sound cricketing technician and England's top all-rounder proved to be so decisive, plus the ever-present wicket-keeping of **Jimmy Binks**, whose keen observations and constructive comment proved invaluable to the skipper as the season progressed.

Ken Taylor, **Doug Padgett** and myself, as the first three batsmen, completed the list of capped professionals, and while we had all had our own periods of individual success, we were still to prove our worth in a professional rebuilding capacity. Our biggest advantage was that we had all played with the skipper in the Second XI. We knew each other very well indeed but, above all, Ron knew that he had our 100 per cent support right from the start.

An additional boost to the dressing-room environment and the skipper's continued confidence had been the previous introduction into the team of senior capped Second XI players who had formed the nucleus of Ron's Second XI Championship-winning side of 1957.

There were **Don Wilson**, **Bob Platt**, **Philip Sharpe** and **Brian Bolus**, followed later by **Dickie Bird**, **Jackie Birkenshaw** and **Mel Ryan**. These talented cricketers not only brought their own individual skills on to the field, but added a character and charisma to the First XI dressing room that none of us had experienced there before and I am sure that none of us will ever forget.

This was all well and good, but as far as the Yorkshire cricket public was concerned we were looked upon as a poor team which had let them down too often in the past — it was results that counted.

The Yorkshire cricket Press were always hopeful but restrained in their comments, and Brian Sellers, our Cricket Chairman, speaking at the opening luncheon, was convinced that such an inexperienced team would need another year or two to progress. As for ourselves, all we could do was to try as hard as we could and see what happened!

The skipper's enthusiasm had not been affected by his experiences in 1958, and he repeated his resolve to get on with the job in hand. The April practices had given him the opportunity to define clearly the ground rules with regard to punctuality and ground arrival times — which in some specific cases had varied a bit the year before! There certainly was no need to remind us of our main responsibility, for we were there first and foremost to play cricket for Yorkshire.

The first few matches convinced us that the skipper had not lost his amazing ability to lose the toss, and we quickly adapted to the everyday requirements of work and effort that two three-day Championship matches per week — plus the inevitable long distance non-motorway travelling — entailed. It was the clear understanding in the dressing room that in the vital interests of team safety, more than team spirit, a

56

certain D B Close should be allowed to leave first on any journey. If this were not possible he should be allowed to overtake at the earliest opportunity, thus ensuring that everyone else arrived in one piece!

The skipper's welcoming and open approach had already made sure that our dressing-room door was always open to our much-respected coaches — **Arthur Mitchell**, * **Morris Leyland** and **Bill Bowes** — plus any past players who could manage to attend. So many did: **Arthur Wood**, **Ellis Robinson**, **Emmott Robinson**, **Abe Waddington**, **Frank Smailes** and **Arthur Booth**. **Herbert Sutcliffe** occasionally would bring **Percy Holmes** who, by his huge smile, so obviously took great enjoyment in being among us all, and, of course, a number of us took the opportunity to talk to **Wilfred Rhodes** at Scarborough.

This very natural acceptance of shared experiences and generous support, coupled with many hilarious anecdotes from such respected members of previous Yorkshire sides, is without doubt the very source of Yorkshire's cricketing tradition and the very reason why our Yorkshire caps are, to this day, an immeasurable treasure.

Also, an excellent and trusting relationship was established with our respected group of Yorkshire cricket-writers. This very experienced band of scribes, having seen many other Yorkshire teams over the years, had viewed our performances to date with various levels of emotion. Exasperation, disappointment, right through to recognition and appreciation and, occasionally, magic moments of sheer enjoyment. They, like us, did not quite know what to expect from one day to the next!

Progressive hard work and continual encouragement for each other had provided many opportunities for each member of the side to contribute on the field. One or two very exciting victories against the odds began to convince some sceptics that we may, after all, be considered worthy of representing Yorkshire. The successful transformation from enthusiastic apprentices to confident tradesmen became apparent as the vital last weeks of the season approached.

Throughout the season, and in a perfect English summer, all our bowlers performed magnificently. Fred, who was rapidly becoming the great fast bowler he was, measured his energy sensibly enough to be able to bowl an amazing 808 overs in all our matches — plus nearly 200 in Test and representative matches.

Bob, taking the other end in support, was having a wonderful season, with 896 overs, beating shin soreness and fatigue to fully deserve the award of his county cap in August — and still, after 50 years of continual lobbying, failing to convince his peers that his 57 not out at Chesterfield should lift him into the all-rounder class!

Raymond, with 830, and Don, with 744, bowled beautifully in very demanding conditions for spin bowlers, and were very well supported by a rapidly improving Jackie on 398 overs. Brian, with 726 overs, bowling spin and medium-pace, continued to break stands and get the vital wickets he did so often, and Ken, on 282, again proving his worth, if proof were ever needed, by "nipping in" when it mattered, particularly his four wickets in the Sussex game. When Test duties took Fred out of the team Mel, on 256, **David Pickles**, on 162, and **Chris Wood**, on 125, blended easily into the side, and gave of their best.

Three excellent victories against Kent and Middlesex (twice) sent us on our final Southern tour top of the table with an eight-point lead over Warwickshire, with Gloucestershire, Surrey and Glamorgan close behind, so we had everything to play for. We were in for a rude awakening! Without Fred and Raymond on Test duty we played well below our standard on a turning pitch at Bath, allowing Somerset to beat us by 16 runs.

Then a disastrous two-and-a-half days at Bristol were enough for **Tony Brown** and **David Smith** to bowl us out for 35 first-innings runs on the way to defeat by an innings and 77 runs. The only bright bit of this game was **Brian Bolus** memorably being told to keep his pads on after making 12 not out at No.5 in the first innings and going back in first to score 91 in the second.

This visit to the South West had cost us dearly, and now, lying a disappointing third, eight points behind Gloucestershire, we made our early move to Worcester. We were in a very serious position, and the whole team accepted that we had to beat Worcestershire to stand any possible chance of winning the Championship. The "early bath" at Bristol enabled one or two of us to visit the brine baths at Droitwich, where bruised and tired limbs and bodies were rejuvenated after a good sleep.

Then followed a truly workmanlike performance from every member of the team for the whole of the three days — which made absolutely sure that we beat a strong and determined Worcestershire side. We set off for Brighton with a lot of hope and expectation, for this would be our last chance to make all our hard work worth while. That Worcestershire victory was a real tonic after Bristol!

So much has been written about our fairytale ending to what were three excellent days of hard-fought, competitive cricket played on a hard and fast Hove pitch under clear, blue skies in front of capacity crowds, which happily included a lot of Yorkshire supporters.

After losing the toss we finished 97 runs in front on first innings, thanks to Ken's four wickets and Raymond's century. We lost the initiative in the Sussex second innings, and needed a breakthrough. The skipper threw the ball to Fred to see if he could manage one last fling before lunch but, understandably, after nearly 1,000 overs in the season his legs had given up on him. By the interval Sussex were well in front with four wickets still to fall. In spite of some very mixed opinions from his own dressing room, **Robin Marlar** — quite rightly in my opinion — continued the innings, challenging us to prove our mettle. As expected, the tail-enders struck away merrily, and wickets fell pretty quickly.

One of my many abiding memories is the sight of a very young Jackie taking four magnificent catches way out on the boundary and under tremendous pressure.

The ground was a cauldron of excited spectators, and as we came off the field two Yorkshire supporters dashed up to me, and asked: "Are we going for them?" The answer, of course, was

Morning after: Bryan Stott, left, and Doug Padgett walk out at Scarborough.
(Photo: Ron Deaton Archive.)

"Yes". There was no doubt in our minds. While padding up I asked **Philip Sharpe**, who was deputising for our regular scorer, **Cyril Turner**, to work out the Sussex over rate in the first innings — and then put up each over as it was bowled, so that we could check our progress from the pitch. From memory, I think we calculated that we would need something like eight runs per over — quite a task!

We got in front from the start, and from then on it was just a case of keeping up the momentum and trying not to lose wickets. Closey caused a bit of a stir early on by knocking the ball out of the ground — and losing us four or five valuable minutes before the umpires produced another ball. When Doug joined me Marlar had a problem deciding how to set his field. He could not, in all fairness, pack all his men on one side, as the left/right-hand combination would demand a complete change nearly every ball. He had to settle on a split field, which helped us considerably, as it created larger gaps.

We quickly decided that every single had to be made into two if possible, so then followed an hour's cricket that neither of us will ever forget — we had never run as fast for so long. It was challenging to both sides, and it was exhausting and exhilarating, the spectators cheering every run and suicide escape but, best of all, it worked! Robert Hudson had been giving the BBC commentary since lunch, and we learned afterwards that thousands of Yorkshiremen from all over England had been glued to their radios. Unfortunately, we have never been able to obtain any of his recordings, and very few photographs of the day either.

So there it was! Good fortune had most certainly favoured the brave and, unbelievably, the Championship was ours at last.

By a unique blend of encouragement, persuasion and an occasional reprimand, but, above all, by an understanding of and a faith in each of the individuals in his side, the skipper had moved his young lions from doubt and disarray in 1958 to determined and dedicated Champions in 1959. We had played 28 three-day Championship matches, which brought 14 wins, seven defeats and seven draws. We finished 18 points in front of the following pack of four counties, who were all within two points of each other. What a summer it had been.

Champagne magically appeared in the dressing room, and our understandably much-delayed departure from Hove was the start of what can only be described as an unforgettable experience for us all.

Glorious memories will never fade as we recall our tumultuous welcome on arriving at Scarborough in small and tired groups in the early hours of the morning after our long car journeys. Scores of jubilant Yorkshire supporters at the Salisbury and Balmoral Hotels would not go to bed until they had seen us home and heard our stories at first hand.

Then, so few hours later, there was an unbelievable crescendo of noise and celebration as first we arrived at the ground, and then as the skipper proudly led us all on to the field. A cheering throng of families, friends, members and supporters formed a huge guard of honour leading from the dressing room to well beyond the pitch. It will come as no surprise that practically every member of this proud team had tears in his eyes by the time we reached the middle. What a memory to share!

The Scarborough Festival had always been dear to the heart of every Yorkshire cricketer. This was one of continual celebration, usually with the skipper in the lead. From Scarborough it was on to The Oval for one final encounter — The Champion County v. The Rest of England. For this game the skipper made a special request that as Vic had not played in many games during the season, and as his long career with the county possibly was nearing its end, he should be invited to play, with Jackie to act as 12th man.

The Committee, presumably because of the cost, had not included Dickie in the London party, so again, in recognition of the part he had played during the year, Ron suggested that we all contribute to the cost of him joining our group for the trip. That both these suggestions were greeted with enthusiasm and successfully accomplished shows the spirit, confidence and companionship generated under Ron's leadership.

Having completed another victory after following on in the first innings, we triumphantly went our separate ways from The Oval, a £100 Championship-winning bonus cheque burning a hole in our pockets, knowing that we had yet another special occasion to come.

Accompanied by our wives and girlfriends, we were invited to celebrate the Championship win with our popular President, Sir William Worsley, and all his family at Hovingham Hall, where his young daughter, now our Patroness, being seated between Ken and myself, was eager to hear the story unfold once again.

Tribute must be paid to our backroom staff of George Alcock, masseur, and Cyril, our scorer. George, fit as a fiddle and immaculately groomed, approached everybody directly and fairly. He had no truck with malingerers, and subsisted all day on pots of hot tea and lashings of sugar. He miraculously kept our bowlers going all season, was a perfect foil for a very boisterous dressing room, was Brian's regular passenger — and had fingers made of iron! We batsmen were rarely allowed anywhere near his table unless it was a dire emergency. Even then, we had to seriously consider our options — either to suffer the pain of the injury or those steely fingers! He was a good friend and a great companion.

Cyril — quiet, observant and with a twinkle in his eye which belied his serious nature, was one of the most respected cricketers of that victorious 1930s side. As an all-rounder and magnificent catcher of the ball, he was a valuable member of that all-powerful team, while never really wanting or seeking public acclamation. He was very much the father figure behind our team, always willing to give advice and help if asked but, above all, a very willing listener. Sometimes the Yorkshire First XI dressing room can be a hard and lonely place, and on such occasions Cyril was always available.

Sadly, Cyril became ill on the last Southern tour, and as he had to travel home he missed experiencing the delight of our Championship win after sharing so many of his own in the 1930s. Thankfully, Philip was able to stay with us as his deputy. I have a lot to thank Cyril for; he was a good friend.

Unbeknown to us all, that game at The Oval would be the last when Ronnie would lead his team on to the field. In November **Brian Sellers**, as Cricket Chairman, presented a future scenario to Ron which, as far as the chairman was concerned, would be resolved only by the skipper standing down. After much discussion and very reluctantly, Ron was forced to agree, so he stood down.

The skipper would now retire, content in the knowledge that he had left behind him a Yorkshire team that not only knew how to win, but now expected to win.

* *Leyland was usually referred to as Maurice, but it later became known that his Christian name was spelt Morris on his birth certificate.*

This award for outstanding service to Yorkshire County Cricket Club was inaugurated in 2008. It was shared between GEOFF HOLMES and VIVIEN STONE, who run the secondhand book stall at Headingley Carnegie on behalf of the John Featherstone Memorial Foundation, and MOLLIE STAINES, a lifelong supporter who became the first woman to serve on the Committee. The recipients tell it in their own words.

BOOKSTALL SUCCESS
IS GOOD NEWS STORY

By Geoff Holmes and Vivien Stone

Ten years ago in 1998 we took over the running of the secondhand bookstall. It coincided with the death of John Featherstone, a dedicated Yorkshire member who had assisted the club in many ways over a long period in a voluntary capacity.

We dedicated it to the John Featherstone Memorial Foundation to support young Yorkshire cricketers in principle and the Club in general. In the first year we set ourselves a target of £1,000 — and were pleasantly surprised to make £1,635. The second year's figure more than doubled it to £3,425.

By publishing a daily running total on a blackboard everyone could see how we were progressing. Without the generous contributions of members, supporters and well-wishers we would not have been able to succeed. Everything we sell has been given by cricket-lovers and, sadly, collections of books donated by the families of members who have died.

All the money we raise is distributed before the next season begins. At the end of the season it is put into a high-interest building-society six-month account, and the accrued interest is added to the total disbursed before the start of the season.

It is very heartening to realise the wonderful spirit of goodwill that exists at Yorkshire CCC, and as a direct result of the generosity of the book-buying members we have been able to award sums to allow several players to tour overseas during the winter. We have given Yorkshire Schools' Cricket Association £3,000, the Under-16s tour to Jersey £2,500, the Joe Lumb Competition £1,000, and the Foundation has also made gifts to the Club.

Five years ago we recruited another member of staff, Robert Stone, Vivien's husband. We jokingly gave him the title of Goods Inward Co-ordinator. He also keeps us all well supplied with drinks.

Up to 2007 we had the arduous task of putting our considerable stock of books into plastic bags at the end of each season to keep them dry during the winter. Then three benefactors gave us a total of £700 to buy plastic containers with lids. All we have to do now lay the books flat, and store them until next spring.

Our best season was 2005, when we raised £8,388 — the South Africa Test match alone raising £1,500. With that in mind — and being in receipt of a £1,200 gift in memory of Kenneth Brook, a dear friend and longstanding member — we hoped to raise £10,000 last summer.

The terrible weather, together with the loss of the Somerset match to Scarborough because of the drainage and levelling work at Headingley Carnegie, meant that we just made £8,000.

This brings the grand total we have raised to £66,000 in our 10 years of trading, starting in a caravan at the end of the Western Terrace before taking over our present location at the end of the West Stand. We hope with these efforts — together with the wonderful support of you, the members — to continue supporting our young cricketers who are the future of our great club.

RICH DIVIDENDS FROM
10s 6d INVESTMENT

By Mollie Staines

It all began on August 11, 1947. With a friend I went to Bradford Park Avenue, where Yorkshire were playing Gloucestershire. The ground was packed, and it was a glorious sunny Bowling Tide Monday. I think I fell in love with Park Avenue that day. I had already started watching league cricket at Hanging Heaton, where I played with a friend — cricket just followed on. The following winter my father offered to buy me a junior membership of Yorkshire. It was 10s.6d. He always said it was the best money he ever spent on me.

So, in May 1948 I used my ticket for the first time, again at Park Avenue, where Yorkshire were playing the Australians. We nearly beat them, too. The Australians were like gods, and the photos of film stars on my bedroom walls came down. Cricketers were real people.

I wrote to the papers quite a bit, because the Yorkshire AGM was held mid-week in a January afternoon. Few members were able to go — we all worked. I kept on writing, suggesting that a Saturday morning would be more suitable. In 1967 I collected 100 signatures on a petition to change the day and time of the AGM, and I took it to John Nash, who was Yorkshire Secretary. There was a referendum — and it worked.

In 1969, on January 27 at 12 noon the AGM took place in the Grand Hotel, Sheffield, and about 250 members attended. I have always thought that it was the best thing I ever did.

By the time the 1970s came, two members — men, of course — spoke to Mr Nash about nominating me for the Committee. First, I had to become a full member, which I duly did. On June 1, 1977, I beat the other two candidates to become the only woman ever to have been elected. Quite a day. I served for seven-and-a-half years, and it certainly was an interesting time.

Retiring in 1989 gave me much more time for cricket, and especially the Second XI, and later the Academy. One day at Harrogate **Doug Padgett** asked: "Why don't you see if you can sell some scorecards?" So I did, and I have been doing it ever since. It's putting a little back for all the pleasure cricket has given me, and all the people I have met, the friends I have made, and the wonderful places I have visited.

Not bad for a 10s 6d investment.

Schools raise £1,320

Yorkshire Schools' Cricket Association raised £1,320 through their Sunday lunch held at the Auctioneers Restaurant, Brighouse. The event was organised by David Crowther, with the assistance of Philip and Patsy Akroyd, and among those present were the association's president, Chris Hassell, and the chairman, Dr Bernard Knowles.

FUTURE IS BRIGHT FOR
TRUE-BLUE JONATHAN

By Bill Bridge

In sport — as in business, politics, the law and the church — it is not unusual for sons to follow in the footprints of their fathers, sometimes successfully, more often less so, but invariably with the unique pressure being "son of" brings. **Jonathan Bairstow**, it seems, does not do pressure.

Red hair, bright-blue eyes, a ready, infectious laugh, affection for sport of all sports and a particular aptitude for cricket — not least keeping wicket — identify the 19-year-old Bairstow as most definitely "son of" David, the Yorkshire and England wicket-keeper who so tragically took his own life in 1997.

David Bairstow joined the Yorkshire dressing-room on the day in 1970 when he rose at dawn to take an A-level examination before making his county debut against Gloucestershire in his native Bradford. His red hair and blue eyes convinced **John Hampshire**, Yorkshire's master-in-charge of nicknames, that the newcomer must have Australian connections. Hence the name "Blue" which was to stay with him for the rest of his life.

So far Jonathan has avoided the sobriquet, but he is fully aware of the impact his father made on Yorkshire cricket. "My father was a great ambassador for Club and country," he says. "Even if I get halfway to being as good as he was it will be quite some achievement. I am aware of the legacy he left behind."

That legacy includes a record of 459 first-class matches, in which he scored 13,961 runs, took 961 catches and made 137 stumpings. He played four Tests and 21 one-day internationals for England, and as a footballer he was good enough to have played with Bradford City.

Jonathan, the younger of David's two sons, has yet to play for Yorkshire's first XI, but already the drums are beating out the message that he is a talent to be nurtured, maybe even the youngster to become the prolific wicket-keeper/batsman — on the lines of Australia's **Andrew Gilchrist** and India's **Mahendra Singh Dhoni** — that England's selectors crave.

The mention of such names and aspirations brings only a dismissive wave from Jonathan. "Like every boy born and brought up in Yorkshire, I want to play for the county. I also wanted to be a footballer and a professional rugby player," he says, "but you can't set targets for yourself; that brings unnecessary pressure. I have everything in front of me; I'm happy to let things take their course."

That means working on his studies at Leeds Metropolitan University, where he is studying for a degree in sports science and performance, playing hockey for the first XI, going to the cinema with his friends, watching Leeds Carnegie play rugby, and spending time with his mother, Janet, and sister, Becky, at home in Dunnington, near York. "We have been through a lot together as a family, and we are still quite close," he says quietly, the smile for once absent.

Apart from one session when the senior squad, second team and Academy players gathered at Headingley Carnegie for a fitness check there was no post-season cricket until nets began in the New Year. Hockey filled Jonathan's sporting void, but he has grown used to going without his physical activity.

From the age of seven he was a member of Leeds United's youth programme — football genes were passed on as well as cricket — and he gave up the game only when Saturday morning school at St Peter's, York, prevented him from getting to Thorp Arch.

Similarly with rugby: he was a fly-half from the age of 11 — St Peter's do not play soccer — who earned selection for Yorkshire, and was in the school team which reached the semi-finals of an Under-15 national knockout competition. He was in the school first XV in the lower sixth, but with cricket taking on more importance he then reluctantly relinquished rugby because of the risk of injury.

"I miss it immensely," he says. "It was hard watching the guys going to train and play matches, but it had been hard giving up football; it was something that had to happen. Things took their natural course. It was always going to be cricket for me; the teachers at school did not put any pressure on me to go down that route."

Jonathan's cricket road began with selection for Leeds Under-11s, and he was spotted quickly by Yorkshire, playing in the county side through the age groups and reaching the York club's first team at the age of 15. He earned a scholarship to Yorkshire, and progressed seamlessly to the Academy; the runs flowed.

He averaged 218 in his first year in the sixth at St Peter's, and was named as *Wisden's* first Schools' Cricketer of the Year. The following season he averaged 175, and his average in five years playing for the school was 60.34 — the highest since the Second World War.

Remarkably, Jonathan's record in the sixth form did not include matches against other schools, which are played on Saturdays at St

Peter's, when he was playing with York or Yorkshire Academy. His flood of runs came against teams like the MCC, Yorkshire Gentlemen and the Saints, made up of league cricketers and including, on one occasion, brother Andrew, who plays for Pudsey Congs in the Bradford League. "I made sure he didn't get me out," he says, the smile back.

Wicket-keeping has been with him all the way through his cricket career, which began as a boy with Ouseburn, where the family lived at the time, and continued at Dunnington, where West Indian Test players **Collis King** and **Alvin Kallicharran** and Yorkshire's **Simon Kellett** were among the players.

"Keeping wicket is another string to my bow," he says. "It seems to be something I'm a natural at. My coaches at school and with Yorkshire have not pushed me into it; we have just let things develop. Yorkshire don't have a wicket-keeping coach at the moment, but **Gerard Brophy** and **Simon Guy**, the county's senior 'keepers, have been supportive. There have been little things they have passed on, but they don't try to complicate things. They tell me to keep it simple, and just enjoy it."

Jonathan last summer had the thrill of being called into Yorkshire's squad to travel to Hove for the last match of the County Championship season against Sussex, but the recovery from injury of **Anthony McGrath** meant that he did not make the XI, having to make do with time as a substitute fielder.

Now his modest sights are on establishing himself as a regular member of the Second XI, then pushing for a place in the senior side "next year or the year after. You can't put timescales on things like this. It's best just to let things flow."

There is a deceptive air of calm about Jonathan Bairstow as he relaxes away from competitive action. Then the penny drops: a midfield player as a footballer, fly-half at rugby, centre-midfield on the hockey pitch and wicket-keeper/batsmen at cricket.

"In control," he says. "I wouldn't have it any other way."

**Bill Bridge is former Sports
Editor of the *Yorkshire Post***

David's mentor dies

Laurie Bennett, who served Bradford and Yorkshire Schools for many years and was the teacher who arranged David Bairstow's early-morning A-level sitting so that he could make his debut for Yorkshire First XI at Bradford Park Avenue against Gloucestershire in 1970, has died aged 96.

THE DAZZLER MAKES
A SHINING EXIT

By David Warner

The curtain came down on **Darren Gough's** first-class career at Scarborough on September 20 — and the great showman made sure that he bowed out in style by summoning up all his energy and experience for one final, memorable burst of fast bowling.

It was also the last morning of Yorkshire's Championship match against Somerset and, with the new ball only six overs old, Darren came running in hard from the Trafalgar Square end, venom and purpose in every stride.

Bowling at full stretch, he began with a no-ball, but his next delivery to makeshift opener Craig Kieswetter plucked his off-stump clean out of the ground. There was even better to come, and a couple of hostile overs later he dismissed his old Test adversary, Justin Langer, with a ball which pitched in line with the stumps — and found the edge of the Australian left-hander's bat as he groped forward.

That turned out to be his last first-class wicket — a fitting scalp for one of Yorkshire and England's greatest personalities and one of the game's most colourful and flamboyant characters.

Darren put everything into that five-over opening burst, which brought him two wickets for 12 runs and, although he came back for a couple of spells later in the day, he could not repeat those earlier dynamics. Indeed, his last two balls of the match were struck for fours by Alfonso Thomas, but the Dazzler had given a sharp reminder of his class ,and he held his cap aloft as he was cheered off the field by each and every spectator at North Marine Road.

It all started 20 seasons ago on a damp late April day in 1989, when Darren made his first-class debut against Middlesex at Lord's. He was not known as the Dazzler in those days. He was an 18-year-old fast bowler from Barnsley who was about to be named among the first intake of youngsters at Yorkshire's new indoor academy at Bradford Park Avenue, and who was filling in at Lord's because three senior pacemen were injured.

Darren's introduction to Yorkshire cricket lasted exactly one over — because after **Paul Jarvis** had opened up with the new ball down came the rain, driving the players back into the pavilion.

Throughout his career Darren has loved to be in the limelight, and he almost claimed a wicket on the resumption with his very first ball, which came desperately close to trapping Paul Downton lbw. He did not have to wait long for his first success: his eighth delivery was again too good for Downton — who could only snick it to first slip, where **Arnie Sidebottom** pulled off an excellent catch.

Jarvis went on to steal the bowling honours with 5-77, but Gough was by no means overshadowed, and he ended up with the excellent figures of 3-44 after getting Keith Brown and Norman Cowans caught behind by **David Bairstow** in the space of eight balls.

Bairstow — whose son, Jonathan, has just signed a three-year junior professional contract with Yorkshire — held on to five catches in that innings to take him beyond the 1,066 dismissals achieved by the great Kent and England wicket-keeper, Godfrey Evans.

The rain-hit game was to fizzle out into a draw, but Darren had not finished: he picked up two more wickets in the second innings, including the formidable Mike Gatting and opener John Carr. Match figures of 5-85 were an early indication that Darren had it in him to become a fine cricketer, but few could have imagined that he would develop into one of England's biggest heroes and one of cricket's all-time superstars.

A back injury — possibly caused by putting everything into his young frame at Lord's — meant that not much was heard of Darren again that season, and his only other first-team appearance was against Warwickshire at Headingley in late August, when he accounted for the visitors' skipper and opening batsman, Andy Lloyd.

His progress after that remained steady for a while, but he still managed to pick up 28 first-class wickets for Yorkshire the following season, Gatting again falling victim when Darren collected six wickets in the match with Middlesex at Headingley.

Darren's real turning point came in 1993 with an electrifying performance against Somerset at Taunton to convince everyone that here was a dynamic fast bowler on his way to the very top. Yorkshire's overseas player at the time, former West Indies captain **Ritchie Richardson**, instilled into Darren the belief that he was a good enough bowler to unsettle and destroy any batsman, no matter what his reputation.

In the first innings he rattled Somerset with 3-54, but in the second he annihilated them with a superb display of fast bowling which brought his Championship-best figures of 7-42, sweeping Yorkshire to victory by 48 runs in a hard-fought encounter which they would not have come anywhere near to winning without his monumental contribution.

Darren continued his rise to fame — and when his England debut came against New Zealand at Old Trafford in 1995 he announced himself by taking a wicket with his sixth ball, as he also went on to do in his first one-day international.

There have been so many highlights for county and country that it is impossible to name them all, but he claimed a hat-trick for Yorkshire against Kent at Headingley in 1995 — when he took four wickets in five balls — and then a hat-trick for England against Australia at Sydney on the 1998-99 tour.

Darren bagged five or more wickets in an innings on nine occasions for England and 17 for Yorkshire, and his 229 Test wickets place him ninth in the list of England's top wicket-takers of all time. In one-day internationals he leads the way among England bowlers with 235.

At county level statistics alone will not show Darren to be among the White Rose elite, because he played in far fewer matches than his predecessors , and his 453 first-class wickets for Yorkshire left him 47 short of joining the 30-strong "500 Club".

Yet with 855 first-class wickets at 27.15 runs apiece and 833 in List A games and one-day internationals, Darren is entitled to put his aching feet up for a while if he wishes. You can bet your bottom dollar, however, that this larger-than-life character will continue to make his presence felt — either in the commentary box or on the dance floor...or doing whatever else he takes a shine to.

DARREN GOUGH

FIRST-CLASS CRICKET FOR YORKSHIRE 1989 TO 2008

Debut: Yorkshire v. Middlesex at Lord's 20 April 1989

Last Match (last day): Yorkshire v. Somerset at Scarborough 20 September 2008

Capped 9 September 1993   Captain 2007-8

BATTING AND FIELDING

Season	M	I	NO	Runs	HS	Avge	100s	50s	Ct
1989	2	2	1	11	9	5.50	0	0	0
1990	14	17	6	123	24	11.18	0	0	1
1991	13	14	3	307	72	27.90	0	2	3
1991/92	1	2	0	19	15	9.50	0	0	1
1992	11	12	4	72	22*	9.00	0	0	3
1992/93	1	2	1	18	16*	18.00	0	0	0
1993	16	24	3	248	39	11.80	0	0	3
1994	9	14	1	209	54	16.07	0	1	1
1995	11	13	1	259	60	21.58	0	1	4
1996	16	25	3	501	121	22.77	1	2	6
1997	8	10	1	179	58	19.88	0	1	0
1998	6	7	0	207	89	29.57	0	2	1
1999	3	5	1	66	33	16.50	0	0	0
2000	3	2	0	28	23	14.00	0	0	1
2001	2	3	1	109	96	54.50	0	1	0
2002	1	Did not bat							
2003	7	10	1	199	83	22.11	0	2	1
2007	14	15	1	219	50	15.64	0	1	2
2008	8	11	1	148	34	14.80	0	0	4
Totals	**146**	**188**	**29**	**2922**	**121**	**18.37**	**1**	**13**	**31**

Century (1)

121   v. Warwickshire at Leeds, 1996

Fifties (13)

96   v. Lancashire at Leeds, 2001
89   v Somerset at Leeds, 1998
83   v Somerset at Leeds, 2003
72   v Northamptonshire at Northampton, 1991
72   v Hampshire at Southampton (Rose Bowl), 2003
60* v Lancashire at Scarborough, 1991
60   v Kent at Leeds, 1995
58   v Kent at Leeds, 1997
58   v Northamptonshire at Northampton, 1998
54   v Glamorgan at Cardiff, 1994
51   v Somerset at Scarborough, 1996
50   v Leicestershire at Bradford, 1996
50   v Durham at Leeds, 2007

BOWLING

Season	Overs	Mdns	Runs	Wkts	Avge	Best	5wI	10wM
1989	65	13	173	6	28.83	3-44	0	0
1990	279.4	49	1037	28	37.03	4-68	0	0
1991	270	55	945	18	52.50	5-41	1	0
1991/92	18	5	40	2	20.00	1-20	0	0
1992	255.1	53	910	25	36.40	4-43	0	0
1992/93	26	8	66	2	33.00	1-18	0	0
1993	507.3	115	1517	57	26.61	7-42	3	1
1994	309	72	960	45	21.33	6-66	3	0
1995	344.5	83	1110	45	24.66	7-28	1	1
1996	573.3	142	1535	67	22.91	6-36	2	0
1997	192.4	43	638	27	23.62	5-56	2	0
1998	179.4	34	577	23	25.08	5-36	1	0
1999	96.5	20	319	17	18.76	4-27	0	0
2000	100.5	22	245	16	15.21	6-63	1	0
2001	88	18	275	8	34.37	4-65	0	0
2002	19	3	85	2	42.50	2-85	0	0
2003	218.1	46	651	19	34.26	3-40	0	0
2007	287.4	74	876	37	23.67	6-47	3	0
2008	149	25	528	9	58.66	2-34	0	0
Totals	**3980.3**	**880**	**12487**	**453**	**27.56**	**7-28**	**17**	**2**

10 Wickets in a Match (2)

10 for 96 (3 for 54 and 7 for 42)   v Somerset at Taunton, 1993
10 for 80 (3 for 52 and 7 for 28)   v Lancashire at Leeds, 1995 (non-championship)

5 Wickets in an Innings (17)

7 for 28   v Lancashire at Leeds, 1995 (non-championship)
7 for 42   v Somerset at Taunton, 1993
6 for 36   v Nottinghamshire at Scarborough, 1996
6 for 47   v Kent at Tunbridge Wells, 2007
6 for 50   v Surrey at Leeds, 2007
6 for 63   v Durham at Chester-le-Street, 2000
6 for 66   v Surrey at Scarborough, 1994
6 for 70   v Hampshire at Leeds, 1994
5 for 36   v Surrey at Middlesbrough, 1996
5 for 36   v Worcestershire at Worcester, 1998
5 for 41   v Lancashire at Scarborough, 1991
5 for 50   v Hampshire at Southampton, 1993
5 for 52   v Warwickshire at Scarborough, 2007
5 for 56   v Glamorgan at Leeds, 1997
5 for 74   v Essex at Ilford, 1997
5 for 75   v Lancashire at Manchester, 1994 (non-championship)
5 for 79   v Durham at Leeds, 1993

Four Wickets in Five Balls
(including the Hat-Trick)

v Kent at Leeds, 1995

R D W

MARK LAWSON experienced some difficult times, both on and off the field, before Yorkshire reluctantly released him towards the end of the season.

It was felt that his opportunities would be severely limited with the development of other spin bowlers like **Adil Rashid**, **David Wainwright**, **Azeem Rafiq** and **James Finch**.

It was a sad end to what had promised to be a glittering career with Yorkshire for the cricketer, now 23, who only two years earlier had created such excitement when he shared the attack with Rashid, the only time in the Club's history that two genuine leg-spinners had bowled in tandem.

Together, they fired out Middlesex in their second innings at Scarborough, Mark claiming the lion's share with 6-88, and he ended that summer with 26 Championship wickets, one more than his partner. While the younger Rashid

MARK LAWSON
Pastures new

continued to flourish, Mark was less successful and, with his confidence affected, he began to fade out of the spotlight. Nevertheless, he can be extremely proud of a career which saw him capture 42 Championship wickets in 15 matches, including two six-wicket and two five-wicket hauls, a start few others have equalled.

Mark joined Derbyshire late last season, but on his debut he broke a finger before he could get on to bowl. Derbyshire have registered him for 2009, and all Yorkshire fans will hope that his luck changes and that he can rebuild his first-class career.

CHRIS ALLINSON, from Guisborough, who was one of Yorkshire's brightest young batting prospects, has left the Academy to take up an apprenticeship with an engineering company concerned with off-shore activities in the oil industry. Chris, 18, marked his Yorkshire Seconds debut in 2006 by scoring 127 and 72 not out against Somerset at Taunton, and he represented England Under-19s. He will continue his cricket this season as the English professional for Marske in the North Yorkshire and South Durham League.

ACTOR RETURNED SAME FIGURES AS FIERY FRED

By David Warner

Whenever Duncan Preston is not down on the farm in top TV soap *Emmerdale* during the summer you can put money on him being either at a Yorkshire match or getting as clued up on the score as he can.

Acting is in the blood of TV and theatre star Duncan — who became a household name through his memorable portrayals in such Victoria Wood classics as *Dinnerladies* and *Acorn Antiques*.

But, being a Bradford lad, born and bred, Duncan's other passion is cricket. He is a loyal and devoted Yorkshire CCC member who considers it a privilege to have become a close friend to so many of the players.

Duncan marvelled at the exuberance and never-say-die attitude of **Darren Gough**, but now that he has ridden off into the sunset the actor could not be more delighted that the captaincy has been passed to fellow Bradfordian **Anthony McGrath**, who lives at Menston, where Duncan also has a place.

The husband of actress Susan Penhaligon, Duncan was born in 1946 at 5 Musgrave Road, Eccleshill, and was a pupil at Wellington Road Infants and Junior School before going on to Bradford Grammar School — where he soon gained a place in the Under-13s team with his left-arm fast bowling.

"I remember getting wickets with my first two deliveries in my first match, and I thought, 'Bloody hell, this is easy'," grinned Duncan as he recalled the moment with obvious pleasure. "I finished up with four wickets for six runs, and in my next game I weighed in with 5-27. I always followed Yorkshire's scores very closely, and I looked in the paper and saw that **Fred Trueman** had also taken 5-27. I wrote and told him that I had also done it on the same day! I didn't get a reply, but as a cricket-mad 12-year-old I was just glad to let him know."

As well as playing for the school Duncan went to watch Yorkshire whenever he could with his elder brother, Martin: "He took me to Bradford Park Avenue a lot, and we used to sit on the rows of wooden seats at the Horton Park end. We also went to Headingley, but it was Park Avenue that I really loved—and still do, to this day.

DUNCAN PRESTON
Emmerdale and cricket

"There · was such a fantastic atmosphere. I remember watching Fred Trueman one day, and when he ran in to bowl he stood on the umpire's foot, and the umpire went hopping up and down. I think it was Frank Chester, but I am not too sure.

"I also have fond boyhood memories of going to the Scarborough Cricket Festival and seeking autographs at the marquee, where the players went for lunch. One day, **Tom Graveney** was walking on to the field after the interval, and as he passed me on the boundary edge he said, 'Will you go and stand at mid-on?' 'No, no, no,' I said, and he just laughed. Tom was only joking, but I was terrified!"

Duncan also turned out for Undercliffe Juniors, and it was while he was there that someone invited him to join Bradford. What persuaded him was the fact that they played at Park Avenue. He was 16 or 17 at the time and playing for Bradford Seconds when something happened which could have seen him in later years starring in *Neighbours* rather than *Emmerdale*!

"My friend, Mick Harrison, who was a really fast bowler and played for Yorkshire Schools, was at Bradford as well, and there was an Aussie called Barry Stegal, who had come over from Victoria to study the wool industry. Barry asked us if we would care to emigrate to Australia and shear sheep on his father's farm, and we said, 'Why not'?

"The assisted-passage scheme was still running, and we paid our £10 and were accepted. At this time I had started doing amateur dramatics at the Bradford Playhouse, and I had gone to audition in

London for the Royal Academy of Dramatic Art (RADA). It was the biggest surprise of my life when they wrote and said I had got in, so I decided to stay at home and make acting my career.

"Mick went, and I think he may still be in Australia but I have lost touch. He was a genuine fast bowler who frightened batsmen to death. He modelled himself on his hero, Fred Trueman, and when he went in to bat he would only hit fours and sixes. He never ran."

While he was with Bradford there was an occasion when Duncan was summoned to bowl to **Geoff Boycott**: "Geoff had been out of the England side through injury, and Bradford groundsman Ron Healey asked teammate Guy Clifford and me if we would come to Park Avenue on a Monday lunchtime to bowl at the great man in the nets. I had a job at the Halifax Building Society, and should have been working, but it was the opportunity of a lifetime.

"I knew I could not miss it, and took the day off work. The third ball I sent down he drove back, and I caught it. I could hardly believe it, but Geoff couldn't have been nicer. He even coached both of us, and was really helpful."

Duncan's main home is in London, where he went after drama school, and he played "friendly, but serious" Sunday afternoon cricket there for a while. He also became involved with an actors' team led by the late William Franklyn — the Schweppes *You Know Who* man — and it was through this that he became well acquainted with Yorkshire players.

"Bill was taking a celebrity team to Acklam Park, Middlesbrough, to play against a Yorkshire side in what I think was a benefit match for one of the players," Duncan said. "Our side included the likes of film director Sam Mendes and actors Robin Asquith and the late Jeremy Sinden, son of Sir Donald Sinden.

"I immediately hit it off with **Phil Carrick**, and we became such close friends that he used to stay with me whenever Yorkshire were in London. I remember that a young Darren Gough was at that first match. Phil pointed to him, and said, 'That lad will go on to play for England one day if he has his head screwed on the right way'.

"Phil was spot on, and I later played golf with Goughie in the Celebrity Masters at Wentworth. He has always been an upbeat guy, and the sort of person who in five minutes after you have met him makes you feel better than five minutes before making his acquaintance. I was quite surprised that so many members of the Yorkshire team who had been my heroes turned out to be quite ordinary blokes, and we got on really well together.

"I went on all sorts of jaunts with Phil, and I loved to hear him talk about the great players such as **Viv Richards**, **Michael Holding** and **Brian Lara**. And when **Sachin Tendulkar** joined Yorkshire, Phil introduced me to him at Canterbury."

It was Carrick who suggested to Duncan that he join Yorkshire and their keenest supporters on the 1992 pre-season tour to South Africa, when they were the first sporting side to visit the country since the ending of apartheid. Duncan had a marvellous time, and his only regret was that he had to return to England just before the official end of the tour to do a TV commercial.

"There was plenty happening out there, and as well as the country's referendum on a free vote it was the time that Yorkshire learned that injury would prevent Australian **Craig McDermott** from becoming their first overseas player. They began negotiations while in Cape Town for Sachin Tendulkar instead."

Duncan is sorry that Gough has finally had to hang up his boots, but he could not be happier that the new man in charge is **Anthony McGrath**: "Maggs has six years' more experience than when he first did the job for a season, and I am certain he will have learned a lot. He's a fantastic batsman, and I am sure that with him and **Martyn Moxon** working closely together Yorkshire will be in good hands."

Steyn leaves his mark

The top 10 wicket-takers in Test matches in 2008 were: D W Steyn (South Africa, 74 dismissals), M G Johnson (Australia, 63), Harbhajan Singh (India, 63), B Lee (Australia, 57), D L Vettori (New Zealand, 54), M Ntini (South Africa, 54), R J Sidebottom (England, 47), J M Anderson (England, 46), M Morkel (South Africa, 43), M Muralitharan (Sri Lanka, 42).

FROM MEMORABILIA TO ILKLEY MOOR BAHT 'AT

By David Hall

The Archives Committee continues to be active on many fronts — and is now starting work in preparation for the opening of the museum at Headingley Carnegie. Completion of the new pavilion will release office space in the East Stand for a visitor reception and museum.

Design contractors have been approached to make proposals for our consideration, and Club directors and Committee members have visited sporting museums to gather ideas. Subject to the space becoming available it is planned to open the facility during the 2010 season. We propose to run ground tours from the museum, and pilot tours have been successfully undertaken to develop our skills in operating these tours.

The Long Room cabinets will feature the 1959 County Championship side and some new bat displays. It is unfortunate that last year's feature on Len Hutton to mark the 70th anniversary of his 364 Test record was marred by the loss of a memorabilia item loaned by the Hutton family. It would be appreciated if members would report any signs of the display cabinets being tampered with.

Among the many items donated to the Archives Committee during the year was a bat that belonged to the Rev E S Carter — who played for Yorkshire between 1876 and 1881, and was responsible for introducing **Lord Hawke** to Yorkshire cricket. Carter, it is said — although he always denied this — was the cricketing cleric who announced on Sunday mornings from the pulpit: "Here endeth the first innings."

Last year we filmed another collection of DVDs recording the career experiences of Yorkshire cricketers. This time they featured **Don Wilson**, **Ken Taylor**, **Bryan Stott**, **Dickie Bird**, **Fred Trueman** and Len Hutton — the last two being possible through the courtesy of the BBC making material available to us, to which we have added interviews with those who played and knew them. These will be available during the season from the club shop.

For every four-day game, Roy Wilkinson and Nigel Pullan will once again produce a brief history and "stat" details of previous encounters with the opposition. These appear on noticeboards in the Long Room and in boxes. We hope this Archives Committee initiative is appreciated by members and visitors.

Memorabilia Inventory work continues to provide more detailed data on the items we hold, and the overseeing of this substantial task is being undertaken by Ron Deaton with the assistance of Committee members.

Ron's considerable knowledge of the subject matter is proving invaluable. This is an ongoing operation taking many hours, week in and week out, with new items arriving and the compilation of displays featuring archival material being rotated at Headingley, Bramall Lane and Skipton Museum creating a constant "in and out" scenario.

Last year we renovated the Club's first minute book that had become dilapidated. This work was undertaken by West Yorkshire Archive Services at considerable cost, which was met by a generous donation

TICKER'S CABINET: Andrew Mitchell, grandson of Yorkshire and England's Arthur "Ticker" Mitchell, stands proudly before a glass case full of items the family loaned for Long Room display in 2008.
(Photo: VAUGHN RIDLEY.)

from Veronica Trueman in memory of Fred. The committee has recently applied to Leeds Civic Trust to install a *Blue Plaque* on the house at Welton Grove, Burley, which was the birthplace of **Hedley Verity**. We hope to have this in place during 2009.

The Club receives numerous inquiries regarding players and the Club's history, which the Archives Committee handles. Some require considerable research, while others seek non-cricket information such as the full verses of Ilkley Moor Baht 'at!

We are extremely fortunate in having a team of committee members who give considerable time, energy and expertise in bringing the numerous projects we undertake to fruition, for which I am most appreciative.

SIR LEN'S PORTRAIT
MOVES BACK HOME

By David Warner

A famous portrait of **Sir Leonard Hutton** was unveiled in the executive suite of the old pavilion at Headingley Carnegie Cricket Ground early last season by his elder son, **Richard Hutton**.

The portrait, owned by Richard and his brother, John, was painted after England's 1950-51 tour of Australia, and has hung in the Long Room at Lord's. Richard and John gave permission for it to be loaned to Yorkshire to mark the 70th anniversary of Sir Leonard's record-breaking 364 against Australia at The Oval.

Yorkshire County Cricket Club Archives Committee also acknowledged Len's splendid achievement by staging an exhibition of Hutton memorabilia in the Headingley Carnegie Long Room throughout the season.

John Hutton also attended the ceremony along with his son, Robert, and Richard's son, Olly. Unveiling the portrait, Richard said it had been commissioned by the *Yorkshire Evening News*, and subscriptions came in from all parts of the county, the names of the subscribers being contained in a book which was now also at Headingley.

The painting had taken pride of place in the Long Room at Lord's following his father's death in 1990 until refurbishment had taken place, when it had been demoted to the bar.

Richard was introduced by Archives Committee chairman David Hall, who said that Yorkshire were extremely fortunate to have persuaded Richard and John to release the portrait of their father from Lord's, and to allow it to be hung at Headingley Carnegie.

*When Yorkshire Archives Committee member Ron Deaton was looking through the book of subscribers' names he spotted that among them was Mollie Staines, who in 2008 was a joint winner of the new President's Medal for outstanding services to Yorkshire cricket.

OUTRAGEOUSLY RUDE
WARM AND GENEROUS

By Martin Howe

On April 12, 2008, at a ceremony at Westoe Rugby Club, County Durham, a plaque was unveiled to the memory of one of the club's members.

It reads: "Alec Coxon (1916-2006). England Cricketer. Westoe Stalwart. His Own Man."

The esteem in which Alec Coxon was held in the North East may be a surprise to those familiar only with his first-class cricket career.

A hostile and whole-hearted fast-medium bowler, Coxon served Yorkshire well in the five seasons after the Second World War, when the main weight of opening the attack fell on his shoulders.

He took 473 wickets in his first-class career at 20.91, and played some

ALEX COXON
His own man

valuable innings for the county. Coxon won one England cap, against Australia in the 1948 Lord's Test, but after the 1950 season — his most successful when he took 131 wickets at 18.60 — Yorkshire dispensed with his services.

Although 34 years old, Coxon was fit and strong, and could have continued to play at the highest level for several more years. To most followers of the game, his departure was a surprise. Yorkshire may have reasoned that with **Bob Appleyard** and **Fred Trueman** now firmly established in the side, they could do without the more senior man.

Coxon joined Sunderland in 1951 as a professional after some coaching in Rhodesia. He took the Durham Senior League by storm — in eight seasons he took 753 wickets at 8.37 and scored 3,764 runs at an average of 34.21. Between 1951 and 1954 Coxon appeared 29 times for Durham in the Minor Counties Championship, taking 127 wickets and scoring 1,047 runs, with two centuries. After leaving Sunderland he had six successful seasons with South Shields, taking 443 wickets at 10.28 and scoring 2,663 runs at 23.63. When South Shields decided not to renew his contract on grounds of age he played for Wearmouth and then Bolden with undiminished enthusiasm until after his 50th birthday.

Coxon opened a cricket school when he finally retired, and later, at the age of 76, he was persuaded to return to South Shields to coach youngsters. The club shares a ground with Westoe Rugby Club, and it was here that Alec developed a passion for rugby football. He was an enthusiastic supporter and a regular spectator at Westoe's matches until the end of his life.

History records that Alec Coxon was a prickly character with a fiery temperament and a harsh manner, ever ready to call a spade a bloody shovel. He had no time for "fancy-dandies". It was rumoured that he had punched **Denis Compton**, the blue-eyed boy of English cricket, in the dressing room at Lord's.

His cricket career, before and after his departure from Yorkshire, was punctuated with brushes with authority. As *Wisden* put it, "he held very high rank in the awkward squad." Combative on the field and in the dressing room, there was another side to him, however, a side revealed only when he settled in the North East, from where his father had moved to Huddersfield before the First World War in search of work.

Coxon's family came first in all things, but after them he revelled in the company of his cricket and rugby chums. He was a man of conflicting moods, who could be outrageously rude, but to those with whom he readily empathised Coxon was a warm and generous friend.

Alec was a great storyteller: he liked to be the centre of attraction, and to hold forth, over a pint or two of beer, about cricket, rugby, politics or life in general. He deplored the permissiveness, lack of discipline and respect for others that he saw in contemporary society. Despite his working-class background Alec was an unashamed fan of Margaret Thatcher. In the cliché, he was a larger-than-life character.

Throughout his life Alec refused to be interviewed on, or to speak about, his first-class career, and since his death his family have faithfully respected his wish that they, too, should remain silent. But in reminiscing with his friends, he did throw light on the story that he had punched Compton and on the reasons for his departure from Yorkshire at the end of the 1950 season.

For Coxon, the Lord's Test started well. He had Barnes caught for a duck in his first over, almost bowled Bradman, and then had a confident lbw appeal against him turned down. Thereafter things went less well for England and for Coxon. No doubt, there was chuntering on the field and harsh words in the dressing room. The story that Coxon had raised a fist to Compton was born, though neither party, nor any likely dressing-room witness, would comment.

In an obituary Clive Crickmer says Coxon told him: "It simply didn't happen. The truth is that we had a difference of opinion and exchanged a few heated words during a drinks break on the field in a festival game. Denis was a very good batsman who made up his own shots, but I can't say I liked him. He had fancy ideas about his own importance. He needed to keep his feet on the ground, and I believe now what I told him that day: that he'd have been all right if he'd been born a Yorkshireman."

Tact was never a strong point with Alec Coxon! The match in question was at Kingston-on-Thames between an England XI, captained by Compton, and a Commonwealth XI, starting August 30, 1950. We do not know the cause of the "few heated words", but it was probably something to do with Compton's captaincy.

As to the ending of Coxon's career with Yorkshire, he indignantly denied that the Committee had sacked him. According to Crickmer, Coxon was disillusioned after his successful season — during which he had been called into the party for the final Test against West Indies as cover for **Trevor Bailey** — at being passed over for the MCC tour of Australia in 1950/51.

Captained by **Freddie Brown**, very much a Lord's establishment man, the tour party included only three new ball bowlers: **Alec Bedser**, Bailey and the uncapped Cambridge captain, **John Warr**. Not without ambition to play again for England, Coxon perhaps had reason to believe that "his face did not fit" at Lord's as at Headingley.

Although he had the compensation of an offer of a salary of £1,000 — a considerable sum in 1950 — to play for Sunderland, if Coxon felt slighted by Warr's selection it would be quite in character for him to walk away from first-class cricket. If this was bloody-mindedness, it was not to be the only example. When in 1959 Sunderland appointed **Ken Biddulph**, of Somerset, as first-team coach without consulting him, Coxon abruptly left the club, declaring he would never set foot in the ground again, and joined their Durham rivals, South Shields.

On his 90th birthday Coxon received a letter of congratulation from Yorkshire. "It means they know I'll soon be dead," he muttered. Alec Coxon always had the last word. He died four weeks later on January 22, 2006.

* This article draws on the writer's longer feature: *Alec Coxon — A Doughty Cricketer, Journal of the Cricket Society, Autumn 2008*, which benefited from obituaries in *Wisden Cricket Monthly* and *The South Shields Gazette* by Clive Crickmer, and from subsequent conversations with him.

TIME TO PLANT OUT MORE
OF THE HOMEGROWN

By Stephen Mann

It is the tea interval on the final day of a County Championship match. The sun, as it has for each of the four days, continues to beat down on the still sizeable crowd.

The match itself is delicately poised, all results still possible. Without exception the spectators agree that thus far it has been a splendid contest, a fine advert for the county game.

"Who needs *Twenty20*?" is the frequently repeated question.

Yet that strange phenomenon, acute pessimism, continues to grip the scene. What a pessimistic lot we followers of the county game are, for each group of supporters feels their side has let the initiative slip in favour of the opponents. From tea break perambulations — or is it a trudge — come the mutterings "thrown it away again" and "snatching defeat from the jaws of victory".

This is, of course, the County Ground, Taunton, in early June 2008, Somerset against Yorkshire in the Championship — a match that witnessed that rarity in another damp summer of four days of uninterrupted play. How delightful to see the covers only at the close of the day.

When **Tim Bresnan** bowled Andy Caddick with little time or overs remaining it sealed a splendid 40-run win for Yorkshire, and concluded a match that had all that is best about the game played in whites. The 21 points for the win were most welcome to Yorkshire — and saw the county head the Championship table as the fixture list determined that it was to be the mid-season break, and the *Twenty20* circus was upon us.

This was a notable victory for a number of reasons. Perhaps the most pleasing aspect was that the Yorkshire side contained nine players who had come through the Academy, no overseas player and just **Jacques Rudolph** as a Kolpak signing. The average age was below 25. How nice it was to hear the Somerset supporters commenting in such favourable terms — and wishing they, also, had a team dominated by homegrown players, not by those from the southern hemisphere.

The question remains as to why so many of the traits so in evidence in this Taunton win were missing for a large part of the season. Why did we not see the leadership on the field, the personal and collective application, team spirit, tight bowling and gritty batting? Where did it go?

At Taunton the batting promised much, with Rudolph crafting a marvellous 155 before a collapse from 315-3 to 372 all out that did not signal a rapid decline to defeat as it was to do on so many other occasions.

**STEPHEN MANN
Players must take
their chances**

From 341-2 to 410 all out at Canterbury is one such collapse that is proving difficult to forget. A gritty second innings 51 from **Richard Pyrah** did much to ensure the setting of a challenging second-innings target for Somerset. Coming in at a crisis score of 104-6 Richard battled through to be ninth out at 202.

Taking 20 wickets at Taunton is never easy, but thanks to some splendid bowling all round — in particular **Steven Patterson**, Yorkshire rose to the challenge in the field. For this observer Patterson was the man of the match: his 3-19 off 12 tight overs in the Somerset first innings was a tremendous effort. His wickets included Trescothick and de Bruyn, followed by Langer, and the stand-breaking capture of Kieswetter in the second innings — this last when the game really was slipping away.

As **George Hirst** once said of a colleague's bowling: They were proper wickets because they were proper batsmen." It is a pity and surprising after such a performance that opportunities for Patterson were to be so limited in the balance of the season.

As the joyful Yorkshire supporters headed north up the M5 who among them would have thought that they had witnessed the last Championship victory of the summer?

A final tally of only two Championship victories compares to that dreadful relegation season of 2002. Since promotion back to the First Division in 2005 only nine victories have been gathered in 48

Championship matches, disappointing statistics. Supporters were left with the winter months to ponder how a team that can amass the highest number of batting points and one of the better bowling hauls could have been so perilously close to relegation.

That prospect of relegation hung ominously over the team as they approached the last match at Hove — a far cry from the final game of 1959 on the same ground when victory achieved in such thrilling fashion saw the Championship return to the broad acres. By the close on a first day restricted by rain and bad light Yorkshire seemed all but doomed to the Second Division as they walked off at 84-6 and much-needed batting points only for the wishful thinkers.

However, this was the same team who had played at Taunton, and they had not been together as an XI since.

What a difference a day makes: 24 hours later Sussex were 25-3, replying to Yorkshire's 400-9 declared. As at Taunton, youth rode to the rescue. Bresnan and **Adil Rashid** began the rebuilding process — and then Rashid and **David Wainwright** put together a stand of 140 for the ninth wicket. Rashid hit a career-best 111 before his partner in the heroics was joined by a doughty-looking **Matthew Hoggard**.

The last pair took Yorkshire to 400 — and to the so welcome fifth batting point, at which juncture **Anthony McGrath** declared. An unbeaten 10th-wicket stand of 82 saw Wainwright finish with a career-best 104 not out, a truly magnificent effort, and Hoggard 28 not out.

Wainwright was not finished — he took 3-9 as Sussex were tumbled out for 207, and were asked to follow on: this they did with greater application, and the match finally petered out to a draw to the satisfaction of both teams as First Division cricket was assured for 2009. Wainwright became yet another man of the match who found first-team opportunities frustratingly limited.

The evidence of Taunton and Hove is clearly that the talent is in the Yorkshire ranks. Opportunity needs to be provided, but it must then be grasped by the player with both hands. The Yorkshire history is littered with talent that has promised much and ultimately disappointed.

If personal application and good cricket thinking can be allied to that homegrown talent the future promises many more days like those experienced at Taunton and Hove in the summer of 2008.

**Stephen Mann is Chairman
of Yorkshire County Cricket Club
Members' Liaison Committee**

FUND-RAISING DINNER
HAILED BIG SUCCESS

By David Warner

Yorkshire Players' Association has continued to thrive since it was formed in 2005, and last year proved to be its most successful yet.

It was decided, not without some trepidation, to stage a dinner at Headingley Carnegie with the purpose of raising funds so that the Association could support fitting cricket projects around the county. Once their committee had agreed to go ahead with the dinner, chairman **Bryan Stott** and secretary **Geoff Cope** worked tirelessly on the arrangements, and the date was fixed for October 15.

Any fears that the event might fall short of expectations were quickly dispelled — and the dinner proved so successful that it was agreed to stage another one this year. The association was able to establish a fund of at least £6,000, a figure which everyone considered quite incredible.

Guest speakers were impressionist Kevin Connelly and local comedian, Billy Bean, who both had the diners doubled up with laughter, while Master of Ceremonies **Mike Cowan**, the former Yorkshire left-arm pace bowler, and Association president **Don Wilson** added to the occasion with fine speeches.

The Association were particularly grateful to their main sponsor, Philip Hodson and Oval Insurance, whose generous support meant so much throughout the year.

One of the Association's chief aims is to go on expanding its membership — with young and old Yorkshire cricketers equally welcome. If some of the younger former players who have not yet joined feel that there is an age gap it should be bridged easily this year with the election as president of **Martyn Moxon**, the former Yorkshire captain and currently the Club's Director of Professional Cricket.

Martyn, who has always been a most popular figure at Headingley, will do everything he can in 2009 to make everyone in the association feel very much at home. There are about 50 former players who are eligible to join but have not yet done so, and Bryan and Geoff would be delighted to hear from them.

The Association's first social event of 2009 was the winter lunch at Fulford Golf Club, while the summer reunion lunch and annual golf events — plus the dinner — are expected to prove as popular as ever.

DESPAIR AND ELATION
IN UNBEATEN CENTURY

By Anthony Bradbury

Previous articles in the *Yearbook* have outlined the history of Yorkshire County Cricket Club's Southern Group, which was founded in 1980 to give a focal point to Yorkshire supporters living in Southern England — or abroad — who had little opportunity to visit Headingley Carnegie or the other home grounds. These supporters are widely spread and, although the group holds two events in London each year, the glue that holds its membership together comes from the quarterly *Southern Group Newsletter* that in 2008 reached its 100th issue.

The *Newsletter* started in March 1984 with typed, and then duplicated, foolscap pages stapled together in the upper left-hand corner. Now, and with welcome sponsorship from Yorkshire Tea, it has graduated to a compact publication which in the latest issue ran to 32 pages with an extra four of coloured photographs.

Many of the photographs arise from the enthusiastic photography of David Hirst, a founder member, and the whole publication is put together under the splendid editorial direction of John Harrison, another founder member. It was fitting that as **Adil Rashid** and **David Wainwright** saved the Yorkshire 2008 season with wonderful centuries at Hove a picture of them together should adorn the front cover of the 100th issue — with Rashid wearing his recently acquired Yorkshire full cap and sweater.

The two summer issues each year feature strongly *The Bosi File*, comprehensive and challenging descriptions of each Yorkshire First XI Championship match. Andrew Bosi has remarkable enthusiasm for Yorkshire cricket: though he lives in London he endeavours from his position behind the bowler's arm to watch almost every ball of every match — and he has unrivalled recall of the performances of vast numbers of Yorkshire cricketers, not just statistically, but in the manner of their making runs or taking wickets.

His articles are rarely the straightforward impartial accounts one might read every year in *Wisden:* his partisanship for the Yorkshire side — often despair, sometimes elation — stands forth in the writing. Here are his opening lines about the wonderful victory which a young

SECOND TIME AROUND: Adil Rashid retains Southern Group's Neil Lloyd Young Cricketer of the Year Award for another season, but for the first time chairman Peter Nutting, left, and committee member David Hirst add a cheque for £250 to the silver salver in this presentation at Headingley Carnegie.

Yorkshire team achieved at Taunton in June 2008: "Next time your sanity is questioned as the fifth pullover and second scarf make no impact, and the umpires seem happy to collude with players' unwillingness to entertain, remember this game. You might wait 20 years to see anything as gripping, but it serves as a reminder that cricket at its best has no equal as a spectator sport."

Andrew will always assume that his readers are well versed in the topography and features of all grounds upon which Yorkshire play, so some of his statements demand further inquiry: when he wrote of this same match that on the fourth day "even the cinema seats with restricted views were occupied by people rather than bags" the reader needs to be aware than at Taunton one stand is full of comfortable armchairs removed from a now closed Somerset cinema. Such information adds to the joy of the reading, and provides a veneer to *Southern Group News* not to be seen elsewhere.

Southern Group members occasionally have the pleasure of meeting in a marquee and enjoying a hospitable lunch, and subsequent reporting may make it plain that the chip butty is not always their chosen food. In a piece of rare writing by Southern Group founder Ernie Taylor about the 1987 game in Glamorgan he wrote of the pleasures in and around the match of indulging in "roast beef and Yorkshire pudding, complemented by Chateau Meaume and Cotes du Rhone". Lunch at Waldo's Positano Italian Pasta and Pizzeria comprising "proscutto melone, lasgne verde and a bottle of 1981 Barolo ensured that we would not be too unhappy in the afternoon." The only reference to a match result was an expression of satisfaction in missing "Tuesday's shambles".

The Southern Group newsletter retains its serious side. Historical analysis and research, not always found elsewhere, have a prominent place. Martin Howe often gives readers an early chance to read articles that may be printed later in fuller form elsewhere, or which remain exclusive to the *Newsletter*. Thus there have been features in recent years on the first President of Yorkshire, T R Barker, and on the players **Cecil Tyson**, **Rockley Wilson**, **Geoffrey Wilson**, and **Harry Halliday**.

Others have written on a variety of subjects — with such recent samples as the London burial place of **W H Woolhouse**, an early Yorkshire administrator and player, Yorkshire's matches as Champion County against the Rest of England, the Hutton family, **Gerald Smithson** — the miner who went from the Yorkshire side to the England team in 1947-8 — and a poignant story of Neil Lloyd, the schoolboy genius who died so young, and after whom the Southern Group name their Young Cricketer of the Year Award. Book reviews have a definite place within the Newsletter, and those cricket books with a specific Yorkshire content nearly always receive welcome publicity.

Southern Group News has in its quarter-century of publication reflected the changing face of cricket as a spectator sport. In 1984 David Wood, then secretary, wrote: "During the season we will have our usual spot at Canterbury opposite the pavilion and a marquee at Bournemouth. We will also have a meeting point at the games at Taunton, Tunbridge Wells, Basingstoke, Northampton, Luton, Lord's The Oval, and Hove. Look out for the SG flag, which we hope will be flying from a new portable flagpole."

Yorkshire will never play again at Bournemouth or Luton — and the holder of a flagpole trying to get into Lord's or The Oval might be charged with possession of an offensive weapon. In 2009 there will be different opportunities for Southern Group and Yorkshire members to express their support for a great Club, and *Southern Group News* will continue to chronicle events and people as it sets out beyond its first century to record more stories, runs and wickets.

Those who would like to read future issues of the *Southern Group Newsletter* — and an address in Yorkshire is no bar to doing that — may join the Southern Group by writing to David Wood, Yorkshire CCC Southern Group, PO Box 6024, Leighton Buzzard LU7 2ZS. Membership is by minimum donation of £7.

TRUMPETING VICTOR
AND 'KING' ARTHUR

By Tony Loffill

They say that to be single-minded is the greatest gift of all, but hindsight must run it close. Flintoff, Gough, Hoggard, Kallis, Vettori and their like: we can see them any day of the week on our screen, familiar visitors to our living room.

Do we romanticise them, paint them in exotic hues, think of them as immortals? Well, hardly. Like the effects of the French Revolution, it is just too early to tell. Yet if the game survives in the form we know and love it — an uncertainty unthinkable till recent times — you can bet that future generations will vote them or their contemporaries equal standing in the annals of cricket's long history.

There is no doubt that distance lends enchantment. Who would resist a peek at the Legends of Long Ago: "Silver Billy" Beldham, Fuller Pilch, Spofforth, the inimitable WG? My pick from those faraway days would be the ill-fated Shrewsbury: "Give me Arthur" was WG's mantra. A Victorian cricketer, born to bat long days at Trent Bridge with his teammate, William Gunn, in Nottinghamshire's sunniest times and encapsulating all the virtues of those long lost days.

When Victor Trumper died he, like Shrewsbury, was a young man. Have you seen the photograph of him jumping out to drive, all skill, balance and courage? When he toured England with Australia in 1902 he set new standards in brilliance and resource against England's finest bowlers, hitting — nay, charming — 100 before lunch at Old Trafford. No wonder he was a hero in his short lifetime who nonetheless caught the Sydney tram to the ground, sharing a seat with his adoring followers. Arthur Mailey, the Australian spinner setting out on a long career, clean bowled him once.

He never forgave himself: "I felt as if I had killed a dove."

One of the bowlers on that Manchester day was Sidney Barnes, simply, surely, the greatest bowler of any age? He played few Test matches, money, alas, being a stronger lure; yet he was taken out of the leagues to tour Australia with unheard-of success. He could bowl on any wicket, and few, indeed, ever mastered him. My grandfather bowled at him in the nets — a sexagenarian still playing for his native

Staffordshire, putting silver threepenny bits on the stumps for any aspiring neophyte to win. The "Joeys" returned safely to the great man's pocket.

So many wonderful names peering at us out of the twilight of cricket's Golden Age. But memory's Desert Island cannot select too many. Not to be left out, though, would be Charlie Macartney, the Australian left-hander who played on both sides of the Great War, and who once scored 345 in under four hours at Trent Bridge. He came to Headingley in 1926, was dropped by the England skipper, Arthur Carr, on two, and went on to reach his 100 before lunch. What a spectacle that must have been! Cardus has him for his Mercutio, "his rapier flashing in the sun".

As his star faded another appeared: Walter Hammond, surely destined to be the finest batsman of the 20th Century. His triumphant tour of Australia under Percy Chapman set him up as the best — until Bradman, lurking in 1928, appeared; and Hammond all his career was in his shadow. Yet what a player he was! He destroyed county attacks year after year, even in 1946 dominating the scene with Gloucestershire. I wish I could have seen that cover-drive, like nothing else in cricket, it is said. Was Bradman as good to watch? I cannot think so. Where the Don had it was his ability and determination never to be kept quiet by any bowler.

If I am allowed just a couple more from the pre-war days I would select Clarrie Grimmett without further thought. Shane Warne's record shines out for itself; but compare his figures with Clarrie, who spun his mysteries from leg for well over a decade. Grimmett and O'Reilly, the twin banes of England in the days before the war that ended too early so many careers. Larwood's own career finished much sooner, cut short by the crass attitudes displayed by Lord's to a player who had brought them spectacular success against Woodfull's 1932-3 team. To have seen his raw pace and control, which were by all accounts just awesome...If he had been born an Aussie...

One of the rarer benefits brought to age: the memory. There is a category of cricketers seen never to be forgotten. Will lovers of the game wish they had set eyes on Ray Lindwall, marvelling at his pace and accuracy and the nonpareil beauty of his lithe, sinuous, soft-footed and oh-so-menacing run to the wicket?

Or Frank Tyson, the Typhoon, the quickest of the quick? Or on peerless Tom Graveney, worth every risk of truant days spent under his spell? Or on the seigneurial disdain shown by Ted Dexter towards any attack when he was in the vein. "Lord Ted" indeed. His innings in the losing 1961 Old Trafford Test against Benaud's Australians expressed unforgettably an Englishman's determination to fight on in adversity.

WHEN THE PEN WAS MIGHTIER

SWEET SUMMERS: The Classic Writing of J M Kilburn. Edited by Duncan Hamilton. (Great Northern Books £16.99.)

At a time when even worthy university professors believe that standard English prose and spelling will have to submit to the mongrelese of e-mail and text language, a collection of Kilburn's work comes as a welcome reminder of the days when writers, sub-editors and publishers all took enormous pride in the style and expression of their work.

Kilburn, along with Neville Cardus and E W Swanton, were famous names in a school of high-class cricket writers who included John Woodcock, Alan Ross and R C Robertson-Glasgow.

Cardus invested the game with an elegance that the cricket of his mid-career did

J M KILBURN
Pride and passion

not always deserve; Swanton always had authority and the ear of Lord's; Kilburn was Yorkshire at a time when Yorkshire county cricket enjoyed a status today captured by Manchester United.

Kilburn's reports and essays reflected the players and game of his era. His daily accounts could be as terse as the opening session of a *Roses* match on a damp morning. Occasionally, just occasionally, he would allow a glimpse of sentiment and nostalgia that could be as suddenly startling as hearing an owl sing like a blackbird. His thoughts on one-day cricket, written down 40 years ago, should be read by every chief executive.

Cricket today is changing more quickly than at any time since its foundation as a national game. Newspapers, themselves in mortal danger from the threat of TV and the internet, have concluded that county-cricket reports are expensive and dispensable, so this collection is not only a tribute to Kilburn's work — but also to the *Yorkshire Post's* devotion to the game, that newspaper's former Deputy Editor and prize-winning author being the compiler. The publisher, too, and designer David Burrill deserve congratulation on a handsome production.

Friends in Worcester will be quick to point out that a Yorkshire ground might have been used for the dustjacket illustration, rather than New Road. Many Yorkshire followers, remembering happy days spent in warm sunshine by the Severn — a yearly delight reduced by two divisions — will have no regrets. Reading these pieces again, some new, some familiar, brings a deep, quiet pleasure afforded by no electronic medium...rather like hearing that lovely old ballad, "Time was..."

And I had a quiet smile at **Geoffrey Boycott's** introduction: "Nowadays, I believe there are too many writers attached to cricket who know bugger all about it and have no opinions, sensible, valid or otherwise, about what's happened on the field." In defence of my fellow hacks I have to point out that most of the opinions expressed in the media about cricket, on or off the field, now come from ex-players.

Derek Hodgson

GEOFFREY BOYCOTT — THE BEST XI.
(Michael Joseph/Penguin Books, £20)

It is rarely dull listening to **Geoffrey Boycott** talk about cricket, whether on the air or off it. There is a chance that you may not agree with what the Yorkshire legend says, but you cannot argue with the fact that he always speaks his mind.

So, you will not be too surprised to learn that Boycott's latest book is hard-hitting. There will certainly be a few players across the world who would not agree with his latest offering if they were to delve beyond the front cover. The *Best XI* is a book in which Boycott picks a squad of his best players from each Test-playing nation from England to Sri Lanka, but the former opening batsman refuses to pick squads for Zimbabwe and Bangladesh.

"I've maintained for some time now that Tests involving these two nations are an embarrassment," he says. "My mum would have scored runs and taken wickets against Bangladesh — and as for the present Zimbabwe side she'd have wanted to bat and bowl at both ends."

He also picks a best world XI of all time.

Boycott — who does not pick himself — has not named any player from the current era, **Sir Ian Botham** being the most recent selected. He explains the reasons for each selection in two or three pages.

You would be shocked if there were not surprise selections: maybe one of the biggest is that legendary Australian captain **Steve Waugh** does not make the grade. And you would be surprised if he were not controversial.

He is sure to divide opinion with his comments on the action of Sri Lankan off-spinner **Muttiah Muralitharan**, the world's leading Test match wicket-taker. There is plenty of Yorkshire involvement, right across the board, although some may have expected more...the likes of **Michael Vaughan** missing out.

Not only does Boycott give his opinions, but he backs up his selections with statistics. Without doubt, this is a book for the avid cricket follower. It is not an easy read, but worth it nonetheless.

Geoffrey Boycott made his Yorkshire debut in 1962, playing his first Test for England two years later. He played in 108 Test matches, notching 22 centuries, and became the first England player to pass 8,000 Test runs.

Graham Hardcastle

NO COWARD SOUL. By Stephen Chalke and Derek Hodgson (Fairfield Books, Bath, £12

This is a glossy, handsome updated paperback version of the *Wisden Book of 2004*, in which Stephen Chalke has included the two years **Bob Appleyard** spent as Yorkshire President, along with a few more instances of his tremendous energy, even past 80 years of age. An intriguing discovery is that Bob has Lancastrian connections.

I have to declare an interest, being a joint author of the first edition. At book-signing sessions after publication I stressed that while I had written a book about a cricketer Stephen had turned it into a book about a man. And what a man.

It is still my firm belief that had Bob entered county cricket at 20, rather than 27, and had sustained good health, he would now be remembered as Yorkshire's greatest-ever bowler, ahead of Rhodes and Trueman. To achieve what he did, with such an incredible number of handicaps, is a story worth a film or TV series.

It is about 150 years since earnest Victorian authors would publish magazines, pamphlets and even books on the virtues of self-help, how to make the best of one's self. Since the 1960s such sentiments have gone out of fashion — but if any parent wishes to inculcate a son or daughter with the principles of how to succeed by effort, imagination, intelligence and resolution this is the book to read.

If I were a director of education I would make it compulsory reading in all my schools.

Derek Hodgson

VIC WILSON

By David Warner

Vic Wilson, 87, who twice led Yorkshire to the County Championship title, died in June, and his funeral service at East Riding Crematorium, Octon, was attended by several former teammates and ex-players.

Vic, who lived at Yedingham, near Malton, was a free-scoring left-hander who impressed fellow cricketers and Yorkshire fans alike with his fiercely determined attitude at the crease. He was appointed Yorkshire captain in 1960 — the year after **Ronnie Burnet** had led the team to the Championship title, so ending the supremacy of Surrey, who had been Champions for the previous seven seasons.

Under Vic's leadership the young and hugely talented *White Rose* team went from strength to strength, retaining the title in 1960 and regaining it in 1962 in his third and final season in charge before retiring and making way for **Brian Close**, the current Yorkshire President.

A quiet and modest man, Vic was respected by all who knew him, and in recent years he had enjoyed meeting several of his former colleagues at functions organised by the Yorkshire Players' Association for past and present players. Indeed, he had been in fine form at the Association's annual lunch early in 2008.

Vic came from farming stock, and learned his cricket at Malton Grammar School before going on to churn out the runs for York and Scarborough. He made his Yorkshire debut in 1947, and went on to play in 477 matches for his native county, scoring 20,548 runs with 29 centuries at an average of 31.66.

His prowess can be gauged by the fact that only 10 other batsmen have scored more runs for Yorkshire — and they include Close and **John Hampshire**, both young members of his side.

Vic's career-best score of 230 was made against Derbyshire at

Bramall Lane in 1952, but on his home ground at Scarborough he hammered 223 not out against Scotland in 1951, sharing in an opening partnership of 228 with **Harry Halliday**.

Vic will be remembered as one of Yorkshire's most brilliant close-in fielders, and during his career he held on to 520 catches — a figure exceeded by only four others. In each of four seasons he took more than 50 catches.

Vic never played in a Test match, but he was selected for MCC's tour of Australia and New Zealand in 1954-55 captained by **Sir Leonard Hutton**.

During the war Vic played in the Bradford League for Undercliffe, scoring 159 not out

VIC WILSON: Only 10 have exceeded his run tally for Yorkshire *(Photo: Yorkshire Post.)*

against Bingley in the Priestley Cup in 1942 and hitting consecutive centuries for them two years later.

Following his successful cricket career, Vic returned to farming, but he went on to lead Wakefield to success in the League and Heavy Woollen Cup in 1968, and he also appeared for Lincolnshire from 1964 to 1966.

Among the many tributes was one from former Yorkshire and England captain **Raymond Illingworth**, who also was a young member of Vic's talented Yorkshire side: "Vic was one of those players you would want in the trenches with you. He was totally reliable, a man who gave 100 per cent and never gave up fighting. If he was beaten by five balls in a row he would lose none of his determination when facing up to the sixth.

"If you have 11 players like Vic Wilson in a team you will never be a bad side. There were also few better close-in fielders than Vic, and with hands the size of shovels he didn't drop many. When he went with MCC to Australia and New Zealand in 1954-55 they had him on as a substitute fielder whenever possible, which was a great compliment to him.

"Basically, Vic was a very good bloke and a fine cricketer, and it is nice when you can say that about someone."

Former Yorkshire President and Chairman Sir Lawrence Byford said in his address at Vic's funeral service: "He made his debut for Yorkshire in 1946, and from 1948 to 1962 he was the stalwart No 3 in Yorkshire's batting line-up, scoring almost 22,000 runs with 29 centuries and two double centuries, passing 1,000 runs per season 14 times and 2,000 runs once. He was a fantastic fielder, and took 521 catches, mainly in the area of short-leg.

"But Vic's main claim to fame was his dependability and absolute loyalty. He concentrated on what was good for the team and, above all, he demanded standards which can often be lacking in sport these days."

Sir Lawrence said that Vic once told him that the best holiday he ever had was when, against the odds, he was selected for Hutton's triumphant tour of Australia and New Zealand in 1954-55: "First-class passages by ship and, as it happened in those days, a prolonged stay Down Under rubbing shoulders with such great players as Hutton, May, Bedser, Graveney, Tyson, Appleyard, Edrich and others."

Like so many others, Sir Lawrence and his wife, Muriel, would miss Vic terribly, especially when in his beloved Scarborough: "I think the proudest episodes for him in his memorable career were not so much his achievements, to which I have referred, but rather his great deeds on the ground he loved most, Scarborough...

"Scarborough and Yorkshire are so proud of this wonderful, unassuming cricketer of great merit. I personally feel honoured to have been his friend and to have been given the opportunity of making this tribute to such an outstanding man, whose cricketing traditions he upheld throughout his life."

John Victor Wilson: **Born Scampston, Malton, January 17, 1921.**
Died Yedingham, Malton, June 4, 2008.

PETER QUINN

Yorkshire Vice-President Peter Quinn, right, who gave many years of service on the former General Committee after winning his place as a North Riding representative in 1984, died at his home in Redcar on October 9, aged 79.

Born in Guisborough, Peter gained his place when the old committee was brought down by the Geoff Boycott revolution, and he was among those who fought successfully for a new contract for Boycott after he had been sacked as a player.

**PETER QUINN
Vice-President**

Peter, who came from Redcar, was one of several Reform Group sympathisers who gained places on the General Committee in 1984 when Reg Kirk took over as Club chairman. He went on to give loyal service — first on the Grounds and Membership Committee, and then in 1985 as chairman of Public Relations, when he was also appointed to the Fund Raising Committee as well as the Rules Revision Committee chaired by the President, Viscount Mountgarret. Peter was Grounds and Membership Committee chairman in 1991, and he also joined the six-strong management committee chaired by new President, Sir Lawrence Byford.

When the committee was reduced from 23 to 12 members in 1992, Peter became one of the three representatives of North District. He went on to serve on the Public Relations and Membership Committee, and later the Finance and Marketing Committee. He decided not to seek re-election in 2000, and he was made a Vice-President in recognition of his outstanding services over 16 years.

Fellow Vice-President Tony Vann, a former Committee colleague, said in tribute: "Peter was a very strong supporter of the Geoff Boycott cause, and he was appalled at the Committee decision to sack him. He rolled his sleeves up, and really got involved in galvanising support in the North East for people who supported his viewpoint.

"Peter worked very hard on the financial side of the Club, and was a sound thinker who could see through the trees to the clear view ahead. He didn't allow prejudices to get in the way of things, and he could appreciate both sides of an argument.

"He had clarity of mind, which served him well on the Committee, and he certainly loved his cricket."

DAVID WARNER

The Players

Anthony McGRATH
Right-hand batsman, right-arm medium bowler
Born: Bradford, 6 October 1975
First-Class cricket:
Debut: Yorkshire v. Glamorgan at Bradford, 1995
Highest score: 188* v. Warwickshire
at Birmingham, 2007
Best bowling: 5 for 39 v. Derbyshire
at Derby, 2004
NatWest/C & G/F P Trophy:
Highest score: 135* v. Lancashire
at Manchester, 2007
Best bowling: 4 for 56 v. Devon at Exmouth, 2004
National League/Pro40:
Highest score: 148 v. Somerset at Taunton, 2006
Best bowling: 4 for 41 v. Surrey at Leeds, 2003

Craig WHITE
Right-hand batsman, right-arm fast-medium bowler
Born: Morley, 16 December 1969
First-Class cricket:
Debut: Yorkshire v. Northamptonshire at Leeds, 1990
Highest score: 186 v. Lancashire at Manchester, 2001
Best bowling: 8 for 55 v. Gloucestershire
at Gloucester, 1998
NatWest/C & G/F P Trophy:
Highest score: 113 v. Ireland at Leeds, 1995
Best bowling: 4 for 35 v. Surrey at Leeds, 2002
National League/Pro40:
Highest score: 73 v. Nottinghamshire
at Nottingham, 2001
Best bowling: 5 for 19 v. Somerset
at Scarborough, 2002

Michael Paul VAUGHAN
Right-hand batsman, right-arm off-break bowler
Born: Salford, 29 October 1974
First-Class cricket:
Debut: Yorkshire v. Lancashire at Manchester, 1993
Highest score: 197 for England v. India at Nottingham,
2002
Highest score for Yorkshire: 183 v. Glamorgan at Cardiff,
1996, and v. Northamptonshire at Northampton, 1996
Best bowling: 4 for 39 v. Oxford University at Oxford,
1994
NatWest/C & G/F P Trophy:
Highest score: 116* v. Lancashire at Manchester, 2004
Best bowling: 1 for 4 v. Yorkshire CB at Harrogate, 2000
National League:
Highest score: 116* v. Kent at Leeds, 2005
Best bowling: 4 for 27 v. Gloucestershire at Bristol, 2000

Matthew James HOGGARD

Right-hand batsman, right-arm fast-medium bowler
Born: Leeds, 31 December 1976

First-Class cricket:
Debut: Yorkshire v South Africa 'A' at Leeds, 1996
Highest score: 89* v. Glamorgan at Leeds, 2004
Best bowling: 7 for 49 v. Somerset at Leeds, 2003

NatWest/C & G/F P Trophy:
Highest score: 7* v. Worcestershire at Worcester, 2003
Best bowling: 5 for 65 v. Somerset at Lord's, 2002

National League:
Highest score: 5* v. Warwickshire
at Birmingham, 2001
Best bowling: 5 for 28 v. Leicestershire
at Leicester, 2000

Timothy Thomas BRESNAN

Right-hand batsman, right-arm medium-fast bowler
Born: Pontefract, 28 February 1985

First-Class cricket:
Debut: v. Northamptonshire at Northampton, 2003
Highest score for Yorkshire: 116 v. Surrey
at The Oval, 2007
Best bowling: 5 for 42 v. Worcestershire
at Worcester, 2005

C & G/F P Trophy:
Highest score: 55 v. Durham
at Chester-le-Street, 2008
Best bowling: 4 for 31 v. Gloucestershire
at Bristol, 2008

National League/Pro40:
Highest score: 61 v. Leicestershire at Leeds, 2003
Best bowling: 2 for 27 v. Derbyshire at Leeds, 2007

Gideon Jacobus KRUIS

Right-hand batsman, right-arm fast-medium bowler
Born: Pretoria, Transvaal, South Africa, 9 May 1974
First-class cricket:
Debut: Northern Transvaal B v Orange Free State B
at Bloemfontein, 1993-94
Debut for Yorkshire: v. Essex at Chelmsford, 2005
Highest score: 59 for Griqualand West v. Bangladeshis
at Kimberley, 2000-01
Highest score for Yorkshire: 50* v. Surrey at Leeds, 2008
Best bowling: 7 for 58 for Griqualand West v. Northerns
at Centurion, 1997-98
Best bowling for Yorkshire: 5 for 47 v Surrey at Leeds, 2008
C & G/F P Trophy:
Highest score: 11 v. Northamptonshire at Leeds, 2005
Best bowling: 3 for 61 v Nottinghamshire
at Nottingham, 2007
National League/Pro40:
Highest score: 31* v. Surrey at The Oval, 2006
Best bowling: 4 for 17 v. Derbyshire at Leeds, 2007

Jacobus (Jacques) Andries RUDOLPH

Left-hand batsman, leg-break/googly bowler
Born: Springs, Transvaal, S A, 4 May 1981

First-Class cricket:
Debut: Northerns B v. Western Province B
at Centurion Park, 1997
Highest score: 222* for South Africa v. Bangladesh
at Chittagong, 2003 (Test debut)
Highest score for Yorkshire: 220 v. Warwickshire
at Scarborough, 2007
Best bowling: 5 for 87 for Northerns B v
Griqualand West B at Centurion Park, 1998

FP Trophy:
Highest score: 100 v. Leicestershire at Leeds, 2007

Pro40:
Highest score: 127 v. Somerset
at Scarborough, 2007

John Joseph SAYERS

Left-hand batsman, right-arm off-break bowler
Born: Leeds, 5 November 1983

First-Class cricket:
Debut: Oxford University v. Worcestershire
at Oxford, 2002
Debut for Yorkshire: v. Leicestershire
at Leicester, 2004
Highest score for Yorkshire: 187 v. Kent
at Tunbridge Wells, 2007

National League/Pro40:
Highest score: 54* v. Derbyshire at Derby, 2005
Best bowling: 1 for 31 v. Warwickshire
at Birmingham, 2005

Gerard Louis BROPHY

Right-hand batsman, wicket-keeper
Born: Welkom, Orange Free State, South Africa,
26 November 1975

First-class cricket:
Debut: Transvaal B v Eastern Province B
at Johannesburg, 1996-97
Highest score: 185 for South African Academy
v. Zimbabwe President's XI at Harare, 1998-99
Highest score for Yorkshire: 100* v Hampshire
at Scarborough, 2007

C & G Trophy/F P:
Highest score for Yorkshire: 61* v. Scotland
at Edinburgh, 2008

National League/Pro40:
Highest score for Yorkshire: 66 v Glamorgan
at Cardiff, 2007

Andrew William GALE

Left-hand batsman
Born: Dewsbury, 28 November 1983

First-Class cricket:
Debut: v. Somerset at Scarborough, 2004
Highest score: 150 v. Surrey
at The Oval, 2008

C & G/F P Trophy:
Highest score: 69* v. Nottinghamshire
at Nottingham, 2007

National League/Pro40:
Highest score: 89 v. Leicestershire
at Leeds, 2008

Adil Usman RASHID

Right-hand batsman, leg-break bowler
Born: Bradford, 17 February 1988

First-Class cricket:
Debut: v. Warwickshire at Scarborough, 2006
Highest score: 111 v. Sussex at Hove, 2008
Best bowling: 7 for 107 v. Hampshire
at Southampton, 2008

F P Trophy:
Highest score: 41* v. Derbyshire at Leeds, 2008
Best bowling: 2 for 21 v. Durham at Leeds, 2008

Pro40:
Highest score: 33* v. Surrey at Guildford, 2008
Best bowling: 3 for 37 v. Derbyshire at Derby, 2008

Simon Mark GUY

Right-hand batsman, wicket-keeper
Born: Rotherham, 17 November 1978

First-Class cricket:
Debut: Yorkshire v. Zimbabweans at Leeds, 2000
Highest score: 52* v. Durham at Leeds, 2006
Most catches in a match: 7 v. Worcestershire
at Leeds, 2005

C & G/F P Trophy:
Highest score: 13 v. Lancashire
at Manchester, 2007

National League/Pro40:
Highest score: 29 v. Leicestershire at Leeds, 2004

Christopher Robert TAYLOR
Right-hand batsman
Born: Rawdon, 21 February 1981
First-Class cricket:
Debut: v. Surrey at Leeds, 2001
Highest score: 121* for Derbyshire v. Glamorgan
at Cardiff, 2006
Highest score for Yorkshire: 52* v. Surrey
at Leeds, 2002
C & G/F P Trophy:
Highest score: 111* for Derbyshire v. Durham
at Derby, 2006
National League/Pro40:
Highest score: 60* for Derbyshire v. Leicestershire
at Derby, 2006
Highest score for Yorkshire: 23 v. Derbyshire
at Derby, 2008

Richard Michael PYRAH
Right-hand batsman, right-arm medium bowler
Born: Dewsbury, 1 November 1982
First-Class cricket:
Debut: v. Glamorgan at Colwyn Bay, 2004
Highest score: 106 v. Loughborough UCCE
at Leeds, 2007
Best bowling: 1 for 4 v. Bangladesh 'A'
at Leeds, 2005
C & G Trophy/F P:
Highest score: 24 v. Scotland at Edinburgh, 2007
Best bowling: 3 for 25 v. Durham at Leeds, 2008
National League/Pro40:
Highest score: 42 v. Durham at Scarborough, 2004
Best bowling: 4 for 35 v. Kent at Scarborough, 2008

David John WAINWRIGHT
Left-hand batsman, left-arm slow bowler
Born: Pontefract, 21 March 1985
First-Class cricket:
Debut: v. Somerset at Taunton, 2004
Highest score: 104* v. Sussex at Hove, 2008
Best bowling: 3 for 9 v. Sussex at Hove, 2008
F P Trophy:
Highest score: 26 v. Surrey at Scarborough, 2007
Best bowling: 2 for 30 v. Surrey
at Scarborough, 2007
Pro40:
Highest score: 13* v. Northamptonshire
at Northampton, 2008
Best bowling: 2 for 33 v. Essex at Chelmsford, 2008

Steven Andrew PATTERSON

Right-hand batsman, right-arm medium-fast bowler
Born: Hull, 3 October 1983

First-Class cricket:
Debut: v. Bangladesh 'A' at Leeds, 2005
Highest score: 46 v. Lancashire at Manchester, 2006
Best bowling: 3 for 19 v. Somerset at Taunton, 2008

C & G/F P Trophy:
Highest score: 3* v. Derbyshire at Leeds, 2006
Best bowling: 3 for 11 for Yorkshire Cricket Board
v. Northamptonshire Cricket Board
at Northampton, 2002

National League/Pro40:
Highest score: 25* v. Worcestershire at Leeds, 2006
Best bowling: 3 for 59 v. Somerset at Taunton, 2006

Ajmal SHAHZAD

Right-hand batsman, right-arm medium-fast bowler
Born: Huddersfield, 27 July 1985

First-Class cricket:
Debut: v. Middlesex at Scarborough, 2006
Highest score: 35 v. Hampshire at Leeds, 2008
Best bowling: 4 for 22 v. Sussex at Leeds, 2007

C & G Trophy/F P:
Highest score: 33 v. Durham
at Chester-le-Street, 2008
Best bowling: 2 for 34 v. Leicestershire
at Leicester, 2006

Pro40:
Highest score: 5 v. Worcestershire at Leeds, 2004
Best bowling: 3 for 30 v. Kent at Scarborough, 2006

Adam LYTH

Left-hand batsman, right-arm medium bowler
Born: Whitby, 25 September 1987

First-Class cricket:
Debut: v. Loughborough UCCE at Leeds, 2007
Highest score: 132 v. Nottinghamshire
at Nottingham, 2008
Best bowling: 1 for 12 v. Loughborough UCCE
at Leeds, 2007

F P Trophy:
Highest score: 38* v. Gloucestershire
at Bristol, 2008

Pro40:
Highest score: 28 v. Surrey at Guildford, 2008

Rana NAVED-UL-HASAN

Right-hand batsman, right-arm fast-medium bowler
Born: Sheikhupura, Punjab, Pakistan,
28 February 1978

First-Class cricket:
Debut: Pakistan A v England A at Multan, 1995
Highest score: 139 for Sussex v Middlesex at Lord's, 2005
Debut for Yorkshire: v Surrey at The Oval, 2008
Highest score for Yorkshire: 22 v Hampshire
at Southampton, 2008
Best bowling for Yorkshire: 4 for 86 v Kent
at Scarborough, 2008
Best bowling: 7 for 49 for Sheikhupura v. Sialkot
at Muridke, 2002

F P Trophy for Yorkshire:
Highest score: 13 v. Essex at Chelmsford, 2008
Best bowling: 2 for 41 v. Essex at Chelmsford, 2008

Pro40 for Yorkshire:
Highest score: 74 v. Derbyshire at Derby, 2008
Best bowling: 2 for 26 v. Glamorgan at Scarborough, 2008

Yorkshire above the ARCHs...

Yorkshire Academy in December completed the second part of a splendid double for the Club by lifting the Academy ARCH Trophy on their tour to Abu Dhabi. Earlier in the year, the first team squad had also triumphed in Abu Dhabi by playing some splendid cricket to win the ARCH Trophy.

The youngsters were in dazzling form — winning all four of their matches for captain **Azeem Rafiq** to be presented with the Trophy, while **Joe Root** received the player-of-the-tournament award for his outstanding 276 runs at an average of 69. Azeem's application for British Citizenship went through in time for the tour — after which he was off again...with England Under-19s to South Africa. Azeem joined up with the Academy shortly after their opening match against United Arab Emirates Under-19s, which the tourists won by 138 runs. **Callum Geldart** hit 91 and Root 80 out of 265-4, and the UAE were bowled out for 127.

The second match was a closer affair — **Chris Allinson** claiming 3-23 as Glamorgan were put out for 181. He then top-scored with 40 out of 186-7, the Academy winning by three wickets.

A convincing victory followed against Guernsey, the Academy winning the toss and reaching 295-2, thanks to **Alex Lees**, 112 not out, and Root, 110. Guernsey were dismissed for 184, **Jack Hughes** grabbing 3-23 and **Jack Hargreaves** 2-21.

The 100 per cent record was completed in the last match when the Academy beat the Sussex Academy by 118 runs. Root top-scored with 75, and there were half-centuries for Hargreaves and **Charlie Roebuck** in a total of 273-6. Sussex were dismissed for 155.

Pro-ARCH Trophy Matches played in Abu Dhabi 2007-8

WINNERS:

Yorkshire

(Day-Night: 50 overs per side)

		P	W	L	T	NR	PTS	NRR
1	**Yorkshire**	4	3	1	0	0	6	1.093
2	Lancashire	4	3	1	0	0	6	1,055
3	Somerset	4	3	1	0	0	6	0.324
4	Essex	4	2	2	0	0	4	-0.312
5	Sussex	4	1	3	0	0	2	-0.585
6	U.A.E.	4	0	4	0	0	0	-1.712

Pre-Season Pro-ARCH Trophy
Yorkshire v. Lancashire

Played at Sheikh Zayed Stadium, Abu Dhabi, on March 21, 2008
Yorkshire won by 41 runs

Toss won by Yorkshire   Yorkshire 2 points; Lancashire 0 points

YORKSHIRE

A W Gale, c Smith b Flintoff	....	32
C White, c Hogg b Marshall	....	29
* A McGrath, c Smith b Marshall	....	41
§ G L Brophy, c Cross b Marshall	....	36
C R Taylor, c Croft b Hogg	....	28
R M Pyrah, c Loye b Horton	....	15
D J Wainwright, b Hogg	....	16
M A K Lawson, st Cross b Marshall	....	16
A Shahzad, c Croft b Newby	....	9
S A Patterson, b Newby	....	0
G J Kruis, not out	....	2
Extras (lb 5, w 7, nb 1)	....	13
Total (48.2 overs)	....	237

Fall of wickets: —

1	2	3	4	5	6	7	8	9	10
66	71	136	154	181	209	210	234	234	237

	O	M	R	W
Chapple	8	0	37	0
Newby	8	0	31	2
Marshall	8.2	0	47	4
Flintoff	4	0	22	1
Hogg	9	1	37	2
Smith	4	0	21	0
Croft	2	0	10	0
Horton	5	0	27	1

LANCASHIRE

M B Loye, c Wainwright b Kruis	....	1
I J Sutcliffe, st Brophy b Patterson	....	28
§ G D Cross, lbw b Shahzad	....	6
P J Horton, c Brophy b Patterson	....	25
* A Flintoff, b Shahzad	....	51
S J Croft, run out (Gale/Brophy)	....	4
G Chapple, st Brophy b Wainwright	....	51
K W Hogg, b Wainwright	....	10
T C Smith, c Gale b Kruis	....	5
S J Marshall, c McGrath b Wainwright	....	3
O J Newby, not out	....	0
Extras (lb 8, w 4)	....	12
Total (47.1 overs)	....	196

Fall of wickets: —

1	2	3	4	5	6	7	8	9	10
7	38	59	76	79	154	188	191	195	196

	O	M	R	W
Kruis	9	1	37	2
Shahzad	10	0	33	2
Patterson	10	1	36	2
Pyrah	8	0	34	0
Lawson	3	0	17	0
Wainwright	7.1	0	31	3

Umpires: Mohammad Ali and Mohammad Asif

Pre-Season Pro-ARCH Trophy
Yorkshire v. Somerset

Played at Sheikh Zayed Stadium, Abu Dhabi, on March 25, 2008
Yorkshire won by 51 runs

Toss won by Yorkshire

Yorkshire 2 points; Somerset 0 points

YORKSHIRE

A W Gale, c Durston b Turner		63
J J Sayers, lbw b Durston		43
§ S M Guy, run out (Durston)		26
A McGrath, c Hildreth b Turner		53
A Lyth, c Hildreth b Durston		7
A U Rashid, not out		35
R M Pyrah, lbw b Jones		6
D J Wainwright, lbw b Jones		6
* D Gough, not out		5
G J Kruis		
O J Hannon-Dalby	Did not bat	
Extras (b 4, lb 5, w 7, nb 4)		20
Total (7 wickets, 50 overs)		264

Fall of wickets: —

1	2	3	4	5	6	7
97	129	150	165	230	241	254

	O	M	R	W
Sutton	3	0	27	0
Jones	10	0	37	2
Phillips	5	0	31	0
Turner	10	0	56	2
Banks	10	0	45	0
Durston	10	0	43	2
Suppiah	2	0	16	0

SOMERSET

C Kieswetter, run out (Lyth)		26
§ C M Gazzard, c Guy b Pyrah		16
A V Suppiah, run out (Hannon-Dalby)		25
J C Hildreth, lbw b Pyrah		13
W J Durston, lbw b Rashid		20
O A C Banks, not out		55
B J Phillips, lbw b Rashid		16
* P S Jones, b Wainwright		17
M L Turner, b Hannon-Dalby		3
A P Sutton, b Hannon-Dalby		0
M K Munday, run out (Rashid/Guy)		1
Extras (b 8, lb 2, w 10, nb 1)		21
Total (47.5 overs)		213

Fall of wickets: —

1	2	3	4	5	6	7	8	9	10
46	58	85	99	127	164	196	205	207	213

	O	M	R	W
Kruis	6	1	17	0
Gough	10	0	56	0
Pyrah	7	2	29	2
Hannon-Dalby	6	0	28	2
Rashid	10	4	23	2
Wainwright	7	0	37	1
McGrath	1.5	0	13	0

Umpires: Mohammad Ali and Mohammad Asif

Pre-Season Pro-ARCH Trophy
Yorkshire v. Sussex

Played at Sheikh Zayed Stadium, Abu Dhabi, on March 26, 2008

Sussex won by 9 runs

Toss won by Sussex   Yorkshire 0 points; Sussex 2 points

SUSSEX

A J Hodd, b Bresnan	18
M A Thornely, c Sayers b Shahzad	49
M H Yardy, run out (Lawson)	39
§ M J Prior, c Lee b Rashid	0
* C J Adams, b Pyrah	23
R J Hamilton-Brown, lbw b Pyrah	15
R S C Martin-Jenkins, not out	34
O P Rayner, c Brophy b Lee	9
R G Aga, c Brophy b Bresnan	6
C J Liddle, not out	6
W A T Beer	Did not bat
Extras (lb 2, w 5, nb 3)	10
Total (8 wickets; 50 overs)	209

Fall of wickets: — 1 2 3 4 5 6 7 8
                36 110 110 110 135 167 179 191

	O	M	R	W
Kruis	9	1	27	0
Shahzad	8	1	35	1
Pyrah	7	0	31	2
Bresnan	6	0	21	2
Lee	7	0	29	1
Rashid	10	1	45	1
Lawson	3	0	19	0

YORKSHIRE

C White, b Yardy	40
J J Sayers, c Prior b Liddle	22
§ G L Brophy, st Prior b Beer	31
A Lyth, c Hodd b Beer	28
A U Rashid, c Prior b Martin-Jenkins	31
T T Bresnan, st Prior b Beer	10
R M Pyrah, lbw b Rayner	0
M A K Lawson, c Beer b Martin-Jenkins	10
A Shahzad, c Yardy b Rayner	5
G J Kruis, not out	3
J E Lee, not out	1
Extras (lb 11, w 8)	19
Total (9 wickets; 50 overs)	200

Fall of wickets: — 1 2 3 4 5 6 7 8 9
            56 90 122 141 169 172 176 194 198

	O	M	R	W
Aga	6	0	30	0
Martin-Jenkins	9	1	27	2
Liddle	6	1	15	1
Thornely	6	0	26	0
Yardy	10	0	42	1
Beer	10	0	34	3
Rayner	3	0	15	2

Umpires: Mohammad Ali and Mohammad Asif

NOTE: The Yorkshire captain was not named

Pre-Season Pro-ARCH Trophy
Yorkshire v. United Arab Emirates

Played at Sheikh Zayed Stadium, Abu Dhabi, on March 28, 2008

Yorkshire won by 4 wickets

Toss won by United Arab Emirates   Yorkshire 2 points; United Arab Emirates 0 points

UNITED ARAB EMIRATES

Amjad Javed, c Lyth b Bresnan	43
Arshad Ali, lbw b Shahzad	10
Alawi Shukri, c McGrath b Sanderson	17
Rashid Khan, c Lyth b Hannon-Dalby	14
I P P Batuwitarachchi, c Bresnan b Lawson	27
* Saqib Ali, lbw b Wainwright	0
§ Abdul Rehman, b Lawson	9
Qasim Zubair, lbw b Hannon-Dalby	37
Fahad Alhashmi, b Lawson	0
Jasim Suwaidi, c Lyth b Bresnan	11
Obaid Hameed, not out	3
Extras (lb 10, w 9)	19
Total (48.1 overs)	190

Fall of wickets: —

1	2	3	4	5	6	7	8	9	10
13	75	77	103	103	127	138	138	186	190

	O	M	R	W
Shahzad	5	0	20	1
Hannon-Dalby	10	2	40	2
Sanderson	6	0	24	1
Bresnan	8.1	0	41	2
Wainwright	10	3	19	1
Lawson	9	1	36	3

YORKSHIRE

A W Gale, c Alawi Shukri b Obaid Hameed	69
G L Wood, c & b Saqib Ali	50
§ S M Guy, c Batuwitarachchi b Jasim Suwaidi	23
* A McGrath, run out (Amjad Javed/Obaid Hameed)	16
A Lyth, not out	14
T T Bresnan, c Abdul Rehman b Jasim Suwaidi	0
D J Wainwright, b Jasim Suwaidi	1
M A K Lawson, not out	4
A Shahzad	
O J Hannon-Dalby Did not bat	
B W Sanderson	
Extras (b 4, lb 4, w 7, nb 1)	16
Total (6 wickets, 24.1 overs)	193

Fall of wickets: —

1	2	3	4	5	6
94	151	153	180	182	184

	O	M	R	W
Qasim Zubair	5	0	37	0
Fahad Alhashmi	1	0	13	0
Amjad Javed	1	0	19	0
Saqib Ali	4	0	37	1
Arshad Ali	4	0	25	0
Batuwitarachchi	2	0	13	0
Obaid Hameed	4	0	24	1
Jasim Suwaidi	3.1	0	17	3

Umpires: Mohammad Ali and Mohammad Asif

HIGHLIGHTS OF 2008

Wins by an innings (1)

Yorkshire (398) beat Hampshire (159 and 212) by an innings and 27 runs at Leeds

Totals of 400 and over (7)

525	versus Surrey at The Oval
457	versus Kent at Scarborough
414 for 9 wkts dec	versus Surrey at Leeds
414	versus Somerset at Scarborough
410	versus Kent at Canterbury
400 for 6 wkts dec	versus Lancashire at Manchester
400 for 9 wkts dec	versus Sussex at Hove

Match aggregates of 1,250 and over (2)

1,292 for 39 wickets: Yorkshire (457 and 175 for 9 wkts) and Kent (227 and 433 at Scarborough

1,290 for 24 wickets: Yorkshire (525) and Surrey (466 for 8 wkts dec and 299 for 6 wkts dec) at The Oval

Century Partnerships (12)

For the 2nd wicket (2)

215	A W Gale and A McGrath versus Lancashire at Manchester
121	A Lyth and A McGrath versus Somerset at Scarborough

For the 3rd wicket (5)

217	A McGrath and J A Rudolph versus Kent at Canterbury
176	A McGrath and J A Rudolph versus Kent at Scarborough
141	A McGrath and J A Rudolph versus Somerset at Scarborough
138	M P Vaughan and A Lyth versus Durham at Leeds
126	J A Rudolph and A W Gale versus Somerset at Taunton

For the 4th wicket (3)

206	J A Rudolph and A W Gale versus Surrey at The Oval
130	J A Rudolph and G L Brophy versus Somerset at Taunton
109	J A Rudolph and A W Gale versus Hampshire at Leeds

For the 6th wicket (1)

106	J A Rudolph and G L Brophy versus Nottinghamshire at Leeds

For the 9th wicket (1)

140	A U Rashid and D J Wainwright versus Sussex at Hove

Centuries (13)

J A Rudolph (5)

155	versus Somerset at Taunton
146	versus Kent at Scarborough
129	versus Kent at Canterbury
121	versus Surrey at The Oval
104*	versus Nottinghamshire at Leeds

A W Gale (3)

150	versus Surrey at The Oval
138	versus Hampshire at Leeds
136	versus Lancashire at Manchester

A McGrath (2)

144	versus Kent at Canterbury
128	versus Somerset at Scarborough

A Lyth (1)

   132   versus Nottinghamshire at Nottingham

A U Rashid (1)

   111   versus Sussex at Hove

D J Wainwright (1)

   104*   versus Sussex at Hove

5 wickets in an innings (7)

A U Rashid (4)

       7 for 107 versus Hampshire at Southampton
       7 for 136 versus Sussex at Hove
       5 for 140 versus Kent at Canterbury
       5 for 95 versus Lancashire at Manchester

T T Bresnan (1)

       5 for 94 versus Durham at Leeds

M J Hoggard (1)

       6 for 57 versus Hampshire at Leeds

G J Kruis (1)

       5 for 47 versus Surrey at Leeds

3 catches in an innings (7)

G L Brophy (6)

     3   versus Nottinghamshire at Leeds
     3   versus Durham at Chester-le-Street
     3   versus Somerset at Taunton
     3   versus Durham at Leeds
     3   versus Nottinghamshire at Nottingham
     3   versus Somerset at Scarborough

J A Rudolph (1)

     3   versus Kent at Canterbury

3 dismissals in an innings (3)

G L Brophy (3)

     4 (3ct, 1st) versus Surrey at The Oval
     4 (3ct, 1st) versus Kent at Canterbury
     3 (1ct, 2st) versus Hampshire at Southampton

5 catches in a match (1)

G L Brophy (1)

     5 (3 + 2) versus Somerset at Scarborough

5 dismissals in a match (2)

G L Brophy (2)

     6 (5ct, 1st) versus Surrey at The Oval
     6 (5ct, 1st) versus Kent at Canterbury

Caps awarded (3)

G L Brophy, A W Gale, A U Rashid

Debuts (5)

In first-class cricket: G S Ballance, O J Hannon-Dalby, B W Sanderson

For Yorkshire, having previously played first-class cricket:

                                      M Morkel, Rana Naved-ul-Hasan

R D W

LV CHAMPIONSHIP FACTFILE

Compiled by Roy D Wilkinson

YORKSHIRE versus HAMPSHIRE at Leeds

1. Yorkshire's win by an innings and 27 runs was their 26th innings victory over Hampshire.
2. A W Gale — 138 off 286 balls in 367 minutes, 19x4; 100 off 201 balls in 261 minutes 14x4.
3. M J Hoggard's 6 for 57 is the best performance for Yorkshire v Hampshire at Leeds since R Appleyard took 6 for 32 in 1951.

YORKSHIRE versus NOTTINGHAMSHIRE at Leeds

1. 422 is the highest Nottinghamshire score at Leeds — exceeding the 393 made in 2004.
2. The partnership of 136 between C M W Read and G P Swann is the record for Nottinghamshire's sixth wicket on this ground — exceed--ing the 107 added by C W Wright and W Attewell in 1894.
3. The partnership of 113 between C M W Read and S C J Broad is the record for Nottinghamshire's seventh wicket on this ground — exceeding the 56 added by C B Harris and A W Carr in 1934.
4. J A Rudolph — 104* off 252 balls in 311 minutes 8x4; 100 off 246 balls in 300 minutes 7x4.
5. M Morkel made his debut for Yorkshire.

YORKSHIRE versus DURHAM at Chester-le-Street

1. Durham's win by 295 runs is the fourth heaviest defeat suffered by Yorkshire by a runs margin.
2. The partnership of 96 between M J Di Venuto and M D Stoneman is the highest for Durham's first wicket versus Yorkshire.
3. M J Di Venuto's 184 is the highest individual score for Durham ver--sus Yorkshire.
4. B W Sanderson made his debut in first-class cricket.

YORKSHIRE versus SURREY at The Oval

1. 525 is the fifth highest score by Yorkshire versus Surrey and their fourth highest at The Oval.
2. The 205 by M A Butcher is the fourth individual innings of over 200 scored for Surrey versus Yorkshire — three of them have been made at The Oval and one at Lord's (J B Hobbs 202 in 1914).
3. His was the 100th century in first-class cricket for Surrey versus Yorkshire.

4. The partnership of 206 between J A Rudolph and A W Gale is the record for Yorkshire's fourth wicket versus Surrey — exceeding the 201* by J H Hampshire and D B Close at Bradford in 1965.

5. J A Rudolph — 121 off 194 balls in 209 minutes 18x4; 100 off 165 balls in 183 minutes 15x4.

6. A W Gale — 150 off 231 balls in 368 minutes 19x4, 1x6; 100 off 168 balls in 232 minutes 12x4, 1x6.

7. Rana Naved-ul-Hasan made his debut for Yorkshire.

8. O J Hannon-Dalby made his debut in first-class cricket.

YORKSHIRE versus LANCASHIRE at Leeds

1. The Lancashire total of 481 for 5 wkts dec is their fifth highest ver- -sus Yorkshire in Championship cricket and the sixth highest over- -all.

2. In the Leeds *Roses* Match in 2007 P J Horton and S G Law added 258 for the 3rd Lancashire wicket — the record partnership for any wicket for Lancashire versus Yorkshire. This was equalled by P J Horton and Mohammad Yousuf in the 2008 encounter.

3. The partnership of 197 between Mohammad Yousuf and S J Croft is the highest for Lancashire's 5th wicket versus Yorkshire.

4. Mohammad Yousuf's 205* is only the third double-century for Lancashire versus Yorkshire in Championship cricket (and the fourth overall). Two of the three have been scored in their two most recent matches at Leeds (S G Law scored 206 in 2007).

5. G L Brophy was awarded his cap on the second day.

YORKSHIRE versus SOMERSET at Taunton

1. J A Rudolph — 155 of 273 balls in 336 minutes 16x4, 1x6; 100 off 169 balls in 210 minutes 11x4, 1x6.

YORKSHIRE versus DURHAM at Leeds

1. The partnership of 143 between P Mustard and L E Plunkett is the highest for Durham's 8th wicket versus Yorkshire — exceeding the 54 by M P Speight and J Wood at Leeds in 1999.

2. The 92 by P Mustard is the fifth innings of 90 to 99 scored for Durham versus Yorkshire. The others have come in 2005, 2006 (two) and 2007.

3. The partnership of 138 between M P Vaughan and A Lyth is the record for Yorkshire's 3rd wicket versus Durham — exceeding the 131 by A McGrath and D S Lehmann at Leeds in 2006.

4. With this win Durham have beaten Yorkshire twice in the same sea son for the second time — the other was in 2003.

LV CHAMPIONSHIP FACTFILE (Continued)

YORKSHIRE versus KENT at Canterbury

1. The Yorkshire innings of 410 is their third highest at Canterbury.

2. The Kent innings of 467 is their third highest versus Yorkshire at Canterbury.

3. The partnership of 217 between A McGrath and J A Rudolph is the highest for Yorkshire's 3rd wicket versus Kent — exceeding the 195 between A McGrath and D S Lehmann at Canterbury in 2000.

4. A McGrath has now scored six centuries versus Kent — the most by any Yorkshire player (L Hutton is second with five). He has scored three centuries in consecutive innings versus Kent (100 at Tunbridge Wells and 120 at Scarborough in 2007 and now 144 at Canterbury).

5. A McGrath — 144 off 226 balls in 286 minutes 16x4, 2x6; 100 off 178 balls in 220 minutes 12x4.

6. J A Rudolph — 129 off 210 balls in 247 minutes 12x4, 1x6; 100 off 143 balls in 144 minutes 12x4, 1x6.

7. G S Ballance made his debut in first-class cricket.

YORKSHIRE versus NOTTINGHAMSHIRE at Nottingham

1. A Lyth — 132 off 266 balls in 375 minutes 19x4; 100 off 218 balls in 294 minutes 14x4.

2. M A Ealham's 7 for 59 is the best bowling performance for Nottinghamshire versus Yorkshire since F D Stephenson took 7 for 38 at Leeds in 1989.

YORKSHIRE versus SURREY at Leeds

1. The Yorkshire total of 414 for 9 wkts dec is their third highest ver--sus Surrey at Leeds.

2. The unfinished partnership of 87 between A U Rashid and G J Kruis is Yorkshire's record 10th wicket versus Surrey — exceeding the 55 by the same players in 2007.

3. M R Ramprakash completed his 100th first-class century. His first was also at Leeds — for Middlesex in 1989.

4. The partnership of 259 between S A Newman and M R Ramprakash is the record for the Surrey 2nd wicket at Leeds — exceeding the 85 added by R Abel and E G Hayes in 1899.

LV CHAMPIONSHIP FACTFILE *(Continued)*

YORKSHIRE versus HAMPSHIRE at Southampton

1. Hampshire scored 108 for 0 wicket to win. This is only the fourth time that Yorkshire have been beaten by 10 wickets with over 100 runs being scored.

2. It is the fourth time Hampshire have beaten Yorkshire by 10 wick--ets (Yorkshire have beaten Hampshire by 10 wickets 12 times, three times in consecutive matches in 1896/97).

3. A U Rashid's 7 for 107 is the best performance for Yorkshire at the Rose Bowl, Southampton, and the best versus Hampshire on any ground since P M Hutchison took 7 for 50 at Portsmouth in 1997.

YORKSHIRE versus LANCASHIRE at Manchester

1. The partnership of 215 between A W Gale and A McGrath is the third highest for Yorkshire's 2nd wicket versus Lancashire (and the second highest at Manchester).

2. A McGrath is the first Yorkshire player to be dismissed for 99 in a Roses Match. A Appleby at Sheffield in 1871 and N H Fairbrother at Manchester in 1990 are the two Lancashire players with 99 ver--sus Yorkshire.

3. A W Gale — 136 off 328 balls in 382 minutes 13x4, 1x6; 100 off 265 balls in 305 minutes 11x4.

YORKSHIRE versus KENT at Scarborough

1. The Yorkshire first innings total of 457 is the second highest versus Kent at Scarborough — exceeded only by the 550 for 9 wkts dec in 2007.

2. The Kent second innings score of 433 is also their second highest at Scarborough — exceeded only by their 486 also in 2007.

3. The partnership of 176 between A McGrath and J A Rudolph is the highest for the 3rd wicket versus Kent at Scarborough — exceeding the 163 added by L Hutton and E I Lester in 1953.

4. For the third consecutive season a Yorkshire player has scored cen--turies home and away versus Kent — D S Lehmann in 2006, A McGrath in 2007 and J A Rudolph in 2008. It was achieved by two other players — M Leyland in 1930 and L Hutton in 1952.

5. J A Rudolph — 146 off 221 balls in 268 minutes 21x4, 1x6; 100 off 146 balls in 186 minutes 15x4, 1x6.

LV CHAMPIONSHIP FACTFILE *(Continued)*

YORKSHIRE versus SOMERSET at Scarborough

1. The Yorkshire total of 414 is their highest score versus Somerset at Scarborough — exceeding the 400 scored in 2000.

2. A McGrath — 128 off 255 balls in 306 minutes 18x4; 100 off 173 balls in 216 minutes 15x4.

3. A W Gale and A U Rashid were awarded their county caps on the second day of the match.

YORKSHIRE versus SUSSEX at Hove

1. The Yorkshire total of 400 for 9 wkts dec is only the fourth time they have reached 400 in an innings at Hove (the others were 461 in 1914, 428 in 1898 and 407 in 1896).

2. For the second successive season a Yorkshire number 10 batsman scored a century. In 2007 J N Gillespie did so versus Surrey at The Oval, and D J Wainwright did so in this match. The only other instance was by G H Hirst with 115* versus Gloucestershire at Bristol in 1894. Interestingly all three remained not out.

3. The partnership of 140 between A U Rashid and D J Wainwright is only the second century partnership for Yorkshire's 9th wicket at Hove — the other being the 173 added by S Haigh and W Rhodes in 1902.

4. The unfinished partnership of 82 between D J Wainwright and M J Hoggard is the record for Yorkshire's 10th wicket versus Sussex — exceeding the 78 added by G A Cope and S Oldham at Hove in 1979.

5. A U Rashid's 7 for 136 is the first time five or more wickets have been taken in an innings for Yorkshire at Hove since P M Hutchison took 7 for 31 in 1998.

6. A U Rashid — 111 off 205 balls in 258 minutes 7x4; 100 off 174 balls in 226 minutes 7x4.

7. D J Wainwright — 104* off 169 balls in 203 minutes 10x4, 1x6; 100 off 166 balls in 196 minutes 10x4, 1x6.

Liverpool Victoria Championship Matches played in 2008

Captain: D Gough

*Captain
§ Wicket-Keeper

Figures in brackets ( ) indicate position in 2nd Innings batting order, where different from 1st Innings.

DETAILS OF PLAYERS WHO APPEARED FOR YORKSHIRE IN 2008
(ALL FIRST-CLASS MATCHES)

Player	Date of Birth	Birthplace	First-Class debut for Yorkshire	Date Capped
D Gough	18 Sept. 1970	Barnsley	20 April 1989	9 Sept. 1993
M P Vaughan	29 Oct. 1974	Salford	19 Aug. 1993	5 Aug. 1995
A McGrath	6 Oct. 1975	Bradford	18 May 1995	20 July 1999
M J Hoggard	31 Dec. 1976	Leeds	3 July 1996	19 July 2000
T T Bresnan	28 Feb. 1985	Pontefract	14 May 2003	19 July 2006
G J Kruis	9 May 1974	Pretoria, S A	13 April 2005	15 Sept. 2006
J A Rudolph	4 May 1981	Transvaal, S A	18 April 2007	25 April 2007
J J Sayers	11 Nov. 1983	Leeds	19 Aug. 2004	16 June 2007
G L Brophy	26 Nov. 1975	Welkom, S A	19 April 2006	31 May 2008
A W Gale	28 Nov. 1983	Dewsbury	21 July 2004	18 Sept. 2008
A U Rashid	17 Feb. 1988	Bradford	19 July 2006	18 Sept. 2008
C R Taylor	21 Feb. 1981	Rawdon	1 Aug. 2001	—
R M Pyrah	1 Nov. 1982	Dewsbury	24 Aug. 2004	—
D J Wainwright	21 Mar. 1985	Pontefract	10 Sept. 2004	—
S A Patterson	3 Oct. 1983	Beverley	3 Aug. 2005	—
A Shahzad	27 July 1985	Huddersfield	30 Aug. 2006	—
A Lyth	25 Sept. 1987	Whitby	16 May 2007	—
M Morkel	6 Oct. 1984	Vereeniging S.A	30 April 2008	—
B W Sanderson	3 Jan. 1989	Sheffield	14 May 2008	—
O J Hannon-Dalby Rana	20 June 1989	Halifax	21 May 2008	—
Naved-ul-Hasan	28 Feb. 1978	Sheikhupura Pak.	21 May 2008	—
G S Ballance	22 Nov. 1989	Harare Zim.	11 July 2008	—

Match-By-Match Reports	**NIGEL PULLAN**
Scorecards	**JOHN POTTER**

LV County Championship Division 1
Yorkshire v. Hampshire

Played at Headingley, Leeds, on April 23, 24, 25, 26, 2008
Yorkshire won an innings and 27 runs at 2.16pm on the Fourth Day

Toss won by Hampshire   Yorkshire 21 points; Hampshire 3 points
Close of play: First Day, Yorkshire 270-6 (Gale 99*, Brophy 4*); Second Day, Hampshire 115-5 (Pothas 36*, Mascarenhas 13*); Third Day, Hampshire 136-4 (Brown 58*, Pothas 28*).

YORKSHIRE

J J Sayers, b Mascarenhas		4
M P Vaughan, c Lamb b Bond		19
*A McGrath, c Brown b Mascarenhas		7
J A Rudolph, c Lumb b Lamb		59
A W Gale, b Tomlinson		138
A U Rashid, c Pothas b Lamb		15
§ G L Brophy, lbw b Tremlett		40
T T Bresnan, c Pothas b Tremlett		21
A Shahzad, c sub (L Dawson) b Lamb		35
M J Hoggard, not out		19
G J Kruis, c Lumb b Tomlinson		8
Extras lb 10, w 7, nb 16		33
Total		398

Bonus points — Yorkshire 4, Hampshire 3

FoW: 1-31 (Vaughan) 2-39 (Sayers) 3-54 (McGrath) 4-163 (Rudolph) 5-199 (Rashid)
   6-265 (Brophy) 7-293 (Bresnan) 8-371 (Gale) 9-371 (Shahzad) 10-398 (Kruis)

	O	M	R	W
Bond	19	2	82	2
Tremlett	32	9	79	2
Mascarenhas	19	5	33	2
Tomlinson	29	2	112	2
Adams	2	0	13	0
Lamb	25	9	69	2

First Innings	HAMPSHIRE		Second Innings	
M A Carberry, c Bresnan b Hoggard		13	c Sayers b Bresnan	14
M J Brown, c Gale b Hoggard		0	c Rudolph b Shahzad	81
J H K Adams, b Hoggard		7	lbw b Bresnan	4
J P Crawley, b Hoggard		25	c Bresnan b McGrath	15
M J Lumb, lbw b Hoggard		11	c Rashid b McGrath	7
§ N Pothas, c Rudolph b Hoggard		36	b Kruis	37
* A D Mascarenhas, c Gale b Shahzad		27	c Brophy b Shahzad	22
G A Lamb, c Rudolph b Kruis		2	c Rudolph b Kruis	8
C T Tremlett, c Sayers b Bresnan		12	c Brophy b Hoggard	8
J A Tomlinson, not out		11	not out	0
S E Bond, c Vaughan b Rashid		1	b Hoggard	1
Extras b1, lb5, nb8		14	Extras b4, lb6, w3, nb2	15
Total		159	Total	212

Bonus points — Yorkshire 3

FoW:	1-7 (Brown) 2-21 (Adams) 3-32 (Carberry) 4-53 (Crawley) 5-82 (Lumb)
1st	6-115 (Pothas) 7-122 (Lamb) 8-145 (Mascarenhas) 9-145 (Tremlett) 10-159 (Bond)
FoW:	1-34 (Carberry) 2-42 (Adams) 3-76 (Crawley) 4-84 (Lumb) 5-158 (Pothas)
2nd	6-190 (Brown) 7-193 (Mascarenhas) 8-209 (Tremlett) 9-209 (Lamb) 10-212 (Bond)

	O	M	R	W		O	M	R	W
Hoggard	19	3	57	6	Hoggard	16.5	4	40	2
Kruis	18	7	36	1	Kruis	19	6	37	2
Shahzad	13	6	21	1	Bresnan	14	2	36	2
Bresnan	14	5	29	1	Shahzad	11	1	43	2
Rashid	6.3	3	10	1	McGrath	13	2	27	2
					Rashid	9	1	19	0

Umpires: M J Harris and P Willey   Scorers: J T Potter and A E Weld

Gale key to innings victory

Hampshire invited Yorkshire to bat on a grey morning, and took advantage of the helpful conditions to reduce them to 54-3.

Bond, the New Zealand Test bowler, generated plenty of pace, and had **Michael Vaughan** caught at

Jacques Rudolph: Decisive catch.

slip. Mascarenhas, an experienced seam bowler, soon replaced the inaccurate Tremlett, and dismissed **Joe Sayers** and **Anthony McGrath** cheaply. A stand of 109 between **Jacques Rudolph** and **Andrew Gale** enabled Yorkshire to survive into the late afternoon as the weather improved, and the quality of the pitch became evident.

Gale's excellent innings was the basis of Yorkshire's winning total: he was 99 not out on the first evening; then he had to contend with another delayed start before he reached his second Championship century. Hampshire were handicapped on the second morning by the loss of Bond, who had injured his ankle in a fall while bowling on Wednesday, and Mascarenhas, who had an injury that prevented him from bowling.

Yorkshire batted with caution, and everyone contributed. Gale was bowled by Tomlinson for 138, including some very effective hooks and pulls, and **Ajmal Shahzad** made a career-best 35. Off spinner Lamb achieved enough turn to have Rudolph caught by Lumb at first slip.

By the close of Day 2 Hampshire were 115-5, and Hoggard had all five. Left out of the England side in New Zealand after the first Test, he now produced a long spell at full pace and with a good deal of movement. His best effort was to bowl Crawley, who seemed in good form, and he had to thank **Tim Bresnan** for an excellent low catch at fourth slip to remove Carberry. The most significant wicket was that of Pothas, caught by Rudolph off the first ball of Day 3, and this enabled the other Yorkshire bowlers to dismiss Hampshire for 159, Hoggard 6-57.

Hampshire followed on. Brown stayed for an admirable 81, but Bresnan claimed Carberry and Adams, while McGrath brought himself on to have Crawley and Lumb caught on the off side. Pothas and Brown resisted on the last morning, but after lunch Hampshire were in trouble. Hoggard took the last two wickets to complete a match analysis of 8-97.

LV County Championship Division 1
Yorkshire v. Nottinghamshire

Played at Headingley, Leeds, on April 30, May 1, 2, 3, 2008
Match drawn at 5.47pm on the Fourth Day

Toss won by Yorkshire — Yorkshire 9 points; Nottinghamshire 12 points
Close of play: First Day, Yorkshire 51-1 (Vaughan 25*, McGrath 14*); Second Day, Nottinghamshire 0-1 (Wood 0*); Third Day, Nottinghamshire 356-6 (Read 115*, Broad 52*).

First Innings	YORKSHIRE		Second Innings	
J J Sayers, b Ealham		9	c Ealham b Sidebottom	8
M P Vaughan, c Patel b Broad		42	b Swann	34
A McGrath, c Read b Shreck		36	c Read b Broad	43
J A Rudolph, not out		104	c Read b Sidebottom	32
A W Gale, lbw b Broad		4	c Ealham b Swann	26
A U Rashid, c Jefferson b Broad		4	c Voges b Sidebottom	4
§ G L Brophy, b Swann		63	c Wagh b Broad	3
T T Bresnan, run out (Sidebottom/Read)		18	not out	12
M Morkel, lbw b Swann		0	c Swann b Patel	8
* D Gough, b Swann		3	not out	8
M J Hoggard, lbw b Swann		12		
Extras lb 4		4	Extras lb8, w1	9
Total		299	Total (8 wkts)	187

Bonus points — Yorkshire 2, Nottinghamshire 3

FoW: 1-33 (Sayers) 2-78 (McGrath) 3-96 (Vaughan) 4-103 (Gale) 5-111 (Rashid)
1st 6-217 (Brophy) 7-269 (Bresnan) 8-271 (Morkel) 9-275 (Gough) 10-299 (Hoggard)
Fow: 1-18 (Sayers) 2-71 (Vaughan) 3-109 (McGrath) 4-140 (Rudolph) 5-149
2nd 6-159 (Gale) 7-159 (Brophy) 8-168 (Morkel)

	O	M	R	W		O	M	R	W
Sidebottom	24	12	45	0	Sidebottom	17	3	39	3
Shreck	33	10	78	1	Shreck	11	2	28	0
Broad	25	5	95	3	Swann	17	2	53	2
Ealham	24	7	52	1	Broad	13	4	26	2
Swann	15.5	4	25	4	Patel	8	4	22	1

NOTTINGHAMSHIRE

W I Jefferson, lbw b Hoggard		0
M J Wood, c Brophy b Bresnan		20
M A Wagh, c Rashid b Gough		56
A C Voges, c Brophy b Morkel		6
S R Patel, b Hoggard		10
* § C M W Read, c & b Bresnan		142
G P Swann, lbw b McGrath		68
S C J Broad, lbw b Rashid		53
M A Ealham, lbw b Bresnan		26
R J Sidebottom, c Brophy b Bresnan		1
C E Shreck, not out		1
Extras b 6, lb 25, nb 8		39
Total		422

Bonus points — Nottinghamshire 5, Yorkshire 3

FoW: 1-0 (Jefferson) 2-43 (Wood) 3-58 (Voges) 4-86 (Patel) 5-115 (Wagh)
6-251 (Swann) 7-364 (Broad) 8-415 (Ealham) 9-419 (Sidebottom) 10-422 (Read)

	O	M	R	W
Hoggard	25	5	92	2
$ Morkel	15.2	4	33	1
Gough	14	0	70	1
$ Bresnan	22.5	4	51	4
McGrath	17	1	57	1
Rashid	25	3	88	1

$ Morkel unable to finish his 16th over. It was completed by Bresnan.

Umpires: S A Garratt and P J Hartley   Scorers: J T Potter and L B Hughes

Yorkshire v. Nottinghamshire
Problem lies with the bowlers

MORNE MORKEL
Short-lived debut

Yorkshire made 299 after a wet first day with the excellent **Jacques Rudolph** unbeaten on 104, and **Gerard Brophy** 63. Rudolph faced 252 balls, and survived some testing bowling with the second new ball.

Nottinghamshire's formidable seam attack of Sidebottom, Broad, Shreck and Ealham bowled well enough to slow Yorkshire's scoring rate — but it was off spinner Swann who took four wickets.

Michael Vaughan made 42, but pulled a ball from Broad into the hands of Patel on the leg-side boundary having batted patiently for three hours.

Day 3 was notable for a fine century from Read, who ended on 115 over four hours, and took it to 142 next morning. Yorkshire had begun in encouraging fashion when, having dismissed Jefferson overnight, they reduced Nottinghamshire to 115-5.

Morne Morkel, a tall South African playing in his first and, as it turned out, his only first-class match for the county, took the wicket of Voges before straining a hamstring. Read received good support from Swann, who passed 50, and they increased the pace of scoring as the pitch eased, Swann showing initiative, and Read the backbone of the innings.

Read and Broad put on 105 at the end of the day to emphasise Yorkshire's problem in bowling sides out.

Nottinghamshire progressed to 422 on the last morning, and then made a valiant attempt to bowl Yorkshire out and win. It appeared as if Yorkshire would survive without alarm as Vaughan, **Anthony McGrath**, Rudolph and **Andrew Gale** took the score to 140-3 and a small lead, but five wickets fell in quick succession, leaving **Tim Bresnan** and skipper **Darren Gough** to defend for 63 deliveries to save the game. It probably would have been beyond Nottinghamshire's capability to hit the runs needed, but credit should go to their bowlers — led by **Ryan Sidebottom** — for their efforts on a slow, unresponsive wicket. The Yorkshire exile took 3-39 in 17 overs.

LV County Championship Division 1
Yorkshire v. Durham

Played at Riverside, Chester-le-Street, on May 14, 15, 16, 2008
Durham won by 295 runs at 6.36pm on the Third Day

Toss won by Durham

Yorkshire 3 points; Durham 22 points

Close of play: First Day, Durham 337-6 (Di Venuto 184*, Wiseman 21*); Second Day, Durham 16-0 (Stoneman 9*, B W Harmison 6*)

First Innings	DURHAM		Second Innings	
M J Di Venuto, lbw b Bresnan	184		(8) not out	45
M D Stoneman, c Sayers b Bresnan	27		(1) lbw b Hoggard	19
K J Coetzer, c McGrath b Bresnan	2		c McGrath b Bresnan	14
N D McKenzie, c Brophy b Gough	5		c Sayers b Hoggard	4
* D M Benkenstein, c Rashid b McGrath	29		not out	86
§ P Mustard, c Brophy b McGrath	6		lbw b Kruis	9
B W Harmison, c Brophy b Bresnan	21		(2) lbw b Bresnan	6
P J Wiseman, c Rudolph b Rashid	60		(7) lbw b Kruis	12
G Onions, c Lyth b Kruis	16			
S J Harmison, c Sayers b Kruis	0			
M Davies, not out	5			
Extras lb 23, w2, nb 26	51		Extras b2, lb 8, w2, nb 6	18
Total	406		Total (6 wkts dec)	205

Bonus points — Yorkshire 3, Durham 5, Yorkshire 3

FoW: 1-96 (Stoneman) 2-118 (Coetzer) 3-141 (McKenzie) 4-239 (Benkenstein) 5-247 (Mustard)
1st 6-292 (B W Harmison) 7-337 (Di Venuto) 8-374 (Onions) 9-384 (S J Harmison) 10-406 (Wiseman)

FoW: 1-18 (B W Harmison) 2-40 (Coetzer) 3-44 (Stoneman) 4-63 (McKenzie) 5-84 (Mustard)
2nd 6-112 (Wiseman)

	O	M	R	W		O	M	R	W
Gough	20	3	78	1	Bresnan	14	3	58	2
Kruis	29	5	98	2	Gough	6	0	21	0
Sanderson	12	4	53	0	Hoggard	14	4	27	2
Bresnan	29	6	73	4	Kruis	10	1	51	2
Rashid	20.2	4	53	1	McGrath	6	0	22	0
McGrath	11	3	28	2	Rashid	4	0	14	0
					Rudolph	1	0	2	0

First Innings	YORKSHIRE		Second Innings	
J J Sayers, c McKenzie b Onions	8		c Coetzer b B W Harmison	22
A Lyth, c McKenzie b S J Harmison	5		lbw b Onions	0
A McGrath, run out (sub: W R S Gidman)	6		lbw b Onions	0
J A Rudolph, c Mustard b S J Harmison	5		c Mustard b Onions	0
A W Gale, c Di Venuto b Onions	13		c Mustard b S J Harmison	19
§ G L Brophy, c Mustard b Onions	4		b Davies	9
A U Rashid, c Mustard b SJ Harmison	70		b B W Harmison	4
T T Bresnan, b Onions	46		not out	32
* D Gough, b Onions	1		b Davies	18
G J Kruis, c McKenzie b Davies	22		(11) b S J Harmison	2
B W Sanderson, not out	0			
M J Hoggard			(10) c sub (G R Breese) b S J Harmison	4
Extras lb 11, w 1	12		Extras b 1, lb 10, w 1	12
Total	194		Total	122

Bonus points — Durham 3

M J Hoggard replaced B W Sanderson before the start of the Third Day

FoW: 1-16 (Lyth) 2-20 (Sayers) 3-29 (McGrath) 4-42 (Gale) 5-50 (Brophy)
1st 6-50 (Rudolph) 7-135 (Bresnan) 8-139 (Gough) 9-194 (Kruis) 10-194 (Rashid)

FoW: 1-0 (Lyth) 2-10 (McGrath) 3-10 (Rudolph) 4-31 (Gale) 5-54 (Sayers)
2nd 6-60 (Rashid) 7-60 (Brophy) 8-101 (Gough) 9-114 (Hoggard) 10-122 (Kruis)

	O	M	R	W		O	M	R	W
S J Harmison	15.1	4	40	3	S J Harmison	17	6	39	3
Onions	20	3	75	5	Onions	12	3	23	3
Davies	13	4	23	1	Davies	10	3	24	2
B W Harmison	6	1	19	0	B W Harmison	6	0	25	2
Wiseman	7	1	26	0					

Umpires: N L Bainton and M J Harris

Scorers: J T Potter and B Hunt

124

Durham v. Yorkshire
Batsmen blamed for defeat

The first ball of the match from **Darren Gough** to di Venuto was a beauty that just missed the edge. By the close di Venuto was 184 not out as he dominated the Durham innings, enabling them to reach 406.

He had dogged support from Stoneman in an opening stand of 96, and Benkenstein added 98 with him for the fourth wicket before Wiseman made a valuable 61.

Yorkshire's best bowler was **Tim Bresnan**, and **Ben Sanderson** — making his first-class debut — was economical until di Venuto hit him for three fours in one over.

Yorkshire's batting failed both times. Onions was the outstanding Durham bowler with a match analysis of 8-98, along with Stephen Harmison — seeking rehabilitation in county cricket — and Davies, a very useful third seamer.

They reduced Yorkshire to 50-6. Both **Joe Sayers** and **Adam Lyth** — on his Championship debut — looked vulnerable, and soon were caught at slip. The more experienced **Jacques Rudolph** and

TIM BRESNAN
All-round effort

Anthony McGrath also went cheaply, McGrath to a run-out. Onions dismissed **Andrew Gale** and **Gerard Brophy**, so it was left to Bresnan and **Adil Rashid** to rebuild the innings with a stand of 85 for the seventh wicket. Onions returned to bowl Bresnan and Gough, and Yorkshire were all out for 194, out of which Rashid made a good 70.

Durham did not enforce the follow-on. **Matthew Hoggard**, omitted from the Lord's Test, replaced Sanderson, and he, **Deon Kruis** and Bresnan bowled well on Friday morning to reduce Durham to 112-6, although crucially Benkenstein was still there: he was joined by di Venuto, batting at No. 8 after a finger injury, and they took Durham to a 417 lead with four and a half sessions left.

Yorkshire lost three second-innings wickets for 10 runs as Lyth, McGrath and Rudolph all failed to score. Stephen Harmison was joined in the attack by his younger brother Ben, who dismissed Sayers and Rashid, while the persistent Davies also took two wickets. It was a poor batting display, and the margin of defeat was 295 runs.

Played at The Oval on May 21, 22, 23, 24, 2008
Match drawn at 4.42pm on the Fourth Day

Toss won by Surrey   Yorkshire 11 points; Surrey 11 points
Close of play: First Day, Surrey 396-5 (Butcher 189*, Nicholson 103*); Second Day, Yorkshire 292-3 (Rudolph 99*, Gale 70*); Third Day, Surrey 56-2 (Newman 26*, Hussain 7*).

SURREY	First Innings		Second Innings	
S A Newman, c Brophy b Bresnan	21		c Brophy b Kruis	31
* M A Butcher, c Rashid b Bresnan	205		c Brophy b Kruis	7
M R Ramprakash, c McGrath b Hannon-Dalby	29		c Gale b McGrath	14
U Afzaal, c Brophy b Kruis	0		(5) st Brophy b Rashid	105
A D Brown, lbw b Kruis	0		b Bresnan	6
§ J N Batty, c Sayers b McGrath	26		(7) not out	54
M J Nicholson, b Bresnan	133		(8) not out	4
J Ormond, b Naved-ul-Hasan	10			
Saqlain Mushtaq, not out	4			
Murtaza Hussain, not out	3		(4) c Brophy b McGrath	56
P T Collins	Did not bat			
Extras b 3, lb 16, nb 16	35		Extras b 1, lb 14, w1, nb 6	22
Total (8 wkts dec)	466		Total (6 wkts dec)	299

Bonus points — Surrey 5, Yorkshire 2

FoW: 1-41 (Newman) 2-112 (Ramprakash) 3-113 (Afzaal) 4-121 (Brown) 5-193 (Batty)
1st 6-425 (Butcher) 7-454 (Nicholson) 8-458 (Ormond)
FoW: 1-13 (Butcher) 2-46 (Ramprakash) 3-70 (Newman) 4-174 (Murtaza Hussain)
2nd 5-183 (Brown) 6-294 (Afzaal)

	O	M	R	W		O	M	R	W
Naved-ul-Hasan	23.4	5	98	1	Kruis	15	6	36	2
Kruis	27	3	98	2	Hannon-Dalby	14	3	56	0
Hannon-Dalby	15	2	58	1	Rashid	37	3	111	2
Bresnan	27	4	102	3	Bresnan	13	2	41	1
Rashid	18	1	51	0	Rudolph	6	1	17	0
McGrath	7	0	25	1	McGrath	16	6	23	1
Rudolph	2	0	15	0	Lyth	0.1	0	0	0

YORKSHIRE

J J Sayers, lbw b Collins	14
A Lyth, c Butcher b Saqlain Mushtaq	40
* A McGrath, lbw b Collins	54
J A Rudolph, lbw b Afzaal	121
A W Gale, c Collins b Nicholson	150
§ G L Brophy, c Nicholson b Saqlain Mushtaq	1
A U Rashid, c Newman b Afzaal	6
T T Bresnan, not out	84
Rana Naved-ul-Hasan, retired hurt	19
G J Kruis, c Ormond b Collins	17
O J Hannon-Dalby, b Collins	1
Extras b 3, lb 8, w 1, nb 6	18
Total	525

Bonus points — Yorkshire 5, Surrey 2. *Naved-ul-Hasan retired hurt with the score 465-7*
FoW: 1-22 (Sayers) 2-101 (McGrath) 3-123 (Lyth) 4-329 (Rudolph) 5-334 (Brophy)
6-343 (Rashid) 7-432 (Gale) 8-513 (Kruis) 9-525 (Hannon-Dalby)

	O	M	R	W
Collins	26.3	2	111	4
Ormond	15	0	69	0
Nicholson	16	1	81	1
Saqlain Mushtaq	39	3	139	2
Murtaza Hussain	16	0	52	0
Afzaal	20	3	62	2

Umpires: G I Burgess and N G C Cowley   Scorers: J T Potter and K R Booth

Surrey v. Yorkshire
Gale and Rudolph do the job

ANDREW GALE
Decisive stand

Highlight of the first morning from Yorkshire's point of view was when **Oliver Hannon-Dalby** — a 6ft 8in fast bowler from Halifax making his debut — had Mark Ramprakash, scorer of 99 first-class centuries, caught by **Anthony McGrath** at second slip.

A distinguished first wicket for Yorkshire, who bowled well to reduce Surrey to 193-5, but the excellent Butcher with 205 and Nicholson with a rapid 133 took command to put Surrey into a strong position.

Butcher, opening again for Surrey after three years, became the fourth Surrey batsman to make a double-century against Yorkshire, taking six and a half hours. **Rana Naved-ul-Hasan**, also on debut, was disappointing, but took the last wicket to fall.

Yorkshire responded to Surrey's large score with their best batting display so far this season: **Jacques Rudolph** was in fine form, and **Andrew Gale** confirmed the good impression he has made this year. Both **Adam Lyth** and McGrath did well — but it was the fourth-wicket stand of 206 between Rudolph and Gale that established the innings. Gale made 150 with 19 fours and a six, his second century of the season, and he exceeded his previous career-best by one run. Rudolph, 99 not out overnight, moved to 121, but then wickets fell to leave Yorkshire precariously on 343-6. **Tim Bresnan**, who must enjoy batting at the Oval, steered Yorkshire into a lead of 59. **Naved-ul-Hasan** pulled a hamstring whilst batting.

Surrey had lost Butcher and Ramprakash by the close on Friday, and they were still three runs behind, but on the last day they had no trouble in avoiding defeat on what had been too placid a pitch. Nightwatchman Murtaza Hussein made a 50, but after the loss of Brown, Afzaal and Batty saw them to safety — Afzaal reaching his century just before an early closure for an inevitable draw.

LV County Championship Division 1
Yorkshire v. Lancashire

Played at Headingley, Leeds, on May 30, 31, June 1, 2, 2008
Match drawn at 4.50pm on the Fourth Day

Toss won by Lancashire — Yorkshire 9 points; Lancashire 12 points
Close of play: First Day, Yorkshire 306-7 (Bresnan 15*, Pyrah 9*); Second Day, Lancashire 243-2 (Horton 137*, Mohammad Yousuf 93*); Third Day, no play.

YORKSHIRE

J J Sayers, lbw b Mahmood	0
A Lyth, c Sutton b Mahmood	19
A McGrath, c Sutton b Mahmood	45
J A Rudolph, c Sutton b Croft	66
A W Gale, c Loye b Keedy	32
§ G L Brophy, c Sutton b Mahmood	59
A U Rashid, c Sutton b Keedy	43
T T Bresnan, not out	64
R M Pyrah, c Cork b Keedy	24
* D Gough, c Sutton b Newby	12
B W Sanderson, c Sutton b Newby	6
Extras lb 14, w 3, nb 8	25
Total	395

Bonus points — Yorkshire 4, Lancashire 3

FoW: 1-0 (Sayers) 2-47 (Lyth) 3-94 (McGrath) 4-171 (Rudolph) 5-177 (Gale) 6-256 (Brophy) 7-297 (Rashid) 8-352 (Pyrah) 9-383 (Gough) 10-395 (Sanderson)

	O	M	R	W
Mahmood	30	8	89	4
Cork	22	6	57	0
Croft	25	4	88	1
Newby	16.4	1	81	2
Keedy	30	5	62	3
du Plessis	1	0	4	0

LANCASHIRE

P J Horton, b Rashid	152
I J Sutcliffe, lbw b Bresnan	0
M B Loye, lbw b Gough	0
Mohammad Yousuf, not out	205
F du Plessis, c Rudolph b Sanderson	0
S J Croft, lbw b Rashid	96
* § L D Sutton, not out	3
D G Cork	
S I Mahmood	Did not bat
O J Newby	
G Keedy	
Extras p 5, lb 11, w 2, nb 4	25
Total (5 wkts dec)	481

Bonus points — Yorkshire 1, Lancashire 5

FoW: 1-0 (Sutcliffe) 2-9 (Loye) 3-267 (Horton) 4-267 (du Plessis) 5-464 (Croft)

	O	M	R	W
Gough	12	5	25	1
Bresnan	29	8	77	1
Pyrah	22	6	86	0
Sanderson	25	3	87	1
Rashid	47	6	133	2
McGrath	5	0	19	0
Lyth	10	0	32	0
Gale	1	0	3	0
Rudolph	0.2	0	0	0

Umpires: J F Steele and P Willey   Scorers: J T Potter and A West

Yorkshire v. Lancashire

258 stand saves *Red Rose*

Too much time was lost for a positive result, with no play possible on Sunday.

Lancashire captain Sutton invited Yorkshire to bat first, but apart from some

Dominic Cork: Catches Richard Pyrah

good bowling by Mahmood, and later by Keedy, his seam bowlers were not as effective in helpful conditions as he might have hoped. Yorkshire's batsmen nearly all contributed, yet no one dominated.

Anthony McGrath and **Jacques Rudolph** led a recovery after **Joe Sayers** and **Adam Lyth** had succumbed to the accurate Mahmood, who achieved disconcerting bounce: he dismissed McGrath with a fine delivery straight after lunch, and Rudolph steered Croft to Cork at slip. **Andrew Gale**, **Adil Rashid**, **Gerard Brophy**, **Richard Pyrah** and **Tim Bresnan** all made useful runs, but Yorkshire fell just short of 400.

Lancashire's ebullient wicket-keeper, Luke Sutton, set a record with seven catches in the innings when he helped Newby to dismiss **Darren Gough** and **Ben Sanderson** at the end.

Yorkshire took the wickets of Sutcliffe and Loye with some alacrity — but Lancashire responded with an excellent stand of 258 between Horton and Mohammad Yousuf that equalled last year's record set in the *Roses* match by Horton and Law. Horton, who confirmed the good impression made with last year's century, has a sound defence, great patience and a good range of offside shots. He had made a career-best 152 when he was bowled by Rashid.

Yousuf, who made 192 for Pakistan in the Headingley Test of 2007, went to an unbeaten 205 off 381 balls with 19 fours and a six. Composed and unhurried, he seemed impregnable as he accumulated runs to take Lancashire into the lead and give himself a Carnegie average of 397. Croft batted with enterprise and some good fortune: as the match lost any competitive purpose his maiden century appeared inevitable, but he slowed down, and was lbw to Rashid for 96.

Adil bowled 47 overs in the Lancashire innings, conceding just under three runs per over on a good batting pitch — while Sanderson took his first wicket in the Championship, dismissing du Plessis for a duck.

LV County Championship Division 1
Yorkshire v. Somerset

Played at The County Ground, Taunton, on June 6, 7, 8, 9, 2008
Yorkshire won by 40 runs at 6.04pm on the Fourth Day

Toss won by Yorkshire   Yorkshire 21 points; Somerset 5 points
Close of play: First Day, Yorkshire 339-6 (Bresnan 5*, Patterson 1*); Second Day, Somerset 220-9 (Kieswetter 53*); Third Day, Somerset Second Innings 12-0 (Trescothick 11*, Edwards 1*).

First Innings	YORKSHIRE		Second Innings	
J A Rudolph, c Kieswetter b Blackwell	155		c Langer b Willoughby	0
A Lyth, c Edwards b Willoughby	4		c Kieswetter b Caddick	0
* A McGrath, c Thomas b Phillips	26		b Thomas	21
A W Gale, b Blackwell	61		lbw b Thomas	58
§ G L Brophy, lbw b Blackwell	70		b Thomas	9
T T Bresnan, lbw b Willoughby	5		c Kieswetter b Blackwell	9
A U Rashid, lbw b de Bruyn	5		c Kieswetter b Willoughby	30
S A Patterson, c Edwards b Phillips	17		(10) not out	13
R M Pyrah, lbw b Willoughby	0		(8) b Thomas	51
D J Wainwright, b Willoughby	5		(9) b Blackwell	5
M J Hoggard, not out	10		b Thomas	2
Extras b 5, lb 4, w 1, nb 4	14		Extras b 2, lb 4, nb 4	10
Total	372		Total	208

Bonus points — Yorkshire 4, Somerset 3

FoW: 1-14 (Lyth) 2-59 (McGrath) 3-185 (Gale) 4-315 (Brophy) 5-330 (Rudolph)
1st 6-335 (Rashid) 7-341 (Bresnan) 8-341 (Pyrah) 9-351 (Wainwright) 10-372 (Patterson)
FoW: 1-0 (Rudolph) 2-0 (Lyth) 3-78 (McGrath) 4-81 (Gale) 5-92 (Bresnan)
2nd 6-104 (Brophy) 7-146 (Rashid) 8-172 (Hoggard) 9-202 (Pyrah) 10-208 (Hoggard)

	O	M	R	W		O	M	R	W
Caddick	22	3	76	0	Willoughby	15	5	29	2
Willoughby	19	3	65	4	Caddick	11	1	34	1
Phillips	14.4	2	58	2	Blackwell	29	5	55	2
Thomas	16	4	57	0	Phillips	4	0	22	0
Blackwell	29	7	68	3	Thomas	18.3	4	46	5
de Bruyn	11	1	39	1	de Bruyn	5	1	16	0

First Innings	SOMERSET		Second Innings	
M E Trescothick, c Rashid b Patterson	51		c Wainwright b Bresnan	12
N J Edwards, lbw b Bresnan	13		c Wainwright b Bresnan	18
* J L Langer, c Brophy b Bresnan	4		c Rudolph b Patterson	10
J C Hildreth, lbw b Pyrah	42		lbw b Hoggard	2
Z de Bruyn, c Brophy b Patterson	12		b Rashid	103
I D Blackwell, b Rashid	1		c Brophy b Hoggard	64
§ C Kieswetter, not out	67		lbw b Patterson	41
B J Phillips, c Brophy b Bresnan	2		b Hoggard	7
A C Thomas, c Lyth b Patterson	28		b Rashid	5
A R Caddick, c Rudolph b Rashid	0		b Bresnan	0
C M Willoughby, c Rudolph b Hoggard	18		not out	0
Extras b 5, lb 9, w 2, nb 4	20		Extras b 8, lb 8, w 2, nb 2	20
Total	258		Total	282

Bonus points — Yorkshire 3, Somerset 2

FoW: 1-20 (Edwards) 2-24 (Langer) 3-98 (Hildreth) 4-130 (Trescothick) 5-130 (de Bruyn)
1st 6-132 (Blackwell) 7-143 (Phillips) 8-201 (Thomas) 9-220 (Caddick) 10-258 (Willoughby)
FoW: 1-25 (Trescothick) 2-33 (Edwards) 3-36 (Hildreth) 4-54 (Langer) 5-142 (Blackwell)
2nd 6-242 (Kieswetter) 7-255 (Phillips) 8-277 (Thomas) 9-282 (de Bruyn) 10-282 (Caddick)

	O	M	R	W		O	M	R	W
Hoggard	17.4	4	69	1	Hoggard	20	2	48	3
Bresnan	23	5	91	3	Bresnan	19.1	5	25	3
Pyrah	9	3	14	1	Rashid	22	3	60	2
Patterson	12	6	19	3	Patterson	16	1	56	2
Rashid	16	2	46	2	Wainwright	10	1	36	0
Wainwright	4	2	5	0	Pyrah	10	0	41	0

Umpires: B Dudleston and T E Jesty   Scorers: J T Potter and G A Stickley

Somerset v. Yorkshire

Well bowled — just in time

A Yorkshire side depleted by injury to bowlers and containing nine locally born and developed players won an evenly contested match.

A first innings of 372 proved to be important after Yorkshire had won the toss and batted. The outstanding contribution came from **Jacques Rudolph** — who made 155 on his debut as Championship opener, well supported by **Andrew Gale** and **Gerard Brophy** as Yorkshire reached 339-6 on Day 1.

Contrary to expectations, the remainder of the match did not see batsmen dominate. Somerset had 50s from Trescothick and Kieswetter, but the six-man Yorkshire attack worked well in

**JACQUES RUDOLPH
155 on debut as opener**

unison. Special praise to **Steven Patterson**, with 3-19, and **Richard Pyrah**, who had a good match as an all rounder. **Adil Rashid** bowled the dangerous hitter, Blackwell, and **Tim Bresnan** dismissed both Edwards and Langer. A last wicket-stand between Kieswetter and Willoughby saved the follow-on, which probably would not have been enforced.

Yorkshire's second innings began with the loss of both Rudolph and **Adam Lyth** without scoring: they were always in difficulties, especially with the swing bowling of Thomas, who took 5-46. Gale provided some durability in making his second 50 of the match. Wickets continued to fall, but Pyrah sustained his concentration to move to 51.

Somerset required 323 to win. It could have gone either way at the start of the last morning, or ended in a draw. Most credit should go to the Yorkshire bowlers who took 10 wickets just in time — but at one stage it looked as if Blackwell, de Bruyn and Kieswetter would win the game for Somerset. It was a good morning for Yorkshire as four batsmen departed — including both Trescothick and Edwards, caught by **David Wainwright** at fine-leg, but the match swung Somerset's way with partnerships of 88 and 100 for the fifth and sixth wickets.

de Bruyn remained implacable, and as prospects of a home win receded he was determined to force a draw. Rashid now intervened to bowl Thomas — and then a crucially pitched leg-break bowled de Bruyn for 103 with four overs remaining. Bresnan yorked Caddick next ball.

131

LV County Championship Division 1
Yorkshire v. Durham

Played at Headingley, Leeds, on June 29, 30, July 1, 2008
Durham won by 8 wickets at 4.52pm on the Third Day

Toss won by Durham   Yorkshire 3 points; Durham 20 points
Close of play: First Day, Durham 59-3 (B W Harmison 21*, Benkenstein 6*); Second Day,
Yorkshire 88-2 (Vaughan 48*, Lyth 33*)

First Innings	YORKSHIRE		Second Innings	
J A Rudolph, c Di Venuto b Plunkett	11		c Mustard b Thorp	3
M P Vaughan, c Mustard b Thorp	0		b S J Harmison	72
A McGrath, lbw b Plunkett	15		c Mustard b Thorp	2
A Lyth, c Collingwood b Thorp	40		c Mustard b SJ Harmison	80
A W Gale, lbw b Plunkett	33		c Mustard b Thorp	32
§ G L Brophy, c Mustard b Collingwood	43		c B W Harmison b Thorp	18
A U Rashid, c Morkel b SJ Harmison	22		c Collingwood b Plunkett	6
T T Bresnan, c Morkel b SJ Harmison	4		c Mustard b Plunkett	10
* D Gough, b Collingwood	0		b Thorp	34
S A Patterson, not out	0		b Plunkett	6
M J Hoggard, b Collingwood	0		not out	0
Extras lb 7, w 1, nb 8	16		Extras b 1, lb 4, w 1, nb 4	10
Total	184		Total	273

Bonus points — Durham 3

FoW: 1-10 (Vaughan) 2-18 (Rudolph) 3-51 (McGrath) 4-109 (Gale) 5-111 (Lyth)
1st   6-166 (Rashid) 7-180 (Brophy) 8-184 (Bresnan) 9-184 (Gough) 10-184 (Hoggard)
FoW: 1-9 (Rudolph) 2-13 (McGrath) 3-151 (Lyth) 4-184 (Vaughan) 5-201 (Gale)
2nd   6-213 (Rashid) 7-233 (Brophy) 8-233 (Bresnan) 9-253 (Patterson) 10-273 (Gough)

	O	M	R	W		O	M	R	W
S J Harmison	15	4	43	2	S J Harmison	20	4	97	2
Thorp	13	4	38	2	Thorp	18.4	3	71	5
Plunkett	15	1	70	3	Plunkett	13	0	49	3
B W Harmison	3	1	9	0	Collingwood	7	1	31	0
Wiseman	1	1	0	0	Wiseman	6	0	15	0
Collingwood	3.5	0	17	3	B W Harmison	1	0	5	0

First Innings	DURHAM		Second Innings	
M J Di Venuto, lbw b Hoggard	0		(2) not out	65
B W Harmison, c Gough b Bresnan	28		(1) c Bresnan b Hoggard	2
W R Smith, c McGrath b Bresnan	20		c Brophy b Hoggard	0
P D Collingwood, c Hoggard b Rashid	5		not out	44
* D M Benkenstein, c Brophy b Patterson	40			
J A Morkel, c Brophy b Gough	37			
§ P Mustard, c Brophy b Bresnan	92			
P J Wiseman, b Bresnan	8			
L E Plunkett, not out	68			
C D Thorp, b Bresnan	1			
S J Harmison, c Lyth b Patterson	17			
Extras b 1, lb 17, w 2, nb 11	31		Extras nb 2	2
Total	347		Total (2 wkts)	113

Bonus points — Yorkshire 3, Durham 3

FoW: 1-0 (Di Venuto) 2-30 (Smith) 3-52 (Collingwood) 4-90 (B W Harmison) 5-127 (Benkenstein)
1st   6-147 (Morkel) 7-161 (Wiseman) 8-304 (Mustard) 9-308 (Thorp) 10-347 (S J Harmison)
2nd: 1-8 (B W Harmison) 2-8 (Smith)

	O	M	R	W		O	M	R	W
Hoggard	25	4	96	1	Hoggard	6	1	22	2
Bresnan	26	2	94	5	Bresnan	8	2	35	0
Gough	16	5	31	1	Patterson	8	3	19	0
Patterson	16.1	4	50	2	Gough	2	1	10	0
Rashid	6	0	26	1	Rashid	3.2	0	27	0
McGrath	5	0	32	0					

Umpires: P J Hartley and N A Mallender   Scorers: J T Potter and B Hunt

The double we did not want

On a gloomy morning Durham invited Yorkshire to bat: they were 88-3 at lunch, but after a long rain break Durham dominated in the evening sunshine.

Test bowlers Stephen Harmison and Plunkett impressed, but Thorp was the most outstanding. He bowled his first three overs to **Michael Vaughan** — dismissing him with the 18th ball. Plunkett accounted for **Jacques Rudolph** and **Anthony McGrath**, but **Adam Lyth** and **Andrew Gale** survived until lunch.

Once they had gone, Yorkshire's innings subsided despite 43 from **Gerard Brophy** as Collingwood took 3-17, but before the close they had three Durham wickets — including that of Collingwood caught by **Matthew Hoggard** at long-on after an injudicious swipe at Rashid.

Having reduced Durham to 161-7 on Day 2 Yorkshire were in a good position, but Durham retaliated with a stand of 143 led by wicket-keeper Mustard supported by Plunkett. This turned the match, and gave Durham an eventual lead of 163.

Mustard demonstrated both determination and fluency, and was disappointed to be out just before tea for 92, caught behind off **Tim Bresnan**. Plunkett then took over in a last-wicket stand with Stephen Harmison worth 39 runs.

**MICHAEL VAUGHAN
Dual with Harmison**

Bresnan earned his 5-94, and **Steven Patterson** would have been pleased to dismiss Blenkenstein.

Yorkshire needed at least one long innings to save the match: Vaughan proceeded carefully to 72, but he was then bowled by the persevering Stephen Harmison. Lyth produced an encouraging career-best 80, but fell to the same bowler. Otherwise, Durham worked their way methodically through the side, and Thorp was rewarded with 5-71.

A score of 273 was reasonable, but the middle and lower order disappointed. Hoggard took two quick wickets before di Venuto and Collingwood took Durham to decisive victory and the double.

LV County Championship Division 1
Yorkshire v. Kent

Played at St Lawrence Ground, Canterbury, on July 11, 12, 13, 14, 2008

Kent won by 3 wickets at 2.15pm on the Fourth Day

Toss won by Yorkshire   Yorkshire 8 points; Kent 22 points

Close of play: First Day, Yorkshire 359-5 (Rudolph 121*, Hoggard 1*); Second Day, Kent 298-6 (Key 122*, Azhar Mahmood 21*); Third Day, Yorkshire 196 all out.

First Innings	YORKSHIRE		Second Innings	
A W Gale, c Stevens b Joseph	10		c Jones b Tredwell	36
A Lyth, lbw b Azhar Mahmood	50		c van Jaarsveld b Yasir Arafat	8
* A McGrath, c van Jaarsveld b Saggers	144		c van Jaarsveld b Azhar Mahmood	25
J A Rudolph, c Jones b Azhar Mahmood	129		c Azhar Mahmood b van Jaarsveld	47
G S Ballance, lbw b Yasir Arafat	1		c van Jaarsveld b Saggers	5
§ G L Brophy, c Stevens b Yasir Arafat	0		lbw b Yasir Arafat	51
M J Hoggard, c Jones b Azhar Mahmood	24		(10) not out	0
A U Rashid, c Kemp b Azhar Mahmood	0		(7) c Kemp b Joseph	4
T T Bresnan, lbw b Azhar Mahmood	10		(8) c Joseph	2
Rana Naved-ul-Hasan, c Stevens b Azhar Mahmood	4		(9) c Denly b Yasir Arafat	8
G J Kruis, not out	5		c Kemp b Yasir Arafat	3
Extras b 4, lb 9, w 2, nb 18	33		Extras b 1, lb 3, w 1, nb 2	7
Total	410		Total	196

Bonus points — Yorkshire 5, Kent 3

FoW: 1-27 (Gale) 2-124 (Lyth) 3-341 (McGrath) 4-344 (Ballance) 5-348 (Brophy)
1st 6-384 (Rudolph) 7-384 (Rashid) 8-395 (Hoggard) 9-399 (Naved-ul-Hasan) 10-410 (Bresnan)
FoW: 1-8 (Lyth) 2-68 (McGrath) 3-72 (Gale) 4-89 (Ballance) 5-173 (Rudolph)
2nd 6-176 (Brophy) 7-182 (Rashid) 8-193 (Naved-ul-Hasan) 9-193 (Bresnan) 10-196 (Kruis)

	O	M	R	W		O	M	R	W
Yasir Arafat	23	3	95	2	Azhar Mahmood	10	1	36	1
Joseph	12	1	66	1	Yasir Arafat	9.1	2	38	4
Azhar Mahmood	24.4	6	55	6	Tredwell	13	4	51	1
Saggers	14	0	59	1	van Jaarsveld	4	0	10	1
Tredwell	29	5	89	0	Saggers	8	2	32	1
Stevens	2	0	15	0	Joseph	7	1	25	2
van Jaarsveld	5	1	18	0					

First Innings	KENT		Second Innings	
J L Denly, lbw b Hoggard	48		c Bresnan b Hoggard	19
* R W T Key, b Rashid	157		c Brophy b Hoggard	15
J C Tredwell, c Gale b Rashid	48		c Rudolph b Rashid	6
M van Jaarsveld, b McGrath	3		lbw b Naved-ul-Hasan	41
D I Stevens, c Rudolph b Rashid	3		st Brophy b Rashid	4
J M Kemp, c Rudolph b Rashid	12		c Brophy b Naved-ul-Hasan	10
§ G O Jones, lbw b Naved-ul-Hasan	10		not out	20
Azhar Mahmood, c Brophy b Bresnan	23		c Brophy b Naved-ul-Hasan	2
Yasir Arafat, not out	90		not out	19
R H Joseph, c Rudolph b Rashid	2			
M J Saggers, c Brophy b Bresnan	33			
Extras b 3, lb 14, nb 21	38		Extras b 4, lb 2	6
Total	467		Total (7 wkts)	142

Bonus points — Yorkshire 3, Kent 5

FoW: 1-68 (Denly) 2-203 (Tredwell) 3-208 (van Jaarsveld) 4-211 (Stevens) 5-235 (Kemp)
1st 6-261 (Jones) 7-305 (Azhar Mahmood) 8-396 (Key) 9-398 (Joseph) 10-467 (Saggers)
FoW: 1-30 (Denly) 2-37 (Key) 3-51 (Tredwell) 4-63 (Stevens) 5-101 (van Jaarsveld)
2nd 6-102 (Kemp) 7-108 (Mahmood)

	O	M	R	W		O	M	R	W
Hoggard	14	0	57	1	Hoggard	11	2	27	2
Naved-ul-Hasan	19	1	102	1	Bresnan	10	1	31	0
Kruis	21	3	82	0	Rashid	9	0	46	2
Bresnan	25	2	51	2	Kruis	4	0	8	0
Rashid	35	2	140	5	Naved-ul-Hasan	4.3	0	24	3
McGrath	7	1	18	1					

Umpires: T E Jesty all days; RA Kettleborough Days 1 and 2; J Halliday Day 3, session 1;
T J Urben Day 3, sessions 2 and 3, and Day 4   Scorers: J T Potter and J C Foley

Batsmen crumble too easily

Yorkshire took advantage of a docile pitch on this handsome ground where Gentlemen of Kent first played in 1847 when Fuller Pilch was groundsman.

The visitors amassed 359-5, based on a fine 144 from **Anthony McGrath** and an unbeaten 120 from **Jacques Rudolph**. **Gary Ballance** on debut made only a single, but **Adam Lyth** made exactly 50.

Yorkshire did not capitalise on their first day. Excellent fast-medium bowling from Azhar Mahmood accounted for all five remaining wickets next morning, and he finished with 6-55.

Kent began apace. They lost Denly at 68 before caption Key and Tredwell took it to 203, but van Jaarsveld and Stephens fell in quick succession while Key held his end in solid defiance. Kent were 305-7 when Arafat joined Key, but the last three wickets saw 162 runs.

Key played an outstanding innings — and it was only when Rashid came round the wicket to bowl him round his legs that Yorkshire broke through.

Arafat was left on 90 not out when Saggers fell to **Tim Bresnan** to end a last-wicket stand of 69. Rashid achieved significant turn, taking five wickets, mostly of top-order batsmen.

Yorkshire's second innings was disappointing. **Andrew Gale** and Rudolph did reasonably well, but no one could

ANTHONY MCGRATH
Amassed fine 144

stay with **Gerard Brophy** as the middle-order submitted too easily to the varied Kent attack. There were some good catches — and Ballance fell to a brilliant one by van Jaarsveld in the slips.

At 101-4 Kent were in control. **Naved-ul-Hasan**, who had had a poor match with bat and ball, and did not bowl before lunch, took wickets with his first and sixth balls afterwards and one in the next over. At 108-7 Yorkshire could win if they could separate Jones and the indomitable Arafat. This pair advanced with trepidation towards a narrow victory.

LV County Championship Division 1
Yorkshire v. Nottinghamshire

Played at Trent Bridge, Nottingham, on July 22, 23, 24, 25, 2008

Nottinghamshire won by 112 runs at 4.09pm on the Fourth Day

Toss won by Nottinghamshire   Yorkshire 3 points; Nottinghamshire 18 points

Close of play: First Day, Yorkshire 72-5 (Brophy 0*, Hoggard 0*); Second Day, Nottinghamshire 146-2 (Wagh 56*, Patel 12*); Third Day, Yorkshire 107-4 (Lyth 35*, Brophy 20*)

NOTTINGHAMSHIRE	First Innings		Second Innings	
M J Wood, c Brophy b Naved-ul-Hasan	58		lbw b Hoggard	14
B M Shafayat, c Bresnan b Hoggard	1		c Naved-ul-Hasan b Hoggard	62
M A Wagh, b Naved-ul-Hasan	33		lbw b Kruis	60
S R Patel, lbw b Naved-ul-Hasan	0		c Rudolph b Bresnan	60
A C Voges, c Bresnan b Hoggard	45		lbw b Bresnan	43
G P Swann, c Brophy b Kruis	27		st Brophy b Rashid	57
* § C M W Read, c Brophy b Bresnan	19		c Taylor b Rashid	26
M A Ealham, c Rudolph b Rashid	14		c Kruis b Hoggard	13
P J Franks, run out (Bresnan/Brophy)	0		b Rashid	4
A R Adams, not out	0		b Rashid	1
C E Shreck, c Lyth b Rashid	0		not out	0
Extras lb 9, nb 6	15		Extras b 1, lb 6, w 1, nb 2	10
Total	213		Total	350

Bonus points — Yorkshire 3, Nottinghamshire 1

FoW: 1-3 (Shafayat) 2-62 (Wagh) 3-62 (Patel) 4-111 (Wood) 5-170 (Swann)
1st   6-189 (Voges) 7-212 (Ealham) 8-212 (Read) 9-213 (Franks) 10-213 (Shreck)
FoW: 1-22 (Wood) 2-125 (Shafayat) 3-150 (Wagh) 4-228 (Voges) 5-265 (Patel)
2nd   6-305 (Read) 7-336 (Swann) 8-344 (Franks) 9-346 (Adams) 10-350 (Ealham)

	O	M	R	W		O	M	R	W
Hoggard	17	3	38	2	Hoggard	25.2	9	62	3
Bresnan	16	2	54	1	Bresnan	24	6	80	2
Kruis	12	2	37	1	$ Naved-ul-Hasan	9.3	3	29	0
Naved-ul-Hasan	16	3	63	3	$ Kruis	22.3	7	61	1
Rashid	7	2	12	2	Rashid	33	5	96	4
					Lyth	4	0	15	0

$ Naved-ul-Hasan unable to complete 10th over.

YORKSHIRE	First Innings		Second Innings	
J J Sayers, c Adams b Shreck	9		c Read b Shreck	2
C R Taylor, c Adams b Shreck	0		lbw b Ealham	48
A Lyth, c Swann b Adams	22		lbw b Adams	132
* J A Rudolph, lbw b Ealham	19		c Read b Ealham	0
A W Gale, lbw b Ealham	4		c Swann b Ealham	0
§ G L Brophy, lbw b Shreck	8		b Ealham	28
M J Hoggard, c Ealham b Adams	1		(9) lbw b Ealham	0
A U Rashid, lbw b Shreck	4		(7) lbw b Swann	21
T T Bresnan, lbw b Ealham	32		(8) lbw b Ealham	36
Rana Naved-ul-Hasan, b Shreck	18		(11) not out	1
G J Kruis, not out	17		(10) lbw b Ealham	6
Extras b 5, lb 3, w 6, nb 8	22		Extras b 4, lb 4, nb 8	16
Total	161		Total	290

Bonus points — Nottinghamshire 3

FoW: 1-1 (Taylor) 2-18 (Sayers) 3-68 (Rudolph) 4-72 (Lyth) 5-72 (Gale)
1st   6-73 (Hoggard) 7-88 (Rashid) 8-95 (Brophy) 9-115 (Naved-ul-Hasan) 10-161 (Bresnan)
FoW: 1-2 (Sayers) 2-75 (Taylor) 3-75 (Rudolph) 4-75 (Gale) 5-139 (Brophy)
2nd   6-190 (Rashid) 7-283 (Lyth) 8-283 (Bresnan) 9-289 (Kruis) 10-290 (Hoggard)

	O	M	R	W		O	M	R	W
Shreck	20	4	58	5	Shreck	26	8	69	1
Adams	18	7	36	2	Adams	17	1	69	1
Franks	8	1	30	0	Franks	9	1	50	0
Ealham	8.2	3	17	3	Ealham	26.4	12	59	7
Swann	5	1	12	0	Swann	18	7	23	1
					Patel	4	1	12	0

Umpires: J H Evans and N J Llong   Scorers: J T Potter and L B Hewes

Nottinghamshire v. Yorkshire

Lyth shines through gloom

Nottinghamshire were out for 213 on Day 1, thanks to a good all-round bowling performance led by **Matthew Hoggard** and **Rana Naved-ul-Hasan**.

Wood and Voges batted well after early wickets, but the hosts lost four more for one run after tea.

Shreck retaliated by dismissing both openers, and Ealham began his depredations by picking up **Jacques Rudolph** and **Andrew Gale** just before the close.

On Wednesday intelligent swing bowling by Shreck

Adam Lyth: Maiden century

ensured that Yorkshire did not recover, as he took 5-58. Naved-ul-Hasan hit him for two fours and a six, but it was only the last-wicket stand of 46 by **Tim Bresnan** and **Deon Kruis** that raised the score to 161.

The match slipped further from Yorkshire's grasp as their bowlers failed to exploit the conditions: they allowed Wagh and Shafayat to add an untroubled 103 for the second wicket before Shafayat fell to a smart catch on the rebound by Naved-ul-Hasan after Hoggard had fumbled a caught-and-bowled chance.

Nottinghamshire consolidated on the third morning, which began with an injury to Naved-ul-Hasan after three balls. Kruis immediately had Wagh lbw, but all the Nottinghamshire middle-order made some contribution to a formidable 350. **Adil Rashid** deserved his late wickets for his persistence and skill. Yorkshire began well, reaching 75-1, but lost three key wickets to Ealham right at the end of the day.

Two outstanding performances embellished a last-day win for Nottinghamshire. **Adam Lyth** made an excellent maiden first-class century, showing patience and resolution, and when he was batting with Bresnan there was a distinct possibility of saving the game. The left-hander from Whitby — playing only his eighth first-class game — displayed good concentration and elegant cover-driving. He and Bresnan fell in successive balls as Ealham went on to claim 7-59, bowling straight and obtaining sufficient movement to disconcert the batsmen.

LV County Championship Division 1
Yorkshire v. Surrey

Played at Headingley, Leeds, on July 30, 31, August 1, 2, 2008
Match drawn at 4.48pm on the Fourth Day

Toss won by Surrey   Yorkshire 12 points; Surrey 8 points

Close of play: First Day, Yorkshire 50-0 (Gale 38*, Taylor 9*); Second Day, Yorkshire 80-0 (Gale 53*, Taylor 23*); Third Day, Yorkshire 414-9 (Rashid 67*, Kruis 50*)

SURREY

First Innings		Second Innings	
S A Newman, lbw b Bresnan	29	b Wainwright	129
S J Walters, c Lyth b Bresnan	40	c Pyrah b Bresnan	0
* M R Ramprakash, b Kruis	6	not out	112
§ J N Batty, c Pyrah b Kruis	0	c Gale Rashid	0
U Afzaal, lbw b Kruis	1	not out	1
M N W Spriegel, b Kruis	29		
M J Nicholson, lbw b Bresnan	25		
C J Jordan, c Rashid b Kruis	7		
Saqlain Mushtaq, not out	22		
J W Dernbach, lbw b Bresnan	1		
P T Collins, run out (Kruis/Rashid)	21		
Extras b 11, lb 7, w 1, nb 4	23	Extras b 7, lb 8, w 1, nb 6	22
Total	204	Total (3 wkts)	264

Bonus points — Yorkshire 3, Surrey 1

FoW: 1-41 (Newman) 2-69 (Ramprakash) 3-69 (Batty) 4-71 (Afzaal) 5-94 (Walters)
1st 6-139 (Nicholson) 7-152 (Jordan) 8-162 (Spriegel) 9-167 (Dernbach) 10-204 (Collins)
2nd: 1-0 (Walters) 2-259 (Newman) 3-260 (Batty)

	O	M	R	W		O	M	R	W
Gough	8	2	36	0	Gough	9	2	31	0
Bresnan	13	5	36	2	Bresnan	10	0	52	1
Kruis	17	5	47	5	Pyrah	4	1	13	0
Pyrah	6	1	27	0	Kruis	12	3	36	0
Rashid	11.1	2	40	2	Rashid	17	1	47	1
Wainwright	1	1	0	0	Wainwright	19	3	59	1
					Lyth	3	1	11	0

YORKSHIRE

A W Gale, c Batty b Dernbach	63
C R Taylor, lbw b Jordan	23
A Lyth, c Batty b Nicholson	36
J A Rudolph, run out (Walters)	64
§ G L Brophy, c Batty b Jordan	23
R M Pyrah, b Collins	12
A U Rashid, not out	67
T T Bresnan, c Jordan b Dernbach	10
D J Wainwright, hit wicket b Collins	19
* D Gough, b Collins	1
G J Kruis, not out	50
Extras p 5, b 4, lb 18, w 3, nb 16	46
Total (9 wkts dec)	414

Bonus points — Yorkshire 5, Surrey 3

FoW: 1-82 (Taylor) 2-104 (Gale) 3-149 (Lyth) 4-220 (Brophy) 5-240 (Rudolph)
6-257 (Pyrah) 7-282 (Bresnan) 8-323 (Wainwright) 9-327 (Gough)

	O	M	R	W
Collins	24	4	74	3
Dernbach	21	3	92	2
Nicholson	21	4	69	1
Saqlain Mushtaq	33	8	77	0
Afzaal	4	0	12	0
Jordan	18	5	53	2
Walters	5	1	10	0

Umpires: R K Illingworth and J W Lloyds   Scorers: J T Potter and K R Booth

Mark Ramprakash 100 100s

Deon Kruis: Last-man 50

A rejuvenated **Deon Kruis** grabbed 5-47, his best figures for Yorkshire, as the home county did very well on the opening day to dismiss Surrey, who had won the toss, for 204.

Kruis bowled Ramprakash with a ball which moved across to take the off bail, then quickly sent back Batty and Afzaal — Batty to a brilliant catch by the agile **Richard Pyrah** at slip.

Walters played a dogged innings, but soon Surrey were 167-9, and only a last-wicket stand by Collins and Saqlain earned them a bonus point. Yorkshire progressed to 80 without loss on a shortened second day — and they spent the third day, which began on time, thanks to valiant efforts by the ground staff, compiling a total of 414 to give them an important lead.

It was good to see an opening stand of 82 from **Andrew Gale** and **Chris Taylor** that was the highest for over a year in the Championship. Gale made 63 and **Jacques Rudolph** 64 before he was run out. The Surrey attack was led by the West Indian Test bowler, Collins, but it was young fast bowler Jordan who caught the eye.

At 327-9 the Yorkshire innings was revived by a remarkable contribution from Kruis — whose unbeaten 50 included six fours and a massive six that threatened the chronometrical version of **Dickie Bird**. **Adil Rashid** kept admiring company with Kruis, and finished on 67 not out.

The last day was memorable for Mark Ramprakash's 100th 100 (see colour plates). He had made his 99th as long ago as May 3, and his first at Headingley in 1989. He regained his composure after a tentative start, and proceeded to a relatively untroubled century. It was a pleasure to witness what may well be the last time this milestone is passed.

Newman also made a good 100, overshadowed perhaps by the occasion, and together they took away any prospect of a Yorkshire victory. **David Wainwright** bowled Newman for 129, some consolation for conceding Ramprakash's 100th run, and then the rain came again.

LV County Championship Division 1
Yorkshire v. Hampshire

Played at The Rose Bowl, Southampton, on August 6, 7, 8, 2008

Hampshire won by 10 wickets at 3.22pm on the Third Day

Toss won by Yorkshire   Yorkshire 4 points; Hampshire 18 points
Close of play: First Day, Yorkshire 206-7 (Rudolph 83*, Wainwright 18*); Second Day, Hampshire 236 all out.

First Innings	YORKSHIRE		Second Innings	
A W Gale, c Mascarenhas b Tremlett		0	b Imran Tahir	31
C R Taylor, c Pothas b Tomlinson		27	lbw b Imran Tahir	23
* A McGrath, lbw b Mascarenhas		3	lbw b Imran Tahir	0
J A Rudolph, c Pothas b Tremlett		89	c Pothas b Tomlinson	2
A Lyth, c & b Mascarenhas		12	lbw b Tomlinson	0
§ G L Brophy, b Tomlinson		36	c Pothas b Tomlinson	0
A U Rashid, c Brown b Tomlinson		2	c Pothas b Tomlinson	6
Rana Naved-ul-Hasan, b Imran Tahir		11	c Carberry b Balcombe	22
D J Wainwright, c Pothas b Tomlinson		25	lbw b Imran Tahir	7
M J Hoggard, c Mascarenhas b Tomlinson		7	c Ervine b Balcombe	0
G J Kruis, not out		3	not out	8
Extras b 2, lb 11, nb 8		21	Extras lb 5, w 3	8
Total		236	Total	107

Bonus points — Yorkshire 1, Hampshire 3

FoW: 1-0 Gale) 2-17 (McGrath) 3-56 (Taylor) 4-82 (Lyth) 5-130 (Brophy) 6-134 (Rashid)
1st   7-145 (Naved-ul-Hasan) 8-220 (Wainwright) 9-220 (Rudolph) 10-236 (Hoggard)
FoW: 1-45 (Gale) 2-45 (McGrath) 3-52 (Rudolph) 4-52 (Lyth) 5-54 (Brophy) 6-66 (Rashid)
     7-85 (Taylor) 8-97 (Wainwright) 9-98 (Hoggard) 10-107 (Naved-ul-Hasan)

	O	M	R	W		O	M	R	W
Tremlett	24	6	61	2	Tremlett	8	1	28	0
Mascarenhas	21	13	23	2	Tomlinson	8	1	31	4
Balcombe	8	2	29	0	Mascarenhas	2	0	5	0
Tomlinson	21.5	8	53	5	Imran Tahir	11	1	37	4
Ervine	7	0	26	0	Balcombe	1.1	0	1	2
Imran Tahir	11	2	30	1					
Carberry	1	0	1	0					

First Innings	HAMPSHIRE		Second Innings	
M A Carberry, c Brophy b Naved-ul-Hasan		46	not out	53
M J Brown, lbw b Rashid		45	not out	46
S M Ervine, st Brophy b Wainwright		43		
M J Lumb, c Lyth b Rashid		21		
C C Benham, lbw b Rashid		0		
§ N Pothas, c Lyth b Rashid		8		
* A D Mascarenhas, lbw b Wainwright		10		
C T Tremlett, st Brophy b Rashid		4		
D J Balcombe, not out		20		
Imran Tahir, c Rudolph b Rashid		4		
J A Tomlinson, c McGrath b Rashid		22		
Extras b 4, lb 6, w 1, nb 2		13	Extras b 4, lb 2, w 1, nb 2	9
Total		236	Total (0 wkts)	108

Bonus points — Yorkshire 3, Hampshire 1

FoW: 1-82 (Brown) 2-108 (Carberry) 3-157 (Lumb) 4-157 (Benham) 5-165 (Ervine) 6-181
(Pothas) 7-190 (Mascarenhas) 8-190 (Tremlett) 9-198 (Imran Tahir) 10-236 (Tomlinson)

	O	M	R	W		O	M	R	W
Hoggard	11	5	23	0	Hoggard	4	0	25	0
Naved-ul-Hasan	13	2	38	1	Naved-ul-Hasan	5	1	7	0
Kruis	12	2	30	0	Rashid	9	0	37	0
Rashid	31.1	1	107	7	Kruis	2	0	7	0
Wainwright	12	4	28	2	Wainwright	4.1	0	26	0

Umpires: R A Kettleborough and N A Mallender   Scorers: J T Potter and A E Weld

Yorkshire batsmen routed

ADIL RASHID
Magnificent seven

Yorkshire won the toss and batted on what was a tedious first day. They did attempt to play sensibly — but with the exception of **Jacques Rudolph** and **David Wainwright** their vulnerability was evident as wickets fell with regularity.

The best Hampshire bowler was Tomlinson, who took 5-58, while Mascarenhas claimed the wickets of **Anthony McGrath** and **Adam Lyth**.

Rudolph began to hit the ball with more confidence after Wainwright joined him at 145-7: without Rudolph's contribution Yorkshire would have been in serious difficulty, and when he was out on Thursday morning the innings was soon concluded.

Hampshire appeared to have established a distinct advantage when they reached 157-2. Lumb and Ervine seemed assured — but **Adil Rashid** and Wainwright were already bowling well on a pitch that rewarded spin.

The turning point came when Rashid turned a ball out of the rough into the left-handed Lumb, and Lyth caught him at short-leg. Next ball Benham misjudged the faster top-spinner, and was lbw. Ervine abandoned caution, but his assault on Wainwright ended in a stumping with the batsman well down. Rashid bowled very well, and deserved his career-best 7-107. After Hampshire's collapse a last-wicket stand between Tomlinson and Balcombe brought their total to exactly the same as Yorkshire's.

The third and last day was a remarkable one: Yorkshire were all out for 107, and Hampshire made 108 to win by 10 wickets. All credit to Tomlinson, whose 4-31 gave him match figures of 9-84, and to Imran Tahir, briefly a Yorkshire player last September, who took 4-37.

Andrew Gale and **Chris Taylor** reached 45 before Imran was introduced, but his fifth ball bowled Gale — and his googly accounted for McGrath next ball. Tomlinson returned after a wayward first spell to take four wickets in five overs, and Yorkshire were 66-6. A vigilant Taylor had survived, playing mostly on the front foot, but succumbed to the top-spinner to be seventh out, and Yorkshire were dismissed for 107.

Hampshire openers Carberry and Brown appeared untroubled by the five bowlers Yorkshire tried.

LV County Championship Division 1
Yorkshire v. Lancashire

Played at Old Trafford, Manchester, on August 12, 13, 14, 15, 2008
Match drawn at 5.15pm on the Fourth Day

Toss won by Lancashire   Yorkshire 12 points; Lancashire 7 points
Close of play: First Day, no play; Second Day, Lancashire 204-8 (Croft 56*, Keedy 11*);
Third Day, Yorkshire 234-2 (Gale 111*, Rudolph 3*)

LANCASHIRE

First Innings		Second Innings	
P J Horton, lbw b Rashid	16	(2) not out	69
I J Sutcliffe, b Hoggard	3	(1) c Brophy b Hoggard	4
* S G Law, c McGrath b Bresnan	37	c Gough b Bresnan	4
F du Plessis, c McGrath b Rashid	38	b Rashid	3
L Vincent, c Brophy b Rashid	4	not out	13
S J Croft, c Naved-ul-Hasan b Rashid	68		
§ L D Sutton, c Brophy b Hoggard	9		
G Chapple, b Hoggard	11		
D G Cork, c Naved-ul-Hasan b Rashid	1		
G Keedy, not out	25		
S I Mahmood, c Bresnan b Rashid	0		
Extras b 8, lb 5, nb 6	19	Extras b 2, lb 7, nb 2	11
Total	231	Total (3 wkts)	104

Bonus points — Lancashire 1, Yorkshire 3

FoW: 1-3 (Sutcliffe) 2-57 (Horton) 3-69 (Law) 4-87 (Vincent) 5-133 (du Plessis)
1st 6-142 (Sutton) 7-164 (Chapple) 8-165 (Cork) 9-231 (Croft) 10-231 (Mahmood)
2nd 1-4 (Sutcliffe) 2-23 (Law) 3-29 (Du Plessis)

	O	M	R	W		O	M	R	W
Hoggard	13	3	26	3	Hoggard	4	0	17	1
Naved-ul-Hasan	12	1	40	0	Bresnan	4	1	7	1
Bresnan	10	1	34	2	Rudolph	4	0	15	0
Gough	8	1	23	0	Rashid	16	6	16	1
Rashid	30.4	4	95	5	Lyth	7	2	22	0
					Naved-ul-Hasan	4	0	11	0
					Gough	3	1	7	0

YORKSHIRE

A W Gale, c Chapple b du Plessis	136
C R Taylor, lbw b Cork	2
A McGrath, lbw b du Plessis	99
J A Rudolph, c Sutton b du Plessis	54
A Lyth, run out (du Plessis/Sutton)	1
T T Bresnan, not out	47
§ G L Brophy, st Sutton b Keedy	14
A U Rashid, not out	15
Rana Naved-ul-Hasan	
M J Hoggard Did not bat	
* D Gough	
Extras b 16, lb 11, w 1, nb 4	32
Total (6 wkts dec)	400

Bonus points — Yorkshire 5, Lancashire 2

FoW: 1-4 (Taylor) 2-219 (McGrath) 3-306 (Gale) 4-312 (Lyth) 5-318 (Rudolph)
6-349 (Brophy)

	O	M	R	W
Chapple	21	6	52	0
Cork	12	2	26	1
Keedy	48.5	7	142	1
Mahmood	12	0	42	0
du Plessis	21	3	61	3
Croft	14	2	50	0

Umpires: G I Burgess and A A Jones   Scorers: J T Potter and A West

Lancashire v. Yorkshire

For the lack of two spinners...

This was a much better match for Yorkshire — who might well have gained that elusive win if so much time had not been lost to the rain.

It was not possible to start until 2.10pm on Day 2, but then the captains and umpires made every effort to stay on the field.

Lancashire won the toss and batted, but the

Andrew Gale: His first *Roses* century.

bowlers — especially **Matthew Hoggard** and **Adil Rashid** — took wickets regularly, sometimes with help from the batsmen. Law and du Plessis got started, but lost their wickets in the 30s, so the most successful batsman was Croft, who was undefeated at the close with 56.

On a bright Day 3 **Andrew Gale** and **Anthony McGrath** batted splendidly in a partnership of 215. Gale made his third first-class century of a good season with some circumspection and many good shots. The tall, strong left-hander from Dewsbury has established himself, and his first *Roses* century was appropriate reward for progress made. Poor McGrath, who had batted so well, was lbw on 99 to du Plessis.

An eventful last day was concluded in gloom as the umpires removed the bails for an early finish. Lancashire made early inroads as Yorkshire decided to go for 400 and a fifth batting point: some thought Yorkshire might have declared after the fourth or even earlier to have more time to bowl at Lancashire. Gale went for 136; **Jacques Rudolph** made a 50 before receiving an unplayable lifter from du Plessis; **Tim Bresnan** was undefeated on 47, and Lancashire took only two bowling points.

The fall of three wickets for 29 raised hopes, but the adhesive Horton and the vigilant New Zealander, Vincent, saw the hosts to safety. Lancashire announced before the match that Cork's contract would not be renewed, and Sutcliffe decided to retire from first-class cricket. Yorkshire took the maximum 12 points for a draw — but may have regretted not including a second spinner, such as **David Wainwright**.

LV County Championship Division 1
Yorkshire v. Kent

Played at North Marine Road, Scarborough, on August 27, 28, 29, 30, 2008
Match drawn at 6.20pm on the Fourth Day

Toss won by Yorkshire   Yorkshire 12 points; Kent 7 points
Close of play: First Day, Yorkshire 85-2 (McGrath 23*, Rudolph 28*); Second Day, Yorkshire 409-7 (Rashid 43*, Gough 12*); Third Day, Kent 273-5 (van Jaarsveld 61*, Jones 4*)

First Innings	KENT		Second Innings	
J L Denly, lbw b Gough	50		c McGrath b Hoggard	66
* R W T Key, c Brophy b Kruis	7		c Rudolph b Hoggard	12
N J Dexter, c McGrath b Kruis	4		b Naved-ul-Hasan	105
M van Jaarsveld, lbw b McGrath	107		c McGrath b Kruis	73
D I Stevens, c McGrath b Naved-ul-Hasan	1		(6) c Gale b Naved-ul-Hasan	0
§ G O Jones, c Brophy b Hoggard	8		(7) b Kruis	0
R McLaren, run out (Lyth)	0		(8) c Brophy b Gough	35
J C Tredwell, lbw b Gough	9		(9) c Rudolph b Rashid	54
A Khan, c Vaughan b Hoggard	5		(10) not out	21
R H Joseph, c Gale b Rashid	7		(11) c Gale b Naved-ul-Hasan	0
M J Saggers, not out	4		(5) b Naved-ul-Hasan	0
Extras lb 16, w 1, nb 8	25		Extras b 5, lb 11, w 1, nb 25	42
Total	227		Total	433

Bonus points — Yorkshire 3, Kent 1

FoW: 1-22 (Key) 2-36 (Dexter) 3-78 (Denly) 4-79 (Stevens) 5-106 (Jones) 6-108 (McLaren)
1st 7-165 (Tredwell) 8-193 (Khan) 9-223 (Joseph) 10-227 (van Jaarsveld)
FoW: 1-23 (Key) 2-155 (Denly) 3-262 (Dexter) 4-268 (Saggers) 5-268 (Stevens)
2nd 6-307 (Jones) 7-316 (van Jaarsveld) 8-394 (McLaren) 9-424 (Tredwell) 10-433 (Joseph)

	O	M	R	W		O	M	R	W
Hoggard	18	4	48	2	Hoggard	21	2	66	2
Kruis	15	4	39	2	Kruis	20	7	56	2
Gough	13	2	34	2	Rashid	37	4	127	1
Naved-ul-Hasan	9	0	53	1	McGrath	5	2	6	0
Rashid	4	0	27	1	Gough	17	0	71	1
McGrath	4.1	0	10	1	Naved-ul-Hasan	21.2	3	86	4
					Lyth	1	0	5	0

First Innings	YORKSHIRE		Second Innings	
A W Gale, b Joseph	10		lbw b Joseph	9
M P Vaughan, c Jones b Joseph	10		c van Jaarsveld b Joseph	0
A McGrath, c Jones b McLaren	52		c van Jaarsveld b Khan	3
J A Rudolph, b Joseph	146		b McLaren	24
A Lyth, c Jones b Saggers	68		c Tredwell b Joseph	52
§ G L Brophy, c van Jaarsveld b Stevens	14		c Saggers b Stevens	14
A U Rashid, lbw b Khan	43		c Tredwell b Stevens	0
Rana Naved-ul-Hasan, c Tredwell b Khan	10		c McLaren b Khan	12
* D Gough, c Key b Tredwell	33		c Key b Khan	32
M J Hoggard, c Stevens b Khan	0		not out	4
G J Kruis, not out	17		not out	1
Extras b 8, lb 8, w 8, nb 30	54		Extras b 7, lb 1, w 6, nb 10	24
Total	457		Total (9 wkts)	175

Bonus points — Yorkshire 5, Kent 2   130-over score:410-8

FoW: 1-19 (Vaughan) 2-37 (Gale) 3-213 (McGrath) 4-273 (Rudolph) 5-303 (Brophy) 6-351
1st (Lyth) 7-373 (Naved-ul-Hasan) 8-410 (Rashid) 9-417 (Hoggard) 10-457 (Gough)
FoW: 1-10 (Vaughan) 2-13 (Gale) 3-25 (McGrath) 4-60 (Rudolph) 5-93 (Brophy)
2nd 6-102 (Rashid) 7-119 (Naved-ul-Hasan) 8-135 (Lyth) 9-166 (Gough)

	O	M	R	W		O	M	R	W
Joseph	33	2	112	3	Khan	12	2	32	3
Khan	26	8	79	3	Joseph	12	1	63	3
Saggers	29	7	97	1	McLaren	15	2	51	1
McLaren	21	4	70	1	Saggers	5	1	6	0
Tredwell	19	4	46	1	Stevens	6	1	12	2
Stevens	10	2	16	1	Tredwell	1	0	3	0
van Jaarsveld	5	0	21	0					

Umpires: J H Evans and R T Robinson   Scorers: J T Potter and J C Foley

Victory? No, the great escape

JACQUES RUDOLPH
Fine display with 146

Yorkshire invited Kent to bat, and took advantage of the conditions. Only van Jaarsveld was able to bat with authority: his excellent 107 included sixes off **Adil Rashid** and **Matthew Hoggard** and 15 fours.

The bowlers shared the wickets as Kent were dismissed for 227. The return of **Michael Vaughan** was not a success, as he was one of two wickets to fall before the close.

Day 2 witnessed a fine batting display — **Jacques Rudolph** making an assured 146, **Anthony McGrath** a four-hour 52, **Adam Lyth** a promising 58 and Rashid 43 not out , contributing to a score of 457 and a lead of 230.

Kent conceded 54 extras, but missed a number of chances, but from now on the match turned their way. Denly and Dexter put on 132 for the second wicket, and Dexter went to his century.

Van Jaarsveld again proved a stern opponent with 73 until he was well caught by McGrath at slip. A hitherto ineffective **Rana Naved-ul-Hasan** took three wickets in 14 balls at the end of the day to leave Kent on 273-5, only 43 ahead, but on the last morning the middle-order all made runs, especially the dependable Tredwell, who made 54 and provided Rashid with his only wicket when he really deserved more.

Yorkshire needed 204 to win — but Joseph removed Vaughan for a duck and **Andrew Gale** for 9. McGrath went at 25; Rudolph and Lyth tried to restore order, but the crucial wicket was when McLaren bowled Rudolph. Wickets continued to fall, although Lyth made a second 50 on his home ground before falling to Joseph. Yorkshire were 135-8 with 15 overs remaining: **Darren Gough** batted very well for 32, as he and Hoggard used up 11 overs before Gough was smartly caught by Key.

Deon Kruis joined Hoggard, and they survived 28 balls balls amidst an encircling cacophony. Hoggard had faced 50 deliveries and Kruis 12 as Yorkshire escaped from a match they must have expected to win.

LV County Championship Division 1
Yorkshire v. Sussex

Played at North Marine Road, Scarborough, on September 3, 4, 5, 6, 2008

Match drawn at 9.45am on the Fourth Day

Toss won by Sussex   Yorkshire 7 points; Sussex 8 points

Close of play: First Day, Sussex 203-4 (Hodd 66*, Hopkinson 1*); Second Day, Yorkshire 133-7 (Brophy 11*, Naved-ul-Hasan 6*); Third and Fourth Days, no play.

SUSSEX

M H Yardy, c Brophy b Patterson		26
C D Nash, c Vaughan b Hoggard		78
§ A J Hodd, lbw b Rashid		81
M W Goodwin, b Patterson		25
* C J Adams, c Rudolph b Rashid		2
C D Hopkinson, lbw b Naved-ul-Hasan		15
R S C Martin-Jenkins, c Rudolph b Rashid		0
O P Rayner, not out		15
Mohammad Sami, lbw b Rashid		9
C D Collymore, run out (Lyth)		3
J D Lewry, b Naved-ul-Hasan		1
Extras lb 2, nb 8		10
Total		265

Bonus points — Yorkshire 3, Sussex 2

FoW: 1-49 (Yardy) 2-150 (Nash) 3-195 (Goodwin) 4-202 (Adams) 5-227 (Hodd) 6-227 (Martin-Jenkins) 7-241 (Hopkinson) 8-258 (Sami) 9-264 (Collymore) 10-265 (Lewry)

	O	M	R	W
Hoggard	12	3	51	1
Kruis	16	5	40	0
Naved-ul-Hasan	16.1	2	55	2
Patterson	15	0	46	2
Rashid	19	0	56	4
McGrath	4	1	15	0

YORKSHIRE

A W Gale, lbw b Lewry		3
M P Vaughan, c Hodd b Lewry		19
* A McGrath, lbw b Collymore		16
J A Rudolph, c Hodd b Rayner		41
A Lyth, c Hodd b Lewry		9
T T Bresnan, b Martin-Jenkins		19
§ G L Brophy, not out		11
A U Rashid, c Rayner b Martin-Jenkins		1
Rana Naved-ul-Hasan, not out		9
M J Hoggard		
G J Kruis Did not bat		
Extras b 4, lb 1		5
Total (7 wkts)		133

Bonus points — Sussex 2

T T Bresnan replaced SA Patterson before the start of play on Day 2.

FoW: 1-4 (Gale) 2-27 (Vaughan) 3-47 (McGrath) 4-60 (Lyth) 5-106 (Bresnan) 6-114 (Rudolph) 7-121 (Rashid)

	O	M	R	W
Lewry	12	4	27	3
Mohammad Sami	9	1	30	0
Collymore	9	2	32	1
Rayner	10	2	28	1
Martin-Jenkins	7	5	11	2

Umpires: S A Garratt and J W Lloyds   Scorers: J T Potter and M J Charman

Yorkshire v. Sussex
Patterson climbs a mountain

There was no play on the last two days as a miserable summer again disrupted cricket.

Sussex gained the advantage after making 265 and reducing Yorkshire to 133-7.

The visitors had a good first day as Hodd and Nash put on 101 for the second wicket, but they lost Adams, in his final season, for 2.

Steven Patterson took the wickets of Yardy, the new Sussex captain, and Goodwin, who was bowled by an off-cutter without playing a shot.

Patterson had been on an expedition to Mount Everest the previous winter — and had played cricket with the sherpas on Gorak Shep Glacier — but he played here only on Wednesday, as he was nominated to be replaced by **Tim Bresnan** when he returned from England duties.

Hodd, the young wicket-keeper/batsman, played a good innings, but the rest of the batting succumbed to **Rana Naved-ul-Hasan** and **Adil Rashid** as they declined

How's that then? Gerard Brophy throws the ball aloft as Steven Patterson celebrates his day of glory.

from 204-4 to 265 all out. Sussex broke through the main Yorkshire batting in two spells before a long break for rain. Lewry claimed three early wickets including **Michael Vaughan**, who had played some good shots, **Andrew Gale** and **Adam Lyth**. Yorkshire lost more wickets after the delay, including the important one of **Jacques Rudolph**, caught by Hodd off the tall off-spinner, Rayner. Martin-Jenkins dismissed Bresnan and Rashid to gain a bonus point and leave Yorkshire with a rearguard action that never happened owing to the continuous rain of Friday.

LV County Championship Division 1
Yorkshire v. Somerset

Played at North Marine Road, Scarborough, on September 17, 18, 19, 20, 2008

Match drawn at 4.21pm on the Fourth Day

Toss won by Yorkshire   Yorkshire 12 points; Somerset 11 points

Close of play: First Day, Somerset 160-3 (Suppiah 58*, Hildreth 29*); Second Day, Yorkshire 121-1 (Lyth 55*, McGrath 50*); Third Day, Somerset 25-0 (Suppiah 14*, Kiesswetter 10*)

SOMERSET

First Innings		Second Innings	
M E Trescothick, c Brophy b Hoggard	0	(8) c sub (Wainwright) b Rudolph	1
A V Suppiah, c Brophy b Hoggard	61	(1) c Brophy b Bresnan	19
* J L Langer, c Hoggard b Rashid	55	c Brophy b Gough	1
Z de Bruyn, lbw b Bresnan	0	c Lyth b Rashid	45
J C Hildreth, c Rudolph b Bresnan	41	c Pyrah b Rashid	63
I D Blackwell, not out	127	c Gough b Lyth	55
§ C Kiesswetter, c Bresnan b Rashid	5	(2) b Gough	10
P D Trego, b Hoggard	51	(7) c Kruis b Rashid	45
A C Thomas, lbw b Hoggard	1	not out	39
A R Caddick, c Brophy b Bresnan	3	not out	9
C M Willoughby, c Gough b Bresnan	14		
Extras b, lb 13, nb 6	22	Extras b 3, lb 7, nb 20	30
Total	380	Total (8 wkts dec)	317

FoW: 1-0 (Trescothick) 2-87 (Langer) 3-91 (de Bruyn) 4-167 (Suppiah) 5-200 (Hildreth)
1st   6-219 (Kiesswetter) 7-318 (Trego) 8-324 (Thomas) 9-360 (Caddick) 10-380 (Willoughby)
FoW: 1-27 (Kiesswetter) 2-35 (Suppiah) 3-39 (Langer) 4-139 (de Bruyn) 5-166 (Hildreth)
  6-236 (Trego) 7-240 (Trescothick) 8-281 (Blackwell)

	O	M	R	W		O	M	R	W
Hoggard	19	5	42	4	Hoggard	7	2	16	0
Kruis	18	2	81	0	Kruis	6	0	23	0
Gough	8	2	39	0	Rashid	29	4	109	3
Bresnan	24	4	78	3	Vaughan	6	0	47	0
Rashid	30	2	116	3	Gough	13	1	52	2
Pyrah	2	0	8	0	Bresnan	14	3	27	1
					Rudolph	5	1	13	1
					Lyth	5	2	20	1

YORKSHIRE

A Lyth, c Caddick b Thomas	65
M P Vaughan, c Blackwell b Willoughby	14
A McGrath, b Thomas	128
J A Rudolph, c Langer b Caddick	98
R M Pyrah, c Kiesswetter b Thomas	2
T T Bresnan, c Kiesswetter b de Bruyn	6
§ G L Brophy, b Thomas	16
A U Rashid, st Kiesswetter b Blackwell	28
* D Gough, lbw b Thomas	6
M J Hoggard, c Hildreth b de Bruyn	15
G J Kruis, not out	24
Extras lb 3, w 1, nb 8	12
Total	414

Bonus points — Yorkshire 5, Somerset 3

FoW: 1-25 (Vaughan) 2-146 (Lyth) 3-287 (McGrath) 4-295 (Pyrah) 5-318 (Bresnan)
  6-324 (Rudolph) 7-357 (Brophy) 8-367 (Gough) 9-375 (Rashid) 10-414 (Hoggard)

	O	M	R	W
Willoughby	23	5	70	1
Caddick	28	6	100	1
Thomas	23	4	84	5
Trego	13	1	50	0
Blackwell	26	6	70	1
Suppiah	2	0	9	0
de Bruyn	11.4	3	28	2

Umpires: P J Hartley and B Leadbeater   Scorers: J T Potter and G A Stickley

Birthday boy's last hurrah!

This was the third consecutive Championship match at Scarborough, as it was moved from Headingley Carnegie because of the drainage work.

Yorkshire invited Somerset to bat — and Hoggard took Trescothick's wicket with the first ball of the match.

Langer dug in with Suppiah until

Farewell party: skipper Darren Gough celebrates his 38th birthday during what was his final match.

lunch. Langer hit **Darren Gough** for five fours off six balls, but an injudicious stroke off **Adil Rashid** ended his innings, and de Bruyn soon followed. Hildreth survived two dropped catches in the slips and one of the easiest of stumpings — he was on his way to the pavilion when he realised that **Gerard Brophy** had missed, and he had to scamper back.

Gough presented Rashid and **Andrew Gale** with their county caps on Thursday morning, and after the dismissal of Suppiah and Hildreth it was Blackwell who dominated the day with a fine 127 not out including 14 fours and a six. With Trego's help he took Somerset to 380, although he might have been stumped at 18.

Yorkshire quickly lost **Michael Vaughan**, but **Adam Lyth** and **Anthony McGrath** batted well on a sunny evening. Next day Lyth went for 65, but McGrath and **Jacques Rudolph** added 141. McGrath made 128, and Rudolph was caught at slip for 98 — just missing his sixth first-class hundred. Thomas beavered away, ending with five wickets, and it required a last-wicket stand of 39 from **Deon Kruis** and **Matthew Hoggard** to gain a critical fifth bonus point.

Gough raised hopes of a win on the last day by bowling Kieswetter and having Langer caught by Brophy — but Somerset's middle-order saw them to safety. Lyth took his first Championship wicket — the illustrious Blackwell. Gough was applauded in at the end of what was to be his last appearance, and players and spectators paid tribute to retiring umpire **Barrie Leadbeater**, who made his debut for Yorkshire at Scarborough in 1966, and has been an efficient umpire for 28 seasons.

LV County Championship Division 1
Yorkshire v. Sussex

Played at The County Ground, Hove, on September 24, 25, 26, 27, 2008
Match drawn at 4.20pm on the Fourth Day

Toss won by Sussex   Yorkshire 12 points; Sussex 8 points
Close of play: First Day, Yorkshire 84-6 (Bresnan 5*, Rashid 4*); Second Day, Sussex 25-3 (Nash 15*, Goodwin 1*); Third Day, Sussex Second Innings 118-2 (Yardy 60*, Goodwin 15*)

YORKSHIRE

A W Gale, c Prior b Mohammad Sami		31
A Lyth, b Lewry		0
* A McGrath, c Rayner b Martin-Jenkins		3
J A Rudolph, b Mohammad Sami		23
§ G L Brophy, b Mohammad Sami		12
T T Bresnan, c Adams b Rayner		39
S A Patterson, lbw b Lewry		0
A U Rashid, lbw b Mohammad Sami		111
R M Pyrah, c Hopkinson b Martin-Jenkins		7
D J Wainwright, not out		104
M J Hoggard, not out		28
Extras b 13, lb 16, w1, nb 12		42
Total (9 wkts dec)		400

Bonus points — Yorkshire 5, Sussex 3

FoW: 1-19 (Lyth) 2-37 (Gale) 3-45 (McGrath) 4-74 (Rudolph) 5-79 (Brophy) 6-80 (Patterson) 7-160 (Bresnan) 8-178 (Pyrah) 9-318 (Rashid)

	O	M	R	W
Lewry	29	3	98	2
Mohammad Sami	35	10	117	4
Martin-Jenkins	28	8	54	2
Wright	5	0	29	0
Rayner	17	2	43	1
Nash	6	0	16	0
Yardy	2.5	0	14	0

SUSSEX

	First Innings		Second Innings	
M H Yardy, lbw b Hoggard		6	c Gale b Rashid	72
C D Nash, c Lyth b Wainwright		106	c Rudolph b Rashid	27
O P Rayner, lbw b Rashid		0	(9) c Brophy b Wainwright	22
C D Hopkinson, b Hoggard		2	(3) lbw b Wainwright	2
M W Goodwin, st Brophy b Patterson		16	(4) c Rudolph b Rashid	118
§ M J Prior, c Pyrah b Patterson		25	(5) c Lyth b Rashid	7
* C J Adams, c Pyrah b Bresnan		0	(6) c Patterson b Rashid	35
L J Wright, not out		40	(7) lbw b Rashid	5
R S C Martin-Jenkins, lbw b Rashid		6	(8) lbw b Rashid	56
Mohammad Sami, c Rudolph b Wainwright		1	not out	28
J D Lewry, c Lyth b Wainwright		0	not out	1
Extras b 2, lb 2, w1		5	Extras b 4, lb 10, w 6	20
Total		207	Total (9 wkts dec)	397

Bonus points — Yorkshire 3, Sussex 1

FoW: 1-15 (Yardy) 2-16 (Rayner) 3-23 (Hopkinson) 4-64 (Goodwin) 5-124 (Prior)
1st   6-129 (Adams) 7-193 (Nash) 8-204 (Martin-Jenkins) 9-207 (Sami) 10-207 (Lewry)
FoW: 1-88 (Nash) 2-97 (Hopkinson) 3-161 (Yardy) 4-177 (Prior) 5-231 (Adams)
    6-248 (Wright) 7-313 (Goodwin) 8-361 (Rayner) 9-383 (Martin-Jenkins)

	O	M	R	W		O	M	R	W
Bresnan	18	2	54	1	Hoggard	8	1	40	0
Hoggard	15	0	48	2	Patterson	16	4	50	0
Rashid	13	0	41	2	Bresnan	14	2	62	0
Patterson	14	4	39	2	Rashid	45	5	136	7
Pyrah	3	0	12	0	Wainwright	30	6	83	2
Wainwright	5	1	9	3	Rudolph	3	0	12	0

Umpires: R J Bailey and R K Illingworth   Scorers: J T Potter and M J Charman

No. 10 the relegation saviour

Yorkshire went down to Hove with relegation a dire probability.

They came home on Saturday evening safe in seventh place after a historic fightback led by young all-rounders **Adil Rashid** and **David Wainwright**.

On a gloomy Wednesday, having been sent in to bat, Yorkshire were a precarious 84-6 and facing imminent defeat.

Lewry, Sami and Martin-Jenkins shared

David Wainwright: Saved Yorkshire from relegation with his maiden first-class century at No. 10.

the wickets of the main batsmen — but by late Thursday afternoon **Anthony McGrath** was able to declare at 400-9 with full batting points after what must have been one of the most remarkable recoveries in the county's history.

First, there was a seventh-wicket partnership of 80 between **Tim Bresnan** and Rashid to take the score to 160 when Bresnan fell to Rayner. **Richard Pyrah** soon followed. Rashid was joined by Wainwright — and they added 140 for the ninth wicket. Rashid played an invaluable innings of 111 — he could not have come in at a more difficult time, and he demonstrated temperament and technique of the highest quality. But the score was only 318 with three bonus points gained when he was lbw to Sami.

The imperturbable **Matthew Hoggard** arrived to present a broad bat as seven Sussex bowlers were tried in desperation...but the senior partner now was Wainwright, a No. 10 batsman of limited first-class experience who gained in confidence as his excellent innings developed. He hit Martin-Jenkins for six to go to 99 — and made his maiden century off 166 balls to remain undefeated when McGrath declared with all five bonus points gathered. The last pair had put on 82 at the declaration.

As conditions had become more conducive to batting Sussex would

Adil Rashid: 111 of highest quality.

have expected to emulate Yorkshire, yet by the close they had lost three wickets for only 25, two of them to Hoggard.

Next day the attack remained in control, except that Nash refused to be dislodged at one end.

Steven Patterson removed Goodwin after a smart stumping by **Gerard Brophy**, and **Richard Pyrah** caught Prior, who had looked in good form.

Good news for both sides was relayed from Canterbury that Kent had failed to gain their third bowling-bonus point.

Yorkshire would be one point ahead of Kent if both drew, but Sussex still needed one batting point for safety. The heroic Nash eventually fell for 106 at 193 amidst Wainwright's spell of 3-9, but Wright took Sussex past 200, giving them one more point than Kent. If Kent did not win against Durham, both Yorkshire and Sussex would survive.

A last day of unbroken sunshine was something of an anti-climax — but there was another exceptional performance as Rashid bowled 45 overs, taking 7-136. He had captured only 15 wickets in the first nine Championship matches — but grabbed 50 in the last nine to end the season on 65, joint second with Stephen Harmison.

Goodwin and Yardy ensured that Sussex did not lose, and Goodwin went on to a fine century. When the players shook hands at 4.20pm both Sussex and Yorkshire had survived: Kent, who lost to Durham, were relegated, and Durham, who did the double over Yorkshire, won their first Championship.

Just how historic was Hove?

A RECORD-BREAKING RECOVERY

In totals of 400 and over

When the Yorkshire innings versus Sussex at Hove last season sank to 80-6 **Tim Bresnan**, **Adil Rashid**, **David Wainwright** and **Matthew Hoggard** helped to take the final total to 400-9 declared. This was a remarkable recovery by any standards.

In fact, it is the lowest score at the fall of the sixth wicket in any innings reaching 400.

There have been 341 occasions in first-class matches when Yorkshire have totalled 400 and over for the loss of at least six wickets. Among those there have been five when the sixth wicket fell for less than 150:

> From **80-6 to 400-9 dec** versus Sussex at Hove 2008 (A U Rashid 111, D Wainwright 104*)
>
> From **123-6 to 401-8 dec** versus Hampshire at Dewsbury in 1919 (D C F Burton 142*, W Rhodes 135)
>
> From **130-6 to 498** versus Nottinghamshire at Nottingham in 1929 (P Holmes 285)
>
> From **134-6 to 439** versus Middlesex at Lord's in 1897 (E Wainwright 171)
>
> From **142-6 to 408** versus Hampshire at Hull in 1925 (W R Allen 95*, W Rhodes 91)

There have been six instances where the fifth wicket fell for less than 100:

> From **75-5 to 515** versus Leicestershire at Leicester (Aylestone Road) in 1905 (G H Hirst 341)
>
> From **79-5 to 400-9 dec** versus Sussex at Hove in 2008. See above
>
> From **83-5 to 425** versus Hampshire at Southampton in 1899 (Lord Hawke 127, E Wainwright 91)
>
> From **90-5 to 498** versus Nottinghamshire at Nottingham in 1929
> See above
>
> From **91-5 to 401 for 8 dec** versus Hampshire at Dewsbury in 1919
> See above
>
> From **94-5 to 456** versus Hampshire at Bradford in 1899 (G H Hirst 131, E Smith 129)

When Yorkshire made their highest total of 887 versus Warwickshire at Birmingham in 1896, the sixth wicket fell at 406, leaving 481 runs to be added for the remaining four wickets! (R Peel 210*, Lord Hawke 166, G H Hirst 85 — earlier in the innings F S Jackson had made 117 and E Wainwright 126).

R D W

LV COUNTY CHAMPIONSHIP 2008

DIVISION 1

	P	W	L	D	Aban.	Bonus Points BAT	Bonus Points BOWL	Pen.	Points
1 Durham (Div 1, 2)	16	6	3	6	1	37	41	0	190
2 Nottinghamshire (Div 2, 2)	16	5	3	7	1	37	43	0	182
3 Hampshire (Div 1, 5)	16	5	4	7	0	33	47	0	178
4 Somerset (Div 2, 1)	16	3	2	11	0	44	44	0	174
5 Lancashire (Div 1, 3)	16	5	2	8	1	24	40	0	170
6 Sussex (Div 1, 1)	16	2	2	12	0	45	38	0	159
7 Yorkshire (Div 1, 6)	**16**	**2**	**5**	**9**	**0**	**50**	**45**	**0**	**159**
8 Kent (Div 1, 7) *	16	4	6	6	0	30	44	0	154
9 Surrey Div 1, 4) *	16	0	5	10	1	45	36	1	124

$ 1 point deducted for each over short in a match based on a rate of 16 overs per hour.
*Relegated to Division 2 for 2009.

DIVISION 2

	P	W	L	D	Aban.	Bonus Points BAT	Bonus Points BOWL	Pen.	Points
1 Warwickshire (Div 1, 8) *	16	5	0	11	0	53	46	0	213
2 Worcestershire (Div 1, 9) *	16	6	2	7	1	40	45	5	196
3 Middlesex (Div 2, 3)	16	4	5	7	0	46	45	0	175
4 Northamptonshire (Div 2, 5) ...	16	3	3	10	0	52	35	0	169
5 Essex (Div 2, 4)	16	5	6	5	0	36	45	3	168
6 Derbyshire (Div 2, 6)	16	4	3	9	0	33	46	4	167
7 Leicestershire (Div 2, 8)	16	3	4	9	0	29	43	0	150
8 Glamorgan (Div 2, 9)	16	3	5	7	1	26	36	0	136
9 Gloucestershire (Div 2, 7)	16	0	5	11	0	42	38	2	122

$ 1 point deducted for each over short in a match based on a rate of 16 overs per hour.
*Promoted to Division 1 for 2009.

(2007 positions in brackets)

LV COUNTY CHAMPIONSHIP

SCORING OF POINTS — 2008

(a) For a win, 14 points plus any points scored in the first innings.

(b) In a tie, each side to score seven points plus any points scored in the first innings.

(c) In a drawn match, each side to score four points plus any points scored in the first innings. (See also Para.(f) below.)

(d) If the scores are equal in a drawn match, the side batting in the fourth innings to score seven points plus any points scored in the first innings, and the opposing side to score four points plus any points scored in the first innings.

(e) **First Innings Points** (awarded only for performances **in the first 130 overs** of each first innings, and retained whatever the result of the match).

    (i) A maximum of five batting points to be available as under:-

            200 to 249 runs — 1 point
            250 to 299 runs — 2 points
            300 to 349 runs — 3 points
            350 to 399 runs — 4 points
            400 runs or over — 5 points

    (ii) A maximum of three bowling points to be available as under:

            3 to 5 wickets taken — 1 point
            6 to 8 wickets taken — 2 points
            9 to 10 wickets taken — 3 points

(f) If play starts when less than eight hours playing time remain, and a one-innings match is played, no first innings points shall be scored. The side winning on the one innings to score 14 points.

(g) The two sides which have the highest aggregate of points gained at the end of the season shall be Champions of their respective division. Should any side in the Championship table be equal on points, the side with most wins will have priority.

Derek Hodgson's History

Cricket writer Derek Hodgson's updated Official History of Yorkshire County Cricket Club, kindly supported by Leeds Metropolitan University, should be hitting the bookshelves around the time that this Yearbook is also in print. Derek retired as Editor of the Yearbook in 2008, and his in-depth knowledge of Yorkshire cricket guarantees that his latest book will be an excellent read. It will be reviewed in these pages next year.

YORKSHIRE AVERAGES 2008

COUNTY CHAMPIONSHIP MATCHES

Played 16   Won 2   Lost 5   Drawn 9

BATTING AND FIELDING

Player	M.	I.	N.O.	Runs	H.S.	Avge	100s	50s	ct/st
J A Rudolph	16	24	1	1292	155	56.17	5	6	24
A W Gale	15	23	0	899	150	39.08	3	3	9
A McGrath	14	21	0	728	144	34.66	2	3	11
T T Bresnan	14	20	5	506	84*	33.73	0	2	9
D J Wainwright	4	6	1	165	104*	33.00	1	0	2
A Lyth	14	21	0	645	132	30.71	1	5	11
G J Kruis	10	14	8	183	50*	30.50	0	1	2
G L Brophy	16	24	1	546	70	23.73	0	4	43/6
A U Rashid	16	24	2	516	111	23.45	1	2	6
M P Vaughan	6	9	0	210	72	23.33	0	1	3
C R Taylor	4	6	0	123	48	20.50	0	0	1
Rana Naved-ul-Hasan	7	10	3	114	22	16.28	0	0	3
R M Pyrah	5	6	0	96	51	16.00	0	1	5
D Gough	8	11	1	148	34	14.80	0	0	4
M J Hoggard	13	17	6	126	28*	11.45	0	0	2
J J Sayers	6	9	0	76	22	8.44	0	0	6

Also batted: S A Patterson (4 matches) 17, 13*, 0*, 6, 0 (1 ct); B W Sanderson (2 matches) 0*, 6; G S Ballance (1 match) 1, 5; M Morkel (1 match) 0, 8; O J Hannon-Dalby (1 match) 1; A Shahzad (1 match) 35.

BOWLING

Player	Overs	Mdns	Runs	Wkts	Avge	Best	5wI	10wM
M J Hoggard	342.5	66	1037	42	24.69	6-57	1	0
S A Patterson	97.1	22	279	11	25.36	3-19	0	0
T T Bresnan	421	77	1278	45	28.40	5-94	1	0
A U Rashid	590.1	64	1886	62	30.41	7-107	4	0
D J Wainwright	85.1	18	246	8	30.75	3-9	0	0
A McGrath	100.1	16	282	9	31.33	2-27	0	0
Rana Naved-ul-Hasan	153.1	21	606	16	37.87	4-86	0	0
G J Kruis	295.3	68	903	22	41.04	5-47	1	0
D Gough	149	25	528	9	58.66	2-34	0	0

Also bowled: A Shahzad 24-7-64-3 (best 2-43); O J Hannon-Dalby 29-5-114-1 (best 1-58); A Lyth 30.1-5-105-1 (best 1-20); M Morkel 15.2-5-33-1 (best 1-33); R M Pyrah 56-11-201-1 (best 1-14); J A Rudolph 21.2-2-74-1 (best 1-13); B W Sanderson 37-7-140-1 (best 1-87); A W Gale 1-0-3-0; M P Vaughan 6-0-47-0.

R D W

University Match (Not First-Class)
Yorkshire v. Leeds/Bradford UCCE

Played at Headingley, Leeds, on April 16, 17, 18, 2008
Match drawn at 3.30pm on the Third Day
Toss won by Yorkshire

Close of play: First Day, Yorkshire 384-6 (Gale 52*, Bresnan 15*); Second Day,
Leeds/Bradford UCCE 120 all out.

First Innings	YORKSHIRE		Second Innings	
J J Sayers, b Wood		87		
M P Vaughan, c Prowting b Gurney		0	b Lambert	2
* A McGrath, c Snell b Browning		52	retired out	80
J A Rudolph, b Gurney		114		
A W Gale, c Prowting b Gurney		60	(6) not out	2
A U Rashid, c Prowting b Lambert		39	(4) c Snell b Woods	9
§ G L Brophy, c Snell b Lambert		11	(5) run out (sub/Prowting)	7
T T Bresnan, c Sutton b Woods		72		
R M Pyrah, b Lambert		10	(1) retired out	74
M J Hoggard, c Campbell b Lambert		33		
G J Kruis, not out		0		
Extras b 8, lb 9, w 1, nb 4		22	Extras b 1, lb 3	4
Total		500	Total (5 wkts dec)	178

FoW: 1-1 (Vaughan) 2-92 (McGrath) 3-249 (Sayers) 4-271 (Rudolph) 5-327 (Rashid)
1st 6-350 (Brophy) 7-403 (Gale) 8-448 (Pyrah) 9-492 (Bresnan) 10-500 (Hoggard)
2nd: 1-12 (Vaughan) 2-160 (Pyrah) 3-160 (McGrath) 4-176 (Rashid) 5-178 (Brophy)

	O	M	R	W		O	M	R	W
Gurney	33	7	116	3	Gurney	4	2	9	0
Browning	10	6	14	1	Lambert	6	3	6	1
Lambert	30	5	115	4	Snell	6	2	32	0
Snell	20	1	95	0	Reddish	5	0	26	0
Campbell	2	0	7	0	Woods	11	0	54	1
Woods	33	1	136	2	Sutton	9.4	0	47	0

LEEDS/BRADFORD UCCE

S J Reddish, c McGrath b Kruis	3
J R A Campbell, lbw b Rashid	60
* R Sutton, c Brophy b Kruis	6
J R Moorhouse, b Kruis	0
N James, lbw b Kruis	0
D G H Snell, lbw b Rashid	19
§ C G Prowting, lbw b Hoggard	23
R J Browning, c Sayers b Hoggard	5
M Lambert, b Rashid	2
H F Gurney, lbw b Rashid	0
D A N Woods, not out	0
Extras nb 2	2
Total (39.3 overs)	120

FoW: 1-7 (Reddish) 2-19 (Sutton) 3-19 (Moorhouse) 4-29 (James) 5-85 (Campbell)
6-88 (Snell) 7-103 (Browning) 8-118 (Lambert) 9-120 (Gurney) 1-120 (Prowting)

	O	M	R	W
Hoggard	11.3	2	29	2
Kruis	8	3	23	4
Pyrah	6	2	24	0
Bresnan	7	1	23	0
Rashid	7	2	21	4

Umpires: B Dudleston and T J Urben   Scorers: J T Potter and H D Galley

Second npower Test Match
England v. South Africa

Played at Headingley, Leeds, on July 18, 19, 20, 21, 2008.
South Africa won by 10 wickets at 6.25pm on the Fourth Day
Toss won by South Africa

Close of play: First Day, South Africa 101-3 (Amla 18*, Prince 9*); Second Day, South Africa 322-4 (Prince 134*, de Villiers 70*); Third Day, England 50-2 (Cook 23*, Anderson 0*)

First Innings	ENGLAND	Second Innings	
A J Strauss, c Boucher b Morkel	27	c Boucher b Ntini	0
A N Cook, c Boucher b Morkel	18	c Amla b Kallis	60
* M P Vaughan, c Smith b Steyn	9	c Boucher b Ntini	21
K P Pietersen, c Smith b Steyn	45	(5) c Boucher b Kallis	13
I R Bell, b Kallis	31	(6) c de Villiers b Morkel	4
§ T R Ambrose, c Boucher b Ntini	12	(7) c Boucher b Steyn	36
A Flintoff, c Boucher b Steyn	17	(8) c Kallis b Morkel	38
S C J Broad, c de Villiers b Morkel	17	(9) not out	67
J M Anderson, not out	17	(4) lbw b Steyn	34
M S Panesar, c de Villiers b Morkel	0	b Steyn	10
D J Pattinson, c Boucher b Steyn	8	b Morkel	13
Extras lb 6, w 6, nb 5	17	Extras b 4, lb 11, w 2, nb 14	31
Total	203	Total	327

FoW: 1-26 (Cook) 2-27 (Vaughan) 3-62 (Strauss) 4-106 (Pietersen) 5-123 (Ambrose)
1st   6-150 (Bell) 7-177 (Flintoff) 8-181 (Broad) 9-186 (Panesar) 10-203 (Pattinson)
FoW: 1-3 (Strauss) 2-50 (Vaughan) 3-109 (Anderson) 4-123 (Pietersen) 5-140 (Bell)
2nd   6-152 (Cook) 7-220 (Ambrose) 8-238 (Flintoff) 9-266 (Panesar) 10-327 (Pattinson)

	O	M	R	W		O	M	R	W
Steyn	18.3	2	76	4	Steyn	28	7	97	3
Ntini	11	0	45	1	Ntini	25	7	69	2
Morkel	15	4	52	4	Morkel	22	4	61	3
Kallis	8	2	24	1	Kallis	17	3	50	2
					Harris	15	5	35	0

First Innings	SOUTH AFRICA	Second Innings	
N D McKenzie, c Flintoff b Anderson	15	(2) not out	6
* G C Smith, c Strauss b Flintoff	44	(1) not out	3
H M Amla, lbw b Pattinson	38		
J H Kallis, b Pattinson	4		
A G Prince, c Ambrose b Pattinson	149		
A B de Villiers, c Flintoff b Broad	174		
§ M V Boucher, b Anderson	34		
M Morkel, b Panesar	0		
P L Harris, c Anderson b Panesar	24		
D W Steyn, not out	10		
M Ntini, c Pietersen b Panesar	1		
Extras b 2, lb 19, w 1, nb 7	29	Extras	0
Total	522	Total (0 wkts)	9

FoW: 1-51 (McKenzie) 2-69 (Smith) 3-76 (Kallis) 4-143 (Amla) 5-355 (Prince)
1st   6-422 (Boucher) 7-427 (Morkel) 8-511 (de Villiers) 9-511 (Harris) 10-522 (Ntini)

	O	M	R	W		O	M	R	W
Anderson	44	9	136	3	Broad	1	0	8	0
Pattinson	30	2	95	2	Pattinson	0.1	0	1	0
Flintoff	40	12	77	1					
Broad	29	2	114	1					
Panesar	29.2	6	65	3					
Pietersen	4	0	14	0					

Man of the match: A G Prince

Umpires: B F Bowden and D J Harper   Scorers: J T Potter and M Snook

158

Friends Provident Trophy Matches Played by Yorkshire in 2008

WINNERS:

Essex, who beat Kent by 5 wickets

WINNERS OF FRIENDS PROVIDENT TROPHY:

2007 **Durham**, who beat Hampshire by 125 runs

WINNERS OF CHELTENHAM & GLOUCESTER TROPHY:

2001 **Somerset**, who beat Leicestershire by 41 runs
2002 **Yorkshire**, who beat Somerset by 6 wickets
2003 **Gloucestershire**, who beat Worcestershire by 7 wickets
2004 **Gloucestershire**, who beat Worcestershire by 8 wickets
2005 **Hampshire**, who beat Warwickshire by 18 runs
2006 **Sussex**, who beat Lancashire by 15 runs

(Winners of the Gillette Cup and NatWest Trophy 1963-2000
are listed in this competition's Records Section)

Match-By-Match Reports	DAVE CALDWELL
Scorecards	JOHN POTTER

Friends Provident Trophy — North Conference
Yorkshire v. Durham

Played at Riverside, Chester-le-Street, on April 20, 2008
Durham won by 5 runs

Toss won by Yorkshire

Yorkshire 0 points; Durham 2points

DURHAM

M J Di Venuto, b Bresnan	2
§ P Mustard, c Rashid b Kruis	25
K J Coetzer, b Shahzad	16
N D McKenzie, run out (Bresnan)	77
* D M Benkenstein, c White b Pyrah	12
B W Harmison, lbw b McGrath	21
G R Breese, c Pyrah b Kruis	2
L E Plunkett, c Brophy b Bresnan	1
G Onions, run out (Rashid/Pyrah)	9
S J Harmison, b Bresnan	16
N Killeen, not out	14
Extras b2, lb 16, w7	25
Total (49.1 overs)	220

FoW: 1-6 (Di Venuto) 2-46 (Mustard) 3-48 (Coetzer) 4-77 (Benkenstein) 5-136 (B W Harmison) 6-155 (Breese) 7-168 (Plunkett) 8-179 (Onions) 9-202 (McKenzie) 10-220 (S J Harmison)

	O	M	R	W
Kruis	10	1	37	2
Bresnan	9.1	0	51	3
Shahzad	9	0	30	1
Pyrah	10	2	46	1
McGrath	7	0	28	1
Rashid	4	0	10	0

YORKSHIRE

A W Gale, st Mustard b Killeen	15
J A Rudolph, c Mustard b Killeen	9
§ G L Brophy, b S J Harmison	13
* A McGrath, lbw b Plunkett	2
A U Rashid, run out (Onions)	0
C White, lbw b B W Harmison	17
A Lyth, st Mustard b Breese	21
T T Bresnan, c Benkenstein b Onions	55
R M Pyrah, c B W Harmison b S J Harmison	18
A Shahzad, c Plunkett b Killeen	33
G J Kruis, not out	3
Extras b 1, lb 14, w 10, nb 4	29
Total (49.5 overs)	215

FoW: 1-26 (Rudolph) 2-33 (Gale) 3-45 (McGrath) 4-49 (Brophy) 5-57 (Rashid) 6-99 (White) 7-105 (Lyth) 8-140 (Pyrah) 9-206 (Shahzad) 10-215 (Bresnan)

	O	M	R	W
Onions	9.5	2	40	1
Killeen	10	2	45	3
Plunkett	10	1	32	1
S J Harmison	10	0	40	2
B W Harmison	4	0	24	1
Breese	6	0	19	1

Umpires: V A Holder and R A Kettleborough

Scorers: J T Potter and B Hunt

Durham v. Yorkshire

Carnegie value for money

With skipper **Darren Gough**, **Morne Morkel** and **Matthew Hoggard** among the absentees, a Yorkshire victory was always going to be improbable against the reigning champions.

In overcast and blustery conditions Carnegie stuck to the task, and made Dynamos work for every run. **Tim Bresnan** "castled" the prolific Di Venuto for two; Mustard's pinch-hitting was curtailed by **Deon Kruis,** and Koetzer had his stumps rearranged by one from the hostile **Ajmal Shazhad** that nipped back.

Durham were 48-3, and Yorkshire looked good value: with Benkenstein caught by **Craig White** off **Richard Pyrah** they were in the ascendency, but South African debutant Neil Mackenzie was Durham's mainstay with a 125-ball 77, including five fours and two sixes.

Ben Harmison helped Mackenzie to add 59 for the fifth wicket, and the remaining batsmen chipped in. Bresnan closed the innings with the last-but-one ball, clean-bowling Ben's brother, Steve, to finish with 3-51, but Shahzad was the pick of the attack with 1-30 in nine overs.

**TIM BRESNAN
Nearly won it.**

Yorkshire's reply was stuttering to say the least. Killeen captured the prize scalp of **Jacques Rudolph** for nine, caught at the wicket by Mustard, and the England wicket-keeper whipped off the bails with **Andrew Gale** short of his ground. **Anthony McGrath** suffered an all-too-familiar early demise, trapped in front for two.

England outcast Steve Harmison joined the attack, and instantly bowled **Gerard Brophy** for 13. White and **Adam Lyth** gave some respectability to the total with dogged innings of 17 and 21 before the game took a distinct about-turn: Bresnan and Shahzad went on the offensive in a last-ditch attempt to haul Yorkshire back into the game.

At 140-8 Carnegie needed 63 off six overs. Killeen returned to the attack with figures of 2-11, but 22 runs from the 47th over gave Durham skipper Benkenstein a severe headache. Shahzad was caught in the deep for a thrilling 33 from 22 balls — and it was all down to Bresnan.

Eleven needed off the last over...six from the final two balls: Bresnan drove a slower ball from Onions to Benkenstein, and was out for a near-match-winning 55 from 58 balls to end a gripping encounter.

Friends Provident Trophy — North Conference
Yorkshire v. Derbyshire

Played at Headingley, Leeds, on April 27, 2008
Yorkshire won by 25 runs

Toss won by Derbyshire   Yorkshire 2 points; Derbyshire 0 points

YORKSHIRE

A W Gale, c Clarke b Lungley		18
§ G L Brophy, c Clarke b Langeveldt		0
M P Vaughan, c Wagg b Lungley		16
A McGrath, c Stubbings b Clare		7
J A Rudolph, c Pipe b Wagg		16
A U Rashid, not out		41
T T Bresnan, c Pipe b Langeveldt		3
A Lyth, c Clarke b Wagg		8
R M Pyrah, not out		2
* D Gough	Did not bat	
G J Kruis		
Extras lb 3, w 5		8
Total (7wkts, 24 overs)		119

FoW: 1-1 (Brophy) 2-36 (Vaughan) 3-41 (Gale) 4-47 (McGrath) 5-83 (Rudolph) 6-88 (Bresnan) 7-115 (Lyth)

	O	M	R	W
Langeveldt	5	0	25	2
Clarke	5	0	25	0
Lungley	4	2	12	2
Clare	5	0	13	1
Wagg	4	0	34	2
Needham	1	0	7	0

DERBYSHIRE

C J L Rogers, b Bresnan		3
S D Stubbings, c Brophy b Kruis		3
J L Sadler, b Bresnan		3
* R Clarke, lbw b Pyrah		1
§ D J Pipe, b Pyrah		20
F D Telo, lbw b McGrath		12
G G Wagg, b McGrath		13
J L Clare, run out (Brophy)		14
T Lungley, b McGrath		3
J Needham, not out		0
C K Langeveldt, c Rashid b Gough		6
Extras b 2, lb 5, w 9		16
Total (22.4 overs)		94

FoW: 1-4 (Rogers) 2-10 (Sadler) 3-10 (Stubbings) 4-27 (Clarke) 5-45 (Pipe) 6-61 (Telo) 7-66 (Wagg) 8-85 (Lungley) 9-85 (Clare) 10-94 (Langeveldt)

	O	M	R	W
Kruis	5	1	18	1
Bresnan	4	1	9	2
Pyrah	5	0	29	2
Gough	4.4	0	15	1
McGrath	4	0	16	3

Umpires: M J Harris and P Willey   Scorers: J T Potter and J M Brown

McGrath snares Phantoms

ADIL RASHID
Struck 41 in 36 balls.

Yorkshire gained a vital first win with relative comfort in a match reduced by rain to 24 overs a side.

Derbyshire Phantoms not surprisingly chose to field first and utilise the seamer-friendly conditions. They were rewarded with the wicket of **Gerard Brophy** without scoring — gaining South African Charl Langeveldt his first wicket for his new club with his fourth ball.

Michael Vaughan and **Andrew Gale** put on 35 before Lungley, bowling beautifully, captured them both — the former England skipper caught on the mid-wicket boundary for 16 — and **Anthony McGrath** followed soon afterwards.

Carnegie were reeling at 47-4. Enter **Adil Rashid** and **Jacques Rudolph**, who mixed thoughtful touch play with controlled aggression: Rudolph was caught at the wicket off Wagg for 16, and it was left to Adil to force the pace at the end. The last three overs yielded 30 runs, which surprisingly did not involve the bowling of Lungley, who had 2-12 from four overs.

Rashid finished with 41 from 36 balls — included a lovely six over mid-wicket off Wagg. Yorkshire's 119-7 from their allocation was just about competitive, taking into the account the overhead conditions and movement off the pitch. Phantoms slipped into the mire at 10-3.

Tim Bresnan forced an inside edge from the dangerous Rogers, then bowled Sadler off his pads. **Deon Kruis** had burly Derbyshire opener Stubbings caught behind for three, and the score was still only 27 when Pyrah's first delivery trapped Clarke in front for a painstaking one run.

Pipe tried to be positive — and quickly reached 20 before he was bowled by Pyrah. McGrath then entered the attack, and Derbyshire's run chase was effectively over as the medium-pacer grabbed 3-16 in four overs and the rate required to climb to double figures and beyond.

Skipper **Darren Gough**, playing in his first game of the season, finished things off with the wicket of Langeveldt, and Phantoms were cut adrift 25 runs short in the 23rd over.

Friends Provident Trophy — North Conference
Yorkshire v. Durham

Played at Headingley, Leeds, on May 5, 2008
Yorkshire won by 5 wickets

Toss won by Yorkshire   Yorkshire 2 points; Durham 0 points

DURHAM

M J Di Venuto, lbw b Bresnan	....	8
§ P Mustard, c Brophy b Gough	....	26
K J Coetzer, b Pyrah	....	61
P D Collingwood, c Brophy b Gough	....	2
N D McKenzie, c Rudolph b Gough	....	1
* D M Benkenstein, st Brophy b Rashid	....	31
B W Harmison, c Rudolph b Pyrah	....	19
G R Breese, not out	....	27
G Onions, run out (Bresnan)	....	0
S J Harmison, c Brophy b Pyrah	....	0
N Killeen, lbw b Rashid	....	0
Extras lb 2, w 6, nb 2	....	10
Total (45.3 overs)	....	185

FoW: 1-14 (Di Venuto) 2-69 (Mustard) 3-71 (Collingwood) 4-81 (McKenzie) 5-134 (Coetzer) 6-136 (Benkenstein) 7-182 (B W Harmison) 8-183 (Onions) 9-184 (S J Harmison) 10-185 (Killeen)

	O	M	R	W
Kruis	10	0	47	0
Bresnan	8	0	34	1
Shahzad	7	0	25	0
Gough	8	0	31	3
Pyrah	6	0	25	3
Rashid	6.3	2	21	2

YORKSHIRE

§ G L Brophy, c Onions b Killeen	....	2
A W Gale, c Breese b SJ Harmison	....	68
M P Vaughan, c Collingwood b Onions	....	22
A McGrath, not out	....	45
J A Rudolph, c Mustard b SJ Harmison	....	34
A U Rashid, c Di Venuto b SJ Harmison	....	0
T T Bresnan, not out	....	10
R M Pyrah		
* D Gough	Did not bat	
A Shahzad		
G J Kruis		
Extras lb 2, w 1, nb 2	....	5
Total (5 wkts, 35.4 overs)	....	186

FoW: 1-14 (Brophy) 2-94 (Gale) 3-94 (Vaughan) 4-152 (Rudolph) 5-152 (Rashid)

	O	M	R	W
Killeen	8	0	28	1
Onions	8	1	44	1
Collingwood	3	0	17	0
S J Harmison	9.4	0	58	3
Breese	7	0	37	0

Umpires: N G C Cowley and P J Hartley   Scorers: J T Potter and B Hunt

Yorkshire v. Durham
Gale pulverises Dynamos

GERARD BROPHY
Stumps Dale Benkenstein.

Carnegie clinched two more valuable points after giving Dynamos first use of a pitch offering lateral movement.

The openers limped to 20-1 off seven overs — the dangerous Di Venuto trapped lbw by **Tim Bresnan** for eight.

The normally aggressive Mustard found it increasingly difficult to negotiate the conditions, and was caught behind chasing a wide ball from **Darren Gough** for 26.

Collingwood went second ball to the same combination, and it was up to Koetzer to anchor his side. McKenzie was snaffled in the slips by **Jacques Rudolph**, again off Gough, but from 81-4 Benkenstein and Koetzer advanced painstakingly to 134 before Koetzer was bowled by **Richard Pyrah** for 61 from 101 deliveries. Benkenstein followed to some nifty glovework by **Gerard Brophy** off **Adil Rashid** for 31, but Ben Harmison and Breese added 46 for the seventh wicket. The last four went down for three runs to leave Breese stranded on 27 from 33 balls.

Brophy was caught brilliantly down at third-man for two, but swashbuckling **Andrew Gale** advanced to 50 in 42 balls, while senior partner **Michael Vaughan** tried to play himself into some form. Gale was taken in the slips at 94 for a pulsating 68 from 50 balls with 10 fours and a six, and with no addition Vaughan, 22, sent a wayward drive into Collingwood's hands at backward-point.

Yorkshire's senior batsmen, **Anthony McGrath** and Rudolph, dug in for a gritty stand of 58, but Rudolph, 34, was caught down the leg side off Steve Harmison — who then produced a first-ball beauty to have Rashid caught behind. Harmison was building a serious head of steam, but McGrath, 45 not out, and the maturing Bresnan weathered the storm to secure the last 34 runs with 86 deliveries still to be bowled.

Friends Provident Trophy — North Conference
Yorkshire v. Lancashire

Played at Old Trafford, Manchester, on May 11, 2008
Lancashire won by 3 wickets (D/L Method)

Toss won by Lancashire   Yorkshire 0 points; Lancashire 2 points

YORKSHIRE

§ G L Brophy, c Sutton b Hogg		18
A W Gale, c Sutton b Hogg		20
A McGrath, lbw b Hogg		2
J A Rudolph, b Marshall		65
A Lyth, c Sutton b Mahmood		2
C White, not out		42
T T Bresnan, c du Plessis b Marshall		21
R M Pyrah, c Cross b Croft		10
D J Wainwright, not out		7
* D Gough		
G J Kruis	Did not bat	
Extras b 2, lb 5, w 6, nb 4		17
Total (7 wkts, 45 overs)		204

FoW: 1-20 (Brophy) 2-39 (McGrath) 3-44 (Gale) 4-58 (Lyth) 5-139 (Rudolph)
6-165 (Bresnan) 7-176 (Pyrah)

	O	M	R	W
Chapple	7	1	30	0
Hogg	10	3	27	3
Mahmood	9	1	47	1
Croft	8	0	42	1
Marshall	7	0	37	2
du Plessis	4	0	14	0

LANCASHIRE

M B Loye, c Lyth b Bresnan		15
G D Cross, b Wainwright		41
* S G Law, c Brophy b Bresnan		0
Mohammad Yousuf, lbw b Gough		2
S J Croft, c & b Gough		5
F du Plessis, not out		77
§ L D Sutton, lbw b Pyrah		17
K W Hogg, c Brophy b Gough		31
G Chapple, not out		13
S J Marshall		
S I Mahmood	Did not bat	
Extras b 1, lb 6, w 8		15
Total (7 wkts, 44 overs)		216

Fow: 1-33 (Loye) 2-34 (Law) 3-40 (Mohammad Yousuf) 4-46 (Croft) 5-76 (Cross)
6-138 (Sutton) 7-195 (Hogg)

	O	M	R	W
Kruis	9	2	22	0
Bresnan	9	1	45	2
Gough	8	0	45	3
Pyrah	8	1	42	1
Wainwright	6	0	33	1
McGrath	4	0	22	0

Umpires: T E Jesty and N A Mallender   Scorers: J T Potter and A West

Lancashire v. Yorkshire
The *Red Rose* by a squeak

The *Red Rose* inched home with six balls to spare: they will argue that they were always just ahead, but they had a few scares in their innings.

They gave their neighbours first use of the pitch — a master stroke as Carnegie were soon 58-4, Kyle Hogg claiming the first three wickets.

Gerard Brophy skied over the leg side to be caught by Sutton, and the same combination accounting for **Andrew Gale**. **Anthony McGrath** and **Adam Lyth** followed cheaply, but **Jacques Rudolph** and **Craig White** carefully rebuilt the innings with a stand of 81.

Rudolph was the main aggressor with a fine 65 from 86 balls, but he fell to Marshall — trying to repeat the six he had hit off the young spinner the ball before.

CRAIG WHITE
Veteran anchorman.

Very heavy rain arrived with Yorkshire on 145-5 after 37 overs, and with an hour's delay five overs were lost. White anchored the innings, while wickets continued to tumble despite cameo performances from **Tim Bresnan** and **Richard Pyrah**. The veteran came in unbeaten on 42 from 76 deliveries as the visitors finished on 204 from their 45 overs.

Lancashire Lightning's answer to a target adjusted to 214 by *Duckworth-Lewis* looked good as Loye and Cross added 33 for the first wicket, but Loye was caught brilliantly at square-leg off a vicious pull from Bresnan — and Law followed first ball, caught at the wicket off a beauty. **Darren Gough** trapped the dangerous Yousuf for two, and with a simple caught-and-bowled despatched Croft.

Lightning were 46-4, but rallied to 76-5 when **David Wainwright** unleashed a snorter to beat Cross's forward lunge and end his 61-ball 41. Francois du Plessis and Luke Sutton steadied the ship with a stand of 62 before Pyrah removed Sutton for 17 — but du Plessis and Hogg then took the game away from Yorkshire with a thrilling partnership of 57.

Hogg was particularly aggressive in his run-a-ball 31, and by the time Gough had him caught behind Lightning's Kolpack South African was well established: with Chapple's help du Plessis took the hosts over the line with six balls remaining, unbeaten himself on 77.

Friends Provident Trophy — North Conference
Yorkshire v. Scotland

Played at Raeburn Place, Edinburgh, on May 18, 2008
Yorkshire won by 7 wickets

Toss won by Yorkshire   Yorkshire 2 points; Scotland 0 points

SCOTLAND

E J M Cowan, c Rudolph b Bresnan		36
* R R Watson, c Brophy b Kruis		22
N S Poonia, b Pyrah		8
§ C J O Smith, c Pyrah b Rashid		30
G M Hamilton, c Pyrah b McGrath		19
D F Watts, c Brophy b Pyrah		17
J A R Blain, c White b Gough		26
G A Rogers, not out		14
G Goudie, b Gough		5
J D Nel		
S D Weeraratna	Did not bat	
Extras b 3, lb 5, w 8		16
Total (8 wkts, 50 overs)		193

FoW: 1-26 (Watson) 2-40 (Poonia) 3-93 (Smith) 4-105 (Cowan) 5-138 (Watts) 6-149 (Hamilton) 7-187 (Blain) 8-193 (Goudie)

	O	M	R	W
Kruis	6	2	29	1
Bresnan	10	3	27	1
Pyrah	8	1	30	2
Gough	10	0	40	2
Rashid	9	0	31	1
Wainwright	3	0	11	0
McGrath	4	0	17	1

YORKSHIRE

A W Gale, c Hamilton b Blain		2
C White, not out		69
A McGrath, lbw b Nel		5
J A Rudolph, c Watson b Blain		48
§ G L Brophy, not out		61
A U Rashid		
T T Bresnan		
R M Pyrah	Did not bat	
D J Wainwright		
* D Gough		
G J Kruis		
Extras lb 8, w 4		12
Total (3 wkts, 47.2 overs)		197

FoW: 1-7 (Gale) 2-18 (McGrath) 3-113 (Rudolph)

	O	M	R	W
Blain	10	3	17	2
Nel	10	1	35	1
Goudie	10	1	31	0
Weeraratna	6	0	44	0
Rogers	8.2	0	48	0
Watson	3	0	14	0

Umpires: S A Garratt and P J Hartley   Scorers: J T Potter and K C Nisbet

Brophy in victory rampage

A vital, yet comfortable, victory kept Carnegie's hopes of a Quarter-Finals berth alive while condemning Saltires to yet another home defeat.

Darren Gough sent Saltires into bat, but the first wicket took longer to arrive than he expected: **Deon Kruis** claimed it, when he had the dangerous skipper, Watson, caught behind for a brisk 22, containing four boundaries.

Poonia was bowled by **Richard Pyrah** as the score slowly advanced towards the half-century mark, but Cowan anchored the innings as he was joined by wicket-keeper Smith.

This pair put on 53, thanks to some ill-disciplined bowling, but the arrival of **Adil Rashid** stopped the spirited Scottish effort as he had Smith smartly caught by Pyrah for 30 from 50

GERARD BROPHY
Blasted 61 in 45 balls.

deliveries. Boundaries were increasingly difficult to come by, and what looked like a slow pitch offered some help to the seamers. Carnegie lacked consistency as the Saltires batsmen kept the scoreboard ticking, although seldom at more than four an over.

Cowan top-scored with 36 from 82 balls, and there were contributions from most of the line-up, but no one could post a score of major significance. Some loose shots ensured that they would fall short of a really challenging total. Gough ended it with a trademark last-ball dismissal.

Carnegie got off to a dreadful start in the face of excellent seam bowling from former teammate **John Blain** and his partner, Nel. **Andrew Gale** was caught for two, and **Anthony McGrath** trapped in front for five. Yorkshire were 18-2, but Scotland lacked depth in their back-up bowling, and the dependable **Jacques Rudolph** and cool veteran **Craig White** proceeded to restore order.

They put on 95 before Blain returned to remove Rudolph for a 72-ball 48 — thus heralding the controlled aggression of **Gerard Brophy**. There was much work to do, but with White playing second fiddle Brophy went on the rampage — blasting nine boundaries and a six in a 45-ball 61. White finished unbeaten on 69 from 142 balls, and Yorkshire crossed the line with 16 balls remaining.

Friends Provident Trophy — North Conference
Yorkshire v. Derbyshire

Played at The County Ground, Derby, on May 25, 2008

No Result

Toss won by Derbyshire

Yorkshire 1 point; Derbyshire 1 points

YORKSHIRE

A W Gale, c Clarke b Wagg		11
C White, c Rogers b Langeveldt		1
A McGrath, c Klokker b Langeveldt		1
J A Rudolph, not out		14
A Lyth, b Lungley		18
§ G L Brophy, not out		0
A U Rashid		
T T Bresnan		
R M Pyrah	Did not bat	
* D Gough		
G J Kruis		
Extras b 1, lb 3, w 10		14
Total (4 wkts, 21.1 overs)		59

FoW: 1-4 (White) 2-6 (McGrath) 3-23 (Gale) 4-56 (Lyth)

	O	M	R	W
Wagg	7	2	22	1
Langeveldt	6	2	10	2
Lungley	4.1	1	12	1
Clare	4	1	11	0

DERBYSHIRE

C J L Rogers	
S D Stubbings	
D J Birch	
* R Clarke	
J L Sadler	
§ F A Klokker	Did not bat
G G Wagg	
J L Clare	
T Lungley	
J Needham	
C K Langeveldt	

Umpires: T E Jesty and N J Llong

Scorers: J T Potter and J M Brown

Derbyshire v. Yorkshire
Heaven helps Carnegie

Andrew Gale: Flourish before rain.

Disappointment all round for both sets of supporters as the North Conference Quarter-Finals qualification was thrown wide open with this washout.

Yorkshire, with their destiny still in their own hands, were probably the happier of the two teams as they were struggling at 59-4 on a green, seaming wicket in very helpful bowling conditions. Derbyshire won the toss, and Yorkshire were soon in trouble with **Craig White** and **Anthony McGrath** both out to Langveldt.

Andrew Gale was caught at the second attempt at mid-wicket by Clarke for 11. **Adam Lyth** followed soon afterwards, clean-bowled by Lungley for 18 — the ball after he had dealt the young left-hander a painful blow a'mid-ships.

Once the rain set in there was going to be only one winner, and play was abandoned at 4pm, with each side taking a point.

Friends Provident Trophy — North Conference
Yorkshire v. Scotland

Played at Headingley, Leeds, on May 26, 2008
Yorkshire won by 7 wickets

Toss won by Scotland   Yorkshire 2 points; Scotland 0 points

SCOTLAND

G M Hamilton, c Pyrah b Rashid	34
* R R Watson, b Gough	54
E J M Cowan, b Rashid	19
§ C J O Smith, b Pyrah	60
D F Watts, lbw b McGrath	34
N F I McCallum, run out (Pyrah)	1
R M Haq, c Pyrah b Gough	16
J A R Blain, b Bresnan	13
C S MacLeod, b Bresnan	1
G Goudie, b Gough	2
J D Nel, not out	4
Extras lb 2, w 4	6
Total (50 overs)	244

FoW: 1-90 (Watson) 2-90 (Hamilton) 3-123 (Cowan) 4-179 (Watts) 5-180 (McCallum) 6-216 (Smith) 7-235 (Haq) 8-237 (Blain) 9-238 (MacLeod) 10-244 (Goudie)

	O	M	R	W
Bresnan	9	1	54	2
$ Kruis	7.2	1	23	0
$ Pyrah	8.4	0	49	1
Gough	10	2	40	3
Rashid	10	1	36	2
Rudolph	1	0	8	0
McGrath	4	0	32	1

$ G J Kruis unable to finish his eighth over.

YORKSHIRE

A W Gale, lbw b Nel	33
C White, c MacLeod b Nel	3
A McGrath, not out	105
J A Rudolph, c Nel b Goudie	82
§ G L Brophy, not out	2
A U Rashid	
A Lyth	
T T Bresnan	Did not bat
R M Pyrah	
* D Gough	
G J Kruis	
Extras b 6, lb 2, w 10, nb 2	20
Total (3 wkts, 40.4 overs)	245

FoW: 1-30 (White) 2-59 (Gale) 3-223 (Rudolph)

	O	M	R	W
Blain	3	0	17	0
Nel	8	0	53	2
Goudie	8.4	1	61	1
MacLeod	7	0	41	0
Haq	9	0	42	0
Watson	5	0	23	0

Umpires: A A Jones and B Leadbeater   Scorers: J T Potter and N J Leitch

McGrath grabs the points

Darren Gough: Dual with Hamilton.

A crucial two points were duly collected by Yorkshire — but not without a scare or two.

Saltires elected to bat first, and they raced towards 100 as Watson and former Yorkshire all-rounder **Gavin Hamilton** put a wayward attack to the sword.

Tim Bresnan and **Deon Kruis** struggled with their lines, and it was left to **Darren Gough** to provide the breakthrough: Watson reached 54 with nine boundaries, tried to cut one that was too close, and Gough bowled him. The skipper then turned to **Adil Rashid** — who stemmed the tide with two wickets for a mere 36 from his 10 overs.

Hamilton's paddle-sweep ended an excellent 34 in 44 balls, when he found the safe hands of **Richard Pyrah**, and Rashid bowled Cowan for 19, although many spectators thought it was a stumping. Wickets tumbled at regular intervals, leaving wicket-keeper Smith to be the mainstay with a 70-ball 60 before he was cleaned up by Pyrah — whose performance was capped with a superb direct hit to run out McCullum.

The visitors were all out on the last ball for a challenging 244, and Carnegie slumped to 59-2 despite **Andrew Gale's** 33 from 36 balls. **Craig White** lobbed an easy catch to Macleod on the leg side off Nel, and Gale was trapped in front by the same bowler.

Now came the big partnership: **Anthony McGrath** started strongly, many of his early runs being dispatched to the on-side boundary, and in partnership with **Jacques Rudolph** he was in imperious form as they built a partnership that oozed class and no little skill.

Rudolph was the more circumspect as his partner crashed boundary after boundary, but at 50 he went into overdrive. He had scored 82 in 96 balls when one big hit too many brought his downfall; he offered Nel a simple catch off Goudie to end a partnership of 164. McGrath completed an excellent century off 97 balls in 121 minutes.

Friends Provident Trophy — North Conference
Yorkshire v. Lancashire

Played at Headingley, Leeds, on May 28, 2008
No Result

Toss won by Lancashire   Yorkshire 1 point; Lancashire 1 point

LANCASHIRE

P J Horton, c McGrath b Patterson		4
I J Sutcliffe, c Rudolph b Gough		16
M B Loye, c Brophy b Patterson		2
Mohammad Yousuf, c Brophy b Bresnan		2
F du Plessis, c Brophy b Gough		9
S J Croft, c Rashid b Pyrah		0
* § L D Sutton, lbw b Pyrah		5
K W Hogg, c Gough b McGrath		25
S I Mahmood, lbw b Gough		0
G Keedy, not out		8
O J Newby, b McGrath		1
Extras lb 7, w 10		17
Total (31.2 overs)		89

FoW: 1-5 (Horton) 2-19 (Loye) 3-28 (Mohammad Yousuf) 4-43 (Sutcliffe) 5-44 (du Plessis) 6-50 (Croft) 7-57 (Sutton) 8-58 (Mahmood) 9-86 (Hogg) 10-89 (Newby)

	O	M	R	W
Bresnan	8	2	16	1
Patterson	8	1	18	2
Gough	8	1	17	3
Pyrah	5	0	23	2
McGrath	2.2	0	8	2

YORKSHIRE

A W Gale, not out		23
C White, not out		8
A McGrath		
J A Rudolph		
§ G L Brophy		
AU Rashid		
A Lyth	Did not bat	
T T Bresnan		
R M Pyrah		
S A Patterson		
* D Gough		
Extras lb 1, w 2		3
Total (4.5 overs)		34

	O	M	R	W
Hogg	2.5	0	19	0
Mahmood	2	0	14	0

Umpires: N B G Cook and I J Gould   Scorers: J T Potter and A West

Yorkshire v. Lancashire
Rain rules out a home draw

Persistent rain robbed Yorkshire of a well deserved victory in this crucial final fixture of the group stages.

A win would have left Carnegie top of the group with a guaranteed home draw in the Quarter-Finals. Instead, Durham claimed the top spot.

Lancashire Lightning stand-in skipper Sutton won the toss, and somewhat

Steven Patterson: Started the rout.

surprisingly opted to bat — a decision that baffled all and sundry, especially an hour into the match. Medium-fast bowler **Steven Patterson**, recalled for his first outing of the season, despatched Horton with his second ball — an outside edge taken at slip by **Anthony McGrath**.

Loye went at 19, when wicket-keeper **Gerard Brophy** held a fantastic one-handed catch from an inside edge, again off Patterson. The ball was seaming around prodigiously, and once the dangerous Yousuf had played across one to give Brophy a simple catch the writing was on the wall for the *Red Rose* county. Sutcliffe was the only top-order batsmen to offer any resistance, and when he was caught by **Jacques Rudolph** off **Darren Gough** for a dogged 16 the innings subsided.

The score was soon 58-8, with **Richard Pyrah** and Gough taking further wickets — but lusty hitting by Hogg provided cheer for the visitors: the tall left-hander added 25 from 23 deliveries, including four boundaries, before he was caught at mid-off from the ever reliable McGrath.

It was McGrath who rapped up the innings for a mere 89 as Newby lost his off stump aiming for something fairly destructive and agricultural. Lightning's innings had lasted a mere 31.2 overs, with only two batsmen reaching double figures.

Only three balls were possible at the start of Carnegie's reply before a nasty bout of rain hit Headingley Carnegie. The players were back after less than an hour, with **Andrew Gale** in particular in no mood to hang around: the sturdy left-hander played some thunderous strokes in an innings of 23 in 19 balls, helping Carnegie to reach 34 in less than five overs, but the rain returned, and play was abandoned at 6pm.

Friends Provident Trophy — Quarter-Final
Yorkshire v. Gloucestershire

Played at The County Ground, Bristol, on June 4, 2008
Yorkshire won by 6 wickets
Toss won by Yorkshire

GLOUCESTERSHIRE

W T S Porterfield, b Bresnan		9
H J H Marshall, c Pyrah b Hoggard		16
A P R Gidman, c Lyth b Hoggard		3
C M Spearman, c & b Bresnan		3
M J North, c Brophy b Hoggard		1
C G Taylor, run out (Pyrah)		54
M A Hardinges, c Brophy b Pyrah		6
§ S J Adshead, c Gough b McGrath		71
* J Lewis, lbw b Bresnan		6
C G Greenidge, c Brophy b Bresnan		7
A J Ireland, not out		7
Extras lb 7, w 7, nb 4		18
Total (45.2 overs)		201

FoW: 1-25 (Porterfield) 2-29 (Marshall) 3-35 (Gidman) 4-35 (Spearman) 5-43 (North) 6-50 (Hardinges) 7-132 (Taylor) 8-157 (Lewis) 9-170 (Greenidge) 10-201 (Adshead)

	O	M	R	W
Bresnan	10	3	31	4
Hoggard	10	2	26	3
Pyrah	8	0	40	1
Gough	8	0	37	0
Rashid	4	0	25	0
McGrath	5.2	0	35	1

YORKSHIRE

A W Gale, b Lewis		12
C White, c Hardinges b Lewis		55
A McGrath, b Hardinges		31
J A Rudolph, not out		53
§ G L Brophy, c Taylor b Hardinges		2
A Lyth, not out		38
A U Rashid		
R M Pyrah		
T T Bresnan	Did not bat	
M J Hoggard		
* D Gough		
Extras lb 2, w 4, nb 8		14
Total (4 wkts, 44.1 overs)		205

FoW: 1-14 (Gale) 2-77 (McGrath) 3-132 (White) 4-139 (Brophy)

	O	M	R	W
Lewis	10	1	21	2
Greenidge	5	0	33	0
Ireland	4	0	33	0
Hardinges	10	1	36	2
Gidman	10	0	35	0
North	4	0	35	0
Marshall	1.1	0	10	0

Umpires: B Dudleston and N J Llong   Scorers: J T Potter and K T Gerrish

Through to the last four

A professional all-round display kept alive Carnegie's hopes of a Lord's final to round off skipper **Darren Gough's** career.

He took his side into the field after winning what turned out to be an important toss. Porterfield and Marshall advanced cautiously into the 20s against after accurate bowling from **Tim Bresnan** and **Matthew Hoggard**.

Bresnan claimed first blood, pegging back Porterfield's stumps at 25 — which soon became 29-2, the dangerous Marshall falling for 16 to a breathtaking catch by **Richard Pyrah** off Hoggard. Matthew dropped a little short outside the off-stump...the Kiwi seized upon the chance of a boundary, but he had not accounted for the agility of Pyrah, who took a superb two-handed, full-length catch at backward-point.

MATTHEW HOGGARD
Lovely away-swingers

Gidman offered an easy leg-side catch to **Adam Lyth** off Hoggard and key batsman Spearman gave a return catch to **Tim Bresnan**. 35-4.

Two lovely away-swingers from Hoggard and Pyrah allowed wicket-keeper **Gerard Brophy** to reduce Gloucester to 50-6, but the batting of Taylor and Adshead was courageous: both set about Yorkshire's seamers until Pyrah raced from deep mid-off to throw down Taylor's stumps. Bresnan came back with two late wickets, and **Anthony McGrath** ended the innings in the last over as Adshead skied to Gough for an incredibly important 71 from 73 balls with seven fours and a six.

Andrew Gale hit three off-side boundaries, but was outfoxed by the canny Lewis. **Craig White** and McGrath now took the sting out of the attack, putting on 63 until McGrath was bowled by Hardinges. White scored singles and twos while **Jacques Rudolph** unfurled the match-winning innings, but there was still time for a mini-collapse.

White miscued a simple catch to Hardinges off Lewis after accumulating 56 in 107 balls, and Brophy played a vicious cut which was taken low down, one-handed and at full stretch by Taylor. 139-4. Rudolph with 63 from 70 balls and **Adam Lyth** with 38 from 24 saw Carnegie home.

177

Friends Provident Trophy — Semi-Final
Yorkshire v. Essex

Played at The County Ground, Chelmsford, on July 5, 2008
Essex won by 87 runs
Toss won by Essex

ESSEX

J E R Gallian, run out (Bresnan)	28
A N Cook, run out (Bresnan)	95
* M L Pettini, c Lyth b Naved-ul-Hasan	12
R S Bopara, c Brophy b Naved-ul-Hasan	37
G R Napier, c McGrath b Bresnan	61
§ J S Foster, c Brophy b Pyrah	10
R N ten Doeschate, c McGrath b Pyrah	1
G W Flower, c Lyth b Bresnan	21
J D Middlebrook, not out	7
D D Masters, not out	3
Danish Kaneria Did not bat	
Extras lb 2, w 8	10
Total (8 wkts, 50 overs)	285

FoW: 1-61 (Gallian) 2-82 (Pettini) 3-180 (Cook) 4-182 (Bopara) 5-208 (Foster) 6-216 (ten Doeschate) 7-270 (Napier) 8-274 (Flower)

	O	M	R	W
Hoggard	6	0	41	0
Bresnan	10	0	58	2
Gough	10	0	56	0
Naved-ul-Hasan	10	1	41	2
Pyrah	8	0	52	2
Rashid	6	0	35	0

YORKSHIRE

A W Gale, run out (ten Doeschate)	64
A Lyth, lbw b Masters	21
A McGrath, c ten Doeschate b Danish Kaneria	53
J A Rudolph, b ten Doeschate	5
§ G L Brophy, lbw b ten Doeschate	0
A U Rashid, c Foster b ten Doeschate	0
T T Bresnan, lbw b Bopara	8
R M Pyrah, st Foster b Danish Kaneria	13
Rana Naved-ul-Hasan, c ten Doeschate b Bopara	13
* D Gough, lbw b Danish Kaneria	1
M J Hoggard, not out	1
Extras lb 6, w 13	19
Total (42.5 overs)	198

FoW: 1-56 (Lyth) 2-140 (Gale) 3-152 (McGrath) 4-152 (Brophy) 5-152 (Rashid) 6-155 (Rudolph) 7-173 (Bresnan) 8-189 (Naved-ul-Hasan) 9-197 (Pyrah) 10-198 Gough)

	O	M	R	W
Masters	9	0	38	1
Napier	6	0	30	0
Bopara	7	0	32	2
Middlebrook	5	0	30	0
Danish Kaneria	8.5	0	32	3
ten Doeschate	7	0	30	3

Umpires: P J Hartley and N J Llong   Scorers: J T Potter and A E Choat

Napier nightmare ends dream

Anthony McGrath: Talisman.

Dreams of Lord's ended as a powerful Essex enjoyed a relatively one-sided outing.

Essex not surprisingly elected to bat on an excellent-looking wicket, and got away to a brisk start.

Matthew Hoggard initially offered too much room for Cook and Gallian, and the score reached 61 when an excellent throw from **Tim Bresnan** found Gallian, 28, well out.

Pettini reached 12 before offering **Adam Lyth** a simple catch off the now fit **Rana Naved-ul-Hassan**, but Bopara joined England teammate Cook in a steady if unspectacular partnership as Carnegie tried to starve their hosts of boundaries. They had put on 98 when Cook was run out for a patient 95: he cut savagely to **Richard Pyrah**, who did well to get a hand to it as it sped towards the third-man fence.

Bresnan picked up — and launched a missile which caught Cook well short on the second run. Cook hit 10 boundaries in his innings of 142 minutes and 127 balls. Bopara, who had struggled for timing all afternoon, was out two runs later for a hard-fought 37, and Yorkshire were back in it — especially when Foster was taken smartly by wicket-keeper **Gerard Brophy** off Pyrah, and the score was 208-5.

Enter man-of-the-moment Napier. Fresh from his record-breaking *Twenty20* heroics, he did not disappoint the capacity crowd: he savaged Carnegie with 61 in 34 balls — including an amazing six sixes. The last 10 overs saw 101 runs as bowlers and fielders started to wilt under such immense stroke play. Bresnan accounted for Napier — but with the total approaching 300 Gough's men faced a stern test. Lyth and **Andrew Gale**

Andrew Gale: Driving hard as Yorkshire's hopes rise.

got away to a half-century partnership, but Lyth went for 21, unluckily adjudged lbw to one that appeared to pitch outside leg stump.

Gale and **Anthony McGrath** patiently built the partnership needed if Carnegie were mount any challenge. The bowling was disciplined, and gave very little away, but McGrath and his junior partner continued to eat away at the 286 target. The asking rate started to climb, and risks would have to be taken.

Both batsmen passed 50...but as the total reached 140 disaster struck. Gale went for a suicidal single to the bowler, and was run out by a country mile for 64; McGrath then spooned an attempted drive to Ten Doeschate — who eventually took the catch after a few juggled attempts — and Yorkshire's talisman was out for 53.

Kaneria was in his element now, weaving a magical spell on all the Yorkshire batsmen: they had no time to block, but they simply had to get on and score quickly. Wickets tumbled frequently, and from 140-1 Yorkshire reeled to 155-6. The contest was over: Essex smelt their prey, moved in for the kill, and the innings subsided to 198 as ten Doeschate finished with 3-30 and Kaneria 3-32.

Friends Provident Trophy

FINAL TABLES

NORTH DIVISION

		P	W	L	T	NR/A	PTS	NRR
1	Durham	8	5	3	0	0	10	0.432
2	**Yorkshire**	8	4	2	0	2	10	**0.544**
3	Derbyshire	8	3	2	0	3	9	-0.141
4	Lancashire	8	3	3	0	2	8	0.243
5	Scotland	8	1	6	0	1	3	-1.090

MIDLANDS DIVISION

		P	W	L	T	NR/A	PTS	NRR
1	Leicestershire	8	5	2	0	1	11	0.692
2	Nottinghamshire	8	4	2	0	2	10	0.017
3	Northamptonshire	8	4	2	0	2	10	0.569
4	Warwickshire	8	2	4	0	2	6	-0.145
5	Ireland	8	1	6	0	1	3	-0.862

SOUTH EAST DIVISION

		P	W	L	T	NR/A	PTS	NRR
1	Kent	8	5	2	0	1	11	0.674
2	Essex	8	4	3	0	1	9	0.310
3	Middlesex	8	3	3	0	2	8	0.064
4	Surrey	8	3	4	0	1	7	-0.627
5	Sussex	8	1	4	0	3	5	-0.534

SOUTH WEST DIVISION

		P	W	L	T	NR/A	PTS	NRR
1	Gloucestershire	8	4	1	0	3	11	0.705
2	Somerset	8	3	2	0	3	9	0.307
3	Worcestershire	8	3	3	0	2	8	-0.121
4	Hampshire	8	3	4	0	1	7	-0.431
5	Glamorgan	8	1	4	0	3	5	-0.219

YORKSHIRE AVERAGES 2008

FRIENDS PROVIDENT TROPHY

Played 10   Won 5   Lost 3   No Result 2

BATTING AND FIELDING

Player	M.	I.	N.O.	Runs	H.S.	Av'ge	100s	50s	ct/st
C White	7	7	3	195	69*	48.75	0	2	2
J A Rudolph	10	9	2	326	82	46.57	0	3	4
A McGrath	10	9	2	251	105*	35.85	1	1	3
A Shahzad	2	1	0	33	33	33.00	0	0	0
A W Gale	10	10	1	266	68	29.55	0	2	0
T T Bresnan	10	5	1	97	55	24.25	0	1	1
A Lyth	8	6	1	108	38*	21.60	0	0	4
M P Vaughan	2	2	0	38	22	19.00	0	0	0
G L Brophy	10	9	3	98	61*	16.33	0	1	17/1
R M Pyrah	10	4	1	43	18	14.33	0	0	6
A U Rashid	9	4	1	41	41*	13.66	0	0	3
Rana Naved-ul-Hasan	1	1	0	13	13	13.00	0	0	0
D Gough	9	1	0	1	1	1.00	0	0	3
D J Wainwright	2	1	1	7	7*	—	0	0	0
G J Kruis	7	1	1	3	3*	—	0	0	0
M J Hoggard	2	1	1	1	1*	—	0	0	0
S A Patterson	1	0	0	0	—	—	0	0	0

BOWLING

Player	Overs	Mdns	Runs	Wkts	Av'ge	Best	4wI	Runs per Over
S A Patterson	8	1	18	2	9.00	2-18	0	2.25
A McGrath	30.4	0	158	9	17.55	3-16	0	5.15
T T Bresnan	77.1	11	325	18	18.05	4-31	1	4.21
D Gough	66.4	3	281	15	18.73	3-17	0	4.21
Rana Naved-ul-Hasan	10	1	41	2	20.50	2-41	0	4.10
M J Hoggard	16	1	67	3	22.33	3-26	0	4.18
R M Pyrah	66.4	4	336	15	22.40	3-25	0	5.04
A U Rashid	39.3	3	158	5	31.60	2-21	0	4.00
G J Kruis	47.2	7	176	4	44.00	2-37	0	3.71
D J Wainwright	9	0	44	1	44.00	1-33	0	4.88
A Shahzad	16	0	55	1	55.00	1-30	0	3.43
J A Rudolph	1	0	8	0	—	0-8	0	8.00

NatWest Pro40 Cricket League Matches Played by Yorkshire in 2008

*Captain
§Wicket Keeper

WINNERS:
SUSSEX

NATIONAL LEAGUE

PREVIOUS WINNERS		Yorkshire's Position
1999	**Lancashire**	5th Div 1
2000	**Gloucestershire**	2nd Div 1
2001	**Kent**	6th Div 1
2002	**Glamorgan**	4th Div 1
2003	**Surrey**	8th Div 1
2004	**Glamorgan**	4th Div 2
2005	**Essex**	8th Div 2
2006	**Essex**	9th Div 2
2007	**Worcestershire**	6th Div 2

SUNDAY LEAGUE

PREVIOUS WINNERS		Yorkshire's Position	PREVIOUS WINNERS		Yorkshire's Position
1969	**Lancashire**	8th	1984	**Essex**	=13th
1970	**Lancashire**	14th	1985	**Essex**	6th
1971	**Worcestershire**	15th	1986	**Hampshire**	8th
1972	**Kent**	4th	1987	**Worcestershire**	=13th
1973	**Kent**	2nd	1988	**Worcestershire**	8th
1974	**Leicestershire**	=6th	1989	**Lancashire**	11th
1975	**Hampshire**	=5th	1990	**Derbyshire**	6th
1976	**Kent**	15th	1991	**Nottinghamshire**	7th
1977	**Leicestershire**	=13th	1992	**Middlesex**	15th
1978	**Hampshire**	7th	1993	**Glamorgan**	9th
1979	**Somerset**	=4th	1994	**Warwickshire**	5th
1980	**Warwickshire**	=14th	1995	**Kent**	12th
1981	**Essex**	=7th	1996	**Surrey**	3rd
1982	**Sussex**	16th	1997	**Warwickshire**	10th
1983	**Yorkshire**	1st	1998	**Lancashire**	9th

Match-By-Match Reports   **DAVE CALDWELL**
Scorecards   **JOHN POTTER**

NatWest Pro40 League Division 2
Yorkshire v. Essex

Played at The County Ground, Chelmsford, on July 16, 2008

Essex won by 5 wickets

Toss won by Yorkshire

Yorkshire 0 points; Essex 2 points

YORKSHIRE

A W Gale, c Foster b Napier	1
§ G L Brophy, lbw b Masters	1
Rana Naved-ul-Hasan, c & b Danish Kaneria	57
A McGrath, c Gallian b Napier	18
J A Rudolph, lbw b Danish Kaneria	8
A Lyth, b Chambers	2
A U Rashid, b Bopara	8
T T Bresnan, run out (Doeschate/Danish Kaneria)	3
R M Pyrah, lbw b ten Doeschate	1
* D Gough, c & b ten Doeschate	33
D J Wainwright, not out	9
Extras lb 8, w8	16
Total (36.2 overs)	157

FoW: 1-4 (Gale) 2-4 (Brophy) 3-43 (McGrath) 4-68 (Rudolph) 5-71 (Lyth)
6-93 (Rashid) 7-111 (Bresnan) 8-111 (Naved-ul-Hasan) 9-113 (Pyrah) 10-157 (Gough)

BOWLING ANALYSIS

	O	M	R	W
Napier	6	0	27	2
Masters	3	0	25	1
Chambers	6	0	26	1
Danish Kaneria	7	1	18	2
Bopara	6	0	22	1
ten Doeschate	7.2	0	25	2
Middlebrook	1	0	6	0

ESSEX

* M L Pettini, lbw b Wainwright	57
J E R Gallian, c Brophy b Naved-ul-Hasan	7
G R Napier, c Rudolph b Pyrah	46
R S Bopara, st Brophy b Rashid	16
G W Flower, not out	10
§ J S Foster, c McGrath b Wainwright	9
R N ten Doeschate, not out	11
J D Middlebrook	
Danish Kaneria	
D D Masters	Did not bat
M A Chambers	
Extras lb 1, w 1	2
Total (5 wkts, 33 overs)	158

FoW: 1-23 (Gallian) 2-86 (Napier) 3-126 (Bopara) 4-130 (Pettini) 5-146 (Foster)

BOWLING ANALYSIS

	O	M	R	W
Bresnan	5	0	23	0
Naved-ul-Hasan	5	0	25	1
$ Pyrah	3.4	0	25	1
$ Gough	0.2	0	2	0
Rashid	8	0	35	1
Wainwright	8	0	33	2
Rudolph	2	0	11	0
Lyth	1	0	3	0

$ D Gough was unable to complete his first over.

Umpires: N L Bainton and R A Kettleborough

Scorers: J T Potter and A E Choat

Hammered by the experts

Carnegie took a fearful beating at the hands of one-day experts.

Skipper **Darren Gough** won the toss, and soon was ruing his decision to bat after losing **Andrew Gale** and **Gerard Brophy**. Gale wafted outside the off-stump to be snapped up by Foster, and his opening partner was trapped in front, lacking foot movement.

The major surprise next was the introduction of **Rana Naved-ul-Hasan** at No. 3 — clearly with instructions to hit the ball as far and as hard as possible, which he did.

Anthony McGrath looked ominous with four early boundaries, but once he was snaffled by Gallian off Napier for 18 the innings had a hollow ring to it. Naved flayed away regardless — and brought up his 50 as **Jacques Rudolph**, **Adam Lyth**, **Tim Bresnan** and **Adil Rashid** all perished.

The batsmen were completely bamboozled by Kaneria, one of the best one-day spinners on the circuit, as he lavishly mixed trickery,

**RANA NAVED-UL-HASAN
Flayed away regardless.**

guile and control. Naved gave him a return catch to end an entertaining 57, and when **Richard Pyrah** departed as swiftly as he had arrived it was 113-9. Gough and **David Wainwright** went on the attack — Gough striking four fours in his 33 as Carnegie reached a totally under-par 157.

Carnegie can be applauded for making the batsmen work — especially as Gough came off after two balls with what appeared to be a back spasm. Naved-ul-Hasan and Bresnan showed great fight, and Naved was rewarded when Gallian edged to Brophy for 7. Essex skipper Pettini employed the minimum of risk while Napier raced to 46 in 43 balls: Napier should have been caught at 14 by Gough, but his innings did not end until Pyrah forced a false stroke to Rudolph at long-off. 86-2.

Wainwright showed immaculate control — snaring Pettini for 57 from 73 balls and having Foster taken in the slips. Unfortunately, ten Doeschate finished the match by lifting him for six.

NatWest Pro40 League Division 2
Yorkshire v. Surrey

Played at Woodbridge Road, Guildford, on July 20, 2008
Yorkshire won by 11 runs

Toss won by Yorkshire   Yorkshire 2 points; Surrey 0 points

YORKSHIRE

A W Gale, b Dernbach	44
J A Rudolph, c Batty b Collins	20
Rana Naved-ul-Hasan, c Afzaal b Dernbach	11
A McGrath, c Roy b Afzaal	37
§ G L Brophy, st Batty b Spriegel	6
A Lyth, c Schofield b Afzaal	28
T T Bresnan, c Spriegel b Afzaal	6
A U Rashid, not out	33
R M Pyrah, not out	26
* D Gough	
D J Wainwright Did not bat	
Extras lb 1, w 14, nb 4	19
Total (7 wkts, 40 overs)	230

FoW: 1-57 (Rudolph) 2-70 (Gale) 3-80 (Naved-ul-Hasan) 4-96 (Brophy) 5-155 (Lyth)
6-164 (McGrath) 7-171 (Bresnan)

BOWLING ANALYSIS

	O	M	R	W
Collins	7	0	42	1
Dernbach	7	0	44	2
Jordan	5	0	38	0
Spriegel	6	0	28	1
Schofield	7	0	34	0
Afzaal	8	0	43	3

SURREY

S A Newman, c McGrath b Bresnan	5
J G E Benning, c & b Bresnan	11
* M R Ramprakash, lbw b Naved-ul-Hasan	1
U Afzaal, c Rudolph b Rashid	41
C J Jordan, lbw b Gough	38
C P Schofield, c Rashid b Gough	58
§ J N Batty, c Pyrah b McGrath	24
J J Roy, b Naved-ul-Hasan	6
M N W Spriegel, not out	5
J W Dernbach, not out	19
P T Collins Did not bat	
Extras b 1, lb 3, w 5, nb 2	11
Total (8 wkts, 40 overs)	219

FoW: 1-7 (Newman) 2-8 (Ramprakash) 3-25 (Benning) 4-90 (Afzaal) 5-136 (Jordan)
6-178 (Batty) 7-194 (Schofield) 8-196 (Roy)

BOWLING ANALYSIS

	O	M	R	W
Naved-ul-Hasan	8	1	34	2
Bresnan	8	1	33	2
Pyrah	4	0	32	0
Gough	8	0	62	2
Wainwright	6	2	18	0
Rashid	5	0	30	1
McGrath	1	0	6	1

Umpires: N J Llong and D J Millns   Scorers: Miss C M Hadley and Mrs J E Booth

Surrey v. Yorkshire
Back in the winning groove

A solid if unspectacular return to winning ways was the tonic needed after a traumatic couple of weeks.

Darren Gough chose to bat, and **Andrew Gale** and **Jacques Rudolph** got away to a swift start. Rudolph ducked into one from Dernbach after nine overs — and Collins found his edge off a back-foot drive at 57.

Carnegie became bogged down. The previously fluent Gale was bowled middle stump by Dernbach for a 44-ball 44, with eight boundaries, and Dernbach had the aggressive **Rana Naved-ul-Hasan** superbly caught by Afzaal at leg-slip for 11. 80-3.

It was 96-4 when **Gerard Brophy** was found short of his ground, but **Anthony McGrath** and **Adam Lyth** took it to 155.

Three wickets toppled swiftly as both partners and then **Tim Bresnan** fell to poor shots off Afzaal, but enter **Adil Rashid** and **Richard Pyrah** to provide stability and impetus: both ended unbeaten

TIM BRESNAN: Real pace.

— 36 runs coming in the last three overs to elevate Yorkshire to a lofty 230. Rashid finished with 33, and Pyrah 26 in a stand of 59.

Newman went to a superb one-handed catch by McGrath at second slip off Bresnan in the second over, and Ramprakash was pinned in front by Naved for a single. 8-2. Benning fought hard, but Bresnan was generating real pace, and a mistimed pull have him an easy return catch. Afzaal and Jordan put on 65 to pull the hosts back into the contest, but **David Wainwright's** first four overs cost only three runs, and the Brown Caps were a long way short of 100 in the 21st over.

Adil Rashid removed Afzaal for 41 off 67 balls, and Jordan was trapped in front by Gough for a hard-working 38. 136-5. Schofield struck 58 from 41 balls with free-flowing drives and lusty blows, and Surrey needed 41 from three overs: Schofield fell to a tumbling catch by Rashid off Gough, and all that remained was clean hitting by Dernbach.

187

NatWest Pro40 League Division 2
Yorkshire v. Leicestershire

Played at Headingley, Leeds, on August 3, 2008
Yorkshire won by 1 run

Toss won by Yorkshire

Yorkshire 2 points; Leicestershire 0 points

YORKSHIRE

A W Gale, run out (Smith)		89
J A Rudolph, c Kruger b Allenby		120
Naved-ul-Hasan, b Smith		10
C R Taylor, c Dippenaar b Allenby		22
§ G L Brophy, not out		32
T T Bresnan, not out		21
A Lyth		
A U Rashid		
R M Pyrah	Did not bat	
D J Wainwright		
* D Gough		
Extras w 9		9
Total (4 wkts, 40 overs)		303

FoW: 1-170 (Gale) 2-187 (Naved-ul-Hasan) 3-245 (Taylor) 4-246 (Rudolph)

BOWLING ANALYSIS

	O	M	R	W
Kruger	4	0	31	0
du Preez	8	0	47	0
Cliff	6	0	47	0
Smith	8	0	46	1
Naik	2	0	17	0
Allenby	8	0	70	2
Henderson	4	0	45	0

LEICESTERSHIRE

H D Ackerman, c Rudolph b Bresnan		0
J du Toit, c Pyrah b Naved-ul-Hasan		15
H H Dippenaar, b Naved-ul-Hasan		20
* § P A Nixon, b Pyrah		47
J Allenby, b Pyrah		18
T C Smith, c Pyrah b Bresnan		52
D du Preez, not out		107
C W Henderson, b Gough		30
J K H Naik, not out		1
S J Cliff		
G J P Kruger	Did not bat	
Extras b 1, lb 3, w 2, nb 6		12
Total (7 wkts, 40 overs)		302

FoW: 1-0 (Ackerman) 2-29 (Dippenaar) 3-42 (du Toit) 4-86 (Allenby) 5-129 (Nixon)
6-198 (Smith) 7-292 (Henderson)

BOWLING ANALYSIS

	O	M	R	W
Bresnan	8	0	63	2
Naved-ul-Hasan	8	0	46	2
Gough	8	0	41	1
Pyrah	8	0	58	2
Wainwright	5	0	50	0
Rashid	3	0	40	0

Umpires: R K Illingworth and W Lloyds

Scorers: J T Potter and G A York

605 runs — and victory by 1

A truly staggering match — with some of the finest clean hitting this writer has seen — culminated in a one-run victory for Carnegie, while keeping alive their promotion hopes.

Darren Gough won the toss, and his now established openers, **Andrew Gale** and **Jacques Rudolph**, immediately set about Foxes' medium-pacers.

The 100 came up in the 16th over — Gale reaching his 50 in 40 balls with blows all round the lush outfield, and Rudolph ran to his half-century in 59 balls. Rudolph was now in complete control, and when a reverse sweep flew over the ropes the floodgates opened.

Gale passed his previous one-day best of 70, but hesitation saw him run out for 89 from 82 balls, with 11 fours and a six. The 170 opening stand was

JACQUES RUDOLPH
Reverse-sweep six.

the highest in this form of the game — beating **Martyn Moxon** and **Ashley Metcalfe's** record at Scarborough in 1991.

Chris Taylor contributed 22 to a stand of 58 until at 245 he gave a simple mid-wicket catch. Rudolph's century arrived in 85 balls, and he flogged the attack to all parts until he was caught in the deep off Allenby for 120 from 96 balls, with 11 fours and four sixes. **Gerard Brophy** and **Tim Bresnan** completed the slaughter with a vicious stand of 57.

Foxes' best batsman, Ackerman, gave Rudolph a routine slip catch off a pumped-up Bresnan second ball. Dippenaar and du Toit steadied the ship, but wickets tumbled as the asking rate climbed to 10 an over. **Richard Pyrah** bowled the dangerous Nixon for 47, but at 129-5 in came du Preez — who with partner Smith added 69 in six overs.

Smith was caught by Pyrah off Bresnan for 52 in 43 balls — with two fours and four sixes — but du Preez unleashed some of the biggest hitting ever witnessed at Headingley: he and Henderson decimated a bewildered attack, and with 88 needed off 10 it was game on. Sixes came from the first three balls of Gough's last-but-one over before he castled Henderson for 30 to end a stand of 94 from 11 overs.

Last over from **Rana Naved-ul-Hasan**: 12 needed. The first ball went for four to bring up du Preez's 61-ball 100, but he then lost the strike. A single off the penultimate ball gave du Preez one last chance — but it had to be six: it went over mid-on, two bounces, for four only.

NatWest Pro40 League Division 2
Yorkshire v. Derbyshire

Played at The County Ground, Derby, on August 21, 2008

Match tied

Toss won by Derbyshire   Yorkshire 1 point; Derbyshire 1 point

YORKSHIRE

A W Gale, c Redfern b Clare	20
J A Rudolph, b Doshi	54
Rana Naved-ul-Hasan, c Smith b Hinds	74
A McGrath, st New b Doshi	2
C R Taylor, c Wagg b Hunter	23
A Lyth, c Clare b Hunter	10
§ S M Guy, c Wagg b Hunter	6
A U Rashid, not out	8
R M Pyrah, not out	1
* D Gough	
G J Kruis Did not bat	
Extras lb 7, w8	15
Total (7 wkts, 34 overs)	213

FoW: 1-48 (Gale) 2-125 (Rudolph) 3-134 (McGrath) 4-178 (Naved-ul-Hasan) 5-194 (Lyth) 6-194 (Taylor) 7-211 (Guy)

BOWLING ANALYSIS

	O	M	R	W
Wagg	7	0	33	0
Hunter	7	0	44	3
Clare	7	0	33	1
Doshi	7	0	47	2
Hinds	6	0	49	1

DERBYSHIRE

* C J L Rogers, lbw b Kruis	19
G M Smith, c Rashid b Naved-ul-Hasan	8
W W Hinds, lbw b Naved-ul-Hasan	0
R Clarke, c McGrath b Rashid	29
J L Sadler, lbw b Rashid	30
D J Redfern, not out	57
G G Wagg, b Rashid	15
§ T J New, not out	28
J L Clare	
I D Hunter Did not bat	
N D Doshi	
Extras b 3, lb 3, w 15, nb 6	27
Total (6 wkts, 34 overs)	213

FoW: 1-12 (Smith) 2-14 (Hinds) 3-49 (Rogers) 4-89 (Clarke) 5-110 (Sadler) 6-128 (Wagg)

BOWLING ANALYSIS

	O	M	R	W
Kruis	7	2	19	1
Naved-ul-Hasan	7	0	62	2
Pyrah	6	0	48	0
Gough	7	0	41	0
Rashid	7	0	37	3

Umpires: N G B Cook and G Sharp   Scorers: J T Potter and J M Brown

Guy's brilliance unmasked

SIMON GUY
Decisive take.

A stunning last-ball take by Yorkshire wicket-keeper **Simon Guy** allowed his side to get out of this nailbiting thriller with a tie.

Play was delayed for an hour by rain, and the match was reduced to 34 overs a side. Derbyshire Phantoms opted to field, but **Andrew Gale** and **Jacques Rudolph** got away to a lively start.

Gale was out for typically pugnacious 20, and **Rana Naved-ul-Hasan**, a powerful striker especially around the mid-wicket to long-on region, set about the attack with gusto. He and Rudolph added 77 before a reverse sweep undid the South African for 54 from 65 balls, but when **Anthony McGrath** was stumped off Doshi it was 134-3.

Naved plundered on until at 178 he holed out on the long-on boundary for a 54-ball 74, with four fours and four sixes. Carnegie rather limped towards the finishing line, but nonetheless reached a challenging total of 213.

Naved with the ball in his hand produced an unpredictable mixture of wides, no-balls, long-hops...and wicket-taking deliveries. Smith hit straight to mid-on, and then Naved trapped Hinds lbw playing almost no stroke.

Deon Kruis beat the outside edge numerous times before he was rewarded with the wicket of Rogers, and Phantoms were struggling at 49-3.

Runs became difficult to come by, and leg-spinner **Adil Rashid** posed many problems: Clarke drove him to cover on 29, and Sadler was lbw trying an expansive leg-side blow. Wagg aimed to repeat his earlier six and was clean bowled — giving Rashid his third wicket.

Teenage batsman Dan Redfern and Wagg had to attempt the near impossible, but Carnegie's out-cricket became ragged, and the runs started to flow. **Darren Gough** and **Richard Pyrah** were struggling with consistency — not helped by dropped catches in the outfield and numerous midfields. Only 45 needed from nine overs, 15 from two.

Gough conceded five plus a leg-bye in a final, good over, and Phantoms needed nine from Naved: the first ball was hammered to the boundary, but only two came from the next three. Two balls, three wanted. A scrambled bye to the wicket-keeper...then the ball flew off New's pads — but only a leg-bye as Guy's brilliance prevented the boundary.

Phantoms hero Redfern finished on 57 from 56 balls.

NatWest Pro40 League Division 2
Yorkshire v. Kent

Played at North Marine Road, Scarborough, on August 25, 2008
Yorkshire won by 7 wickets

Toss won by Yorkshire   Yorkshire 2 points; Kent 0 points

KENT

J L Denly, c Brophy b Kruis	....	22
* R W T Key, c Rudolph b Bresnan	....	9
M van Jaarsveld, c Brophy b Kruis	....	0
J M Kemp, c Rudolph b Pyrah	....	36
S J Cook, b Pyrah	....	42
D I Stevens, not out	....	60
R McLaren, c Brophy b Pyrah	....	0
§ G O Jones, c Brophy b Pyrah	....	8
J C Tredwell, c Lyth b Rashid	....	1
A Khan, b Naved-ul-Hasan	....	4
R H Joseph, not out	....	1
Extras lb 3, w 3	....	6
Total (9 wkts, 40 overs)	....	189

FoW: 1-20 (Key) 2-21 (van Jaarsveld) 3-44 (Denly) 4-90 (Kemp) 5-120 (Cook)
6-120 (McLaren) 7-143 (Jones) 8-146 (Tredwell) 9-172 (Khan)

BOWLING ANALYSIS

	O	M	R	W
Kruis	8	0	35	2
Bresnan	5	1	10	1
Naved-ul-Hasan	7	0	34	1
Gough	6	0	41	0
Pyrah	8	0	35	4
Rashid	6	0	31	1

YORKSHIRE

A W Gale, c Stevens b McLaren	....	14
J A Rudolph, c Jones b Joseph	....	41
Rana Naved-ul-Hasan, c Jones b McLaren	....	0
A McGrath, not out	....	85
§ G L Brophy, not out	....	38
T T Bresnan		
A Lyth		
A U Rashid	Did not bat	
R M Pyrah		
* D Gough		
G J Kruis		
Extras lb 5, w 7	....	12
Total (3 wkts, 33.1 overs)	....	190

FoW: 1-39 (Gale) 2-39 (Naved-ul-Hasan) 3-114 (Rudolph)

BOWLING ANALYSIS

	O	M	R	W
Khan	5	0	26	0
Joseph	8	0	45	1
McLaren	5	1	16	2
Cook	5.1	0	38	0
Tredwell	8	0	52	0
Stevens	2	0	8	0

Umpires: M J D Bodenham and J H Evans   Scorers: J T Potter and J C Foley

Pyrah shoots down Spitfires

Carnegie outclassed Kent Spitfires in what was never going to be their day from the moment **Darren Gough** put them in under helpful cloud cover.

Skipper Key survived two big shouts before edging a good one to **Jacques Rudolph** at slip off **Tim Bresnan** for 9.

The crowd had barely finished . their applause when the dangerous Van Jaarsveld was caught behind without scoring off a resurgent Deon Kruis.

Carnegie were now in the hot seat, where they were to remain. In-form Denly left at 44, and despite a rally of sorts from Kemp and Cook the

RICHARD PYRAH: Career best.

visitors could not get the run rate much above four. Kemp, who called for a runner, took out his frustrations on **Rana Naved-ul-Hasan**, pulling numerous short-pitched deliveries in a bright 36, but a miscued drive was caught superbly on the boundary by Rudolph off **Richard Pyrah**.

A vicious in-swinging yorker from Pyrah despatched Cook for a gutsy 42, and next ball McLaren got an inside edge. Spitfires 120-6, with 10 overs to go. They owed much to Stevens — who in an unbeaten 60 hit 17 in Gough's last over, and was harsh with **Adil Rashid**, his 50 coming in 38 balls. Pyrah finished with a career best 4-35.

Kent's total looked competitive compared with 10 overs before — but with 39 runs to Carnegie in six overs the signs were ominous. McLaren had **Andrew Gale** caught on the drive for 14, and Naved nibbled one outside the off stump — but Rudolph was in imperious form, and **Anthony McGrath** provided the calm before the storm.

McLaren and Cook slowed the scoring until McGrath hit Cook for 19 in one over, and the stand was worth 75 when Joseph found Rudolph's edge to end his 56-ball 41. McGrath held centre-stage, and in tandem with Brophy took the game beyond Kent's reach: the vice-captain put off-spinner Treadwell to destructive use as he raced to 85 in 80 balls.

NatWest Pro40 League Division 2
Yorkshire v. Glamorgan

Played at North Marine Road, Scarborough, on August 31, 2008
Yorkshire won by 49 runs (D/L method)

Toss won by Yorkshire   Yorkshire 2 points; Glamorgan 0 points

YORKSHIRE

A W Gale, lbw b Harris		7
J A Rudolph, b Harris		84
Rana Naved-ul-Hasan, c Powell b Gillespie		24
A McGrath, c Powell b Gillespie		73
§ G L Brophy, c Wallace b Wharf		4
A Lyth, c Hemp b Wharf		14
R M Pyrah, not out		8
D J Wainwright		
A U Rashid	Did not bat	
* D Gough		
G J Kruis		
Extras lb 3, w 13		16
Total (6 wkts, 40 overs)		230

FoW: 1-9 (Gale) 2-37 (Naved-ul-Hasan) 3-201 (Rudolph) 4-204 (McGrath) 5-207 (Brophy) 6-230 (Lyth)

BOWLING ANALYSIS

	O	M	R	W
Gillespie	8	0	40	2
Harris	8	0	40	2
Wharf	8	0	42	2
Croft	8	0	56	0
Cosker	6	0	36	0
Dalrymple	2	0	13	0

GLAMORGAN

R D B Croft, c Gough b Naved-ul-Hasan		25
* D L Hemp, b Pyrah		38
M J Powell, c Pyrah b Naved-ul-Hasan		6
T L Maynard, b Kruis		2
J W M Dalrymple, b Gough		0
B J Wright, c Rashid b Pyrah		20
§ M A Wallace, not out		20
A G Wharf, c Brophy b Gough		9
J A R Harris, not out		0
J N Gillespie		
D A Cosker	Did not bat	
Extras lb 7, w 8		15
Total (7 wkts, 29.2 overs)		135

FoW: 1-35 (Croft) 2-45 (Powell) 3-55 (Maynard) 4-71 (Dalrymple) 5-97 (Hemp) 6-116 (Wright) 7-135 (Wharf)

BOWLING ANALYSIS

	O	M	R	W
Kruis	8	0	26	1
Naved-ul-Hasan	6	0	26	2
Gough	4.2	0	20	2
Pyrah	7	0	31	2
Rashid	4	0	25	0

Umpires: J H Evans and R T Robinson   Scorers: J T Potter and A J Hignell

Carnegie promotion charge

ANTHONY MCGRATH
Straight down ground.

Promotion hopes were very much alive after a resounding victory as **Anthony McGrath** and **Jacques Rudolph** forged yet another match-winning partnership.

Carnegie took first use of the pitch, but **Andrew Gale** was trapped in front by a superb Harris in-swinger. **Rana Naved-ul-Hasan** got the board moving with four fours and a towering six off former Yorkshire fast bowler **Jason Gillespie**, but the one-time Australian star had him caught in the slips by Powell for a 13-ball 24.

Rudolph and McGrath then embarked on another superb stand — the vice-captain the main aggressor at first, but Rudolph never letting the bowlers get on top.

McGrath was magnificent throughout — especially down the ground where his straight, lofted drives were a delight. He reached his 50 in 69 balls and Rudolph, now moving through the gears, reached his landmark in 72 deliveries.

A hundred for both seemed nailed on, but Rudolph was bowled by Harris for 84 off 93 balls, with 11 fours and a six, and McGrath fell to the Powell/Gillespie combination for 73. Their stand of 164 had propelled Carnegie to 201, but a late flurry of wickets prevented them from reaching the 250 they had expected.

Croft and Hemp started brightly, but Croft was to become Naved's first wicket when he miscued to **Darren Gough** at mid-on for 25. Naved had Powell caught by Pyrah; **Deon Kruis** bowled Maynard, and Gough uprooted Dalrymple's stumps for a duck.

Hemp was playing a determined captain's innings, but Pyrah's slightly quicker ball breached his defences after he had made 38 from 62 balls. His departure in rapidly fading light effectively ended the contest: Glamorgan had reached 135-7 after a breezy knock from wicket-keeper Wallace when the umpires called a halt with 10 overs to be bowled.

Duckworth/Lewis indicated that the Dragons were 49 runs adrift.

NatWest Pro40 League Division 2
Yorkshire v. Warwickshire

Played at Headingley, Leeds, on September 9, 2008
No result

Toss won by Warwickshire   Yorkshire 1 point; Warwickshire 1 point

WARWICKSHIRE

I J L Trott, c Brophy b Kruis		11
N M Carter, not out		12
J O Troughton, not out		2
* D L Maddy		
§ T R Ambrose		
I J Westwood		
R Clarke	Did not bat	
A G Botha		
C R Woakes		
T D Groenewald		
C S Macleod		
Extras lb 1, w 2		3
Total (1 wkt, 6 overs)		28

FoW: 1-22 (Trott)

BOWLING ANALYSIS

	O	M	R	W
Kruis	3	0	12	1
Bresnan	3	0	15	0

YORKSHIRE

A W Gale
J A Rudolph
Rana Naved-ul-Hasan
A McGrath
§ G L Brophy
A Lyth
T T Bresnan
A U Rashid
R M Pyrah
* D Gough
G J Kruis

Umpires: N L Bainton and A A Jones   Scorers: J T Potter and D E Wainwright

Yorkshire v. Warwickshire
Will we? Won't we?

SKIPPER DARREN GOUGH
Soggy farewell to Headingley.

Darren Gough's sad farewell match at Headingley Carnegie ended after only six overs of play when persistent rain left the crowd and both teams equally frustrated.

Yorkshire now knew that automatic promotion was out of their hands — and even a win at Northampton might not be enough to gain second spot.

Play began at 5.45pm after a mass mop-up of the sodden outfield, and the match was reduced to 33 overs a side.

Trott and Carter began with a flourish — collecting boundaries from some wayward bowling by **Deon Kruis** and **Tim Bresnan**.

The Warwickshire pair had reached 22 in the fifth over when Kruis induced a faint edge to **Gerard Brophy**, and Trott was out for 11.

Soon afterwards the rain returned and play was halted. The teams did not return.

NatWest Pro40 League Division 2
Yorkshire v. Northamptonshire

Played at The County Ground, Northampton, on September 13, 2008
Yorkshire won by 4 runs

Toss won by Yorkshire   Yorkshire 2 points; Northamptonshire 0 points

YORKSHIRE

A W Gale, c Brown b Crook		9
J A Rudolph, lbw b Lucas		22
Rana Naved-ul-Hasan, c Lucas b Boje		23
A McGrath, b Brown		23
§ G L Brophy, c White b Boje		59
T T Bresnan, lbw b Panesar		7
A U Rashid, c Wessels b Brown		11
R M Pyrah, st O'Brien b Boje		4
D J Wainwright, not out		13
* D Gough, not out		4
G J Kruis	Did not bat	
Extras lb 3, w 4		7
Total (8 wkts, 40 overs)		182

FoW: 1-18 (Gale) 2-40 (Rudolph) 3-68 (Naved-ul-Hasan) 4-97 (McGrath) 5-130 (Bresnan) 6-155 (Rashid) 7-161 (Pyrah) 8-172 (Brophy)

BOWLING ANALYSIS

	O	M	R	W
Crook	6	0	24	1
Lucas	8	0	44	1
Wigley	3	0	19	0
Boje	7	0	34	3
Brown	8	0	33	2
Panesar	8	1	25	1

NORTHAMPTONSHIRE

D J G Sales, b Kruis		88
§ N J O'Brien, c Rashid b Bresnan		24
M H Wessels, c Bresnan b Gough		8
R A White, lbw b Naved-ul-Hasan		1
M A G Nelson, b Rashid		24
* N Boje, b Naved-ul-Hasan		21
S P Crook, c McGrath b Kruis		1
D S Lucas, run out (Rashid/Naved-ul-Hasan)		4
M S Panesar, b Kruis		1
D H Wigley, b Kruis		0
J F Brown, not out		1
Extras w 3, nb 2		5
Total (34.4 overs)		178

FoW: 1-34 (O'Brien) 2-58 (Wessels) 3-59 (White) 4-104 (Nelson) 5-157 (Boje) 6-158 (Crook) 7-163 (Lucas) 8-169 (Panesar) 9-169 (Wigley) 10-178 (Sales)

BOWLING ANALYSIS

	O	M	R	W
Kruis	6.4	0	32	4
Bresnan	5	1	16	1
Gough	5	1	22	1
Naved-ul-Hasan	7	0	39	2
Wainwright	4	0	21	0
Rashid	5	0	28	1
Pyrah	2	0	20	0

Umpires: M J Harris and P J Hartley   Scorers: J T Potter and A C Kingston

Promotion — thanks to Kruis

DEON KRUIS
Four wickets in 15 balls.

A nailbiting and at times improbable victory took Yorkshire back into the top flight of *Pro40* cricket.

With Essex defeating Kent at Chelmsford **Darren Gough** could leave the Yorkshire captaincy with something to celebrate. He won the toss again, decided to bat, but at 68-3 this might have been questioned.

The dismissals of **Andrew Gale** and **Jacques Rudolph** were followed by a typical cameo from **Rana Naved-ul-Hasan**, but with three spinners on a slow pitch boundaries were difficult to get.

Panesar, Brown and Boje all asked testing questions, and without the big scores of **Anthony McGrath** and **Jacques Rudolph** the middle-order had a brittle look.

McGrath dropped anchor, while **Gerard Brophy** played more extravagantly. McGrath was bowled round his legs for 23, and despite dogged efforts from **David Wainwright**, **Tim Bresnan** and **Adil Rashid** it was left to Brophy to do most of the run-scoring: he ran to his 50 with a colossal six over mid-wicket — but Boje had his man caught by White for 59 from 69 balls. Without a *Pro40* win this year, Steelbacks had nothing to lose.

O'Brien attacked Bresnan and **Deon Kruis** from the off: Bresnan had him caught by Rashid for 22, and Wessels holed out to mid-on off Gough. White was lbw to Naved second ball, but skipper Sales and Nelson began a partnership that was to add 45 until Rashid bowled Nelson. Then Boje added 53 with his skipper before Naved bowled him.

Could Sales do it? He was striking the ball cleanly all round the ground — but Kruis had Crook caught by McGrath, and Lucas was run out. Kruis bowled Panesar with an in-swinging yorker, and he was on fire as he despatched Wigley. With something akin to a volcanic eruption Kruis summoned up one last yorker — and Sales was out for 88. Kruis was the saviour with a meteoric spell of four wickets in 15 balls.

NATWEST PRO40 COMPETITION 2008

DIVISION 1

		P	W	L	T	NR/A	PTS	NRR
1	Sussex Sharks (Div 1, 5)	8	5	1	0	2	12	-0.106
2	Hampshire Hawks (Div 1, 4)	8	4	2	0	2	10	0.633
3	Durham Dynamos (Div 2, 1)	8	4	3	0	1	9	0.369
4	Nottinghamshire Outlaws (Div 1, 2)	8	4	4	0	0	8	0.250
5	Gloucestershire Gladiators (Div 1, 6)	8	3	3	0	2	8	-0.460
6	Somerset Sabres (Div 2, 2)	8	3	4	1	0	7	0.154
7	Worcestershire Royals (Div 1, 1) **	8	2	3	1	2	7	0.110
8	Lancashire Lightning (Div 1, 3) *	8	1	3	0	4	6	-0.815
9	Middlesex Crusaders (Div 2, 3) *	8	2	5	0	1	5	-0.138

* Relegated to Division 2 for 2009.

** Worcestershire Royals defeated Glamorgan Dragons by 103 runs in the play-off, and so remain in Division 1.

DIVISION 2

		P	W	L	T	NR/A	PTS	NRR
1	Essex Eagles (Div 1, 9) *	8	6	0	1	1	14	1.479
2	**Yorkshire Carnegie (Div 2, 6) ***	**8**	**5**	**1**	**1**	**1**	**12**	**0.250**
3	Glamorgan Dragons (Div 2, 9) **	8	5	3	0	0	10	0.113
4	Kent Spitfires (Div 2, 5)	8	4	2	0	2	10	1.629
5	Surrey Brown Caps (Div 2, 4)	8	4	4	0	0	8	-0.444
6	Warwickshire Bears (Div 1, 8)	8	3	3	0	2	8	-0.242
7	Leicestershire Foxes (Div 2, 7)	8	1	4	1	2	5	-0.463
8	Derbyshire Phantoms (Div 2, 8)	8	1	6	1	0	3	-0.892
9	Northamptonshire Steelbacks (Div 1, 7)	8	0	6	0	2	2	-0.993

* Promoted to Division 1 for 2009.

** Remaining in Division 2 after losing the play-off with Worcestershire Royals.

(2007 positions in brackets)

YORKSHIRE AVERAGES 2008

NatWest Pro40 Cricket League Division 2

Played 8   Won 5   Tied 1   Lost 1   No result 1

BATTING AND FIELDING

Player	M.	I.	N.O.	Runs	H.S.	Avge	100s	50s	ct/st
J A Rudolph	8	7	0	349	120	49.85	1	2	5
A McGrath	7	6	1	238	85*	47.60	0	2	4
D Gough	8	2	1	37	33	37.00	0	0	1
G L Brophy	7	6	2	140	59	35.00	0	1	7/1
A U Rashid	8	4	2	60	33*	30.00	0	0	4
Rana Naved-ul-Hasan	8	7	0	199	74	28.42	0	2	0
A W Gale	8	7	0	184	89	26.28	0	1	0
C R Taylor	2	2	0	45	23	22.50	0	0	0
R M Pyrah	8	5	3	40	26*	20.00	0	0	4
A Lyth	7	4	0	54	28	13.50	0	0	1
T T Bresnan	6	4	1	37	21*	12.33	0	0	2
S M Guy	1	1	0	6	6	6.00	0	0	0
D J Wainwright	5	2	2	22	13*	—	0	0	0
G J Kruis	5	0	0	0	—	—	0	0	0

BOWLING

Player	Overs	Mdns	Runs	Wkts	Avge	Best	4wI	Runs per Over
A McGrath	1	0	6	1	6.00	1-6	0	6.00
G J Kruis	32.4	2	124	9	13.77	4-32	1	3.79
Rana Naved-ul-Hasan	48	1	266	12	22.16	2-26	0	5.54
T T Bresnan	34	3	160	6	26.66	2-33	0	4.70
R M Pyrah	38.4	0	249	9	27.66	4-35	1	6.43
A U Rashid	38	0	226	7	32.28	3-37	0	5.94
D Gough	38.4	1	229	6	38.16	2-20	0	5.92
D J Wainwright	23	2	122	2	61.00	2-33	0	5.30
J A Rudolph	2	0	11	0	—	0-11	0	5.50
A Lyth	1	0	3	0	—	0-3	0	3.00

YORKSHIRE AVERAGES 2008

ALL LIMITED-OVERS MATCHES
(Friends Provident Trophy and NatWest Pro40 Cricket League)
(Twenty20 Cup matches NOT included)

Played 18   Won 10   Lost 4   Tied 1   No result 3

BATTING AND FIELDING

Player	M.	I.	N.O.	Runs	H.S.	Avge	100s	50s	ct/st
C White	7	7	3	195	69*	48.75	0	2	2
J A Rudolph	18	16	2	675	120	48.21	1	5	9
A McGrath	17	15	3	489	105*	40.75	1	3	7
A Shahzad	2	1	0	33	33	33.00	0	0	0
A W Gale	18	17	1	450	89	28.12	0	3	0
Rana Naved-ul-Hasan	9	8	0	212	74	26.50	0	2	0
G L Brophy	17	15	5	238	61*	23.80	0	2	24/2
C R Taylor	2	2	0	45	23	22.50	0	0	0
A U Rashid	17	8	3	101	41*	20.20	0	0	7
T T Bresnan	16	9	2	134	55	19.14	0	1	3
D Gough	17	3	1	38	33	19.00	0	0	4
M P Vaughan	2	2	0	38	22	19.00	0	0	0
A Lyth	15	10	1	162	38*	18.00	0	0	5
R M Pyrah	18	9	4	83	26*	16.60	0	0	10
S M Guy	1	1	0	6	6	6.00	0	0	0
D J Wainwright	7	3	3	29	13*	—	0	0	0
G J Kruis	12	1	1	3	3*	—	0	0	0
M J Hoggard	2	1	1	1	1*	—	0	0	0
S A Patterson	1	0	0	0	—	—	0	0	0

BOWLING

Player	Overs	Mdns	Runs	Wkts	Avge	Best	4wI	Runs per Over
S A Patterson	8	1	18	2	9.00	2-18	0	2.25
A McGrath	31.4	0	164	10	16.40	3-16	0	5.17
T T Bresnan	111.1	14	485	24	20.20	4-31	1	4.36
Rana Naved-ul-Hasan	58	2	307	14	21.92	2-26	0	5.29
M J Hoggard	16	2	67	3	22.33	3-26	0	4.18
G J Kruis	80	9	300	13	23.07	4-32	1	3.75
D Gough	105.2	4	510	21	24.28	3-17	0	4.84
R M Pyrah	105.2	4	585	24	24.37	4-35	1	5.55
A U Rashid	77.3	3	384	12	32.00	3-37	0	4.95
A Shahzad	16	0	55	1	55.00	1-30	0	3.43
D J Wainwright	32	2	166	3	55.33	2-33	0	5.18
J A Rudolph	3	0	19	0	—	0-8	0	6.33
A Lyth	1	0	3	0	—	0-3	0	3.00

NatWest Series — Match One
England v. South Africa

Played at Headingley, Leeds, on August 22, 2008
England won by 20 runs
Toss won by England

ENGLAND

I R Bell, c de Villiers b Kallis		35
§ M J Prior, c de Villiers b Kallis		42
O A Shah, c Philander b Botha		12
* K P Pietersen, not out		90
A Flintoff, b Steyn		78
L J Wright, not out		2
R S Bopara		
S R Patel		
S C J Broad	Did not bat	
S J Harmison		
J M Anderson		
Extras b 4, lb 5, w 6, nb 1		16
Total (4 wkts, 50 overs)		275

FoW: 1-77 (Bell) 2-86 (Prior) 3-113 (Shah) 4-271 (Flintoff)

BOWLING ANALYSIS

	O	M	R	W
Steyn	10	0	67	1
Ntini	9	0	38	0
Nel	10	1	53	0
Kallis	5	0	25	2
Botha	7	0	33	1
Philander	9	0	50	0

SOUTH AFRICA

H H Gibbs, b Patel		37
* G C Smith, c Prior b Harmison		21
J H Kallis, run out (Bell/Pietersen)		52
A B de Villiers, c Bell b Pietersen		24
J P Duminy, c Prior b Harmison		18
§ M V Boucher, st Prior b Pietersen		16
J Botha, c sub (T T Bresnan) b Broad		26
V D Philander, run out (Broad)		23
A Nel, b Flintoff		10
D W Steyn, not out		3
M Ntini, b Flintoff		2
Extras b 4, lb 8, w 11		23
Total (49.4 overs)		255

FoW: 1-50 (Smith) 2-93 (Gibbs) 3-142 (de Villiers) 4-149 (Kallis) 5-168 (Boucher) 6-202 (Duminy) 7-219 (Botha) 8-245 (Philander) 9-249 (Nel) 10-255 (Ntini)

BOWLING ANALYSIS

	O	M	R	W
Broad	10	0	61	1
Anderson	3	0	18	0
Harmison	10	1	43	2
Flintoff	9.4	1	46	2
Patel	10	0	42	1
Bopara	2	0	11	0
Pietersen	5	0	22	2

Man of the match: K P Pietersen

Umpires: I J Gould and S J A Taufel   Scorers: J T Potter and M Snook

Twenty20 Cup Matches Played by Yorkshire in 2008

WINNERS:

Middlesex, who beat Kent by 3 runs

PREVIOUS WINNERS

2003 **Surrey,** who beat Warwickshire by 9 wickets
2004 **Leicestershire,** who beat Surrey by 7 wickets
2005 **Somerset,** who beat Lancashire by 7 wickets
2006 **Leicestershire,** who beat Nottinghamshire by 4 runs
2007 **Kent,** who beat Gloucestershire by 4 wickets

NORTH DIVISION

		P	W	L	T	NR	PTS	NRR
1	Durham Dynamos (5) *	10	6	1	1	2	15	0.984
2	Lancashire Lightning (2) *	10	6	3	0	1	13	0.921
3	**Yorkshire Carnegie (3) **	**10**	**5**	**3**	**1**	**1**	**10**	**-0.312**
4	Nottinghamshire Outlaws (1)	10	4	5	0	1	9	0.027
5	Derbyshire Phantoms (6)	10	3	7	0	0	6	-0.421
6	Leicestershire Foxes (4)	10	2	7	0	1	5	-0.893

MID/WEST/WALES DIVISION

		P	W	L	T	NR	PTS	NRR
1	Warwickshire Bears (1) *	10	6	1	1	2	15	0.694
2	Northamptonshire Steelbacks (4) *	10	6	3	0	1	13	0.431
3	Glamorgan Dragons (6) *	10	3	3	0	4	10	-0.176
4	Somerset Sabres (5)	10	3	4	0	3	9	0.313
5	Worcestershire Royals (3)	10	3	6	0	1	7	-0.488
6	Gloucestershire Gladiators (2)	10	1	5	1	3	6	-0.931

SOUTH DIVISION

		P	W	L	T	NR	PTS	NRR
1	Middlesex Crusaders (5) *	10	8	2	0	0	16	0.732
2	Essex Eagles (4) *	10	6	3	1	0	13	0.937
3	Kent Spitfires (2) *	10	6	4	0	0	12	0.640
4	Hampshire Hawks (6)	10	5	4	1	0	11	-0.505
5	Sussex Sharks (1)	10	2	8	0	0	4	-0.876
6	Surrey Brown Caps (3)	10	2	8	0	0	4	-0.905

* Qualified for the Quarter Finals.
** Deducted 2 points for fielding an unregistered player.

(2007 divisional positions in brackets)

Match-By-Match Reports   **DAVE CALDWELL**
Scorecards   **JOHN POTTER**

Twenty20 Cup — North Division
Yorkshire v. Derbyshire

Played at Headingley, Leeds, on June 12, 2008
Derbyshire won by 47 runs

Toss won by Derbyshire   Yorkshire 0 points; Derbyshire 2 points

DERBYSHIRE

D J Birch, c & b Bresnan		12
G M Smith, not out		100
W W Hinds, run out (Pyrah/Bresnan)		61
* R Clarke, not out		1
J L Sadler		
§ D J Pipe		
G G Wagg		
J L Clare	Did not bat	
C K Langeveldt		
J Needham		
N D Doshi		
Extras lb 2, w 1, nb 4		7
Total (2 wkts, 20 overs)		181

FoW: 1-29 (Birch) 2-178 (Hinds)

	O	M	R	W
Hoggard	4	0	28	0
Bresnan	4	0	32	1
Wainwright	3	0	39	0
Gough	4	0	21	0
Rashid	1	0	13	0
Pyrah	2	0	26	0
Vaughan	2	0	20	0

YORKSHIRE

A W Gale, c Doshi b Wagg		4
M P Vaughan, c Smith b Langeveldt		0
A McGrath, c Sadler b Needham		55
J A Rudolph, c Clarke b Wagg		13
§ G L Brophy, st Pipe b Doshi		25
T T Bresnan, c Clarke b Langeveldt		15
A U Rashid, b Clarke		2
R M Pyrah, b Langeveldt		5
D J Wainwright, not out		3
* D Gough, c Needham b Langeveldt		4
M J Hoggard	Did not bat	
Extras lb 4, w 2, nb 2		8
Total (9 wkts, 20 overs)		134

FoW: 1-4 (Gale) 2-6 (Vaughan) 3-30 (Rudolph) 4-100 (Brophy) 5-101 (McGrath)
6-107 (Rashid) 7-124 (Bresnan) 8-124 (Pyrah) 9-134 (Gough)

	O	M	R	W
Wagg	3	0	25	2
Langeveldt	4	0	9	4
Clare	1	0	15	0
Needham	4	0	35	1
Doshi	4	0	24	1
Clarke	4	0	22	1

Man of the match: G M Smith

Umpires: NGC Cowley and J W Lloyds   Scorers: J T Potter and J M Brown

62-ball 100 batters Carnegie

Carnegie's campaign got off to a terrible start when they were comprehensively despatched by a workmanlike Derbyshire.

Phantoms elected to bat — and a lusty century from Greg Smith led the way. Fours flowed from the word go, but Smith several times got away with miscued leg-side shots.

Birch fell to a sharp caught and bowled by **Tim Bresnan** for 12 — but this brought former West Indies batsmen Hinds to the crease,

70 in eight overs: Gerard Brophy, left, and Anthony McGrath.

and luck clearly was on both batsmen's side: they edged and deflected the ball to unmanned areas, and offered a fair few chances to a ragged Yorkshire outfit. **Andrew Gale** dropped Smith on 66, and the rest of the over went for 24 off a clearly shaken **David Wainwright**.

Adil Rashid put down Hinds on the cover boundary, when the left-hander had made only three, and the batsmen grew in confidence. Smith was now destructive and fluid, Hinds strong backward of square on both sides of the wicket. They added 149 in 16 overs before Hinds was run out for a 43-ball 61, with four sixes and three fours, after good work by **Richard Pyrah** in the deep. Smith went to his 100 of the last-but-one ball of the innings in 62 deliveries, with two sixes and 12 fours.

Gale fell in the first over, and **Michael Vaughan** — playing his first game in this format for Yorkshire — slashed his second ball to Smith at backward point. **Anthony McGrath** and **Jacques Rudolph** were not to provide the crucial partnership this time: Rudolph skied a simple chance to skipper Clarke for 13, and it was 30-3. McGrath and **Gerard Brophy** had a real chase at this large target — adding 70 in eight overs, McGrath completing his 50 in 41 deliveries. Brophy was snared by the experienced slow left-armer Doshi for 25, and McGrath was caught in the deep next over for 55. The dreaded collapse was on, and Langeveldt collected four wickets in an astonishing four overs for nine runs.

Twenty20 Cup — North Division
Yorkshire v. Nottinghamshire

Played at Headingley, Leeds, on June 13, 2008
Nottinghamshire won by 4 wickets

Toss won by Yorkshire

Yorkshire 0 points; Nottinghamshire 2 points

YORKSHIRE

A W Gale, c Adams b Shreck		6
C White, c Adams b Patel		26
M P Vaughan, c Patel b Shreck		17
A McGrath, c Voges b Patel		32
J A Rudolph, c Shafayat b Ealham		23
§ G L Brophy, b Clough		0
T T Bresnan, c Jefferson b Adams		7
A U Rashid, run out (Voges/Read)		10
R M Pyrah, not out		1
* D Gough, not out		1
M J Hoggard	Did not bat	
Extras lb 9, w 5, nb 4		18
Total (8 wkts, 15 overs)		141

FoW: 1-12 (Gale) 2-41 (Vaughan) 3-75 (White) 4-99 (McGrath) 5-105 (Brophy) 6-127 (Bresnan) 7-137 (Rudolph) 8-140 (Rashid)

	O	M	R	W
Shreck	3	1	20	2
Pattinson	2	0	17	0
Adams	3	0	25	1
Ealham	3	0	34	1
Patel	2	0	24	2
Clough	2	0	12	1

NOTTINGHAMSHIRE

W I Jefferson, c McGrath b Vaughan		40
A R Adams, c Rashid b Bresnan		1
S R Patel, c Pyrah b Gough		21
A C Voges, not out		40
C L Cairns, b Pyrah		5
* § C M W Read, b Pyrah		25
M A Ealham, c & b Pyrah		0
B M Shafayat, not out		0
G D Clough		
D J Pattinson	Did not bat	
C E Shreck		
Extras lb 10, w 1		11
Total (6 wkts, 14.2 overs)		143

FoW: 1-2 (Adams) 2-62 (Jefferson) 3-69 (Patel) 4-97 (Cairns) 5-137 (Read) 6-137 (Ealham)

	O	M	R	W
Hoggard	3	0	25	0
Bresnan	3	0	29	1
Vaughan	2	0	21	1
Gough	3	0	24	1
Pyrah	3	0	28	3
McGrath	0.2	0	6	0

Man of the match: W I Jefferson

Umpires: N G C Cowley and J W Lloyds

Scorers: J T Potter and L B Hewes

Yorkshire v. Nottinghamshire
Pyrah almost robs Outlaws

The hosts crashed to another defeat — even though they set Outlaws a stiff target in a 15-over match, and **Richard Pyrah** almost robbed them at the death.

Carnegie took strike, but at 12 lost **Andrew Gale**. **Michael Vaughan** and **Craig White** got into their stride, Vaughan setting off with real intent: he hit Pattinson for six over cover, and planted Shreck over mid-wicket before a sliced drive ended his quickfire 17.

White kept the board moving, allowing **Anthony McGrath** for the second game in succession to provide the main thrust: McGrath's 32 came from 19 balls, with three fours and a six, and White contributed a near run-a-ball 26 before the usual flurry of wickets and occasional big shots brought the close.

Outlaws would need an impressive 9.5 runs an over: Adams holed out to **Adil Rashid** at mid-on off **Tim Bresnan**, but Jefferson and Patel added 60 runs in four overs, with both **Matthew Hoggard** and Bresnan taking some serious tap.

Jefferson in fading light launched Vaughan's first delivery into orbit before planting a similar one into the safe hands of McGrath on the edge. He had made 40 from 19 balls, with six fours and two sixes, in a little over 15 minutes.

Patel was caught in the deep off Gough for an equally vital 21 from 14 balls, and Pyrah cleaned up Cairns. At 97 with six wickets in hand the run rate was creeping up, and Voges and Read took it away from Yorkshire with a thrilling stand of 40.

MICHAEL VAUGHAN
Two cleared the ring.

Pyrah struck twice in the last-but-one over, bowling Read for 25 and catching and bowling Ealham next ball, and the Outlaws needed five from the last over. The ball was tossed to McGrath...but his second ball to Voges flew over mid-wicket for six.

Twenty20 Cup — North Division
Yorkshire v. Derbyshire

Played at Queen's Park, Chesterfield, on June 15, 2008
Yorkshire won by 11 runs

Toss won by Yorkshire   Yorkshire 2 points; Derbyshire 0 points

YORKSHIRE

A W Gale, c Langeveldt b Clarke		25
C White, b Langeveldt		0
M P Vaughan, c Telo b Hinds		31
A McGrath, not out		72
J A Rudolph, run out (Clarke)		5
§ G L Brophy, c Birch b Clarke		13
TT Bresnan, not out		13
R M Pyrah		
D J Wainwright	Did not bat	
* D Gough		
M J Hoggard		
Extras lb 4, w 6		10
Total (5 wkts, 20 overs)		169

FoW: 1-9 (White) 2-35 (Gale) 3-67 (Vaughan) 4-80 (Rudolph) 5-139 (Brophy)

	O	M	R	W
Langeveldt	4	0	27	1
Wagg	4	0	27	0
Clarke	4	0	32	2
Doshi	3	0	25	0
Hinds	2	0	7	1
Sadler	1	0	13	0
Needham	2	0	34	0

DERBYSHIRE

F D Telo, c Brophy b Bresnan		12
G M Smith, run out (Hoggard/Wainwright)		68
W W Hinds, c Gough b White		12
* R Clarke, c McGrath b Pyrah		2
§ D J Pipe, c Pyrah b Gough		17
D J Birch, not out		17
J L Sadler, c Pyrah b McGrath		1
G G Wagg, not out		18
C K Langeveldt		
J Needham	Did not bat	
N D Doshi		
Extras b 1, lb 6, w 4		11
Total (6 wkts, 20 overs)		158

FoW: 1-26 (Telo) 2-91 (Smith) 3-97 (Hinds) 4-104 (Clarke) 5-121 (Pipe)
6-125 (Sadler)

	O	M	R	W
Hoggard	4	0	37	0
Bresnan	4	0	35	1
Gough	4	0	31	1
Pyrah	4	0	18	1
McGrath	3	0	24	1
$ Wainwright	0.5	0	6	0
$ White	0.1	0	0	1

$ D J Wainwright was unable to complete his over.

Man of the match: A McGrath

Umpires: G I Burgess and R T Robinson   Scorers: J T Potter and J M Brown

McGrath starts victory run

Victory at last! **Anthony McGrath** once again was Carnegie's star performer as they opened their account in this format.

Anthony produced one of his finest knocks, but it was the Queen's Park home crowd who cheered first as **Craig White** left in the first over, aiming an expansive drive off Langeveldt.

Michael Vaughan and **Andrew Gale** struggled to pierce the field, only 17 coming in the first five overs, and at 35 Gale tried to ignite the innings: he fell to a fine catch in the deep

Sheer class: Anthony McGrath hammers 72 with never a slog.

for 25 from 29 balls. Vaughan and McGrath added 32 before Vaughan, 31, sent a simple catch to the mid-wicket fence. 67-3. Nine overs to go.

McGrath produced an innings of sheer class — no aimless slogging or desperation shots. Repeatedly, he hit high and straight, Clarke and Doshi in particular coming in for harsh treatment. Rudolph was run out cheaply backing up — but cameos from **Gerard Brophy** and **Tim Bresnan** kept McGrath company as he raced to his 50 in 29 balls. He and Brophy put on 59 in five overs, a six off Wagg in the last over taking him to an unbeaten 72 in 42 deliveries, with three fours and six sixes.

Derbyshire, needing 170 at 8.5 an over, lost Telo, caught behind off Bresnan, but Smith's 50 came in 33 balls — one over from McGrath going for 16 runs. The game turned on the dismissal of Smith, attempting a suicidal run to **Matthew Hoggard**, for a 42-ball 68. **David Wainwright** joined the attack and left it as a vicious straight-drive from Clarke damaged the left-armer's bowling hand.

One ball from Wainwright's over remained — and White dragged it half way down for Hinds to pull it to fine leg, where **Darren Gough** took a superb catch. Clarke gave **Richard Pyrah** a wicket he richly deserved for four tight overs, and the run rate was climbing steadily. The valiant Pipe and Sadler perished in the safe hands of Pyrah, and Phantoms entered the last over needing 25. Wagg enjoyed a few lusty blows, but 170 had always been a bridge too far.

Twenty20 Cup — North Division
Yorkshire v. Leicestershire

Played at Grace Road, Leicester, on June 17, 2008
Yorkshire won by 6 wickets

Toss won by Leicestershire   Yorkshire 2 points; Leicestershire 0 points

LEICESTERSHIRE

H D Ackerman, not out		57
J du Toit, c Gale b Hoggard		15
J Allenby, lbw b Rashid		29
* § P A Nixon, c Hoggard b Rashid		15
D du Preez, not out		33
H H Dippenaar		
M A G Boyce		
J N Snape	Did not bat	
C W Henderson		
M N Malik		
D T Rowe		
Extras lb 4, w 1		5
Total (3 wkts, 20 overs)		154

FoW: 1-16 (du Toit) 2-78 (Allenby) 3-110 (Nixon)

	O	M	R	W
Bresnan	4	0	19	0
Hoggard	3	0	30	1
Pyrah	3	0	31	0
Gough	3	0	23	0
Rashid	4	0	28	2
Vaughan	3	0	19	0

YORKSHIRE

§ G L Brophy, c Nixon b Malik		3
A W Gale, retired hurt		15
M P Vaughan, run out (du Toit/du Preez)		1
J A Rudolph, b du Preez		56
A McGrath, c Rowe b Allenby		59
C R Taylor, not out		10
T T Bresnan, not out		2
R M Pyrah		
A U Rashid	Did not bat	
* D Gough		
M J Hoggard		
Extras b 2, lb 6, w 4		12
Total (4 wkts, 20 overs)		158

A W Gale retired hurt with the score 20-2

FoW: 1-17 (Brophy) 2-20 (Vaughan) 3-141 (McGrath) 4-148 (Rudolph)

	O	M	R	W
du Preez	4	0	33	1
Malik	4	1	17	1
Rowe	2	0	16	0
Allenby	4	0	32	1
Henderson	4	0	31	0
Snape	2	0	21	0

Man of the match: J A Rudolph

Umpires: N A Mallender and G Sharp   Scorers: J T Potter and G A York

Leicestershire v. Yorkshire
Taylor the last-ball hero

CHRIS TAYLOR: Victory six.

Chris Taylor — playing his first senior game of the season — clubbed the last ball of the match for six to give Carnegie their second win of the campaign and keep their knockout aspirations truly alive.

Foxes opted for first use, and du Toit was going well when he was caught by **Andrew Gale** off **Matthew Hoggard**. Ackerman struggled to break the infield, but Allenby carved runs to all corners of the ground until he was trapped in front by **Adil Rashid** for a quickfire 29.

Nixon got the board moving, but **Matthew Hoggard's** catch in the deep gave Rashid his second wicket. A late flourish from du Preez with 33 from 24 balls gave Foxes hope, but the bowlers — unspectacular but disciplined — restricted the hosts to 154-3, Ackerman finishing with 57 from 51 balls.

Carnegie got off to a poor start: **Gerard Brophy** was caught behind off Malik, and the run-out of England skipper **Michael Vaughan** made it 20-2. Vaughan turned for a routine second run — only to find his partner, **Andrew Gale**, lying on the floor with a turned ankle. They came off together as two new batsmen emerged, with Carnegie second favourites. How many times did **Jacques Rudolph** and **Anthony McGrath** turn proceedings on their head this season? This was another.

McGrath in particular was really developing a liking for this format, and after a steady start the runs began to accumulate. They enjoyed a superb stand of 121 before falling in successive overs: McGrath had 59 from 46 deliveries when he presented Rowe with a deep-field catch off Allenby, and Rudolph, with 59 from 46 balls, was bowled by du Preez.

Tim Bresnan and Taylor at the crease: seven needed off the last over. Victory a formality? Four runs from the first five balls, and it looked anything but. Allenby, with an excellent last over under his belt so far, ran in to bowl to Taylor with three still wanted. Taylor launched it over long on, and Carnegie had reignited their hopes.

Twenty20 Cup — North Division
Yorkshire v. Lancashire

Played at Headingley, Leeds, on June 18, 2008
Yorkshire won by 2 wickets

Toss won by Yorkshire   Yorkshire 2 points; Lancashire 0 points

LANCASHIRE

L Vincent, c Pyrah b Hoggard	3
M B Loye, c Pyrah b McGrath	43
* S G Law, b Pyrah	23
F du Plessis, c Gale b Pyrah	10
S J Croft, b Pyrah	2
§ G D Cross, not out	42
K W Hogg, b Bresnan	14
D G Cork, not out	2
S J Marshall	
S I Mahmood	Did not bat
T C Smith	
Extras b 5, lb 3, w 1, nb 2	11
Total (6 wkts, 20 overs)	150

FoW: 1-8 (Vincent) 2-48 (Law) 3-74 (du Plessis) 4-83 (Croft) 5-91 (Loye)
6-136 (Hogg)

	O	M	R	W
Hoggard	3	0	25	1
Bresnan	4	0	32	1
Pyrah	4	0	20	3
Gough	4	0	29	0
Rashid	3	0	22	0
McGrath	2	0	14	1

YORKSHIRE

A W Gale, b Hogg	0
§ G L Brophy, b Marshall	28
M P Vaughan, b Smith	21
A McGrath, b Mahmood	46
J A Rudolph, st Cross b du Plessis	16
C R Taylor, lbw b du Plessis	0
T T Bresnan, c Smith b Croft	3
A U Rashid, not out	5
R M Pyrah, c Cork b Mahmood	1
* D Gough, not out	20
M J Hoggard	Did not bat
Extras b 5, lb 7, w 2	14
Total (8 wkts, 19.4 overs)	154

FoW: 1-6 (Gale) 2-47 (Vaughan) 3-60 (Brophy) 4-86 (Rudolph) 5-86 (Taylor)
6-114 (Bresnan) 7-119 (McGrath) 8-121 (Pyrah)

	O	M	R	W
Hogg	3	0	27	1
Cork	3	0	36	0
Mahmood	4	0	13	2
Smith	3.4	0	21	1
Marshall	2	0	12	1
Croft	2	0	20	1
du Plessis	2	0	13	2

Man of the match: A McGrath

Umpires: N L Bainton and J W Holder   Scorers: J T Potter and A West

Yorkshire v. Lancashire
Dazzler flashes winning blade

Carnegie grabbed their third successive victory as the *Red Rose* retreated across the Pennines after a battle which ebbed and flowed until skipper **Darren Gough** snatched victory from the jaws of defeat — this time with the bat.

Chasing 151 in rapidly fading light, Carnegie were sliding towards defeat at 121-8 after Mahmood had decimated the middle-order. Cork took the 18th over: four leg-byes, and then **Adil Rashid** got to the non-striker's end with a scrambled single.

Gough proceeded to carve his old England teammate for three consecutive fours — and 17 had come from the over. Seven came from the 19th, and six were needed from the last, bowled by Smith.

First ball no run...then a sprinted single...four leg-byes...and an expansive cover-drive from

RICHARD PYRAH
Economy and wickets.

'Dazzler' Gough settled it. Carnegie's bowling again impressed — **Richard Pyrah** taking the bulk of the plaudits as he showed variation in pace and kept very disciplined lines, giving the batsmen little room for invention. His brisk medium-pace brought him 3-20.

Pyrah's first victim was Law, who was bowled trying to fashion some room after he had put on 35 with Loye. **Anthony McGrath** had the dangerous Loye caught in the deep for 43 from 33 balls, and Pyrah accounted for du Plessis and Croft. Wicket-keeper Cross broke the stranglehold with a six off **Tim Bresnan**, and sent Gough's last three balls of the innings to the ropes to finish on 42 from 24 balls.

Carnegie had got off to another shaky start as **Andrew Gale** was bowled in the first over, but **Michael Vaughan** put on 41 with the dashing **Gerard Brophy** before he was bowled for a 12-ball 21. Brophy went for 28 — but McGrath's sticking-plaster 46 from 39 balls was vital to Yorkshire's quest as Gough stole the headlines.

215

Twenty20 Cup — North Division
Yorkshire v. Lancashire

Played at Old Trafford, Manchester, on June 20, 2008
Yorkshire won by 4 runs

Toss won by Yorkshire   Yorkshire 2 points; Lancashire 0 points

YORKSHIRE

A W Gale, run out (du Plessis)	....	0
§ G L Brophy, c Cross b Keedy	....	44
M P Vaughan, b Mahmood	....	0
A McGrath, c Marshall b Croft	....	25
J A Rudolph, c Flintoff b Marshall	....	23
S M Guy, c Law b Marshall	....	7
T T Bresnan, not out	....	13
A U Rashid, c Cross b Chapple	....	1
R M Pyrah, c du Plessis b Marshall	....	8
* D Gough, not out	....	1
M J Hoggard	Did not bat	
Extras lb 7, w 4, nb 2	....	13
Total (8 wkts, 20 overs)	....	135

FoW: 1-0 (Gale) 2-8 (Vaughan) 3-67 (Brophy) 4-85 (McGrath) 5-104 (Rudolph) 6-108 (Guy) 7-111 (Rashid) 8-130 (Pyrah)

	O	M	R	W
Chapple	4	0	22	1
Mahmood	3	0	22	1
Hogg	4	0	29	0
Croft	3	0	25	1
Keedy	3	0	19	1
Marshall	3	0	11	3

LANCASHIRE

M B Loye, c Brophy b Hoggard	....	17
* S G Law, c Guy b Bresnan	....	1
A Flintoff, lbw b Bresnan	....	0
F du Plessis, c McGrath b Gough	....	42
S J Croft, c Bresnan b Rashid	....	29
§ G D Cross, not out	....	11
K W Hogg, b Gough	....	22
G Chapple, not out	....	4
S I Mahmood		
S J Marshall	Did not bat	
G Keedy		
Extras b 2, lb 2, w 1	....	5
Total (6 wkts, 20 overs)	....	131

FoW: 1-11 (Law) 2-12 (Flintoff) 3-20 (Loye) 4-88 (Croft) 5-94 (du Plessis) 6-120 (Hogg)

	O	M	R	W
Bresnan	4	0	12	2
Hoggard	4	0	31	1
Pyrah	3	0	16	0
Rashid	4	0	25	1
Gough	4	0	31	2
Vaughan	1	0	12	0

Man of the match: T T Bresnan

Umpires: B Dudleston and V A Holder   Scorers: J T Potter and A West

Four in a row for Carnegie

Superb bowling and outcricket helped Carnegie to complete the double over their arch-rivals and to secure the perfect springboard to qualify for the Quarter-Finals.

The margin of victory appeared close, but the Lightening run chase faltered badly in the face

GERARD BROPHY: Chose aerial route.

of tremendous bowling by **Tim Bresnan**, **Richard Pyrah** and **Adil Rashid**. **Darren Gough** gave his batsmen first knock, but **Andrew Gale** was run out for a duck after great work by du Plessis at backward point — and **Gerard Brophy** nearly went the same way next ball.

Michael Vaughan played on off the inside edge for a three-ball duck, but **Anthony McGrath** and Brophy took on the challenge as they added 59 in eight overs. Brophy went for the aerial route, but he was caught behind for 44 off 36 balls, and McGrath was caught in the deep soon afterwards for 25. **Jacques Rudolph** showed inventiveness with 23 in 15 balls before giving Marshall his first wicket, and Marshall grabbed two more wickets, Carnegie's 135 looking a long way short of par.

With 11 on the board Lightning skipper Law was caught by **Simon Guy** off **Tim Bresnan's** brisk away-swinger, but enter the returning Flintoff: he was back in the pavilion one ball later, lbw to Bresnan on a slightly dubious decision. Loye gave a routine catch to Brophy off **Matthew Hoggard**, but du Plessis and Croft set about the task with determination and a few breezy strokes. The run rate was slowing up, and after a partnership of 68 the pair were separated in consecutive overs: Croft holed out to Bresnan off **Adil Rashid** for 29 from 34 balls, and Gough accounted for du Plessis for 42 in 38 balls.

The runs dried up as Rashid and Gough provided excellent "death" bowling, and Bresnan sent down yorker-length deliveries almost at will. Lightning needed 44 from four overs, and then 35 from three, but despite Hogg's spirited power hitting 12 were needed off the last over. Only eight were obtained, as Carnegie ran to their fourth win on the trot.

Twenty20 Cup — North Division
Yorkshire v. Durham

Played at Headingley, Leeds, on June 22, 2008
Match tied

Toss won by Durham

Yorkshire 1 point; Durham 1 point

YORKSHIRE

A W Gale, b Plunkett		7
§ G L Brophy, c Mustard b Pollock		2
M P Vaughan, c BW Harmison b SJ Harmison		34
A McGrath, c Di Venuto b SJ Harmison		65
J A Rudolph, lbw b Plunkett		33
T T Bresnan, c Breese b SJ Harmison		0
S M Guy, c Di Venuto b SJ Harmison		4
R M Pyrah, not out		1
A U Rashid, not out		0
* D Gough		
M J Hoggard	Did not bat	
Extras lb 5, w 6, nb 2		13
Total (7 wkts, 20 overs)		159

FoW: 1-11 (Brophy) 2-17 (Gale) 3-78 (Vaughan) 4-152 (Rudolph) 5-154 (McGrath)
6-154 (Bresnan) 7-158 (Guy)

	O	M	R	W
Plunkett	4	0	24	2
Pollock	4	0	30	1
Breese	4	0	33	0
S J Harmison	4	0	38	4
B W Harmison	2	0	16	0
Benkenstein	2	0	13	0

DURHAM

M J Di Venuto, b Hoggard		12
§ P Mustard, lbw b Pyrah		40
W R Smith, c Rudolph b Hoggard		3
* D M Benkenstein, c Bresnan b Pyrah		8
J A Morkel, c Hoggard b Pyrah		17
S M Pollock, c Vaughan b Pyrah		5
B W Harmison, b Gough		21
G R Breese, not out		21
L E Plunkett, not out		13
G T Park		
S J Harmison	Did not bat	
Extras b 4, lb 7, w 5, nb 3		19
Total (7 wkts, 20 overs)		159

FoW: 1-49 (Di Venuto) 2-57 (Smith) 3-67 (Mustard) 4-88 (Benkenstein) 5-88 (Morkel)
6-94 (Pollock) 7-133 (B W Harmison)

	O	M	R	W
Hoggard	4	1	22	2
Bresnan	4	0	47	0
Gough	4	0	26	1
Pyrah	4	0	20	4
Rashid	3	0	29	0
McGrath	1	0	4	0

Man of the match: R M Pyrah

Umpires: B Dudleston and A A Jones

Scorers: J T Potter and B Hunt

Field-set tangle ends in a tie

RICHARD PYRAH
4-20 Man of the Match

Neither side could be separated as Breese hit the last ball for six to grab an unlikely point and keep Dynamos ahead of Carnegie at the top of the table.

Inserted Yorkshire again proved to be a near one-man show with the bat as **Anthony McGrath** provided the top score and stability.

Andrew Gale was bowled by Plunkett for seven, and **Gerard Brophy** gave Mustard a catch off Pollock. At 17-2 Carnegie needed another herculean effort from McGrath to get anywhere near a competitive total. **Michael Vaughan** helped Yorkshire's talisman to add 61 for the third wicket, and he had 34 from 24 deliveries, when he was caught by Ben Harmison to give brother Steve his first wicket.

Jacques Rudolph joined McGrath to add 74 in nine overs, and 170-plus looked in sight when Rudolph was lbw to Plunkett for 33. Steve Harmison then bundled back McGrath, **Tim Bresnan** and **Simon Guy** in minutes as Carnegie slid from 155-3 to 158-7. McGrath made 65 from 58 balls, and Steve Harmison finished with 4-38.

Carnegie will feel this was a game they should have won: Dynamos were 146-7 with one over to go, and Bresnan had the ball. Plunkett took two from the first ball, but the next two were dots. Plunkett smashed the fourth through the leg-side for four...but could only scramble a single to leave Breese on strike with six to tie: the stocky right-hander obliged with a maximum over extra-cover, and the match was all square.

The result was especially hard on Man-of-the-Match **Richard Pyrah**, whose 4-20 was due tribute not only to the medium-pacer's economy rate, but the timing of his wickets and the quality of his scalps. Di Venuto fell first to an improving **Matthew Hoggard**, who soon followed with Smith. Mustard was particularly brutal on Bresnan — but Pyrah trapped his man lbw for 40 from 28 balls, and it was 88-4 as Pyrah had Benkenstein caught on the off-side. Morkel and Pollock both fell to Pyrah — but Ben Harmsion, Breese and Plunkett all batted courageously to earn a share of the spoils.

Crucially, Yorkshire were punished by a no-ball in the last-but-one over for not having sufficient fielders in the circle. It cost three runs.

Twenty20 Cup — North Division
Yorkshire v. Durham

Played at Riverside, Chester-le-Street, on June 24, 2008
Durham won by 39 runs (D/L Method)

Toss won by Yorkshire

Durham 2 points; Yorkshire 0 points

DURHAM

M J Di Venuto, c Brophy b Bresnan		17
§ P Mustard, c Brophy b Pyrah		49
W R Smith, c Rashid b Pyrah		20
* D M Benkenstein, c Hoggard b Pyrah		29
J A Morkel, c Brophy b Gough		11
S M Pollock, run out (Bresnan/Brophy/McGrath)		6
G R Breese, c Brophy b Gough		13
L E Plunkett, st Brophy b McGrath		1
G T Park, not out		9
B W Harmison, not out		0
S J Harmison	Did not bat	
Extras b 3, lb 4		7
Total (8 wkts, 20 overs)		162

FoW: 1-35 (Di Venuto) 2-80 (Smith) 3-97 (Mustard) 4-123 (Benkenstein) 5-134 (Morkel) 6-138 (Pollock) 7-151 (Plunkett) 8-161 (Breese)

	O	M	R	W
Hoggard	4	0	28	0
Bresnan	3	0	18	1
Rashid	2	0	21	0
Pyrah	4	0	32	3
McGrath	3	0	28	1
Gough	4	0	28	2

YORKSHIRE

§ G L Brophy, b Pollock		5
A U Rashid, run out (B W Harmison/Mustard)		0
A McGrath, c BW Harmison b Plunkett		8
J A Rudolph, not out		22
A Lyth, b S J Harmison		0
T T Bresnan, c Mustard b S J Harmison		5
A W Gale, not out		4
R M Pyrah		
S M Guy		
* D Gough	Did not bat	
M J Hoggard		
Extras lb 3, w 2		5
Total (5 wkts, 10 overs)		49

FoW: 1-3 (Rashid) 2-9 (Brophy) 3-27 (McGrath) 4-29 (Lyth) 5-39 (Bresnan)

	O	M	R	W
Pollock	3	0	15	1
Plunkett	3	0	10	1
S J Harmison	2	0	7	2
B W Harmison	1	0	10	0
Breese	1	0	4	0

Man of the match: P Mustard

Umpires: M J D Bodenham and G I Burgess

Scorers: J T Potter and B Hunt

Dynamos have the power

Carnegie's tremendous run came to a soggy end half way through their reply when *Duckworth/Lewis* gave a comfortable victory to Dynamos.

Yorkshire had limped towards 50 while losing five wickets — and the asking rate was nearly 11 an over.

Darren Gough opted to field, but once again Mustard made the bowlers rue the decision: he got off to a flying start with Di Venuto before the Australian-born opener was caught at the wicket off **Tim Bresnan** for 17.

Mustard continued his assault, not deterred by losing Smith for 20: he had reached 49 from 37 balls when he skied **Richard Pyrah** straight up in the air and wicket-keeper **Gerard Brophy** got under it.

Pyrah, again the pick of the bowlers, was backed up ably by

DARREN GOUGH
Excellent counter-attack.

his Gough — who recovered from a first-over mauling to produce excellent figures. Pyrah had Benkenstein caught at long-on for 29 to finish with 3-32, and Gough, whose first over went for 16, came off with a commendable 2-28. Carnegie never quite had Dynamos under control, and their total of 162 in fading light was always a fraction out of reach.

Adil Rashid was sent back going for a second run by Brophy, and departed without facing, and the wicket-keeper was bowled playing expansively to the leg-side after a 14-ball struggle for five. **Anthony McGrath** had a rare failure when he was caught for eight, and at 27-3 Carnegie were not in the hunt. Steve Harmison — by now bowling at a fearsome pace — was nigh on unplayable, and he blew away **Adam Lyth** and **Tim Bresnan**.

Jacques Rudolph stood firm on 22, but the rain came with the game a long way from Yorkshire's grasp. They need to win both of their last two qualifying matches to stand any chance of a Quarter-Final place, and with the bad weather this season that is by no means a formality.

Twenty20 Cup — North Division

Yorkshire v. Leicestershire

At Headingley, Leeds, on June 26, 2008
Match abandoned without a ball bowled
Yorkshire 1 point; Leicestershire 1 point

Yorkshire v. Nottinghamshire

Played at Trent Bridge, Nottingham, on June 27, 2008
Yorkshire won by 9 wickets
Toss won by Nottinghamshire   Yorkshire 0 points; Nottinghamshire 0 points
(The result and individual performances in the match stand, but all points were declared void when it was realised that Yorkshire had fielded an unregistered player)

NOTTINGHAMSHIRE

W I Jefferson, c Rashid b Bresnan		19
M J Wood, b Hoggard		10
A C Voges, st Brophy b Rashid		39
S R Patel, c Bresnan b Rashid		18
C L Cairns, lbw b Rashid		9
* § C M W Read, run out (Guy/Brophy)		31
M A Ealham, st Brophy b Rashid		3
A R Adams, c McGrath b Gough		0
P J Franks, not out		2
D J Pattinson		
R S Ferley	Did not bat	
Extras lb 2, w 3		5
Total (8 wkts, 20 overs)		136

FoW: 1-30 (Wood) 2-32 (Jefferson) 3-76 (Patel) 4-99 (Cairns) 5-106 (Voges)
6-114 (Ealham) 7-117 (Adams) 8-136 (Read)

	O	M	R	W
Bresnan	4	0	20	1
Hoggard	3	0	25	1
Azeem Rafiq	2	0	18	0
Pyrah	3	0	18	0
Rashid	4	0	24	4
Gough	4	0	29	1

YORKSHIRE

A W Gale, c Jefferson b Ferley		45
§ G L Brophy, not out		57
A McGrath, not out		30
Extras lb 5		5
Total (1 wkt, 18 overs)		137

Did not bat: J A Rudolph, S M Guy, T T Bresnan, R M Pyrah,
Azeem Rafiq, A U Rashid, * D Gough and M J Hoggard

FoW: 1-99 (Gale)

	O	M	R	W
Adams	3	0	28	0
Pattinson	3	0	16	0
Ealham	3	0	23	0
Ferley	4	0	33	1
Patel	4	0	24	0
Voges	1	0	8	0

Man of the match: A U Rashid

Umpires: S A Garratt and T E Jesty   Scorers: J T Potter and L B Hewes

Yorkshire expected to play Durham in a Quarter-Final at Chester-le-Street on July 7, but this match was cancelled by direction of the England and Wales Cricket Board. The effect of an appeal decision was that Yorkshire no longer had sufficient points to qualify.

Triumph and tragedy

No result from the total abandonment of
Yorkshire's home fixture with
Leicestershire meant that their chance of
qualifying for the Quarter-Finals
depended on the last round of matches.

A superb all-round display brought
victory — **Adil Rashid** heading the
wicket-takers before batsmen **Andrew
Gale**, **Gerard Brophy** and **Anthony
McGrath** romped home.

The Outlaws got off to a positive
start, Jefferson battering the Carnegie
seamers, but Wood was bowled by
Matthew Hoggard and Adil caught
Jefferson on the square-leg boundary to
give **Tim Bresnan** a deserved wicket.

From 32-2 Voges and Patel staged a
comeback — the third umpire giving
Voges the benefit on seven when he
looked short of his ground: Carnegie
debutant **Azeem Rafiq** was judged to
have broken the stumps minus the ball.
They had put on 44 when Bresnan
caught Patel at deep mid-wicket, and
Rashid had the first of his four scalps.

Cairns was out lbw to a lovely Rashid
top-spinner, and his flighted leg-spinners
were to prove too much for Voges and

ANDREW GALE
Real entertainment.

Ealham as Brophy whipped off the bails each time. Voges made 39
from 28 balls, but with his departure ended any hopes of a competitive
total. Read offered a typically audacious cameo of 31 in 25 balls, but
Rashid came in with 4-24, and the Outlaws looked way below par.

Brophy and Gale provided some real entertainment with shots all
around the wicket in a record opening stand of 99 — and Brophy
equalled his previous best of 57 from 45 balls with six boundaries.
Gale, with a slightly more circumspect 45 in 48 deliveries, was the
only man out — to a falling catch by Jefferson off Ferley — and
McGrath polished off the proceedings with 30 in 15 balls: two overs
were still to be bowled when he finished it with a drive over cover.

Carnegie were to face a stiff examination at the Riverside in a
Quarter-Final clash with Durham Dynamos, but that was when the
non-registration of Azeem was realised; the points won in this match
were declared void, and Yorkshire no longer had sufficient to qualify.

YORKSHIRE AVERAGES 2008

TWENTY20 CUP

Played 10   Won 5   Tied 1   Lost 3   Abandoned 1

BATTING AND FIELDING

Player	M.	I.	N.O.	Runs	H.S.	Av'ge	100s	50s	ct/st
A McGrath	9	9	2	392	72*	56.00	0	4	4
J A Rudolph	9	8	1	191	56	27.28	0	1	1
D Gough	9	4	3	26	20*	26.00	0	0	1
G L Brophy	9	9	1	177	57*	22.12	0	1	6/3
A W Gale	9	9	2	106	45	15.14	0	0	2
M P Vaughan	7	7	0	104	34	14.85	0	0	1
C White	2	2	0	26	26	13.00	0	0	0
T T Bresnan	9	8	3	58	15	11.60	0	0	4
C R Taylor	2	2	1	10	10*	10.00	0	0	0
S M Guy	4	2	0	11	7	5.50	0	0	1
RM Pyrah	9	5	2	16	8	5.33	0	0	6
A U Rashid	8	6	2	18	10	4.50	0	0	3
A Lyth	1	1	0	0	0	0.00	0	0	0
D J Wainwright	2	1	1	3	3*	—	0	0	0
M J Hoggard	9	0	0	0	—	—	0	0	3
Azeem Rafiq	1	0	0	0	—	—	0	0	0

BOWLING

Player	Overs	Mdns	Runs	Wkts	Avge	Best	4wI	Runs per Over
C White	0.1	0	0	1	0.00	1-0	0	0.00
R M Pyrah	30	0	209	14	14.92	4-20	1	6.96
A U Rashid	21	0	162	7	23.14	4-24	1	7.71
A McGrath	9.2	0	76	3	25.33	1-14	0	8.14
D Gough	34	0	242	8	30.25	2-28	0	7.11
T T Bresnan	34	0	244	8	30.50	2-12	0	7.17
M J Hoggard	32	1	251	6	41.83	2-22	0	7.84
M P Vaughan	8	0	72	1	72.00	1-21	0	9.00
D J Wainwright	3.5	0	45	0	—	0-6	0	11.74
Azeem Rafiq	2	0	18	0	—	0-18	0	9.00

Second Eleven Championship Matches played in 2008

DETAILS OF PLAYERS WHO APPEARED FOR YORKSHIRE 2nd XI IN 2008
(excluding 1st XI capped players)

Player	Date of Birth	Birthplace	Type
S M Guy*	17 November 1978	Rotherham	RHB/WK
C R Taylor*	21 February 1981	Rawdon	RHB
R M Pyrah*	1 November 1982	Dewsbury	RHB/RM
M A K Lawson*	24 October 1985	Leeds	RHB/LB
S A Patterson*	3 October 1983	Beverley	RHB/RMF
D J Wainwright*	21 March 1985	Pontefract	LHB/SLA
A Shahzad*	27 July 1985	Huddersfield	RHB/RFM
A Lyth*	25 September 1987	Whitby	LHB/RM
G L Wood	2 December 1988	Dewsbury	LHB/WK
J M Finch	17 November 1988	Leeds	RHB/OS
J E Lee	23 December 1988	Sheffield	LHB/RFM
B W Sanderson	3 January 1989	Sheffield	RHB/RM
O J Hannon-Dalby	20 June 1989	Halifax	RHB/RM
C A Allinson	19 April 1990	Guisborough	LHB
M S Chadwick	24 May 1989	Leeds	RHB/RM
J M Bairstow	26 September 1989	Bradford	RHB/WK
J E Root	30 December 1990	Sheffield	RHB/OB
G S Ballance	22 November 1989	Harare, Zim.	LHB/LB
C G Roebuck	14 August 1991	Huddersfield	RHB/RM
Azeem Rafiq	27 February 1991	Karachi, Pak.	RHB/OB
P S E Sandri	14 January 1983	Cape Town, S A	RHB/RMF
D G H Snell	30 July 1986	York	LHB/LM

*2nd XI Cap

225

SECOND ELEVEN

HIGHLIGHTS OF 2008

Wins by an innings (2)

Yorkshire (419) beat Nottinghamshire (263 and 101) by an innings and 55 runs at Stamford Bridge

Yorkshire (334) beat Derbyshire (143 and 183) by an innings and 8 runs at Barnsley

Total of 400 and over (1)

419   versus Nottinghamshire at Stamford Bridge

Opponents dismissed for under 100 (1)

49   Leicestershire at Leicester

Century Partnerships (9)

For the 1st wicket (3)

199   A Lyth and C White versus Leicestershire at Leicester

170   A Lyth and C R Taylor versus Nottinghamshire at Stamford Bridge

115   J J Sayers and G S Ballance versus Worcestershire at Leeds

For the 2nd wicket (1)

117   C White and C G Roebuck versus Somerset at Todmorden

For the 3rd wicket (1)

201   J J Sayers and G L Wood versus Scotland A at Sheffield

For the 4th wicket (2)

173   J M Bairstow and S M Guy versus Worcestershire at Leeds

102   C White and S M Guy versus Somerset at Todmorden

For the 6th wicket (1)

176   S M Guy and Azeem Rafiq versus Somerset at Todmorden

For the 8th wicket (1)

101   J M Bairstow and D J Wainwright versus Warwickshire at Stamford Bridge

Centuries (8)

A Lyth (2)

137*   versus Leicestershire at Leicester

127   versus Nottinghamshire at Stamford Bridge

S M Guy (2)

143   versus Sussex at Horsham

122   versus Somerset at Todmorden

J M Bairstow (1)

139*   versus Worcestershire at Leeds

J J Sayers (1)

132   versus Scotland A at Sheffield

Centuries *(Continued)*

C White (l)

    109   versus Somerset at Todmorden

G L Wood (1)

    114   versus Scotland A at Sheffield

5 wickets in an innings (4)

S A Patterson (l)

    5 for 53 versus Sussex at Horsham

Azeem Rafiq (1)

    5 for 51 versus Lancashire at Leeds

B W Sanderson (1)

    6 for 30 versus Nottinghamshire at Stamford Bridge

Ajmal Shahzad (1)

    6 for 42 versus Derbyshire at Barnsley

10 wickets in a match (1)

B W Sanderson (1)

    10 for 81 (4 for 51 and 6 for 30) versus Nottinghamshire at Stamford Bridge

3 catches in an innings (5)

S M Guy (2)

    4   versus Leicestershire at Leicester

    3   versus Worcestershire at Leeds

M A K Lawson (1)

    3   versus Nottinghamshire at Stamford Bridge

C White (1)

    3   versus Lancashire at Leeds

G L Wood (1)

    3   versus Nottinghamshire at Stamford Bridge

Debuts (5)

G S Ballance, Azeem Rafiq, P S E Sandri, D G H Snell, C G Roebuck

R D W

Yorkshire 2nd XI v. Leicestershire 2nd XI

Played at Grace Road, Leicester, on April 22, 23, 24, 2008
Yorkshire won by 8 wickets at 7.21pm on the Second Day
Toss won by Leicestershire   Yorkshire 22 points; Leicestershire 2 points
Close of play: First Day, Leicestershire, Second Innings 75-1 (Foster 51*, Pope 5*).

First Innings	LEICESTERSHIRE		Second Innings	
E J Foster, c Guy b Gough	1		c Lawson b Hannon-Dalby	51
G P Smith, c Guy b Gough	2		c Wainwright b Lawson	13
N J Ferraby, lbw b Gough	0		(4) lbw b Lawson	38
G T Cairns, c Sanderson b Hannon-Dalby	10		(5) lbw b Sanderson	0
S B Patel, c Guy b Lee	7		(6) c Lee b Lawson	55
J Augustus, lbw b Hannon-Dalby	0		(7) run out	47
C S Yates, run out	5		(8) b Hannon-Dalby	42
§ J I Pope, c Guy b Lee	2		(3) lbw b Sanderson	34
* J K H Naik, lbw b Lee	6		lbw b Wainwright	11
J J C Lawson, lbw b Lee	4		b Gough	23
S J Cliff, not out	7		not out	5
Extras (lb 1, nb 6)	7		Extras (b 3, lb 5, nb 8)	16
Total (25.5 overs)	49		Total (87 overs)	335

Twelfth man: Zafran Ali

FoW: 1-3 (Smith), 2-3 (Ferraby), 3-4 (Foster), 4-18 (Cairns), 5-22 (Augustus),
1st   6-26 (Patel), 7-26 (Pope), 8-32 (Naik), 9-36 (Lawson), 10-49 (Yates)
FoW: 1-63 (Smith), 2-75 (Foster), 3-136 (Pope), 4-136 (Cairns), 5-148 (Ferraby),
2nd   6-219 (Augustus), 7-281 (Patel), 8-298 (Naik), 9-327(Yates), 10-335(Lawson)

	O	M	R	W		O	M	R	W
Gough	6	3	15	3	Gough	15	2	84	1
Hannon-Dalby	7	1	8	2	Hannon-Dalby	18	2	58	2
Lee	7	2	20	4	Wainwright	18	4	43	1
Sanderson	5.5	3	5	0	Lawson	15	0	76	3
					Lee	7	1	31	0
					Sanderson	11	6	24	2
					Allinson	3	1	11	0

First Innings	YORKSHIRE		Second Innings	
A Lyth, not out	137		c Augustus b Lawson	31
C White, c & b Naik	77		c & b Naik	23
C A Allinson, c Smith b Yates	8		not out	15
G L Wood, c Cairns b Lawson	19		not out	7
§ S M Guy, c Naik b Yates	6			
D J Wainwright, c Foster b Yates	0			
M A K Lawson, c Naik b Yates	1			
* D Gough, not out	7			
J E Lee				
B W Sanderson	Did not bat			
O J Hannon-Dalby				
Extras (b 8, lb 5, nb 32)	45		Extras (nb 12)	12
Total (6 wkts dec, 56.0 overs)	300		Total (2 wkts, 19.4 overs)	88

FoW: 1-199 (White), 2-214 (Allinson), 3-261 (Wood), 4-282 (Guy), 5-282 (Wainwright)
1st   6-284 (Lawson)
2nd   1-61 (Lyth), 2-76 (White)

	O	M	R	W		O	M	R	W
Lawson	14	3	65	1	Lawson	6	2	24	1
Cliff	6	1	32	0	Cliff	4	0	17	0
Zafran Ali	4	0	44	0	Zafran Ali	3	0	22	0
Ferraby	2	0	10	0	Yates	5	0	16	0
Naik	12	1	54	1	Naik	1.4	0	9	1
Yates	18	1	82	4					

Umpires: N A Mallender and I M Armitage   Scorers : M Snook and D Ayriss

Yorkshire 2nd XI v. Glamorgan 2nd XI

Played at Ffosyrefail Ground, Pontarddulais, on April 29, 30, May 1, 2008
Match drawn. No further play was possible after 3:35pm on the First Day

Toss won by Glamorgan   Yorkshire 7 points; Glamorgan 4 points

GLAMORGAN

R N Grant, lbw b Ajmal Shahzad	0
M P O'Shea, b Hannon-Dalby	1
T L Maynard, c Guy b Sanderson	18
B J Wright, lbw b Lee	8
Imran Hassan, c White b Hannon-Dalby	15
M J Fisher, b Lee	1
* D A Cosker, lbw b Hannon-Dalby	2
R F Evans, not out	10
H T Waters, not out	4
§ G Slade	
C P Ashling Did not bat	
Extras (lb 1, nb 16)	17
Total (7 wkts, 51.4 overs)	76

Twelfth man: A I Jones

FoW: 1-0 (Grant), 2-4 (O'Shea), 3-29 (Maynard), 4-35 (Wright), 5-41 (Fisher)
1st 6-50 (Cosker), 7-51 (Imran Hassan)

	O	M	R	W
Ajmal Shahzad	5	5	0	1
Hannon-Dalby	13	5	27	3
Pyrah	15	7	30	0
Sanderson	12	9	3	1
Lee	6	0	15	2
Lawson	0.4	0	0	0

YORKSHIRE

* C White
C R Taylor
A Lyth
R M Pyrah
§ S M Guy
D J Wainwright
M A K Lawson
G L Wood
B W Sanderson
Ajmal Shahzad
O J Hannon-Dalby

Twelfth man: J E Lee

Umpires: J H James and S J Malone   Scorers: M Snook and B Jones

Second Eleven Championship
Yorkshire 2nd XI v. Nottinghamshire 2nd XI

Played at Low Catton Road, Stamford Bridge, on May 7, 8, 9, 2008

Yorkshire won by an innings and 55 runs at 12.47pm on the Third Day

Toss won by Nottinghamshire   Yorkshire 22 points; Nottinghamshire 7 points

Close of play: First Day, Yorkshire 39-0 (Lyth 17*, Taylor 16*); Second Day, Nottinghamshire 25-4 (Fletcher 1*).

NOTTINGHAMSHIRE

	First Innings		Second Innings	
A D Hales,	c Lawson b Lee	2	c Pyrah b Sanderson	11
C P Marsden,	c Lyth b Sanderson	62	c Lyth b Sanderson	3
W A Sabey,	c Wainwright b Hannon-Dalby	14	c Wood b Sanderson	6
G D Clough,	c Lawson b Sanderson	6	(5) c Wood b Sanderson	0
* P J Franks,	c Lawson b Sanderson	8	(6) c Wood b Hannon-Dalby	7
R S Ferley,	c Guy b Pyrah	5	(7) c Wainwright b Pyrah	6
§ J A Simpson,	st Guy b Wainwright	48	(8) b Sanderson	6
L J Fletcher,	lbw b Lawson	15	(4) lbw b Sanderson	1
A J Harris,	b Sanderson	58	not out	41
I D Saxelby,	c & b Wainwright	30	b Pyrah	0
A Carter,	not out	5	c White b Wainwright	12
	Extras (lb 6, w 2, nb 2)	10	Extras (lb 6, nb 2)	8
	Total (95 overs)	263	Total (39.5 overs)	101

FoW: 1-5 (Hales), 2-34 (Sabey), 3-50 (Clough), 4-64 (Franks), 5-76 (Ferley), 6-122
1st   (Marsden), 7-150 (Fletcher), 8-174 (Simpson), 9-249 (Saxelby), 10-263 (Harris)
FoW: 1-13 (Hales), 2-24 (Marsden), 3-25 (Sabey), 4-25 (Clough), 5-32 (Franks), 6-32
2nd   (Fletcher), 7-42 (Simpson), 8-58 (Ferley), 9-64 (Saxelby), 10-101 (Carter)

	O	M	R	W		O	M	R	W
Hannon-Dalby	16	4	45	1	Hannon-Dalby	9	3	14	1
Lee	15	2	50	1	Sanderson	12	2	30	6
Sanderson	16	2	51	4	Lawson	2	1	2	0
Pyrah	16	5	41	1	Pyrah	7	1	12	2
Lawson	13	2	36	1	Wainwright	7.5	1	32	1
Wainwright	19	9	34	2	Lee	2	1	5	0

YORKSHIRE

A Lyth, lbw b Ferley		127
C R Taylor, c Clough b Franks		86
* C White, c Ferley b Franks		5
G L Wood, c Simpson b Carter		0
R M Pyrah, c Clough b Ferley		36
§ S M Guy, c & b Ferley		46
D J Wainwright, c Carter b Clough		28
M A K Lawson, run out (Clough)		2
B W Sanderson, c Sabey b Harris		26
J E Lee, b Franks		24
O J Hannon-Dalby, not out		0
Extras (b 4, lb 6, w 1, nb 28)		39
Total (97.1 overs)		419

FoW: 1-170 (Taylor), 2-178 (White), 3-183 (Wood), 4-266 (Pyrah), 5-292 (Lyth), 6-347
1st   (Guy), 7-358 (Lawson), 8-362 (Wainwright), 9-419 (Sanderson), 10-419 (Lee)

	O	M	R	W
Harris	18	1	93	1
Franks	11.1	0	58	3
Fletcher	13	3	35	0
Ferley	29	3	110	3
Clough	12	1	52	1
Carter	14	1	61	1

Umpires: J H Evans and I Dawood   Scorers: M Snook and R Marshall

Second Eleven Championship
Yorkshire 2nd XI v. Lancashire 2nd XI

Played at Headingley, Leeds, on May 13, 14, 15, 16, 2008
Lancashire won by 251 runs at 2.28pm on the Fourth Day

Toss won by Lancashire   Yorkshire 4 points; Lancashire 21 points
Close of play: First Day, Lancashire 354-9 (Parry 43*, Kerrigan 1*); Second Day, Lancashire 59-0 (Brown 15*, Sutcliffe 44*0); Third Day, Yorkshire 44-4 (White 22*, Guy 0*).

First Innings	LANCASHIRE		Second Innings	
K R Brown, c Hannon-Dalby b Azeem Rafiq	155		c Pyrah b Hannon-Dalby	24
*I J Sutcliffe, c Roebuck b Lawson	49		run out (Sandri)	128
S J Marshall, c White b Sandri	48		b Wainwright	16
§ G D Cross, c White b Azeem Rafiq	13		c & b Chadwick	1
I A Cockbain, c White b Azeem Rafiq	10		c Guy b Wainwright	38
S D Parry, c Wood b Hannon-Dalby	50		run out (Pyrah)	28
L A Proctor, lbw b Azeem Rafiq	0		(8) not out	12
L M Reece, c & b Wainwright	2		(9) not out	10
S P Cheetham, b Azeem Rafiq	5			
S D Lees, c Wood b Hannon-Dalby	6			
S C Kerrigan, not out	1			
V Tripathi	Did not bat		(7) c Lawson b Wainwright	12
Extras (b 1, lb 9, w 6, nb 6)	22		Extras (b 6, lb 9, w 8, nb 4)	27
Total (105 overs)	361		Total (7 wkts dec, 91 overs)	296

Lancashire's Twelfth Man, S C Kerrigan, was allowed to bat in place of V Tripathi, whose arrival was delayed by his college studies. S M Guy kept wicket during Lancashire's second innings.

FoW: 1-127 (Sutcliffe), 2-218 (Marshall), 3-252 (Cross), 4-291 (Brown), 5-293 (Cockbain),
1st   6-293 (Proctor), 7-300 (Reece), 8-323 (Cheetham), 9-342 (Lees), 10-361 (Parry)
FoW: 1-80 (Brown), 2-114 (Marshall), 3-115 (Cross), 4-211 (Cockbain), 5-238 (Sutcliffe)
2nd   6-256 (Tripathi), 7-262 (Parry)

	O	M	R	W		O	M	R	W
Hannon-Dalby	17	1	46	2	Hannon-Dalby	10	0	35	1
Lee	14	1	75	0	Lee	13	0	63	0
Pyrah	8	2	25	0	Pyrah	10	1	29	0
Sandri	9	0	54	1	Wainwright	32	9	73	3
Lawson	14	1	44	1	Lawson	5	0	23	0
Wainwright	27	5	56	1	Chadwick	6	1	17	1
Azeem Rafiq	16	2	51	5	Azeem Rafiq	10	2	21	0
					Sandri	5	1	20	0

First Innings	YORKSHIRE		Second Innings	
§ G L Wood, c Cockbain b Cheetham	62		c Cross b Cheetham	20
* C White, c Cross b Marshall	27		lbw b Cheetham	30
C G Roebuck, c Tripathi b Kerrigan	41		c Marshall b Cheetham	5
R M Pyrah, lbw b Parry	29		(5) b Cheetham	0
S M Guy, b Kerrigan	17		(6) c & b Kerrigan	36
D J Wainwright, b Parry	12		(7) lbw b Kerrigan	40
M A K Lawson, c Cross b Parry	23		(4) c Marshall b Cheetham	0
Azeem Rafiq, b Kerrigan	2		c & b Kerrigan	0
J E Lee, c Cross b Parry	7		b Parry	2
P S E Sandri, b Kerrigan	0		c Cockbain b Kerrigan	13
O J Hannon-Dalby, not out	0		not out	4
Extras (b 11, lb 3)	14		Extras (b 15, lb 6, w 1)	22
Total (80.1 overs)	234		Total (77.2 overs)	172

Twelfth man: M S Chadwick

FoW: 1-62 (White), 2-102 (Wood), 3-163 (Pyrah), 4-169 (Roebuck), 5-188 (Wainwright)
1st   6-198 (Guy), 7-212 (Azeem Rafiq), 8-221 (Lee), 9-232 (Lawson), 10-234 (Sandri)
FoW: 1-30 (Wood), 2-50 (White), 3-50 (Roebuck), 4-54 (Pyrah), 5-81 (White) 6-112
2nd   (Guy), 7-118 (Azeem Rafiq), 8-133 (Lee), 9-163 (Wainwright), 10-172 (Sandri)

	O	M	R	W		O	M	R	W
Cheetham	15	2	55	1	Cheetham	19	6	36	5
Reece	6	1	18	0	Reece	4	1	13	0
Marshall	18	5	43	1	Parry	18	2	48	1
Parry	23	7	44	4	Marshall	10	3	17	0
Kerrigan	18.1	3	60	4	Kerrigan	22.2	8	33	4
					Lees	4	2	4	0

Umpires: K Coburn and M A Eggleston   Scorers: M Snook and D M White

Second Eleven Championship
Yorkshire 2nd XI v. Somerset 2nd XI

Played at Centre Vale, Todmorden, on May 20, 21, 22, 2008
Somerset won by 5 wickets at 5.58pm on the Third Day

Toss won by Somerset

Yorkshire 6 points; Somerset 21 points

Close of play: First Day, Somerset 39-0 (Suppiah 15*, Francis 20*); Second Day, Yorkshire 119-5 (Guy 43*, Azeem Rafiq 14*).

First Innings	YORKSHIRE		Second Innings	
G L Wood, b Sutton	27		c Gazzard b Thomas	8
* C White, b Thomas	109		b Thomas	4
C G Roebuck, c Lansdale b Sutton	64		c Francis b Thomas	31
D G H Snell, c Thomas b Waller	60		lbw b Sutton	5
§ S M Guy, b Thomas	60		st Gazzard b Suppiah	122
C A Allinson, b Turner	18		lbw b Thomas	7
Azeem Rafiq, b Sutton	13		b Thomas	83
B W Sanderson, not out	0		run out	4
S A Patterson, not out	4		not out	0
J M Finch				
M S Chadwick	Did not bat			
Extras (b 12, lb 7, w 7, nb 2)	28		Extras (b 9, lb 4)	13
Total (7 wkts dec, 94 overs)	334		Total (8 wkts dec, 70.4 overs)	277

FoW: 1st 1-31 (Wood), 2-148 (Roebuck), 3-188 (Snell), 4-290 (White), 5-295 (Guy) 6-321 (Allinson), 7-330 (Azeem Rafiq)

FoW: 2nd 1-10 (Wood), 2-31 (White), 3-52 (Roebuck), 4-56 (Snell), 5-69 (Allinson) 6-245 (Guy), 7-273 (Sanderson), 8-277 (Azeem Rafiq)

	O	M	R	W		O	M	R	W
Thomas	23	6	64	2	Thomas	17.4	8	43	5
Turner	17	4	68	1	Turner	16	3	51	0
Sutton	16	2	56	3	Sutton	9	0	41	1
Parsons	5	1	13	0	Durston	7	0	34	0
Davis	3	0	12	0	Banks	6	1	20	0
Banks	9	1	35	0	Suppiah	8	1	36	1
Durston	9	4	22	0	Waller	7	0	39	0
Waller	12	3	45	1					

First Innings	SOMERSET		Second Innings	
A V Suppiah, b Patterson	36		c Guy b Sanderson	42
J D Francis, lbw b Allinson	49		c sub b Sanderson	18
W J Durston, lbw b Finch	96		not out	132
O A C Banks, c Finch b Snell	5		c Guy b Snell	43
§ C M Gazzard, lbw b Sanderson	28		c Chadwick b Snell	9
* K A Parsons, not out	49		run out	8
W R Lansdale, b Finch	9		not out	41
D F Davis, not out	31			
A C Thomas				
M L Turner	Did not bat			
M T C Waller				
Extras (b 6, lb 8)	14		Extras (lb 2)	2
Total (6 wkts dec, 80 overs)	317		Total (5 wkts, 53.1 overs)	295

Twelfth man: A P Sutton

FoW: 1st 1-81 (Suppiah), 2-127 (Francis), 3-143 (Banks), 4-210 (Gazzard), 5-242 (Durston) 6-356 (Lansdale)

FoW: 1st 1-60 (Suppiah), 2-65 (Francis), 3-168 (Banks), 4-184 (Gazzard), 5-204 (Parsons)

	O	M	R	W		O	M	R	W
Sanderson	17	5	60	1	Sanderson	15	2	77	2
Patterson	22	6	61	1	Patterson	15	0	89	0
Allinson	7	0	34	1	Chadwick	8.1	0	43	0
Chadwick	11	1	48	0	Snell	12	0	57	2
Snell	3	1	15	1	Finch	1	0	6	0
Azeem Rafiq	9	1	55	0	Azeem Rafiq	2	0	21	0
Finch	11	5	30	2					

Umpires: D J Millns and R S Jakeman

Scorers: M Snook and H J Thorne

Second Eleven Championship
Yorkshire 2nd XI v. Derbyshire 2nd XI

Played at The Racecourse Ground, Derby, on May 27, 28, 29, 2008

Match drawn at 5.16pm on the Third Day

Toss won by Yorkshire — Yorkshire 4 points; Derbyshire 10 points
Close of play: First Day, Yorkshire 93-4 (Guy 15*, Allinson 6*); Second Day, Yorkshire 142-8 (Lee 0*, Finch 0*).

First Innings	YORKSHIRE		Second Innings		
* J J Sayers, c Guthrie b Whiteley	9				
G S Ballance, c Smith b Whiteley	38		(1) not out		20
§ G L Wood, c Gouldstone b Whiteley	7		(2) c Guthrie b White		4
C G Roebuck, c Thompson b Jones	7		(3) not out		3
S M Guy, lbw b Hunter	15				
C A Allinson, c Redfern b Hunter	20				
M A K Lawson, c Brown b Hunter	14				
B W Sanderson, c & b Hunter	7				
J E Lee, not out	0				
J M Finch, c Smith b White	1				
O J Hannon-Dalby, c Whiteley b White	2				
Extras (b 5, lb 13, w 5, nb 2)	25		Extras (b 1, lb 4, w 1, nb 2)		8
Total (56 overs)	145		Total (1 wkt, 19 overs)		35

Twelfth man: M S Chadwick

FoW: 1-41 (Sayers), 2-60 (Ballance), 3-61 (Wood), 4-79 (Roebuck), 5-101 (Guy), 6-123
1st (Lawson), 7-133 (Allinson), 8-142 (Sanderson), 9-143 (Finch), 10-145 (Hannon-Dalby)
2nd: 1-13 (Wood)

	O	M	R	W		O	M	R	W
White	15	6	27	2	White	8	3	11	1
Hunter	20	6	46	4	Hunter	5	1	12	0
Whiteley	9	2	31	3	Brown	4	2	2	0
Jones	8	2	23	1	Redfern	2	0	5	0
Doshi	2	2	0	0					
Brown	2	2	0	0					

DERBYSHIRE

C E J Thompson, not out		120
§ J M Guthrie, c Sanderson b Chadwick		55
* G M Smith, not out		30
S J Marillier		
D J Redfern		
M Gouldstone		
W A White	Did not bat	
R A Whiteley		
I D Hunter		
E P Jones		
N D Doshi		
Extras (lb 10, w 1, nb 2)		13
Total (1 wkt dec, 58 overs)		218

Twelfth man: M J Brown

FoW: 1-148 (Guthrie)

	O	M	R	W
Hannon-Dalby	12	3	26	0
Sanderson	12	5	19	0
Lee	8	0	46	0
Chadwick	10	2	39	1
Allinson	6	1	22	0
Lawson	6	0	37	0
Finch	4	0	19	0

Umpires: D J Millns and B F Mayhew   Scorers: M Snook and T M Cottam

Second Eleven Championship
Yorkshire 2nd XI v. Scotland A

Played at Abbeydale Park, Sheffield, on June 17, 18, 19, 2008
Match drawn at 6.51pm on the Third Day

Toss won by Yorkshire   Yorkshire 12 points; Scotland 10 points
Close of play: First Day, Scotland 21-2 (MacRae 7*, Kerr 5*); Second Day, Scotland 236-5 (Sheikh 103*, Haq 6*).

First Innings	YORKSHIRE		Second Innings	
* J J Sayers, lbw b Weeraratna	132		lbw b Weeraratna	7
A Lyth, c Goudie b Parker	33		c Farooq b Goudie	26
C G Roebuck, c & b Haq	20		c Knox b Weeraratna	27
G L Wood, c Flanagan b Farooq	114		c Knox b Parker	44
§ S M Guy, c Kerr b Weeraratna	10			
Ajmal Shahzad, c Hussain b Goudie	10		(5) c Hussain b Parker	16
M A K Lawson, run out	29		(6) b Haq	4
B W Sanderson, c Farooq b Goudie	7		b Haq	1
J E Lee, not out	13		not out	8
J M Finch				
P E S Sandri	Did not bat			
J M Bairstow			(7) st Kerr b Haq	9
Extras (b 2, lb 5, w 2, nb 2)	11		Extras (b 4, lb 2)	6
Total (8 wkts dec, 90 overs)	379		Total (8 wkts dec, 25 overs)	148

NOTE: *S M Guy was called up for First Eleven duties at the start of the Second Day. He was replaced by J M Bairstow, and G L Wood kept wicket for the rest of the match.*

FoW: 1-66 (Lyth), 2-105 (Roebuck), 3-306 (Sayers), 4-306 (Wood), 5-316 (Guy)
1st 6-332 (Ajmal Shahzad), 7-352 (Sanderson), 8-379 (Lawson)
FoW: 1-25 (Sayers), 2-39 (Lyth), 3-102 (Roebuck), 4-111 (Wood), 5-124 (Lawson)
2nd 6-138 (Ajmal Shahzad), 7-139 (Bairstow), 8-148 (Sanderson)

	O	M	R	W		O	M	R	W
Goudie	21	0	99	2	Goudie	8	0	44	1
Weeraratna	11	1	60	2	Weeraratna	8	1	56	2
Parker	12	4	42	1	Haq	5	0	15	3
Farooq	11	1	35	1	Parker	4	0	27	2
Haq	21	5	75	1					
Bashir	14	2	61	0					

First Innings	SCOTLAND		Second Innings	
* S T Knox, run out	1		c Wood b Sanderson	4
R F Flanagan, lbw b Ajmal Shahzad	4		c sub b Lee	16
N J MacRae, c Lee b Finch	55		c Wood b Sanderson	0
§ J A M Kerr, lbw b Ajmal Shahzad	8		(9) b Finch	0
M Q Sheikh, c Wood b Lee	104		(4) c Lawson b Sandri	1
R O Hussain, c Sayers b Finch	43		(5) lbw b Lawson	56
R M Haq, c Wood b Sandri	11		(6) c Bairstow b Finch	63
M A Parker, b Sandri	1		(7) not out	5
S D Weeraratna, not out	13		(8) c Lee b Lawson	5
G Goudie, run out	5		c Lawson b Finch	0
Z Bashir, lbw b Lee	5		not out	2
Extras (lb 6, nb 10)	16		Extras (b 4, lb 7)	11
Total (81.5 overs)	266		Total (9 wkts, 49 overs)	163

Twelfth man: A K Farooq

FoW: 1-3 (Knox), 2-11 (Flanagan), 3-25 (Kerr), 4-139 (MacRae), 5-213 (Hussain)
1st 6-236 (Sheikh), 7-238 (Parker), 8-255 (Haq), 9-260 (Goudie), 10-266 (Bashir)
FoW: 1-11 (Knox), 2-13 (MacRae), 3-18 (Sheikh), 4-32 (Flanagan), 5-137 (Hussain)
2nd 6-153 (Haq), 7-158 (Kerr), 8-161 (Kerr), 9-161 (Goudie)

	O	M	R	W		O	M	R	W
Ajmal Shahzad	17	7	41	2	Ajmal Shahzad	9	2	16	0
Sanderson	17	7	24	0	Sanderson	8	3	12	2
Sandri	10	0	38	2	Sandri	7	1	20	1
Lawson	9	0	47	0	Lee	5	1	19	1
Lee	7.5	1	29	2	Finch	12	4	50	3
Finch	15	1	65	2	Lyth	2	0	6	0
Lyth	6	1	16	0	Lawson	6	2	29	2

Umpires: J W Lloyds and A Bullock   Scorers: M Snook and D J Love

Second Eleven Championship
Yorkshire 2nd XI v. Warwickshire 2nd XI

Played at Low Catton Road, Stamford Bridge, on July 22, 23, 24, 25, 2008
Warwickshire won by 6 wickets at 12.17pm on the Fourth Day

Toss won by Yorkshire   Yorkshire 3 points; Warwickshire 17 points
Close of play: First day, Warwickshire 38-2 (Benton 4*, McMahon 15*); Second Day, Yorkshire 58-5 (Guy 21*, Bairstow 1*); Third Day, Warwickshire 145-3 (Piolet 35*, Ord 58*).

YORKSHIRE

First Innings		Second Innings	
G S Ballance, c Johnson b Tahir	58	lbw b Tahir	8
G L Wood, c Johnson b Groenewald	0	(3) b Groenewald	1
R M Pyrah, b McMahon	49	(4) c Johnson b Daggett	5
* § S M Guy, c & b McMahon	0	(5) c MacLeod b Daggett	35
J E Root, c MacLeod b Tahir	13	(2) c Johnson b Groenewald	12
J M Bairstow, not out	58	(7) b McMahon	50
Ajmal Shahzad, b Tahir	0	(8) c McLeod b Groenewald	6
D J Wainwright, c & b McMahon	14	(9) b McMahon	65
S A Patterson, b McMahon	2	(6) lbw b Daggett	0
J E Lee, c & b McMahon	0	c Groenewald b McMahon	2
J M Finch, lbw b McMahon	0	not out	9
Extras (b 1, lb 1, w 1, nb 2)	5	Extras (b 6, lb 9, w 1, nb 6)	22
Total (81.5 overs)	199	Total (75.1 overs)	215

Twelfth man: O J Hannon-Dalby

FoW: 1-4 (Wood), 2-94 (Pyrah), 3-94 (Guy), 4-120 (Ballance), 5-121 (Root), 6-121
1st (Ajmal Shahzad), 7-163 (Wainwright), 8-171 (Patterson), 9-177 (Lee), 10-199 (Finch)
FoW: 1-17 (Ballance), 2-18 (Wood), 3-27 (Root), 4-55 (Pyrah), 5-57 (Patterson), 6-82 (Guy)
2nd 7-95 (Ajmal Shahzad), 8-196 (Bairstow), 9-198 (Lee), 10-215 (Wainwright)

	O	M	R	W		O	M	R	W
Daggett	9	2	48	0	Tahir	13	3	39	1
Groenewald	14	5	28	1	Groenewald	19	4	47	3
MacLeod	9	0	39	0	Daggett	12	2	37	3
Tahir	14	4	23	3	McMahon	16.1	4	46	3
Miller	8	1	16	0	Miller	7	2	14	0
McMahon	27.5	9	43	6	James	2	1	2	0
					MacLeod	6	1	15	0

WARWICKSHIRE

First Innings		Second Innings	
S R Benton, c Guy b Patterson	17	c Guy b Patterson	6
N A James, b Ajmal Shahzad	9	b Pyrah	25
* L C Parker, b Patterson	3	c Guy b Hannon-Dalby	18
P J McMahon, lbw b Hannon-Dalby	15		
S A Piolet, c Wainwright b Pyrah	48	(4) lbw b Wainwright	37
J E Ord, b Pyrah	14	(5) not out	105
T D Groenewald, c Guy b Patterson	16	(6) not out	29
§ R M Johnson, c & b Wainwright	14		
C S MacLeod, c Bairstow b Wainwright	16		
N Tahir, c Root b Ajmal Shahzad	20		
L M Daggett, not out	5		
Extras (b 1, lb 8, nb 6)	15	Extras (lb 3)	3
Total (82.5 overs)	192	Total (4 wkts, 65 overs)	223

Twelfth man: A S Miller

FoW: 1-15 (James), 2-20 (Parker), 3-38 (McMahon), 4-70 (Benton), 5-106 (Ord),
1st 6-132 (Groenewald), 7-139 (Piolet), 8-156 (Johnson), 9-175 (MacLeod), 10-192 (Tahir)
2nd: 1-24 (Benton), 2-45 (James), 3-53 (Parker), 4-148 (Piolet)

	O	M	R	W		O	M	R	W
Shahzad	13.5	3	44	2	Patterson	12	3	40	1
Patterson	17	7	30	3	Shahzad	7	0	33	0
Wainwright	18	8	19	2	Pyrah	11	3	27	1
Hannon-Dalby	6	2	17	1	Hannon-Dalby	9	3	20	1
Lee	4	1	12	0	Lee	3	0	17	0
Pyrah	10	3	25	2	Wainwright	20	4	69	1
Finch	14	5	36	0	Finch	2	0	11	0
					Ballance	1	0	3	0

Umpires: D J Millns and R S Jakeman   Scorers: M Snook and S Smith

Second Eleven Championship
Yorkshire 2nd XI v. Worcestershire 2nd XI

Played at Headingley, Leeds, on August 6, 7, 8, 2008

Match drawn at 5.50pm on the Third Day

Toss won by Worcestershire   Yorkshire 12 points; Worcestershire 6 points

Close of play: First Day, Worcestershire 176-6 (Knappett 42*, Shantry 28*); Second Day, Yorkshire 311-3 (Bairstow 93*, Guy 56*).

WORCESTERSHIRE			
First Innings		Second Innings	
M M Ali, c Ballance b Azeem Rafiq	26	lbw b Azeem Rafiq	22
O M Ali, c White b Patterson	19	c Guy b Lawson	7
D A Wheeldon, b Hannon-Dalby	12	c sub b Patterson	48
U-K S Birkenstock, c Guy b Patterson	28	c sub b Chadwick	53
P W Harrison, lbw b Hannon-Dalby	1	lbw b Patterson	15
* § J P T Knappett, c & b Chadwick	47	lbw b Azeem Rafiq	13
C S Sandri, lbw b Lawson	11	lbw b Patterson	0
J D Shantry, c Guy b Ajmal Shahzad	35	lbw b Patterson	8
R A Jones, c Guy b Ajmal Shahzad	0	not out	7
C D Whelan, not out	2	not out	6
M Ahmed, b Chadwick	0		
Extras (b 1, lb 9, nb 2)	12	Extras (b 13, lb 9, w 5)	27
Total (74.4 overs)	193	Total (8 wkts, 83 overs)	206

Twelfth man: A S Dhindsa

FoW: 1st   1-38 (O M Ali), 2-53 (Wheeldon), 3-60 (Birkenstock), 4-71 (M M Ali), 5-99 (Harrison), 6-126 (Sandri), 7-190 (Shantry), 8-190 (Knappett), 9-192 (Jones), 10-193 (Ahmed)

FoW: 2nd   1-30 (O M Ali), 2-39 (M M Ali), 3-128 (Birkenstock), 4-161 (Wheeldon), 5-168 (Harrison), 6-168 (Sandri), 7-184 (Shantry), 8-188 (Knappett)

	O	M	R	W		O	M	R	W
Shahzad	16.4	6	38	2	Hannon-Dalby	9	2	30	0
Hannon-Dalby	16	5	49	2	Shahzad	10	2	31	0
Patterson	15.2	7	26	2	Lawson	2	0	8	1
Azeem Rafiq	8	1	23	1	Patterson	24	9	35	4
Lawson	14	0	41	1	Azeem Rafiq	33	13	54	2
Chadwick	4.4	0	6	2	Chadwick	3	1	21	1
					Ballance	2	0	5	0

Shahzad was unable to complete his 13th over.

YORKSHIRE	
J J Sayers, c & b Dhindsa	45
G S Ballance, c Knappett b M M Ali	61
* C White, b Shantry	31
J M Bairstow, not out	139
§ S M Guy, b M M Ali	78
Ajmal Shahzad, lbw b M M Ali	13
Azeem Rafiq	
M A K Lawson	
S A Patterson Did not bat	
O J Hannon-Dalby	
M S Chadwick	
Extras (b 3, lb 8, w 13, nb 4)	28
Total (5 wkts dec, 108 overs)	395

FoW: 1-115 (Ballance), 2-121 (Sayers), 3-200 (White), 4-373 (Guy), 5-395 (Ajmal Shahzad)

	O	M	R	W
Whelan	21	0	79	0
Jones	8.4	2	40	0
Ahmed	17.2	5	52	0
M M Ali	33	4	102	3
Dhindsa	16	3	53	1
Sandri	3	0	9	0
Shantry	8	1	44	1
O M Ali	1	0	5	0

R A Jones was unable to complete his ninth over.

Umpires: M A Gough and R S Jakeman   Scorers: M Snook and Mrs D E Pugh

NOTE: G L Wood, who was nominated to play for Yorkshire, was taken ill during Worcestershire's first innings, and was replaced by M S Chadwick.

Second Eleven Championship
Yorkshire 2nd XI v. Surrey 2nd XI

Played at Clifton Park, York, on August 12, 13, 14, 15, 2008
Surrey won by 85 runs at 5.19pm on the Fourth Day

Toss won by Yorkshire

Yorkshire 3 points; Surrey 17 points

Close of play: First Day, no play; Second Day, Surrey 309-9 (Hodgson 82*, Meaker 23*); Third Day, no play.

First Innings	SURREY		Second Innings	
C P Murtagh, c Sayers b Patterson	36		not out	18
§ P W Harrison, c Pyrah b Ajmal Shahzad	2		not out	13
L J Evans, c Guy b Hannon-Dalby	16			
* J G E Benning, b Hannon-Dalby	0			
A Harinath, c Finch b Patterson	49			
J J Roy, lbw b Azeem Rafiq	41			
L J Hodgson, c Bairstow b Hannon-Dalby	85			
A J Tudor, b Ajmal Shahzad	12			
Murtaza Hussain, b Finch	27			
S J King, c sub b Pyrah	8			
S C Meaker, not out	23			
Extras (b 1, lb 4, w 2, nb 6)	13		Extras (w 5, nb 2)	7
Total (85.2 overs)	312		Total (0 wkts dec, 1.3 overs)	38

Twelfth man: T E Linley

FoW: 1-3 (Harrison), 2-24 (Evans), 3-24 (Benning), 4-109 (Murtagh), 5-118 (Harinath) 6-170 (Roy), 7-187 (Tudor), 8-222 (Murtaza Hussain), 9-244 (King), 10-312 (Hodgson)

	O	M	R	W		O	M	R	W
Ajmal Shahzad	18	2	57	2	White	1	0	25	0
Patterson	25	7	71	2	Bairstow	0.3	0	13	0
Hannon-Dalby	18.2	1	62	3					
Pyrah	10	1	47	1					
Azeem Rafiq	9	0	51	1					
Finch	5	1	19	1					

YORKSHIRE Second Innings*

J J Sayers, c Benning b Hodgson	35
G S Ballance, lbw b Hodgson	14
* C White, c Harinath b King	23
R M Pyrah, c Harrison b Tudor	50
J M Bairstow, b Hodgson	2
§ S M Guy, c Linley b Tudor	63
Ajmal Shahzad, c Harrison b Hodgson	13
Azeem Rafiq, c Linley b Murtaza Hussain	1
S A Patterson, c Linley b Murtaza Hussain	18
J M Finch, c Linley b Murtaza Hussain	11
O J Hannon-Dalby, not out	0
Extras (lb 7, w 2, nb 26)	35
Total (77.4 overs)	265

Yorkshire forfeited their first innings.

FoW: 1-29 (Ballance), 2-86 (White), 3-122 (Sayers), 4-124 (Bairstow), 5-203 (Pyrah), 6-220
2nd: (Guy), 7-228 (Azeem Rafiq), 8-236 (Ajmal Shahzad), 9-259 (Finch), 10-265 (Patterson)

	O	M	R	W
Tudor	17	4	48	2
Meaker	0.2	0	12	0
Hodgson	17.4	5	44	4
Linley	11	1	39	0
Benning	4	0	21	0
King	11	3	29	1
Murtaza Hussain	16.4	4	65	3

S C Meaker was taken off during his first over, which was completed by L J Hodgson

Umpires: M A Gough and A Bullock

Scorers: M Snook and Mrs J E Booth

Second Eleven Championship
Yorkshire 2nd XI v. Sussex 2nd XI

Played at Cricketfield Road, Horsham, on August 27, 28, 29, 2008
Yorkshire won by 9 wickets at 1.55pm on the Third Day

Toss won by Sussex
Close of play: First Day, Sussex 52-1 (Beeny 35*, Hamilton-Brown 16*); Second Day, Sussex (Second Innings) 100-5 (Gould 13*, T M J Smith 3*).

Yorkshire 22 points; Sussex 5 points

YORKSHIRE First Innings		Second Innings	
J J Sayers, c Thornely b Liddle	47	lbw b Aga	3
G S Ballance, c D R Smith b Rudge	1	not out	20
* C White, b Liddle	16	not out	2
G L Wood, c & b Liddle	0		
J M Bairstow, c Hamilton-Brown b Jones	26		
§ S M Guy, c Liddle b Rudge	143		
Ajmal Shahzad, lbw b T M J Smith	35		
Azeem Rafiq, lbw b T M J Smith	8		
S A Patterson, c Hamilton-Brown b T M J Smith	36		
B W Sanderson, c Brown b Rollings	1		
O J Hannon-Dalby, not out	1		
Extras (lb 8, w 7, nb 8)	23	Extras (lb 1, w 2)	3
Total (89.1 overs)	337	Total (1 wkt, 5.5 overs)	28

FoW: 1-4 (Ballance), 2-27 (White), 3-27 (Wood), 4-91 (Bairstow), 5-107 (Sayers), 6-198
1st (Ajmal Shahzad), 7-238 (Azeem Rafiq), 8-306 (Guy), 9-321 (Sanderson) 10-337 (Patterson
2nd 1-14 (Sayers)

	O	M	R	W		O	M	R	W
Aga	8	1	21	0	Aga	3	0	4	1
Rudge	12	2	52	2	D R Smith	2.5	0	23	0
Liddle	19	5	71	3					
D R Smith	10	3	35	0					
Hamilton-Brown	6	1	13	0					
Rollings	8	0	32	1					
T M J Smith	15.1	4	45	3					
Jones	8	1	31	1					
Thornely	3	0	29	0					

SUSSEX First Innings		Second Innings	
J W K Beeny, lbw b Patterson	47	lbw b Ajmal Shahzad	34
M A Thornely, c Guy b Patterson	0	lbw b Hannon-Dalby	34
R J Hamilton-Brown, b Patterson	28	lbw b Patterson	3
§ B C Brown, c Ballance b Sanderson	0	c Bairstow b Patterson	6
D R Smith, c Ajmal Shahzad b Sanderson	27	c Sayers b Hannon-Dalby	1
M J T Gould, c Bairstow b Hannon-Dalby	25	b Hannon-Dalby	25
* T M J Smith, not out	41	lbw b Patterson	9
R G Aga, c Guy b Ajmal Shahzad	1	not out	34
C J Liddle, lbw b Ajmal Shahzad	1	c Wood b Azeem Rafiq	22
W D Rudge, c Sayers b Patterson	7	run out	0
J N J Rollings, b Patterson	0	b Ajmal Shahzad	0
Extras (lb 2, nb 2)	4	Extras (b 2, lb 7, w 2, nb 2)	13
Total (57.3 overs)	181	Total (73.3 overs)	181

Twelfth man: D H Jones J M Bairstow kept wicket in Sussex's second innings.

FoW: 1-4 (Thornely), 2-70 (Hamilton-Brown), 3-71 (Brown), 4-85 (Beeny), 5-109 (D R Smith)
1st 6-147 (Gould), 7-152 (Aga), 8-154 (Liddle), 9-177 (Rudge), 10-181 (Rollings)
FoW: 1-67 (Beeny), 2-74 (Thornely), 3-74 (Hamilton-Brown), 4-75 (D R Smith), 5-89 (Brown)
2nd 6-110 (T M J Smith), 7-128 (Gould), 8-180 (Liddle), 9-181 (Rudge), 10-181 (Rollings)

	O	M	R	W		O	M	R	W
Shahzad	18	2	59	2	Patterson	25	9	48	3
Patterson	18	6	53	5	Sanderson	14	3	23	0
Hannon-Dalby	12	1	38	1	Azeem Rafiq	7	0	36	1
Sanderson	9	0	29	2	Shahzad	10.3	0	40	2
					Hannon-Dalby	16	7	23	3
					Ballance	1	0	2	0

Umpires: R R Garland, T J Urben (Days 1 & 2) and I R E Farrell (Day 3).

Scorers: M Snook and R H Brearley

Second Eleven Championship
Yorkshire 2nd XI v. Lancashire 2nd XI

At Centre Vale, Todmorden, on September 3, 4, 5, 2008
Match abandoned without a ball being bowled
Note that this was Lancashire's home fixture　　　　Yorkshire 4 points; Lancashire 4 points

Yorkshire 2nd XI v. Derbyshire 2nd XI

Played at Shaw Lane, Barnsley, on September 10, 11, 12, 2008
Yorkshire won by an innings and 8 runs at 2.30pm on the Third Day
Toss won by Derbyshire　　　　　　　　　　　Yorkshire 22 points; Derbyshire 4 points
Close of play: First Day, Yorkshire 251-8 (Bairstow 1*, Ajmal Shahzad 7*); Second Day, Derbyshire (Second Innings) 24-2 (Stubbings 5*, Telo 0*).

YORKSHIRE

J J Sayers, c Jones b White	....	7
G S Ballance, c Poynton b White	....	0
J E Root, c Patel b Needham	....	30
C G Roebuck, c Sadler b Paget	....	41
J M Bairstow, c Borrington b Needham	....	24
§ S M Guy, b Paget	....	1
Ajmal Shahzad, c Needham b Sadler	....	57
D J Wainwright, b Sheikh	....	52
B W Sanderson, not out	....	36
J E Lee, c White b Paget	....	50
O J Hannon-Dalby, c Sheikh b Paget	....	2
Extras (b 11, lb 10, w 3, nb 10)	....	34
Total (90.1 overs)		334

Twelfth man: * C White
FoW: 1-10 (Ballance), 2-11 (Sayers), 3-93 (Root), 4-97 (Roebuck), 5-103 (Guy), 6-147 (Bairstow) 7-232 (Ajmal Shahzad), 8-247 (Wainwright), 9-331 (Lee), 10-334 (Hannon-Dalby)

	O	M	R	W
White	8	3	25	2
Whiteley	18	6	25	0
Needham	26	2	96	2
Jones	5	0	31	0
Paget	17.1	2	77	4
Sheikh	11	2	41	1
Sadler	5	1	18	1

DERBYSHIRE

First Innings				Second Innings		
* S D Stubbings, c Ballance b Wainwright	.....	6		(2) c Guy b Shahzad	....	5
P M Borrington, lbw b Lee		32		(1) c Bairstow b Shahzad	......	1
J L Sadler, c Sanderson b Wainwright		17		c Sayers b Root	....	10
F D Telo, b Lee		11		b Shahzad		33
A Patel, c Wainwright b Hannon-Dalby	....	18		b Shahzad		8
J Needham, c Shahzad b Hannon-Dalby		4		(7) b Wainwright		21
W A White, c Guy b Hannon-Dalby		7		(6) b Shahzad		0
C D Paget, lbw b Wainwright		5		c Lee b Root		12
§ T J Poynton, lbw b Shahzad		6		b Sanderson		27
R A Whiteley, not out		29		b Shahzad		47
E P Jones, c Wainwright b Sanderson		2		not out		0
Extras (w 2, nb 4)		6		Extras (b 8, lb 7, nb 4)		19
Total (65.1 overs)	....	143		Total (68 overs)	....	183

Twelfth man: A Sheikh　　　　*J M Bairstow kept wicket in Derbyshire's second innings*
FoW: 1-13 (Stubbings), 2-37 (Sadler), 3-68 (Telo), 4-77 (Borrington), 5-82 (Needham)
1st 6-94 (White), 7-102 (Paget), 8-106 (Patel), 9-129 (Poynton), 10-143 (Jones)
FoW: 1-10 (Borrington), 2-24 (Sadler), 3-25 (Stubbings), 4-59 (Patel), 5-59 (White)
2nd 6-66 (Telo), 7-96 (Needham), 8-106 (Paget), 9-166 (Poynton), 10-183 (Whiteley)

	O	M	R	W		O	M	R	W
Shahzad	18	5	35	1	Shahzad	16	2	42	6
Sanderson	10.1	3	21	1	Sanderson	14	5	46	1
Wainwright	22	8	59	3	Wainwright	23	9	36	1
Lee	7	4	11	2	Root	2	1	1	2
Hannon-Dalby	8	1	17	3	Lee	5	1	21	0
					Hannon-Dalby	6	1	18	0
					Ballance	2	1	4	0

Umpires: D J Millns and H Evans　　　　　　Scorers : M Snook and T M Cottam

Second Eleven Championship
Yorkshire 2nd XI v. Durham 2nd XI

At Hornby Park, Seaton Carew, on September 15, 16, 17, 2008
Match abandoned without a ball being bowled
Yorkshire 4 points; Durham 4 points

SECOND ELEVEN CHAMPIONSHIP 2008

FINAL TABLE

		P	W	L	D	Bonus BT	Bonus BO	Ded Pts	Avge	Runs per wicket scored	Runs per wicket against
1	Durham (5)	15	8	0	7	42	38	0.0	220	14.67	42.64	18.97
2	Middlesex (6)	13	5	2	6	35	40	0.0	169	13.00	35.36	28.62
3	Somerset (2)	11	3	1	7	31	35	1.0	135	12.27	39.35	30.77
4	Worcestershire (18) .	12	4	3	5	20	34	1.5	128.5	10.71	26.30	29.86
5	**Yorkshire (10)**	**14**	**4**	**4**	**6**	**29**	**38**	**0.0**	**147**	**10.50**	**31.65**	**25.94**
6	Surrey (11)	15	4	1	10	32	29	1.0	156	10.40	34.25	29.87
7	Sussex (1)	13	3	1	9	26	29	0.0	133	10.23	31.58	27.04
8	Kent (20)	7	1	1	5	15	18	0.5	69.5	9.93	32.72	28.52
9	Warwickshire (8) . . .	13	3	3	7	22	36	0.0	128	9.85	26.51	26.69
10	Nottinghamshire (12)	11	2	3	6	20	36	0.0	108	9.82	22.87	27.77
11	Essex (17)	10	3	3	4	17	30	7.5	97.5	9.75	28.13	29.40
12	Gloucestershire (16)	11	3	4	4	17	30	0.0	105	9.55	29.46	29.97
13	Northamptonshire (13)	11	2	3	6	20	33	0.5	104.5	9.50	27.30	30.21
14	Lancashire (4)	15	3	5	7	31	35	0.0	136	9.07	34.06	31.68
15	Hampshire (3)	11	2	0	9	19	18	6.0	95	8.64	31.35	34.59
16	Derbyshire (9)	14	2	4	8	21	38	0.0	119	8.50	28.64	29.25
17	Glamorgan (19)	11	1	5	5	23	27	0.0	84	7.64	30.33	37.49
18	Leicestershire (7) . . .	12	1	5	6	14	29	2.0	79	6.58	23.66	31.13
19	Scotland (15)	6	0	3	3	5	22	0.0	39	6.50	18.67	38.04
20	MCC YC (14)	15	1	4	10	18	25	0.0	97	6.47	25.69	42.17

(2007 final positions in brackets)

SECOND ELEVEN CHAMPIONS

(In the seasons in which Yorkshire have competed)

Season	Champions	Yorkshire's Position	Season	Champions	Yorkshire's Position
1959	Gloucestershire 2nd XI	7th	**1991**	**Yorkshire 2nd XI**	**1st**
1960	Northamptonshire 2nd XI	14th	1992	Surrey 2nd XI	5th
1961	Kent 2nd XI	11th	1993	Middlesex 2nd XI	3rd
1975	Surrey 2nd XI	4th	1994	Somerset 2nd XI	2nd
1976	Kent 2nd XI	5th	1995	Hampshire 2nd XI	5th
1977	**Yorkshire 2nd XI**	**1st**	1996	Warwickshire 2nd XI	4th
1978	Sussex 2nd XI	5th	1997	Lancashire 2nd XI	2nd
1979	Warwickshire 2nd XI	3rd	1998	Northamptonshire 2nd XI	9th
1980	Glamorgan 2nd XI	5th	1999	Middlesex 2nd XI	14th
1981	Hampshire 2nd XI	11th	2000	Middlesex 2nd XI	5th
1982	Worcestershire 2nd XI	14th	2001	Hampshire 2nd XI	2nd
1983	Leicestershire 2nd XI	2nd	2002	Kent 2nd XI	3rd
1984	**Yorkshire 2nd XI**	**1st**	**2003**	**Yorkshire 2nd XI**	**1st**
1985	Nottinghamshire 2nd XI	12th	2004	Somerset 2nd XI	8th
1986	Lancashire 2nd XI	5th	2005	Kent 2nd XI	10th
1987	**Yorkshire & Kent 2nd XIs**	**1st**	2006	Kent 2nd XI	3rd
1988	Surrey 2nd XI	9th	2007	Sussex 2nd XI	10th
1989	Middlesex 2nd XI	9th	2008	Durham 2nd XI	5th
1990	Sussex 2nd XI	17th			

SECOND ELEVEN CHAMPIONSHIP

Played 14   Won 4   Lost 4   Drawn 4   Abandoned 2

BATTING AND FIELDING

Player	M.	I.	N.O.	Runs	H.S.	Avge	100s	50s	ct/st
A Lyth	4	5	1	354	137*	88.50	2	0	2
J M Bairstow	6	7	2	308	139*	61.60	1	2	6/0
S M Guy	12	14	0	632	143	45.14	2	3	22/1
J J Sayers	6	8	0	285	132	35.62	1	0	5
C White	9	11	1	347	109	34.70	1	1	6
G S Ballance	6	9	2	220	61	31.42	0	2	3
D J Wainwright	6	7	0	211	65	30.14	0	2	9
C G Roebuck	5	9	1	239	64	29.87	0	1	1
R M Pyrah	5	6	0	169	50	28.16	0	1	3
G L Wood	9	14	1	313	114	24.07	1	1	10/0
Ajmal Shahzad	7	8	0	150	57	18.75	0	1	2
Azeem Rafiq	5	6	0	107	83	17.83	0	1	0
J E Lee	8	9	3	106	50	17.66	0	1	4
S A Patterson	5	6	2	60	36	15.00	0	0	0
B W Sanderson	8	8	2	82	36*	13.66	0	0	3
M A K Lawson	7	7	0	73	29	10.42	0	0	7
J M Finch	5	4	1	21	11	7.00	0	0	2
O J Hannon-Dalby	10	7	5	9	4*	4.50	0	0	1

Also batted: C A Allinson (3 matches) 8, 15*, 18, 7, 20; J E Root (2 matches) 13, 12, 30 (1 catch); P S E Sandri (2 matches) 0, 13; C R Taylor (2 matches) 86; D Gough (1 match) 7*; D G H Snell (1 match) 11, 5.

Did not bat: M S Chadwick (4 matches).

BOWLING

Player	Overs	Mdns	Runs	Wkts	Avge	Best	5wI	10wM
B W Sanderson	173	55	424	22	19.27	6-30	1	1
O J Hannon-Dalby	202.2	42	533	26	20.50	3-17	0	0
S A Patterson	173.5	54	453	21	21.57	5-53	1	0
Ajmal Shahzad	159	36	436	20	21.80	6-42	1	0
D J Wainwright	186.5	57	421	15	28.06	3-59	0	0
J M Finch	64	16	236	8	29.50	3-50	0	0
Azeem Rafiq	94	19	312	10	31.20	5-51	1	0
R M Pyrah	87	23	236	7	33.71	2-12	0	0
J E Lee	103.5	15	414	12	34.50	4-20	0	0
M S Chadwick	42.5	5	174	5	34.80	2-6	0	0
M A K Lawson	86.4	6	343	9	38.11	3-76	0	0

Also bowled: D Gough 21-5-99-4; P S E Sandri 31-2-132-4; D G H Snell 15-1-72-3; J E Root 2-1-1-2; C A Allinson 16-2-67-1; A Lyth 8-1-22-0; G S Ballance 6-1-14-0; C White 1-0-25-0; J M Bairstow 0.3-0-13-0.

SECOND ELEVEN TROPHY

2008

A ZONE – FINAL TABLE

	Played	Won	Lost	No result	Net run rate	Points
1 Leicestershire (5)	8	6	1	1	0.782	13
2 Durham (2)	8	5	0	3	1.661	13
3 Lancashire (1)	8	1	4	3	-0.290	5
4 Yorkshire (3)	**8**	**1**	**4**	**3**	**-1.230**	**5**
5 Derbyshire (4)	8	1	5	2	-1.027	4

(2007 final positions in brackets)

FINAL

Hampshire beat Essex by 7 runs

PREVIOUS WINNERS:

1986	**Northamptonshire**, who beat Essex by 14 runs
1987	**Derbyshire**, who beat Hampshire by 7 wickets
1988	**Yorkshire**, who beat Kent by 7 wickets
1989	**Middlesex**, who beat Kent by 6 wickets
1990	**Lancashire**, who beat Somerset by 8 wickets
1991	**Nottinghamshire**, who beat Surrey by 8 wickets
1992	**Surrey**, who beat Northamptonshire by 8 wickets
1993	**Leicestershire**, who beat Sussex by 142 runs
1994	**Yorkshire**, who beat Leicestershire by 6 wickets
1995	**Leicestershire**, who beat Gloucestershire by 3 runs
1996	**Leicestershire**, who beat Durham by 46 runs
1997	**Surrey**, who beat Gloucestershire by 3 wickets
1998	**Northamptonshire**, who beat Derbyshire by 5 wickets
1999	**Kent**, who beat Hampshire by 106 runs.
2000	**Leicestershire**, who beat Hampshire by 25 runs.
2001	**Surrey**, who beat Somerset by 6 wickets
2002	**Kent**, who beat Hampshire by 5 wickets
2003	**Hampshire**, who beat Warwickshire by 8 wickets
2004	**Worcestershire**, who beat Essex by 8 wickets
2005	**Sussex**, who beat Nottinghamshire by 6 wickets
2006	**Warwickshire**, who beat Yorkshire by 93 runs
2007	**Middlesex**, who beat Somerset by 1 run

Second XI Trophy
Yorkshire 2nd XI v. Leicestershire 2nd XI

Played at Wagon Lane, Bingley, on June 25, 2008
Leicestershire won by 17 runs at 6.40pm

Toss won by Leicestershire   Yorkshire 0 points; Leicestershire 2 points

LEICESTERSHIRE

* T J New, st Wood b Sanderson	....	100
J Augustus, c Wood b Kruis	....	25
G P Smith, c Kruis b Azeem Rafiq	....	37
E J Foster, lbw b Azeem Rafiq	....	4
R J A Malcolm-Hansen, b Patterson	....	26
N J Ferraby, not out	....	44
§ J I Pope, not out	....	37
D T Rowe		
H F Gurney	Did not bat	
C S Yates		
Zafran Ali		
Extras (lb 3, w 7)	....	10
Total (5 wkts, 50 overs)	....	283

FoW: 1-47 (Augustus), 2-155 (Smith), 3-160 (Foster), 4-191 (New), 5-221 (Malcolm-Hansen)

	O	M	R	W
Kruis	10	0	64	1
Shahzad	6	0	37	0
Patterson	10	0	55	1
Sanderson	8	0	54	1
Azeem Rafiq	10	0	41	2
Lyth	6	0	29	0

YORKSHIRE

A W Gale, c Smith b Gurney	....	46
* J J Sayers, c Pope b Rowe	....	1
A Lyth, c Foster b Gurney	....	0
C R Taylor, b Rowe	....	11
§ G L Wood, c Foster b Gurney	....	8
J M Bairstow, c Pope b Malcolm-Hansen	....	27
Ajmal Shahzad, c Smith b Yates	....	91
Azeem Rafiq, b Malcom-Hansen	....	16
S A Patterson, c New b Malcolm-Hansen	....	37
G J Kruis, c New b Malcolm-Hansen	....	10
B W Sanderson, not out	....	1
Extras (lb 10, w 4, nb 4)	....	18
Total (49 overs)	....	266

FoW: 1-7 (Sayers), 2-9 (Lyth), 3-47 (Taylor), 4-60 (Wood), 5-83 (Gale), 6-139 (Bairstow), 7-177 (Azeem Rafiq), 8-245 (Ajmal Shahzad), 9-265 (Kruis), 10-266 (Patterson)

	O	M	R	W
Rowe	9	1	47	2
Gurney	10	0	44	3
Zafran Ali	4	0	16	0
Ferraby	7	0	46	0
Malcolm-Hansen	9	0	54	4
Yates	10	1	49	1

Umpires: M A Gough and A Clark   Scorers: M Snook and D Ayriss

Second XI Trophy
Yorkshire 2nd XI v. Durham 2nd XI

Played at Hornby Park, Seaton Carew, on June 27, 2008
Durham won by 7 wickets at 4.24pm

Toss won by Durham   Yorkshire 0 points; Durham 2 points

YORKSHIRE

* J J Sayers, c Goddard b Claydon	6
J E Root, c Claydon b Onions	1
§ G L Wood, c Goddard b Claydon	0
C R Taylor, c Claydon b Gidman	48
J M Bairstow, c Muchall b Davies	7
C G Roebuck, st Goddard b Turner	0
Ajmal Shahzad, c Goddard b Claydon	27
Rana Naved-ul-Hasan, c Stoneman b Davies	3
D J Wainwright, b Davies	40
G J Kruis, b Wiseman	4
B W Sanderson, not out	10
Extras (lb 3,w 5)	8
Total (42.4 overs)	154

FoW: 1-8 (Root), 2-8 (Wood), 3-9 (Sayers), 4-65 (Taylor), 5-68 (Bairstow), 6-68 (Roebuck) 7-89 (Rana Naved-ul-Hasan), 8-107 (Ajmal Shahzad), 9-130 (Kruis) 10-154 (Wainwright)

	O	M	R	W
Claydon	10	3	17	3
Onions	10	1	32	1
Gidman	7	0	39	1
Davies	5.4	1	23	3
Turner	2	1	15	1
Wiseman	8	3	25	1

DURHAM

M D Stoneman, b Shahzad		83
K Turner, b Kruis		1
K J Coetzer, b Shahzad		10
* G J Muchall, not out		33
U Mahomed, not out		22
W R S Gidman		
§ L J Goddard		
P J Wiseman	Did not bat	
G Onions		
A M Davies		
M E Claydon		
Extras (lb 2, w 4)		6
Total (3 wkts, 27.4 overs)		155

FoW: 1-3 (Turner), 2-89 (Coetzer), 3-104 (Stoneman)

	O	M	R	W
Naved-ul-Hasan	9	0	56	0
Kruis	9	0	36	1
Sanderson	4.4	0	37	0
Shahzad	5	1	24	2

Umpires: M A Gough and J W Crockatt   Scorers: M Snook and R V Hilton

Second XI Trophy
Yorkshire 2nd XI v. Derbyshire 2nd XI

Played at The Copper Yard, Denby, on July 1, 2008
Yorkshire won by 16 runs at 6.08pm

Toss won by Derbyshire   Yorkshire 2 points; Derbyshire 0 points

YORKSHIRE

* J J Sayers, c & b Whiteley		4
G S Ballance, c Poynton b Hunter		21
§ S M Guy, c Poynton b Whiteley		1
C R Taylor, b Whiteley		84
R M Pyrah, lbw b Whiteley		0
J M Bairstow, run out		47
Ajmal Shahzad, c Redfern b Whiteley		12
Rana Naved-ul-Hasan, run out		48
D J Wainwright, c White b Whiteley		12
Azeem Rafiq, run out		0
G J Kruis, not out		0
Extras (lb 7, w 14, nb 10)		31
Total (48.1 overs)		260

FoW: 1-29 (Ballance), 2-33 (Guy), 3-37 (Sayers), 4-37 (Pyrah), 5-147 (Bairstow), 6-177 (Ajmal Shahzad), 7-194 (Taylor), 8-244 (Wainwright), 9-260 (Azeem Rafiq) 10-260 (Rana Naved-ul-Hasan)

	O	M	R	W
White	9	0	49	0
Hunter	9.1	1	50	1
Whiteley	10	0	74	6
Doshi	10	2	23	0
Paget	8	0	42	0
Patel	2	0	15	0

DERBYSHIRE

F A Klokker, c Guy b Naved-ul-Hasan		103
P M Borrington, run out		54
* J L Sadler, c Sayers b Pyrah		21
D J Redfern, c Naved-ul-Hasan b Azeem Rafiq		14
A Patel, c Naved-ul-Hasan b Azeem Rafiq		9
W A White, b Pyrah		10
R A Whiteley, b Naved-ul-Hasan		1
§ T J Poynton, b Naved-ul-Hasan		5
C D Paget, not out		3
I D Hunter, c Sayers b Pyrah		0
N D Doshi, not out		5
Extras (b 1, lb 3, w 9, nb 6)		19
Total (9 wkts, 50 overs)		244

FoW: 1-131 (Borrington), 2-167 (Sadler), 3-199 (Redfern), 4-215 (Patel), 5-229 (Klokker) 6-230 (White), 7-232 (Whiteley), 8-237 (Poynton), 9-238 (Hunter)

	O	M	R	W
Naved-ul-Hasan	10	0	40	3
Kruis	10	4	28	0
Pyrah	10	0	49	3
Shahzad	3	0	27	0
Wainwright	10	0	58	0
Azeem Rafiq	7	0	38	2

Umpires : A Hicks and N R Roper   Scorers : M Snook and T M Cottam

Second XI Trophy
Yorkshire 2nd XI v. Leicestershire 2nd XI

Played at Leicester Road, Hinckley, on July 2, 2008
Leicestershire won by 96 runs (D/L Method) at 6.28pm

Toss won by Leicestershire   Yorkshire 0 points; Leicestershire 2 points

LEICESTERSHIRE

* § T J New, c Guy b Pyrah		94
M A G Boyce, lbw b Pyrah		38
G P Smith, run out		95
E J Foster, c Ballance b Azeem Rafiq		17
R J A Malcolm-Hansen, not out		14
J I Pope, c Guy b Naved-ul-Hasan		0
D T Rowe, run out		13
J H K Naik		
S J Cliff	Did not bat	
H F Gurney		
R A G Cummins		
Extras (b 1, lb 2, w 13, nb 6)		22
Total (6 wkts, 50 overs)		293

FoW: 1-85 (Boyce), 2-197 (New), 3-228 (Foster), 4-272 (Smith), 5-273 (Pope), 6-293 (Rowe)

	O	M	R	W
Naved-ul-Hasan	10	1	59	1
Kruis	9	1	46	0
Shahzad	7	0	30	0
Pyrah	9	0	78	2
Wainwright	7	0	39	0
Azeem Rafiq	8	0	38	1

YORKSHIRE

* J J Sayers, b Rowe	24
G S Ballance, c New b Naik	42
§ S M Guy, lbw b Rowe	0
C R Taylor, c Cliff b Malcolm-Hansen	29
R M Pyrah, run out	1
J M Bairstow, st New b Naik	4
Rana Naved-ul-Hasan, c New b Naik	0
Ajmal Shahzad, b Malcolm-Hansen	2
D J Wainwright, b Naik	1
Azeem Rafiq, c Cummins b Malcolm-Hansen	7
G J Kruis, not out	8
Extras (w 6)	6
Total (24.5 overs)	124

FoW: 1-50 (Sayers), 2-50 (Guy), 3-83 (Ballance), 4-85 (Pyrah), 5-105 (Bairstow), 6-105 (Rana Naved-ul-Hasan), 7-107 (Taylor), 8-107 (Ajmal Shahzad), 9-110 (Wainwright), 10-124 (Azeem Rafiq)

	O	M	R	W
Cummins	6	1	16	0
Rowe	4	1	17	2
Cliff	3	0	17	0
Gurney	2	0	20	0
Malcolm-Hansen	5.5	0	38	3
Naik	4	0	16	4

Umpires: K Coburn and C W Whittaker   Scorers: M Snook and D Ayriss

Second XI Trophy
Yorkshire 2nd XI v. Derbyshire 2nd XI

Played at Bawtry Road, Sheffield, on July 8, 2008
Match abandoned. No Result

Toss won by Derbyshire   Yorkshire 1 point; Derbyshire 1 point

YORKSHIRE

*J J Sayers, not out	....	11
C R Taylor, not out	....	5
G S Ballance		
§ S M Guy		
J M Bairstow		
G L Wood		
Ajmal Shahzad	Did not bat	
D J Wainwright		
S A Patterson		
G J Kruis		
J E Lee		
Extras (lb 1, w 4)	....	5
Total (0 wkts, 5 overs)	....	21

	O	M	R	W
White	3	1	9	0
Hunter	2	0	11	0

DERBYSHIRE

C J L Rogers
D J Birch
* J L Sadler
S D Stubbings
G M Smith
A Patel
§ T J Poynton
R A Whiteley
I D Hunter
N D Doshi
W A White

Umpires: S A Garrett and I Dawood   Scorers: M Snook and T M Cottam

Yorkshire 2nd XI v. Lancashire 2nd XI

At Weetwood, Leeds, on July 10, 2008
Match abandoned without a ball being bowled
Yorkshire 1 point; Lancashire 1 point

Yorkshire 2nd XI v. Lancashire 2nd XI

At Old Trafford, Manchester, on July 11, 2008
Match abandoned without a ball being bowled
Yorkshire 1 point; Lancashire 1 point

Second XI Trophy
Yorkshire 2nd XI v. Durham 2nd XI

Played at Weetwood, Leeds, on July 14, 2008
Durham won by 4 wickets at 5.32pm

Toss won by Durham   Yorkshire 0 points; Durham 2 points

YORKSHIRE

* J J Sayers, c Park b Gidman	....	11
C R Taylor, c Goddard b Gidman	....	23
G L Wood, c Park b Breese	....	26
R M Pyrah, b Park	....	16
§ S M Guy, b Breese	....	8
D J Wainwright, b Park	....	3
J M Bairstow, b Claydon	....	34
Ajmal Shahzad, run out	....	16
Azeem Rafiq, c & b Breese	....	4
J E Lee, run out	....	1
O J Hannon-Dalby, not out	....	1
Extras (lb 7, w 11, nb 2)		20
Total (49.4 overs)		163

FoW: 1-40 (Taylor), 2-42 (Sayers), 3-86 (Pyrah), 4-94 (Wood), 5-95 (Guy), 6-100 (Wainwright), 7-130 (Ajmal Shahzad), 8-146 (Azeem Rafiq), 9-148 (Lee) 10-163 (Bairstow)

	O	M	R	W
Killeen	9	3	13	0
Claydon	6.4	1	19	1
Davies	7	1	18	0
Gidman	6	0	24	2
Park	5	1	29	2
Breese	10	0	26	3
Borthwick	6	0	27	0

DURHAM

G M Scott, b Shahzad	....	14
K J Coetzer, c Guy b Lee	....	31
* G J Muchall, lbw b Hannon-Dalby	....	0
G T Park, c Pyrah b Lee	....	11
G R Breese, b Hannon-Dalby	....	51
W R S Gidman, not out	....	41
§ L J Goddard, lbw b Hannon-Dalby	....	0
S G Borthwick, not out	....	3
M E Claydon		
A M Davies	Did not bat	
N Killeen		
Extras (w 12, nb 2)		14
Total (6 wkts, 37.4 overs)		165

FoW: 1-22 (Scott), 2-23 (Muchall), 3-61 (Coetzer), 4-73 (Park), 5-151 (Breese) 6-151 (Goddard)

	O	M	R	W
Shahzad	9	1	33	1
Hannon-Dalby	7.4	1	40	3
Pyrah	6	2	17	0
Lee	5	0	23	2
Wainwright	5	0	24	0
Azeem Rafiq	5	0	28	0

Umpires: P J Hartley and D O Oslear   Scorers: M Snook and R V Hilton

YORKSHIRE AVERAGES 2008

SECOND ELEVEN TROPHY

Played 8   Won 1   Lost 4   Abandoned 3

BATTING AND FIELDING

Player	M.	I.	N.O.	Runs	H.S.	Avge	100s	50s	ct/st
C R Taylor	6	6	1	200	84	40.00	0	1	0
G S Ballance	3	2	0	63	42	31.50	0	0	1
Ajmal Shahzad	6	5	0	148	91	29.60	0	1	0
J M Bairstow	6	5	0	119	47	23.80	0	0	0
Rana Naved-ul-Hasan	3	3	0	51	48	17.00	0	0	2
D J Wainwright	5	4	0	56	40	14.00	0	0	0
J J Sayers	6	6	1	57	24	11.40	0	0	2
G L Wood	4	3	0	34	26	11.33	0	0	1/1
G J Kruis	5	4	2	22	10	11.00	0	0	1
Azeem Rafiq	4	4	0	27	16	6.75	0	0	0
R M Pyrah	3	3	0	17	16	5.66	0	0	1
S M Guy	4	3	0	9	8	3.00	0	0	4/0

Also batted: J E Lee (2 matches) 1; S A Patterson (2 matches) 37; B W Sanderson (2 matches) 1*, 10*; A W Gale (1 match) 46; O J Hannon-Dalby (1 match) 1*; A Lyth (1 match) 0; C G Roebuck (1 match) 0; J E Root (1 match) 1.

BOWLING

Player	Overs	Mdns	Runs	Wkts	Avge	Best	4wI
J E Lee	5	0	23	2	11.50	2-23	0
O J Hannon-Dalby	7.4	1	40	3	13.33	3-40	0
R M Pyrah	25	2	144	5	28.80	3-49	0
Azeem Rafiq	30	0	145	5	29.00	2-38	0
Rana Naved-ul-Hasan	29	1	155	4	38.75	3-40	0
Ajmal Shahzad	30	2	151	3	50.33	2-24	0
S A Patterson	10	0	55	1	55.00	1-55	0
G J Kruis	38	5	174	2	87.00	1-36	0
B W Sanderson	12.4	0	91	1	91.00	1-54	0
D J Wainwright	22	0	121	0	—	—	0
A Lyth	6	0	29	0	—	—	0

Also bowled: O J Hannon-Dalby 7.4-1-40-3; J E Lee 5-0-23-2; A Lyth 6-0-29-0.

Other Second Eleven Matches
Yorkshire 2nd XI v. Durham 2nd XI

At The Racecourse, Durham, on April 16, 2008
Match abandoned without a ball being bowled

Yorkshire 2nd XI v. Durham 2nd XI

At The Racecourse, Durham, on April 17, 2008
Match abandoned without a ball being bowled

Yorkshire 2nd XI v. Durham 2nd XI

At Roseworth Terrace, Gosforth, on April 18, 2008
Match abandoned without a ball being bowled

Yorkshire 2nd XI v. A Kent-Northamptonshire XII

Played at Worsley Bridge Road, Beckenham, on June 3, 4, 5, 6, 2008
Match drawn at 1pm on the Second Day
Toss won by A Kent-Northamptonshire XII
Close of play: First Day, Yorkshire 53-4 (Roebuck 16*, Azeem Rafiq 0*).

YORKSHIRE

C A Allinson, lbw b Saggers	9
G L Wood, b Saggers	5
C G Roebuck, c & b Saggers	29
Ashley Lyth, lbw b Saggers	0
* § S M Guy, c Crook b Saggers	17
Azeem Rafiq, not out	27
J M Finch, c Walker b Saggers	0
B W Sanderson, c Crook b Saggers	9
J E Lee, c Crook b Saggers	4
P S E Sandri, c Barber b Saggers	0
O J Hannon-Dalby, not out	3
Extras (lb 6, nb 10)	16
Total (9 wkts, 43 overs)	119

Twelfth man: M A K Lawson

FoW: 1-15 (Wood), 2-16 (Allinson), 3-16 (Ashley Lyth), 4-46 (Guy), 5-71 (Roebuck)
6-71 (Finch), 7-97 (Sanderson), 8-109 (Lee), 9-109 (Sandri)

	O	M	R	W
Saggers	22	6	62	9
Wigley	14	2	35	0
Logan	7	0	16	0

A KENT-NORTHAMPTONSHIRE XII

N J Dexter *(Kent)*
A R Crook *(Northamptonshire)*
A G Wakeley *(Northamptonshire)*
* M J Walker *(Kent)*
M A G Nelson *(Northamptonshire)*
C R Hemphrey *(Kent)*
G G White *(Northamptonshire)*
§ A M J Barber *(Kent)*
D H Wigley *(Northamptonshire)*
M J Saggers *(Kent)*
R J Logan *(Northamptonshire)*
W W Lee *(Kent)*

Umpires: T J Urben and K G Amos   Scorers: M Snook and C A Booth

NOTE: N J Dexter (Kent) was called to First XI duties at the start of the second day, and was replaced by A J Blake (Kent). The match was abandoned at lunchtime on the second day when the ground was requisitioned for the Kent v. Somerset Friends' Provident Quarter-Final, which was transferred from a waterlogged Canterbury, and was to be played the following day.

YORKSHIRE ECB COUNTY PREMIER LEAGUE 2008

*	P	CW	IW1	IW2	IW3	IL1	IL2	IL3	CL	T	C	A	Pts
York	26	8	3	2	3	0	2	2	1	1	3	1	130
Castleford	26	11	1	1	1	0	0	1	5	0	4	2	124
Rotherham Town	26	9	0	0	4	0	1	2	5	0	4	1	112
Doncaster Town	26	7	1	1	5	0	0	4	4	0	2	2	110
Barnsley	26	9	0	0	2	1	1	4	5	0	3	1	99
Yorkshire Academy ...	**26**	**6**	**0**	**0**	**5**	**1**	**0**	**2**	**6**	**0**	**5**	**1**	**98**
Hull & YPI	26	6	0	0	4	1	1	4	3	1	5	1	97
Cleethorpes	26	4	1	1	5	3	1	1	5	0	3	2	96
Scarborough	26	6	0	1	2	1	1	0	7	0	6	2	93
Sheffield Collegiate ..	26	5	2	3	0	0	1	5	4	0	5	1	89
Driffield Town	26	7	0	1	1	1	0	3	7	1	4	1	89
Sheffield United	26	3	0	1	3	0	2	2	9	1	4	1	69
Appleby Frodingham ..	26	5	0	0	0	0	2	1	13	1	2	2	58
Harrogate	26	0	1	1	1	1	0	4	12	1	6	0	36

* P = Played; CW = Complete win (8 points); IW1 = Incomplete win (6 points); IW2 = Incomplete
win (6 points); IW3 = Incomplete win (6 points); IL1 = Incomplete loss (2 points); IL2 = Incomplete
loss (1 point); IL3 = Incomplete loss (0 points); CL = Complete loss (0 points); T = Tied (4 points);
C = Cancelled (3 points); A = Abandoned (3 points); Pts = Total Points.

Yorkshire ECB County Premier League Cup: 2008 Final was postponed to Saturday, April 18,
2009, because of fixture congestion. York are to play Castleford.

YORKSHIRE ACADEMY BATTING AVERAGES
IN ECB COUNTY PREMIER LEAGUE

	I	NO	HS	Runs	Avge	Ct/St
G Ballance	10	1	176	591	65.67	7
J Root	12	2	90*	459	45.90	1
J Bairstow	16	2	80	490	35.00	15/5
C Geldart	10	1	93	263	29.22	2
J Morgan	14	1	76	343	26.38	4/1
C Roebuck	12	1	109	230	20.91	5
C Allinson	14	3	47	202	18.36	7
M Chadwick	10	6	18*	69	17.25	5
B Sanderson	4	2	14*	27	13.50	—
A Rafiq	5	0	32	64	12.80	—
D Sharp	14	3	31*	140	12.73	7
R Wilkinson	4	1	24	27	9.00	2
J Lee	10	2	20	61	7.63	5
D Girling	3	1	6	15	7.50	—
G Rhodes	2	0	13	15	7.50	—
G Randhawa	10	1	25	60	6.67	4
A Lilley	6	2	10	23	5.75	1
O Hannon-Dalby	5	1	1*	2	0.50	2

YORKSHIRE ACADEMY BOWLING AVERAGES
IN ECB COUNTY PREMIER LEAGUE

	O	M	Runs	Wkts	Best	Avge
G Balance	1	0	1	1	1-1	1.00
J Root	7	1	17	3	3-17	5.67
B Sanderson	53.1	14	132	14	4-40	9.43
O Hannon Dalby	102	14	270	16	5-10	16.88
A Rafiq	194.4	43	599	35	5-12	17.11
J Lee	95	11	336	19	5-15	17.68
R Wilkinson	45.5	13	117	6	2-3	19.50
A Lilley	29	3	133	5	3-17	26.60
G Randhawa	115.1	11	479	17	3-61	28.18
M Chadwick	120	15	377	13	3-18	29.00
C Allinson	53	5	216	6	2-23	36.00
D Girling	22	3	80	0	0-10	—
G Rhodes	15	1	54	0	0-16	—
D Sharp	3	0	23	0	0.23	—

RECORDS SECTION

(All records in this section relate to First-Class Yorkshire matches only — except where otherwise stated)

HONOURS

County Champions (32)
1867, 1870, 1893, 1896, 1898, 1900, 1901, 1902, 1905, 1908, 1912, 1919, 1922, 1923, 1924, 1925, 1931, 1932, 1933, 1935, 1937, 1938, 1939, 1946, 1959, 1960, 1962, 1963, 1966, 1967, 1968, 2001.

Joint Champions (2)
1869, 1949

Promoted to Division 1
2005

Gillette Cup Winners (2)
1965, 1969

Cheltenham & Gloucester Trophy (1)
2002

Benson & Hedges Cup Winners (1)
1987

John Player Special League Winners (1)
1983

Fenner Trophy Winners (3)
1972, 1974, 1981

Asda Challenge Winners (1)
1987

Ward Knockout Cup (1)
1989

Joshua Tetley Festival Trophy (7)
1991, 1992 (Joint), 1993, 1994, 1996, 1997 and 1998

Tilcon Trophy Winners (2)
1978 and 1988

Pro-Arch Trophy (1)
2007-08

Second Eleven Champions (4)
1977, 1984, 1991, 2003

Joint Champions (1)
1987

Minor Counties Champions (5)
1947, 1957, 1958, 1968, 1971

Under-25 Competition Winners (3)
1976, 1978, 1987

Bain Clarkson Trophy Winners (2)
1988 and 1994

252

YORKSHIRE'S CHAMPIONSHIP CAPTAINS

1867 to 2001

R Iddison (2)	1867, 1870
Lord Hawke (8)	1893, 1896, 1898, 1900, 1901, 1902, 1905, 1908
Sir Archibald White (1)	1912
D C F Burton (1)	1919
G Wilson (3)	1922, 1923, 1924
A W Lupton (1)	1925
F E Greenwood (2)	1931, 1932
A B Sellers (6)	1933, 1935, 1937, 1938, 1939, 1946
J R Burnet (1)	1959
J V Wilson (2)	1960, 1962
D B Close (4)	1963, 1966, 1967, 1968
D Byas (1)	2001

Joint Champions

R Iddison (1)	1869
N W D Yardley (1)	1949

RECORDS SECTION

INDEX

CHAMPION COUNTIES SINCE 1873

		Yorkshire's Position
1873	Gloucestershire / Nottinghamshire	7th
1874	Gloucestershire	4th
1875	Nottinghamshire	4th
1876	Gloucestershire	3rd
1877	Gloucestershire	7th
1878	Middlesex	6th
1879	Nottinghamshire/Lancashire	6th
1880	Nottinghamshire	5th
1881	Lancashire	3rd
1882	Nottinghamshire/Lancashire	3rd
1883	Nottinghamshire	2nd
1884	Nottinghamshire	3rd
1885	Nottinghamshire	2nd
1886	Nottinghamshire	4th
1887	Surrey	3rd
1888	Surrey	2nd
1889	Surrey/Lancashire / Nottinghamshire	7th
1890	Surrey	3rd
1891	Surrey	8th
1892	Surrey	6th
1893	**Yorkshire**	**1st**
1894	Surrey	2nd
1895	Surrey	3rd
1896	**Yorkshire**	**1st**
1897	Lancashire	4th
1898	**Yorkshire**	**1st**
1899	Surrey	3rd
1900	**Yorkshire**	**1st**
1901	**Yorkshire**	**1st**
1902	**Yorkshire**	**1st**
1903	Middlesex	3rd
1904	Lancashire	2nd
1905	**Yorkshire**	**1st**
1906	Kent	2nd
1907	Nottinghamshire	2nd
1908	**Yorkshire**	**1st**
1909	Kent	3rd
1910	Kent	8th
1911	Warwickshire	7th
1912	**Yorkshire**	**1st**
1913	Kent	2nd
1914	Surrey	4th
1919	**Yorkshire**	**1st**
1920	Middlesex	4th
1921	Middlesex	3rd
1922	**Yorkshire**	**1st**
1923	**Yorkshire**	**1st**
1924	**Yorkshire**	**1st**

		Yorkshire's Position
1925	**Yorkshire**	**1st**
1926	Lancashire	2nd
1927	Lancashire	3rd
1928	Lancashire	4th
1929	Nottinghamshire	2nd
1930	Lancashire	3rd
1931	**Yorkshire**	**1st**
1932	**Yorkshire**	**1st**
1933	**Yorkshire**	**1st**
1934	Lancashire	5th
1935	**Yorkshire**	**1st**
1936	Derbyshire	3rd
1937	**Yorkshire**	**1st**
1938	**Yorkshire**	**1st**
1939	**Yorkshire**	**1st**
1946	**Yorkshire**	**1st**
1947	Middlesex	7th
1948	Glamorgan	4th
1949	**Yorkshire/Middlesex**	**1st**
1950	Lancashire/Surrey	3rd
1951	Warwickshire	2nd
1952	Surrey	2nd
1953	Surrey	12th
1954	Surrey	2nd
1955	Surrey	2nd
1956	Surrey	7th
1957	Surrey	3rd
1958	Surrey	11th
1959	**Yorkshire**	**1st**
1960	**Yorkshire**	**1st**
1961	Hampshire	2nd
1962	**Yorkshire**	**1st**
1963	**Yorkshire**	**1st**
1964	Worcestershire	5th
1965	Worcestershire	4th
1966	**Yorkshire**	**1st**
1967	**Yorkshire**	**1st**
1968	**Yorkshire**	**1st**
1969	Glamorgan	13th
1970	Kent	4th
1971	Surrey	13th
1972	Warwickshire	10th
1973	Hampshire	14th
1974	Worcestershire	11th
1975	Leicestershire	2nd
1976	Middlesex	8th
1977	Kent/Middlesex	12th
1978	Kent	4th
1979	Essex	7th
1980	Middlesex	6th
1981	Nottinghamshire	10th

		Yorkshire's Position			Yorkshire's Position
1982	Middlesex	10th	1996	Leicestershire	6th
1983	Essex	17th	1997	Glamorgan	6th
1984	Essex	14th	1998	Leicestershire	3rd
1985	Middlesex	11th	1999	Surrey	6th
1986	Essex	10th	2000	Surrey	3rd
1987	Nottinghamshire	8th	**2001**	**Yorkshire**	**1st**
1988	Worcestershire	13th	2002	Surrey	9th
1989	Worcestershire	16th	2003	Sussex	Div 2, 4th
1990	Middlesex	10th	2004	Warwickshire	Div 2, 7th
1991	Essex	14th	2005	Nottinghamshire	Div 2, 3rd
1992	Essex	16th	2006	Sussex	Div 1, 6th
1993	Middlesex	12th	2007	Sussex	Div 1, 6th
1994	Warwickshire	13th	2008	Durham	Div 1, 7th
1995	Warwickshire	8th			

£500,000 Championship bonanza

Yorkshire have an even bigger incentive this summer for clinching the First Division title of the LV Championship because prize-money for the winners has been increased to £500,000 in an attempt by the ECB to reassert the status of first-class cricket. When Yorkshire won the title in 2001 — for the first time in 33 years — they received £105,000.

100TH 100 FOR MARK RAMPRAKASH

SPOT THE BALL: It is on the crease line to the extreme right of VAUGHN RIDLEY'S action picture as Mark Ramprakash's square cut off left-arm spinner David Wainwright whistles through point to bring Mark, 38, his 100th first-class century during the last session of Yorkshire's LV Championship match against Surrey at Headingley Carnegie on August 2. It was Mark's seventh century against Yorkshire. In 1993 he and Mike Gatting set a Middlesex third-wicket record against Yorkshire of 321 at Scarborough, and at Headingley in 1995 he plundered 235.

CHAMPAGNE AND SILVER: Former Yorkshire Chairman Geoff Cope presented Mark with a bottle of champagne and a congratulatory letter, and Surrey coach Alan Butcher gave him a silver salver and another bottle of champagne.

PRESIDENT'S MEDAL: Outgoing President Bob Appleyard awards the first President's Medals for outstanding services to Yorkshire County Cricket Club to joint winners GEOFF HOLMES, extreme left, and VIVIEN STONE, who run the book-stall at Headingley Carnegie on behalf of the John Featherstone Memorial Foundation. *(Photo: SIMON WILKINSON.)*

PRESIDENT'S MEDAL: Incoming President Brian Close honours MOLLIE STAINES, a lifelong supporter who became the first woman to serve on the Yorkshire Committee. *(Photo VAUGHN RIDLEY.)*

ROSES CAP: Wicket-keeper/batsman Gerard Brophy, above right, will always remember the 2008 *Roses* match at Headingley Carnegie for the award of his county cap by skipper Darren Gough. Extreme left is Jacques Rudolph, Yorkshire Vice-Captain in 2009. BELOW: Consolation for injured batsman Andrew Gale, left, comes at Scarborough when he is capped in company with leg-spinning all-rounder Adil Rashid.

CHIP OFF THE OLD BLOCK: Jonathan Bairstow, promising wicket-keeper/batsman son of David, receives his *Wisden* Schools Cricketer of the Year 2008 Trophy and Book.
BELOW: The player of two halves. *(Photos: VAUGHN RIDLEY.)*

DIGGING FOR VICTORY: Geoffrey Boycott, of the YCCC Management Board, cuts the first sod for the installation of the new Headingley Carnegie drainage system and complete relaying of the outfield. Geoffrey is flanked by, left to right, Jacques Rudolph, Yorkshire Vice-Captain in 2009; Brian Close, Yorkshire President, and Anthony McGrath, Yorkshire Captain.

YORKSHIRE — 1909

Back row, left to right: C H Hardisty, W E Bates, J T Newstead, J W Rothery, H Myers and J Hoyland (Scorer).
Front row: W H Wilkinson, S Haigh, G H Hirst, Lord Hawke (Captain), D Hunter, D Denton and W Rhodes.
(Photo: RON DEATON Archive.)

PLAYER TO WATCH: Steven Patterson, who has played cricket on the slopes of Everest, made the most of his limited first-team opportunities with Yorkshire last season, taking 11 Championship wickets at a respectable average of 25.36. The 25-year-old paceman is eager to get his Yorkshire career on a firm footing— and to go on climbing up the national averages.

ARCH DOUBLE: Anthony McGrath accepts the 2008 ARCH Trophy in Abu Dhabi on behalf of winners Yorkshire and, below, skipper Azeem Rafiq and Ian Dews, Director of Cricket Operations, lift the Academy ARCH Trophy later in the year.

SEASON-BY-SEASON RECORD OF ALL FIRST-CLASS
MATCHES PLAYED BY YORKSHIRE 1863-2008

Season	Played	Won	Lost	Drawn	Abd§	Season	Played	Won	Lost	Drawn	Abd§
1863	4	2	1	1		1921	30	17	5	8	
1864	7	2	4	1		1922	33	20	2	11	
1865	9	—	7	2		1923	35	26	1	8	
1866	3	—	2	1		1924	35	18	4	13	
1867	7	7	—	—		1925	36	22	—	14	
1868	7	4	3	—		1926	35	14	—	21	1
1869	5	4	1	—		1927	34	11	3	20	1
1870	7	6	—	1		1928	32	9	—	23	
1871	7	3	3	1		1929	35	11	2	22	
1872	10	2	7	1		1930	34	13	3	18	2
1873	13	7	5	1		1931	33	17	1	15	1
1874	14	10	3	1		1932	32	21	2	9	2
1875	12	6	4	2		1933	36	21	5	10	
1876	12	5	3	4		1934	35	14	7	14	
1877	14	2	7	5		1935	36	24	2	10	
1878	20	10	7	3		1935-6	3	1	—	2	
1879	17	7	5	5		1936	35	14	2	19	
1880	20	6	8	6		1937	34	22	3	9	1
1881	20	11	6	3		1938	36	22	2	12	
1882	24	11	9	4		1939	34	23	4	7	1
1883	19	10	2	7		1945	2	—	—	2	
1884	20	10	6	4		1946	31	20	1	10	
1885	21	8	3	10		1947	32	10	9	13	
1886	21	5	8	8		1948	31	11	6	14	
1887	20	6	5	9		1949	33	16	3	14	
1888	20	7	7	6		1950	34	16	6	12	1
1889	16	3	11	2	1	1951	35	14	3	18	
1890	20	10	4	6		1952	34	17	3	14	
1891	17	5	11	1	2	1953	35	7	7	21	
1892	19	6	6	7		1954	35	16	3	16*	
1893	23	15	5	3		1955	33	23	6	4	
1894	28	18	6	4	1	1956	35	11	7	17	
1895	31	15	10	6		1957	34	16	5	13	1
1896	32	17	6	9		1958	33	10	8	15	2
1897	30	14	7	9		1959	35	18	8	9	
1898	30	18	3	9		1960	38	19	7	12	
1899	34	17	4	13		1961	39	19	5	15	
1900	32	19	1	12		1962	37	16	5	16	
1901	35	23	2	10	1	1963	33	14	4	15	
1902	31	15	3	13	1	1964	33	12	4	17	
1903	31	16	5	10		1965	33	12	4	17	
1904	32	10	2	20	1	1966	32	16	6	10	1
1905	33	21	4	8		1967	31	16	5	10	2
1906	33	19	6	8		1968	32	13	4	15	
1907	31	14	5	12	2	1969	29	4	7	18	
1908	33	19	—	14		1970	26	10	5	11	
1909	30	12	5	13		1971	27	5	8	14	
1910	31	11	8	12		1972	21	4	5	12	1
1911	32	16	9	7		1973	22	3	5	14*	
1912	35	14	3	18	1	1974	22	6	7	9	1
1913	32	16	5	11		1975	21	11	1	9	
1914	31	16	4	11	2	1976	22	7	7	8	
1919	31	12	5	14		1977	23	7	5	11	1
1920	30	17	6	7		1978	24	10	3	11	1

Season	Played	Won	Lost	Drawn	Abd§	Season	Played	Won	Lost	Drawn	Abd§
1979	22	6	3	13	1	1995	20	8	8	4	
1980	24	5	4	15		1995-6	2	2	—	—	
1981	24	5	9	10		1996	19	8	5	6	
1982	22	5	1	16	1	1997	20	7	4	9	
1983	23	1	5	17	1	1998	19	9	3	7	
1984	24	5	4	15		1999	17	8	6	3	
1985	25	3	4	18	1	2000	18	7	4	7	
1986	25	4	6	15		2001	16	9	3	4	
1986-7	1	—	—	1		2002	16	2	8	6	
1987	24	7	4	13	1	2003	17	4	5	8	
1988	24	5	6	13		2004	16	3	4	9	
1989	22	3	9	10		2005	17	6	1	10	
1990	24	5	9	10		2006	16	3	6	7	
1991	24	4	6	14		2007	17	5	4	8	
1991-2	1	—	1	—		2008	16	2	5	9	
1992	22	4	6	12	1						
1992-3	1	—	—	1			3463	1466	635	1362	38
1993	19	6	4	9							
1994	20	7	6	7		*Includes one tie in each season.					

§ All these matches were abandoned without a ball being bowled, except Yorkshire v Kent at Harrogate, 1904, which was abandoned under Law 9. The two in 1914 and the one in 1939 were abandoned due to war. All these matches are excluded from the total played.

Of the 1,466 matches won, 504 have been by an innings margin, 81 by 200 runs or more, and 129 by 10 wickets. Of the 635 matches lost, 107 have been by an innings margin, 12 by 200 runs or more, and 33 by 10 wickets.

ANALYSIS OF RESULTS VERSUS ALL
FIRST-CLASS TEAMS 1863-2008
COUNTY CHAMPIONSHIP

Opponents	Played	Won	Lost	Drawn	Tied
Derbyshire	201	101	19	81	—
Durham	22	11	6	5	—
Essex	156	82	25	49	—
Glamorgan	109	52	13	44	—
Gloucestershire	198	100	43	55	—
Hampshire	157	71	19	67	—
Kent	196	84	38	74	—
Lancashire	247	74	50	123	—
Leicestershire	164	83	15	65	1
Middlesex	225	78	54	92	1
Northamptonshire	138	65	26	47	—
Nottinghamshire	240	86	46	108	—
Somerset	159	87	18	54	—
Surrey	238	85	67	86	—
Sussex	189	82	32	75	—
Warwickshire	176	78	30	68	—
Worcestershire	134	66	21	47	—
Cambridgeshire	8	3	4	1	—
Totals	2957	1288	526	1141	2

OTHER FIRST-CLASS MATCHES

Opponents	Played	Won	Lost	Drawn	Tied
Derbyshire	2	1	1	0	—
Essex	2	2	0	0	—
Hampshire	1	0	0	1	—
Lancashire	12	5	3	4	—
Leicestershire	2	1	1	0	—
Middlesex	1	1	0	0	—
Nottinghamshire	2	1	1	0	—
Surrey	1	0	0	1	—
Sussex	2	0	0	2	—
Warwickshire	2	0	0	2	—
Totals	**27**	**11**	**6**	**10**	**—**
Australians	55	6	19	30	—
Indians	14	5	1	8	—
New Zealanders	10	2	0	8	—
Pakistanis	4	1	0	3	—
South Africans	17	1	3	13	—
Sri Lankans	3	0	0	3	—
West Indians	17	3	7	7	—
Zimbabweans	2	0	1	1	—
Bangladesh 'A'	1	1	0	0	—
India 'A'	1	0	0	1	—
Pakistan 'A'	1	1	0	0	—
South Africa 'A'	1	0	0	1	—
Totals	**126**	**20**	**31**	**75**	**—**
Cambridge University	87	42	17	28	—
Canadians	1	1	0	0	—
Combined Services	1	0	0	1	—
England XI's	6	1	2	3	—
Hon. M.B. Hawke's XI	1	0	1	0	—
International XI	1	1	0	0	—
Ireland	3	3	0	0	—
Jamaica	3	1	0	2	—
Liverpool and District*	3	2	1	0	—
Loughborough UCCE	1	1	—	—	—
MCC	153	54	39	60	—
Mashonaland	1	1	0	0	—
Matabeleland	1	1	0	0	—
Minor Counties	1	1	0	0	—
Oxford University	44	21	3	20	—
Philadelphians	1	0	0	1	—
Rest of England	16	4	5	7	—
Royal Air Force	1	0	0	1	—
Scotland**	11	7	0	4	—
South of England	2	1	0	1	—
C. I. Thornton's XI	5	2	0	3	—
United South of England	1	1	0	0	—
Western Province	2	0	1	1	—
Windward Islands	1	0	0	1	—
I Zingari	6	2	3	1	—
Totals	**353**	**147**	**72**	**134**	**—**
Grand Totals	**3463**	**1466**	**635**	**1360**	**2**

*Matches played in 1889, 1891, 1892 and 1893 are excluded. **Match played in 1878 is included

ABANDONED MATCHES (38)

1889	v. MCC at Lord's
1891 (2)	v. MCC at Lord's
	v. MCC at Scarborough
1894	v. Kent at Bradford
1901	v. Surrey at The Oval
1902	v. Leicestershire at Leicester (AR)
1904	v. Kent at Harrogate (Law 9 — now Law 10)
1907 (2)	v. Derbyshire at Sheffield
	v. Nottinghamshire at Huddersfield
1912	v. Surrey at Sheffield
1914 (2)	v. England at Harrogate (due to war)
	v. MCC at Scarborough (due to war)
1926	v. Nottinghamshire at Leeds
1927	v. Kent at Bradford
1930 (2)	v. Derbyshire at Chesterfield*
	v. Northamptonshire at Harrogate*
1931	v. Sussex at Hull
1932 (2)	v. Derbyshire at Chesterfield
	v. Kent at Sheffield
1937	v. Cambridge University at Bradford
1939	v. MCC at Scarborough (due to war)
1950	v. Cambridge University at Cambridge
1957	v. West Indians at Bradford
1958 (2)	v. Nottinghamshire at Hull
	v. Worcestershire at Bradford
1966	v. Oxford University at Oxford
1967 (2)	v. Leicestershire at Leeds
	v. Lancashire at Manchester
1972	v. Australians at Bradford
1974	v. Hampshire at Bournemouth
1977	v. Gloucestershire at Bristol
1978	v. Pakistan at Bradford
1979	v. Nottinghamshire at Sheffield (AP)
1982	v. Nottinghamshire at Harrogate
1983	v. Middlesex at Lord's
1985	v. Essex at Sheffield (AP)
1987	v. Sussex at Hastings
1992	v. Oxford University at Oxford

*Consecutive matches

ANALYSIS OF RESULTS ON GROUNDS IN YORKSHIRE USED IN 2008

FIRST-CLASS MATCHES

Ground	Played	Won	Lost	Drawn	Tied
Leeds Headingley 1891-2008	397	154 (38.8%)	71 (17.9%)	172 (43.3%)	0 (0.0%)
Scarborough North Marine Road 1874-2008	237	94 (39.7%)	34 (14.3%)	109 (46.0%)	0 (0.0%)

HIGHEST MATCH AGGREGATES – OVER 1350 RUNS

Runs	Wkts	
1665	33	Yorkshire (351 and 481) lost to Warwickshire (601:9 dec and 232:4) by 6 wkts at Birmingham, 2002
1473	17	Yorkshire (600:4 dec. and 231:3 dec.) drew with Worcestershire (453:5 dec. and 189:5) at Scarborough, 1995.
1442	29	Yorkshire (501:6 dec. and 244:6 dec.) beat Lancashire (403:7 dec. and 294) by 48 runs at Scarborough, 1991.
1439	32	Yorkshire (536:8 dec. and 205:7 dec.) beat Glamorgan (482: 7 dec. and 216) by 43 runs at Cardiff, 1996.
1417	33	Yorkshire (422 and 193:7) drew with Glamorgan (466 and 336:6 dec) at Colwyn Bay, 2003
1406	37	Yorkshire (354 and 341:8) drew with Derbyshire (406 and 305:9 dec) at Derby, 2004
1400	32	Yorkshire (299 and 439: 4 dec.) drew with Hampshire (296 and 366:8) at Southampton, 2007
1393	35	Yorkshire (331 and 278) lost to Kent (377 and 407:5 dec) by 175 runs at Maidstone, 1994.
1390	34	Yorkshire (431: 8 dec. and 265:7) beat Hampshire (429 and 265) by 3 wkts at Southampton, 1995.
1376	33	Yorkshire (531 and 158:3) beat Lancashire (373 and 314) by 7 wkts at Leeds, 2001
1376	20	Yorkshire (677: 7 dec.) drew with Durham (518 and 181:3 dec.) at Leeds, 2006
1374	36	Yorkshire (594: 9 dec. and 266:7 dec.) beat Surrey (344 and 170) by 346 runs at The Oval, 2007
1373	36	Yorkshire (520 and 114:6) drew with Derbyshire (216 and 523) at Derby, 2005
1364	35	Yorkshire (216 and 433) lost to Warwickshire (316 and 399:5 dec.) by 66 runs at Birmingham, 2006
1359	25	Yorkshire (561 and 138:3 dec.) drew with Derbyshire (412:4 dec. and 248:8) at Sheffield, 1996.
1353	18	Yorkshire (377:2 dec. and 300:6) beat Derbyshire (475:7 dec. and 201:3 dec.) by 4 wkts at Scarborough, 1990.

LOWEST MATCH AGGREGATES – UNDER 225 RUNS IN A COMPLETED MATCH

Runs	Wkts	
165	30	Yorkshire (46 and 37:0) beat Nottinghamshire (24 and 58 by 10 wkts at Sheffield, 1888.
175	29	Yorkshire (104) beat Essex (30 and 41) by an innings and 33 runs at Leyton, 1901.
182	15	Yorkshire (4:0 dec. and 88.5) beat Northamptonshire (4:0 dec. and 86) by 5 wkts at Bradford, 1931.
193	29	Yorkshire (99) beat Worcestershire (43 and 51) by an innings and 5 runs at Bradford, 1900.
219	30	Yorkshire (113) beat Nottinghamshire (71 and 35) by an innings and 7 runs at Nottingham, 1881.
222	32	Yorkshire (98 and 14:2) beat Gloucestershire (68 and 42) by 8 wkts at Gloucester, 1924.
223	40	Yorkshire (58 and 51) lost to Lancashire (64 and 50) by 5 runs at Manchester, 1893.

LOWEST MATCH AGGREGATES – UNDER 325 RUNS
IN A MATCH IN WHICH ALL 40 WICKETS FELL

Runs	Wkts	
223	40	Yorkshire (58 and 51) lost to Lancashire (64 and 50) by 5 runs at Manchester, 1893.
288	40	Yorkshire (55 and 68) lost to Lancashire (89 and 76) by 42 runs at Sheffield, 1872.
295	40	Yorkshire (71 and 63) lost to Surrey (56 and 105) by 27 runs at The Oval, 1886.
303	40	Yorkshire (109 and 77) beat Middlesex (63 and 54) by 69 runs at Lord's, 1891.
318	40	Yorkshire (96 and 96) beat Lancashire (39 and 87) by 66 runs at Manchester, 1874.
318	40	Yorkshire (94 and 104) beat Northamptonshire (61 and 59) by 78 runs at Bradford, 1955.
319	40	Yorkshire (84 and 72) lost to Derbyshire (106 and 57) by 7 runs at Derby, 1878.
320	40	Yorkshire (98 and 91) beat Surrey (72 and 59) by 58 runs at Sheffield, 1893.
321	40	Yorkshire (88 and 37) lost to I Zingari (103 and 93) by 71 runs at Scarborough, 1877.
321	40	Yorkshire (80 and 67) lost to Derbyshire (129 and 45) by 27 runs at Sheffield, 1879.

LARGE MARGINS OF VICTORY – BY AN INNINGS
AND OVER 250 RUNS

Inns and 397 runs	Yorkshire (548:4 dec.) beat Northamptonshire (58 and 93) at Harrogate, 1921
Inns and 387 runs	Yorkshire (662) beat Derbyshire (118 and 157) at Chesterfield, 1898.
Inns and 343 runs	Yorkshire (673:8 dec) beat Northamptonshire (184 and 146) at Leeds, 2003
Inns and 321 runs	Yorkshire (437) beat Leicestershire (58 and 58) at Leicester, 1908.
Inns and 314 runs	Yorkshire (356:8 dec) beat Northamptonshire (27 and 15) at Northampton, 1908. (Yorkshire's first match v. Northamptonshire).
Inns and 313 runs	Yorkshire (555:1 dec) beat Essex (78 and 164) at Leyton, 1932.
Inns and 307 runs	Yorkshire (681:5 dec.) beat Sussex (164 and 210) at Sheffield, 1897.
Inns and 302 runs	Yorkshire (660) beat Leicestershire (165 and 193) at Leicester, 1896.
Inns and 301 runs	Yorkshire (499) beat Somerset (125 and 73) at Bath, 1899.
Inns and 294 runs	Yorkshire (425:7 dec.) beat Gloucestershire (47 and 84) at Bristol, 1964.

LARGE MARGINS OF VICTORY – BY AN INNINGS
AND OVER 250 RUNS *(Continued)*

Inns and 284 runs   Yorkshire (467:7 dec) beat Leicestershire (111 and 72)
at Bradford, 1932.

Inns and 282 runs   Yorkshire (481:8 dec) beat Derbyshire (106 and 93)
at Huddersfield, 1901.

Inns and 280 runs   Yorkshire (562) beat Leicestershire (164 and 118)
at Dewsbury, 1903.

Inns and 271 runs   Yorkshire (460) beat Hampshire (128 and 61) at Hull, 1900.

Inns and 271 runs   Yorkshire (495:5 dec) beat Warwickshire (99 and 125)
at Huddersfield, 1922.

Inns and 266 runs   Yorkshire (352) beat Cambridgeshire (40 and 46)
at Hunslet, 1869.

Inns and 260 runs   Yorkshire (521: 7dec.) beat Worcestershire (129 and 132)
at Leeds, 2007.

Inns and 258 runs   Yorkshire (404:2 dec) beat Glamorgan (78 and 68)
at Cardiff, 1922.
(Yorkshire's first match v. Glamorgan).

Inns and 256 runs   Yorkshire (486) beat Leicestershire (137 and 93)
at Sheffield, 1895.

Inns and 251 runs   Yorkshire (550) beat Leicestershire (154 and 145)
at Leicester, 1933.

LARGE MARGINS OF VICTORY – BY OVER 300 RUNS

389 runs   Yorkshire (368 and 280:1 dec) beat Somerset (125 and 134)
at Bath, 1906.

370 runs   Yorkshire (194 and 274) beat Hampshire (62 and 36)
at Leeds, 1904.

351 runs   Yorkshire (280 and 331) beat Northamptonshire (146 and 114)
at Northampton, 1947.

346 runs   Yorkshire (594: 9 dec. and 266: 7 dec.) beat Surrey (344 and 179)
at The Oval, 2007.

328 runs   Yorkshire (186 and 318:1 dec) beat Somerset (43 and 133)
at Bradford, 1930.

328 runs   Yorkshire (280 and 277:7 dec) beat Glamorgan (104 and 105)
at Swansea, 2001.

320 runs   Yorkshire (331 and 353:9 dec) beat Durham (150 and 214)
at Chester-le-Street, 2004

308 runs   Yorkshire (89 and 420) beat Warwickshire (72 and 129)
at Birmingham, 1921.

LARGE MARGINS OF VICTORY – BY 10 WICKETS
(WITH OVER 100 RUNS SCORED IN THE 4th INNINGS)

4th Innings

167:0 wkt	Yorkshire (247 and 167:0) beat Northamptonshire 233 and 180) at Huddersfield, 1948.
147:0 wkt	Yorkshire (381 and 147:0) beat Middlesex (384 and 142) at Lord's, 1896.
142:0 wkt	Yorkshire (304 and 142:0) beat Sussex (254 and 188) at Bradford, 1887.
139:0 wkt	Yorkshire (163:9 dec and 139:0) beat Nottinghamshire (234 and 67) at Leeds, 1932.
138:0 wkt	Yorkshire (293 and 138:0) beat Hampshire (251 and 179) at Southampton, 1897.
132:0 wkt	Yorkshire (328 and 132:0) beat Northamptonshire (281 and 175) at Leeds, 2005
127:0 wkt	Yorkshire (258 and 127:0) beat Cambridge University (127 and 257) at Cambridge, 1930.
119:0 wkt	Yorkshire (109 and 119:0) beat Essex (108 and 119) at Leeds, 1931.
118:0 wkt	Yorkshire (121 and 118:0) beat MCC (125 and 113) at Lord's, 1883.
116:0 wkt	Yorkshire (147 and 116:0) beat Hampshire (141 and 120) at Bournemouth, 1930.
114:0 wkt	Yorkshire (135 and 114:0) beat Hampshire (71 and 176) at Bournemouth, 1948.

HEAVY DEFEATS – BY AN INNINGS
AND OVER 250 RUNS

Inns and 272 runs	Yorkshire (78 and 186) lost to Surrey (536) at The Oval, 1898.
Inns and 261 runs	Yorkshire (247 and 89) lost to Sussex (597: 8 dec.) at Hove, 2007.
Inns and 255 runs	Yorkshire (125 and 144) lost to All England XI (524) at Sheffield, 1865.

HEAVY DEFEATS – BY OVER 300 RUNS

324 runs	Yorkshire (247 and 204) lost to Gloucestershire (291 and 484) at Cheltenham, 1994.
305 runs	Yorkshire (119 and 51) lost to Cambridge University (312 and 163) at Cambridge, 1906.

HEAVY DEFEATS – BY 10 WICKETS
(WITH OVER 100 RUNS SCORED IN THE 4th INNINGS)

4th Innings

148:0 wkt	Yorkshire (83 and 216) lost to Lancashire (154 and 148:0) at Manchester, 1875.
119:0 wkt	Yorkshire (92 and 109) lost to Nottinghamshire (86 and 119:0 wkt) at Leeds, 1989.
108:0 wkt	Yorkshire (236 and 107) lost to Hampshire (236 and 108:0 wkt) at Southampton, 2008
100:0 wkt	Yorkshire (95 and 91) lost to Gloucestershire (88 and 100:0) at Bristol, 1956.

NARROW VICTORIES – BY 1 WICKET

Yorkshire (70 and 91:9) beat Cambridgeshire (86 and 74) at Wisbech, 1867.
Yorkshire (91 and 145:9) beat MCC (73 and 161) at Lord's, 1870.
Yorkshire (265 and 154:9) beat Derbyshire (234 and 184) at Derby, 1897.
Yorkshire (177 and 197:9) beat MCC (188 and 185) at Lord's, 1899.
Yorkshire (391 and 241:9) beat Somerset (349 and 281) at Taunton, 1901.
Yorkshire (239 and 168:9) beat MCC (179 and 226) at Scarborough, 1935.
Yorkshire (152 and 90:9) beat Worcestershire (119 and 121) at Leeds, 1946.
Yorkshire (229 and 175:9) beat Glamorgan (194 and 207) at Bradford, 1960.
Yorkshire (265.9 dec and 191:9) beat Worcestershire (227 and 227) at Worcester, 1961.
Yorkshire (329:6 dec and 167:9) beat Essex (339.9 dec and 154) at Scarborough, 1979.
Yorkshire (Innings forfeited and 251:9 beat Sussex (195 and 55.1 dec) at Leeds, 1986.
Yorkshire (314 and 150:9) beat Essex (200 and 261) at Scarborough, 1998.

NARROW VICTORIES – BY 5 RUNS OR LESS

By 1 run	Yorkshire (228 and 214) beat Middlesex (206 and 235) at Bradford, 1976.
By 1 run	Yorkshire (383 and inns forfeited) beat Loughborough UCCE (93: 3 dec. and 289) at Leeds, 2007.
By 2 runs	Yorkshire (108 and 122) beat Nottinghamshire (56 and 172) at Nottingham, 1870.
By 2 runs	Yorkshire (304:9 dec and 135) beat Middlesex (225:2 dec and 212) at Leeds, 1985.
By 3 runs	Yorkshire (446:9 dec and 172:4 dec) beat Essex (300:3 dec and 315) at Colchester, 1991.
By 5 runs	Yorkshire (271 and 147:6 dec) beat Surrey (198 and 215) at Sheffield, 1950.
By 5 runs	Yorkshire (151 and 176) beat Hampshire (165 and 157) at Bradford, 1962.
By 5 runs	Yorkshire (376:4 and 106) beat Middlesex (325:8 and 152) at Lord's, 1975
By 5 runs	Yorkshire (323:5 dec and inns forfeited) beat Somerset (inns forfeited and 318) at Taunton, 1986.

NARROW DEFEATS – BY 1 WICKET

Yorkshire (224 and 210) lost to Australian Imperial Forces XI (265 and 170:9) at Leeds, 1985.
Yorkshire (101 and 159) lost to Warwickshire (45 and 216:9) at Scarborough, 1934.
Yorkshire (239 and 184:9 dec.) lost to Warwickshire (125 and 302:9) at Birmingham, 1983.
Yorkshire (289 and 153) lost to Surrey (250:2 dec and 193:9) at Guildford, 1991.
Yorkshire (341 and Inns forfeited) lost to Surrey (39:1 dec and 306:9) at Bradford, 1992.

NARROW DEFEATS – BY 5 RUNS OR LESS

By 1 run	Yorkshire (135 and 297) lost to Essex (139 and 294) at Huddersfield, 1897.
By 1 run	Yorkshire (159 and 232) lost to Gloucestershire (164 and 228) at Bristol, 1906.
By 1 run	Yorkshire (126 and 137) lost to Worcestershire (101 and 163) at Worcester, 1968.
By 1 run	Yorkshire (366 and 217) lost to Surrey (409 and 175) at The Oval, 1995.
By 2 runs	Yorkshire (172 and 107) lost to Gloucestershire (157 and 124) at Sheffield, 1913.
By 2 runs	Yorkshire (179:9 dec and 144) lost to MCC (109 and 216) at Lord's, 1957.
By 3 runs	Yorkshire (126 and 181) lost to Sussex (182 and 128) at Sheffield, 1883.
By 3 runs	Yorkshire (160 and 71) lost to Lancashire (81 and 153) at Huddersfield, 1889.
By 3 runs	Yorkshire (134 and 158) lost to Nottinghamshire (200 and 95) at Leeds, 1923.
By 4 runs	Yorkshire (169 and 193) lost to Middlesex (105 and 261) at Bradford, 1920.
By 5 runs	Yorkshire (58 and 51) lost to Lancashire (64 and 50) at Manchester, 1893.
By 5 runs	Yorkshire (119 and 115) lost to Warwickshire (167 and 72) at Bradford, 1969.

HIGH FOURTH INNINGS SCORES – 300 AND OVER

By Yorkshire

To Win:	406:4	beat Leicestershire by 6 wkts at Leicester, 2005.
	400:4	beat Leicestershire by 6 wkts at Scarborough, 2005
	331:8	beat Middlesex by 2 wkts at Lord's, 1910.
	327:6	beat Nottinghamshire by 4 wkts at Nottingham, 1990.*
	323:5	beat Nottinghamshire by 5 wkts at Nottingham, 1977.
	318:3	beat Glamorgan by 7 wkts at Middlesbrough, 1976.
	309:7	beat Somerset by 3 wkts at Taunton, 1984.
	305:8	beat Nottinghamshire by 2 wkts at Worksop, 1982.
	305:3	beat Lancashire by 7 wickets at Manchester, 1994.
	304:4	beat Derbyshire by 6 wkts at Chesterfield, 1959.
	300:4	beat Derbyshire by 6 wkts at Chesterfield, 1981.
	300:6	beat Derbyshire by 4 wkts at Scarborough, 1990.*
To Draw:	341:8	(set 358) drew with Derbyshire at Derby, 2004.
	316:6	(set 326) drew with Oxford University at Oxford, 1948.
	316:7	(set 320) drew with Somerset at Scarborough, 1990.
To Lose:	433	(set 500) lost to Warwickshire by 66 runs at Birmingham, 2006
	380	(set 406) lost to MCC. by 25 runs at Lord's, 1937.
	324	(set 485) lost to Northamptonshire by 160 runs at Luton, 1994.
	322	(set 344) lost to Middlesex by 21 runs at Lord's, 1996.
	309	(set 400) lost to Middlesex by 90 runs at Lord's 1878.

Consecutive matches

By Opponents:

To Win:	404:5	Hampshire won by 5 wkts at Leeds, 2006
	392:4	Gloucestershire won by 6 wkts at Bristol, 1948.
	354:5	Nottinghamshire won by 5 wkts at Scarborough, 1990.
	337:4	Worcestershire won by 6 wkts at Kidderminster, 2007.
	334:6	Glamorgan won by 4 wkts at Harrogate, 1955.
	329:5	Worcestershire won by 5 wkts at Worcester, 1979.
	306:9	Surrey won by 1 wkt at Bradford, 1992.
	305:7	Lancashire won by 3 wkts at Manchester, 1980.
	302:9	Warwickshire won by 1 wkt at Birmingham, 1983.

HIGH FOURTH INNINGS SCORES – 300 AND OVER *(Continued)*

By Opponents:

To Draw:			
	366:8	(set 443) Hampshire drew at Southampton, 2007.	
	334:7	(set 339) MCC. drew at Scarborough, 1911.	
	322:9	(set 334) Middlesex drew at Leeds, 1988.	
	317:6	(set 355) Nottinghamshire drew at Nottingham, 1910.	
	300:9	(set 314) Northamptonshire drew at Northampton, 1990.	

To Lose:		
	370	(set 539) Leicestershire lost by 168 runs at Leicester, 2001
	319	(set 364) Gloucestershire lost by 44 runs at Leeds, 1987.
	318	(set 324) Somerset lost by 5 runs at Taunton, 1986.
	315	(set 319) Essex lost by 3 runs at Colchester, 1991.
	314	(set 334) Lancashire lost by 19 runs at Manchester, 1993.
	310	(set 417) Warwickshire lost by 106 runs at Scarborough, 1939.
	306	(set 413) Kent lost by 106 runs at Leeds, 1952.
	300	(set 330) Middlesex lost by 29 runs at Sheffield, 1930.

TIE MATCHES

Yorkshire (351:4 dec and 113) tied with Leicestershire (328 and 136) at Huddersfield, 1954.
Yorkshire (106:9 dec and 207) tied with Middlesex (102 and 211) at Bradford, 1973.

HIGHEST SCORES BY AND AGAINST YORKSHIRE

Yorkshire versus: —

	By Yorkshire:	**Against Yorkshire:**
Derbyshire:		
In Yorkshire:	570 at Leeds, 2005	491 at Bradford, 1949
Away:	662 at Chesterfield, 1898	523 at Derby, 2005
Durham:		
In Yorkshire:	677:7 dec. at Leeds, 2006	518 at Leeds, 2006
Away:	448 at Chester-le-Street, 2003	481 at Chester-le-Street, 2007
Essex:		
In Yorkshire:	512:9 dec. at Sheffield, 1928	622:8 dec. at Leeds, 2005
Away:	555:1 dec. at Leyton, 1932	521 at Leyton, 1905
Glamorgan:		
In Yorkshire:	580:9 dec at Scarborough, 2001	498 at Leeds, 1999
Away:	536:8 dec. at Cardiff, 1996	482:7 dec. at Cardiff, 1996
Gloucestershire:		
In Yorkshire:	504:7 dec. at Bradford, 1905	411 at Leeds, 1992
Away:	494 at Bristol, 1897	574 at Cheltenham, 1990
Hampshire:		
In Yorkshire:	493:1 dec. at Sheffield, 1939	456:2 dec. at Leeds, 1920
Away:	585:3 dec. at Portsmouth, 1920	521:8 dec. at Portsmouth, 1927
Kent:		
In Yorkshire:	550:9 dec. at Scarborough, 1995	486 at Scarborough, 2007
Away:	559 at Canterbury, 1887	580: 9 dec. at Maidstone, 1998
Lancashire:		
In Yorkshire:	590 at Bradford, 1887	517 at Leeds, 2007.
Away:	528:8 dec. at Manchester, 1939	537 at Manchester, 2005

Yorkshire versus: —

Leicestershire:	**By Yorkshire:**	**Against Yorkshire:**
In Yorkshire	562 { at Scarborough, 1901 / at Dewsbury, 1903	681:7 dec. at Bradford, 1996
Away:	660 at Leicester, 1896	425 at Leicester, 1906

Middlesex:

In Yorkshire:	575:7 dec. at Bradford, 1899	527 at Huddersfield, 1887
Away:	538:6 dec. at Lord's, 1925	488 at Lord's, 1899

Northamptonshire:

In Yorkshire:	673:8 dec. at Leeds, 2003	517:7 dec. at Scarborough, 1999
Away:	523:8 dec. at Wellingborough, 1949	531:4 at Northampton, 1996

Nottinghamshire:

In Yorkshire:	562 at Bradford, 1899	492:5 dec. at Sheffield, 1949
Away:	520:7 dec. at Nottingham, 1928	490 at Nottingham, 1897

Somerset:

In Yorkshire:	525:4 dec. at Leeds, 1953	630 at Leeds, 1901
Away:	589:5 dec at Bath, 2001	592 at Taunton, 1892

Surrey:

In Yorkshire:	582:7 dec. at Sheffield, 1935	510 at Leeds, 2002
Away:	704 at The Oval, 1899	560:6 dec. at The Oval, 1933

Sussex:

In Yorkshire:	681:5 dec. at Sheffield, 1897	566 at Sheffield, 1937
Away:	522:7 dec. at Hastings, 1911	597:8 dec. at Hove, 2007

Warwickshire:

In Yorkshire:	561:7 dec. at Scarborough, 2007	459 at Scarborough, 1994
Away:	887 at Birmingham, 1896	601:9 dec. at Birmingham, 2002
	(Highest score by a First-Class county)	

Worcestershire:

In Yorkshire:	600: 4 dec. at Scarborough, 1995	453:5 dec. at Scarborough, 1995
Away:	560:6 dec. at Worcester, 1928	456:8 at Worcester, 1904

Australians:

In Yorkshire:	377 at Sheffield, 1953	470 at Bradford, 1893

Indians:

In Yorkshire:	385 at Hull, 1911	490:5 dec. at Sheffield, 1946

New Zealanders:

In Yorkshire:	419 at Bradford, 1965	370:7 dec. at Bradford, 1949

Pakistanis:

In Yorkshire:	433:9 dec. at Sheffield, 1954	356 at Sheffield, 1954

South Africans:

In Yorkshire:	579 at Sheffield, 1951	454:8 dec at Sheffield, 1951

Sri Lankans:

In Yorkshire:	314:8 dec. at Leeds, 1991	422:8 dec. at Leeds, 1991

West Indians:

In Yorkshire:	312:5 dec. at Scarborough, 1973	426 at Scarborough, 1995

Zimbabweans:

In Yorkshire:	298:9 dec at Leeds, 1990	235 at Leeds, 2000

Cambridge University:

In Yorkshire:	359 at Scarborough, 1967	366 at Leeds, 1998
Away:	540 at Cambridge, 1938	425:7 at Cambridge, 1929

HIGHEST SCORES BY AND AGAINST YORKSHIRE *(Continued)*

Yorkshire versus: —

MCC:	By Yorkshire:	Against Yorkshire:
In Yorkshire:	557:8 dec. at Scarborough, 1933	478:8 at Scarborough, 1904
Away:	528:8 dec. at Lord's, 1919	488 at Lord's, 1919

Oxford University:

In Yorkshire:	209:7 at Leeds, 1998	260:7 dec. at Leeds, 1998
Away:	468:6 dec. at Oxford, 1978	422:9 dec. at Oxford, 1953

LOWEST SCORES BY AND AGAINST YORKSHIRE

Yorkshire versus:

Derbyshire:

	By Yorkshire:	Against Yorkshire:
In Yorkshire:	50 at Sheffield, 1894	20 at Sheffield, 1939
Away:	44 at Chesterfield, 1948	26 at Derby, 1880

Durham:

In Yorkshire:	93 at Leeds, 2003	125 at Harrogate, 1995
Away:	108 at Durham, 1992	74 at Chester-le-Street, 1998

Essex:

In Yorkshire:	31 at Huddersfield, 1935	52 at Harrogate, 1900
Away:	98 at Leyton, 1905	30 at Leyton, 1901

Glamorgan:

In Yorkshire:	83 at Sheffield, 1946	52 at Hull, 1926
Away:	92 at Swansea, 1956	48 at Cardiff, 1924

Gloucestershire:

In Yorkshire:	61 at Leeds, 1894	36 at Sheffield, 1903
Away:	35 at Bristol, 1959	42 at Gloucester, 1924

Hampshire:

In Yorkshire:	23 at Middlesbrough, 1965	36 at Leeds, 1904
Away:	96 at Bournemouth, 1971	36 at Southampton, 1898

Kent:

In Yorkshire:	30 at Sheffield, 1865	39 { at Sheffield, 1882 / at Sheffield, 1936
Away:	62 at Maidstone, 1889	63 at Canterbury, 1901

Lancashire:

In Yorkshire:	33 at Leeds, 1924	30 at Holbeck, 1868
Away:	51 { at Manchester, 1888 / at Manchester, 1893	39 at Manchester, 1874

Leicestershire:

	By Yorkshire:	Against Yorkshire:
In Yorkshire:	93 at Leeds, 1935	34 at Leeds, 1906
Away:	47 at Leicester, 1911	57 at Leicester, 1898

Middlesex:

In Yorkshire:	45 at Leeds, 1898	45 at Huddersfield, 1879
Away:	43 at Lord's, 1888	49 at Lord's in 1890

Northamptonshire:

In Yorkshire:	85 at Sheffield, 1919	51 at Bradford, 1920
Away	64 at Northampton, 1959	15 at Northampton, 1908 (and 27 in first innings)

269

Yorkshire versus:

Nottinghamshire:	**By Yorkshire:**	**Against Yorkshire:**
In Yorkshire:	32 at Sheffield, 1876	24 at Sheffield, 1888
Away:	43 at Nottingham, 1869	13 at Nottingham, 1901
	(second smallest total by a First-Class county)	

Somerset:
In Yorkshire:	73 at Leeds, 1895	43 at Bradford, 1930
Away:	83 at Wells, 1949	35 at Bath, 1898

Surrey:
In Yorkshire:	54 at Sheffield, 1873	31 at Holbeck, 1883
Away:	26 at The Oval, 1909	44 at The Oval, 1935

Sussex:
In Yorkshire:	61 at Dewsbury, 1891	20 at Hull, 1922
Away:	42 at Hove, 1922	24 at Hove, 1878

Warwickshire:
In Yorkshire:	49 at Huddersfield, 1951	35 at Sheffield, 1979
Away:	54 at Birmingham, 1964	35 at Birmingham, 1963

Worcestershire:
In Yorkshire:	62 at Bradford, 1907	24 at Huddersfield, 1903
Away:	72 at Worcester, 1977	65 at Worcester, 1925

Australians:
In Yorkshire:	48 at Leeds, 1893	23 at Leeds, 1902

Indians:
In Yorkshire:	146 at Bradford, 1959	66 at Harrogate, 1932

New Zealanders:
In Yorkshire:	189 at Harrogate, 1931	134 at Bradford, 1965

Pakistanis:
In Yorkshire:	137 at Bradford, 1962	150 at Leeds, 1967

South Africans:
In Yorkshire:	113 at Bradford, 1907	76 at Bradford, 1951

Sri Lankans:
In Yorkshire:	Have not been dismissed.	287:5 dec at Leeds, 1988
	Lowest is 184:1 dec at Leeds, 1991	

West Indians:
In Yorkshire:	50 at Harrogate, 1906	58 at Leeds, 1928

Zimbabweans:
In Yorkshire:	124 at Leeds, 2000	68 at Leeds, 2000

Cambridge University:
In Yorkshire:	110 at Sheffield, 1903	39 at Sheffield, 1903
Away:	51 at Cambridge, 1906	30 at Cambridge, 1928

MCC:
In Yorkshire:	46 { at Scarborough, 1876 at Scarborough, 1877	31 at Scarborough, 1877
Away:	44 at Lord's, 1880	27 at Lord's, 1902

Oxford University:
In Yorkshire:	Have not been dismissed.	
	Lowest is 115:8 at Harrogate, 1972	133 at Harrogate, 1972
Away:	141 at Oxford, 1949	46 at Oxford, 1956

INDIVIDUAL INNINGS OF 150 AND OVER

A complete list of all First-class Centuries up to and including 2007 is to be found in the 2008 edition

W BARBER (7)

162	v Middlesex	Sheffield	1932
168	v MCC	Lord's	1934
248	v Kent	Leeds	1934
191	v Sussex	Leeds	1935
255	v Surrey	Sheffield	1935
158	v Kent	Sheffield	1936
157	v Surrey	Sheffield	1938

M G BEVAN (2)

153*	v Surrey	The Oval	1995
160*	v Surrey	Middlesbrough	1996

H D BIRD (1)

181*	v Glamorgan	Bradford	1959

R J BLAKEY (3)

204*	v Gloucestershire	Leeds	1987
196	v Oxford University	Oxford	1991
223*	v Northamptonshire	Leeds	2003

G BLEWETT (1)

190	v Northamptonshire	Scarborough	1999

M W BOOTH (1)

210	v Worcestershire	Worcester	1911

G BOYCOTT (32)

165*	v Leicestershire	Scarborough	1963
151	v Middlesex	Leeds	1964
151*	v Leicestershire	Leicester	1964
177	v Gloucestershire	Bristol	1964
164	v Sussex	Hove	1966
220*	v Northamptonshire	Sheffield	1967
180*	v Warwickshire	Middlesbrough	1968
260*	v Essex	Colchester (Garrison Ground)	1970
169	v Nottinghamshire	Leeds	1971
233	v Essex	Colchester (Garrison Ground)	1971
182*	v Middlesex	Lord's	1971
169	v Lancashire	Sheffield	1971
151	v Leicestershire	Bradford	1971
204*	v Leicestershire	Leicester	1972
152*	v Worcestershire	Worcester	1975
175*	v Middlesex	Scarborough	1975
201*	v Middlesex	Lord's	1975
161*	v Gloucestershire	Leeds	1976
207*	v Cambridge University	Cambridge	1976
156*	v Glamorgan	Middlesbrough	1976
154	v Nottinghamshire	Nottingham	1977

271

151*	v Derbyshire	Leeds	1979
167	v Derbyshire	Chesterfield	1979
175*	v Nottinghamshire	Worksop	1979
154*	v Derbyshire	Scarborough	1980
159	v Worcestershire	Sheffield (Abbeydale Park)	1982
152*	v Warwickshire	Leeds	1982
214*	v Nottinghamshire	Worksop	1983
163	v Nottinghamshire	Bradford	1983
169*	v Derbyshire	Chesterfield	1983
153*	v Derbyshire	Harrogate	1984
184	v Worcestershire	Worcester	1985

J T BROWN (8)

168*	v Sussex	Huddersfield	1895
203	v Middlesex	Lord's	1896
311	v Sussex	Sheffield	1897
300	v Derbyshire	Chesterfield	1898
150	v Sussex	Hove	1898
168	v Cambridge University	Cambridge	1899
167	v Australians	Bradford	1899
192	v Derbyshire	Derby	1899

D BYAS (5)

153	v Nottinghamshire	Worksop	1991
156	v Essex	Chelmsford	1993
181	v Cambridge University	Cambridge	1995
193	v Lancashire	Leeds	1995
213	v Worcestershire	Scarborough	1995

D B CLOSE (5)

164	v Combined Services	Harrogate	1954
154	v Nottinghamshire	Nottingham	1959
198	v Surrey	The Oval	1960
184	v Nottinghamshire	Scarborough	1960
161	v Northamptonshire	Northampton	1963

D DENTON (11)

153*	v Australians	Bradford	1905
165	v Hampshire	Bournemouth	1905
172	v Gloucestershire	Bradford	1905
184	v Nottinghamshire	Nottingham	1909
182	v Derbyshire	Chesterfield	1910
200*	v Warwickshire	Birmingham	1912
182	v Gloucestershire	Bristol	1912
221	v Kent	Tunbridge Wells	1912
191	v Hampshire	Southampton	1912
168*	v Hampshire	Southampton	1914
209*	v Worcestershire	Worcester	1920

A W GALE (1)

150	v Surrey	The Oval	2008

196	v Worcestershire	Worcester	1934
163	v Surrey	Leeds	1936
161	v MCC	Lord's	1937
271*	v Derbyshire	Sheffield	1937
153	v Leicestershire	Hull	1937
180	v Cambridge University	Cambridge	1938
158	v Warwickshire	Birmingham	1939
280*	v Hampshire	Sheffield	1939
151	v Surrey	Leeds	1939
177	v Sussex	Scarborough	1939
183*	v Indians	Bradford	1946
171*	v Northamptonshire	Hull	1946
197	v Glamorgan	Swansea	1947
197	v Essex	Southend-on-Sea	1947
270*	v Hampshire	Bournemouth	1947
176*	v Sussex	Sheffield	1948
155	v Sussex	Hove	1948
167	v New Zealanders	Bradford	1949
201	v Lancashire	Manchester	1949
165	v Sussex	Hove	1949
269*	v Northamptonshire	Wellingborough	1949
156	v Essex	Colchester (Castle Park)	1950
153	v Nottinghamshire	Nottingham	1950
156	v South Africans	Sheffield	1951
151	v Surrey	The Oval	1951
194*	v Nottinghamshire	Nottingham	1951
152	v Lancashire	Leeds	1952
189	v Kent	Leeds	1952
178	v Somerset	Leeds	1953
163	v Combined Services	Harrogate	1954
194	v Nottinghamshire	Nottingham	1955

R A HUTTON (1)

189	v Pakistanis	Bradford	1971

R ILLINGWORTH (2)

150	v Essex	Colchester (Castle Park)	1959
162	v Indians	Sheffield	1959

Hon F S JACKSON (3)

160	v Gloucestershire	Sheffield	1898
155	v Middlesex	Bradford	1899
158	v Surrey	Bradford	1904

P A JAQUES (5)

243	v Hampshire	Southampton (Rose Bowl)	2004
173	v Glamorgan	Leeds	2004
176	v Northamptonshire	Leeds	2005
219	v Derbyshire	Leeds	2005
172	v Durham	Scarborough	2005

R KILNER (5)

169	v Gloucestershire	Bristol	1914
206*	v Derbyshire	Sheffield	1920
166	v Northamptonshire	Northampton	1921
150	v Northamptonshire	Harrogate	1921
150	v Middlesex	Lord's	1926

F LEE (1)

165	v Lancashire	Bradford	1887

D S LEHMANN (13)

177	v Somerset	Taunton	1997
163*	v Leicestershire	Leicester	1997
182	v Hampshire	Portsmouth	1997
200	v Worcestershire	Worcester	1998
187*	v Somerset	Bath	2001
252	v Lancashire	Leeds	2001
193	v Leicestershire	Leicester	2001
216	v Sussex	Arundel	2002
187	v Lancashire	Leeds	2002
150	v Warwickshire	Birmingham	2006
193	v Kent	Canterbury	2006
172	v Kent	Leeds	2006
339	v Durham	Leeds	2006

E I LESTER (5)

186	v Warwickshire	Scarborough	1949
178	v Nottinghamshire	Nottingham	1952
157	v Cambridge University	Hull	1953
150	v Oxford University	Oxford	1954
163	v Essex	Romford	1954

M LEYLAND (17)

191	v Glamorgan	Swansea	1926
204*	v Middlesex	Sheffield	1927
247	v Worcestershire	Worcester	1928
189*	v Glamorgan	Huddersfield	1928
211*	v Lancashire	Leeds	1930
172	v Middlesex	Sheffield	1930
186	v Derbyshire	Leeds	1930
189	v Middlesex	Sheffield	1932
153	v Leicestershire	Leicester (Aylestone Road)	1932
166	v Leicestershire	Bradford	1932
153*	v Hampshire	Bournemouth	1932
192	v Northamptonshire	Leeds	1933
210*	v Kent	Dover	1933
263	v Essex	Hull	1936
163*	v Surrey	Leeds	1936
167	v Worcestershire	Stourbridge	1937
180*	v Middlesex	Lord's	1939

E LOCKWOOD (1)

208	v Kent	Gravesend	1883

J D LOVE (4)

163	v Nottinghamshire	Bradford	1976
170*	v Worcestershire	Worcester	1979
161	v Warwickshire	Birmingham	1981
154	v Lancashire	Manchester	1981

F A LOWSON (10)

155	v Kent	Maidstone	1951
155	v Worcestershire	Bradford	1952
166	v Scotland	Glasgow	1953
259*	v Worcestershire	Worcester	1953
165	v Sussex	Hove	1954
164	v Essex	Scarborough	1954
150*	v Kent	Dover	1954
183*	v Oxford University	Oxford	1956
154	v Somerset	Taunton	1956
154	v Cambridge University	Cambridge	1957

R G LUMB (2)

159	v Somerset	Harrogate	1979
165*	v Gloucestershire	Bradford	1984

A McGRATH (6)

165	v Lancashire	Leeds	2002
174	v Derbyshire	Derby	2004
165*	v Leicestershire	Leicester	2005
173*	v Worcestershire	Leeds	2005
158	v Derbyshire	Derby	2005
188*	v Warwickshire	Birmingham	2007

D R MARTYN (1)

238	v Gloucestershire	Leeds	2003

A METCALFE (7)

151	v Northamptonshire	Luton	1986
151	v Lancashire	Manchester	1986
152	v MCC	Scarborough	1987
216*	v Middlesex	Leeds	1988
162	v Gloucestershire	Cheltenham	1990
150*	v Derbyshire	Scarborough	1990
194*	v Nottinghamshire	Nottingham	1990

A MITCHELL (7)

189	v Northamptonshire	Northampton	1926
176	v Nottinghamshire	Bradford	1930
177*	v Gloucestershire	Bradford	1932
150*	v Worcestershire	Worcester	1933
158	v MCC	Scarborough	1933
152	v Hampshire	Bradford	1934
181	v Surrey	Bradford	1934

F MITCHELL (2)

194	v Leicestershire	Leicester	1899
162*	v Warwickshire	Birmingham	1901

M D MOXON (14)

153	v Lancashire	Leeds	1983
153	v Somerset	Leeds	1985
168	v Worcestershire	Worcester	1985
191	v Northamptonshire	Scarborough	1989
162*	v Surrey	The Oval	1989
218*	v Sussex	Eastbourne	1990
200	v Essex	Colchester (Castle Park)	1991
183	v Gloucestershire	Cheltenham	1992
171*	v Kent	Leeds	1993
161*	v Lancashire	Manchester	1994
274*	v Worcestershire	Worcester	1994
203*	v Kent	Leeds	1995
213	v Glamorgan	Cardiff (Sophia Gardens)	1996
155	v Pakistan 'A'	Leeds	1997

E OLDROYD (5)

151*	v Glamorgan	Cardiff	1922
194	v Worcestershire	Worcester	1923
162*	v Glamorgan	Swansea	1928
168	v Glamorgan	Hull	1929
164*	v Somerset	Bath	1930

D E V PADGETT (1)

161*	v Oxford University	Oxford	1959

R PEEL (2)

158	v Middlesex	Lord's	1889
210*	v Warwickshire	Birmingham	1896

W RHODES (8)

196	v Worcestershire	Worcester	1904
201	v Somerset	Taunton	1905
199	v Sussex	Hove	1909
176	v Nottinghamshire	Harrogate	1912
152	v Leicestershire	Leicester (Aylestone Road)	1913
167*	v Nottinghamshire	Leeds	1920
267*	v Leicestershire	Leeds	1921
157	v Derbyshire	Leeds	1925

P E ROBINSON (2)

150*	v Derbyshire	Scarborough	1990
189	v Lancashire	Scarborough	1991

J W ROTHERY (1)

161	v Kent	Dover	1908

J A RUDOLPH (2)

220	v Warwickshire	Scarborough	2007
155	v Somerset	Taunton	2008

H RUDSTON (1)

164	v Leicestershire	Leicester (Aylestone Rd)	1904

J J SAYERS (1)

187	v Kent	Tunbridge Wells	2007

A B SELLERS (1)

204	v Cambridge University	Cambridge	1936

K SHARP (2)

173	v Derbyshire	Chesterfield	1984
181	v Gloucestershire	Harrogate	1986

P J SHARPE (4)

203*	v Cambridge University	Cambridge	1960
152	v Kent	Sheffield	1960
197	v Pakistanis	Leeds	1967
172*	v Glamorgan	Swansea	1971

G A SMITHSON (1)

169	v Leicestershire	Leicester	1947

W B STOTT (2)

181	v Essex	Sheffield	1957
186	v Warwickshire	Birmingham	1960

H SUTCLIFFE (39)

174	v Kent	Dover	1919
232	v Surrey	The Oval	1922
213	v Somerset	Dewsbury	1924
160	v Sussex	Sheffield	1924
255*	v Essex	Southend-on-Sea	1924
235	v Middlesex	Leeds	1925
206	v Warwickshire	Dewsbury	1925
171	v MCC	Scarborough	1925
200	v Leicestershire	Leicester (Aylestone Road)	1926
176	v Surrey	Leeds	1927
169	v Nottinghamshire	Bradford	1927
228	v Sussex	Eastbourne	1928
150	v Northamptonshire	Northampton	1929
150*	v Essex	Dewsbury	1930
173	v Sussex	Hove	1930
173*	v Cambridge University	Cambridge	1931
230	v Kent	Folkestone	1931
183	v Somerset	Dewsbury	1931
195	v Lancashire	Sheffield	1931
187	v Leicestershire	Leicester (Aylestone Road)	1931
153*	v Warwickshire	Hull	1932
313	v Essex	Leyton	1932
270	v Sussex	Leeds	1932
182	v Derbyshire	Leeds	1932
194	v Essex	Scarborough	1932
205	v Warwickshire	Birmingham	1933
177	v Middlesex	Bradford	1933

H SUTCLIFFE (Continued)

174	v Leicestershire	Leicester (Aylestone Road)	1933
152	v Cambridge University	Cambridge	1934
166	v Essex	Hull	1934
203	v Surrey	The Oval	1934
187*	v Worcestershire	Bradford	1934
200*	v Worcestershire	Sheffield	1935
212	v Leicestershire	Leicester (Aylestone Road)	1935
202	v Middlesex	Scarborough	1936
189	v Leicestershire	Hull	1937
165	v Lancashire	Manchester	1939
234*	v Leicestershire	Hull	1939
175	v Middlesex	Lord's	1939

W H H SUTCLIFFE (3)

171*	v Worcestershire	Worcester	1952
181	v Kent	Canterbury	1952
161*	v Glamorgan	Harrogate	1955

K TAYLOR (8)

168*	v Nottinghamshire	Nottingham	1956
159	v Leicestershire	Sheffield	1961
203*	v Warwickshire	Birmingham	1961
178*	v Oxford University	Oxford	1962
163	v Nottinghamshire	Leeds	1962
153	v Lancashire	Manchester	1964
160	v Australians	Sheffield	1964
162	v Worcestershire	Kidderminster	1967

T L TAYLOR (1)

156	v Hampshire	Harrogate	1901

J TUNNICLIFFE (2)

243	v Derbyshire	Chesterfield	1898
158	v Worcestershire	Worcester	1900

G ULYETT (1)

199*	v Derbyshire	Sheffield	1887

M P VAUGHAN (7)

183	v Glamorgan	Cardiff (Sophia Gardens)	1996
183	v Northamptonshire	Northampton	1996
161	v Essex	Ilford	1997
177	v Durham	Chester-le-Street	1998
151	v Essex	Chelmsford	1999
153	v Kent	Scarborough	1999
155*	v Derbyshire	Leeds	2000

E WAINWRIGHT (3)

171	v Middlesex	Lord's	1897
153	v Leicestershire	Leicester	1899
228	v Surrey	The Oval	1899

W WATSON (7)

153*	v Surrey	The Oval	1947
172	v Derbyshire	Scarborough	1948
162*	v Somerset	Leeds	1953
163	v Sussex	Sheffield	1955
174	v Lancashire	Sheffield	1955
214*	v Worcestershire	Worcester	1955
162	v Northamptonshire	Harrogate	1957

C WHITE (6)

181	v Lancashire	Leeds	1996
172*	v Worcestershire	Leeds	1997
186	v Lancashire	Manchester	2001
183	v Glamorgan	Scarborough	2001
161	v Leicestershire	Scarborough	2002
173*	v Derbyshire	Derby	2003

B B WILSON (2)

150	v Warwickshire	Birmingham	1912
208	v Sussex	Bradford	1914

J V WILSON (7)

157*	v Sussex	Leeds	1949
157	v Essex	Sheffield	1950
166*	v Sussex	Hull	1951
223*	v Scotland	Scarborough	1951
154	v Oxford University	Oxford	1952
230	v Derbyshire	Sheffield	1952
165	v Oxford University	Oxford	1956

M J WOOD (5)

200*	v Warwickshire	Leeds	1998
157	v Northamptonshire	Leeds	2003
207	v Somerset	Taunton	2003
155	v Hampshire	Scarborough	2003
202*	v Bangladesh 'A'	Leeds	2005

N W D YARDLEY (2)

177	v Derbyshire	Scarborough	1947
183*	v Hampshire	Leeds	1951

YOUNUS KHAN (2)

202*	v Hampshire	Southampton (Rose Bowl)	2007
217*	v Kent	Scarborough	2007

CENTURIES BY CURRENT PLAYERS

A complete list of all First-class Centuries up to and including 2007 is to be found in the 2008 edition

T T BRESNAN (2)

116	v Surrey	The Oval	2007
101*	v Warwickshire	Scarborough	2007

G L BROPHY (1)

100*	v Hampshire	Southampton	2007

A W GALE (4)

149	v Warwickshire	Scarborough	2006
138	v Hampshire	Leeds	2008
150	v Surrey	The Oval	2008
136	v Lancashire	Manchester	2008

A LYTH (1)

132	v Nottinghamshire	Nottingham	2008

A McGRATH (26)

101	v Kent	Canterbury	1996
137	v Hampshire	Harrogate	1996
105*	v Oxford University	Oxford	1997
141	v Worcestershire	Leeds	1997
142*	v Middlesex	Leeds	1999
133	v Kent	Canterbury	2000
116*	v Surrey	The Oval	2001
165	v Lancashire	Leeds	2002
127*	v Glamorgan	Colwyn Bay	2003
126	v Durham	Chester-le-Street	2004
174	v Derbyshire	Derby	2004
109	v Derbyshire	Leeds	2004
165*	v Leicestershire	Leicester	2005
133*	v Durham	Chester-le-Street	2005
134	v Derbyshire	Leeds	2005
173*	v Worcestershire	Leeds	2005
158	v Derbyshire	Derby	2005
123*	v Kent	Canterbury	2006
127	v Hampshire	Leeds	2006
140*	v Durham	Chester-le-Street	2006
102	v Lancashire	Manchester	2006
100	v Kent	Tunbridge Wells	2007
188*	v Warwickshire	Birmingham	2007
120	v Kent	Scarborough	2007
144	v Kent	Canterbury	2008
128	v Somerset	Scarborough	2008

R M PYRAH (1)

106	v Loughborough UCCE	Leeds	2007

CENTURIES BY CURRENT PLAYERS *(Continued)*

A U RASHID (2)

108	v Worcestershire	Kidderminster	2007
111	v Sussex	Hove	2008

J A RUDOLPH (9)

122	v Surrey	The Oval	2007
129*	v Worcestershire	Leeds	2007
111	v Durham	Chester-le-Street	2007
220	v Warwickshire	Scarborough	2007
104*	v Nottinghamshire	Leeds	2008
121	v Surrey	The Oval	2008
155	v Somerset	Taunton	2008
129	v Kent	Canterbury	2008
146	v Kent	Scarborough	2008

J J SAYERS (6)

104	v Leicestershire	Scarborough	2005
115	v Bangladesh 'A'	Leeds	2005
122*	v Middlesex	Scarborough	2006
149*	v Durham	Leeds	2007
123	v Worcestershire	Leeds	2007
187	v Kent	Tunbridge Wells	2007

M P VAUGHAN (20)

106*	v Oxford University	Oxford	1994
105	v Somerset	Bradford	1994
117	v Northamptonshire	Luton	1994
106	v Matebeleland	Bulawayo	1995/96
183	v Glamorgan	Cardiff	1996
135	v Surrey	Middlesbrough	1996
183	v Northamptonshire	Northampton	1996
109	v Oxford University	Oxford	1997
161	v Essex	Ilford	1997
105	v Lancashire	Manchester	1997
177	v Durham	Chester-le-Street	1998
107	v Middlesex	Lord's	1998
100	v Essex (1st inns)	Chelmsford	1999
151	v Essex (2nd inns)	Chelmsford	1999
153	v Kent	Scarborough	1999
155*	v Derbyshire	Leeds	2000
118	v Durham	Leeds	2000
133	v Northamptonshire	Leeds	2001
113	v Essex	Scarborough	2001
103	v Northamptonshire	Northampton	2003

D J WAINWRIGHT (1)

104*	v Sussex	Hove	2008

CENTURIES BY CURRENT PLAYERS *(Continued)*

C WHITE (19)

146	v Durham	Leeds	1993
108*	v Essex	Leeds	1994
107	v Leicestershire	Leicester	1995
110	v Northamptonshire	Sheffield	1995
107*	v Worcestershire	Scarborough	1995
181	v Lancashire	Leeds	1996
172*	v Worcestershire	Leeds	1997
104*	v Surrey	Leeds	1998
186	v Lancashire	Manchester	2001
183	v Glamorgan	Scarborough	2001
104	v Kent	Canterbury	2002
161	v Leicestershire	Scarborough	2002
173*	v Derbyshire	Derby	2003
135*	v Durham	Chester-le-Street	2003
110*	v Lancashire	Manchester	2005
104	v Sussex	Arundel	2006
116	v Lancashire	Manchester	2006
147	v Nottinghamshire	Leeds	2006
117	v Surrey	The Oval	2007

CENTURIES

(Including highest score)

112	H Sutcliffe	313 v Essex	at Leyton	1932
103	G Boycott	260* v Essex	at Colchester (Garrison Gd)	1970
85	L Hutton	280* v Hampshire	at Sheffield	1939
62	M Leyland	263 v Essex	at Hull	1936
61	D Denton	221 v Kent	at Tunbridge Wells	1912
60	P Holmes	315* v Middlesex	at Lord's	1925
56	G H Hirst	341 v Leicestershire	at Leicester (Aylestone Rd)	1905
46	W Rhodes	267* v Leicestershire	at Leeds	1921
41	M D Moxon	274* v Worcestershire	at Worcester	1994
39	A Mitchell	189 v Northamptonshire	at Northampton	1926
37	E Oldroyd	194 v Worcestershire	at Worcester	1923
34	J H Hampshire	183* v Sussex	at Hove	1971
33	D B Close	198 v Surrey	at The Oval	1960
30	F A Lowson	259* v Worcestershire	at Worcester	1953
29	D E V Padgett	161* v Oxford University	at Oxford	1959
29	J V Wilson	230 v Derbyshire	at Sheffield	1952
28	D Byas	213 v Worcestershire	at Scarborough	1995
27	W Barber	255 v Surrey	at Sheffield	1935
26	D S Lehmann	339 v Durham	at Leeds	2006
26	A McGrath	188* v Warwickshire	at Birmingham	2007
26	W Watson	214* v Worcestershire	at Worcester	1955
25	A A Metcalfe	216* v Middlesex	at Leeds	1988
24	E I Lester	186 v Warwickshire	at Scarborough	1949
23	J T Brown	311 v Sussex	at Sheffield	1897
23	P J Sharpe	203* v Cambridge University	at Cambridge	1960
22	R J Lumb	165* v Gloucestershire	at Bradford	1984
22	J Tunnicliffe	243 v Derbyshire	at Chesterfield	1898
21	Hon F S Jackson	160 v Gloucestershire	at Sheffield	1898

283

20	M P Vaughan	183	v Glamorgan	at Cardiff (Sophia Gardens)	1996
	and	183	v Northamptonshire	at Northampton	1996
19	C White	186	v Lancashire	at Manchester	2001
18	E Wainwright	228	v Surrey	at The Oval	1899
17	W B Stott	186	v Warwickshire	at Birmingham	1960
17	N W D Yardley	183*	v Hampshire	at Leeds	1951
16	K Taylor	203*	v Warwickshire	at Birmingham	1961
16	M J Wood	207	v Somerset	at Taunton	2003
15	R Kilner	206*	v Derbyshire	at Sheffield	1920
15	G Ulyett	199*	v Derbyshire	at Sheffield	1887
15	B B Wilson	208	v Sussex	at Bradford	1914
14	R Illingworth	162	v Indians	at Sheffield	1959
13	J D Love	170*	v Worcestershire	at Worcester	1979
12	R J Blakey	223*	v Northamptonshire	at Leeds	2003
12	H Halliday	144	v Derbyshire	at Chesterfield	1950
11	K Sharp	181	v Gloucestershire	at Harrogate	1986
10	C W J Athey	134	v Derbyshire	at Derby	1982
10	Lord Hawke	166	v Warwickshire	at Birmingham	1896
10	F Mitchell	194	v Leicestershire	at Leicester	1899
9	D L Bairstow	145	v Middlesex	at Scarborough	1980
9	M G Bevan	160*	v Surrey	at Middlesbrough	2004
9	L Hall	160	v Lancashire	at Bradford	1887
9	J A Rudolph	220	v Warwickshire	at Scarborough	2007
8	W Bates	136	v Sussex	at Hove	1886
8	M J Lumb	144	v Middlesex	at Southgate	2006
8	T L Taylor	156	v Hampshire	at Harrogate	1901
7	J B Bolus	146*	v Hampshire	at Portsmouth	1960
7	P A Jaques	243	v Hampshire	at Southampton (Rose Bowl)	2004
7	E Robinson	135*	v Leicestershire	at Leicester (Aylestone Rd)	1921
7	P E Robinson	189	v Lancashire	at Scarborough	1991
7	E Lockwood	208	v Kent	at Gravesend	1883
6	R Peel	210*	v Warwickshire	at Birmingham	1896
6	J J Sayers	187	v Kent	at Tunbridge Wells	2007
6	W H H Sutcliffe	181	v Kent	at Canterbury	1952
5	C M Old	116	v Indians	at Bradford	1974
4	A W Gale	150	v Surrey	at The Oval	2008
4	I Grimshaw	129*	v Cambridge University	at Sheffield	1885
4	S Haigh	159	v Nottinghamshire	at Sheffield	1901
4	S N Hartley	114	v Gloucestershire	at Bradford	1982
4	R A Hutton	189	v Pakistanis	at Bradford	1971
4	A B Sellers	204	v Cambridge University	at Cambridge	1936
3	P Carrick	131*	v Northamptonshire	at Northampton	1980
3	A J Dalton	128	v Middlesex	at Leeds	1972
3	A Drake	147*	v Derbyshire	at Chesterfield	1911
3	F Lee	165	v Lancashire	at Bradford	1887
3	G G Macaulay	125*	v Nottinghamshire	at Nottingham	1921
3	R Moorhouse	113	v Somerset	at Taunton	1896
3	J W Rothery	161	v Kent	at Dover	1908
3	J Rowbotham	113	v Surrey	at The Oval	1873
3	T F Smailes	117	v Glamorgan	at Cardiff	1938
3	Younus Khan	217*	v Kent	at Scarborough	2007
2	M W Booth	210	v Worcestershire	at Worcester	1911
2	T T Bresnan	116	v Surrey	at The Oval	2007
2	D C F Burton	142*	v Hampshire	at Dewsbury	1919
2	K R Davidson	128	v Kent	at Maidstone	1934

2	P A Gibb	157*	v Nottinghamshire	at Sheffield	1935
2	P J Hartley	127*	v Lancashire	at Manchester	1988
2	I J Harvey	209*	v Somerset	at Leeds	2005
2	C Johnson	107	v Somerset	at Sheffield	1973
2	S A Kellett	125*	v Derbyshire	at Chesterfield	1991
2	N Kilner	112	v Leicestershire	at Leeds	1921
2	B Parker	138*	v Oxford University	at Oxford	1997
2	A U Rashid	111	v Sussex	at Hove	2008
2	A Sellers	105	v Middlesex	at Lord's	1893
2	E Smith (Morley)	129	v Hampshire	at Bradford	1899
2	G A Smithson	169	v Leicestershire	at Leicester	1947
2	G B Stevenson	115*	v Warwickshire	at Birmingham	1982
2	F S Trueman	104	v Northamptonshire	at Northampton	1963
2	C Turner	130	v Somerset	at Sheffield	1936
2	T A Wardall	106	v Gloucestershire	at Gloucester (Spa Ground)	1892
1	A T Barber	100	v England XI	at Sheffield	1929
1	H D Bird	181*	v Glamorgan	at Bradford	1959
1	T J D Birtles	104	v Lancashire	at Sheffield	1914
1	G S Blewett	190	v Northamptonshire	at Scarborough	1999
1	G L Brophy	100*	v Hampshire	at Southampton (Rose Bowl)	2007
1	M T G Elliott	127	v Warwickshire	at Birmingham	2002
1	T Emmett	104	v Gloucestershire	at Clifton	1873
1	G M Fellows	109	v Lancashire	at Manchester	2002
1	J N Gillespie	123*	v Surrey	at The Oval	2007
1	D Gough	121	v Warwickshire	at Leeds	1996
1	A K D Gray	104	v Somerset	at Taunton	2003
1	A P Grayson	100	v Worcestershire	at Worcester	1994
1	F E Greenwood	104*	v Glamorgan	at Hull	1929
1	G M Hamilton	125	v Hampshire	at Leeds	2000
1	W E Harbord	109	v Oxford University	at Oxford	1930
1	R Iddison	112	v Cambridgeshire	at Hunslet	1869
1	W G Keighley	110	v Surrey	at Leeds	1951
1	R A Kettleborough	108	v Essex	at Leeds	1996
1	B Leadbeater	140*	v Hampshire	at Portsmouth	1976
1	A Lyth	138	v Nottinghamshire	at Nottingham	2008
1	D R Martyn	238	v Gloucestershire	at Leeds	2003
1	J T Newstead	100*	v Nottinghamshire	at Nottingham	1908
1	R M Pyrah	106	v Loughborough UCCE	at Leeds	2007
1	R B Richardson	112	v Warwickshire	at Birmingham	1993
1	H Rudston	164	v Leicestershire	at Leicester (Aylestone Rd)	1904
1	A Sidebottom	124	v Glamorgan	at Cardiff (Sophia Gardens)	1977
1	I G Swallow	114	v MCC	at Scarborough	1987
1	S R Tendulkar	100	v Durham	at Durham	1992
1	J Thewlis	108	v Surrey	at The Oval	1868
1	C T Tyson	100*	v Hampshire	at Southampton	1921
1	H Verity	101	v Jamaica	at Kingston (Sabina Park)	1935/36
1	A Waddington	114	v Worcestershire	at Leeds	1927
1	D J Wainwright	104*	v Sussex	at Hove	2008
1	W A I Washington	100*	v Surrey	at Leeds	1902
1	H Wilkinson	113	v MCC	at Scarborough	1904
1	W H Wilkinson	103	v Sussex	at Sheffield	1909
1	E R Wilson	104*	v Essex	at Bradford	1913
1	A Wood	123*	v Worcestershire	at Sheffield	1935
1	J D Woodford	101	v Warwickshire	at Middlesbrough	1971

SUMMARY OF CENTURIES
FOR AND AGAINST YORKSHIRE 1863-2008

FOR YORKSHIRE				AGAINST YORKSHIRE		
Total	In Yorkshire	Away		Total	In Yorkshire	Away
105	62	43	Derbyshire	54	25	29
15	7	8	Durham	11	8	3
71	31	40	Essex	42	20	22
68	38	30	Glamorgan	23	13	10
85	41	44	Gloucestershire	52	27	25
83	35	48	Hampshire	50	21	29
80	36	44	Kent	57	27	30
104	54	50	Lancashire	108	56	52
94	51	43	Leicestershire	44	22	22
89	45	44	Middlesex	84	36	48
77	33	44	Northamptonshire	52	25	27
113	53	60	Nottinghamshire	79	30	49
88	46	42	Somerset	49	19	30
111	47	64	Surrey	104	37	67
85	39	46	Sussex	62	26	36
96	33	63	Warwickshire	65	24	41
67	28	39	Worcestershire	37	12	25
1	1	—	Cambridgeshire	—	—	—
1432	**680**	**752**	**Totals**	**973**	**428**	**545**
9	9	—	Australians	16	16	—
9	9	—	Indians	7	7	—
8	8	—	New Zealanders	3	3	—
5	5	—	Pakistanis	1	1	—
9	9	—	South Africans	7	7	—
5	5	—	Sri Lankans	1	1	—
5	5	—	West Indians	6	6	—
1	1	—	Zimbabweans	—	—	—
3	3	—	Bangladesh 'A'	1	1	—
—	—	—	India 'A'	1	1	—
1	1	—	Pakistan 'A'	1	1	—
45	1	44	Cambridge University	20	2	18
2	2	—	Combined Services	—	—	—
4	3	1	England XI's	3	2	1
—	—	—	International XI	1	1	—
1	—	1	Ireland	—	—	—
3	—	3	Jamaica	3	—	3
1	—	1	Liverpool & District	—	—	—
1	1	—	Loughborough UCCE	1	1	—
1	—	1	Mashonaland	—	—	—
2	—	2	Matebeleland	1	—	1
52	38	14	MCC	52	34	18
39	—	39	Oxford University	11	—	11
6	—	6	Rest of England	15	—	15
9	5	4	Scotland	1	—	1
3	3	—	C I Thornton's XI	4	4	—
—	—	—	Western Province	1	—	1
1	1	—	I Zingari	1	1	—
225	**109**	**116**	**Totals**	**158**	**89**	**69**
1657	**789**	**868**	**Grand Totals**	**1131**	**517**	**614**

FOUR CENTURIES IN ONE INNINGS

		F S Jackson	117
		E Wainwright	126
1896	v. Warwickshire	Lord Hawke	166
	at Birmingham	R Peel	....................*210

(First instance in First-Class cricket)

THREE CENTURIES IN ONE INNINGS

		L Hall	116
1884	v. Cambridge University	W Bates	133
	at Cambridge	I Grimshaw	115
		G Ulyett	124
1887	v. Kent	L Hall	110
	at Canterbury	F Lee	119
		J T Brown	311
1897	v. Sussex	J Tunnicliffe	147
	at Sheffield	E Wainwright	...............*104
		F S Jackson	155
1899	v. Middlesex	D Denton	113
	at Bradford	F Mitchell	121
		D Denton	105
1904	v. Surrey	G H Hirst	104
	at The Oval	J Tunnicliffe	...............*139
		H Sutcliffe	118
1919	v. Gloucestershire	D Denton	122
	at Leeds	R Kilner	...................*115
		P Holmes	130
1925	v. Glamorgan	H Sutcliffe	121
	at Huddersfield	E Robinson	...............*108
		P Holmes	105
1928	v. Middlesex	E Oldroyd	108
	at Lord's	A Mitchell	105
		H Sutcliffe	129
1928	v. Essex	P Holmes	136
	at Leyton	M Leyland	...............*133
		E Oldroyd	168
1929	v. Glamorgan	W Barber	114
	at Hull	F E Greenwood	...............*104
		H Sutcliffe	107
1933	v. MCC	A Mitchell	158
	at Scarborough	M Leyland	133
		H Sutcliffe	129
1936	v. Surrey	L Hutton	163
	at Leeds	M Leyland	...............*163
		H Sutcliffe	189
1937	v. Leicestershire	L Hutton	153
	at Hull	M Leyland	...............*118
		L Hutton	137
1947	v. Leicestershire	N W D Yardley	100
	at Leicester	G.A Smithson	169
		J H Hampshire	...............*116
1971	v. Oxford University	R A Hutton	101
	at Oxford	A J Dalton	111

287

			G Boycott 141
1975	v.	Gloucestershire	R G Lumb 101
		at Bristol	J H Hampshire *106
			M D Moxon 130
1995	v.	Cambridge University	D Byas 181
		at Cambridge	M G Bevan *113
			M J Wood 102
2001	v.	Leicestershire	M J Lumb 122
		at Leeds	D S Lehmann 104
			C White 183
2001	v.	Glamorgan	M J Wood 124
		at Scarborough	D Byas 104
			J A Rudolph 122
2007	v.	Surrey	T T Bresnan 116
		at The Oval	J N Gillespie *123

CENTURY IN EACH INNINGS

D Denton	107 and 109*	v. Nottinghamshire at Nottingham, 1906
G H Hirst	111 and 117*	v. Somerset at Bath, 1906
D Denton	133 and 121	v. MCC at Scarborough, 1908
W Rhodes	128 and 115	v. MCC at Scarborough, 1911
P Holmes	126 and 111*	v. Lancashire at Manchester, 1920
H Sutcliffe	107 and 109*	v. MCC at Scarborough, 1926
H Sutcliffe	111 and 100*	v. Nottinghamshire at Nottingham, 1928
E I Lester	126 and 142	v. Northamptonshire at Northampton, 1947
L Hutton	197 and 104	v. Essex at Southend, 1947
E I Lester	125* and 132	v. Lancashire at Manchester, 1948
L Hutton	165 and 100	v. Sussex at Hove, 1949
L Hutton	103 and 137	v. MCC at Scarborough, 1952
G Boycott	103 and 105	v. Nottinghamshire at Sheffield, 1966
G Boycott	163 and 141*	v. Nottinghamshire at Bradford, 1983
M D Moxon	123 and 112*	v. Indians at Scarborough, 1986
A A Metcalfe	194* and 107	v. Nottinghamshire at Nottingham, 1990
M P Vaughan	100 and 151	v. Essex at Chelmsford, 1999
Younus Khan	106 and 202*	v. Hampshire at Southampton, 2007

HIGHEST INDIVIDUAL SCORES
FOR AND AGAINST YORKSHIRE

Highest For Yorkshire:
341 G H Hirst v. Leicestershire at Leicester, 1905

Highest Against Yorkshire:
318* W G Grace for Gloucestershire at Cheltenham, 1876

Yorkshire versus:

Derbyshire	*For Yorkshire:*	300 — J T Brown at Chesterfield, 1898
	Against:	219 — J D Eggar at Bradford, 1949
Most Centuries	*For Yorkshire:*	G Boycott 9
	Against:	K J Barnett and W Storer 4 each
Durham	*For Yorkshire:*	339 — D S Lehmann at Leeds, 2006
	Against:	184 — M J di Venuto at Chester-le-Street, 2008
Most Centuries	*For Yorkshire:*	D S Lehmann 3
	Against:	D M Benkenstein 2
Essex	*For Yorkshire:*	313 — H Sutcliffe at Leyton, 1932
	Against:	219* — D J Insole at Colchester, 1949
Most Centuries	*For Yorkshire:*	H Sutcliffe 9
	Against:	F L Fane, K W R Fletcher, G A Gooch and D J Insole 3 each

Yorkshire versus

Glamorgan

	For Yorkshire:	213 — M D Moxon at Cardiff, 1996
	Against:	202*— H Morris at Cardiff, 1996
Most Centuries	*For Yorkshire:*	G Boycott, P Holmes and H Sutcliffe 5 each
	Against:	H Morris 5

Gloucestershire

	For Yorkshire:	238 — D R Martyn at Leeds, 2003
	Against:	318*— W G Grace at Cheltenham, 1876
Most Centuries	*For Yorkshire:*	G Boycott 6
	Against:	W G Grace 9

Hampshire

	For Yorkshire:	302*— P Holmes at Portsmouth, 1920
	Against:	268— E G Wynyard at Southampton, 1896
Most Centuries	*For Yorkshire:*	H Sutcliffe 6
	Against:	C P Mead 10

Kent

	For Yorkshire:	248— W Barber at Leeds, 1934.
	Against:	207— D P Fulton at Maidstone, 1998
Most Centuries	*For Yorkshire:*	A McGrath 6
	Against:	F E Woolley 5

Lancashire

	For Yorkshire:	252— D S Lehmann at Leeds, 2001
	Against:	225— G D Lloyd at Leeds, 1997 (Non-Championship)
		206 — S G Law at Leeds, 2007
Most Centuries	*For Yorkshire:*	G Boycott and H Sutcliffe 6 each
	Against:	M A Atherton and C H Lloyd 6 each.

Leicestershire

	For Yorkshire:	341— G H Hirst at Leicester, 1905
	Against:	218— J J Whitaker at Bradford, 1996
Most Centuries	*For Yorkshire:*	H Sutcliffe 10
	Against:	J J Whitaker and C J B Wood 5 each

Middlesex

	For Yorkshire:	315*— P Holmes at Lord's, 1925
	Against:	243*— A J Webbe at Huddersfield, 1887
Most Centuries	*For Yorkshire:*	P Holmes and H Sutcliffe 7 each
	Against:	M W Gatting 8

Northamptonshire

	For Yorkshire:	277*— P Holmes at Harrogate, 1921
	Against:	235—A J Lamb at Leeds, 1990
Most Centuries	*For Yorkshire:*	H Sutcliffe 5
	Against:	W Larkins 5

Nottinghamshire

	For Yorkshire:	285—P Holmes at Nottingham, 1929
	Against:	220*— R T Robinson at Nottingham, 1990
Most Centuries	*For Yorkshire:*	G Boycott 15
	Against:	R T Robinson 6

Somerset

	For Yorkshire:	213 — H Sutcliffe at Dewsbury, 1924
	Against:	297— M J Wood at Taunton, 2005
Most Centuries	*For Yorkshire:*	G Boycott 6
	Against:	L C H Palairet and IVA. Richards 5 each

Surrey

	For Yorkshire:	255— W Barber at Sheffield, 1935
	Against:	273— T W Hayward at The Oval, 1899
Most Centuries	*For Yorkshire:*	H Sutcliffe 9
	Against:	J B Hobbs 8

Sussex

	For Yorkshire:	311— J T Brown at Sheffield, 1897
	Against:	253*— A P Wells at Middlesbrough, 1991
Most Centuries	*For Yorkshire:*	L Hutton 8
	Against:	C B Fry 7

Warwickshire

	For Yorkshire:	275 — P Holmes at Bradford, 1928
	Against:	225 — D P Ostler at Birmingham, 2002
Most Centuries	*For Yorkshire:*	G Boycott and H Sutcliffe 8
	Against:	D L Amiss, H E Dollery, R B Khanhai and W G Quaife 4 each.

Yorkshire versus

Worcestershire	*For Yorkshire:*	274* — M D Moxon at Worcester, 1994
	Against:	259 — D Kenyon at Kidderminster, 1956
Most Centuries	*For Yorkshire:*	M Leyland 6
	Against:	D Kenyon and G M Turner 5 each
Australians	*For Yorkshire:*	167 — J T Brown at Bradford, 1899
	Against:	193* — B C Booth at Bradford, 1964
Most Centuries	*For Yorkshire:*	G Boycott and D Denton 2 each
	Against:	N C O'Neill 2
Indians	*For Yorkshire:*	183* — L Hutton at Bradford, 1946
	Against:	244* — V S Hazare at Sheffield, 1946
Most Centuries	*For Yorkshire:*	M D Moxon 2
	Against:	V S Hazare, VMankad, PR Umrigar
		D K Gaekwad, G A Parkar and R Lamba 1 each
New Zealanders	*For Yorkshire:*	175 — P Holmes at Bradford, 1927
	Against:	126 — W M Wallace at Bradford, 1949
Most Centuries	*For Yorkshire:*	L Hutton and DB Close 2 each
	Against:	H G Vivian, WM Wallace and J G Wright 1 each
Pakistanis	*For Yorkshire:*	197 — P J Sharpe at Leeds, 1967
	Against:	139 — A H Kardar at Sheffield, 1954
Most Centuries	*For Yorkshire:*	P J Sharpe 2
	Against:	A H Kardar 1
South Africans	*For Yorkshire:*	156 — L Hutton at Sheffield, 1951
	Against:	168 — I J Seidle at Sheffield, 1929
Most Centuries	*For Yorkshire:*	L Hutton 2
	Against:	H B Cameron, J D Lindsay, B Mitchell,
		D P B Morkel, I J Seidle, L J Tancred,
		C B van Ryneveld 1 each
Sri Lankans	*For Yorkshire:*	132 — M D Moxon at Leeds, 1988
	Against:	112 — S A R Silva at Leeds, 1988
Most Centuries	*For Yorkshire:*	K Sharp 2
	Against:	S A R Silva 1
West Indians	*For Yorkshire:*	112* — D Denton at Harrogate, 1906
	Against:	164 — S F A Bacchus at Leeds, 1980
Most Centuries	*For Yorkshire:*	M G Bevan, D Denton, L Hutton, R G Lumb
		and A A Metcalfe 1 each
	Against:	S F A Bacchus, C O Browne, S Chanderpaul
		P A Goodman, C L Hooper and G St A Sobers
		1 each
Zimbabweans	*For Yorkshire:*	113 — M D Moxon at Leeds, 1990
	Against:	89 — G J Whittall at Leeds, 2000
Most Centuries	*For Yorkshire:*	M D Moxon 1
	Against:	None
Cambridge	*For Yorkshire:*	207* — G Boycott at Cambridge, 1976
University	*Against:*	171* — G L Jessop at Cambridge, 1899
		171 — P B H May at Cambridge, 1952
Most Centuries	*For Yorkshire:*	H Sutcliffe 4
	Against:	G M Kemp 2
MCC	*For Yorkshire:*	180* — G H Hirst at Lord's, 1919
	Against:	214 — E Hendren at Lord's, 1919
Most Centuries	*For Yorkshire:*	L Hutton 8
	Against:	R E S Wyatt 5
Oxford University	*For Yorkshire:*	196 — R J Blakey at Oxford, 1991
	Against:	201 — J E Raphael at Oxford, 1904
Most Centuries	*For Yorkshire:*	M Leyland 4
	Against:	A A Baig and Nawab of Pataudi (Jun.) 2 each

J B Hobbs scored 11 centuries against Yorkshire – the highest by any individual (8 for Surrey and 3 for the Rest of England).

Three players have scored 10 centuries against Yorkshire – W G Grace (9 for Gloucestershire and 1 for MCC). E H Hendren (6 for Middlesex, 3 for MCC and 1 for the Rest of England) and C P Mead (all 10 for Hampshire).

CARRYING BAT THROUGH A COMPLETED INNINGS

Batsman	Score	Total	Against	Season
G R Atkinson	30*	73	Nottinghamshire at Bradford	1865
L Hall	31*	94	Sussex at Hove	1878
L Hall	124*	331	Sussex at Hove	1883
L Hall	128*	285	Sussex at Huddersfield	1884
L Hall	32*	81	Kent at Sheffield	1885
L Hall	79*	285	Surrey at Sheffield	1885
L Hall	37*	96	Derbyshire at Derby	1885
L Hall	50*	173	Sussex at Huddersfield	1886
L Hall	74*	172	Kent at Canterbury	1886
G Ulyett	199*	399	Derbyshire at Sheffield	1887
L Hall	119*	334	Gloucestershire at Dewsbury	1887
L Hall	82*	218	Sussex at Hove	1887
L Hall	34*	104	Surrey at The Oval	1888
L Hall	129*	461	Gloucestershire at Clifton	1888
L Hall	85*	259	Middlesex at Lord's	1889
L Hall	41*	106	Nottinghamshire at Sheffield	1891
W Rhodes	98*	184	MCC at Lord's	1903
W Rhodes	85*	152	Essex at Leyton	1910
P Holmes	145*	270	Northamptonshire at Northampton	1920
H Sutcliffe	125*	307	Essex at Southend	1920
P Holmes	175*	377	New Zealanders at Bradford	1927
P Holmes	110*	219	Northamptonshire at Bradford	1929
H Sutcliffe	104*	170	Hampshire at Leeds	1932
H Sutcliffe	114*	202	Rest of England at The Oval	1933
H Sutcliffe	187*	401	Worcestershire at Bradford	1934
H Sutcliffe	135*	262	Glamorgan at Neath	1935
H Sutcliffe	125*	322	Oxford University at Oxford	1939
L Hutton	99*	200	Leicestershire at Sheffield	1948
L Hutton	78*	153	Worcestershire at Sheffield	1949
F A Lowson	76*	218	MCC at Lord's	1951
W B Stott	144*	262	Worcestershire at Worcester	1959
D E V Padgett	115*	230	Gloucestershire at Bristol	1962
G Boycott	114*	297	Leicestershire at Sheffield	1968
G Boycott	53*	119	Warwickshire at Bradford	1969
G Boycott	182*	320	Middlesex at Lord's	1971
G Boycott	138*	232	Warwickshire at Birmingham	1971
G Boycott	175*	360	Nottinghamshire at Worksop	1979
G Boycott	112*	233	Derbyshire at Sheffield	1983
G Boycott	55*	183	Warwickshire at Leeds	1984
G Boycott	55*	131	Surrey at Sheffield	1985
M J Wood	60*	160	Somerset at Scarborough	2004
J J Sayers	122*	326	Middlesex at Scarborough	2006
J J Sayers	149*	414	Durham at Leeds	2007

43 instances, of which L Hall (14 times), G Boycott (8) and H Sutcliffe (6) account for 28 between them.

The highest percentage of an innings total is 61.17 by H. Sutcliffe (104* v. Hampshire at Leeds in 1932) but P Holmes was absent ill, so only 9 wickets fell.

Other contributions exceeding 55% are:

59.48%	G Boycott	(138*	v. Warwickshire at Birmingham, 1971)
56.87%	G Boycott	(182*	v. Middlesex at Lord's, 1971)
56.43%	H Sutcliffe	(114*	v. Rest of England at The Oval, 1933)
55.92%	W Rhodes	(85*	v. Essex at Leyton, 1910)

2,000 RUNS IN A SEASON

Batsman	Season	M	I	NO	Runs	HS	Avge	100s
G H Hirst	1904	32	44	3	2257	157	55.04	8
D Denton	1905	33	52	2	2258	172	45.16	8
G H Hirst	1906	32	53	6	2164	169	46.04	6
D Denton	1911	32	55	4	2161	137*	42.37	6
D Denton	1912	36	51	4	2088	221	44.23	6
P Holmes	1920	30	45	6	2144	302*	54.97	7
P Holmes	1925	35	49	9	2351	315*	58.77	6
H Sutcliffe	1925	34	48	8	2236	235	55.90	7
H Sutcliffe	1928	27	35	5	2418	228	80.60	11
P Holmes	1928	31	40	4	2093	275	58.13	6
H Sutcliffe	1931	28	33	8	2351	230	94.04	9
H Sutcliffe	1932	29	41	5	2883	313	80.08	12
M Leyland	1933	31	44	4	2196	210*	54.90	7
A Mitchell	1933	34	49	10	2100	158	53.84	6
H Sutcliffe	1935	32	47	3	2183	212	49.61	8
L Hutton	1937	28	45	6	2448	271*	62.76	8
H Sutcliffe	1937	32	52	5	2054	189	43.70	4
L Hutton	1939	29	44	5	2316	280*	59.38	10
L Hutton	1947	19	31	2	2068	270*	71.31	10
L Hutton	1949	26	44	6	2640	269*	69.47	9
F A Lowson	1950	31	54	5	2067	141*	42.18	5
D E V Padgett	1959	35	60	8	2158	161*	41.50	4
W B Stott	1959	32	56	2	2034	144*	37.66	3
P J Sharpe	1962	36	62	8	2201	138	40.75	7
G Boycott	1971	18	25	4	2221	233	105.76	11
A A Metcalfe	1990	23	44	4	2047	194*	51.17	6

1,000 RUNS IN A SEASON

Batsman		Runs scored	Runs scored	Runs scored
C W J Athey	(2)	1113 in 1980	1339 in 1982	—
D L Bairstow	(3)	1083 in 1981	1102 in 1983	1163 in 1985
W Barber	(8)	1000 in 1932	1595 in 1933	1930 in 1934
		1958 in 1935	1466 in 1937	1455 in 1938
		1501 in 1939	1170 in 1946	—
M G Bevan	(2)	1598 in 1995	1225 in 1996	—
R J Blakey	(5)	1361 in 1987	1159 in 1989	1065 in 1992
		1236 in 1994	1041 in 2002	—
J B Bolus	(2)	1245 in 1960	1970 in 1961	—
M W Booth	(2)	1189 in 1911	1076 in 1913	—
G Boycott	(19)	1628 in 1963	1639 in 1964	1215 in 1965
		1388 in 1966	1530 in 1967	1004 in 1968
		1558 in 1970	2221 in 1971	1156 in 1972
		1478 in 1974	1915 in 1975	1288 in 1976
		1259 in 1977	1074 in 1978	1160 in 1979
		1913 in 1982	1941 in 1983	1567 in 1984
		1657 in 1985	—	—
J T Brown	(9)	1196 in 1894	1260 in 1895	1755 in 1896
		1634 in 1897	1641 in 1898	1375 in 1899
		1181 in 1900	1627 in 1901	1291 in 1903
D Byas	(5)	1557 in 1991	1073 in 1993	1297 in 1994
		1913 in 1995	1319 in 1997	—
D B Close	(13)	1192 in 1952	1287 in 1954	1131 in 1955
		1315 in 1957	1335 in 1958	1740 in 1959
		1699 in 1960	1821 in 1961	1438 in 1962
		1145 in 1963	1281 in 1964	1127 in 1965
		1259 in 1966	—	—

Batsman		*Runs scored*	*Runs scored*	*Runs scored*
K R Davidson	(1)	1241 in 1934	—	—
D Denton	(20)	1028 in 1896	1357 in 1897	1595 in 1899
		1378 in 1900	1400 in 1901	1191 in 1902
		1562 in 1903	1919 in 1904	2258 in 1905
		1905 in 1906	1128 in 1907	1852 in 1908
		1765 in 1909	1106 in 1910	2161 in 1911
		2088 in 1912	1364 in 1913	1799 in 1914
		1213 in 1919	1324 in 1920	—
A Drake	(2)	1487 in 1911	1029 in 1913	—
A P Grayson	(1)	1046 in 1994	—	—
S Haigh	(1)	1031 in 1904	—	—
L Hall	(1)	1120 in 1887	—	—
H Halliday	(4)	1357 in 1948	1484 in 1950	1351 in 1952
		1461 in 1953	—	—
J H Hampshire	(12)	1236 in 1963	1280 in 1964	1424 in 1965
		1105 in 1966	1244 in 1967	1133 in 1968
		1079 in 1970	1259 in 1971	1124 in 1975
		1303 in 1976	1596 in 1978	1425 in 1981
Lord Hawke	(1)	1005 in 1895	—	—
G H Hirst	(19)	1110 in 1896	1248 in 1897	1546 in 1899
		1752 in 1900	1669 in 1901	1113 in 1902
		1535 in 1903	2257 in 1904	1972 in 1905
		2164 in 1906	1167 in 1907	1513 in 1908
		1151 in 1909	1679 in 1910	1639 in 1911
		1119 in 1912	1431 in 1913	1655 in 1914
		1312 in 1919	—	—
P Holmes	(14)	1876 in 1919	2144 in 1920	1458 in 1921
		1614 in 1922	1884 in 1923	1610 in 1924
		2351 in 1925	1792 in 1926	1774 in 1927
		2093 in 1928	1724 in 1929	1957 in 1930
		1431 in 1931	1191 in 1932	—
L Hutton	(12)	1282 in 1936	2448 in 1937	1171 in 1938
		2316 in 1939	1322 in 1946	2068 in 1947
		1792 in 1948	2640 in 1949	1581 in 1950
		1554 in 1951	1956 in 1952	1532 in 1953
R Illingworth	(5)	1193 in 1957	1490 in 1959	1029 in 1961
		1610 in 1962	1301 in 1964	—
F S Jackson	(4)	1211 in 1896	1300 in 1897	1442 in 1898
		1468 in 1899	—	—
P A Jaques	(2)	1118 in 2004	1359 in 2005	—
S A Kellett	(2)	1266 in 1991	1326 in 1992	—
R Kilner	(10)	1586 in 1913	1329 in 1914	1135 in 1919
		1240 in 1920	1137 in 1921	1132 in 1922
		1265 in 1923	1002 in 1925	1021 in 1926
		1004 in 1927	—	—
D S Lehmann	(5)	1575 in 1997	1477 in 2000	1416 in 2001
		1136 in 2002	1706 in 2006	—
E I Lester	(6)	1256 in 1948	1774 in 1949	1015 in 1950
		1786 in 1952	1380 in 1953	1330 in 1954
M Leyland	(17)	1088 in 1923	1203 in 1924	1560 in 1925
		1561 in 1926	1478 in 1927	1554 in 1928
		1407 in 1929	1814 in 1930	1127 in 1931
		1821 in 1932	2196 in 1933	1228 in 1934
		1366 in 1935	1621 in 1936	1120 in 1937
		1640 in 1938	1238 in 1939	—

Batsman	Runs scored	Runs scored	Runs scored
J D Love	(2) 1161 in 1981	1020 in 1983	—
F A Lowson	(8) 1678 in 1949	2067 in 1950	1607 in 1951
	1562 in 1952	1586 in 1953	1719 in 1954
	1082 in 1955	1428 in 1956	
M J Lumb	(1) 1038 in 2003	—	—
R G Lumb	(5) 1002 in 1973	1437 in 1975	1070 in 1978
	1465 in 1979	1223 in 1980	—
A McGrath	(1) 1425 in 2005	1293 in 2006	
A A Metcalfe	(6) 1674 in 1986	1162 in 1987	1320 in 1988
	1230 in 1989	2047 in 1990	1210 in 1991
A Mitchell	(10) 1320 in 1928	1633 in 1930	1351 in 1932
	2100 in 1933	1854 in 1934	1530 in 1935
	1095 in 1936	1602 in 1937	1305 in 1938
	1219 in 1939	—	—
F Mitchell	(2) 1678 in 1899	1801 in 1901	
R Moorhouse	(1) 1096 in 1895	—	—
M D Moxon	(11) 1016 in 1984	1256 in 1985	1298 in 1987
	1430 in 1988	1156 in 1989	1621 in 1990
	1669 in 1991	1314 in 1992	1251 in 1993
	1458 in 1994	1145 in 1995	—
E Oldroyd	(10) 1473 in 1921	1690 in 1922	1349 in 1923
	1607 in 1924	1262 in 1925	1197 in 1926
	1390 in 1927	1304 in 1928	1474 in 1929
	1285 in 1930	—	—
D E V Padgett	(12) 1046 in 1956	2158 in 1959	1574 in 1960
	1856 in 1961	1750 in 1962	1380 in 1964
	1220 in 1965	1194 in 1966	1284 in 1967
	1163 in 1968	1078 in 1969	1042 in 1970
R Peel	(1) 1193 in 1896	—	—
W Rhodes	(17) 1251 in 1904	1353 in 1905	1618 in 1906
	1574 in 1908	1663 in 1909	1355 in 1910
	1961 in 1911	1030 in 1912	1805 in 1913
	1325 in 1914	1138 in 1919	1329 in 1921
	1368 in 1922	1168 in 1923	1030 in 1924
	1256 in 1925	1071 in 1926	—
E Robinson	(2) 1104 in 1921	1097 in 1929	—
P E Robinson	(3) 1173 in 1988	1402 in 1990	1293 in 1991
J A Rudolph	(2) 1078 in 2007	1292 in 2008	—
A B Sellers	(1) 1109 in 1938	—	—
K Sharp	(1) 1445 in 1984	—	—
P J Sharpe	(10) 1039 in 1960	1240 in 1961	2201 in 1962
	1273 in 1964	1091 in 1965	1352 in 1967
	1256 in 1968	1012 in 1969	1149 in 1970
	1320 in 1973	—	—
W B Stott	(5) 1362 in 1957	1036 in 1958	2034 in 1959
	1790 in 1960	1409 in 1961	—

Batsman	*Runs scored*	*Runs scored*	*Runs scored*
H Sutcliffe .... (21)	†1839 in 1919	1393 in 1920	1235 in 1921
	1909 in 1922	1773 in 1923	1720 in 1924
	2236 in 1925	1672 in 1926	1814 in 1927
	2418 in 1928	1485 in 1929	1636 in 1930
	2351 in 1931	2883 in 1932	1986 in 1933
	1511 in 1934	2183 in 1935	1295 in 1936
	2054 in 1937	1660 in 1938	1416 in 1939

† First season in First-Class cricket – The record for a debut season.

W H H Sutcliffe .... (1)	1193 in 1955	—	—
K Taylor .... (6)	1306 in 1959	1107 in 1960	1494 in 1961
	1372 in 1962	1149 in 1964	1044 in 1966
T L Taylor .... (2)	1236 in 1901	1373 in 1902	—
S R Tendulkar .... (1)	1070 in 1992	—	—
J Tunnicliffe .... (12)	1333 in 1895	1368 in 1896	1208 in 1897
	1713 in 1898	1434 in 1899	1496 in 1900
	1295 in 1901	1274 in 1902	1650 in 1904
	1096 in 1905	1232 in 1906	1195 in 1907
C Turner .... (1)	1153 in 1934	—	—
G Ulyett .... (4)	1083 in 1878	1158 in 1882	1024 in 1885
	1285 in 1887	—	—
M P Vaughan .... (4)	1066 in 1994	1235 in 1995	1161 in 1996
	1161 in 1998	—	—
E Wainwright .... (3)	1492 in 1897	1479 in 1899	1044 in 1901
W A I Washington .... (1)	1022 in 1902	—	—
W Watson .... (8)	1331 in 1947	1352 in 1948	1586 in 1952
	1350 in 1953	1347 in 1954	1564 in 1955
	1378 in 1956	1455 in 1957	—
W H Wilkinson .... (1)	1282 in 1908	—	—
B B Wilson .... (5)	1054 in 1909	1455 in 1911	1453 in 1912
	1533 in 1913	1632 in 1914	—
B B Wilson .... (5)	1054 in 1909	1455 in 1911	1453 in 1912
J V Wilson .... (12)	1460 in 1949	1548 in 1950	1985 in 1951
	1349 in 1952	1531 in 1953	1713 in 1954
	1799 in 1955	1602 in 1956	1287 in 1957
	1064 in 1960	1018 in 1961	1226 in 1962
A Wood .... (1)	1237 in 1935	—	—
M J Wood .... (4)	1080 in 1998	1060 in 2001	1432 in 2003
	1005 in 2005	—	—
N W D Yardley .... (4)	1028 in 1939	1299 in 1947	1413 in 1949
	1031 in 1950	—	—

PLAYERS WHO HAVE SCORED CENTURIES
FOR AND AGAINST YORKSHIRE

Player		For	Venue	Season
C W J Athey (5)	114*	Gloucestershire	Bradford	1984
(10 for Yorkshire)	101	Gloucestershire	Gloucester	1985
	101*	Gloucestershire	Leeds	1987
	112	Sussex	Scarborough	1993
	100	Sussex	Eastbourne	1996
M G Bevan (1)	142	Leicestershire	Leicester	2002
(9 for Yorkshire)				
J B Bolus (2)	114	Nottinghamshire	Bradford	1963
(7 for Yorkshire)	138	Derbyshire	Sheffield	1973
D B Close (1)	102	Somerset	Taunton	1971
(33 for Yorkshire)				
M T G Elliott (1)	125	Glamorgan	Leeds	2004
(1 for Yorkshire)				
P A Gibb (1)	107	Essex	Brentwood	1951
(2 for Yorkshire)				
P A Jaques (1)	222	Northamptonshire	Northampton	2003
(7 for Yorkshire)				
N Kilner (2)	119	Warwickshire	Hull	1932
(2 for Yorkshire)	197	Warwickshire	Birmingham	1933
P J Sharpe (1)	126	Derbyshire	Chesterfield	1976
(23 for Yorkshire)				

Matthew Wood retires

Former Yorkshire batsman **Matthew Wood**, who was born in Huddersfield, has made the difficult decision to retire from first-class cricket. Matthew had another year to run on his contract with Glamorgan, where he went after leaving Yorkshire at the end of the 2007 season, but has decided to call it a day. Matthew, who played for Yorkshire from 1997 to 2007, will be remembered as one of the Club's most loyal players. He scored 6,742 first-class runs for the county, with 16 centuries, and in one-day cricket he amassed 3,209 runs, with five centuries.

BATSMEN WHO HAVE SCORED OVER 10,000 RUNS

Player	M	I	NO	Runs	HS	Av'ge	100s
H Sutcliffe	602	864	96	38558	313	50.20	112
D Denton	676	1058	61	33282	221	33.38	61
G Boycott	414	674	111	32570	260*	57.85	103
G H Hirst	717	1050	128	32024	341	34.73	56
W Rhodes	883	1195	162	31075	267*	30.08	46
P Holmes	485	699	74	26220	315*	41.95	60
M Leyland	548	720	82	26180	263	41.03	62
L Hutton	341	527	62	24807	280*	53.34	85
D B Close	536	811	102	22650	198	31.94	33
J H Hampshire	456	724	89	21979	183*	34.61	34
J V Wilson	477	724	75	20548	230	31.66	29
D E V Padgett	487	774	63	20306	161*	28.55	29
J Tunnicliffe	472	768	57	19435	243	27.33	22
M D Moxon	277	476	42	18973	274*	43.71	41
A Mitchell	401	550	69	18189	189	37.81	39
P J Sharpe	411	666	71	17685	203*	29.72	23
E Oldroyd	383	509	58	15891	194	35.23	37
J T Brown	345	567	41	15694	311	29.83	23
W Barber	354	495	48	15315	255	34.26	27
R Illingworth	496	668	131	14986	162	27.90	14
D Byas	268	449	42	14398	213	35.37	28
G Ulyett	355	618	31	14157	199*	24.11	15
R J Blakey	339	541	30	14150	223*	30.96	12
W Watson	283	430	65	13953	214*	38.22	26
F A Lowson	252	404	31	13897	259*	37.25	30
Lord Hawke	510	739	91	13133	166	20.26	10
R Kilner	365	478	46	13018	206*	30.13	15
D L Bairstow	429	601	113	12985	145	26.60	9
K Taylor	303	505	35	12864	203*	27.37	16
N W D Yardley	302	420	56	11632	183*	31.95	17
R G Lumb	239	395	30	11525	165*	31.57	22
E Wainwright	352	545	30	11092	228	21.53	18
S Haigh	513	687	110	10993	159	19.05	4
A McGrath	183	309	24	10868	188*	38.13	26
E I Lester	228	339	27	10616	186	34.02	24
A A Metcalfe	184	317	19	10465	216*	35.11	25
C White	221	350	45	10376	186	34.01	19
Hon F S Jackson	207	328	22	10371	160	33.89	21
J D Love	247	388	58	10263	170*	31.10	13

RECORD PARTNERSHIPS FOR YORKSHIRE

1st wkt	555	P Holmes (224*) and H Sutcliffe (313) v. Essex at Leyton, 1932
2nd wkt	346	W Barber (162) and M Leyland (189) v. Middlesex at Sheffield, 1932
3rd wkt	323*	H Sutcliffe (147*) and M Leyland (189*) v. Glamorgan at Huddersfield, 1928
4th wkt	358	D S Lehmann (339) and M J Lumb (98) v. Durham at Leeds, 2006
5th wkt	340	E Wainwright (228) and G H Hirst (186) v. Surrey at The Oval, 1899
6th wkt	276	M Leyland (191) and E Robinson (124*) v. Glamorgan at Swansea, 1926
7th wkt	254	W Rhodes (135) and D C F Burton (142*) v. Hampshire at Dewsbury, 1919
8th wkt	292	R Peel (210*) and Lord Hawke (166) v. Warwickshire at Birmingham, 1896
9th wkt	246	T T Bresnan (116) and J N Gillespie (123*) v. Surrey at The Oval, 2007
10th wkt	149	G Boycott (79) and G B Stevenson (115*) v. Warwickshire at Birmingham, 1982

RECORD PARTNERSHIPS AGAINST YORKSHIRE

1st wkt	372	R R Montgomerie (127) and M B Loye (205) for Northamptonshire at Northampton, 1996
2nd wkt	417	K J Barnett (210*) and TA Tweats (189) for Derbyshire at Derby, 1997
3rd wkt	393	A Fordham (206*) and A J Lamb (235) for Northamptonshire at Leeds, 1990
4th wkt	447	R Abel (193) and T Hayward (273) for Surrey at The Oval, 1899
5th wkt	261	W G Grace (318*) and W O Moberley (103) for Gloucestershire at Cheltenham, 1876
6th wkt	294	D R Jardine (157) and P G H Fender (177) for Surrey at Bradford, 1928
7th wkt	315	D M Benkenstein (151) and O D Gibson (155) for Durham at Leeds, 2006
8th wkt	178	A P Wells (253*) and B T P Donelan (59) for Sussex at Middlesbrough, 1991
9th wkt	160	D R Wilcox (64) and R Smith (86*) for Essex at Southend, 1947
10th wkt	132	A Hill (172*) and M Jean-Jacques (73) for Derbyshire at Sheffield, 1986

CENTURY PARTNERSHIPS FOR THE FIRST WICKET IN BOTH INNINGS

128	108	G Ulyett (82 and 91) and L Hall (87 and 37) v. Sussex at Hove, 1885
		(First instance in First-Class cricket)
138	147*	J T Brown (203 and 81*) and J Tunnicliffe (62 and 63*) v. Middlesex at Lord's, 1896
		(Second instance in First-Class cricket)
105	265*	P Holmes (51 and 127*) and H Sutcliffe (71 and 131*) v. Surrey at The Oval, 1926
184	210*	P Holmes (83 and 101*) and H Sutcliffe (111 and 100*) v. Nottinghamshire at Nottingham, 1928
110	117	L Hutton (95 and 86) and W Watson (34 and 57) v. Lancashire at Manchester, 1947
122	230	W B Stott (50 and 114) and K Taylor (79 and 140) v. Nottinghamshire at Nottingham, 1957
136	138	J B Bolus (108 and 71) and K Taylor (89 and 75) v. Cambridge University at Cambridge, 1962
105	105	G Boycott (38 and 64) and K Taylor (85 and 49) v. Leicestershire at Leicester, 1963
116	112*	K Taylor (45 and 68) and J H Hampshire (68 and 67*) v. Oxford University at Oxford, 1964
104	104	G Boycott (117 and 49*) and R G Lumb (47 and 57) v. Sussex at Leeds, 1974
134	185*	M D Moxon (57 and 89*) and A A Metcalfe (216* and 78*) v. Middlesex at Leeds, 1988

CENTURY PARTNERSHIPS FOR THE FIRST WICKET
IN BOTH INNINGS BUT WITH CHANGE OF PARTNER

109		W H H Sutcliffe (82) and F A Lowson (46)
	143	W H H Sutcliffe (88) and W Watson (52) v. Canadians at Scarborough, 1954
109		G Boycott (70) and R G Lumb (44)
	135	G Boycott (74) and JH Hampshire (58) v. Northamptonshire at Bradford, 1977

CENTURY PARTNERSHIPS

FIRST WICKET (Qualification 200 runs)

555	P Holmes (224*) and H Sutcliffe (313) v. Essex at Leyton, 1932
554	J T Brown (300) and J Tunnicliffe (243) v. Derbyshire at Chesterfield, 1898
378	J T Brown (311) and J Tunnicliffe (147) v. Sussex at Sheffield, 1897
362	M D Moxon (213) and M P Vaughan (183) v. Glamorgan at Cardiff, 1996
351	G Boycott (184) and M D Moxon (168) v. Worcestershire at Worcester, 1985
347	P Holmes (302*) and H Sutcliffe (131) v. Hampshire at Portsmouth, 1920
323	P Holmes (125) and H Sutcliffe (195) v. Lancashire at Sheffield, 1931
315	H Sutcliffe (189) and L Hutton (153) v. Leicestershire at Hull, 1937
315	H Sutcliffe (116) and L Hutton (280*) v. Hampshire at Sheffield, 1939
309	P Holmes (250) and H Sutcliffe (129) v. Warwickshire at Birmingham, 1931
309	C White (186) and M J Wood (115) v. Lancashire at Manchester, 2001
290	P Holmes (179*) and H Sutcliffe (104) v. Middlesex at Leeds, 1928
288	G Boycott (130*) and R G Lumb (159) v. Somerset at Harrogate, 1979
286	L Hutton (156) and F A Lowson (115) v. South Africans at Sheffield, 1951
282	M D Moxon (147) and A A Metcalfe (151) v. Lancashire at Manchester, 1986
281*	W B Stott (138*) and K Taylor (130*) v. Sussex at Hove, 1960
279	P Holmes (133) and H Sutcliffe (145) v. Northamptonshire at Northampton, 1919
274	P.Holmes (199) and H Sutcliffe (139) v. Somerset at Hull, 1923
274	P Holmes (180) and H Sutcliffe (134) v. Gloucestershire at Gloucester, 1927
272	P Holmes (194) and H Sutcliffe (129) v. Leicestershire at Hull, 1925
272	M J Wood (202*) and J J Sayers (115) v. Bangladesh 'A' at Leeds, 2005
268	P Holmes (136) and H Sutcliffe (129) v. Essex at Leyton, 1928
267	W Barber (248) and L Hutton (70) v. Kent at Leeds, 1934
265*	P Holmes (127*) and H Sutcliffe (131*) v. Surrey at The Oval, 1926
264	G Boycott (161*) and R G Lumb (132) v. Gloucestershire at Leeds, 1976
253	P Holmes (123) and H Sutcliffe (132) v. Lancashire at Sheffield, 1919
248	G Boycott (163) and A A Metcalfe (122) v. Nottinghamshire at Bradford, 1983
245	L Hutton (152) and F A Lowson (120) v. Lancashire at Leeds, 1952
241	P Holmes (142) and H Sutcliffe (123*) v. Surrey at The Oval, 1929
240	G Boycott (233) and P J Sharpe (92) v. Essex at Colchester, 1971
238*	P Holmes (126*) and H Sutcliffe (105*) v. Cambridge University at Cambridge, 1923
236	G Boycott (131) and K Taylor (153) v. Lancashire at Manchester, 1964
236	P Holmes (130) and H Sutcliffe (132*) v. Glamorgan at Sheffield, 1930
233	G Boycott (141*) and R G Lumb (90) v. Cambridge University at Cambridge, 1973
233	H Halliday (116) and W Watson (108) v. Northamptonshire at Northampton, 1948
231	M P Vaughan (151) and D Byas (90) v. Essex at Chelmsford, 1999
230	H Sutcliffe (129) and L Hutton (163) v. Surrey at Leeds, 1936
230	W B Stott (114) and K Taylor (140*) v. Nottinghamshire at Nottingham, 1957
228	H Halliday (90) and J V Wilson (223*) v. Scotland at Scarborough, 1951
228	G Boycott (141) and R G Lumb (101) v. Gloucestershire at Bristol, 1975
227	P Holmes (110) and H Sutcliffe (119) v. Leicestershire at Leicester, 1928
225	R G Lumb (101) and C W J Athey (125*) v. Gloucestershire at Sheffield, 1980
224	C W J Athey (114) and J D Love (104) v. Warwickshire at Birmingham, 1980

222	W B Stott (141) and K Taylor (90) v. Sussex at Bradford, 1958
221	P Holmes (130) and H Sutcliffe (121) v. Glamorgan at Huddersfield, 1925
221	M D Moxon (141) and A A Metcalfe (73) v. Surrey at The Oval, 1992
219	P Holmes (102) and A Mitchell (130*) v. Somerset at Bradford, 1930
218	M Leyland (110) and H Sutcliffe (235) v. Middlesex at Leeds, 1925
218	R G Lumb (145) and M D Moxon (111) v. Derbyshire at Sheffield, 1981
210*	P Holmes (101*) and H Sutcliffe (100*) v. Nottinghamshire at Nottingham, 1928
210	G Boycott (128) and P J Sharpe (197) v. Pakistanis at Leeds, 1967
209	F A Lowson (115) and D E V Padgett (107) v. Scotland at Hull, 1956
208	A Mitchell (85) and E Oldroyd (111) v. Cambridge University at Cambridge, 1929
207	A Mitchell (90) and W Barber (107) v. Middlesex at Lord's, 1935
206	G Boycott (118) and R G Lumb (87) v. Glamorgan at Sheffield, 1978
204	M D Moxon (66) and A A Metcalfe (162) v. Gloucestershire at Cheltenham, 1990
203	L Hutton (119) and F A Lowson (83) v. Somerset at Huddersfield, 1952
203	M D Moxon (117) and S A Kellett (87) v. Somerset at Middlesbrough, 1992
203	M D Moxon (134) and M P Vaughan (106) v. Matebeleland at Bulawayo, 1996
200*	P Holmes (107*) and H Sutcliffe (80*) v. Oxford University at Oxford, 1930

Note: P Holmes and H Sutcliffe shared 69 century opening partnerships for Yorkshire; G Boycott and R G Lumb 29; L Hutton and F A Lowson 22; M D Moxon and A A Metcalfe 21; J T Brown and J Tunnicliffe 19; H Sutcliffe and L Hutton 15, and L Hall and G Ulyett 12.

SECOND WICKET (Qualification 200 runs)

346	W Barber (162) and M Leyland (189) v. Middlesex at Sheffield, 1932
343	F A Lowson (183*) and J V Wilson (165) v. Oxford University at Oxford, 1956
333	P Holmes (209) and E Oldroyd (138*) v. Warwickshire at Birmingham, 1922
314	H Sutcliffe (255*) and E Oldroyd (138) v. Essex at Southend-on-Sea, 1924
305	J W.Rothery (134) and D Denton (182) v. Derbyshire at Chesterfield, 1910
302	W Watson (172) and J V Wilson (140) v. Derbyshire at Scarborough, 1948
301	P J Sharpe (172*) and D E V Padgett (133) v. Glamorgan at Swansea, 1971
288	H Sutcliffe (165) and A Mitchell (136) v. Lancashire at Manchester, 1939
280	L Hall (160) and F Lee (165) v. Lancashire at Bradford, 1887
266*	K Taylor (178*) and D E V Padgett (107*) v. Oxford University at Oxford, 1962
261*	L Hutton (146*) and J V Wilson (110*) v. Scotland at Hull, 1949
260	R G Lumb (144) and K Sharp (132) v. Glamorgan at Cardiff, 1984
258	H Sutcliffe (230) and E Oldroyd (93) v. Kent at Folkestone, 1931
253	B B Wilson (150) and D Denton (200*) v. Warwickshire at Birmingham, 1912
248	H Sutcliffe (200) and M. Leyland (116) v. Leicestershire at Leicester, 1926
244	P. Holmes (138) and E Oldroyd (151*) v. Glamorgan at Cardiff, 1922
243	G Boycott (141) and J D Love (163) v. Nottinghamshire at Bradford, 1976
243	C White (183) and M J Wood (124) v. Glamorgan at Scarborough, 2001
237	H Sutcliffe (118) and D Denton (122) v. Gloucestershire at Leeds, 1919
237	M D Moxon (132) and K Sharp (128) v. Sri Lankans at Leeds, 1988
236	F A Lowson (112) and J V Wilson (157) v. Essex at Leeds, 1950
235	M D Moxon (130) and D Byas (181) v. Cambridge University at Cambridge, 1995
230	L Hutton (180) and A Mitchell (100) v. Cambridge University at Cambridge, 1938
230	M P Vaughan (109) and B Parker (138*) v. Oxford University at Oxford, 1997.
227	M J Wood (102) and M J Lumb (122) v. Leicestershire at Leeds, 2001
225	H Sutcliffe (138) and E Oldroyd (97) v. Derbyshire at Dewsbury, 1928
223	M D Moxon (153) and R J Blakey (90) v. Somerset at Leeds, 1985
222	H Sutcliffe (174) and D Denton (114) v. Kent at Dover, 1919
219	F S Jackson (155) and D Denton (113) v. Middlesex at Bradford, 1899
217	R G Lumb (107) and J D Love (107) v. Oxford University at Oxford, 1978
216	M P Vaughan (105) and D Byas (102) v. Somerset at Bradford, 1994

CENTURY PARTNERSHIPS *(Continued)*

215	A W Gale (136) and A McGrath (99) v. Lancashire at Manchester, 2008
207	P A Jaques (115) and A McGrath (93) v. Essex at Chelmsford, 2004
206	J Tunnicliffe (102) and F S Jackson (134*) v. Lancashire at Sheffield, 1898
206	H Sutcliffe (187) and M Leyland (90) v. Leicestershire at Leicester, 1931
205	H Sutcliffe (174) and A Mitchell (95) v. Leicestershire at Leicester, 1933
205	G Boycott (148) and P J Sharpe (108) v. Kent at Sheffield, 1970
203	A T Barber (100) and E Oldroyd (143) v. An England XI at Sheffield, 1929
203	J J Sayers (187) and A McGrath (100) v. Kent at Tunbridge Wells, 2007
202*	W Rhodes (115*) and G H Hirst (117*) v. Somerset at Bath, 1906
202	G Boycott (113) and C W J Athey (114) v. Northamptonshire at Northampton, 1978

THIRD WICKET (Qualification 200 runs)

323*	H Sutcliffe (147*) and M Leyland (189*) v. Glamorgan at Huddersfield, 1928
317	A McGrath (165) and D S Lehmann (187) v. Lancashire at Leeds, 2002
310	A McGrath (134) and P A Jaques (219) v. Derbyshire at Leeds, 2005
301	H Sutcliffe (175) and M Leyland (180*) v. Middlesex at Lord's, 1939
293*	A A Metcalfe (150*) and P E Robinson (150*) v. Derbyshire at Scarborough, 1990
269	D Byas (101) and R J Blakey (196) v. Oxford University at Oxford, 1991
258*	J T Brown (134*) and F Mitchell (116*) v. Warwickshire at Bradford, 1901
252	D E V Padgett (139*) and D B Close (154) v. Nottinghamshire at Nottingham, 1959
249	D E V Padgett (95) and D B Close (184) v. Nottinghamshire at Scarborough, 1960
248	C Johnson (102) and J H Hampshire (155*) v. Gloucestershire at Leeds, 1976
247	P Holmes (175*) and M Leyland (118) v. New Zealanders at Bradford, 1927
244	D E V Padgett (161*) and D B Close (144) v. Oxford University at Oxford, 1959
240	L Hutton (151) and M Leyland (95) v. Surrey at Leeds, 1939
236	H Sutcliffe (107) and R Kilner (137) v. Nottinghamshire at Nottingham, 1920
236	M J Wood (94) and D S Lehmann (200) v. Worcestershire at Worcester, 1998
234*	D Byas (126*) and A McGrath (105*) v. Oxford University at Oxford, 1997.
233	L Hutton (101) and M Leyland (167) v. Worcestershire at Stourbridge, 1937
230	D Byas (103) and M J Wood (103) v. Derbyshire at Leeds, 1998
229	L Hall (86) and R Peel (158) v. Middlesex at Lord's, 1889
228	A Mitchell (142) and M Leyland (133) v. Worcestershire at Sheffield, 1933
228	W Barber (141) and M Leyland (114) v. Surrey at The Oval, 1939
228	J V Wilson (132*) and D E V Padgett (115) v. Warwickshire at Birmingham, 1955
226	D E V Padgett (117) and D B Close (198) v. Surrey at The Oval, 1960
224	J V Wilson (110) and D B Close (114) v. Cambridge University at Cambridge, 1955
224	G Boycott (140*) and K Sharp (121) v. Gloucestershire at Cheltenham, 1983
221	A Mitchell (138) and M Leyland (134) v. Nottinghamshire at Bradford, 1933
219	L Hall (116) and W Bates (133) v. Cambridge University at Cambridge, 1884
217	A McGrath (144) and J A Rudolph (129) v. Kent at Canterbury, 2008
216	R G Lumb (118) and J H Hampshire (127) v. Surrey at The Oval, 1975
215	A Mitchell (73) and M Leyland (139) v. Surrey at Bradford, 1928
213	E Oldroyd (168) and W Barber (114) v. Glamorgan at Hull, 1929
208	J V Wilson (157*) and E I Lester (112) v. Sussex at Leeds, 1949
205*	E Oldroyd (122*) and M Leyland (100*) v. Hampshire at Harrogate, 1924
205	F S Jackson (124) and D Denton (112) v. Somerset at Taunton, 1897
205	D E V Padgett (83) and D B Close (128) v. Somerset at Bath, 1959
204	M P Vaughan (113) and A McGrath (70) v. Essex at Scarborough, 2001
203	D Denton (132) and J Tunnicliffe (102) v. Warwickshire at Birmingham, 1905
203	A A Metcalfe (216*) and P E Robinson (88) v. Middlesex at Leeds, 1988
201	J Tunnicliffe (101) and T L Taylor (147) v. Surrey at The Oval, 1900
201	H Sutcliffe (87) and W Barber (130) v. Leicestershire at Leicester, 1938
200	M D Moxon (274*) and A P Grayson (100) v. Worcestershire at Worcester, 1994

FOURTH WICKET (Qualification 175 runs)

358	D S Lehmann (339) and M J Lumb (98) v. Durham at Leeds, 2006	
330	M J Wood (116) and D R Martyn (238) v. Gloucestershire at Leeds, 2003	
312	D Denton (168*) and G H Hirst (146) v. Hampshire at Southampton, 1914	
299	P Holmes (277*) and R Kilner (150) v. Northamptonshire at Harrogate, 1921	
272	D Byas (138) and A McGrath (137) v. Hampshire at Harrogate, 1996	
271	B B Wilson (208) and W Rhodes (113) v. Sussex at Bradford, 1914	
259	A Drake (115) and G H Hirst (218) v. Sussex at Hastings, 1911	
258	J Tunnicliffe (128) and G H Hirst (152) v. Hampshire at Portsmouth, 1904	
258	P E Robinson (147) and D Byas (117) v. Kent at Scarborough, 1989	
249	W B Stott (143) and G Boycott (145) v. Lancashire at Sheffield, 1963	
247*	R G Lumb (165*) and S N Hartley (104*) v. Gloucestershire at Bradford, 1984	
247	M Leyland (263) and L Hutton (83) v. Essex at Hull, 1936	
238	D S Lehmann (216) and M J Lumb (92) v. Sussex at Arundel, 2002	
233	D Byas (120) and P E Robinson (189) v. Lancashire at Scarborough, 1991.	
226	W H Wilkinson (89) and G H Hirst (140) v. Northamptonshire at Hull, 1909	
225	C H Grimshaw (85) and G H Hirst (169) v. Oxford University at Oxford, 1906	
212	B B Wilson (108) and G H Hirst (166*) v. Sussex at Hastings, 1913	
212	G Boycott (260*) and J H Hampshire (80) v. Essex at Colchester, 1970	
211	J V Wilson (120) and W Watson (108) v. Derbyshire at Harrogate, 1951	
210*	A Mitchell (150*) and M Leyland (117*) v. Worcestershire at Worcester, 1933	
210	E I. Lester (178) and W Watson (97) v. Nottinghamshire at Nottingham, 1952	
207	D Byas (213) and C White (107*) v. Worcestershire at Scarborough, 1995	
206	J A Rudolph (121) and A W Gale (150) v. Surrey at The Oval, 2008	
205*	G Boycott (151*) and P J Sharpe (79*) v. Leicestershire at Leicester, 1964	
205	E Oldroyd (121) and R Kilner (117) v. Worcestershire at Dudley, 1922	
205	W Watson (162*) and E I Lester (98) v. Somerset at Leeds, 1953	
201*	J H Hampshire (105*) and D B Close (101*) v. Surrey at Bradford, 1965	
201	W H H Sutcliffe (181) and L Hutton (120) v. Kent at Canterbury, 1952	
200	J V Wilson (92) and W Watson (122) v. Somerset at Taunton, 1950	
198	A A Metcalfe (138) and D Byas (95) v. Warwickshire at Leeds, 1989	
197	N W D Yardley (177) and A Coxon (58) v. Derbyshire at Scarborough, 1947	
196	M D Moxon (130) and D L Bairstow (104) v. Derbyshire at Harrogate, 1987	
193	A Drake (85) and G H Hirst (156) v. Lancashire at Manchester, 1911	
192	J V Wilson (132) and W Watson (105) v. Essex at Bradford, 1955	
191	M Leyland (114) and C Turner (63) v. Essex at Ilford, 1938	
188	H Myers (60) and G H Hirst (158) v. Cambridge University at Cambridge, 1910	
187	E Oldroyd (168) and F E Greenwood (104*) v. Glamorgan at Hull, 1929	
187	K Taylor (203*) and W B Stott (57) v. Warwickshire at Birmingham, 1961	
186	D S Lehmann (193) and D Byas (100) v. Leicestershire at Leicester, 2001	
184	J H Hampshire (96) and R Illingworth (100*) v. Leicestershire at Sheffield, 1968	
182*	E I Lester (101*) and W Watson (103*) v. Nottinghamshire at Bradford, 1952	
180*	G Boycott (207*) and B Leadbeater (50*) v. Cambridge University at Cambridge, 1976	
180	J Tunnicliffe (139*) and G H Hirst (108) v. Surrey at The Oval, 1904	
179	J H Hampshire (179) and S N Hartley (63) v. Surrey at Harrogate, 1981	
179	M D Moxon (171*) and R J Blakey (71) v. Kent at Leeds, 1993	
178	E I Lester (186) and J V Wilson (71) v. Warwickshiire at Scarborough, 1949	
177	J D Love (105*) and J H Hampshire (89) v. Lancashire at Manchester, 1980	
175	L Hutton (177) and W Barber (84) v. Sussex at Scarborough, 1939	
175	A McGrath (188*) and J A Rudolph (82) v. Warwickshire at Birmingham, 2007	

CENTURY PARTNERSHIPS (Continued)

IFTH WICKET (Qualification 150 runs)

40	E Wainwright (228) and G H Hirst (186) v. Surrey at The Oval, 1899	
29	F Mitchell (194) and E Wainwright (153) v. Leicestershire at Leicester, 1899	
76	W Rhodes (104*) and R Kilner (166) v. Northamptonshire at Northampton, 1921	
73	L Hutton (270*) and N W D Yardley (136) v. Hampshire at Bournemouth, 1947	
45*	H Sutcliffe (107*) and W Barber (128*) v. Northamptonshire at Northampton, 1939	
29	D S Lehmann (193) and C White (79) v. Kent at Canterbury, 2006	
17	D B Close (140*) and R Illingworth (107) v. Warwickshire at Sheffield, 1962	
98	E Wainwright (145) and R Peel (111) v. Sussex at Bradford, 1896	
98	W Barber (168) and K R Davidson (101*) v. MCC at Lord's, 1934	
96*	R Kilner (115*) and G H Hirst (82*) v. Gloucestershire at Leeds, 1919	
95	M J Lumb (93) and C White (173*) v. Derbyshire at Derby, 2003	
94*	Younus Khan (202*) and G L Brophy (100*) v. Hampshire at Southampton, 2007	
93	A Mitchell (189) and W Rhodes (88) v. Northamptonshire at Northampton, 1926	
93	J D Love (106) and S N Hartley (108) v. Oxford University at Oxford, 1985	
92	C W J Athey (114*) and J D Love (123) v. Surrey at The Oval, 1982	
91*	L Hutton (271*) and C Turner (81*) v. Derbyshire at Sheffield, 1937	
91	M G Bevan (105) and A A Metcalfe (100) v. West Indians at Scarborough, 1995	
90*	R J Blakey (204*) and J D Love (79*) v. Gloucestershire at Leeds, 1987	
88	D E V Padgett (146) and J V Wilson (72) v. Sussex at Middlesbrough, 1960	
88	J V Wilson (230) and H Halliday (74) v. Derbyshire at Sheffield, 1952	
85	G Boycott (104*) and K Sharp (99) v. Kent at Tunbridge Wells, 1984	
82	E Lockwood (208) and E Lumb (40) v. Kent at Gravesend, 1882	
82	B B Wilson (109) and W Rhodes (111) v. Sussex at Hove, 1910	
82	D B Close (164) and J V Wilson (55) v. Combined Services at Harrogate, 1954	
81	A A Metcalfe (149) and J D Love (88) v. Glamorgan at Leeds, 1986	
77	Hon F S Jackson (87) and G H Hirst (232*) v. Surrey at The Oval, 1905	
76	L Hutton (176*) and A Coxon (72) v. Sussex at Sheffield, 1948	
75	A Drake (108) and R Kilner (77) v. Cambridge University at Cambridge, 1913	
73	H Sutcliffe (206) and R Kilner (124) v. Warwickshire at Dewsbury, 1925	
70	W Rhodes (157) and R Kilner (87) v. Derbyshire at Leeds, 1925	
70	J V Wilson (130*) and N W D Yardley (67) v. Lancashire at Manchester, 1954	
69	W Watson (147) and A B Sellers (92) v. Worcestershire at Worcester, 1947	
68	A T Barber (63) and A Mitchell (122*) v. Worcestershire at Worcester, 1929	
65	E Oldroyd (143) and W Rhodes (110) v. Glamorgan at Leeds, 1922	
65	K Sharp (100*) and P Carrick (73) v. Middlesex at Lord's, 1980	
64	A A Metcalfe (151) and D L Bairstow (88) v. Northamptonshire at Luton, 1986	
159*	J D Love (170*) and D L Bairstow (52*) v. Worcestershire at Worcester, 1979	
159	D B Close (128) and R Illingworth (74) v. Lancashire at Sheffield, 1959	
159	J H Hampshire (183*) and C Johnson (53) v. Sussex at Hove, 1971	
158*	G Boycott (153*) and P E Robinson (74*) v. Derbyshire at Harrogate, 1984	
157	T L Taylor (135*) and G H Hirst (72) v. An England XI at Hastings, 1901	
157	G H Hirst (142) and F Smith (51) v. Somerset at Bradford, 1903	
157	W Barber (87) and N W D Yardley (101) v. Surrey at The Oval, 1937	
156	A McGrath (158) and I J Harvey (103) v. Derbyshire at Derby, 2005	
153	S N Hartley (87) and M D Moxon (112*) v. Indians at Scarborough, 1986	
152	J H Hampshire (83) and S N Hartley (106) v. Nottinghamshire at Nottingham, 1981	
151*	G H Hirst (102*) and R Kilner (50*) v. Kent at Bradford, 1913	
151	G H Hirst (120) and F Smith (55) v. Kent at Leeds, 1903	
151	W Rhodes (57) and R Kilner (90) v. Nottinghamshire at Nottingham, 1925	

CENTURY PARTNERSHIPS *(Continued)*

SIXTH WICKET (Qualification 150 runs)

276	M Leyland (191) and E Robinson (124*) v. Glamorgan at Swansea, 1926
252	C White (181) and R J Blakey (109*) v. Lancashire at Leeds, 1996
233	M W Booth (210) and G H Hirst (100) v. Worcestershire at Worcester, 1911
229	W Rhodes (267*) and N Kilner (112) v. Leicestershire at Leeds, 1921
225	E Wainwright (91) and Lord Hawke (127) v. Hampshire at Southampton, 1899
217*	H Sutcliffe (200*) and A Wood (123*) v. Worcestershire at Sheffield, 1935
214	W Watson (214*) and N W D Yardley (76) v. Worcestershire at Worcester, 1955
205	G H Hirst (125) and S Haigh (159) v. Nottinghamshire at Sheffield, 1901
200	D Denton (127) and G H Hirst (134) v. Essex at Bradford, 1902
198	M Leyland (247) and W Rhodes (100*) v. Worcestershire at Worcester, 1928
190	W Rhodes (126) and M Leyland (79) v. Middlesex at Bradford, 1923
190	J A Rudolph (122) and A U Rashid (86) v. Surrey at The Oval, 2007
188	W Watson (174) and R Illingworth (53) v. Lancashire at Sheffield, 1955
188	M P Vaughan (161) and R J Blakey (92) v. Essex at Ilford, 1997.
184	R Kilner (104) and M W Booth (79) v. Leicestershire at Leeds, 1913
183	G H Hirst (131) and E Smith (129) v. Hampshire at Bradford, 1899
183	W Watson (139*) and R Illingworth (78) v. Somerset at Harrogate, 1956
178*	D Denton (108*) and G H Hirst (112*) v. Lancashire at Manchester, 1902
178*	N W D Yardley (100*) and R Illingworth (71*) v. Gloucestershire at Bristol, 1955
178	E Robinson (100) and D C F Burton (83) v. Derbyshire at Hull, 1921
178	H Sutcliffe (135) and P A Gibb (157*) v. Nottinghamshire at Sheffield, 1935
175	G M Fellows (88) and R J Blakey (103) v. Warwickshire at Birmingham, 2002
174	D S Lehmann (136) and G M Hamilton (73) v. Kent at Maidstone, 1998
172	A J Dalton (119*) and D L Bairstow (62) v. Worcestershire at Dudley, 1971
169	W Barber (124) and H Verity (78*) v. Warwickshire at Birmingham, 1933
169	R Illingworth (162) and J Birkenshaw (37) v. Indians at Sheffield, 1959
166	E Wainwright (116) and E Smith (61) v. Kent at Catford, 1900
166	D B Close (161) and F S Trueman (104) v. Northamptonshire at Northampton, 1963
162*	G Boycott (220*) and J G Binks (70*) v. Northamptonshire at Sheffield, 1967
161*	D L Bairstow (100*) and P Carrick (59*) v. Middlesex at Leeds, 1983
159*	D S Lehmann (187*) and R J Blakey (78*) v. Somerset at Bath, 2001
156	W Rhodes (82*) and E Robinson (94) v. Derbyshire at Chesterfield, 1919
154	C Turner (84) and A Wood (79) v. Glamorgan at Swansea, 1936
153*	J A Rudolph (92*) and A U Rashid (73*) v. Worcestershire at Kidderminster, 2007
151	D Denton (91) and W Rhodes (76) v. Middlesex at Sheffield, 1904
151	G Boycott (152*) and P Carrick (75) v. Warwickshire at Leeds, 1982
150	G Ulyett (199*) and J M Preston (93) v. Derbyshire at Sheffield, 1887

SEVENTH WICKET (Qualification 125 runs)

254	W Rhodes (135) and D C F Burton (142*) v. Hampshire at Dewsbury, 1919
247	P Holmes (285) and W Rhodes (79) v. Nottinghamshire at Nottingham, 1929
215	E Robinson (135*) and D C F Burton (110) v. Leicestershire at Leicester, 1921
185	E Wainwright (100) and G H Hirst (134) v. Gloucestershire at Bristol, 1897
183	G H Hirst (341) and H Myers (57) v. Leicestershire at Leicester, 1905
183	J A Rudolph (220) and T T Bresnan (101*) v. Warwickshire at Scarborough, 2007
180	C Turner (130) and A Wood (97) v. Somerset at Sheffield, 1936
170	G S Blewett (190) and G M Hamilton (84*) v. Northamptonshire at Scarborough, 1999
166	R Peel (55) and I Grimshaw (122*) v. Derbyshire at Holbeck, 1886
162	E Wainwright (109) and S Haigh (73) v. Somerset at Taunton, 1900
162	R J Blakey (90) and R K J Dawson (87) v. Kent at Canterbury, 2002
162	A W Gale (149) and G L Brophy (97) v. Warwickshire at Scarborough, 2006

CENTURY PARTNERSHIPS *(Continued)*

161   R G Lumb (118) and C M Old (89) v. Worcestershire at Bradford, 1980
160   J Tunnicliffe (158) and D Hunter (58*) v. Worcestershire at Worcester, 1900
157*   F A Lowson (259*) and R Booth (53*) v. Worcestershire at Worcester, 1953
155   D Byas (122*) and P Carrick (61) v. Leicestershire at Leicester.1991.
154*   G H Hirst (76*) and J T Newstead (100*) v. Nottinghamshire at Nottingham, 1908
148   J Rowbotham (113) and J Thewlis (50) v. Surrey at The Oval, 1873
147   E Wainwright (78) and G Ulyett (73) v. Somerset at Taunton, 1893
147   M P Vaughan (153) and R J Harden (64) v. Kent at Scarborough, 1999
143   C White (135*) and A K D Gray (60) v. Durham at Chester-le-Street, 2003
141   G H Hirst (108*) and S Haigh (48) v. Worcestershire at Worcester, 1905
141   J H Hampshire (149*) and J G Binks (72) v. MCC at Scarborough, 1965
140   E Wainwright (117) and S Haigh (54) v. CI Thornton's XI at Scarborough, 1900
140   D Byas (67) and P J Hartley (75) v. Derbyshire at Chesterfield, 1990
138   D Denton (78) and G H Hirst (103*) v. Sussex at Leeds, 1905
136   GH Hirst (93) and S Haigh (130) v. Warwickshire at Birmingham, 1904
136   E Robinson (77*) and A Wood (65) v. Glamorgan at Scarborough, 1931
133*   W Rhodes (267*) and M Leyland (52*) v. Leicestershire at Leeds, 1921
133*   E I Lester (86*) and A B Sellers (73*) v. Northamptonshire at Northampton, 1948
133   D Byas (100) and P W Jarvis (80*) v. Northamptonshire at Scarborough, 1992
132   W Rhodes (196) and S Haigh (59*) v. Worcestershire at Worcester, 1904
131*   D L Bairstow (79*) and A Sidebottom (52*) v. Oxford University at Oxford, 1981
130   P J Sharpe (64) and J V Wilson (134) v. Warwickshire at Birmingham, 1962
128   W Barber (66) and T F Smailes (86) v. Cambridge University at Cambridge, 1938
128   D B Close (88*) and A Coxon (59) v. Essex at Leeds, 1949
126   E Wainwright (171) and R Peel (46) v. Middlesex at Lord's, 1897
126   W Rhodes (91) and G G Macaulay (63) v. Hampshire at Hull, 1925
126   J C Balderstone (58) and J G Binks (95) v. Middlesex at Lord's, 1964
125   A B Sellers (109) and T F Smailes (65) v. Kent at Bradford, 1937

EIGHTH WICKET (Qualification 125 runs)

292   R Peel (210*) and Lord Hawke (166) v. Warwickshire at Birmingham, 1896
238   I J Harvey (209*) and T T Bresnan (74) v. Somerset at Leeds, 2005
192*   W Rhodes (108*) and G G Macaulay (101*) v. Essex at Harrogate, 1922
180   W Barber (191) and T F Smailes (89) v. Sussex at Leeds, 1935
165   S Haigh (62) and Lord Hawke (126) v. Surrey at The Oval, 1902
163   G G Macaulay (67) and A Waddington (114) v. Worcestershire at Leeds, 1927
159   E Smith (95) and W Rhodes (105) v. MCC at Scarborough, 1901
152   W Rhodes (98) and J W Rothery (70) v. Hampshire at Portsmouth, 1904
151   W Rhodes (201) and Lord Hawke (51) v. Somerset at Taunton, 1905
151   R J Blakey (80*) and P J Hartley (89) v. Sussex at Eastbourne, 1996
147   J P G Chadwick (59) and F S Trueman (101) v. Middlesex at Scarborough, 1965
146   S Haigh (159) and Lord Hawke (89) v. Nottinghamshire at Sheffield, 1901
138   E Wainwright (100) and Lord Hawke (81) v. Kent at Tonbridge, 1899
137   E Wainwright (171) and Lord Hawke (75) v. Middlesex at Lord's, 1897
133   P W Jarvis (55) and P J Hartley (69) v. Nottinghamshire at Scarborough, 1992
133   R Illingworth (61) and F S Trueman (74) v. Leicestershire at Leicester, 1955
132   G H Hirst (103) and E Smith (59) v. Middlesex at Sheffield, 1904
132   W Watson (119) and J H Wardle (65) v. Leicestershire at Leicester, 1949
131   P E Robinson (85) and P Carrick (64) v. Surrey at Harrogate, 1990
130   E Smith (98) and Lord Hawke (54) v. Lancashire at Leeds, 1904
128   H Verity (96*) and T F Smailes (77) v. Indians at Bradford, 1936
128   D L Bairstow (145) and G B Stevenson (11) v. Middlesex at Scarborough, 1980

CENTURY PARTNERSHIPS *(Continued)*

127	E Robinson (70*) and A Wood (62) v. Middlesex at Leeds, 1928
126	R Peel (74) and E Peate (61) v. Gloucestershire at Bradford, 1883
126	M W Booth (56) and E R Wilson (104*) v. Essex at Bradford, 1913
126	J D Middlebrook (84) and C E W Silverwood (70) v. Essex at Chelmsford, 2001
126	M J Lumb (115*) and D Gough (72) v. Hampshire at Southampton, 2003

NINTH WICKET (Qualification 100 runs)

246	T T Bresnan (116) and J N Gillespie (123*) v. Surrey at The Oval, 2007
192	G H Hirst (130*) and S Haigh (85) v. Surrey at Bradford, 1898
179	R A Hutton (189) and G A Cope (30*) v. Pakistanis at Bradford, 1971
176*	R Moorhouse (59*) and G H Hirst (115*) v. Gloucestershire at Bristol, 1894
173	S Haigh (85) and W Rhodes (92*) v. Sussex at Hove, 1902
167	H Verity (89) and T F Smailes (80) v. Somerset at Bath, 1936
162	W Rhodes (94*) and S Haigh (84) v. Lancashire at Manchester, 1904
161	E Smith (116*) and W Rhodes (79) v. Sussex at Sheffield, 1900
149*	R J Blakey (63*) and A K D Gray (74*) v. Leicestershire at Scarborough, 2002
149	G H Hirst (232*) and D Hunter (40) v. Surrey at The Oval, 1905
146	G H Hirst (214) and W Rhodes (53) v. Worcestershire at Worcester, 1901
144	T T Bresnan (91) and J N Gillespie (44) v. Hampshire at Leeds, 2006
140	A U Rashid (111) and D J Wainwright (104) v. Sussex at Hove, 2008
136	R Peel (210*) and G H Hirst (85) v. Warwickshire at Birmingham, 1896
125*	L Hutton (269*) and A Coxon (65*) v. Northamptonshire at Wellingborough, 1949
124	P J Hartley (87*) and P W Jarvis (47) v. Essex at Chelmsford, 1986
120	G H Hirst (138) and W Rhodes (38) v. Nottinghamshire at Nottingham, 1899
119	A B Sellers (80*) and E P Robinson (66) v. Warwickshire at Birmingham, 1938
118	S Haigh (96) and W Rhodes (44) v. Somerset at Leeds, 1901
114	E Oldroyd (194) and A Dolphin (47) v. Worcestershire at Worcester, 1923
114	N Kilner (102*) and G G Macaulay (60) v. Gloucestershire at Bristol, 1923
113	G G Macaulay (125*) and A Waddington (44) v. Nottinghamshire at Nottingham, 1921
113	A Wood (69) and H.Verity (45*) v. MCC at Lord's, 1938
112	G H Hirst (78) and Lord Hawke (61*) v. Essex at Leyton, 1907
109	Lees Whitehead (60) and W Rhodes (81*) v. Sussex at Harrogate, 1899
108	A McGrath (133*) and C E W Silverwood (80) v. Durham at Chester-le-Street, 2005
105	J V Wilson (134) and A G Nicholson (20*) v. Nottinghamshire at Leeds, 1962
105	C M Old (100*) and H P Cooper (30) v. Lancashire at Manchester, 1978
105	C White (74*) and J D Batty (50) v. Gloucestershire at Sheffield, 1993
104	L Hall (129*) and R Moorhouse (86) v. Gloucestershire at Clifton, 1888
100	G Pollitt (51) and Lees Whitehead (54) v. Hampshire at Bradford, 1899

TENTH WICKET (Qualification 100 runs)

149	G Boycott (79) and G B Stevenson (115*) v. Warwickshire at Birmingham, 1982
148	Lord Hawke (107*) and D Hunter (47) v. Kent at Sheffield, 1898
144	A Sidebottom (124) and A L Robinson (30*) v. Glamorgan at Cardiff, 1977
121	J T Brown (141) and D Hunter (25*) v. Liverpool & District at Liverpool, 1894
118	Lord Hawke (110*) and D Hunter (41) v. Kent at Leeds, 1896
113	P J Hartley (88*) and R D Stemp (22) v. Middlesex at Lord's, 1996
110	C E W Silverwood (45*) and R D Stemp (65) v. Durham at Chester-le-Street, 1996
108	Lord Hawke (79) and Lees Whitehead (45*) v. Lancashire at Manchester, 1903
108	G Boycott (129) and M K Bore (37*) v. Nottinghamshire at Bradford, 1973
106	A B Sellers (79) and D V Brennan (30) v. Worcestershire at Worcester, 1948
103	A Dolphin (62*) and E Smith (49) v. Essex at Leyton, 1919
102	D Denton (77*) and D Hunter (45) v. Cambridge University at Cambridge, 1895

FIFTEEN WICKETS OR MORE IN A MATCH

A complete list of 12, 13 and 14 wickets in a match up to and including 2007 is to be found in the 2008 edition

W E BOWES (1)

16 for 35 (8 for 18 and 8 for 17) v. Northamptonshire at Kettering, 1935

A DRAKE (1)

15 for 51 (5 for 16 and 10 for 35) v. Somerset at Weston-super-Mare, 1914

T EMMETT (1)

16 for 38 (7 for 15 and 9 for 23) v. Cambridgeshire at Hunslet, 1869

G H HIRST (1)

15 for 63 (8 for 25 and 7 for 38) v. Leicestershire at Hull, 1907

R ILLINGWORTH (1)

15 for 123 (8 for 70 and 7 for 53) v. Glamorgan at Swansea, 1960

R PEEL (1)

15 for 50 (9 for 22 and 6 for 28) v. Somerset at Leeds, 1895

W RHODES (1)

15 for 56 (9 for 28 and 6 for 28) v. Essex at Leyton, 1899

H VERITY (4)

17 for 91 (8 for 47 and 9 for 44) v. Essex at Leyton, 1933
15 for 129 (8 for 56 and 7 for 73) v. Oxford University at Oxford, 1936
15 for 38 (6 for 26 and 9 for 12) v. Kent at Sheffield, 1936
15 for 100 (6 for 52 and 9 for 48) v. Essex at Westcliffe-on-Sea, 1936

J H WARDLE (1)

16 for 112 (9 for 48 and 7 for 64) v. Sussex at Hull, 1954

TEN WICKETS IN A MATCH
(including best analysis)

61	W Rhodes	15 for	56	v Essex	at Leyton	1899
48	H Verity	17 for	91	v Essex	at Leyton	1933
40	G H Hirst	15 for	63	v Leicestershire	at Hull	1907
31	G G Macaulay	14 for	92	v Gloucestershire	at Bristol	1926
28	S Haigh	14 for	43	v Hampshire	at Southampton	1898
27	R Peel	14 for	33	v Nottinghamshire	at Sheffield	1888
25	W E Bowes	16 for	35	v Northamptonshire	at Kettering	1935
25	J H Wardle	16 for	112	v Sussex	at Hull	1954
22	E Peate	14 for	77	v Surrey	at Huddersfield	1881
20	F S Trueman	14 for	123	v Surrey	at The Oval	1960
19	T Emmett	16 for	38	v Cambridgeshire	at Hunslet	1869
17	R Appleyard	12 for	43	v Essex	at Bradford	1951
15	E Wainwright	14 for	77	v Essex	at Bradford	1896
11	R Illingworth	15 for	123	v Glamorgan	at Swansea	1960
10	A Waddington	13 for	48	v Northamptonshire	at Northampton	1920
9	M W Booth	14 for	160	v Essex	at Leyton	1914
9	R Kilner	12 for	55	v Sussex	at Hove	1924
8	W Bates	11 for	47	v Nottinghamshire	at Nottingham	1881
8	G Freeman	13 for	60	v Surrey	at Sheffield	1869
7	E P Robinson	13 for	115	v Lancashire	at Leeds	1939
7	D Wilson	13 for	52	v Warwickshire	at Middlesbrough	1967

6 G A Cope	12 for 116	v Glamorgan	at Cardiff (Sophia Gardens)	1968
6 A Hill	12 for 59	v Surrey	at The Oval	1871
6 T F Smailes	14 for 58	v Derbyshire	at Sheffield	1939
5 P Carrick	12 for 89	v Derbyshire	at Sheffield (Abbeydale Pk)	1983
5 J M Preston	13 for 63	v MCC	at Scarborough	1888
5 E Robinson	12 for 95	v Northamptonshire	at Huddersfield	1927
4 J T Newstead	11 for 72	v Worcestershire	at Bradford	1907
3 T W Foster	11 for 93	v Liverpool & District	at Liverpool	1894
3 G P Harrison	11 for 76	v Kent	at Dewsbury	1883
3 F S Jackson	12 for 80	v Hampshire	at Southampton	1897
3 P W Jarvis	11 for 92	v Middlesex	at Lord's	1986
3 S P Kirby	13 for 154	v Somerset	at Taunton	2003
3 A G Nicholson	12 for 73	v Glamorgan	at Leeds	1964
3 R K Platt	10 for 87	v Surrey	at The Oval	1959
3 A Sidebottom	11 for 64	v Kent	at Sheffield (Abbeydale Pk)	1980
3 G Ulyett	12 for 102	v Lancashire	at Huddersfield	1889
2 T Armitage	13 for 46	v Surrey	at Sheffield	1876
2 R Aspinall	14 for 65	v Northamptonshire	at Northampton	1947
2 J T Brown (Darfield)	12 for 109	v Gloucestershire	at Huddersfield	1899
2 R O Clayton	12 for 104	v Lancashire	at Manchester	1877
2 D B Close	11 for 116	v Kent	at Gillingham	1965
2 M J Cowan	12 for 87	v Warwickshire	at Birmingham	1960
2 A Coxon	10 for 57	v Derbyshire	at Chesterfield	1949
2 D Gough	10 for 80	v Lancashire	at Leeds	1995
2 G M Hamilton	11 for 72	v Surrey	at Leeds	1998
2 P J Hartley	11 for 68	v Derbyshire	at Chesterfield	1995
2 R A Hutton	11 for 62	v Lancashire	at Manchester	1971
2 E Leadbeater	11 for 162	v Nottinghamshire	at Nottingham	1950
2 M A Robinson	12 for 124	v Northamptonshire	at Harrogate	1993
2 M Ryan	10 for 77	v Leicestershire	at Bradford	1962
2 E Smith (Morley)	10 for 97	v MCC	at Scarborough	1893
2 G B Stevenson	11 for 74	v Nottinghamshire	at Nottingham	1980
2 S Wade	11 for 56	v Gloucestershire	at Cheltenham	1886
2 E R Wilson	11 for 109	v Sussex	at Hove	1921
1 A B Bainbridge	12 for 111	v Essex	at Harrogate	1961
1 J Birkenshaw	11 for 134	v Middlesex	at Leeds	1960
1 A Booth	10 for 91	v Indians	at Bradford	1946
1 H P Cooper	11 for 96	v Northamptonshire	at Northampton	1976
1 A Drake	15 for 51	v Somerset	at Weston-Super-Mare	1914
1 L Greenwood	11 for 71	v Surrey	at The Oval	1867
1 P M Hutchison	11 for 102	v Pakistan 'A'	at Leeds	1997
1 L Hutton	10 for 101	v Leicestershire	at Leicester (Aylestone Rd)	1937
1 R Iddison	10 for 68	v Surrey	at Sheffield	1864
1 M Leyland	10 for 94	v Leicestershire	at Leicester (Aylestone Rd)	1933
1 J D Middlebrook	10 for 170	v Hampshire	at Southampton	2000
1 F W Milligan	12 for 110	v Sussex	at Sheffield	1897
1 H Myers	12 for 109	v Gloucestershire	at Dewsbury	1904
1 C M Old	11 for 46	v Gloucestershire	at Middlesbrough	1969
1 D Pickles	12 for 133	v Somerset	at Taunton	1957
1 W Ringrose	11 for 135	v Australians	at Bradford	1905
1 R J Sidebottom	11 for 43	v Kent	at Leeds	2000
1 C E W Silverwood	12 for 148	v Kent	at Leeds	1997
1 W Slinn	12 for 53	v Nottinghamshire	at Nottingham	1864
1 J Waring	10 for 63	v Lancashire	at Leeds	1966
1 F Wilkinson	10 for 129	v Hampshire	at Bournemouth	1938
1 A C Williams	10 for 66	v Hampshire	at Dewsbury	1919

TEN WICKETS IN AN INNINGS

Bowler			*Year*
A Drake . . . . 10 for 35	v.	Somerset at Weston-super-Mare	1914
H Verity . . . . 10 for 36	v.	Warwickshire at Leeds	1931
*H Verity . . . . 10 for 10	v.	Nottinghamshire at Leeds	1932
T F Smailes . . . . 10 for 47	v.	Derbyshire at Sheffield	1939

*Includes the hat trick.

EIGHT WICKETS OR MORE IN AN INNINGS

(Ten wickets in an innings also listed above)

A complete list of seven wickets in an innings up to and including 2007 is to be found in the 2008 edition

R APPLEYARD (1)

8 for 76 v. MCC at Scarborough, 1951

R ASPINALL (1)

8 for 42 v. Northamptonshire at Northampton, 1947

W BATES (2)

8 for 45 v. Lancashire at Huddersfield, 1878
8 for 21 v. Surrey at The Oval, 1879

M W BOOTH (4)

8 for 52 v. Leicestershire at Sheffield, 1912
8 for 47 v. Middlesex at Leeds, 1912
8 for 86 v. Middlesex at Sheffield, 1913
8 for 64 v. Essex at Leyton, 1914

W E BOWES (9)

8 for 77 v. Leicestershire at Dewsbury, 1929
8 for 69 v. Middlesex at Bradford, 1930
9 for 121 v. Essex at Scarborough, 1932
8 for 62 v. Sussex at Hove, 1932
8 for 69 v. Gloucestershire at Gloucester, 1933
8 for 40 v.Worcestershire at Sheffield, 1935
8 for 18 v. Northamptonshire at Kettering, 1935
8 for 17 v. Northamptonshire at Kettering, 1935
8 for 56 v. Leicestershire at Scarborough, 1936

J T BROWN (Darfield) (1)

8 for 40 v. Gloucestershire at Huddersfield, 1899

P CARRICK (2)

8 for 33 v. Cambridge University at Cambridge, 1973
8 for 72 v. Derbyshire at Scarborough, 1975

R O CLAYTON (1)

8 for 66 v. Lancashire at Manchester, 1877

D B CLOSE (2)

8 for 41 v. Kent at Leeds, 1959
8 for 43 v. Essex at Leeds, 1960

H P COOPER (1)

8 for 62 v. Glamorgan at Cardiff, 1975

EIGHT WICKETS OR MORE IN AN INNINGS *(Continued)*

G A COPE (1)

8 for 73 v. Gloucestershire at Bristol, 1975

M J COWAN (1)

9 for 43 v. Warwickshire at Birmingham, 1960

A COXON (1)

8 for 31 v. Worcestershire at Leeds, 1946

A DRAKE (2)

8 for 59 v. Gloucestershire at Sheffield, 1913
10 for 35 v. Somerset at Weston-super-Mare, 1914

T EMMETT (8)

9 for 34 v. Nottinghamshire at Dewsbury, 1868
9 for 23 v. Cambridgeshire at Hunslet, 1869
8 for 31 v. Nottinghamshire at Sheffield, 1871
8 for 46 v. Gloucestershire at Clifton, 1877
8 for 16 v. MCC at Scarborough, 1877
8 for 22 v. Surrey at The Oval, 1881
8 for 52 v. MCC at Scarborough, 1882
8 for 32 v. Sussex at Huddersfield, 1884

S D FLETCHER (1)

8 for 58 v. Essex at Sheffield, 1988

T W FOSTER (1)

9 for 59 v. MCC at Lord's, 1894

G FREEMAN (2)

8 for 11 v. Lancashire at Holbeck, 1868
8 for 29 v. Surrey at Sheffield, 1869

L GREENWOOD (1)

8 for 35 v. Cambridgeshire at Dewsbury, 1867

S HAIGH (5)

8 for 78 v. Australians at Bradford, 1896
8 for 35 v. Hampshire at Harrogate, 1896
8 for 21 v. Hampshire at Southampton, 1898
8 for 33 v. Warwickshire at Scarborough, 1899
9 for 25 v. Gloucestershire at Leeds, 1912

P J HARTLEY (2)

8 for 111 v. Sussex at Hove, 1992
9 for 41 v. Derbyshire at Chesterfield, 1995

G H HIRST (8)

8 for 59 v. Warwickshire at Birmingham, 1896
8 for 48 v. Australians at Bradford, 1899
8 for 25 v. Leicestershire at Hull, 1907
9 for 45 v. Middlesex at Sheffield, 1907
9 for 23 v. Lancashire at Leeds, 1910
8 for 80 v. Somerset at Sheffield, 1910
9 for 41 v. Worcestershire at Worcester, 1911
9 for 69 v. MCC at Lord's, 1912

EIGHT WICKETS OR MORE IN AN INNINGS *(Continued)*

R ILLINGWORTH (5)

8 for 69 v. Surrey at The Oval, 1954
9 for 42 v. Worcestershire at Worcester, 1957
8 for 70 v. Glamorgan at Swansea, 1960
8 for 50 v. Lancashire at Manchester, 1961
8 for 20 v. Worcestershire at Leeds, 1965

R KILNER (2)

8 for 26 v. Glamorgan at Cardiff, 1923
8 for 40 v. Middlesex at Bradford, 1926

S P KIRBY (1)

8 for 80 v. Somerset at Taunton, 2003

E LEADBEATER (1)

8 for 83 v. Worcestershire at Worcester, 1950

M LEYLAND (1)

8 for 63 v. Hampshire at Huddersfield, 1938

G G MACAULAY (3)

8 for 43 v. Gloucestershire at Bristol, 1926
8 for 37 v. Derbyshire at Hull, 1927
8 for 21 v. Indians at Harrogate, 1932

H MYERS (1)

8 for 81 v. Gloucestershire at Dewsbury, 1904

A G NICHOLSON (2)

9 for 62 v. Sussex at Eastbourne, 1967
8 for 22 v. Kent at Canterbury, 1968

E PEATE (6)

8 for 24 v. Lancashire at Manchester, 1880
8 for 30 v. Surrey at Huddersfield, 1881
8 for 69 v. Sussex at Hove, 1881
8 for 32 v. Middlesex at Sheffield, 1882
8 for 5 v. Surrey at Holbeck, 1883
8 for 63 v. Kent at Gravesend, 1884

R PEEL (6)

8 for 12 v. Nottinghamshire at Sheffield, 1888
8 for 60 v. Surrey at Sheffield, 1890
8 for 54 v. Cambridge University at Cambridge, 1893
9 for 22 v. Somerset at Leeds, 1895
8 for 27 v. South of England XI at Scarborough, 1896
8 for 53 v. Kent at Halifax, 1897

J M PRESTON (2)

8 for 27 v. Sussex at Hove, 1888
9 for 28 v. MCC at Scarborough, 1888

EIGHT WICKETS OR MORE IN AN INNINGS *(Continued)*

W RHODES (18)

9 for 28 v. Essex at Leyton, 1899
8 for 38 v. Nottinghamshire at Nottingham, 1899
8 for 68 v. Cambridge University at Cambridge, 1900
8 for 43 v. Lancashire at Bradford, 1900
8 for 23 v. Hampshire at Hull, 1900
8 for 72 v. Gloucestershire at Bradford, 1900
8 for 28 v. Essex at Harrogate, 1900
8 for 53 v. Middlesex at Lord's, 1901
8 for 55 v. Kent at Canterbury, 1901
8 for 26 v. Kent at Catford, 1902
8 for 87 v. Worcestershire at Worcester, 1903
8 for 61 v. Lancashire at Bradford, 1903
8 for 90 v. Warwickshire at Birmingham, 1905
8 for 92 v. Northamptonshire at Northampton, 1911
8 for 44 v. Warwickshire at Bradford, 1919
8 for 39 v. Sussex at Leeds, 1920
8 for 48 v. Somerset at Huddersfield, 1926
9 for 39 v. Essex at Leyton, 1929

W RINGROSE (1)

9 for 76 v. Australians at Bradford, 1905

E ROBINSON (3)

9 for 36 v. Lancashire at Bradford, 1920
8 for 32 v. Northamptonshire at Huddersfield, 1927
8 for 13 v. Cambridge University at Cambridge, 1928

E P ROBINSON (2)

8 for 35 v. Lancashire at Leeds, 1939
8 for 76 v. Surrey at The Oval, 1946

M A ROBINSON (1)

9 for 37 v. Northamptonshire at Harrogate, 1993

A SIDEBOTTOM (1)

8 for 72 v. Leicestershire at Middlesbrough, 1986

T F SMAILES (2)

8 for 68 v. Glamorgan at Hull, 1938
10 for 47 v. Derbyshire at Sheffield, 1939

G B STEVENSON (2)

8 for 65 v. Lancashire at Leeds, 1978
8 for 57 v. Northamptonshire at Leeds, 1980

F S TRUEMAN (8)

8 for 70 v. Minor Counties at Lord's, 1949
8 for 68 v. Nottinghamshire at Sheffield, 1951
8 for 53 v. Nottinghamshire at Nottingham, 1951
8 for 28 v. Kent at Dover, 1954
8 for 84 v. Nottinghamshire at Worksop, 1962
8 for 45 v. Gloucestershire at Bradford, 1963
8 for 36 v. Sussex at Hove, 1965
8 for 37 v. Essex at Bradford, 1966

EIGHT WICKETS OR MORE IN AN INNINGS *(Continued)*

H VERITY (20)

9 for 60 v. Glamorgan at Swansea, 1930
10 for 36 v. Warwickshire at Leeds, 1931
8 for 33 v. Glamorgan at Swansea, 1931
8 for 107 v. Lancashire at Bradford, 1932
8 for 39 v. Northamptonshire at Northampton, 1932
10 for 10 v. Nottinghamshire at Leeds, 1932
8 for 47 v. Essex at Leyton, 1933
9 for 44 v. Essex at Leyton, 1933
9 for 59 v. Kent at Dover, 1933
8 for 28 v. Leicestershire at Leeds, 1935
8 for 56 v. Oxford University at Oxford, 1936
8 for 40 v. Worcestershire at Stourbridge, 1936
9 for 12 v. Kent at Sheffield, 1936
9 for 48 v. Essex at Westcliff-on-Sea, 1936
8 for 42 v. Nottinghamshire at Bradford, 1936
9 for 43 v. Warwickshire at Leeds, 1937
8 for 80 v. Sussex at Eastbourne, 1937
8 for 43 v. Middlesex at The Oval, 1937
9 for 62 v. MCC at Lord's, 1939
8 for 38 v. Leicestershire at Hull, 1939

A WADDINGTON (3)

8 for 34 v. Northamptonshire at Leeds, 1922
8 for 39 v. Kent at Leeds, 1922
8 for 35 v. Hampshire at Bradford, 1922

E WAINWRIGHT (3)

8 for 49 v. Middlesex at Sheffield, 1891
9 for 66 v. Middlesex at Sheffield, 1894
8 for 34 v. Essex at Bradford, 1896

J H WARDLE (4)

8 for 87 v. Derbyshire at Chesterfield, 1948
8 for 26 v. Middlesex at Lord's, 1950
9 for 48 v. Sussex at Hull, 1954
9 for 25 v. Lancashire at Manchester, 1954

C WHITE (1)

8 for 55 v. Gloucestershire at Gloucester, 1998

A C WILLIAMS (1)

9 for 29 v. Hampshire at Dewsbury, 1919

R WOOD (1)

8 for 45 v. Scotland at Glasgow, 1952

SIX WICKETS IN AN INNINGS AT LESS THAN FOUR RUNS EACH

A complete list of 5 wickets at less than 4 runs each up to and including 2007 is to be found in the 2008 edition

R APPLEYARD (2)

6 for 17 v. Essex at Bradford, 1951

6 for 12 v. Hampshire at Bournemouth, 1954

T ARMITAGE (1)

6 for 20 v. Surrey at Sheffield, 1876

R ASPINALL (1)

6 for 23 v. Northamptonshire at Northampton, 1947

W BATES (5)

6 for 11 v. Middlesex at Huddersfield, 1879

6 for 22 v. Kent at Bradford, 1881

6 for 17 v. Nottinghamshire at Nottingham, 1881

6 for 12 v. Kent at Sheffield, 1882

6 for 19 v. Lancashire at Dewsbury, 1886

A BOOTH (1)

6 for 21 v. Warwickshire at Birmingham, 1946

W E BOWES (4)

6 for 17 v. Middlesex at Lord's, 1934

6 for 16 v. Lancashire at Bradford, 1935

6 for 20 v. Gloucestershire at Sheffield, 1936

6 for 23 v. Warwickshire at Birmingham, 1947

J T BROWN (Darfield) (1)

6 for 19 v. Worcestershire at Worcester, 1899

R.O CLAYTON (1)

6 for 20 v. Nottinghamshire at Sheffield, 1876

A COXON (1)

6 for 17 v. Surrey at Sheffield, 1948

T EMMETT (6)

6 for 7 v. Surrey at Sheffield, 1867

6 for 13 v. Lancashire at Holbeck, 1868

6 for 21 v. Middlesex at Scarborough, 1874

6 for 12 v. Derbyshire at Sheffield, 1878

6 for 19 v. Derbyshire at Bradford, 1881

6 for 22 v. Australians at Bradford, 1882

H FISHER (1)

6 for 11 v. Leicestershire at Bradford, 1932

SIX WICKETS IN AN INNINGS AT LESS THAN FOUR
RUNS EACH *(Continued)*

S HAIGH (10)

6 for 18 v. Derbyshire at Bradford, 1897
6 for 22 v. Hampshire at Southampton, 1898
6 for 21 v. Surrey at The Oval, 1900
6 for 23 v. Cambridge University at Cambridge, 1902
6 for 19 v. Somerset at Sheffield, 1902
6 for 22 v. Cambridge University at Sheffield, 1903
6 for 21 v. Hampshire at Leeds, 1904
6 for 21 v. Nottinghamshire at Sheffield, 1905
6 for 13 v. Surrey at Leeds, 1908
6 for 14 v. Australians at Bradford, 1912

A HILL (2)

6 for 9 v. United South of England XI at Bradford, 1874
6 for 18 v. MCC at Lord's, 1881

G H HIRST (7)

6 for 23 v. MCC at Lord's, 1893
6 for 20 v. Lancashire at Bradford, 1906
6 for 12 v. Northamptonshire at Northampton, 1908
6 for 7 v. Northamptonshire at Northampton, 1908
6 for 23 v. Surrey at Leeds, 1908
6 for 23 v. Lancashire at Manchester, 1909
6 for 20 v. Surrey at Sheffield, 1909

R ILLINGWORTH (2)

6 for 15 v. Scotland at Hull, 1956
6 for 13 v. Leicestershire at Leicester, 1963

F S JACKSON (1)

6 for 19 v. Hampshire at Southampton, 1897

R KILNER (5)

6 for 22 v. Essex at Harrogate, 1922
6 for 13 v. Hampshire at Bournemouth, 1922
6 for 14 v. Middlesex at Bradford, 1923
6 for 22 v. Surrey at Sheffield, 1923
6 for 15 v. Hampshire at Portsmouth, 1924

G G MACAULAY (10)

6 for 10 v. Warwickshire at Birmingham, 1921
6 for 3 v. Derbyshire at Hull, 1921
6 for 8 v. Northamptonshire at Northampton, 1922
6 for 12 v. Glamorgan at Cardiff, 1922
6 for 18 v. Northamptonshire at Bradford, 1923
6 for 19 v. Northamptonshire at Northampton, 1925
6 for 22 v. Leicestershire at Leeds, 1926
6 for 11 v. Leicestershire at Hull, 1930
6 for 22 v. Leicestershire at Bradford, 1933
6 for 22 v. Middlesex at Leeds, 1934

SIX WICKETS IN AN INNINGS AT LESS THAN FOUR
RUNS EACH *(Continued)*

E PEATE (5)

6 for 14 v. Middlesex at Huddersfield, 1879
6 for 12 v. Derbyshire at Derby, 1882
6 for 13 v. Gloucestershire at Moreton-in-Marsh, 1884
6 for 16 v. Sussex at Huddersfield, 1886
6 for 16 v. Cambridge University at Sheffield, 1886

R PEEL (4)

6 for 21 v. Nottinghamshire at Sheffield, 1888
6 for 19 v. Australians at Huddersfield, 1888
6 for 22 v. Gloucestershire at Bristol, 1891
6 for 19 v. Leicestershire at Scarborough, 1896

A C RHODES (1)

6 for 19 v. Cambridge University at Cambridge, 1932

W RHODES (12)

6 for 21 v. Somerset at Bath, 1898
6 for 16 v. Gloucestershire at Bristol, 1899
6 for 4 v. Nottinghamshire at Nottingham, 1901
6 for 15 v. MCC at Lord's, 1902
6 for 16 v. Cambridge University at Cambridge, 1905
6 for 9 v. Essex at Huddersfield, 1905
6 for 22 v. Derbyshire at Glossop, 1907
6 for 17 v. Leicestershire at Leicester, 1908
6 for 13 v. Sussex at Hove, 1922
6 for 23 v. Nottinghamshire at Leeds, 1923
6 for 22 v. Cambridge University at Cambridge, 1924
6 for 20 v. Gloucestershire at Dewsbury, 1927

W RINGROSE (1)

6 for 20 v. Leicestershire at Dewsbury, 1903

R J SIDEBOTTOM (1)

6 for 16 v. Kent at Leeds, 2000

W SLINN (1)

6 for 19 v. Nottinghamshire at Nottingham, 1864

G B STEVENSON(1)

6 for 14 v. Warwickshire at Sheffield, 1979

F S TRUEMAN (4)

6 for 23 v. Oxford University at Oxford, 1955
6 for 23 v. Oxford University at Oxford, 1958
6 for 18 v. Warwickshire at Birmingham, 1963
6 for 20 v. Leicestershire at Sheffield, 1968

H VERITY (5)

6 for 11 v. Surrey at Bradford, 1931
6 for 21 v. Glamorgan at Swansea, 1931
6 for 12 v. Derbyshire at Hull, 1933
6 for 10 v. Essex at Ilford, 1937
6 for 22 v. Hampshire at Bournemouth, 1939

SIX WICKETS IN AN INNINGS AT LESS THAN FOUR
RUNS EACH *(Continued)*

A WADDINGTON (2)

6 for 21 v. Northamptonshire at Harrogate, 1921
6 for 21 v. Northamptonshire at Northampton, 1923

S WADE (1)

6 for 18 v. Gloucestershire at Dewsbury, 1887

E WAINWRIGHT (4)

6 for 16 v. Sussex at Leeds, 1893
6 for 23 v. Sussex at Hove, 1893
6 for 18 v. Sussex at Dewsbury, 1894
6 for 22 v. MCC at Scarborough, 1894

J H WARDLE (8)

6 for 17 v. Sussex at Sheffield, 1948
6 for 10 v. Scotland at Edinburgh, 1950
6 for 12 v. Gloucestershire at Hull, 1950
6 for 20 v. Kent at Scarborough, 1950
6 for 23 v. Somerset at Sheffield, 1951
6 for 21 v. Glamorgan at Leeds, 1951
6 for 18 v. Gloucestershire at Bristol, 1951
6 for 6 v. Gloucestershire at Bristol, 1955

D WILSON (3)

6 for 22 v. Sussex at Bradford, 1963
6 for 15 v. Gloucestershire at Middlesbrough, 1966
6 for 22 v. Middlesex at Sheffield, 1966

FOUR WICKETS IN FOUR BALLS

A Drake v. Derbyshire at Chesterfield, 1914

FOUR WICKETS IN FIVE BALLS

F S Jackson v. Australians at Leeds, 1902
A Waddington v. Northamptonshire at Northampton, 1920
G G Macaulay v. Lancashire at Manchester, 1933
P J Hartley v. Derbyshire at Chesterfield, 1995
D Gough v. Kent at Leeds, 1995
J D Middlebrook v. Hampshire at Southampton, 2000

BEST BOWLING ANALYSES IN A MATCH
FOR AND AGAINST YORKSHIRE

Best For Yorkshire:
17 for 91 (8 for 47 and 9 for 44) H Verity v Essex at Leyton, 1933

Against Yorkshire:
17 for 91 (9 for 62 and 8 for 29) H Dean for Lancashire at Liverpool, 1913
(non-championship)

County Championship
16 for 114 (8 for 48 and 8 for 66) G Burton for Middlesex at Sheffield, 1888

Yorkshire versus:

Derbyshire	*For Yorkshire:*	14 for 58 (4 for 11 and 10 for 47) T F Smailes at Sheffield, 1939
	Against:	13 for 65 (7 for 33 and 6 for 32) W Mycroft at Sheffield, 1879
Most 10 wickets *in a match*	*For Yorkshire:* *Against:*	P Carrick and E Peate 4 each W Mycroft 3
Durham	*For Yorkshire:*	10 for 101 (6 for 57 and 4 for 44) M A Robinson at Durham, 1992
	Against:	10 for 144 (7 for 81 and 3 for 63) O D Gibson at Chester-le-Street, 2007
Most 10 wickets *in a match*	*For Yorkshire:* *Against:*	M A Robinson 1 G R Breese and O D Gibson 1 each
Essex	*For Yorkshire:*	17 for 91 (8 for 47 and 9 for 44) H Verity at Leyton, 1933
	Against:	14 for 127 (7 for 37 and 7 for 90) W Mead at Leyton, 1899
Most 10 wickets *in a match*	*For Yorkshire:* *Against:*	W Rhodes 7 J K Lever, W Mead 2 each
Glamorgan	*For Yorkshire:*	15 for 123 (8 for 70 and 7 for 53) R Illingworth at Swansea. 1960
	Against:	12 for 76 (7 for 30 and 5 for 46) D J Shepherd at Cardiff, 1957
Most 10 wickets *in a match*	*For Yorkshire:* *Against:*	H Verity 5 D J Shepherd, J S Pressdee 1 each
Gloucestershire	*For Yorkshire:*	14 for 64 (7 for 58 and 7 for 6) R Illingworth at Harrogate, 1967
	Against:	15 for 79 (8 for 33 and 7 for 46) W G Grace at Sheffield, 1872
Most 10 wickets *in a match*	*For Yorkshire:* *Against:*	W Rhodes 8 E G Dennett 5
Hampshire	*For Yorkshire:*	14 for 43 (8 for 21 and 6 for 22) S Haigh at Southampton, 1898
	Against:	12 for 145 (7 for 78 and 5 for 67) D Shackleton at Bradford, 1962
Most 10 wickets *in a match*	*For Yorkshire:* *Against:*	W Rhodes, E Robinson, H Verity 3 each A S Kennedy 3

BEST BOWLING ANALYSES IN A MATCH
FOR AND AGAINST YORKSHIRE *(continued)*

Yorkshire versus

Kent	For Yorkshire:	15 for 38 (6 for 26 and 9 for 12)
		H Verity at Sheffield, 1936
	Against:	13 for 48 (5 for 13 and 8 for 35)
		A Hearne at Sheffield, 1885
Most 10 wickets	For Yorkshire:	E Peate and J H Wardle 4 each
in a match	*Against:*	C Blythe 6
Lancashire	For Yorkshire:	14 for 80 (6 for 56 and 8 for 24)
		E Peate at Manchester, 1880
	Against:	17 for 91 (9 for 62 and 8 for 29)
		H Dean at Liverpool, 1913 (non-championship)
		14 for 90 (6 for 47 and 8 for 43)
		R Tattersall at Leeds, 1956 (championship)
Most 10 wickets	For Yorkshire:	T Emmett 5
in a match	*Against:*	J Briggs 8
Leicestershire	For Yorkshire:	15 for 63 (8 for 25 and 7 for 38)
		G H Hirst at Hull, 1907
	Against:	12 for 139 (8 for 85 and 4 for 54)
		A D Pougher at Leicester, 1895
Most 10 wickets	For Yorkshire:	G H Hirst 5
in a match	*Against:*	A D Pougher 2
Middlesex	For Yorkshire:	13 for 94 (6 for 61 and 7 for 33)
		S Haigh at Leeds, 1900
	Against:	16 for 114 (8 for 48 and 8 for 66)
		G Burton at Sheffield, 1888
Most 10 wickets	For Yorkshire:	W Rhodes 5
in a match	*Against:*	J T Hearne 7
Northamptonshire	For Yorkshire:	16 for 35 (8 for 18 and 8 for 17)
		W E Bowes at Kettering, 1935
	Against:	15 for 31 (7 for 22 and 8 for 9)
		G E Tribe at Northampton, 1958
Most 10 wickets	For Yorkshire:	W E Bowes, G G Macaulay, H Verity,
in a match		A Waddington 3 each
	Against:	G E Tribe 3
Nottinghamshire	For Yorkshire:	14 for 33 (8 for 12 and 6 for 21)
		R Peel at Sheffield, 1888
	Against:	14 for 94 (8 for 38 and 6 for 56)
		F Morley at Nottingham, 1878
Most 10 wickets	For Yorkshire:	G H Hirst 5
in a match	*Against:*	F Morley, J C Shaw 4 each
Somerset	For Yorkshire:	15 for 50 (9 for 22 and 6 for 28)
		R Peel at Leeds, 1895
	Against:	15 for 71 (6 for 30 and 9 for 41)
		L C Braund at Sheffield, 1902
Most 10 wickets	For Yorkshire:	G H Hirst 7
in a match	*Against:*	L C Braund 3

Yorkshire versus

Surrey	*For Yorkshire:*	14 for 77 (6 for 47 and 8 for 30) E Peate at Huddersfield, 1881
	Against:	15 for 154 (7 for 55 and 8 for 99) T Richardson at Leeds, 1897
Most 10 wickets	*For Yorkshire:*	W Rhodes 7
in a match	*Against:*	G A Lohmann, T Richardson 6 each
Sussex	*For Yorkshire:*	16 for 112 (9 for 48 and 7 for 64) J H Wardle at Hull, 1954
	Against:	12 for 110 (6 for 71 and 6 for 39) G R Cox at Sheffield, 1907
Most 10 wickets	*For Yorkshire:*	R Peel, E Wainwright 3 each
in a match	*Against:*	Twelve players 1 each
Warwickshire	*For Yorkshire:*	14 for 92 (9 for 43 and 5 for 49) H Verity at Leeds, 1937
	Against:	12 for 55 (5 for 21 and 7 for 34) T W Cartwright at Bradford, 1969
Most 10 wickets	*For Yorkshire:*	S Haigh 4
in a match	*Against:*	E F Field 4
Worcestershire	*For Yorkshire:*	14 for 211 (8 for 87 and 6 for 124) W Rhodes at Worcester, 1903
	Against:	13 for 76 (4 for 38 and 9 for 38) J A Cuffe at Bradford, 1907
Most 10 wickets	*For Yorkshire:*	S Haigh, G G Macaulay 4 each
in a match	*Against:*	N Gifford 2
Australians	*For Yorkshire:*	13 for 149 (8 for 48 and 5 for 101) G H Hirst at Bradford, 1902
	Against:	13 for 170 (6 for 91 and 7 for 79) J M Gregory at Sheffield, 1919
Most 10 wickets	*For Yorkshire:*	S Haigh 2
in a match	*Against:*	C V Grimmett, F R Spofforth, C T B Turner, H Trumble 2 each

BEST BOWLING ANALYSES IN AN INNINGS
FOR AND AGAINST YORKSHIRE

Best For Yorkshire:
10 for 10 H Verity v Nottinghamshire at Leeds, 1932

Against Yorkshire:
10 for 37 C V Grimmett for Australians at Sheffield, 1930
(non-championship)

County Championship
10 for 51 H Howell for Warwickshire at Birmingham, 1923

Yorkshire versus:

Derbyshire	*For Yorkshire:*	10 for 47	T F Smailes at Sheffield, 1939
	Against:	9 for 27	J J Hulme at Sheffield, 1894
Most 5 wickets	*For Yorkshire:*	S Haigh, E Peat, W Rhodes 11 each	
in an innings	*Against:*	W Mycroft 10	

BEST BOWLING ANALYSES IN AN INNINGS
FOR AND AGAINST YORKSHIRE *(continued)*

Yorkshire versus

Durham

	For Yorkshire:	6 for 37	R D Stemp at Durham, 1994
	Against:	7 for 58	J Wood at Leeds, 1999
Most 5 wickets	*For Yorkshire:*	D Gough 2	
in an innings	*Against:*	G R Breese and S J E Brown 2 each	

Essex

	For Yorkshire:	9 for 28	W Rhodes at Leyton, 1899
	Against:	8 for 44	F G Bull at Bradford, 1896
Most 5 wickets	*For Yorkshire:*	W Rhodes 18	
in an innings	*Against:*	W Mead 14	

Glamorgan

	For Yorkshire:	9 for 60	H Verity at Swansea, 1930
	Against:	9 for 43	J S Pressdee at Swansea, 1965
Most 5 wickets	*For Yorkshire:*	H Verity 12	
in an innings	*Against:*	D J Shepherd 6	

Gloucestershire

	For Yorkshire:	9 for 25	S Haigh at Leeds, 1912
	Against:	9 for 36	C W L Parker at Bristol, 1922
Most 5 wickets	*For Yorkshire:*	W Rhodes 22	
in an innings	*Against:*	T W J Goddard 17	

Hampshire

	For Yorkshire:	9 for 29	A C Williams at Dewsbury, 1919
	Against:	8 for 49	O W Herman at Bournemouth, 1930
Most 5 wickets	*For Yorkshire:*	G H Hirst 10	
in an innings	*Against:*	A S Kennedy 10	

Kent

	For Yorkshire:	9 for 12	H Verity at Sheffield, 1936
	Against:	8 for 35	A Hearne at Sheffield, 1885
Most 5 wickets	*For Yorkshire:*	W Rhodes 12	
in an innings	*Against:*	A P Freeman 14	

Lancashire

	For Yorkshire:	9 for 23	G H Hirst at Leeds, 1910
	Against:	9 for 41	A Mold at Huddersfield, 1890
Most 5 wickets	*For Yorkshire:*	T Emmett 16	
in an innings	*Against:*	J Briggs 19	

Leicestershire

	For Yorkshire:	8 for 25	G H Hirst at Hull, 1907
	Against:	9 for 63	C T Spencer at Huddersfield, 1954
Most 5 wickets	*For Yorkshire:*	G H Hirst 15	
in an innings	*Against:*	H A Smith 7	

Middlesex

	For Yorkshire:	9 for 45	G H Hirst at Sheffield 1907
	Against:	9 for 57	F A Tarrant at Leeds, 1906
Most 5 wickets	*For Yorkshire:*	W Rhodes 18	
in an innings	*Against:*	J T Hearne 21	

Northamptonshire

	For Yorkshire:	9 for 37	M A Robinson at Harrogate, 1993
	Against:	9 for 30	A E Thomas at Bradford, 1920
Most 5 wickets	*For Yorkshire:*	G G Macaulay 14	
in an innings	*Against:*	G E Tribe, W Wells 7 each	

Nottinghamshire

	For Yorkshire:	10 for 10	H Verity at Leeds, 1932
	Against:	8 for 32	J C Shaw at Nottingham, 1865
Most 5 wickets	*For Yorkshire:*	W Rhodes 17	
in an innings	*Against:*	F Morley 17	

BEST BOWLING ANALYSES IN AN INNINGS
FOR AND AGAINST YORKSHIRE *(continued)*

Yorkshire versus

Somerset	*For Yorkshire:*	10 for 35	A Drake at Weston-super-Mare, 1914
	Against:	9 for 41	L C Braund at Sheffield, 1902
Most 5 wickets	*For Yorkshire:*	G H Hirst 16	
in an innings	*Against:*	E J Tyler 8	
Surrey	*For Yorkshire:*	8 for 5	E Peate at Holbeck, 1883
	Against:	9 for 47	T Richardson at Sheffield, 1893
Most 5 wickets	*For Yorkshire:*	W Rhodes 17	
in an innings	*Against:*	W Southerton 19	
Sussex	*For Yorkshire:*	9 for 48	J H Wardle at Hull, 1954
	Against:	9 for 34	James Langridge at Sheffield, 1934
Most 5 wickets	*For Yorkshire:*	W Rhodes 14	
in an innings	*Against:*	G R Cox, J A Snow 6 each	
Warwickshire	*For Yorkshire:*	10 for 36	H Verity at Leeds, 1930
	Against:	10 for 51	H Howell at Birmingham, 1923
Most 5 wickets	*For Yorkshire:*	W Rhodes 18	
in an innings	*Against:*	E F Field, W E Hollies 7 each	
Worcestershire	*For Yorkshire:*	9 for 41	G H Hirst at Worcester, 1911
	Against:	9 for 38	J A Cuffe at Bradford, 1907
Most 5 wickets	*For Yorkshire:*	S Haigh, W Rhodes 11 each	
in an innings	*Against:*	R T D Perks 7	
Australians	*For Yorkshire:*	9 for 76	W Ringrose at Bradford, 1905
	Against:	10 for 37	C V Grimmett at Sheffield, 1930
Most 5 wickets	*For Yorkshire:*	R Peel 7	
in an innings	*Against:*	F R Spofforth 7	

HAT-TRICKS

G Freeman v. Lancashire at Holbeck, 1868
G Freeman v. Middlesex at Sheffield, 1868
A Hill v. United South of England XI at Bradford, 1874
A Hill v. Surrey at The Oval, 1880
E Peate v. Kent at Sheffield, 1882
G Ulyett v. Lancashire at Sheffield, 1883
E Peate v. Gloucestershire at Moreton-in-Marsh, 1884
W Fletcher v. MCC at Lord's, 1892
E Wainwright v. Sussex at Dewsbury, 1894
G H Hirst v. Leicestershire at Leicester, 1895
J T Brown v. Derbyshire at Derby, 1896
R Peel v. Kent at Halifax, 1897
S Haigh v. Derbyshire at Bradford, 1897
W Rhodes v. Kent at Canterbury, 1901
S Haigh v. Somerset at Sheffield, 1902
H A Sedgwick v. Worcestershire at Hull, 1906
G Deyes v. Gentlemen of Ireland at Bray, 1907
G H Hirst v. Leicestershire at Hull, 1907
J T Newstead v. Worcestershire at Bradford, 1907
S Haigh v. Lancashire at Manchester, 1909
M W Booth v. Worcestershire at Bradford, 1911
A Drake v. Essex at Huddersfield, 1912

HAT-TRICKS *(Continued)*

M W Booth v. Essex at Leyton, 1912
A Drake v. Derbyshire at Chesterfield, 1914 (4 in 4)
W Rhodes v. Derbyshire at Derby, 1920
A Waddington v. Northamptonshire at Northampton, 1920 (4 in 5)
G G Macaulay v. Warwickshire at Birmingham, 1923
E Robinson v. Sussex at Hull, 1928
G G Macaulay v. Leicestershire at Hull, 1930
E Robinson v. Kent at Gravesend, 1930
H Verity v. Nottinghamshire at Leeds, 1932
H Fisher v. Somerset at Sheffield, 1932 (all lbw)
G G Macaulay v. Glamorgan at Cardiff, 1933
G G Macaulay v. Lancashire at Manchester, 1933 (4 in 5)
M.Leyland v. Surrey at Sheffield, 1935
E Robinson v. Kent at Leeds, 1939
A Coxon v. Worcestershire at Leeds, 1946
F S Trueman v. Nottinghamshire at Nottingham, 1951
F S Trueman v. Nottinghamshire at Scarborough, 1955
R Appleyard v. Gloucestershire at Sheffield, 1956
F S.Trueman v. MCC at Lord's, 1958
D Wilson v. Nottinghamshire at Middlesbrough, 1959
F S Trueman v. Nottinghamshire at Bradford, 1963
D Wilson v. Nottinghamshire at Worksop, 1966
D Wilson v. Kent at Harrogate, 1966
G A Cope v. Essex at Colchester, 1970
A L Robinson v. Nottinghamshire at Worksop, 1974
P W Jarvis v. Derbyshire at Chesterfield, 1985
P J Hartley v. Derbyshire at Chesterfield, 1995 (4 in 5)
D Gough v. Kent at Leeds, 1995 (4 in 5)
C White v. Gloucestershire at Gloucester, 1998

51 Hat-Tricks: G G Macaulay and F S Trueman took four each, S Haigh and D Wilson three each. There have been seven hat-tricks versus Kent and Nottinghamshire, and six versus Derbyshire.

200 WICKETS IN A SEASON

Bowler	Season	Overs	Maidens	Runs	Wickets	Average
W Rhodes	1900	1366.4	411	3054	240	12.72
W Rhodes	1901	1455.3	474	3497	233	15.00
G H Hirst	1906	1111.1	262	3089	201	15.36
G G Macaulay	1925	1241.2	291	2986	200	14.93
R Appleyard†	1951	1323.2	394	2829	200	14.14

† First full season in First-Class cricket.

100 WICKETS IN A SEASON

Bowler		Wickets taken	Wickets taken	Wickets taken
R Appleyard	(3)	200 in 1951	141 in 1954	110 in 1956
A Booth	(1)	111 in 1946	—	—
M W Booth	(3)	104 in 1912	167 in 1913	155 in 1914
W E Bowes	(8)	117 in 1931	168 in 1932	130 in 1933
		109 in 1934	154 in 1935	113 in 1936
		106 in 1938	107 in 1939	—

Bowler		Wickets taken	Wickets taken	Wickets taken
D B Close	(2)	105 in 1949	114 in 1952	—
A Coxon	(2)	101 in 1949	129 in 1950	—
A Drake	(2)	115 in 1913	158 in 1914	—
T Emmett	(1)	112 in 1886	—	—
S Haigh	(10)	100 in 1898	160 in 1900	154 in 1902
		102 in 1903	118 in 1904	118 in 1905
		161 in 1906	120 in 1909	100 in 1911
		125 in 1912	—	—
G H Hirst	(12)	150 in 1895	171 in 1901	121 in 1903
		114 in 1904	100 in 1905	201 in 1906
		169 in 1907	164 in 1908	138 in 1910
		130 in 1911	113 in 1912	100 in 1913
R Illingworth	(5)	103 in 1956	120 in 1961	116 in 1962
		122 in 1964	105 in 1968	—
R Kilner	(4)	107 in 1922	143 in 1923	134 in 1924
		123 in 1925	—	—
G G Macaulay	(10)	101 in 1921	130 in 1922	163 in 1923
		184 in 1924	200 in 1925	133 in 1926
		130 in 1927	117 in 1928	102 in 1929
		141 in 1933	—	—
J T Newstead	(1)	131 in 1908	—	—
A G Nicholson	(2)	113 in 1966	101 in 1967	—
E Peate	(3)	131 in 1880	133 in 1881	165 in 1882
R Peel	(6)	118 in 1888	132 in 1890	106 in 1892
		134 in 1894	155 in 1895	108 in 1896
W Rhodes	(22)	141 in 1898	153 in 1899	240 in 1900
		233 in 1901	174 in 1902	169 in 1903
		118 in 1904	158 in 1905	113 in 1906
		164 in 1907	100 in 1908	115 in 1909
		105 in 1911	117 in 1914	155 in 1919
		156 in 1920	128 in 1921	100 in 1922
		127 in 1923	102 in 1926	111 in 1928
		100 in 1929	—	—
E Robinson	(1)	111 in 1928	—	—
E P Robinson	(4)	104 in 1938	120 in 1939	149 in 1946
		108 in 1947	—	—
T F Smailes	(4)	105 in 1934	125 in 1936	120 in 1937
		104 in 1938	—	—
F S Trueman	(8)	129 in 1954	140 in 1955	104 in 1959
		150 in 1960	124 in 1961	122 in 1962
		121 in 1965	107 in 1966	—
H Verity	(9)	169 in 1931	146 in 1932	168 in 1933
		100 in 1934	199 in 1935	185 in 1936
		185 in 1937	137 in 1938	189 in 1939
A Waddington	(5)	100 in 1919	140 in 1920	105 in 1921
		132 in 1922	105 in 1925	—
E Wainwright	(3)	114 in 1893	157 in 1894	102 in 1896
J H Wardle	(10)	148 in 1948	100 in 1949	172 in 1950
		122 in 1951	169 in 1952	126 in 1953
		122 in 1954	159 in 1955	146 in 1956
		106 in 1957	—	—
D Wilson	(3)	100 in 1966	107 in 1968	101 in 1969

BOWLERS WHO HAVE TAKEN OVER 500 WICKETS

Player	M	Runs	Wkts	Av'ge	Best
W Rhodes	883	57634	3598	16.01	9 for 28
G H Hirst	717	44716	2481	18.02	9 for 23
S Haigh	513	29289	1876	15.61	9 for 25
G G Macaulay	445	30554	1774	17.22	8 for 21
F S Trueman	459	29890	1745	17.12	8 for 28
H Verity	278	21353	1558	13.70	10 for 10
J H Wardle	330	27917	1539	18.13	9 for 25
R Illingworth	496	26806	1431	18.73	9 for 42
W E Bowes	301	21227	1351	15.71	9 for 121
R Peel	318	20638	1311	15.74	9 for 22
T Emmett	299	15465	1216	12.71	9 for 23
D Wilson	392	22626	1104	20.49	7 for 19
P Carrick	425	30530	1018	29.99	8 for 33
E Wainwright	352	17744	998	17.77	9 for 66
D B Close	536	23489	967	24.29	8 for 41
Emmott Robinson	413	19645	893	21.99	9 for 36
A G Nicholson	282	17296	876	19.74	9 for 62
R Kilner	365	14855	857	17.33	8 for 26
A Waddington	255	16201	835	19.40	8 for 34
T F Smailes	262	16593	802	20.68	10 for 47
E Peate	154	9986	794	12.57	8 for 5
Ellis P Robinson	208	15141	735	20.60	8 for 35
C M Old	222	13409	647	20.72	7 for 20
R Appleyard	133	9903	642	15.42	8 for 76
W Bates	202	10692	637	16.78	8 for 21
G A Cope	230	15627	630	24.80	8 for 73
P J Hartley	195	17438	579	30.11	9 for 41
A Sidebottom	216	13852	558	24.82	8 for 72
M W Booth	144	11017	557	19.17	8 for 47
A Hill	140	7002	542	12.91	7 for 14
Hon F S Jackson	207	9690	506	19.15	7 for 42

BOWLERS UNCHANGED IN A MATCH

(IN WHICH THE OPPONENTS WERE DISMISSED TWICE)

**There have been 31 instances. The first and most recent are listed below.
A complete list is to be found in the 2008 edition.**

First: L Greenwood (11 for 71) and G Freeman (8 for 73) v. Surrey
at The Oval, 1867
Yorkshire won by an innings and 111 runs

Most Recent: E Robinson (8 for 65) and G G Macaulay (12 for 50) v. Worcestershire
at Leeds, 1927
Yorkshire won by an innings and 106 runs

FIELDERS (IN MATCHES FOR YORKSHIRE)

MOST CATCHES IN AN INNINGS

6	E P Robinson v. Leicestershire at Bradford, 1938
5	J Tunnicliffe v. Leicestershire at Leeds, 1897
5	J Tunnicliffe v. Leicestershire at Leicester, 1900
5	J Tunnicliffe v. Leicestershire at Scarborough, 1901
5	A B Sellers v. Essex at Leyton, 1933
5	D Wilson v. Surrey at The Oval, 1969
5	R G Lumb v. Gloucestershire at Middlesbrough, 1972

FIELDERS IN MATCHES FOR YORKSHIRE *(Continued)*

MOST CATCHES IN A MATCH

7	J Tunnicliffe v. Leicestershire at Leeds, 1897
7	J Tunnicliffe v. Leicestershire at Leicester, 1900
7	A B Sellers v Essex at Leyton, 1933
7	E P Robinson v. Leicestershire at Bradford, 1938
7	D Byas v. Derbyshire at Leeds, 2000

MOST CATCHES IN A SEASON

70	J Tunnicliffe in 1901
70	P J Sharpe in 1962
61	J Tunnicliffe in 1895
60	J Tunnicliffe in 1904
59	J Tunnicliffe in 1896
57	J V Wilson in 1955
54	J V Wilson in 1961
53	J V Wilson in 1957
51	J V Wilson in 1951

MOST CATCHES IN A CAREER

665	J Tunnicliffe (1.40 per match)
586	W Rhodes (0.66 per match)
564	D B Close (1.05 per match)
525	P J Sharpe (1.27 per match)
520	J V Wilson (1.09 per match)
518	G H Hirst (0.72 per match)

WICKET-KEEPERS IN MATCHES FOR YORKSHIRE

MOST DISMISSALS IN AN INNINGS

7	(7ct)	D L Bairstow v. Derbyshire at Scarborough, 1982
6		J Hunter v. Gloucestershire at Gloucester, 1887
6	(5ct,1st)	D Hunter v. Surrey at Sheffield, 1891
6	(6ct)	D Hunter v. Middlesex at Leeds, 1909
6	(2ct,4st)	W R Allen v. Sussex at Hove, 1921
6	(5ct,1st)	J G Binks v. Lancashire at Leeds, 1962
6	(6ct)	D L Bairstow v. Lancashire at Manchester, 1971
6	(6ct)	D L Bairstow v. Warwickshire at Bradford, 1978
6	(5ct,1st)	D L Bairstow v. Lancashire at Leeds, 1980
6	(6ct)	D L Bairstow v. Derbyshire at Chesterfield, 1984
6	(6ct)	R J Blakey v. Sussex at Eastbourne, 1990
6	(5ct,1st)	R J Blakey v. Gloucestershire at Cheltenham, 1992
6	(5ct,1st)	R J Blakey v. Glamorgan at Cardiff, 1994
6	(6ct)	R J Blakey v. Glamorgan at Leeds, 2003

MOST DISMISSALS IN A MATCH

11	(11ct)	D L Bairstow v. Derbyshire at Scarborough, 1982
		(Equalled World Record)
9	(9ct)	J.Hunter v. Gloucestershire at Gloucester, 1887
9	(8ct,1st)	A Dolphin v. Derbyshire at Bradford, 1919
9	(9ct)	D L Bairstow v. Lancashire at Manchester, 1971
9	(9ct)	R J Blakey v. Sussex at Eastbourne, 1990
8	(2ct,6st)	G Pinder v. Lancashire at Sheffield, 1872
8	(2ct,6st)	D Hunter v. Surrey at Bradford, 1898
8	(7ct,1st)	A Bairstow v. Cambridge University at Cambridge, 1899
8	(8ct)	A Wood v. Northamptonshire at Huddersfield, 1932
8	(8ct)	D L Bairstow v. Lancashire at Leeds, 1978
8	(7ct,1st)	D L Bairstow v. Derbyshire at Chesterfield, 1984
8	(6ct,2st)	D L Bairstow v. Derbyshire at Chesterfield, 1985
8	(8ct)	R J Blakey v. Hampshire at Southampton, 1989
8	(8ct)	R J Blakey v. Northamptonshire at Harrogate, 1993

MOST DISMISSALS IN A SEASON

107	(96ct,11st)	J G Binks, 1960
94	(81ct,13st)	JG Binks, 1961
89	(75ct,14st)	A Wood, 1934
88	(80ct,8st)	J G Binks, 1963
86	(70ct,16st)	J G Binks, 1962
82	(52ct,30st)	A Dolphin, 1919
80	(57ct,23st)	A. Wood, 1935

MOST DISMISSALS IN A CAREER

1186	(863ct,323st)	D Hunter (2.29 per match)
1044	(872ct,172st)	J G Binks (2.12 per match)
1038	(907ct,131st)	D L Bairstow (2.41 per match)
855	(612ct,243st)	A Wood (2.09 per match)
829	(569ct,260st)	A Dolphin (1.94 per match)
824	(768ct, 56st)	R J Blakey (2.43 per match)

YORKSHIRE PLAYERS WHO HAVE COMPLETED THE "DOUBLE"

(all First-Class matches)

Player	Year	Runs	Average	Wickets	Average
M W Booth (1)	1913	1,228	27.28	181	18.46
D B Close (2)	†1949	1,098	27.45	113	27.87
	1952	1,192	33.11	114	24.08
A Drake (1)	1913	1,056	23.46	116	16.93
S Haigh (1)	1904	1,055	26.37	121	19.85
G H Hirst (14)	1896	1,122	28.20	104	21.64
	1897	1,535	35.69	101	23.22
	1901	1,950	42.39	183	16.38
	1903	1,844	47.28	128	14.94
	1904	2,501	54.36	132	21.09
	1905	2,266	53.95	110	19.94
	††1906	2,385	45.86	208	16.50
	1907	1,344	28.38	188	15.20
	1908	1,598	38.97	114	14.05
	1909	1,256	27.30	115	20.05
	1910	1,840	32.85	164	14.79
	1911	1,789	33.12	137	20.40
	1912	1,133	25.75	118	17.37
	1913	1,540	35.81	101	20.13
R Illingworth (6)	1957	1,213	28.20	106	18.40
	1959	1,726	46.64	110	21.46
	1960	1,006	25.79	109	17.55
	1961	1,153	24.53	128	17.90
	1962	1,612	34.29	117	19.45
	1964	1,301	37.17	122	17.45
F S Jackson (1)	1898	1,566	41.21	104	15.67
R Kilner (4)	1922	1,198	27.22	122	14.73
	1923	1,404	32.24	158	12.91
	1925	1,068	30.51	131	17.92
	1926	1,187	37.09	107	22.52
R Peel (1)	1896	1,206	30.15	128	17.50
W Rhodes (16)	1903	1,137	27.07	193	14.57
	1904	1,537	35.74	131	21.59
	1905	1,581	35.93	182	16.95
	1906	1,721	29.16	128	23.57
	1907	1,055	22.93	177	15.57
	1908	1,673	31.56	115	16.13
	1909	2,094	40.26	141	15.89
	1911	2,261	38.32	117	24.07
	1914	1,377	29.29	118	18.27
	1919	1,237	34.36	164	14.42
	1920	1,123	28.07	161	13.18
	1921	1,474	39.83	141	13.27
	1922	1,511	39.76	119	12.19
	1923	1,321	33.02	134	11.54
	1924	1,126	26.18	109	14.46
	1926	1,132	34.30	115	14.86
T F Smailes (1)	1938	1,002	25.05	113	20.84
E Wainwright (1)	1897	1,612	35.82	101	23.06

† First season in First-Class cricket.
†† The only instance in First-Class cricket of 2,000 runs and 200 wickets in a season.

H Sutcliffe (194) and M Leyland (45) hit 102 off six consecutive overs for Yorkshire v. Essex at Scarborough in 1932.

From 1898 to 1930 inclusive, Wilfred Rhodes took no less than 4,187 wickets, and scored 39,969 runs in First-Class cricket at home and abroad, a remarkable record. He also took 100 wickets and scored 1,000 in a season 16 times, and G H Hirst 14 times.

Of players with a qualification of not less than 50 wickets, Wilfred Rhodes was first in bowling in First-Class cricket in 1900, 1901, 1919, 1920, 1922, 1923 and 1926; Schofield Haigh in 1902, 1905, 1908 and 1909; Mr E R Wilson in 1921; G G Macaulay in 1924; H Verity in 1930, 1933, 1935, 1937 and 1939; W E Bowes in 1938; A Booth in 1946; R Appleyard in 1951 and 1955, and F S Trueman in 1952 and 1963.

The highest aggregate of runs made in one season in First-Class cricket by a Yorkshire player is 3,429 by L Hutton in 1949. This total has been exceeded three times, viz: D C S Compton 3,816 and W J Edrich 3,539 in 1947, and 3,518 by T Hayward in 1906. H Sutcliffe scored 3,336 in 1932.

Three players have taken all 10 Yorkshire wickets in an innings. G Wootton, playing for All England XI at Sheffield in 1865, took all 10 wickets for 54 runs. H Howell performed the feat for Warwickshire at Edgbaston in 1923 at a cost of 51 runs; and C V Grimmett, Australia, took all 10 wickets for 37 runs at Sheffield in 1930.

The match against Sussex at Dewsbury on June 7th and 8th, 1894, was brought to a summary conclusion by a remarkable bowling performance on the part of Edward Wainwright. In the second innings of Sussex, he took the last five wickets in seven balls, including the "hat trick". In the whole match he obtained 13 wickets for only 38 runs.

M D Moxon has the unique distinction of scoring a century in each of his first two First-Class matches in Yorkshire — 116 (2nd inns.) v. Essex at Leeds and 111 (1st inns.) v. Derbyshire at Sheffield, June 1981).

In the Yorkshire v. Norfolk match — played on the Hyde Park Ground, Sheffield, on July 14th to 18th, 1834 — 851 runs were scored in the four innings, of which no fewer than 128 were extras: 75 byes and 53 wides. At that time wides were not run out, so that every wide included in the above total represents a wide actually bowled. This particular achievement has never been surpassed in the annals of county cricket.

L Hutton reached his 1,000 runs in First-Class cricket in 1949 as early as June 9th.

W Barber reached his 1,000 runs in 1934 on June 13th. P Holmes reached his 1,000 in 1925 on June 16th, as also did H Sutcliffe in 1932. J T Brown reached his 1,000 in 1899 on June 22nd. In 1905, D Denton reached his 1,000 runs on June 26th; and in 1906 G H Hirst gained the same total on June 27th.

In 1912, D Denton scored over 1,000 runs during July, while M Leyland and H Sutcliffe both scored over 1,000 runs in August 1932.

L Hutton scored over 1,000 in June and over 1,000 runs in August in 1949.

H Verity took his 100th wicket in First-Class cricket as early as June 19th in 1936 on June 27th in 1935. In 1900, W Rhodes obtained his 100th wicket on June 21st, and again on the same date in 1901, while G H Hirst obtained his 100th wicket on June 28th, 1906.

In 1930, Yorkshiremen (H Sutcliffe and H Verity) occupied the first places by English players in the batting and bowling averages of First-Class cricket, which is a record without precedent. H Sutcliffe was also first in the batting averages in 1931 and 1932.

G Boycott was the first player to have achieved an average of over 100 in each of two English seasons. In 1971, he scored 2,503 runs for an average of 100.12, and in 1979 he scored 1,538 runs for an average of 102.53.

FIRST-CLASS MATCHES BEGUN AND FINISHED IN ONE DAY

Yorkshire v. Somerset, at Huddersfield, July 9th, 1894.
Yorkshire v. Hampshire, at Southampton, May 27th, 1898.
Yorkshire v. Worcestershire, at Bradford, May 7th, 1900

For England

YORKSHIRE TEST CRICKETERS 1877-2008 (Correct to December 31, 2008)

Player	M.	I	NO	Runs	HS.	Av'ge	100s	50s	Balls	R	W	Av'ge	Best	5wI	10wM	c/st
APPLEYARD, R ...1954-56	9	9	6	51	19*	17.00	—	—	1596	554	31	17.87	5-51	1	—	4
ARMITAGE, T ...1877	2	3	0	33	21	11.00	—	—	12	15	0	—	—	—	—	—
ATHEY, C W J ...1980-88	23	41	1	919	123	22.97	1	4	—	—	—	—	—	—	—	13
BAIRSTOW, D L ...1979-81	4	7	1	125	59	20.83	—	1	—	—	—	—	—	—	—	12/1
BARBER, W ...1935	2	4	0	83	44	20.75	—	—	2	0	1	0.00	1-0	—	—	1
BATES, W ...1881-87	15	26	2	656	64	27.33	—	5	2364	821	50	16.42	7-28	4	1	9
BINKS, J G ...1964	2	4	0	91	55	22.75	—	1	—	—	—	—	—	—	—	8/—
BLAKEY, R J ...1993	2	4	0	7	6	1.75	—	—	—	—	—	—	—	—	—	2/—
BOOTH, M W ...1913-14	2	2	0	46	32	23.00	—	—	312	130	7	18.57	4-49	—	—	2
BOWES, W E ...1932-46	15	11	5	28	10*	4.66	—	—	3655	1519	68	22.33	6-33	6	—	33
†BOYCOTT, G ...1964-82	108	193	23	8114	246*	47.72	22	42	944	382	7	54.57	3-47	—	—	—/1
BRENNAN, D V ...1951	2	2	0	16	16	8.00	—	—	—	—	—	—	—	—	—	7
BROWN, J T ...1894-99	8	16	3	470	140	36.15	1	1	35	22	0	—	—	—	—	7
†CLOSE, D B ...1949-76	22	37	2	887	70	25.34	—	4	1212	532	18	29.55	4-35	—	—	24
COPE, G A ...1977-78	3	3	1	40	22	13.33	—	—	864	277	8	34.62	3-102	—	—	1
COXON, A ...1948	1	2	0	19	19	9.50	—	—	378	172	3	57.33	2-90	—	—	—
DAWSON, R K J ...2002-03	7	13	3	114	19*	11.40	—	—	1116	677	11	61.54	4-134	—	—	3
DENTON, D ...1905-10	11	22	1	424	104	20.19	1	1	—	—	—	—	—	—	—	8
DOLPHIN, A ...1921	1	2	0	1	1	0.50	—	—	—	—	—	—	—	—	—	1/—
EMMETT, T ...1877-82	7	13	1	160	48	13.33	—	—	728	284	9	31.55	7-68	1	—	9
GIBB, P A ...1938-46	8	13	0	581	120	44.69	2	3	—	—	—	—	—	—	—	3/1
GOUGH, D ...1994-2003	58	86	18	855	65	12.57	—	2	11821	6503	229	28.39	6-42	9	—	13
GREENWOOD, A ...1877	2	4	0	77	49	19.25	—	—	—	—	—	—	—	—	—	2
HAIGH, S ...1899-1912	11	18	3	113	25	7.53	—	—	1294	622	24	25.91	6-11	1	—	8

YORKSHIRE TEST CRICKETERS 1877-2008 (Continued)

Player	M.	I	NO	Runs	HS.	Av'ge	100s	50s	Balls	R	W	Av'ge	Best	5wI	10wM	c/st
HAMILTON, G.M. 1999	1	2	0	0	0	0.00	—	—	90	63	0	—	—	—	—	—
HAMPSHIRE, J H ...1969-75	8	16	1	403	107	26.86	1	2	—	—	—	—	—	—	—	9
†HAWKE, LORD ...1896-99	5	8	1	55	30	7.85	—	—	—	—	—	—	—	—	—	3
HILL, A 1877	2	4	2	101	49	50.50	—	—	340	130	7	18.57	4-27	—	—	1
HIRST, G H ...1897-1909	24	38	3	790	85	22.57	—	5	3967	1770	59	30.00	5-48	3	—	18
HOGGARD, M J .2000-2008	67	92	27	473	38	7.27	—	—	13909	7564	248	30.50	7-61	7	1	24
HOLMES, P 1921-32	7	14	1	357	88	27.46	—	4	—	—	—	—	—	—	—	3
HUNTER, J 1884-85	5	7	2	93	39*	18.60	—	—	—	—	—	—	—	—	—	8/3
†HUTTON, L ...1937-55	79	138	15	6971	364	56.67	19	33	260	232	3	77.33	1-2	—	—	57
HUTTON, R A 1971	5	8	2	219	81	36.50	—	2	738	257	9	28.55	3-72	—	—	9
†ILLINGWORTH, R .1958-73	61	90	11	1836	113	23.24	2	5	11934	3807	122	31.20	6-29	3	—	45
†JACKSON, Hon F S1893-1905	20	33	4	1415	144*	48.79	5	6	1587	799	24	33.29	5-52	1	—	10
JARVIS, P W 1988-93	9	15	2	132	29*	10.15	—	—	1912	965	21	45.95	4-107	—	—	2
KILNER, R 1924-26	9	8	1	233	74	33.28	—	2	2368	734	24	30.58	4-51	—	—	6
LEADBEATER, E .1951-52	2	2	0	40	38	20.00	—	—	289	218	2	109.00	1-38	—	—	3
LEYLAND, M ...1928-38	41	65	5	2764	187	46.06	9	10	1103	585	6	97.50	3-91	—	—	13
LOWSON, F A. ..1951-55	7	13	0	245	68	18.84	—	2	—	—	—	—	—	—	—	5
McGRATH, A 2003	4	5	0	201	81	40.20	—	2	102	56	4	14.00	3-16	—	—	3
MACAULAY, G G .1923-33	8	10	4	112	76	18.66	—	1	1701	662	24	27.58	5-64	1	—	5
MILLIGAN, F W 1899	2	4	0	58	38	14.50	—	—	45	29	0	—	—	—	—	1
MITCHELL, A. ..1933-36	6	10	0	298	72	29.80	—	2	6	4	0	—	—	—	—	9
*MITCHELL, F 1899	2	4	0	88	41	22.00	—	—	—	—	—	—	—	—	—	2
MOXON, M D ...1986-89	10	17	1	455	99	28.43	—	3	48	30	0	—	—	—	—	10
OLD, C M 1972-81	46	66	9	845	65	14.82	—	2	8858	4020	143	28.11	7-50	4	—	22
PADGETT, D E V 1960	2	4	0	51	31	12.75	—	—	12	8	0	—	—	—	—	—

YORKSHIRE TEST CRICKETERS 1877-2008 (Continued)

Player	M.	I	NO	Runs	HS.	Av'ge.	100s	50s	Balls	R	W	Av'ge	Best	5wI	10wM	c/st
PEATE, E 1881-86	9	14	8	70	13	11.66	—	—	2096	682	31	22.00	6-85	2	—	2
PEEL, R 1884-96	20	33	4	427	83	14.72	—	3	5216	1715	101	16.98	7-31	5	1	17
RHODES, W ...1899-1930	58	98	21	2325	179	30.19	2	11	8231	3425	127	26.96	8-68	6	1	60
SHARPE, P J 1963-69	12	21	4	786	111	46.23	1	4								17
SIDEBOTTOM, A 1985	1	1	0	2	2	2.00	—	—	112	65	1	65.00	1-65	—	—	—
SIDEBOTTOM, R J ..2001-8	18	27	10	266	31	15.64	—	—	4272	1952	76	25.68	7-47	5	1	5
SILVERWOOD, CEW1997-2003	6	7	3	29	10	7.25	—	—	828	444	11	40.36	5-91	1	—	2
SMAILES, T F 1946	1	1	0	25	25	25.00	—	—	120	62	3	20.66	3-44	—	—	—
SMITHSON, G A 1948	2	3	0	70	35	23.33	—	—								—
†STANYFORTH, R T 1927-28	4	6	1	13	6*	2.60	—	—								7/2
STEVENSON, G B ..1980-81	2	2	1	28	27*	28.00	—	—	312	183	5	36.60	3-111	—	—	—
SUTCLIFFE, H 1924-35	54	84	9	4555	194	60.73	16	23								23
TAYLOR, K 1959-64	3	5	0	57	24	11.40	—	—	12	6	0					1
TRUEMAN, F S ...1952-65	67	85	14	981	39*	13.81	—	—	15178	6625	307	21.57	8-31	17	3	64
ULYETT, G 1877-90	25	39	0	949	149	24.33	1	7	2627	1020	50	20.40	7-36	1	—	19
†VAUGHAN M P .1999-2008	82	147	9	5719	197	41.44	18	18	978	561	6	93.50	2-71	—	—	44
VERITY, H 1931-39	40	44	12	669	66*	20.90	—	3	11173	3510	144	24.37	8-43	5	2	30
WADDINGTON, A ..1920-21	2	4	0	16	7	4.00	—	—	276	119	1	119.00	1-35	—	—	1
WAINWRIGHT, E ..1893-98	5	9	0	132	49	14.66	—	—	127	73	0					2
WARDLE, J H 1948-57	28	41	8	653	66	19.78	—	2	6597	2080	102	20.39	7-36	5	—	12
WATSON, W ...1951-59	23	37	3	879	116	25.85	2	3								8
WHITE, C 1994-2002	30	50	7	1052	121	24.46	1	5	3959	2220	59	37.62	5-32	3	—	14
WILSON, C E M 1899	2	4	1	42	18	14.00	—	—								—
WILSON, D 1964-71	6	7	1	75	42	12.50	—	—	1472	466	11	42.36	2-17	—	—	1
WILSON, E R 1921	1	2	0	10	5	5.00	—	—	123	36	3	12.00	2-28	—	—	—

YORKSHIRE TEST CRICKETERS 1877-2008 (Continued)

For England

Player	M.	I	NO	Runs	HS.	Av'ge	100s	50s	Balls	R	W	Av'ge	Best	5wI	10wM	c/st
WOOD, A 1938-39	4	5	1	80	53	20.00	—	1	—	—	—	—	—	—	—	10/1
†YARDLEY, N W D ...1938-50	20	34	2	812	99	25.37	—	4	1662	707	21	33.66	3-67	—	—	14

†Captained England
*Also represented and captained South Africa

For South Africa

Player	M.	I	NO	Runs	HS.	Av'ge	100s	50s	Balls	R	W	Av'ge	Best	5wI	10wM	c/st
†MITCHELL, F 1912	3	6	0	28	12	4.66	—	—	—	—	—	—	—	—	—	—

†Captained South Africa

Overseas Players

(Qualification: 24 first-class matches for Yorkshire)

For Australia

Player	M.	I	NO	Runs	HS.	Av'ge	100s	50s	Balls	R	W	Av'ge	Best	5wI	10wM	c/st
BEVAN, M G 1994-98	18	30	3	785	91	29.07	—	6	1285	703	29	24.24	6-82	1	1	8
GILLESPIE, J N 1996-2006	71	93	28	1218	201*	18.73	1	2	14234	6770	259	26.13	7-37	8	—	27
JAQUES, P A 2005-2008	11	19	0	902	150	47.47	3	6	—	—	—	—	—	—	—	7
LEHMANN, D S ..1999-2004	27	42	2	1798	177	44.95	5	10	974	412	15	27.46	3-42	—	—	11

CENTURIES FOR ENGLAND

C W J ATHEY (1)
123 v Pakistan at Lord's, 1987

G BOYCOTT (22)

113	v. Australia at The Oval, 1964	112	v West Indies at Port-of-Spain, 1974
117	v. South Africa at Port Elizabeth, 1965	107	v. Australia at Nottingham, 1977
246*	v. India at Leeds, 1967	191	v. Australia at Leeds, 1977
116	v. West Indies at Georgetown, 1968	100*	v. Pakistan at Hyderabad, 1978
128	v. West Indies at Manchester, 1969	131	v. New Zealand at Nottingham, 1978
106	v. West Indies at Lord's, 1969	155	v. India at Birmingham, 1979
142*	v. Australia at Sydney, 1971	125	v. India at The Oval, 1979
119*	v. Australia at Adelaide, 1971	128*	v. Australia at Lord's, 1980
121*	v. Pakistan at Lord's, 1971	104*	v. West Indies at St John's, 1981
112	v. Pakistan at Leeds, 1971	137	v. Australia at The Oval, 1981
115	v. New Zealand at Leeds, 1973	105	v. India at Delhi, 1981

J T BROWN (1)
140 v. Australia at Melbourne, 1895

D DENTON (1)
104 v. South Africa at Old Wanderers, Johannesburg, 1910

P A GIBB (2)
106 v. South Africa at Old Wanderers, Johannesburg, 1938
120 v. South Africa at Kingsmead, Durban, 1939

J H HAMPSHIRE (1)
107 v. West Indies at Lord's, 1969

L HUTTON (19)

100	v. New Zealand at Manchester, 1937	206	v. New Zealand at The Oval, 1949
100	v. Australia at Nottingham, 1938	202*	v. West Indies at The Oval, 1950
364	v. Australia at The Oval, 1938	156*	v. Australia at Adelaide, 1951
196	v. West Indies at Lord's, 1939	100	v. South Africa at Leeds, 1951
165*	v. West Indies at The Oval, 1939	150	v. India at Lord's, 1952
122*	v. Australia at Sydney, 1947	104	v. India at Manchester, 1952
100	v. South Africa at Leeds, 1947	145	v. Australia at Lord's, 1953
158	v. South Africa at Ellis Park, J'b'rg, 1948	169	v. West Indies at Georgetown, 1954
123	v. South Africa at Ellis Park, J'b'rg, 1949	205	v. West Indies at Kingston, 1954
101	v. New Zealand at Leeds, 1949		

R ILLINGWORTH (2)
113 v. West Indies at Lord's, 1969
107 v. India at Manchester, 1971

Hon. F S JACKSON (5)

103	v. Australia at The Oval, 1893	144*	v. Australia at Leeds, 1905
118	v. Australia at The Oval, 1899	113	v. Australia at Manchester, 1905
128	v. Australia at Manchester, 1902		

M LEYLAND (9)

137	v. Australia at Melbourne, 1929	161	v. South Africa at The Oval, 1935
102	v. South Africa at Lord's, 1929	126	v. Australia at Woolloongabba, Brisbane, 1936
109	v. Australia at Lord's, 1934		
153	v. Australia at Manchester, 1934	111*	v. Australia at Melbourne, 1937
110	v. Australia at The Oval, 1934	187	v. Australia at The Oval, 1938

CENTURIES FOR ENGLAND

W RHODES (2)

179 v. Australia at Melbourne, 1912
152 v. South Africa at Old Wanderers, Johannesburg, 1913

P J SHARPE (1)

111 v. New Zealand at Nottingham, 1969

H SUTCLIFFE (16)

122	v. South Africa at Lord's, 1924	114	v. South Africa at Birmingham, 1929
115	v. Australia at Sydney, 1924	100	v. South Africa at Lord's, 1929
176	v. Australia at Melbourne, 1925 (1st Inns)	104	v. South Africa at The Oval, 1929 (1st inns)
127	v. Australia at Melbourne, 1925 (2nd Inns)	109*	v. South Africa at The Oval, 1929 (2nd inns)
143	v. Australia at Melbourne, 1925	161	v. Australia at The Oval, 1930
161	v. Australia at The Oval, 1926	117	v. New Zealand at The Oval, 1931
102	v. South Africa at Old Wanderers, Jbg.1927	109*	v. New Zealand at Manchester, 1931
135	v. Australia at Melbourne, 1929	194	v. Australia at Sydney, 1932

G ULYETT (1)

149 v. Australia at Melbourne, 1882

M P VAUGHAN (18)

120	v. Pakistan at Manchester, 2001	105	v. Sri Lanka at Kandy, 2003
115	v. Sri Lanka at Lord's, 2002	140	v. West Indies at Antigua, 2004
100	v. India at Lord's, 2002	103	v. West Indies at Lord's (1st inns) 2004
197	v. India at Nottingham, 2002	101*	v. West Indies at Lord's (2nd inns) 2004
195	v. India at The Oval, 2002	120	v. Bangladesh at Lord's, 2005
177	v. Australia at Adelaide, 2002	166	v. Australia at Manchester,2005
145	v. Australia at Melbourne, 2002	103	v. West Indies at Leeds, 2007
183	v. Australia at Sydney, 2003	124	v. India at Nottingham, 2007
156	v. South Africa at Birmingham, 2003	106	v. New Zealand at Lord's, 2008

W WATSON (2)

109 v. Australia at Lord's, 1953   116 v. West Indies at Kingston, 1954

C WHITE (1)

121 v. India at Ahmedabad, 2001

Summary of the Centuries

versus	Total	In England	Away
Australia	40	21	19
Bangladesh	1	1	0
India	12	10	2
New Zealand	9	9	—
Pakistan	5	4	1
South Africa	18	10	8
Sri Lanka	2	1	1
West Indies	17	10	7
Totals	104	66	38

For Australia

J N GILLESPIE (1)

201* v. Bangladesh at Chittagong, 2006

P A JAQUES (3)

100 v. Sri Lanka at Brisbane, 2007   108 v. West Indies at Bridgetown, 2008
150 v. Sri Lanka at Hobart, 2007

D S LEHMANN (5)

160 v. West Indies at Port of Spain, 2003   129 v. Sri Lanka at Galle, 2004
110 v. Bangladesh at Darwin, 2003   153 v. Sri Lanka at Columbo, 2004
177 v. Bangladesh at Cairns, 2003

10 WICKETS IN A MATCH FOR ENGLAND

W BATES (1)
14 for 102 (7 for 28 and 7 for 74) v. Australia at Melbourne, 1882

M J HOGGARD (1)
12 for 205 (5 for 144 and 7 for 61) v. South Africa at Johannesburg, 2005

R PEEL (1)
11 for 68 (7 for 31 and 4 for 37) v. Australia at Mancester, 1888

Note: The scorebook for the Australia v. England Test match at Sydney in February 1888 shows that the final wicket to fall was taken by W Attewell, and not by Peel

Peel therefore took 9, and not 10 wickets, in the match

His career totals have been amended to take account of this alteration

W RHODES (1)
15 for 124 (7 for 56 and 8 for 68) v. Australia at Melbourne, 1904

R J SIDEBOTTOM (1)
10 for 139 (4 for 90 and 6 for 49) v. New Zealand at Hamilton, 2008

F S TRUEMAN (3)
11 for 88 (5 for 58 and 6 for 30) v. Australia at Leeds, 1961
11 for 152 (6 for 100 and 5 for 52) v. West Indies at Lord's, 1963*
12 for 119 (5 for 75 and 7 for 44) v. West Indies at Birmingham, 1963*
consecutive Tests

H VERITY (2)
11 for 153 (7 for 49 and 4 for 104) v. India at Chepauk, Madras, 1934
15 for 104 (7 for 61 and 8 for 43) v. Australia at Lord's, 1934

J H WARDLE (1)
12 for 89 (5 for 53 and 7 for 36) v. South Africa at Cape Town, 1957

Summary of Ten Wickets in a Match

versus	Total	In England	Away
Australia	5	3	2
India	1	—	1
New Zealand	1	—	1
Pakistan	—	—	—
South Africa	2	—	2
Sri Lanka	—	—	—
West Indies	2	2	—
Totals	11	5	6

For Australia

M G BEVAN (1)
10 for 113 (4 for 31and 6 for 82) v. West Indies at Adelaide, 1997

5 WICKETS IN AN INNINGS FOR ENGLAND

R APPLEYARD (1)
5 for 51 v. Pakistan at Nottingham, 1954

W BATES (4)
7 for 28 v. Australia at Melbourne, 1882   5 for 31 v. Australia at Adelaide, 1884
7 for 74 v. Australia at Melbourne, 1882   5 for 24 v. Australia at Sydney, 1885

5 WICKETS IN AN INNINGS FOR ENGLAND *(Continued)*

W E BOWES (6)

6 for 34 v. New Zealand at Auckland, 1933
6 for 142 v. Australia at Leeds, 1934*
5 for 55 v. Australia at The Oval, 1934*

5 for 100 v. South Africa at Manchester, 1935
5 for 49 v. Australia at The Oval, 1938
6 for 33 v. West Indies at Manchester, 1939

consecutive Test matches

T EMMETT (1)

7 for 68 v. Australia at Melbourne, 1879

D GOUGH (9)

6 for 49 v. Australia at Sydney, 1995
5 for 40 v. New Zealand at Wellington, 1997
5 for 149 v. Australia at Leeds, 1997
6 for 42 v. South Africa at Leeds, 1998
5 for 96 v. Australia at Melbourne, 1998

5 for 70 v. South Africa at Johannesburg, 1999
5 for 109 v. West Indies at Birmingham, 2000
5 for 61 v. Pakistan at Lord's, 2001
5 for 103 v. Australia at Leeds, 2001

S HAIGH (1)

6 for 11 v. South Africa at Cape Town, 1909

G H HIRST (3)

5 for 77 v. Australia at The Oval, 1902
5 for 48 v. Australia at Melbourne, 1904

5 for 58 v. Australia at Birmingham, 1909

M J HOGGARD (7)

7 for 63 v. New Zealand at Christchurch, 2002
5 for 92 v. Sri Lanka at Birmingham, 2002
5 for 144 v. South Africa at Johannesburg, 2005*
7 for 61 v. South Africa at Johannesburg, 2005*

5 for 73 v. Bangladesh at Chester-le-Street, 2005
6 for 57 v. India at Nagpur, 2006
7 for 104 v. Australia at Adelaide, 2006

Consecutive Test innings

R ILLINGWORTH (3)

6 for 29 v. India at Lord's, 1967
6 for 87 v. Australia at Leeds, 1968

5 for 70 v. India at The Oval, 1971

Hon F S JACKSON (1)

5 for 52 v. Australia at Nottingham, 1905

G G MACAULAY (1)

5 for 64 v. South Africa at Cape Town, 1923

C M OLD (4)

5 for 113 v. New Zealand at Lord's, 1973
5 for 21 v. India at Lord's, 1974

6 for 54 v. New Zealand at Wellington, 1978
7 for 50 v. Pakistan at Birmingham, 1978

E PEATE (2)

5 for 43 v. Australia at Sydney, 1882

6 for 85 v. Australia at Lord's, 1884

R PEEL (5)

5 for 51 v. Australia at Adelaide, 1884
5 for 18 v. Australia at Sydney, 1888
7 for 31 v. Australia at Manchester, 1888

6 for 67 v. Australia at Sydney, 1894
6 for 23 v. Australia at The Oval, 1896

W RHODES (6)

7 for 17 v. Australia at Birmingham, 1902
5 for 63 v. Australia at Sheffield, 1902
5 for 94 v. Australia at Sydney, 1903*

7 for 56 v. Australia at Melbourne, 1904*
8 for 68 v. Australia at Melbourne, 1904*
5 for 83 v. Australia at Manchester, 1909

consecutive Test innings

5 WICKETS IN AN INNINGS FOR ENGLAND *(Continued)*

C E W SILVERWOOD (1)

5 for 91 v. South Africa, at Cape Town, 2000

R J SIDEBOTTOM (5)

5 for 88 v. West Indies at Chester-le-Street, 2007 7 for 47 v. New Zealand at Napier, 2008
6 for 49 v. New Zealand at Hamilton, 2008 6 for 47 v. New Zealand at Nottingham, 2008
5 for 105 v. New Zealand at Wellington, 2008

F S TRUEMAN (17)

8 for 31 v. India at Manchester, 1952 6 for 31 v. Pakistan at Lord's, 1962
5 for 48 v. India at The Oval, 1952 5 for 62 v. Australia at Melbourne, 1963
5 for 90 v. Australia at Lord's, 1956 7 for 75 v. New Zealand at Christchurch, 1963
5 for 63 v. West Indies at Nottingham, 1957 6 for 100 v. West Indies at Lord's, 1963*
5 for 31 v. New Zealand at Birmingham, 1958 5 for 52 v. West Indies at Lord's, 1963*
5 for 35 v. West Indies at Port-of-Spain, 1960 5 for 75 v. West Indies at Birmingham, 1963*
5 for 27 v. South Africa at Nottingham, 1960 7 for 44 v. West Indies at Birmingham, 1963*
5 for 58 v. Australia at Leeds, 1961* 5 for 48 v. Australia at Lord's, 1964
6 for 30 v. Australia at Leeds, 1961*

G ULYETT (1)

7 for 36 v. Australia at Lord's, 1884

H VERITY (5)

5 for 33 v. Australia at Sydney 1933 8 for 43 v. Australia at Lord's, 1934*
7 for 49 v. India at Chepauk, Madras, 1934 5 for 70 v. South Africa at Cape Town, 1939
7 for 61 v. Australia at Lord's, 1934*

J H WARDLE (5)

7 for 56 v. Pakistan at The Oval, 1954 7 for 36 v. South Africa at Cape Town, 1957*
5 for 79 v. Australia at Sydney, 1955 5 for 61 v. South Africa at Kingsmead,
5 for 53 v. South Africa at Cape Town, 1957* Durban, 1957*

C WHITE (3)

5 for 57 v. West Indies at Leeds, 2000 5 for 32 v. West Indies at The Oval, 2000
5 for 127 v. Australia at Perth, 2002

*consecutive Test innings

Summary of Five Wickets in an Innings

versus	Total	In England	Away
Australia	42	22	20
Bangladesh	1	1	—
India	7	5	2
New Zealand	11	3	8
Pakistan	5	5	—
South Africa	13	3	10
Sril Lanka	1	1	—
West Indies	11	10	1
Totals	91	50	41

For Australia

M G BEVAN (1)

6 for 82 v. West Indies at Adelaide, 1997

5 WICKETS IN AN INNINGS

J N GILLESPIE (8)

5 for 54	v.	South Africa at Port Elizabeth, 1997
7 for 37	v.	England at Leeds, 1997
5 for 88	v.	England at Perth, 1998
5 for 89	v.	West Indies at Adelaide, 2000
6 for 40	v.	West Indies at Melbourne, 2000
5 for 53	v.	England at Lord's, 2001
5 for 39	v.	West Indies at Georgetown, 2003
5 for 56	v.	India at Nagpur, 2004

HAT-TRICKS

W Bates v. Australia at Melbourne, 1882
D Gough v. Australia at Sydney, 1998
M J Hoggard v. West Indies at Bridgetown, 2004
R J Sidebottom v. New Zealand at Hamilton, 2008

FOUR WICKETS IN FIVE BALLS

C M Old v. Pakistan at Birmingham, 1978

THREE WICKETS IN FOUR BALLS

R Appleyard v. New Zealand at Auckland, 1955
D Gough v. Pakistan at Lord's, 2001

YORKSHIRE PLAYERS WHO PLAYED ALL THEIR TEST CRICKET AFTER LEAVING YORKSHIRE

For England

Player	M.	I	NO	Runs	HS.	Av'ge.	100s	50s	Balls	R	W	Av'ge	Best	5wI	10wM	c/st
BALDERSTONE, J C ..1976	2	4	0	39	35	9.75	—	—	96	80	1	80.00	1:80	—	—	1
BATTY, G J ..2003	4	7	1	136	38	22.66	—	—	992	504	8	63.00	3:55	—	—	—
BIRKENSHAW, J ..1973-74	5	7	1	148	64	21.14	—	1	1017	469	13	36.07	5:57	1	—	3
BOLUS, J B ..1963-64	7	12	0	496	88	41.33	—	4	18	16	0	—	—	—	—	2
†PARKIN, C H ..1920-24	10	16	3	160	36	12.30	—	—	2095	1128	32	35.25	5:38	2	—	3
RHODES, S J ..1994-95	11	17	5	294	65*	24.50	—	1	—	—	—	—	—	—	—	46/3
†SUGG, F H ..1888	2	2	0	55	31	27.50	—	—	—	—	—	—	—	—	—	1
WARD, A ..1893-95	7	13	0	487	117	37.46	1	3	—	—	—	—	—	—	—	6
WOOD, B ..1972-78	12	21	0	454	90	21.61	—	2	98	50	0	—	—	—	—	—

For South Africa

Player	M.	I	NO	Runs	HS.	Av'ge.	100s	50s	Balls	R	W	Av'ge	Best	5wI	10wM	c/st
THORNTON, P G ..1902	1	1	1	1	1*	—	—	—	24	20	1	20.00	1:20	—	—	1

†Born outside Yorkshire

CENTURIES FOR ENGLAND

A WARD (1)
117 v. Australia at Sydney, 1894

5 WICKETS IN AN INNINGS FOR ENGLAND

J BIRKENSHAW (1)
5 : 57 v. Pakistan at Karachi, 1973

C H PARKIN (2)
5 : 60 v. Australia at Adelaide, 1921
5 : 38 v. Australia at Manchester, 1921

YORKSHIRE'S TEST CRICKET RECORDS

R APPLEYARD

Auckland 1954-55: took 3 wickets in 4 balls as New Zealand were dismissed for the lowest total in Test history (26).

C W J ATHEY

Perth 1986-87: shared an opening stand of 223 with B C Broad – England's highest for any wicket at the WACA Ground.

W BATES

Melbourne 1882-83 (Second Test): achieved the first hat-trick for England when he dismissed P S McDonnell, G Giffen and G J Bonnor in Australia's first innings. Later in the match, he became the first player to score a fifty (55) and take 10 or more wickets (14 for 102) in the same Test.

W E BOWES

Melbourne 1932-33: enjoyed the unique satisfaction of bowling D G Bradman first ball in a Test match (his first ball to him in Test cricket).

G BOYCOTT

Leeds 1967: scored 246 not out off 555 balls in 573 minutes to establish the record England score against India. His first 100 took 341 minutes (316 balls) and he was excluded from the next Test as a disciplinary measure; shared in hundred partnerships for three successive wickets.

Adelaide 1970-71: with J H Edrich, became the third opening pair to share hundred partnerships in both innings of a Test against Australia.

Port-of-Spain 1973-74: first to score 99 and a hundred in the same Test.

Nottingham 1977: with A P E Knott, equalled England v. Australia sixth-wicket partnership record of 215 – the only England v. Australia stand to be equalled or broken since 1938. Batted on each day of the five-day Test (second after M L Jaisimha to achieve this feat).

Leeds 1977: first to score his 100th First Class hundred in a Test; became the fourth England player to be on the field for an entire Test.

Perth: 1978-79: eighth to score 2,000 runs for England against Australia.

Birmingham 1979: emulated K F Barrington by scoring hundreds on each of England's six current home grounds.

Perth: 1979-80: fourth to carry his bat through a completed England innings (third v. Australia) and the first to do so without scoring 100; first to score 99 not out in a Test.

Lord's 1981: 100th Test for England – second after M C Cowdrey (1968).

The Oval, 1981: second after Hon F S Jackson to score five hundreds v. Australia in England.

Gained three Test records from M C Cowdrey: exceeded England aggregate of 7,624 runs in 11 fewer Tests (Manchester 1981); 61st fifty – world record (The Oval 1981); 189th innings – world record (Bangalore 1981-82).

Delhi, 4.23 p.m. on 23 December 1981: passed G St.A Sobers' world Test record of 8,032 runs, having played 30 more innings and batted over 451 hours (cf. 15 complete five-day Tests); his 22nd hundred equalled the England record.

J T BROWN

Melbourne 1894-95: his 28-minute fifty remains the fastest in Test cricket, and his 95-minute hundred was a record until 1897-98; his third-wicket stand of 210 with A Ward set a Test record for any wicket.

D B CLOSE

Manchester 1949: at 18 years 149 days he became – and remains – the youngest to represent England.

Melbourne 1950-51: became the youngest (19 years 301 days) to represent England against Australia.

T EMMETT

Melbourne 1878-79: first England bowler to take seven wickets in a Test innings.

P A GIBB

Johannesburg 1938-39: enjoyed a record England debut, scoring 93 and 106 as well as sharing second-wicket stands of 184 and 168 with E Paynter.

Durban 1938-39: shared record England v. South Africa second-wicket stand of 280 with W J Edrich, his 120 in 451 minutes including only two boundaries.

D GOUGH

Sydney 1998-99: achieved the 23rd hat-trick in Test cricket (ninth for England and first for England v. Australia since 1899).

Lord's 2001: took 3 wickets in 4 balls v. Pakistan.

S HAIGH

Cape Town 1898-99: bowled unchanged through the second innings with A E Trott, taking 6 for 11 as South Africa were dismissed for 35 in the space of 114 balls.

J H HAMPSHIRE

Lord's 1969: became the first England player to score 100 at Lord's on his debut in Tests.

A HILL

Melbourne 1876-77: took the first wicket to fall in Test cricket when he bowled N Thompson, and held the first catch when he dismissed T P Horan.

G H HIRST

The Oval 1902: helped to score the last 15 runs in a match-winning tenth-wicket partnership with W Rhodes.

Birmingham 1909: shared all 20 Australian wickets with fellow left-arm spinner C Blythe (11 for 102).

M J HOGGARD

Bridgetown 2004: became the third Yorkshire player to take a hat-trick in Test cricket (see W Bates and D Gough). It was the 10th hat-trick for England and the third for England versus West Indies.

L HUTTON

Nottingham 1938: scored 100 in his first Test against Australia.

The Oval 1938: his score (364) and batting time (13 hours 17 minutes – the longest innings in English First-Class cricket) remain England records, and were world Test records until 1958. It remains the highest Test score at The Oval. His stand of 382 with M Leyland is the England second-wicket record in all Tests and the highest for any wicket against Australia. He also shared a record England v. Australia sixth-wicket stand of 216 with J Hardstaff Jr. – the first instance of a batsman sharing in two stands of 200 in the same Test innings. 770 runs were scored during his innings (Test record) which was England's 100th century against Australia, and contained 35 fours. England's total of 903 for 7 declared remains the Ashes Test record.

Lord's 1939: added 248 for the fourth wicket with D C S Compton in 140 minutes.

The Oval 1939: shared (then) world-record third-wicket stand of 264 with W R Hammond, which remains the record for England v. West Indies. Hutton's last eight Tests had brought him 1,109 runs.

The Oval 1948: last out in the first innings, he was on the field for all but the final 57 minutes of the match.

Johannesburg 1948-49: shared (then) world-record first-wicket stand of 359 in 310 minutes with C Washbrook on the opening day of Test cricket at Ellis Park; it remains England's highest opening stand in all Tests.

The Oval 1950: scored England's first 200 in a home Test v. West Indies, and remains alone in carrying his bat for England against them; his 202 not out (in 470 minutes) is the highest score by an England batsman achieving this feat.

L HUTTON (Continued)

Adelaide 1950-51: only England batsman to carry his bat throughout a complete Test innings twice, and second after R Abel (1891-92) to do so for any country against Australia.

Manchester 1951: scored 98 not out, just failing to become the first to score his 100th First Class hundred in a Test match.

The Oval 1951: became the only batsman to be out 'obstructing the field' in Test cricket.

1952: first professional to be appointed captain of England in the 20th Century.

The Oval 1953: first captain to win a rubber after losing the toss in all five Tests.

Kingston 1953-54: scored the first 200 by an England captain in a Test overseas.

R ILLINGWORTH

Manchester 1971: shared record England v. India eighth-wicket stand of 168 with P. Lever.

Hon. F S JACKSON

The Oval 1893: his 100 took 135 minutes, and was the first in a Test in England to be completed with a hit over the boundary (then worth only four runs).

The Oval 1899: his stand of 185 with T W Hayward was then England's highest for any wicket in England, and the record opening partnership by either side in England v. Australia Tests.

Nottingham 1905: dismissed M A Noble, C Hill and J Darling in one over (W01W0W).

Leeds 1905: batted 268 minutes for 144 not out – the first hundred in a Headingley Test.

Manchester 1905: first to score five Test hundreds in England.

The Oval 1905: first captain to win every toss in a five-match rubber.

M LEYLAND

Melbourne 1928-29: scored 137 in his first innings against Australia.

1934: first to score three hundreds in a rubber against Australia in England.

Brisbane 1936-37: scored England's only 100 at 'The Gabba' before 1974-75.

The Oval 1938: contributed 187 in 381 minutes to the record Test total of 903 for 7 declared, sharing in England's highest stand against Australia (all wickets) and record second-wicket stand in all Tests: 382 with L Hutton. First to score hundreds in his first and last innings against Australia.

G G MACAULAY

Cape Town 1922-23: fourth bowler (third for England) to take a wicket (G A L Hearne) with his first ball in Test cricket. Made the winning hit in the fourth of only six Tests to be decided by a one-wicket margin.

Leeds 1926: shared a match-saving ninth-wicket stand of 108 with G Geary.

C M OLD

Birmingham 1978: took 4 wickets in 5 balls in his 19th over (0WW no-ball WW1) to emulate the feat of M J C Allom.

R PEEL

Took his 50th wicket in his ninth Test and his 100th in his 20th Test – all against Australia.

W RHODES

Birmingham 1902: his first-innings analysis of 7 for 17 remains the record for all Tests at Edgbaston.

The Oval 1902: helped to score the last 15 runs in a match-winning tenth-wicket partnership with G H Hirst.

Sydney 1903-04: shared record England v. Australia tenth-wicket stand of 130 in 66 minutes with R E Foster.

Melbourne 1903-04: first to take 15 wickets in England v. Australia Tests; his match analysis of 15 for 124 remains the record for all Tests at Melbourne.

Melbourne 1911-12: shared record England v. Australia first-wicket stand of 323 in 268 minutes with J B Hobbs.

Johannesburg 1913-14: took his 100th wicket and completed the first 'double' for England (in 44 matches).

Sydney 1920-21: first to score 2,000 runs and take 100 wickets in Test cricket.

Adelaide 1920-21: third bowler to take 100 wickets against Australia.

The Oval 1926: set (then) record of 109 wickets against Australia.

Kingston 1929-30: ended the world's longest Test career (30 years 315 days) as the oldest Test cricketer (52 years 165 days).

H SUTCLIFFE

Birmingham 1924: shared the first of 15 three-figure partnerships with J B Hobbs at the first attempt.

Lord's 1924: shared stand of 268 with J B Hobbs, which remains the first-wicket record for all Lord's Tests, and was then the England v. South Africa record.

Sydney 1924-25: his first opening stands against Australia with J B Hobbs realised 157 and 110.

Melbourne 1924-25 (Second Test): with J B Hobbs achieved the first instance of a batting partnership enduring throughout a full day's Test match play; they remain the only England pair to achieve this feat, and their stand of 283 in 289 minutes remains the longest for the first wicket in this series. Became the first to score 100 in each innings of a Test against Australia, and the first Englishman to score three successive hundreds in Test cricket.

Melbourne 1924-25 (Fourth Test): first to score four hundreds in one rubber of Test matches; it was his third 100 in successive Test innings at Melbourne. Completed 1,000 runs in fewest Test innings (12) – since equalled.

Sydney 1924-25: his aggregate of 734 runs was the record for any rubber until 1928-29.

The Oval 1926: shared first-wicket stand of 172 with J B Hobbs on a rain-affected pitch.

The Oval 1929: first to score hundreds in each innings of a Test twice; only England batsman to score four hundreds in a rubber twice.

Sydney 1932-33: his highest England innings of 194 overtook J B Hobbs's world record of 15 Test hundreds.

F S TRUEMAN

Leeds 1952: reduced India to 0 for 4 in their second innings by taking 3 wickets in 8 balls on his debut.

Manchester 1952: achieved record England v. India innings analysis of 8 for 31.

The Oval 1952: set England v. India series record with 29 wickets.

Leeds 1961: took 5 for 0 with 24 off-cutters at a reduced pace v. Australia.

Lord's 1962: shared record England v. Pakistan ninth-wicket stand of 76 with T W Graveney,

Christchurch 1962-63: passed J B Statham's world Test record of 242 wickets; his analysis of 7 for 75 remains the record for Lancaster Park Test and for England in New Zealand.

Birmingham 1963: returned match analysis (12 for 119) against West Indies in England and for any Birmingham Test, ending with a 6 for 4 spell from 24 balls.

The Oval 1963: set England v. West Indies series record with 34 wickets.

The Oval 1964: first to take 300 wickets in Tests.

G ULYETT

Sydney 1881-82: with R G Barlow shared the first century opening partnership in Test cricket (122).

Melbourne 1881-82: his 149 was the first Test hundred for England in Australia, and the highest score for England on the first day of a Test in Australia until 1965-66.

M P VAUGHAN

Scored 1481 runs in 2002 – more than any other England player in a calendar year, surpassing the 1379 scored by D L Amiss in 1979. It was the fourth highest in a calendar year.

Scored 633 runs in the 2002-3 series versus Australia – surpassed for England in a five Test series versus Australia only by W R Hammond, who scored 905 runs in 1928-29, H Sutcliffe (734 in 1924-25), J B Hobbs (662 in 1911-12) and G Boycott (657 in 1970-71), when he played in five of the six Tests.

Scored six Test Match centuries in 2002 to equal the record set for England by D C S Compton in 1947.

Lord's 2004: scored a century in each innings (103 and 101*) versus West Indies and so became the third player (after G A Headley and G A Gooch) to score a century in each innings of a Test match at Lord's.

Lord's 2005: only the second player (J B Hobbs is the other) to have scored centuries in three consecutive Test match innings at Lord's. Scored the 100th century for England by a Yorkshire player.

H VERITY

Lord's 1934: took 14 for 80 on the third day (six of them in the final hour) to secure England's first win against Australia at Lord's since 1896. It remains the most wickets to fall to one bowler in a day of Test cricket in England. His match analysis of 15 for 104 was then the England v. Australia record, and has been surpassed only by J C Laker.

W WATSON

Lord's 1953: scored 109 in 346 minutes in his first Test against Australia.

N W D YARDLEY

Melbourne 1946-47: dismissed D G Bradman for the third consecutive innings without assistance from the field. Became the first to score a fifty in each innings for England and take five wickets in the same match.

Nottingham 1947: shared record England v. South Africa fifth-wicket stand of 237 with D C S Compton.

* * *

Facts adapted by Bill Frindall from his *England Test Cricketers – The Complete Record from 1877* (Collins Willow, 1989). With later additions.

TEST MATCHES AT HEADINGLEY, LEEDS 1899-2008

1899 **Australia 172** (J Worrall 76) and 224 (H Trumble 56, J T Hearne hat-trick). **England 220** (A F A Lilley 55, H Trumble 5 for 60) and **19 for 0 wkt.**
Match drawn
Toss: Australia

1905 **England 301** (Hon F S Jackson 144*) and **295 for 5 wkts dec** (J T Tyldesley 100, T W Hayward 60, W. W. Armstrong 5 for 122). **Australia 195** (W W Armstrong 66, A R Warren 5 for 57) and **224 for 7 wkts** (M A Noble 62).
Toss: England

1907 **England 76** (G A Faulkner 6 for 17) and **162** (C B Fry 54). **South Africa 110** (C Blythe 8 for 59) and **75** (C Blythe 7 for 40).
England won by 53 runs
Toss: England

1909 **Australia 188** and **207** (S F Barnes 6 for 63). **England 182** (J Sharp 61, J T Tyldesley 55, C G Macartney 7 for 58) and **87** (A Cotter 5 for 38).
Australia won by 126 runs
Toss: Australia

1912 **England 242** (F E Woolley 57) and **238** (R H Spooner 82, J B Hobbs 55). **South Africa 147** (S F Barnes 6 for 52) and **159.**
England won by 174 runs
Toss: England

1921 **Australia 407** (C G Macartney 115, W W Armstrong 77, C E Pellew 52, J M Taylor 50) and **273 for 7 wkts dec** (T J E Andrew 92). **England 259** (J W H T Douglas 75, Hon L H Tennyson 63, G Brown 57) and **202.**
Australia won by 219 runs
Toss: Australia

1924 **England 396** (E H Hendren 132, H Sutcliffe 83) and **60 for 1 wkt. South Africa 132** (H W Taylor 59*, M W Tate 6 for 42) and **323** (H W Taylor 56, R H Catterall 56).
England won by 9 wickets
Toss: England

1926 **Australia 494** (C G Macartney 151, W M Woodfull 141, A J Richardson 100). **England 294** (G G Macaulay 76, C V Grimmett 5 for 88) and **254 for 3 wkts** (H Sutcliffe 94, J B Hobbs 88).
Match drawn
Toss: England

1929 **South Africa 236** (R H Catterall 74, C L Vincent 60, A P Freeman 7 for 115) and **275** (H G Owen-Smith 129). **England 328** (F E Woolley 83, W R Hammond 65, N A Quinn 6 for 92) and **186 for 5 wkts** (F E Woolley 95*).
England won by 5 wickets
Toss: South Africa

1930 **Australia 566** (D G Bradman 334, A F Kippax 77, W M Woodfull 50, M W Tate 5 for 124). **England 391** (W R Hammond 113, C V Grimmett 5 for 135) and **95 for 3 wkts.**
Match drawn
Toss: Australia

1934 **England 200** and **229 for 6 wkts. Australia 584** (D G Bradman 304, W H Ponsford 181, W E Bowes 6 for 142).
Match drawn
Toss: England

1935 **England 216** (W R Hammond 63, A Mitchell 58) and **294 for 7 wkts dec** (W R Hammond 87*, A Mitchell 72, D Smith 57). **South Africa 171** (E A B Rowan 62) and **194 for 5 wkts** (B Mitchell 58).
Match drawn
Toss: England

1938 **England 223** (W R Hammond 76, W .J O'Reilly 5 for 66) and **123** (.W J O'Reilly 5 for 56). **Australia 242** (D G Bradman 103, B A Barnett 57) and **107 for 5 wkts.**
Australia won by 5 wickets
Toss: Australia

1947 **South Africa 175** (B Mitchell 53, A Nourse 51) and **184** (A D Nourse 57). **England 317 for 7 wkts dec** (L Hutton 100, C Washbrook 75) and **47 for 0 wkt.**
England won by 10 wickets
Toss: South Africa

1948 **England 496** (C Washbrook 143, W .J Edrich 111, L Hutton 81, A V Bedser 79) and **365 for 8 wkts dec** (D C S. Compton 66, C Washbrook 65, L Hutton 57, W J Edrich 54). **Australia 458** (R N Harvey 112, S J E Loxton 93, R R Lindwall 77, K R Miller 58) and 404 for 3 wkts (A R Morris 182, D G Bradman 173*).
Australia won by 7 wickets
Toss: England

1949 **England 372** (D C S Compton 114, L Hutton 101, T B Burtt 5 for 97, J Cowie 5 for 127) and **267 for 4 wkts dec** (C Washbrook 103*, W J Edrich 70). **New Zealand 341** (F B Smith 96, M P Donnelly 64, T E Bailey 6 for 118) and **195 for 2 wkts** (B Sutcliffe 82, F Smith 54*).
Match drawn   Toss: England

1951 **South Africa 538** (E A B Rowan 236, P N F Mansell 90, C B. van Ryneveld 83, R A McLean 67) and **87 for 0 wkt** (E A B Rowan 60*). **England 505** (P B H May 138, L Hutton 100, T E Bailey 95, F A Lowson 58, A M B Rowan 5 for 174).
Match drawn   Toss: South Africa

1952 **India 293** (V L Manjrekar 133, V S Hazare 89) and 165 (D G Phadkar 64, V S Hazare 56). **England 334** (T W Graveney 71, T G Evans 66, Ghulam Ahmed 5 for 100) and **128 for 3 wkts** (R T Simpson 51).
England won by 7 wickets   Toss: India

1953 **England 167** (T W Graveney 55, R R Lindwall 5 for 54) and **275** (W J Edrich 64, D C S Compton 61). **Australia 266** (R N Harvey 71, G B Hole 53, A V Bedser 5 for 95) and **147 for 4 wkts.**
Match drawn   Toss: Australia

1955 **South Africa 171** and **500** (D J McGlew 133, W R Endean 116*, T L Goddard 74, H J Keith 73). **England 191** (D C S Compton 61) and **256** (P B H May 97, T L Goddard 5 for 69, H J Tayfield 5 for 94).
South Africa won by 224 runs   Toss: South Africa

1956 **England 325** (P B H May 101, C Washbrook 98). **Australia 143** (J C Laker 5 for 58) and **140** (R N Harvey 69, J C Laker 6 for 55).
England won by an innings and 42 runs   Toss: England

1957 **West Indies 142** (P J Loader 6 for 36, including hat-trick) and **132**. **England 279** (P B H May 69, M C Cowdrey 68, Rev D S Sheppard 68, F M M Worrell 7 for 70).
England won by an innings and 5 runs   Toss: West Indies

1958 **New Zealand 67** (J C Laker 5 for 17) and **129** (G A R Lock 7 for 51). **England 267 for 2 wkts dec** (P B H May 113*, C A Milton 104*).
England won by an innings and 71 runs   Toss: New Zealand

1959 **India 161** and **149**. **England 483 for 8 wkts dec** (M C Cowdrey 160, K F Barrington 80, W G A Parkhouse 78, G Pullar 75).
England won by an innings and 173 runs   Toss: India

1961 **Australia 237** (R N Harvey 73, C C McDonald 54, F S Trueman 5 for 58) and **120** (R N Harvey 53, F S Trueman 6 for 30); **England 299** (M C Cowdrey 93, G Pullar 53, A K Davidson 5 for 63) and **62 for 2 wkts.**
England won by 8 wickets   Toss: Australia

1962 **England 428** (P H Parfitt 119, M J Stewart 86, D A Allen 62, Munir Malik 5 for 128). **Pakistan 131** (Alimuddin 50) and **180** (Alimuddin 60, Saeed Ahmed 54).
England won by an innings and 117 runs   Toss: Pakistan

1963 **West Indies 397** (G St A Sobers 102, R B Kanhai 92, J S Solomon 62) and **229** (B F Butcher 78, G St.A Sobers 52). **England 174** (G A R Lock 53, C C Griffith 6 for 36) and **231** (J M Parks 57, D B Close 56).
West Indies won by 221 runs   Toss: West Indies

1964 **England 268** (J M Parks 68, E R Dexter 66, N J N Hawke 5 for 75) and 229 (K F Barrington 85). **Australia 389** (P J P Burge 160, W M Lawry 78) and **111 for 3 wkts** (I R Redpath 58*).
Australia won by 7 wickets   Toss: England

1965 **England 546 for 4 wkts dec** (J H Edrich 310*, K F Barrington 163). **New Zealand 193** (J R Reid 54) and **166** (V Pollard 53, F J Titmus 5 for 19).
England won by an innings and 187 runs   Toss: England

1966 **West Indies 500 for 9 wkts dec** (G.St.A Sobers 174, S M Nurse 137). **England 240** (B L D'Oliveira 88, G.St.A Sobers 5 for 41) and **205** (R W Barber 55, L R Gibbs 6 for 39).
West Indies won by an innings and 55 runs   Toss: West Indies

1967 **England 550 for 4 wkts dec** (G Boycott 246*, B L D'Oliveira 109, K F Barrington 93, T W Graveney 59) and **126 for 4 wkts. India 164** (Nawab of Pataudi jnr 64) and **510** (Nawab of Pataudi jnr 148, A L Wadekar 91, F M Engineer 87, Hanumant Singh 73). **England won by 6 wickets** Toss: England

1968 **Australia 315** (I R Redpath 92, I M Chappell 65) and **312** (I M Chappell 81, K D Walters 56, R Illingworth 6 for 87). **England 302** (R M Prideaux 64, J H Edrich 62, A N Connolly 5 for 72) and **230 for 4 wkts** (J H Edrich 65). **Match drawn** Toss: Australia

1969 **England 223** (J H Edrich 79) and **240** (G.St A Sobers 5 for 42). **West Indies 161** and **272** (B F Butcher 91, G S Camacho 71). **England won by 30 runs** Toss: England

1971 **England 316** (G Boycott 112, B L D'Oliveira 74) and **264** (B L D'Oliveira 72, D L Amiss 56) **Pakistan 350** (Zaheer Abbas 72, Wasim Bari 63, Mushtaq Mohammad 57) and **205** (Sadiq Mohammad 91). **England won by 25 runs** Toss: England

1972 **Australia 146** (K R Stackpole 52) and **136** (D L Underwood 6 for 45). **England 263** (R Illingworth 57, A A Mallett 5 for 114) and **21 for 1 wkt.** **England won by 9 wickets** Toss: Australia

1973 **New Zealand 276** (M G Burgess 87, V Pollard 62) and **142** (G M Turner 81, G G Arnold 5 for 27). **England 419** (G Boycott 115, K W R Fletcher 81, R Illingworth 65, RO Collinge 5 for 74). **England won by an innings and 1 run** Toss: New Zealand

1974 **Pakistan 285** (Majid Khan 75, Safraz Nawaz 53) and **179. England 183** and **238 for 6 wkts** (J H Edrich 70, K W R Fletcher 67*). **Match drawn** Toss: Pakistan

1975 **England 288** (D S Steele 73, J H Edrich 62, A W Greig 51, G J Gilmour 6 for 85) and **291** (D S Steele 92). **Australia 135** (P H Edmonds 5 for 28) and **220 for 3 wkts** (R B McCosker 95*, I M Chappell 62). **Match drawn** Toss: England

1976 **West Indies 450** (C G Greenidge 115, R C Fredericks 109, I V A Richards 66, L G Rowe 50) and **196** (C L King 58, R G D Willis 5 for 42). **England 387** (A W Greig 116, A P E Knott 116) and **204** (A W Greig 76*). **West Indies won by 55 runs** Toss: West Indies

1977 **England 436** (G Boycott 191, A P E Knott 57). **Australia 103** (I T Botham 5 for 21) and **248** (R W Marsh 63). **England won by an innings and 85 runs** Toss: England

1978 **Pakistan 201** (Sadiq Mohammad 97). **England 119 for 7 wkts** (Safraz Nawaz 5 for 39). **Match drawn** Toss: Pakistan

1979 **England 270** (I T Botham 137). **India 223 for 6 wkts** (S M Gavaskar 78, D B Vengsarkar 65*). **Match drawn** Toss: England

1980 **England 143 and 227 for 6 wkts dec** (G A Gooch 55). **West Indies 245.** **Match drawn** Toss: West Indies

1981 **Australia 401 for 9 wkts dec** (J Dyson 102, K J Hughes 89, G N Yallop 58, I T Botham 6 for 95) and **111** (R G D Willis 8 for 43). **England 174** (I T Botham 50) and **356** (I T Botham 149*, G R Dilley 56, T M Alderman 6 for 135). **England won by 18 runs** Toss: Australia

1982 **Pakistan 275** (Imran Khan 67*, Mudassar Nazar 65, Javed Miandad 54) and **199** (Javed Miandad 52, I T Botham 5 for 74). **England 256** (D I Gower 74, I T Botham 57, Imran Khan 5 for 49) and **219 for 7 wkts** (G Fowler 86). **England won by 3 wickets** Toss: Pakistan

1983 **England 225** (C J Tavaré 69, A J Lamb 58, B L Cairns 7 for 74) and **252** (D I Gower 112*, E J Chatfield 5 for 95). **New Zealand 377** (J G Wright 93, B A Edgar 84, R J Hadlee 75) and **103 for 5 wkts** (R G D Willis 5 for 35). **New Zealand won by 5 wickets** Toss: New Zealand

1984 **England 270** (A J Lamb 100) and **159** (G Fowler 50, M D Marshall 7 for 53). **West Indies 302** (H A Gomes 104*, M A Holding 59, P J W Allott 6 for 61) and **131 for 2 wkts.**
West Indies won by 8 wickets   Toss: England

1985 **Australia 331** (A M J Hilditch 119) and **324** (W B Phillips 91, A M J Hilditch 80, K C Wessels 64, J E Emburey 5 for 82). **England 533** (R T Robinson 175, I T Botham 60, P R Downton 54, M W Gatting 53) and **123 for 5 wkts.**
England won by 5 wickets   Toss: Australia

1986 **India 272** (D B Vengsarkar 61) and **237** (D B Vengsarkar 102*). **England 102** (R M H Binny 5 for 40) and **128.**
India won by 279 runs   Toss: India

1987 **England 136** (D J Capel 53) and **199** (D I Gower 55, Imran Khan 7 for 40). **Pakistan 353** (Salim Malik 99, Ijaz Ahmed 50, N A Foster 8 for 107).
Pakistan won by an innings and 18 runs   Toss: England

1988 **England 201** (A J Lamb 64*) and **138** (G A Gooch 50). **West Indies 275** (R A Harper 56, D L Haynes 54, D R Pringle 5 for 95) and **67 for 0 wkt.**
West Indies won by 10 wickets   Toss: West Indies

1989 **Australia 601 for 7 wkts dec** (S R Waugh 177*, M A Taylor 136, D M Jones 79, M G Hughes 71, A R Border 66) and **230 for 3 wkts dec** (M A Taylor 60, A R Border 60*). **England 430** (A J Lamb 125, K J Barnett 80, R A Smith 66, T M Alderman 5 for 107) and **191.** (G A Gooch 68, T M Alderman 5 for 44).
Australia won by 210 runs   Toss: England

1991 **England 198** (R A Smith 54) and **252** (G A Gooch 154*, C E L Ambrose 6 for 52). **West Indies 173** (I V A Richards 73) and **162** (R B Richardson 68).
England won by 115 runs   Toss: West Indies

1992 **Pakistan 197** (Salim Malik 82*) and **221** (Salim Malik 84*, Ramiz Raja 63, N A Mallinder 5 for 50). **England 320** (G A Gooch 135, M A Atherton 76, Waqar Younis 5 for 117) and **99 for 4 wkts.**
England won by 6 wickets   Toss: Pakistan

1993 **Australia 653 for 4 wkts dec** (A R Border 200*, S R Waugh 157*, D C Boon 107, M J Slater 67, M E Waugh 52). **England 200** (G A Gooch 59, M A Atherton 55, P R Reiffel 5 for 65) and **305** (A J Stewart 78, M A Atherton 63).
Australia won by an innings and 148 runs   Toss: Australia

1994 **England 477 for 9 wkts dec** (M A Atherton 99, A J Stewart 89, G P Thorpe 72, S J Rhodes 65*) and **267 for 5 wkts dec** (G A Hick 110, G P Thorpe 73). **South Africa 447** (P N Kirsten 104, B M McMillan 78, C R Matthews 62*) and **116 for 3 wkts** (G Kirsten 65).
Match drawn   Toss: England

1995 **England 199** (M A Atherton 81, I R Bishop 5 for 32) and **208** (G P Thorpe 61). **West Indies 282** (S L Campbell 69, J C Adams 58, B C Lara 53) and **129 for 1 wkt** (C L Hooper 73*).
West Indies won by 9 wickets   Toss: West Indies

1996 **Pakistan 448** (Ijaz Ahmed 141, Mohin Khan 105, Salim Malik 55, Asif Mujtaba 51, D G Cork 5 for 113) and **242 for 7 wkts dec** (Inzamam-ul-Haq 65, Ijaz Ahmed sen 52) **England 501** (A J Stewart 170, N V Knight 113, J P Crawley 53).
Match drawn   Toss: England

1997 **England 172** (J N. Gillespie 7 for 37) and **268** (N Hussain 105, J P Crawley 72, P R Reiffel 5 for 49). **Australia 501 for 9 wkts dec** (M T G Elliott 199, R T Ponting 127, P R Reiffel 54*, D Gough 5 for 149).
Australia won by an innings and 61 runs   Toss: Australia

1998 **England 230** (M A Butcher 116) and **240** (N Hussain 94, S M Pollock 5 for 53, A A Donald 5 for 71). **South Africa 252** (W J. Cronje 57, A R C Fraser 5 for 42) and **195** (J N Rhodes 85, B M McMillan 54, D Gough 6 for 42).
England won by 23 runs   Toss: England

2000 **West Indies 172** (R R Sarwan 59*, C White 5 for 57) and **61** (A R Caddick 5 for 14). **England 272** (M P Vaughan 76, G A Hick 59).
England won by an innings and 39 runs   Toss: West Indies

2001 **Australia 447** (R T Ponting 144, D R Martyn 118, M E Waugh 72, D Gough 5 for 103) and **176 for 4 wkts dec** (R T Ponting 72). **England 309** (A J Stewart 76*, G D McGrath 7 for 76) and **315 for 4 wkts** (M A Butcher 173*, N Hussain 55).
England won by 6 wickets   Toss: Australia

2002 **India 628 for 8 wkts dec** (S R Tendulkar 193, R S Dravid 148, S C Ganguly 128, S B Bangar 68). **England 273** (A J Stewart 78*, M P Vaughan 61) and **309** (N Hussain 110.)
India won by an innings and 46 runs   Toss: India

2003 **South Africa 342** (G Kirsten 130, M Zondeki 59, J A Rudolph 55) and **365** (A J Hall 99*, G Kirsten 60). **England 307** (M A Butcher 77, M E Trescothick 59, A Flintoff 55) and **209** (M A Butcher 61, A Flintoff 50, J H Kallis 6 for 54.)
South Africa won by 191 runs   Toss: South Africa

2004 **New Zealand 409** (S P Fleming 97, M H W Papps 86, B B McCullum 54) and **161.** **England 526** (M E Trescothick 132, G O Jones 100, A Flintoff 94, A J Strauss 62) and **45 for 1 wkt**
England won by 9 wickets   Toss: England

2006 **England 515** (K P Pietersen 135, I R Bell 119, Umar Gul 5 for 123) and **345** (A J Strauss 116, M E Trescothick 58, C M W Reid 55). **Pakistan 538** (Mohammad Yousuf 192, Younis Khan 173) and **155.**
England won by 167 runs   Toss: England

2007 **England 570 for 7 wkts dec** (K P Pietersen 226, M P Vaughan 103, M J Prior 75). **West Indies 146** and **141** (D J Bravo 52).
England won by an innings and 283 runs   Toss: England

2008 **England 203** and **327** (S C J Broad 67*, A N Cook 60). **South Africa 522** (A B de Villiers 174, A G Prince 149) and **9 for 0 wkt**.
South Africa won by 10 wickets   Toss: South Africa

SUMMARY OF RESULTS

ENGLAND	First played	Last played	Played	Won	Lost	Drawn
v. Australia	1899	2001	23	7	8	8
v. India	1952	2002	6	3	2	1
v. New Zealand	1949	2004	6	4	1	1
v. Pakistan	1962	2006	9	5	1	3
v. South Africa	1907	2008	12	6	3	3
v. West Indies	1957	2007	12	5	6	1
Totals	1899	2008	68	30	21	17

SIX HIGHEST AGGREGATES

Runs	Wkts	
1723	31	in 1948 (England 496 and 365 for 8 wkts dec; Australia 458 and 404 for 3 wkts)
1553	40	in 2006 (England 515 and 345; Pakistan 538 and 155)
1452	30	in 1989 (Australia 601 for 7 wkts dec and 230 for 3 wkts dec; England 430 and 191)
1350	28	in 1967 (England 550 for 4 wkts dec and 126 for 4 wkts; India 164 and 510)
1311	35	in 1985 (Australia 331 and 324; England 533 and 123 for 5 wkts)
1307	28	in 1994 (England 477 and 267 for 5 wkts dec; South Africa 447 and 116 for 3 wkts)

Note: The highest aggregate prior to the Second World War

| 1141 | 37 | in 1921 (Australia 407 and 272 for 7 wkts dec; England 259 and 202) |

SIX LOWEST AGGREGATES

Runs	Wkts	
423	40	in 1907 (England 76 and 162; South Africa 110 and 75)
463	22	in 1958 (New Zealand 67 and 129; England 267 for 2 wkts)
505	30	in 2000 (West Indies 172 and 61; England 272)
553	30	in 1957 (West Indies 142 and 132; England 279)
566	31	in 1972 (Australia 146 and 136; England 263 and 21 for 1 wkt)
608	30	in 1956 (England 325; Australia 143 and 140)

SIX HIGHEST TOTALS

653 for 4 wkts dec	Australia v. England, 1993
608 for 8 wkts dec	India v. England, 2002
601 for 7 wkts dec	Australia v. England, 1989
584	Australia v. England, 1934
570 for 7 wkts dec	England v. West Indies, 2007
566	Australia v. England, 1930

SIX LOWEST TOTALS

61	West Indies v. England, 2000
67	New Zealand v. England, 1958
75	South Africa v. England, 1907
76	England v. South Africa, 1907
87	England v. Australia, 1909
102	England v. India, 1986

SIX HIGHEST INDIVIDUAL SCORES

For England

310*	J H Edrich versus New Zealand, 1965
246*	G Boycott versus India, 1967
226	K P Pietersen versus West Indies, 2007
191	G Boycott versus Australia, 1977
175	R T Robinson versus Australia, 1985
173*	M A Butcher versus Australia, 2001

For Australia

334	D G Bradman, 1930
304	D G Bradman, 1934
200*	A R Border, 1993
199	M T G Elliott, 1997
182	A R Morris, 1948
181	W H Ponsford, 1934

For Pakistan

192	Mohammad Yousuf, 2006
173	Younis Khan, 2006
141	Ijaz Ahmed, 1996
105	Moin Khan, 1996
99	Salim Malik, 1987
97	Sadiq Mohammad, 1978

For India

193	S R Tendulkar, 2002
148	Nawab of Pataudi jnr, 1967
148	R S Dravid, 2002
133	V L Manjrekar, 1952
128	S C Gangulay, 2002
102*	D B Vengsarkar, 1986

For South Africa

236	E A B Rowan, 1951
174	A B de Villiers, 2008
149	A G Prince, 2008
133	D J McGlew, 1955
130	G Kirsten, 2003
129	H G Owen-Smith, 1929

For New Zealand

97	S P Fleming, 2004
96	F B Smith, 1949
93	J G Wright, 1983
87	M G Burgess, 1973
86	M H W Papps, 2004
84	B A Edgar, 1983

For West Indies

174	G St.A Sobers, 1966
137	S M Nurse, 1966
115	C G. Greenidge, 1976
109	R C Fredericks, 1976
104*	H A Gomes, 1984
102	G St A Sobers, 1963

HUNDRED BEFORE LUNCH

First day

112*   C G Macartney for Australia, 1926
105*   D G Bradman for Australia, 1930

Third day

102   (from 27* to 129) H G Owen-Smith for South Africa, 1929

CARRYING BAT THROUGH A COMPLETED INNINGS

154* out of 252 G A Gooch, England v. West Indies, 1991

MOST CENTURIES IN AN INNINGS

3	1926	C G Macartney (151), W M Woodfull (141) and A J Richardson for Australia
3	1993	A R Border (200*), S R Waugh (157*) and D C Boon (107) for Australia
3	2002	S R Tendulkar (193), R S Dravid (148) and S C Ganguly (128) for India

MOST CENTURIES IN A MATCH

5	1948	C Washbrook (143) and W J Edrich (111) for England; R N Harvey (112), A R Morris (182) and D G Bradman (173*) for Australia
5	2006	K P Pietersen (135), I R Bell (119) and A J Strauss (116) for England: Younis Khan (173) and Mohammad Yousuf (192) for Pakistan
4	1976	C G Greenidge (115) and R C Fredericks (109) for West Indies; A W Greig (116) and A P E Knott (116) for England
4	1996	Ijaz Ahmed (141) and Moin Khan (105) for Pakistan; A J Stewart (170) and N V Knight (113) for England
4	2002	S R Tendulkar (193), R S Dravid (148) and S C Ganguly (128) for India; N Hussain (110) for England

CENTURY PARTNERSHIPS

For England
(six highest)
For the 1st wicket

168	L Hutton (81) and C Washbrook (143) v. Australia, 1948 (1st inns)
168	G A Gooch (135) and M A Atherton (76) v. Pakistan, 1992
158	M E Trescothick (58) and A J Strauss (116) v. Pakistan, 2006
156	J B Hobbs (88) and H Sutcliffe (94) v. Australia, 1926
153	M E Trescothick (132) and A J Strauss (62) v. New Zealand, 2004
146	W G A Parkhouse (78) and G Pullar (75) v. India, 1959

For all other wickets

369	(2nd wkt) J H Edrich (310*) and K F Barrington (163) v. New Zealand, 1965
252	(4th wkt) G Boycott (246*) and B L D'Oliveira (109) v. India, 1967
194*	(3rd wkt) C A Milton (104*) and P B H May (113*) v. New Zealand, 1958
193	(4th wkt) M C Cowdrey (160) and K F Barrington (80) v. India, 1959
187	(4th wkt) P B H May (101) and C Washbrook (98) v. Australia, 1956
181	(3rd wkt) M A Butcher (173*) and N Hussain (55) v. Australia, 2001

For Australia
(six highest)
For the 1st wkt – none

For all other wickets

388	(4th wkt) W H Ponsford (181) and D G Bradman (304), 1934
332*	(5th wkt) A R Border (200*) and S R Waugh (157*), 1993
301	(2nd wkt) A R Morris (182) and D G Bradman (173*), 1948
268	(5th wkt) M T G Elliott (199) and R T Ponting (127), 1997
235	(2nd wkt) W M Woodfull (141) and C G Macartney (151), 1926
229	(3rd wkt) D G Bradman (334) and A F Kippax (77), 1930

CENTURY PARTNERSHIPS
(in total)

For India

249	(4th wkt) S R Tendulkar (193) and S C Ganguly (128), 2002	
222	(4th wkt) V S Hazare (89) and V L Manjrekar (133), 1952	
170	(2nd wkt) S B Bangar (68) and R S Dravid (148), 2002	
168	(2nd wkt) F M Engineer (87) and A L Wadekar (91), 1967	
150	(3rd wkt) R S Dravid (148) and S R Tendulkar (193), 2002	
134	(5th wkt) Hanumant Singh (73) and Nawab of Pataudi jnr (148), 1967	
105	(6th wkt) V S Hazare (56) and D G Phadkar (64), 1952	

For New Zealand

169	(2nd wkt) M H W Papps (86) and S P Fleming (97), 2004
120	(5th wkt) M P Donnelly (64) and F B Smith (96), 1949
116	(2nd wkt) J G Wright (93) and M D Crowe (37), 1983
112	(1st wkt) B Sutcliffe (82) and V J Scott (43), 1949
106	(5th wkt) M G Burgess (87) and V Pollard (62), 1973

For Pakistan

363	(3rd wkt) Younis Khan (173) and Mohammad Yousuf (192), 2006
130	(4th wkt) Ijaz Ahmed (141) and Salim Malik (55), 1996
129	(3rd wkt) Zaheer Abbas (72) and Mushtaq Mohammed (57), 1971
112	(7th wkt) Asif Mujtaba (51) and Moin Khan (105), 1996
100	(3rd wkt) Mudassar Nazar (65) and Javed Miandad (54), 1982
100	(4th wkt) Majid Khan (75) and Zaheer Abbas (48), 1974

For South Africa

212	(5th wkt) A G Prince (149) and A B de Villiers (174), 2008
198	(2nd wkt) E A B Rowan (236) C B van Ryneveld (83), 1951
176	(1st wkt) D J McGlew (133) and T L Goddard (74), 1955
150	(8th wkt) G Kirsten (130) and M Zondeki (59), 2003
117	(6th wkt) J N Rhodes (85) and B M McMillan (54), 1998
115	(7th wicket) P N Kirsten (104) and B M McMillan (78), 1994
108	(5th wkt) E A B Rowan (236) and R A McLean (67), 1951
103	(10th wkt) H G Owen-Smith (129) and A J Bell (26*), 1929

For West Indies

265	(5th wkt) S M Nurse (137) and G St A Sobers (174), 1966
192	(1st wkt) R C Fredericks (109) and C G Greenidge (115), 1976
118*	(2nd wkt) C L Hooper (73*) and B C Lara (48*), 1995
143	(4th wkt) R B Kanhai (92) and G St A Sobers (102), 1963
108	(3rd wkt) G S Camacho (71) and B F Butcher (91), 1969
106	(1st wkt) C G Greenidge (49) and D L Haynes (43), 1984

6 BEST INNINGS ANALYSES

For England

8 for 43	R G D Willis v. Australia, 1981
8 for 59	C Blythe v. South Africa, 1907 (1st inns)
8 for 107	N A Foster v. Pakistan, 1987
7 for 40	C Blythe v. South Africa, 1907 (2nd inns)
7 for 51	G A R Lock v. New Zealand, 1958
7 for 115	A P Freeman v. South Africa, 1929

For Australia

7 for 37	J N Gillespie, 1997
7 for 58	C G Macartney, 1909
7 for 76	G D McGrath, 2001
6 for 85	G J Gilmour, 1975
6 for 135	T M Alderman, 1981
5 for 38	A Cotter, 1909

5 WICKETS IN AN INNINGS

	For India (2)			**For South Africa (7)**
5 for 40	R M H Binny, 1986		6 for 17	G A Faulkner, 1907
5 for 100	Ghulam Ahmed, 1952		6 for 92	N A Quinn, 1929
			6 for 54	J H Kallis, 2003
	For New Zealand (5)		5 for 53	S M Pollock, 1998
7 for 74	B L Cairns, 1983		5 for 69	T L Goddard, 1955
5 for 74	R O Collinge, 1973		5 for 71	A A Donald, 1998
5 for 95	E J Chatfield, 1983		5 for 94	H J Tayfield, 1955
5 for 97	T B Burtt, 1949		5 for 174	A M B Rowan, 1951
5 for 127	J Cowie, 1949			
				For West Indies (8)
			7 for 53	M D Marshall, 1984
	For Pakistan (6)		7 for 70	F M Worrell, 1957
7 for 40	Imran Khan, 1987		6 for 36	C C Griffith, 1963
5 for 39	Sarfraz Nawaz, 1978		6 for 39	L R Gibbs, 1996
5 for 49	Imran Khan, 1982		6 for 52	C E L Ambrose, 1991
5 for 117	Waqar Younis, 1992		5 for 32	I R Bishop, 1995
5 for 123	Umar Gul, 2006		5 for 41	G.St.A Sobers, 1966
5 for 128	Munir Malik, 1962		5 for 42	G.St A Sobers, 1969

10 WICKETS IN A MATCH

For England (7)

15 for 99	(8 for 59 and 7 for 40)	C Blythe v. South Africa, 1907
11 for 65	(4 for 14 and 7 for 51)	G A R Lock v. New Zeland, 1958
11 for 88	(5 for 58 and 6 for 30)	F S Trueman v. Australia, 1961
11 for 113	(5 for 58 and 6 for 55)	J C Laker v. Australia, 1956
10 for 82	(4 for 37 and 6 for 45)	D L Underwood v. Australia, 1972
10 for 115	(6 for 52 and 4 for 63)	S F Barnes v. South Africa, 1912
10 for 207	(7 for 115 and 3 for 92)	A P Freeman v. South Africa, 1929

For Australia (3)

11 for 85	(7 for 58 and 4 for 27)	C G Macartney, 1909
10 for 122	(5 for 66 and 5 for 56)	W J O'Reilly, 1938
10 for 151	(5 for 107 and 5 for 44)	T M Alderman, 1989

For New Zealand (1)

10 for 144	(7 for 74 and 3 for 70)	B L Cairns, 1983

For Pakistan (1)

10 for 77	(3 for 37 and 7 for 40)	Imran Khan, 1987

Note: Best bowling in a match for:
- India: 7 for 58 (5 for 40 and 2 for 18) R M H Binney, 1986
- South Africa: 9 for 75 (6 for 17 and 3 for 58) G A Faulkner, 1907
- West Indies: 9 for 81 (6 for 36 and 3 for 45) C C Griffith, 1963

HAT-TRICKS

J T Hearne v. Australia, 1899
P J Loader v. West Indies, 1957

TEST MATCH AT BRAMALL LANE, SHEFFIELD 1902

1902 **Australia 194** (S F Barnes 6 for 49) and **289** (C Hill 119, V T Trumper 62, W Rhodes 5 for 63) **England 145** (J V Saunders 5 for 50, M A Noble 5 for 51) and **195** (A C MacLaren 63, G L Jessop 55, M A Noble 6 for 52).
Australia won by 143 runs
Toss: Australia

LIMITED-OVERS INTERNATIONAL MATCHES
AT HEADINGLEY, LEEDS 1973-2008

1973 **West Indies 181** (54 overs) (R B Kanhai 55). **England 182 for 9 wkts** (54.3 overs) (M H Denness 66).
England won by 1 wicket   **Award: M H Denness**

1974 **India 265** (53.5 overs) (B P Patel 82, A L Wadekar 67). **England 266 for 6 wkts** (51.1 overs) (J H Edrich 90).
England won by 4 wickets   **Award: J H Edrich**

1975 **Australia 278 for 7 wkts** (60 overs) (R Edwards 80*). **Pakistan 205** (53 overs) (Majid Khan 65, Asif Iqbal 53, D K Lillee 5 for 34).
Australia won by 73 runs   **Award: D K Lillee**

1975 **East Africa 120** (55.3 overs). **India 123 for 0 wkt** (29.5 overs) (S M Gavaskar 65* F M Engineer 54*).
India won by 10 wickets   **Award: F M Engineer**

1975 **England 93** (36.2 overs) (G J Gilmour 6 for 14). **Australia 94 for 6 wkts** (28.4 overs).
Australia won by 4 wickets   **Award: G J Gilmour**

1979 **Canada 139 for 9 wkts** (60 overs). **Pakistan 140 for 2 wkts** (40.1 overs) (Sadiq Mohammed 57*).
Pakistan won by 8 wickets   **Award: Sadiq Mohammed**

1979 **India 182** (55.5 overs) (S M Gavaskar 55). **New Zealand 183 for 2 wkts** (57 overs) (B A Edgar 84*).
New Zealand won by 8 wickets   **Award: B A Edgar**

1979 **England 165 for 9 wkts** (60 overs). **Pakistan 151** (56 overs) (Asif Iqbal 51, M Hendrick 4 for 15)
England won by 14 runs   **Award: M Hendrick**

1980 **West Indies 198** (55 overs) (C G Greenidge 78). **England 174** (51.2 overs) (C J Tavaré 82*).
West Indies won by 24 runs   **Award: C J Tavaré**

1981 **Australia 236 for 8 wkts** (55 overs) (G M Wood 108). **England 165** (46.5 overs) (R M Hogg 4 for 29).
Australia won by 71 runs   **Award: G M Wood**

1982 **India 193** (55 overs) (Kapil Dev 60, I T Botham 4 for 56). **England 194 for 1 wkt** (50.1 overs) (B Wood 78*, C J Tavaré 66).
England won by 9 wickets   **Award: B Wood**

1983 **West Indies 252 for 9 wkts** (60 overs) (H A Gomes 78). **Australia 151** (30.3 overs) (W W Davis 7 for 51).
West Indies won by 101 runs   **Award: W W Davis**

1983 **Pakistan 235 for 7 wkts** (60 overs) (Imran Khan 102*, Shahid Mahboob 77, A L F de Mel 5 for 39). **Sri Lanka 224** (58.3 overs) (S Wettimuny 50, Abdul Qadir 5 for 44).
Pakistan won by 11 runs   **Award: Abdul Qadir**

1983 **Sri Lanka 136** (50.4 overs). **England 137 for 1 wkt** (24.1 overs) (G Fowler 81*).
England won by 9 wickets   **Award: R G D Willis**

1986 **New Zealand 217 for 8 wkts** (55 overs) (J J Crowe 66). **England 170** (48.2 overs).
New Zealand won by 47 runs   **Award: J J Crowe**

1988 **England 186 for 8 wkts** (55 overs). **West Indies 139** (46.3 overs).
England won by 47 runs   **Award: D R Pringle**

1990 **England 295 for 6 wkts** (55 overs) (R A Smith 128, G A Gooch 55). **New Zealand 298 for 6 wkts** (54.5 overs) (M J Greatbatch 102*, J G Wright 52, A H Jones 51).
New Zealand won by 4 wickets   **Award: M J Greatbatch**

1990 **England 229** (54.3 overs) (A J Lamb 56, D I Gower 50). **India 233 for 4 wkts** (53 overs) (S V Manjrekar 82, M Azharuddin 55*)
India won by 6 wickets   **Award: A Kumble**

1996 **India 158** (40.2 overs). **England 162 for 4 wkts** (39.3 overs) (G P Thorpe 79*).
England won by 6 wickets   **Award: G P Thorpe**

1997 **Australia 170 for 8 wkts** (50 overs). **England 175 for 4 wkts** (40.1 overs) (G P Thorpe 75*, A J Hollioake 66*).
England won by 6 wickets   **Award: G P Thorpe**

1998 **South Africa 205 for 8 wkts** (50 overs) (S M Pollock 56). **England 206 for 3 wkts** (35 overs) (A D Brown 59, N V Knight 51).
England won by 7 wickets   **Award: A D Brown**

1999 **Pakistan 275 for 8 wkts** (50 overs) (Inzamam-ul-Haq 81, Abdur Razzaq 60). **Australia 265** (49.5 overs) (M G Bevan 61, Wasim Akram 4-40).
Pakistan won by 10 runs   **Award: Inazmam-ul-Haq**

1999 **Zimbabwe 175** (49.3 overs) (M A Goodwin 57). **New Zealand 70 for 3 wkts** (15 overs).
No result   **No Award**

1999 **South Africa 271 for 7 wkts** (50 overs) (H H Gibbs 101, D J Cullinan 50). **Australia 275 for 5 wkts** (49.4 overs) (S R. Waugh 120*, R T Ponting 69).
Australia won by 5 wickets   **Award: S R Waugh**

2001 **England 156 (45.2 overs)** (B C Hollioake 53, Waqar Younis 7 for 36). **Pakistan 153 for 4 wkts** (39.5 overs) (Abdur Razzaq 75).
Pakistan won — England conceding the match following a pitch invasion.
                                                      Award: Waqar Younis

2002 **Sri Lanka 240 for 7 wkts** (32 overs) (S T Jayasuriya 112). **England 241 for 7 wkts** (31.2 overs) (M E Trescothick 82).
England won by 3 wkts   **Award: S T Jayasuriya**

2003 **England 81 for 4 wkts. Zimbabwe did not bat.**
No result   **No Award**

2004 **West Indies 159** (40.1 overs). **England 160 for 3 wkts** (22 overs) (M E Trescothick 55).
England won by 7 wickets   **Award: S J Harmison**

2005 **Bangladesh 208 for 7 wkts** (50 overs) (Belim 81, A Flintoff 4-29). **England 209 for 5 wkts** (38.5 overs) (A J Strauss 98)
England won by 5 wickets   **Award: A J Strauss**

    Australia 219 for 7 wkts (50 overs) (P D Collingwood 4-34). **England 221 for 1 wkt** (46 overs) (M E Trescothick 104*, M P Vaughan 59*).
England won by 9 wickets   **Award: M E Trescothick**

2006 **England 321 for 7 wkts** (50 overs) (M E Trescothick 121, S L Malinga 4-44). **Sri Lanka 324 for 2 wkts** (37.3 overs) (S T Jayasuriya 152, W U Tharanga 109).
Sri Lanka won by 8 wickets   **Award: S T Jayasuriya**

2007 **India 324 for 6 wkts** (50 overs) (Yuvraj Singh 72, S R Tendulkar 71, S C Ganguly 59, G Gambhir 51). **England 242 for 8 wkts** (39 overs) (P D Collingwood 91*)
India won by 38 runs *(D/L Method)*   **Award: S C Ganguly**

2008 **England 275 for 4 wkts** (50 overs) (K P Pietersen 90*, A Flintoff 78). **South Africa 255** (J H Kallis 52).
England won by 20 runs   **Award: K P Pietersen**

SUMMARY OF RESULTS

ENGLAND	Played	Won	Lost
v. Australia	4	2	2
v. Bangladesh	1	1	0
v. India	5	3	2
v. New Zealand	2	0	2
v. Pakistan	2	1	1
v. South Africa	2	2	0
v. Sri Lanka	3	2	1
v. West Indies	4	3	1
v. Zimbabwe	1*	0	0
Totals	24	14	9

*No result

AUSTRALIA	Played	Won	Lost
v. England	4	2	2
v. Pakistan	2	1	1
v. South Africa	1	1	0
v. West Indies	1	0	1
Totals	8	4	4

BANGLADESH	Played	Won	Lost
v. England	1	0	1

INDIA	Played	Won	Lost
v. England	5	2	3
v. East Africa	1	1	0
v. New Zealand	1	0	1
Totals	7	3	4

NEW ZEALAND	Played	Won	Lost
v. England	2	2	0
v. India	1	1	0
v. Zimbabwe	1*	0	0
Totals	4	3	0

*No result

PAKISTAN	Played	Won	Lost
v. Australia	2	1	1
v. Canada	1	1	0
v. England	2	1	1
v. Sri Lanka	1	1	0
Totals	6	4	2

SOUTH AFRICA	Played	Won	Lost
v. Australia	1	0	1
v. England	2	0	2
Totals	3	0	3

SRI LANKA	Played	Won	Lost
v. England	3	1	2
v. Pakistan	1	0	1
Totals	4	1	3

SUMMARY OF RESULTS *(Continued)*

WEST INDIES	Played	Won	Lost
v. Australia	1	1	0
v. England	4	1	3
Totals	5	2	3

ZIMBABWE	Played	Won	Lost
v. England	1*	0	0
v. New Zealand	1*	0	0
Totals	2*	0	0

*No result

CANADA	Played	Won	Lost
v. Pakistan	1	0	1

EAST AFRICA	Played	Won	Lost
v. India	1	0	1

CENTURIES

152	S J Jayasuriya for Sri Lanka v. England, 2006
128	R A Smith for England v. New Zealand, 1990
121	M E Trescothick for England v. Sri Lanka, 2006
120*	S R Waugh for Australia v. South Africa, 1999
112	S J Jayasuriya for Sri Lanka v. England, 2002
109	W U Tharanga for Sri Lanka v. England, 2006
108	G M Wood for Australia v. England, 1981
104*	M E Trescothick for England v. Australia, 2005
102*	Imran Khan for Pakistan v. Sri Lanka, 1983
102*	M J Greatbatch for New Zealand v. England, 1990
101	H H Gibbs for South Africa v. Australia,1999

4 WICKETS IN AN INNINGS

7 for 36	Waqar Younis for Pakistan v. England, 2001
7 for 51	W W Davis for West Indies v. Australia, 1983
6 for 14	G J Gilmour for Australia v. England, 1975
5 for 34	D K Lillee for Australia v. Pakistan, 1975
5 for 39	A L F de Mel for Sri Lanka v. Pakistan, 1983
5 for 44	Abdul Qadir for Pakistan v. Sri Lanka, 1983
4 for 15	M Hendrick for England v. Pakistan, 1979
4 for 29	R M Hogg for Australia v England, 1981
4 for 29	A Flintoff for England v. Bangladesh, 2005
4 for 34	P D Collingwood for England v. Australia, 2005
4 for 40	Wasim Akram for Pakistan v. Australia, 1999
4 for 44	S L Malinga for Sri Lanka v. England, 2006
4 for 56	I T Botham for England v. India, 1982

LIMITED-OVERS INTERNATIONAL MATCHES
AT NORTH MARINE ROAD, SCARBOROUGH 1976-1978

1976 **England 202 for 8 wkts** (55 overs) (G D Barlow 80*, A M E Roberts 4 for 32).
West Indies 207 for 4 wkts (41 overs) (I V A Richards 119*).
West Indies won by 6 wickets　　　　　　　　　　**Award: I V A Richards**

1978 **England 206 for 8 wkts** (55 overs) (G A Gooch 94, B L Cairns 5 for 28).
New Zealand 187 for 8 wkts (55 overs) (B E Congdon 52*).
England won by 19 runs　　　　　　　　　　　　**Award: G A Gooch**

LIST OF PLAYERS AND CAREER AVERAGES IN ALL FIRST-CLASS MATCHES FOR YORKSHIRE 1863-2008

Based on research by the late Anthony Woodhouse and Roy D. Wilkinson

R D W

The Editor will welcome any information which will help in keeping this list up to date. In recent years some statisticians have sought to alter the classification of a number of matches, including some involving Yorkshire. The present compiler, in common with Anthony Woodhouse and many others, does not believe we should alter the status from that determined at the time they were played. Therefore, these averages include the match versus Gentlemen of Scotland in 1878, and exclude the matches versus Liverpool and District played in 1889, 1891, 1892 and 1893 in line with what appear to be decisions taken by the County Club at the time.

* Played as an amateur   © Awarded County Cap   § Born outside Yorkshire

Player	Date of Birth	Date of Death (if known)	First Played	Last Played	M	Inns	NO	Runs	HS	Av'ge	100s	Runs	Wkts	Av'ge	Ct/St
Ackroyd, A *	Aug. 29, 1858	Oct. 3, 1927	1879	1879	1	1	1	—	2*	—	0	7	—	—	—
Allen, S *	Dec 20, 1893	Oct 9, 1978	1924	1924	1	2	1	8	6	4.00	0	116	2	58.00	—
Allen, W R	Apr14, 1893	Oct 14, 1950	1921	1925	30	32	10	475	95*	21.59	0	—	0	—	45/21
Ambler, J	Feb 12, 1860	Feb 10 1899	1886	1886	4	7	0	68	21	9.71	0	22	—	—	2
Anderson, G	Jan 20, 1826	Nov 27, 1902	1851	1869	19	31	0	520	99*	20.80	0	—	—	—	19
Anderson, P N	Apr. 28, 1966		1988	1988	1	1	0	0	0	0.00	0	47	1	47.00	1
Anson, C E *	Oct 14, 1889	Mar 26, 1969	1924	1924	1	2	0	27	14	13.50	0	—	—	—	1
Appleton, C *	May15, 1844	Feb 26, 1925	1865	1865	3	6	1	56	18	11.20	0	—	—	—	1
Appleyard, R	© June 27, 1924		1950	1958	133	122	43	679	63	8.59	0	9,903	642	15.42	70
Armitage, C1 *	Apr 24, 1849	Apr 24, 1917	1873	1878	3	5	0	26	12	5.20	0	29	0	—	—
Armitage, T	Apr 25, 1848	Sept 21, 1922	1872	1878	52	85	8	1,053	95	13.67	0	1,614	107	15.08	20
Ash, D L	Feb 18, 1944		1965	1965	3	3	0	22	12	7.33	0	22	0	—	—
Ashman, J R	© May 20, 1926		1951	1951	1	1	1	0	0*	—	0	116	4	29.00	—
Aspinall, R	Oct 26, 1918	Aug 16, 1999	1946	1950	36	48	8	763	75*	19.07	0	2,670	131	20.38	18
Aspinall, W	Mar 24, 1858	Not known	1880	1880	2	3	0	16	14	5.33	0	—	—	—	1
Asquith, F T	Feb 5, 1870	Jan 11, 1916	1903	1903	1	1	0	0	0	0.00	0	—	—	—	2
Athey, C W J	© Sept 27, 1957		1976	1983	151	246	21	6,320	134	28.08	10	1,003	21	47.76	144/2
Atkinson, G R	Sept 21, 1830	May 3, 1906	1861	1870	27	38	8	399	44	13.30	0	1,146	54	21.22	14
Atkinson, H	Feb 1, 1881	Dec 22, 1959	1903	1907	1	2	0	0	0	0.00	0	17	0	—	—
Backhouse, E N	May 13, 1901	Nov 1, 1936	1931	1931	1	1	0	2	2	2.00	0	4	0	—	—
Badger, H D *	Mar 7, 1900	Aug 10, 1975	1921	1922	2	4	2	6	6*	3.00	0	145	6	24.16	1

LIST OF PLAYERS AND CAREER AVERAGES IN ALL FIRST-CLASS MATCHES FOR YORKSHIRE (Continued)

Player	Date of Birth	Date of Death (if known)	First Played	Last Played	M	Inns	NO	Runs	HS	Av'ge	100s	Runs	Wkts	Av'ge	Ct/St
Bainbridge, A B	Oct 15, 1932		1961	1963	5	10	0	93	24	9.30	0	358	20	17.90	3
Baines, F E *	June 18, 1864	Nov 17, 1948	1888	1888	1	1	0	0	0	0.00	0	—	—	—	—
Bairstow, A	Aug 14, 1868	Dec 7, 1945	1896	1900	24	24	10	69	12	4.92	0	—	—	—	41/18
Bairstow, D L	@ Sept 1, 1951	Jan 5, 1998	1970	1990	429	601	113	12,985	145	26.60	9	192	6	32.00	907/131
Baker, G R	Apr 18, 1862	Feb 6, 1938	1884	1884	7	11	1	42	13	4.20	0	—	—	—	5
Baker, R *	July 13, 1849	June 21, 1896	1874	1875	3	5	1	45	22	11.25	0	43	0	—	3
Balderstone, J C	Nov 16, 1940	Mar 6, 2000	1961	1969	68	81	6	1,332	82	17.76	0	790	37	21.35	24
§ Ballance, A T *	@ Nov 22, 1989		2008	2008	1	2	0	6	5	3.00	0	—	—	—	—
Barber, A T *	@ June 17, 1905	Mar 10, 1985	1929	1930	42	54	3	1,050	125	20.58	1	0	0	—	40
Barber, W	Apr 18, 1901	Sept 10, 1968	1926	1947	354	495	48	15,315	255	34.26	27	404	14	28.85	169
Barraclough, E S	Mar 30, 1923	May 21, 1999	1949	1950	2	4	2	43	24*	21.50	0	136	4	34.00	—
Bates, W	Nov 19, 1855	Jan 8, 1900	1877	1887	202	331	12	6,499	136	20.37	8	10,692	637	16.78	163
Bates, W E	@ Mar 5, 1884	Jan 17, 1957	1907	1913	113	167	15	2,634	81	17.32	0	57	2	28.50	64
Batty G J	@ Oct 13, 1977		1997	1997	1	2	0	18	18	9.00	0	70	2	35.00	—
Batty, J D	May 15, 1971		1989	1994	64	67	20	703	51	14.95	0	5,286	140	37.75	25
Bayes, G W	Feb 27, 1884	Dec 6, 1960	1910	1921	18	24	11	165	36	12.69	0	1,534	48	31.95	11
Beaumont, H	Oct 14, 1916	Nov. 15, 2003	1946	1947	28	46	6	716	60	17.90	0	236	9	26.22	11
Beaumont, J	Sept 16, 1855	May 1, 1920	1877	1878	5	9	1	60	24	7.50	0	50	2	25.00	—
Bedford, H	July 17, 1907	July 5, 1968	1928	1928	5	5	1	57	24	14.25	0	179	8	22.37	—
Bedford, W	Feb 24, 1879	July 28, 1939	1903	1903	2	2	1	38	30*	38.00	0	117	2	58.50	1
Bell, J T	June 16, 1895	Aug 8, 1971	1921	1923	7	8	1	125	54	17.85	0	—	—	—	—
Berry, John	Jan 10, 1823	Feb 26, 1895	1849	1867	18	32	2	492	78	16.40	0	149	8	18.62	12
Berry, Joseph	Nov 29, 1824	Apr 20, 1894	1861	1867	3	4	0	68	30	17.00	0	—	—	—	1
Berry, P J	Dec 28, 1966		1986	1990	2	4	1	76	31*	25.33	0	401	7	57.28	2
Betts, G	Sept 19, 1843	Sept 26, 1902	1873	1874	2	2	1	56	44*	56.00	0	—	—	—	—
§ Bevan, M G	@ May 8, 1970		1995	1996	32	56	8	2,823	160*	58.81	9	720	10	72.00	24
Binks, J G	@ Oct 5, 1935		1955	1969	491	587	128	6,745	95	14.69	0	66	0	—	872/172
Binns, J	Mar 31, 1870	Dec 8, 1934	1898	1898	1	1	0	4	4	4.00	0	—	—	—	0/3
Bird, H D	Apr 19, 1933		1956	1959	14	25	2	613	181*	26.65	1	—	—	—	3
Birkenshaw, J	Nov 13, 1940		1958	1960	30	42	7	588	42	16.80	0	1,819	69	26.36	21
Birtles, T J D	Oct 26, 1886	Jan 13, 1971	1913	1924	37	57	11	876	104	19.04	1	20	0	—	19

LIST OF PLAYERS AND CAREER AVERAGES IN ALL FIRST-CLASS MATCHES FOR YORKSHIRE (Continued)

Player	Date of Birth	Date of Death (if known)	First Played	Last Played	M	Inns	NO	Runs	HS	Av'ge	100s	Runs	Wkts	Av'ge	Ct/St
Blackburn, J D H *	Oct 27, 1956	Feb 19, 1987	1956	1956	1	2	0	18	15	9.00	0	173	7	24.71	4
Blackburn, J S	Sept 24, 1852	July 8, 1922	1876	1877	7	11	1	102	28	10.20	0	1,113	45	24.73	9
§ Blackburn, W E *	Nov 24, 1888	June 3, 1941	1919	1920	10	13	6	26	6*	3.71	0	1,292	38	34.00	4
§ Blain, J A R	Jan 4, 1979		2004	2006	14	17	7	137	28*	13.70	0	17	1	17.00	—
Blake, W	Nov 29, 1854	Not known	1880	1880	2	3	0	44	21	14.66	0	68	1	68.00	—
◉ Blakey, R J	Jan 15, 1967		1985	2003	339	541	84	14,150	223*	30.96	12	—	—	—	768/56
Blamires, E	July 31, 1850	Mar 22, 1886	1877	1877	1	2	0	23	17	11.50	0	82	5	16.40	5
§ Blewett, G S	Oct 29, 1971		1999	1999	12	23	2	655	190	31.19	1	212	5	42.40	2
Bloom, G R	Sept 13, 1941		1964	1964	1	2	0	14	11	7.00	0	—	—	—	—
Bocking, H	Dec 10, 1835	Feb 22, 1907	1865	1865	1	1	0	6	6	6.00	0	—	—	—	—
Boden, J G *	Dec 27, 1848	Jan 3, 1928	1878	1878	1	—	—	—	—	—	—	—	—	—	—
Bolton, B C *	Sept 23, 1862	Nov 18, 1910	1890	1891	4	6	0	25	11	4.16	0	252	13	19.38	1
Bolus, J B	Jan 31, 1934		1956	1962	107	179	18	4,712	146*	29.26	7	407	13	31.30	45
Booth, A	Nov 3, 1902	Aug 17, 1974	1931	1947	36	36	16	114	29	5.70	0	1,684	122	13.80	10
Booth, M W	Dec 10, 1886	July 1, 1916	1908	1914	144	218	31	4,244	210	22.69	2	11,017	557	19.17	114
Booth, P A	Sept 5, 1965		1982	1989	23	28	8	193	33*	9.65	0	1,517	35	43.34	—
Booth, R K	Oct 1, 1926		1951	1955	65	76	28	730	53*	15.20	0	—	—	—	79/29
Bore, M K	June 2, 1947		1969	1977	74	78	21	481	37*	8.43	0	4,866	162	30.03	27
Borrill, P D	July 4, 1951		1971	1971	4	7	1	20	7	3.33	0	61	5	12.20	2
Bosomworth, W E	Mar 8, 1847	June 7, 1891	1872	1880	1	—	—	—	—	—	—	140	9	15.55	1
Bottomley, I H *	Apr 9, 1855	Apr 23, 1922	1878	1880	9	12	0	166	32	13.83	0	75	1	75.00	5
Bottomley, J	Dec 26, 1910	Feb 19, 1977	1934	1935	6	7	0	142	51	20.28	0	188	1	188.00	—
Bower, W H	Oct 17, 1857	Jan 31, 1943	1883	1883	1	—	—	—	—	—	—	—	—	—	—
Bowes, W E	July 25, 1908	Sept 4, 1987	1929	1947	301	257	117	1,251	43*	8.93	0	21,227	1,351	15.71	118
◉ Boycott, G	Oct 21, 1940		1962	1986	414	674	111	32,570	260*	57.85	103	665	28	23.75	200
Brackin, T	Jan 5, 1859	Oct 7, 1924	1882	1882	3	6	0	12	9	2.00	0	104	3	34.66	—
Brayshay, P B *	Oct 14, 1916	July 6, 2004	1952	1952	2	3	0	20	13	6.66	0	—	—	—	—
Brearley, W *	June 26, 1913	Aug 14, 2007	1937	1937	6	2	0	17	9	8.50	0	—	—	—	—
Brennan, D V *	Feb 16, 1920	Jan 9, 1985	1947	1953	204	221	66	1,653	47	10.66	0	—	—	—	280/100
◉ Bresnan, T T	**Feb 28, 1985**		**2003**	**2008**	**68**	**93**	**18**	**1,871**	**116**	**24.94**	**2**	**5,583**	**177**	**31.54**	**27**
Britton, G	Feb 7, 1843	Jan 3, 1910	1867	1867	1	1	0	3	3	1.50	0	—	—	—	—

LIST OF PLAYERS AND CAREER AVERAGES IN ALL FIRST-CLASS MATCHES FOR YORKSHIRE (Continued)

Player	Date of Birth	Date of Death (if known)	First Played	Last Played	M	Inns	NO	Runs	HS	Av'ge	100s	Runs	Wkts	Av'ge	Ct/St
Broadbent, A	June 7, 1879	July 19, 1958	1909	1910	3	5	0	66	29	13.20	0	252	5	50.40	1
Broadhead, W B	May 31, 1903	Apr 2, 1986	1929	1929	2	2	0	5	3	2.50	0	—	—	—	1
Broadhurst, M	June 20, 1974		1991	1994	5	3	0	7	6	2.33	0	231	7	33.00	—
§ **Brophy, G L**	© Nov 26, 1975		2006	2008	39	59	2	1,390	100*	24.38	1	—	—	—	104/12
Brook, J W	Feb 1, 1897	Mar.3 1989	1923	1923	1	1	0	0	0	0.00	0	—	—	—	—
Brooke, B	Mar 3, 1930		1950	1950	2	4	0	16	14	4.00	0	191	2	95.50	—
Broughton, P N	Oct 22, 1935		1956	1956	6	5	2	19	12	6.33	0	365	16	22.81	2
Brown, A	June 10, 1854	Nov 2, 1900	1872	1872	2	3	0	9	5	3.00	0	47	3	15.66	1
Brown, J T (Driffield) ©	Aug 20, 1869	Nov 4, 1904	1889	1904	345	567	41	15,694	311	29.83	23	5,183	177	29.28	188
Brown, J T (Darfield) ©	Nov 24, 1874	Apr 12, 1950	1897	1903	30	32	3	333	37*	11.48	0	2,071	97	21.35	18
Brown, W	Nov 19, 1876	July 27, 1945	1902	1908	14	20	3	185	25	10.88	0	84	4	21.00	7
Brownhill, T	Oct 10, 1838	Jan 6, 1915	1861	1871	2	1	0	2	2	2.00	0	—	—	—	—
Brumfitt, J *	Feb. 18, 1917	Mar 16, 1987	1938	1938	1	1	0	9	9	9.00	0	—	—	—	—
Buller, J S	Aug 23, 1909	Aug 7, 1970	1930	1930	1	1	0	5	5	5.00	0	—	—	—	2
Bulmer, J R L	Dec 28, 1867	Jan 20, 1917	1891	1891	1	2	0	5	3	2.50	0	79	1	79.00	—
Burgess, T	Oct 1, 1859	Feb 22, 1922	1895	1895	1	2	1	0	0*	0.00	0	—	—	—	—
Burgin, E	Jan 4, 1924		1952	1953	12	10	3	92	32	13.14	0	795	31	25.64	—
Burman, J	Oct 5, 1838	May 14, 1900	1867	1867	1	2	1	1	1*	1.00	0	—	—	—	—
Burnet, J R *	© Oct 11, 1918	Mar 7, 1999	1958	1959	54	75	6	889	54	12.88	0	26	1	26.00	31
§ Burrows, M	Aug 18, 1855	May 29, 1893	1880	1880	10	10	0	82	23	8.20	0	—	—	—	2
Burton, D C F *	Sept 13, 1887	Sept 24, 1971	1907	1921	104	130	15	2,273	142*	19.76	2	—	—	—	44
Burton, R C *	Apr 11, 1891	Apr 30, 1971	1914	1914	2	2	0	47	47	23.50	0	—	—	—	—
Butterfield, E B *	Oct 22, 1848	May 6, 1899	1870	1870	1	2	0	18	10	9.00	0	73	6	12.16	—
Byas, D ©	© Aug 26, 1963		1986	2001	268	449	42	14,398	213	35.37	28	727	12	60.58	351
Byrom, J L *	July, 20, 1851	Aug 24, 1931	1874	1874	2	4	0	19	11	4.75	0	—	—	—	1
Cammish, J W	May 21, 1921	July 16, 1974	1954	1954	2	1	0	0	0	0.00	0	155	3	51.66	—
Carrick, P ©	© July, 16 1952	Jan 11, 2000	1970	1993	425	543	102	9,994	131*	22.66	3	30,530	1,018	29.99	183
Carter, Rev E S *	Feb 3, 1845	May 23, 1923	1876	1881	14	21	2	210	39*	11.05	0	104	8	13.00	4
Cartman, W H	June 20, 1861	Jan 16, 1935	1891	1891	3	6	0	57	49	9.50	0	—	—	—	—
Cawthray, G	Sept 28, 1913	Jan 5, 2000	1939	1952	4	6	0	114	30	19.00	0	304	4	76.00	1

LIST OF PLAYERS AND CAREER AVERAGES IN ALL FIRST-CLASS MATCHES FOR YORKSHIRE (Continued)

Player	Date of Birth	Date of Death (if known)	First Played	Last Played	M	Inns	NO	Runs	HS	Av'ge	100s	Runs	Wkts	Av'ge	Ct/St
Chadwick, J P G	Nov 8, 1934	—	1960	1965	6	9	3	106	59	17.66	0	67	2	33.50	7
Champion, A	Dec 27, 1851	June 30, 1909	1876	1879	14	23	4	148	29	7.78	0	17	1	17.00	7
Chapman, C A	June 8, 1971	—	1990	1998	8	13	2	238	80	21.63	0	—	—	—	13/3
Charlesworth, A P	Feb 19, 1865	May 11, 1926	1894	1895	7	12	1	241	63	21.90	0	—	—	—	2
§ Chichester-Constable, R C J *	Dec 21, 1890	May 26, 1963	1919	1919	1	1	0	0	0	0.00	0	—	—	—	—
Clarkson, A	Sept 5, 1939	—	1963	1963	6	8	1	80	30	11.42	0	6	0	—	5
Claughton, H M	Dec 24, 1891	Oct 17, 1980	1914	1919	4	6	0	39	15	6.50	0	92	5	18.40	1
§ Claydon, M E	Nov 25, 1982	—	2005	2006	3	2	0	38	38	19.00	0	176	3	58.66	—
§ Clayton, R O	Jan 1, 1844	Nov 26, 1901	1870	1879	70	115	23	992	62	10.78	0	263	3	87.66	26
§ Cleary, M F	July 19, 1980	—	2005	2005	2	2	0	23	12	11.50	0	250	8	31.25	—
Clegg, H	Dec 8, 1850	Dec 30, 1920	1881	1881	6	8	1	63	25*	9.00	0	—	—	—	2
Clifford, C C	◎ July 5, 1942	—	1972	1972	11	12	1	39	12*	4.87	0	666	26	25.61	5
Close, D B	◎ Feb 24, 1931	—	1949	1970	536	811	102	22,650	198	31.94	33	23,489	967	24.29	564
Clough, G D	May 23, 1978	—	1998	1998	1	2	0	34	33	17.00	0	11	0	—	1
Collinson, R W *	Nov 6, 1875	Dec 26, 1963	1897	1897	2	3	0	58	34	19.33	0	—	—	—	—
Cooper, H P	Apr 17, 1949	—	1971	1980	98	107	29	1,159	56	14.85	0	6,327	227	27.87	60
Cooper, P E *	Feb 19, 1885	May 21, 1950	1910	1910	1	2	0	0	0	0.00	0	—	—	—	1
Cope, G A	◎ Feb 23, 1947	—	1966	1980	230	249	89	2,241	78	14.00	0	15,627	630	24.80	64
Corbett, A M	Nov 25, 1855	Oct 7, 1934	1881	1881	1	2	0	31	18	15.50	0	—	—	—	1
Coverdale, S P	Nov 20, 1954	—	1973	1980	6	4	2	2	19*	1.00	0	—	—	—	11/4
Coverdale, A *	July 8, 1862	Sept 23, 1934	1888	1888	1	2	1	19	19*	19.00	0	—	—	—	2
Cowan, M J	◎ June 10, 1933	—	1953	1962	91	84	48	170	19*	4.72	0	6,389	266	24.01	37
Cownley, J M	Feb 24, 1929	Nov 7, 1998	1952	1952	2	2	1	19	19*	19.00	0	119	—	—	—
Coxon, A	◎ Jan 18, 1916	Jan 22, 2006	1945	1950	142	182	33	2,747	83	18.43	0	9,528	464	20.53	124
Craven, V J	July 31, 1980	—	2000	2004	33	55	6	1,206	81*	24.61	0	584	15	38.93	18
Crawford, G H	Dec 15, 1890	June 28, 1975	1914	1926	9	8	0	46	21	5.75	0	541	21	25.76	3
Crawford, M G *	July 30, 1920	—	1951	1951	4	2	0	22	13	11.00	0	—	—	—	1
Creighton, E	July 9, 1859	Feb 17, 1931	1888	1888	4	6	0	33	10	5.50	0	—	—	—	—
Crick, H	Jan 29, 1910	Feb 10, 1960	1937	1947	8	10	0	88	20	8.80	0	181	10	18.10	—
Crookes, R	Oct 9, 1846	Feb 15, 1897	1879	1879	8	2	1	2	2*	2.00	0	14	0	—	18/4

LIST OF PLAYERS AND CAREER AVERAGES IN ALL FIRST-CLASS MATCHES FOR YORKSHIRE (Continued)

Player	Date of Birth	Date of Death (if known)	First Played	Last Played	M	Inns	NO	Runs	HS	Av'ge	100s	Runs	Wkts	Av'ge	Ct/St
Crossland, S M	Aug 16, 1851	April 11, 1906	1883	1886	4	6	2	32	20	8.00	0	—	—	—	3/5
Crowther, A	Aug 1, 1878	June 4, 1946	1905	1905	1	2	0	0	0	0.00	0	—	—	—	—
Cuttell, W	Jan 28, 1835	June 10, 1896	1862	1871	21	27	6	271	56	12.90	0	596	36	16.55	4
Dalton, A J	Mar 14, 1947		1969	1972	21	31	2	710	128	24.48	3	—	—	—	6
§ Darnton, T	Feb 12, 1836	Oct 25, 1874	1864	1868	13	22	1	314	81*	14.95	0	349	12	29.08	3
Davidson, K R ©	Dec 24, 1905	Dec 25, 1954	1933	1935	30	46	5	1,331	128	32.46	2	—	—	—	18
Dawes, J	Feb 14, 1836	Not known	1865	1865	5	9	2	93	28*	13.28	0	196	5	39.20	3
Dawood, I	July 23, 1976		2004	2005	20	31	7	636	75	26.50	0	—	—	—	46/3
Dawson, E	May 1, 1835	Dec 1, 1888	1863	1874	16	25	1	224	20	9.33	0	—	—	—	5
Dawson, R K J ©	Aug 4, 1980		2001	2006	72	106	9	2,179	87	22.46	0	6,444	157	41.04	39
Dawson, W A *	Dec 3, 1850	Mar 6, 1916	1870	1870	1	2	0	0	0	0.00	0	—	—	—	1
Day, A G *	Sept 20, 1865	Oct 16, 1908	1885	1888	6	10	0	78	25	7.80	0	—	—	—	3
Dennis, F	© June 11, 1907	Nov 21, 2000	1928	1933	89	100	28	1,332	67	18.50	0	4,517	156	28.95	58
Dennis, S J	Oct 18, 1960		1980	1988	67	62	24	338	53*	8.89	0	5,548	173	32.06	19
Denton, D	© July 4, 1874	Feb 16, 1950	1894	1920	676	1,058	61	33,282	221	33.38	61	957	34	28.14	360/1
Denton, J	Feb 3, 1865	July 19, 1946	1887	1888	15	24	2	222	59	9.65	0	—	—	—	6
Dewse, G	Feb 23, 1836	Jan 8, 1910	1873	1873	1	2	0	14	12	7.00	0	15	0	—	1
Deyes, G	Feb 11, 1879	Jan 11, 1963	1905	1907	17	24	4	44	12	2.20	0	944	41	23.02	6
Dick, R D *	Apr 16, 1889	Dec 14, 1983	1911	1911	2	2	1	2	2	2.00	0	37	2	18.50	1
Dobson, A	Feb 22, 1854	Sept 17, 1932	1879	1879	1	3	0	2	1	0.33	0	—	—	—	—
Doidge, M J	July 2, 1970		1990	1990	1	—	—	—	—	—	—	—	—	—	—
Dolphin, A	© Dec 24, 1885	Oct 23, 1942	1905	1927	427	446	157	3,325	66	11.50	0	106	0	—	569/260
Douglas, J S	Apr 4, 1903	Dec 27, 1971	1925	1934	23	26	8	125	19	6.94	0	28	1	28.00	14
Drake, A	© Apr 16, 1884	Feb 14, 1919	1909	1914	156	244	24	4,789	147*	21.76	3	8,623	479	18.00	93
Drake, J	Sept 1, 1893	May 22, 1967	1923	1924	3	4	1	21	10	7.00	0	117	1	117.00	2
Driver, J	May 16, 1861	Dec 10, 1946	1889	1889	3	4	1	24	8	8.00	0	—	—	—	2
Dury, T S *	June 12, 1854	Mar 20, 1932	1878	1881	13	24	1	329	46	14.30	0	21	0	—	3
Dyson, W L	Dec 11, 1857	May 1, 1936	1887	1887	2	4	0	8	6	2.00	0	—	—	—	2
Earnshaw, W	Sept 20, 1867	Nov 24, 1941	1893	1896	6	7	3	44	23	11.00	0	—	—	—	6/2
Eastwood, D	Mar 30, 1848	May 17, 1903	1870	1877	29	51	2	591	68	12.06	0	349	11	31.72	16

LIST OF PLAYERS AND CAREER AVERAGES IN ALL FIRST-CLASS MATCHES FOR YORKSHIRE (Continued)

Player	Date of Birth	Date of Death (if known)	First Played	Last Played	M	Inns	NO	Runs	HS	Av'ge	100s	Runs	Wkts	Av'ge	Ct/St
Eckersley, R	Sept 4, 1925		1945	1945	1	1	1	9	9*	—	0	62	0	—	—
Elam, F W *	Sept 13, 1871	Mar 19, 1943	1900	1902	2	3	1	48	28	24.00	0	—	—	—	—
§ Elliott, M T G	Sept 28, 1971		2002	2002	5	10	1	487	127	54.11	1	77	1	77.00	7
Ellis, J E	Nov 10, 1864	Dec 1, 1927	1888	1892	11	15	6	14	4*	1.55	0	—	—	—	11/10
Ellis, S *	Nov 23, 1851	Oct 28, 1930	1880	1880	2	3	0	12	9	4.00	0	—	—	—	2
Elms, J E	Dec 24, 1874	Nov 1, 1951	1905	1905	1	2	0	20	20	10.00	0	28	1	28.00	1
Elstub, C J	Feb 3, 1981		2000	2002	6	7	6	28	18*	28.00	0	356	9	39.55	2
Emmett, T	©Sept 3, 1841	June 30, 1904	1866	1888	299	484	65	6,315	104	15.07	1	15,465	1,216	12.71	179
Farrar, A	Apr 29, 1884	Dec 25, 1954	1906	1906	1	1	0	2	2	2.00	0	—	—	—	1
Fearnley, M C	Aug 21, 1936	July 7, 1979	1962	1964	3	4	2	19	11*	9.50	0	133	6	22.16	—
Featherby, W D	Aug 18, 1888	Nov 20, 1958	1920	1920	2	1	1	—	—	—	0	12	—	—	—
Fellows, G M	July 30, 1978		1998	2003	46	71	6	1,526	109	23.47	1	1,202	32	37.56	23
Fidding, K	Oct 13, 1917	June 19, 1992	1938	1946	18	24	1	182	25	10.11	0	—	—	—	24/13
Firth, A *	Sept 3, 1847	Jan 16, 1927	1869	1869	1	1	0	4	4	4.00	0	—	—	—	—
Firth, Rev E B *	Apr 11, 1863	July 25, 1905	1894	1894	1	1	0	1	1	1.00	0	—	—	—	—
Firth, J	June 27, 1918	Sept 7, 1981	1949	1950	8	8	5	134	76*	44.66	0	—	—	—	14/2
Fisher, H	©Aug 3, 1903	Apr 16, 1974	1928	1936	52	58	14	681	76*	15.47	0	2,621	93	28.18	22
Fisher, I D	Mar 31, 1976		1996	2001	24	32	9	545	68*	23.69	0	1,382	43	32.13	1
Flaxington, S	Oct 14, 1860	Mar 10, 1895	1882	1882	2	4	0	121	57	15.12	0	—	—	—	—
§ Fleming, S P	Apr 1, 1973		2003	2003	7	14	2	469	98	39.08	0	—	—	—	13
Fletcher, S D	©June 8, 1964		1983	1991	107	91	31	414	28*	6.90	0	7,966	234	34.04	25
Fletcher, W	Feb 16, 1866	June 1, 1935	1892	1892	5	8	1	80	31*	11.42	0	157	7	22.42	4
Foord, C W	June 11, 1924		1947	1953	51	34	16	114	35	6.33	0	3,412	126	27.07	19
Foster, E	Nov 23, 1873		1901	1901	1	1	0	2	2	2.00	0	—	—	—	27
Foster, M J	Sept 17, 1972		1993	1994	5	7	1	165	63*	27.50	0	156	6	25.00	6
§ Foster, T W	Nov 12, 1871	April 16, 1956	1894	1895	14	20	5	138	25	9.20	0	952	58	16.41	3
Frank, J *	Dec 17, 1857	Jan 31, 1947	1881	1881	1	2	0	10	7	5.00	0	17	1	17.00	—
Frank R W *	©May 29, 1864	Oct 22, 1940	1889	1903	18	28	4	298	58	12.41	0	9	—	—	8
Freeman, G	©July 27, 1843	Nov 18, 1895	1865	1880	32	54	2	752	53	14.46	0	2,079	209	9.94	16
Gale, A W	©Nov 28, 1983		2004	2008	**30**	**47**	**0**	**1419**	**150**	**30.19**	**4**	**36**	**1**	**36.00**	**18**

Player	Date of Birth	Date of Death (if known)	First Played	Last Played	M	Inns	NO	Runs	HS	Av'ge	100s	Runs	Wkts	Av'ge	Ct/St
Gibb, P A *	© July 11, 1913	Dec 7, 1977	1935	1946	36	54	7	1,545	157*	32.87	3	82	3	27.33	25/8
§ Gifkins, C J *	Feb 19, 1856	Not known	1880	1880	2	3	0	30	23	10.00	0	—	0	—	1
Gilbert, C R	Apr 16, 1984		2007	2007	1	1	0	64	64	64.00	0	11	0	—	1
Gill, F	Sept 3, 1883	Nov 1, 1917	1906	1906	2	4	0	18	11	4.50	0	—	—	—	1
§ Gillespie, J N	©April 19, 1975		2006	2007	26	34	11	640	123*	27.82	1	2,013	59	34.11	4
Gillhouley, K	Aug 8, 1934		1961	1961	24	31	7	323	56*	13.45	0	1,702	77	22.10	16
Gough, D	© Sept 18, 1970		1989	2008	146	188	29	2,922	121	18.37	1	12,487	453	27.56	30
Goulder, A	Aug 16, 1907		1929	1929	2	1		3	3	3.00	0	90	3	30.00	—
§ Gray, A K D	May 19, 1974		2001	2004	18	26	3	649	104	28.21	1	1,357	30	45.23	16
Grayson, A P	Mar 31, 1971		1990	1995	52	80	10	1,958	100	27.97	1	846	13	65.07	36
Greenwood, A	Aug 20, 1847	Feb 12, 1889	1869	1880	95	166	12	2,762	91	17.93	0	9	0	—	33
Greenwood, F E *	© Sept 28, 1905	July 30, 1963	1929	1932	57	66	8	1,458	104*	25.13	1	36	2	18.00	37
Greenwood, L	July 13, 1834	Nov 1, 1909	1861	1874	50	84	12	885	83	12.29	0	1,615	85	19.00	24
Grimshaw, C H	May 12, 1880	Sept 25, 1947	1904	1908	54	75	7	1,219	85	17.92	0	221	7	31.57	42
Grimshaw, I	May 4, 1857	Jan 18, 1911	1880	1887	125	194	14	3,354	129*	18.63	4	—	—	—	76/3
Guy, S M	**Nov 17, 1978**		**2000**	**2008**	**36**	**50**	**6**	**727**	**52***	**16.52**	**0**	**8**	**0**	**—**	**97/12**
Haggas, S	Apr 18, 1856	Mar 14, 1926	1878	1882	31	47	3	478	43	10.86	0	—	—	—	10
Haigh, S	© Mar 19, 1871	Feb 27, 1921	1895	1913	513	687	110	10,993	159	19.05	4	29,289	1,876	15.61	276
Hall, B	Sept 16, 1929	Feb 27, 1989	1952	1952	1	2	0	14	10	7.00	0	55	1	55.00	—
Hall, C H	Apr 5, 1906	Dec 11, 1976	1928	1934	23	22	9	67	15*	5.15	0	1,226	45	27.24	11
§ Hall, J	Nov 11, 1818	Apr 17, 1888	1844	1863	1	2	0	4	4	2.00	0	—	—	—	—
Hall, L	© Nov 1, 1852	Nov 19, 1915	1873	1894	275	477	58	9,757	144	23.28	9	781	15	52.06	173
Halliday, H	© Feb 9, 1920	Aug 27, 1967	1938	1953	182	279	18	8,361	144	32.03	12	3,119	101	30.88	140
Halliday, C	Dec 5, 1852	Mar 23, 1929	1872	1872	3	5	0	27	17	5.40	0	—	—	—	2
Hamer, A	Dec 8, 1916	Nov 3, 1993	1938	1938	3	2	0	3	3	1.50	0	—	—	—	2
§ Hamilton, G M	© Sept 16, 1974		1994	2003	73	108	18	2,228	125	24.75	1	5,479	222	24.68	25
Hampshire, A W	Oct 18, 1950		1975	1975	1	2	0	18	17	9.00	0	64	2	32.00	2
Hampshire, J	Oct 5, 1913	May 23, 1997	1937	1937	3	2	0	5	5	2.50	0	—	—	—	2
Hampshire, J H	© Feb 10, 1941		1961	1981	456	724	89	21,979	183*	34.61	34	109	5	21.80	368
Hannon-Dalby, O J	**© June 20, 1989**		**2008**	**2008**	**1**	**1**	**0**	**1**	**1***	**1.00**	**0**	**1,108**	**24**	**46.16**	**—**

Player	Date of Birth	Date of Death (if known)	First Played	Last Played	M	Inns	NO	Runs	HS	Av'ge	100s	Runs	Wkts	Av'ge	Ct/St
§ Harbord, W E *	Dec 15, 1908	July 28, 1992	1929	1935	16	21	1	411	109	20.55	1	—	—	—	7
§ Harden, R J *	Aug 16, 1965		1999	2000	12	22	3	439	69	23.10	0	—	—	—	2
Hardisty, C H	Dec 10, 1885		1906	1909	38	55	5	991	84	19.82	0	—	—	—	18
Hargreaves, H S	Mar 22, 1913	Sept 29, 1990	1934	1938	18	20	6	51	9	3.64	0	—	—	—	3
Harris, W	Nov 21, 1861		1884	1887	4	8	2	45	25	7.50	0	1,145	55	20.81	3
Harrison, G P ...©	Feb 11, 1862	Sept 14, 1940	1883	1892	59	87	26	407	28	6.67	0	3,276	226	14.49	36
Harrison, H	Jan 26, 1885	Feb 11, 1962	1907		2	3	1	4	4*		0	39	2	19.50	1
Harrison, W H	May 27, 1863	July 15, 1939	1888	1888	3	6	1	12	7	2.40	0	—	—	—	—
Hart, H W *	Sept 21, 1859	Nov 2, 1895	1888	1888	1	2	0	6	6	3.00	0	32	2	16.00	2
Hart, P R	Jan 12, 1947		1981	1981	3	5	0	23	11	4.60	0	140	2	70.00	1
Hartington, H E	Sept 18, 1881	Feb 16, 1950	1910	1911	10	10	4	51	16	8.50	0	764	23	33.21	2
Hartley, P J ...©	Apr 18, 1960		1985	1997	195	237	51	3,844	127*	20.66	2	17,438	579	30.11	60
Hartley, S N ...©	Mar 18, 1956		1978	1988	133	199	27	4,193	114	24.37	4	2,052	42	48.85	47
§ Harvey, I J	Apr 10, 1972		2004	2005	20	31	1	1,045	209*	36.03	2	831	37	22.45	12
Hatton, A G	Mar 25, 1937		1960	1961	3	3	1	4	4*		0	202	6	33.66	1
§ Hawke, Lord * ...©	Aug 16, 1860	Oct 10, 1938	1881	1911	510	739	91	13,133	166	20.26	10	16	0	—	159
Hayley, H	Feb 22, 1860	June 3, 1922	1884	1898	7	12	1	122	24	11.09	0	48	0	—	3
Haywood, W J	Feb 25, 1841	Jan 7, 1912	1878	1878	1	2	0	7	7	3.50	0	14	1	14.00	—
Hicks, J	Dec 10, 1850	June 10, 1912	1872	1876	15	25	3	313	66	14.22	0	17	0	—	12
Higgins, J	Mar 13, 1871	July 19, 1954	1901	1905	9	14	5	93	28*	10.33	0	—	—	—	10/3
Hill, A	Nov 14, 1843	Aug 29, 1910	1871	1882	140	223	25	1,705	49	8.61	0	7,002	542	12.91	91
Hill, H *	Nov 29, 1858	Aug 14, 1935	1888	1891	14	27	2	337	34	13.48	0	—	—	—	10
Hill, L G *	Nov 2, 1860	Aug 27, 1940	1882	1882	1	2	0	13	8	6.50	0	—	—	—	1
Hirst, E T *	May 6, 1857	Oct 26, 1914	1877	1881	21	33	2	328	87*	10.58	0	—	—	—	7
Hirst, E W *	Feb 27, 1855	Oct 24, 1933	1881	1881	2	3	0	33	28	11.00	0	3	0	—	—
Hirst, G H ...©	Sept 7, 1871	May 10, 1954	1891	1921*	717	1,050	128	32,024	341	34.73	56	44,716	2,481	18.02	518
Hirst, T H	May 21, 1865	Apr 3, 1927	1899	1899	1	1	0	5	5*	4.00	0	27	0	—	0/2
Hodgson, G	July 24, 1938		1964	1964	1	1	0	4	4	4.00	0	—	—	—	—
Hodgson, I	Nov 15, 1828	Nov 24, 1867	1855	1866	21	35	14	164	21*	7.80	0	1,537	88	17.46	11
Hodgson, P	Sept 21, 1935		1954	1956	13	6	2	33	8*	8.25	0	648	22	29.45	6
Hoggard, M J ...©	**Dec 31, 1976**		**1996**	**2008**	**86**	**103**	**30**	**761**	**89***	**10.42**	**0**	**7,470**	**285**	**26.21**	**18**

366

LIST OF PLAYERS AND CAREER AVERAGES IN ALL FIRST-CLASS MATCHES FOR YORKSHIRE (Continued)

Player	Date of Birth	Date of Death (if known)	First Played	Last Played	M	Inns	NO	Runs	HS	Av'ge	100s	Runs	Wkts	Av'ge	Ct/St
Holdsworth, W E N	Sept 17, 1928		1952	1953	27	26	12	111	22*	7.92	0	1,598	53	30.15	15
Holgate, G	June 23, 1839	July 11, 1895	1865	1867	12	19	0	174	38	9.15	0				17/1
Holmes, P ...©	Nov 25, 1886	Sept 3, 1971	1913	1933	485	699	74	26,200	315*	41.95	60	124	1	124.00	319
Horner, N F	May 10, 1926	Dec 24, 2003	1950	1950	2	4	0	114	43	28.50	0				2
Houseman I J	Oct 12, 1969		1989	1991	5	2	1	18	18	18.00	0	311	3	103.66	
Hoyle, T H	Mar 19, 1884	June 2, 1953	1919	1919	1	2	0	7	7	3.50	0				0/1
Hudson, D	June 29, 1852	Nov 11, 1901	1880	1880	3	4	0	13	7	3.25	0				2
Hunter, D ...©	Feb 23, 1860	Jan 11, 1927	1888	1909	517	681	323	4,177	58*	11.66	0	43	0		863/323
Hunter, J	Aug 3, 1855	Jan 4, 1891	1878	1888	143	213	61	1,183	60*	7.78	0				207/102
Hutchison, P M ...©	June 9, 1977		1996	2001	39	39	23	187	30	11.68	0	3,244	143	22.68	8
Hutton, L ...©	June 23, 1916	Sept. 6, 1990	1934	1955	341	527	62	24,807	280*	53.34	85	4,221	154	27.40	278
Hutton, R A ...©	Sept 6, 1942		1962	1974	208	292	45	4,986	189	20.18	4	10,254	468	21.91	160
Iddison, R	Sept 15, 1834	Mar 19, 1890	1855	1876	72	108	15	1,916	112	20.60	0	1,540	102	15.09	70
Illingworth, R ...©	June 8, 1932		1951	1983	496	668	131	14,986	162	27.90	14	26,806	1,431	18.73	286
§ Imran Tahir	Mar 27, 1979		2007	2007	1	2	0	5	5	2.50	0	141	0		
Ingham, P G	Sept 28, 1956		1979	1981	8	14	0	290	64	20.71	0				1
Inglis, J W	Oct 19, 1979		2000	2000	1	2	0	4	2	2.00	0				
§ Inzamam-ul-Haq	Mar 3, 1970		2007	2007	3	4	0	89	51	22.25	0				5
Jackson, Hon F S * ...©	Nov 21, 1870	Mar 9, 1947	1890	1907	207	328	22	10,371	160	33.89	21	9,690	506	19.15	129
Jackson, S R *	July 15, 1859	July 19, 1941	1891	1891	1	2	0	9	9	4.50	0				
Jacques, T A	Feb 19, 1905	Feb 23, 1995	1927	1936	28	20	7	162	33*	12.46	0				12
Jakeman, F	Jan 10, 1920	May 18, 1986	1946	1947	10	16	2	262	51	18.71	0	1,786	57	31.33	3
James, B	Apr 21, 1934		1954	1954	4	5	3	22	11*	11.00	0				1
§ Jaques, P A ...©	May 3, 1979		2004	2005	24	42	3	2,477	243	61.92	7	228	8	28.50	25
Jarvis, P W ...©	June 29, 1965**		1981	1993	138	160	46	1,898	80	16.64	0	11,990	449	26.70	36
Johnson, C	Sept 5, 1947		1969	1979	100	152	14	2,960	107	21.44	2	265	4	66.25	50
Johnson, J	May 16, 1916		1936	1939	3	3	2	5	4*	5.00	0	27	5	5.40	1
Johnson, M	Apr 23, 1958		1981	1981	4	4	2	2	2	1.00	0	301	7	43.00	1

**At 16 years, 75 days the youngest to appear for Yorkshire in First-Class Cricket

LIST OF PLAYERS AND CAREER AVERAGES IN ALL FIRST-CLASS MATCHES FOR YORKSHIRE (Continued)

Player	Date of Birth	Date of Death (if known)	First Played	Last Played	M	Inns	NO	Runs	HS	Av'ge	100s	Runs	Wkts	Av'ge	Ct/St
Joy, J	Sept 29, 1826	Sept 27, 1889	1849	1867	3	5	0	107	74	21.40	0		0	—	3
Judson, A	July 10, 1885	Apr 8, 1975	1920	1920	1	—	—	—	—	—	—		0	—	—
§ Katich, S M	Aug 21, 1975		2002	2002	1	2	0	37	21	18.50	0	25	0	—	1
Kaye, Harold S *	May 9, 1882	Nov 6, 1953	1907	1908	18	25	1	243	37	10.12	0	—	—	—	9
Kaye, Haven	June 11, 1846	Jan 24, 1892	1872	1873	8	14	0	117	33	8.35	0	—	—	—	3
Keedy,	Nov 27, 1974		1994	1994	1	1	0	1	1	1.00	0	—	—	—	—
§ Keighley, W G *	Jan 10, 1925	June 14, 2005	1947	1951	35	51	5	1,227	110	26.67	1	18	0	—	12
Kellett, S A	Oct 16, 1967		1989	1995	86	147	10	4,204	125*	30.68	7	7	0	—	74
Kennie, G	May 17, 1904	Apr 11, 1994	1927	1927	1	2	0	6	6	3.00	0	—	—	—	—
Kettleborough, R A	Mar 15, 1973		1994	1997	13	19	2	446	108	26.23	1	153	3	51.00	9
Kilburn, S	Oct 16, 1868	Sept 25, 1940	1896	1896	1	1	0	8	8	8.00	0	—	—	—	—
Kilner, N	July 21, 1895	Apr 28, 1979	1919	1923	69	73	7	1,253	112	18.98	2	—	—	—	34
Kilner, R	Oct 17, 1890	Apr 5, 1928	1911	1927	365	478	46	13,018	206*	30.13	15	14,855	857	17.33	231
King, A M	Oct 8, 1932		1955	1955	1	1	0	12	12	12.00	0	279	8	34.87	—
Kippax, P J	Oct 15, 1940		1961	1962	4	7	1	37	12	7.40	0	5,143	182	28.25	11
§ Kirby, S P	Oct 4, 1977		2001	2004	47	61	14	342	57	7.27	0	4,615	132	34.96	10
§ Kruis, G J	May 9, 1974		2005	2008	45	55	29	486	50*	18.69	0	—	—	—	—
§ Lambert, G A	Jan 1, 1980		2000	2000	2	3	2	6	3*	6.00	0	133	4	33.25	—
Lancaster, W W	Feb 4, 1873	Dec 30, 1938	1895	1895	7	10	0	163	51	16.30	0	29	0	—	1
§ Landon, C W *	May 30, 1850	Mar 5, 1903	1878	1882	9	13	0	51	18	3.92	0	74	0	—	7
§ Law, W *	Apr 9, 1851	Dec 20, 1892	1871	1873	4	7	0	51	22	7.28	0	—	—	—	3
Lawson, M A K	Oct 24, 1985		2004	2007	15	21	5	197	44	12.31	0	1,699	42	40.45	7
Leadbeater, B	Aug 14, 1943		1966	1979	144	236	27	5,247	140*	25.10	1	5	1	5.00	80
Leadbeater, E	Aug 15, 1927		1949	1956	81	94	29	898	91	13.81	0	5,657	201	28.14	49
Leadbeater, H *	Dec 31, 1863	Oct 9, 1928	1884	1890	6	10	2	141	65	17.62	0	11	0	—	4
Leatham, G A B *	Apr 30, 1851	June 19, 1932	1874	1886	12	18	5	61	14	4.69	0	—	—	—	21/7
Leather, R S *	Aug 17, 1880	Jan 31, 1913	1906	1906	1	2	0	19	14	9.50	0	—	—	—	—
Lee, C	Mar 17, 1924	Sept 4, 1999	1952	1952	2	4	0	98	74	24.50	0	—	—	—	1
Lee, F	Nov 18, 1856	Sept 13, 1896	1882	1890	105	182	10	3,622	165	21.05	3	—	—	—	53/1
Lee, G H	Aug 24, 1854	Oct 4, 1919	1879	1879	1	2	0	13	9	6.50	0	—	—	—	—

LIST OF PLAYERS AND CAREER AVERAGES IN ALL FIRST-CLASS MATCHES FOR YORKSHIRE (Continued)

Player	Date of Birth	Date of Death (if known)	First Played	Last Played	M	Inns	NO	Runs	HS	Av'ge	100s	Runs	Wkts	Av'ge	Ct/St
Lee, Herbert	July 2, 1856	Feb 4, 1908	1885	1885	5	6	0	20	12	3.33	0	—	—	—	2
Lee, J E *	Mar 23, 1838	Apr 2, 1880	1867	1867	3	3	0	9	6	3.00	0	—	—	—	—
Lee, J E	**Dec 23, 1988**		**2006**	**2006**	**1**	**2**	**1**	**22**	**21***	**22.00**	**0**	—	—	—	—
Legard, A D *	June 19, 1878	Aug 15, 1939	1910	1910	4	5	0	26	15	10.00	0	36	0	—	1
Lehmann, D S ©	Feb 5, 1970		1997	2006	88	137	8	8,871	339	68.76	26	1,952	61	32.00	35
Lester, E I ©	Feb 18, 1923		1945	1956	228	339	27	10,616	186	34.02	24	160	3	53.33	106
Leyland, M ©	July 20, 1900	Jan 1, 1967	1920	1946	548	720	82	26,180	263	41.03	62	11,079	409	27.08	204
Linaker, L	Apr 8, 1885	Nov 17, 1961	1909	1909	1	2	1	0	0	0.00	0	—	—	—	1
Lister, B	Dec 9, 1850	Dec 3, 1919	1874	1878	7	11	1	36	10	3.60	0	64	1	64.00	2
§ Lister-Kaye, K A *	Mar 27, 1892	Feb 28, 1955	1928	1928	1	2	1	13	7*	13.00	0	—	—	—	2
Lister, J *	May 14, 1930	Jan 28, 1991	1954	1954	2	4	0	35	16	8.75	0	—	—	—	2
Lockwood, E	Apr 4, 1845	Dec 19, 1921	1868	1884	214	364	29	7,789	208	23.25	6	2,265	141	16.06	164/2
Lockwood, H	Oct 20, 1855	Feb 18, 1930	1877	1882	16	27	2	408	90	16.32	0	37	0	—	8
Lodge, J T	Apr 16, 1921		1948	1948	2	3	0	48	30	16.00	0	17	0	—	—
Love, J D ©	Apr 22, 1955		1975	1989	247	388	58	10,263	170*	31.10	13	835	12	69.58	123
Lowe, G E	Jan 12, 1878	Aug 15, 1932	1902	1902	1	1	0	5	5	5.00	0	—	—	—	—
Lowson, F A ©	July 1, 1925	Sept 8, 1984	1949	1958	252	404	31	13,897	259*	37.25	30	15	0	—	180
§ Loxley-Firth, E *	Mar 7, 1886	Jan 8, 1949	1912	1912	1	4	0	43	37	10.75	0	—	—	—	1
Lucas, D S	Aug 19, 1978		2005	2005	1	—	—	—	—	—	—	—	—	—	—
Lumb, E * ©	Sept 12, 1852	Apr 5, 1891	1872	1886	14	23	4	311	70*	16.36	0	84	8	10.50	5
§ Lumb, M J ©	Feb 12, 1980		2000	2006	78	135	12	4,194	144	34.09	8	199	5	39.80	43
Lumb, R G ©	Feb 27, 1950		1970	1984	239	395	30	11,525	165*	31.57	22	5	0	—	129
Lupton, A W * ©	Feb 23, 1879	Apr 14, 1944	1908	1927	104	79	15	668	43*	10.43	0	88	0	—	25
Lynas, G G	Sept 7, 1832	Dec 8, 1896	1867	1867	2	3	1	4	4*	2.00	0	—	—	—	2
Lyth, A	**Sept 25, 1987**		**2007**	**2008**	**15**	**22**	**1**	**676**	**132**	**30.72**	**1**	**117**	**2**	**58.50**	**11**
Macaulay, G G ©	Dec 7, 1897	Dec 13, 1940	1920	1935	445	430	112	5,717	125*	17.97	3	30,554	1,774	17.22	361
McGrath, A ©	**Oct 6, 1975**		**1995**	**2008**	**183**	**309**	**24**	**10,868**	**188***	**38.13**	**26**	**3,601**	**103**	**34.96**	**131**
McHugh, F P	Nov 15, 1925		1949	1949	3	1	0	2	2	2.00	0	147	4	36.75	—
Marshall, A	July 10, 1849	Aug 3, 1891	1874	1874	1	2	0	2	2	1.00	0	11	0	—	—
§ Martyn, D R ©	Oct 21, 1971		2003	2003	1	2	0	342	238	171.00	1	—	—	—	2

LIST OF PLAYERS AND CAREER AVERAGES IN ALL FIRST-CLASS MATCHES FOR YORKSHIRE (Continued)

Player	Date of Birth	Date of Death (if known)	First Played	Last Played	M	Inns	NO	Runs	HS	Av'ge	100s	Runs	Wkts	Av'ge	Ct/St
Mason, A	May 2, 1921		1947	1950	18	19	3	105	22	6.56	0	1,473	51	28.88	6
Maude, E *	Dec 31, 1839	July 2, 1876	1866	1866	2	2	0	17	16	8.50	0	—	—	—	—
© Metcalfe, A A	Dec 25, 1963		1983	1995	184	317	19	10,465	216*	35.11	25	344	3	114.66	—
72 Micklethwait, W H *	Dec 13, 1885	Oct 7, 1947	1911	1911	1	1	0	44	44	44.00	0	—	—	—	—
Middlebrook, J D	May 13, 1977		1998	2001	23	31	3	485	84	17.32	0	1,458	49	29.75	14
Middlebrook, W	May 23, 1858	Apr 26, 1919	1888	1889	17	27	7	88	19*	4.40	0	895	50	17.90	17
Midgley, C A *	Nov 11, 1877	June 24, 1942	1906	1906	4	6	2	115	59*	28.75	0	149	8	18.62	3
Milburn, S M	Sept 29, 1972		1992	1995	6	8	2	22	7	3.66	0	431	14	30.78	—
§ Milligan, F W *	Mar 19, 1870	Mar 31, 1900	1894	1898	81	113	10	1,879	74	18.24	0	2,736	112	24.42	40
© Mitchell, A	Sept 13, 1902	Dec 25, 1976	1922	1945	401	550	69	18,189	189	37.81	39	291	5	58.20	406
© Mitchell, F *	Aug 13, 1872	Oct 11, 1935	1894	1904	83	125	5	4,104	194	34.20	10	16	1	16.00	52
Monks, G D	Sept 3, 1929		1952	1952	1	1	0	3	3	3.00	0	—	—	—	—
© Moorhouse, R	Sept 7, 1866	Jan 7, 1921	1888	1899	206	315	45	5,217	113	19.32	3	1,232	43	28.65	92
§ Morkel, R	Oct 6, 1984		2008	2008	2	2	0	8	8	4.00	0	33	1	33.00	—
Morris, A C	Oct 4, 1976		1995	1997	16	23	2	362	60	17.23	0	508	9	56.44	12
Mosley, H	Mar 8, 1852	Nov 29, 1933	1881	1881	2	4	0	1	8	0.25	0	34	3	11.33	—
Motley, A *	Feb 5, 1858	Sept 28, 1897	1879	1879	2	2	1	10	8*	10.00	0	135	7	19.28	—
© Mounsey, J T	Aug 30, 1871	Apr 6, 1949	1891	1897	92	145	21	1,939	64	15.63	0	444	10	44.40	45
© Moxon, M D	May 4, 1960		1981	1997	277	476	42	18,973	274*	43.71	41	1,213	22	55.13	190
Myers, H	Jan 2, 1875	June 12, 1944	1901	1910	201	289	46	4,450	91	18.31	0	7,095	282	25.15	106
Myers, M	Apr 12, 1847	Dec 8, 1919	1876	1878	22	40	4	537	49	14.91	0	7	0	—	11
§ Naved-ul-Hasan, Rana	Feb 28, 1978		2008	2008	7	10	3	114	22	16.28	0	606	16	37.87	3
Naylor, J E	Dec 11, 1930	June 26, 1996	1953	1953	1	—	—	—	—	—	—	88	0	—	1
© Newstead, J T	Sept 8, 1877	Mar 25, 1952	1903	1913	96	128	17	1,791	100*	16.13	1	5,555	297	18.70	75
© Nicholson, A G	June 25, 1938	Nov 3, 1985	1962	1975	282	267	125	1,667	50	11.73	0	17,296	876	19.74	85
Nicholson, N G	Oct 17, 1963		1988	1989	5	8	3	134	56*	26.80	0	25	0	—	5/1
Oates, William	Jan 2, 1852	Dec 9, 1940	1874	1875	7	13	7	34	14*	5.66	0	—	—	—	—
Oates, W F	June 11, 1929	May 15, 2001	1956	1956	3	3	0	20	9	6.66	0	—	—	—	—
© Old, C M	Dec 22, 1948		1966	1982	222	262	56	4,785	116	23.22	5	13,409	647	20.72	131
Oldham, S	July 26, 1948		1974	1985	59	39	18	212	50	10.09	0	3,849	130	29.60	18

LIST OF PLAYERS AND CAREER AVERAGES IN ALL FIRST-CLASS MATCHES FOR YORKSHIRE (Continued)

Player	Date of Birth	Date of Death (if known)	First Played	Last Played	M	Inns	NO	Runs	HS	Av'ge	100s	Runs	Wkts	Av'ge	Ct/St
Oldroyd, E ©	Oct 1, 1888	Dec 29, 1964	1910	1931	383	509	58	15,891	194	35.23	37	1,658	42	39.47	203
Oyston, C	May 12, 1869	July 15, 1942	1900	1909	15	21	8	96	22	7.38	0	872	31	28.12	3
Padgett, D E V ©	July 20, 1934		1951	1971	487	774	63	20,306	161*	28.55	29	208	6	34.66	250
Padgett, G H	Oct 9, 1931		1952	1952	6	7	4	56	32*	18.66	0	336	4	84.00	5
Padgett, J	Nov 21, 1860	Aug 2, 1943	1882	1889	6	9	0	92	22	10.22	0	—	—	—	2
Parker, B	June 23, 1970		1992	1998	44	71	10	1,839	138*	30.14	2	3	0	—	19
§ Parkin, C H	Feb 18, 1886	June 15, 1943	1906	1906	1	1	0	0	0	0.00	0	25	2	12.50	—
Parratt, J	Mar 24, 1859	May 6, 1905	1888	1890	2	2	0	11	11	5.50	0	75	1	75.00	—
§ Parton, J W	Jan 31, 1863	Jan. 30, 1906	1889	1889	1	2	0	16	14	8.00	0	4	1	4.00	4
Patterson, S A	**Oct. 3, 1983**		**2005**	**2008**	**11**	**12**	**3**	**121**	**46**	**13.44**	**0**	**574**	**15**	**38.26**	**3**
Pearson, H E	Aug 7, 1851	July 8, 1903	1878	1880	4	7	5	31	10*	15.50	0	90	5	18.00	1
Pearson, J H	May 14, 1915		1934	1936	3	3	0	54	44	18.00	0	—	—	—	—
© Peate, E	Mar 2, 1855	Mar 11, 1900	1879	1887	154	226	61	1,793	95	10.86	0	9,986	794	12.57	97
Peel, R	Feb 12, 1857	Aug 12, 1941	1882	1897	318	510	42	9,322	210*	19.91	6	20,638	1,311	15.74	141
Penny, J H	July 29, 1856	July 29, 1902	1891	1891	1	1	1	8	8*	—	0	31	2	15.50	1
Pickles, C S	Jan 30, 1966		1985	1992	58	76	21	1,336	66	24.29	0	3,638	83	43.83	24
Pickles D	Nov 16, 1935		1957	1960	41	40	20	74	12	3.70	0	2,062	96	21.47	10
Pinder, G	July 15, 1841	Jan 15, 1903	1867	1880	125	199	44	1,639	57	10.57	0	325	19	17.10	145/102
© Platt, R K	Dec 26, 1932		1955	1963	96	103	47	405	57*	7.23	0	6,389	282	22.65	35
Pollard, D	June 3, 1835	Mar 26, 1909	1865	1865	1	2	0	3	3	1.50	0	19	0	—	—
Pollitt, D	June 3, 1874	Not known	1899	1899	1	1	0	51	51	51.00	0	—	—	—	1
Prest, C H *	Dec 9, 1841	Mar 4, 1875	1864	1864	2	4	0	57	57	14.25	0	—	—	—	3
© Preston, J M	Aug 23, 1864	Nov 26, 1890	1885	1889	79	134	11	1,935	93	15.73	0	3,232	178	18.15	36
Pride, T	July 23, 1864	Feb 16, 1919	1887	1889	1	1	0	1	1	1.00	0	—	—	—	4/3
Priestley, I M	Sept 25, 1967		1989	1989	2	4	2	25	23	12.50	0	119	4	29.75	—
Pullan, P	Mar 29, 1857	Mar 3, 1901	1884	1884	1	1	0	14	14	14.00	0	5	0	—	—
Pyrah, R M	**Nov 1, 1982**		**2004**	**2008**	**12**	**17**	**1**	**438**	**106**	**27.37**	**1**	**278**	**5**	**55.60**	**6**
§ Radcliffe, E J R H * ©	Jan 27, 1884	Nov 23, 1969	1909	1911	64	89	13	826	54	10.86	0	134	2	67.00	21
Ramage, A	Nov 29, 1957		1979	1983	23	22	9	219	52	16.84	0	1,649	44	37.47	1
Ramsden, G	Mar 2, 1983		2000	2000	1	1	1	0	0*	—	0	68	1	68.00	0

Player	Date of Birth	Date of Death (if known)	First Played	Last Played	M	Inns	NO	Runs	HS	Av'ge	100s	Runs	Wkts	Av'ge	Ct/St
Raper, J R S *	Aug 9, 1909	Mar 9, 1997	1936	1947	3	4	0	24	15	6.00	0	4,093	127	32.22	16
Rashid, A U ......©	Feb 17, 1988		2006	2008	36	51	6	1,421	111	31.57	2	498	21	23.71	2
Rawlin, E R	Oct 4, 1897		1927	1936	8	10	1	72	35	8.00	0	258	11	23.45	13
Rawlin, J T	Nov 10, 1856	Jan 19, 1924	1880	1885	27	36	2	274	31	8.05	0	62	5	12.40	16
Rawlinson, E B ..	Apr 10, 1837	Feb 17, 1892	1867	1875	37	68	5	991	55	15.73	0	—	—	—	—
Redfearn, J	May 13, 1862	Jan 14, 1931	1890	1890	1	1	0	5	5	5.00	0	—	—	—	—
Render, G W A ..	Jan 5, 1887	Sept 17, 1922	1919	1919	1	1	0	5	5	5.00	0	—	—	—	—
Rhodes, A C .....©	Oct 14, 1906	May 21, 1957	1932	1934	61	70	19	917	64*	17.98	0	3,026	107	28.28	45
§ Rhodes, H E * ..	Jan 11, 1852	Sept 10, 1889	1878	1883	10	16	1	269	64	17.93	0	—	—	—	4
Rhodes, S J	June 17, 1964		1981	1984	3	2	1	41	35	41.00	0	—	—	—	3
Rhodes, Wilfred ©	Oct 29, 1877	July 8, 1973	1898	1930	883	1,195	162	31,075	267*	30.08	46	57,634	3,598	16.01	586
Rhodes, William ..	Mar 4, 1883	Aug 5, 1941	1911	1911	1	—	—	—	1*	—	0	40	1	40.00	—
Richardson, J A *	Aug 4, 1908	Apr 2, 1985	1936	1947	7	12	1	308	61	30.80	0	90	2	45.00	3
§ Richardson, R B ©	Jan 12, 1962		1993	1994	7	13	2	310	112	34.47	0	23	1	23.00	18
§ Richardson, S A	Sept 5, 1977		2000	2003	13	23	1	377	69	17.95	0	—	—	—	11
Riley, H	Aug 17, 1875	Nov 6, 1922	1895	1900	4	5	1	36	25*	9.00	0	54	1	54.00	—
Riley, M *	Apr 5, 1851	June 1, 1899	1878	1882	17	28	1	361	92	13.37	0	10	—	—	3
Ringrose, W .....©	Sept 2, 1871	Sept 14, 1943	1901	1906	57	66	9	353	23	6.19	0	3,224	155	20.80	25
Robinson, A L ...	Aug 17, 1946		1971	1977	84	69	31	365	30*	9.60	0	4,927	196	25.13	48
Robinson, Edward *	Dec 27, 1862	Sept 3, 1942	1887	1887	1	2	1	23	23	23.00	0	—	—	—	—
Robinson, Emmott ©	Nov 16, 1883	Nov 17, 1969	1919	1931	413	455	77	9,651	135*	25.53	7	19,645	893	21.99	318
Robinson, E P ....©	Aug 10, 1911	Nov 10, 1998	1934	1949	208	253	46	2,596	75*	12.54	0	15,141	735	20.60	189
Robinson, H	May 12, 1858	Dec 14, 1909	1879	1879	1	2	0	5	4	2.50	0	20	1	20.00	—
Robinson, M A ...©	Nov 23, 1966		1991	1995	90	93	36	240	23	4.21	0	6,866	218	31.49	17
Robinson, P E ....©	Aug 3, 1963		1984	1991	132	217	31	6,668	189	35.84	7	238	1	238.00	96
Robinson, W	Nov 29, 1851	Aug 14, 1919	1876	1880	7	14	1	151	68	11.61	0	—	—	—	3
Roper, E *	Apr 8, 1851	Apr 27, 1921	1878	1877	5	7	1	85	68	14.16	0	—	—	—	2
Rothery, J W ....©	Sept 5, 1877	June 2, 1919	1903	1910	150	236	18	4,614	161	21.16	0	44	2	22.00	45
Rowbotham, J	July 8, 1831	Dec 22, 1899	1861	1876	94	162	9	2,624	113	17.15	0	37	3	12.33	52
§ Rudolph, J A ...©	May 4, 1981		2007	2008	31	46	4	2,370	220	56.42	9	129	1	129.00	43
Rudston, H	Nov 22, 1879	April 14, 1962	1902	1907	21	30	0	609	164	20.30	0	—	—	—	3

LIST OF PLAYERS AND CAREER AVERAGES IN ALL FIRST-CLASS MATCHES FOR YORKSHIRE (Continued)

Player	Date of Birth	Date of Death (if known)	First Played	Last Played	M	Inns	NO	Runs	HS	Av'ge	100s	Runs	Wkts	Av'ge	Ct/St
Ryan, M	©June 23, 1933		1954	1965	150	149	58	682	26*	7.49	0	9,466	413	22.92	59
Ryder, L	Aug 28, 1899	Jan 24, 1955	1924	1924	2	2	1	1	1	1.00	0	151	4	37.75	2
Sanderson, B W	**Jan 3, 1989**		**2008**	**2008**	**2**	**2**	**1**	**6**	**6**	**6.00**	**0**	**140**	**1**	**140.00**	**—**
Savile, G*	Apr 26, 1847	Sept 4, 1904	1867	1874	5	7	0	—	—	—	0	—	—	—	2
Sayers, J J	**©Nov 11, 1983**		**2004**	**2008**	**48**	**78**	**7**	**2,213**	**187**	**31.16**	**6**	**42**	**0**	**—**	**29**
Schofield, C J	Mar 21, 1976		1996	1996	1	1	0	25	25	25.00	0	—	—	—	—
Schofield, D	Oct 9, 1947		1970	1974	3	4	4	13	6*	—	0	112	5	22.40	—
Scott, E	July 6, 1834	Dec 3, 1898	1864	1864	1	1	0	8	8	8.00	0	27	2	13.50	—
Sedgwick, H A	Apr 8, 1883	Dec 28, 1957	1906	1906	3	5	2	53	34	17.66	0	327	16	20.43	1
Sellers, Arthur*	©May 31, 1870	Sept 25, 1941	1890	1899	49	88	1	1,643	105	18.88	2	84	2	42.00	40
Sellers, A B*	©Mar 5, 1907	Feb 20, 1981	1932	1948	334	437	51	8,949	204	23.18	4	653	8	81.62	264
Shackleton, W A	Mar 9, 1908	Nov 16, 1971	1928	1934	8	6	0	49	25	8.16	0	130	6	21.66	3
Shahzad, Ajmal	**July 27, 1985**		**2006**	**2008**	**8**	**9**	**3**	**102**	**35**	**17.00**	**0**	**452**	**12**	**37.66**	**3**
Sharp, K	©Apr. 6, 1959		1976	1990	195	320	35	8,426	181	29.56	11	836	12	69.66	95
§ Sharpe, C M*	Sept 6, 1851	June 25, 1935	1875	1875	1	1	0	15	15	15.00	0	17	0	—	—
Sharpe, P J	Dec 27, 1936		1958	1974	411	666	71	17,685	203*	29.72	23	140	2	70.00	525
Shaw C	Feb 17, 1964		1984	1988	61	58	27	340	31	10.96	0	4,101	123	33.34	9
Shaw, J	Jan 22, 1865	Jan 22, 1921	1896	1897	3	3	0	8	7	2.66	0	181	7	25.85	2
Sheepshanks, E R*	Mar 22, 1910	Dec 31, 1937	1929	1929	1	1	0	26	26	26.00	0	—	—	—	—
Shepherd, D A*	Mar 10, 1916		1938	1938	1	2	0	0	0	0.00	0	26	0	—	—
Shotton, W	Dec 1, 1840	May 26, 1909	1865	1874	4	6	2	13	7	3.25	0	—	—	—	—
Sidebottom, A	Apr 1, 1954		1973	1991	216	249	50	4,243	124*	22.33	0	13,852	558	24.82	60
Sidebottom, R J	©Jan 15, 1978		1997	2003	54	72	23	582	54	11.87	0	4,096	163	25.12	22
Sidgwick, R*	Aug 7, 1851	1934	1882	1882	9	13	0	64	17	4.92	0	—	—	—	—
Silverwood, C E W*	©Mar 3, 1975		1993	2005	131	179	33	2,369	84	16.22	0	11,413	413	27.62	30
Silvester, S	Mar 12, 1951		1976	1977	6	7	4	30	10	10.00	0	313	12	26.08	2
Simpson, E T B*	Mar 5, 1867	Mar 20, 1944	1889	1889	1	2	0	1	1	0.50	0	—	—	—	—
§ Simpson, Rev H M*	Mar 15, 1853	Oct 5, 1885	1875	1877	5	10	1	109	35*	12.11	0	—	—	—	—
Slinn, W	Dec 13, 1826	June 19, 1888	1861	1864	9	14	3	22	11	2.00	0	742	48	15.45	5
Smailes, T F	©Mar 27, 1910	Dec 1, 1970	1932	1948	262	339	42	5,686	117	19.14	3	16,593	802	20.68	153

LIST OF PLAYERS AND CAREER AVERAGES IN ALL FIRST-CLASS MATCHES FOR YORKSHIRE (Continued)

Player	Date of Birth	Date of Death (if known)	First Played	Last Played	M	Inns	NO	Runs	HS	Av'ge	100s	Runs	Wkts	Av'ge	Ct/St
Smales, K	Sept 15, 1927		1948	1950	13	19	3	165	45	10.31	0	766	22	34.81	4
Smith, A F	Mar 7, 1847	Jan 6, 1915	1868	1874	28	49	4	692	89	15.37	0	—	—	—	11
Smith, E (Barnsley)	July 11, 1888	Jan 2, 1972	1914	1926	16	21	5	169	49	10.56	0	1,090	46	23.69	5
Smith, Ernest (Morley) *©	Oct 19, 1869	Feb 9, 1945	1888	1907	154	234	18	4,453	129	20.61	2	6,278	248	25.31	112
Smith, Fred (Idle)	Dec 26, 1885	Not known	1911	1911	1	1	0	11	11	11.00	0	45	2	22.50	—
Smith, Fred (Yeadon)	Dec 18, 1879	Oct 20, 1905	1903	1903	13	19	1	292	55	16.22	0	—	—	—	3
Smith, G	Jan 13, 1876	Jan 16, 1929	1901	1906	2	1	0	7	7	7.00	0	62	0	—	3
Smith, J	Mar 23, 1833	Feb 12, 1909	1865	1865	2	3	0	28	16	9.33	0	72	6	12.00	3
Smith, N	Apr 1, 1949	Mar 4, 2003	1970	1971	8	11	5	82	20	13.66	0	—	—	—	14/3
Smith, R	Apr 6, 1944		1969	1970	5	9	4	99	59	19.80	0	—	—	—	3
Smith, Walker	Aug 14, 1847	July 7, 1900	1874	1874	5	9	0	152	90	16.88	0	—	—	—	8
§ Smith, William	Nov 1, 1839	Apr 19, 1897	1865	1874	11	19	3	260	59	16.25	0	84	1	84.00	21
Smithson, G A ©	Nov 1, 1926	Sept 6, 1970	1946	1950	39	60	5	1,449	169	26.34	2	237	12	19.75	4
Smurthwaite, J	Oct 17, 1916	Oct 20, 1989	1938	1939	7	9	5	29	20*	7.25	0	—	—	—	1
Sowden, A	Dec 1, 1853	July 5, 1921	1878	1887	8	11	0	137	37	12.45	0	22	0	—	—
Squire, D	Dec 31, 1864	Apr 28, 1922	1893	1893	1	2	0	0	0	0.00	0	25	0	—	—
Squires, P J	Aug 4, 1951		1972	1976	49	84	8	1,271	70	16.72	0	32	0	—	14
Stanley, H C *	Feb 16, 1888	May 18, 1934	1911	1913	8	13	0	155	42	11.92	0	—	—	—	6
§ Stanyforth, R T *	May 30, 1892	Feb 21, 1964	1928	1928	3	3	0	26	10	8.66	0	—	—	—	2
Stead, B	June 21, 1939	Apr 15, 1980	1959	1959	2	3	0	8	8	2.66	0	115	7	16.42	—
Stemp, R D	Dec 11, 1967		1993	1998	104	135	36	1,267	67	12.79	0	8,557	241	35.50	49
Stephenson, R D	June 5, 1832	July 5, 1898	1861	1873	36	61	5	803	60	14.33	0	—	—	—	30/27
Stephenson, G B J S *	Nov 10, 1903	Oct 7, 1975	1923	1926	16	19	5	182	60	13.00	0	65	0	—	6
Stevenson, G B ©	Dec 16, 1955		1973	1986	177	217	32	3,856	115*	20.84	2	13,254	464	28.56	73
Stott, W B ©	July 18, 1934		1952	1963	187	309	19	9,168	186	31.61	17	112	7	16.00	89
Stringer, P M	Feb 23, 1943		1967	1969	19	17	8	101	15*	11.22	0	696	32	21.75	7
Stuchbury, S	June 22, 1954		1978	1981	3	3	2	7	4*	7.00	0	236	8	29.50	—
§ Sugg, F H	Jan 11, 1862	May 29, 1933	1883	1883	8	12	4	80	13*	10.00	0	—	—	—	4/1
§ Sugg, J H B *	May 21, 1860	May 21, 1933	1881	1881	1	1	0	9	9	9.00	0	43	0	—	—
Sullivan, J H B ©	Sept 21, 1890	Feb 8, 1932	1912	1912	1	2	0	41	26	20.50	0	—	—	—	—
Sutcliffe, H ©	Nov 24, 1894	Jan 22, 1978	1919	1945	602	864	96	38,558	313	50.20	112	381	8	47.62	402

LIST OF PLAYERS AND CAREER AVERAGES IN ALL FIRST-CLASS MATCHES FOR YORKSHIRE (Continued)

Player	Date of Birth	Date of Death (if known)	First Played	Last Played	M	Inns	NO	Runs	HS	Av'ge	100s	Runs	Wkts	Av'ge	Ct/St
§ Sutcliffe, W H H *	Oct 10, 1926	Sept 16, 1998	1948	1957	177	273	34	6,247	181	26.13	6	152	6	25.33	80
Swallow, I G	Dec 18, 1962		1983	1989	61	82	18	1,296	114	20.25	1	3,270	64	51.09	28
§ Swanepoel, P J	Mar 30, 1977		2003	2003	2	3	0	20	17	6.66	0	129	3	43.00	1
§ Tait, T	Oct 7, 1872	Sept 6, 1954	1898	1899	2	3	1	7	3	3.50	0				
Tasker, J *	Feb 4, 1887	Aug 24, 1975	1912	1913	31	43	4	586	67	15.02	0				14
Tattersall, G *	Apr 21, 1882	June 29, 1972	1905	1905	2	2	0	26	26	13.00	0				
Taylor, C R	Feb 21, 1981		2001	2005	16	27	3	416	52*	17.33	0				8
Taylor, H	Dec 18, 1900	Oct 28, 1988	1924	1925	9	13	0	153	36	11.76	0				1
Taylor, H S	Dec 11, 1856	Nov 16, 1856	1879	1879	3	5	0	36	22	7.20	0				
© Taylor, J	Apr 2, 1850	May 27, 1924	1880	1881	9	13	1	107	44	8.91	0				4
© Taylor, K	Aug 21, 1935		1953	1968	303	505	35	12,864	203*	27.37	16	3,680	129	28.52	146
Taylor, N S	June 2, 1963		1982	1983	6	6	1	10	6	2.00	0	720	22	32.72	2
© Taylor, T L *	May 25, 1878	Mar. 16, 1960	1899	1906	82	122	10	3,933	156	35.11	8				47/2
§ © Tendulkar, S R	Apr 24, 1973		1992	1992	16	25	2	1,070	100	46.52	1	195	4	48.75	10
Thewlis, H	Aug 31, 1865	Nov 30, 1920	1888	1888	2	4	1	4	2*	1.33	0				
Thewlis, John Jun.	Sept 21, 1850	Aug 9, 1901	1879	1879	3	4	0	21	10	5.25	0				21/1
Thewlis, John Sen.	June 30, 1828	Dec 29, 1899	1861	1875	44	80	3	1,280	108	16.62	1	545	16	34.06	2
Thornicroft, N D	Jan 23, 1985		2002	2007	7	10	4	50	30	8.33	0				2
Thornton, A	July 20, 1854	Apr 18, 1915	1881	1881	3	4	0	21	7	5.25	0				
Thornton, G *	Dec 24, 1867	Jan 31, 1939	1891	1891	3	4	0	21	16	5.25	0	74	2	37.00	2
Thorpe, G	Feb 20, 1834	Mar 2, 1899	1864	1864	1	2	1	14	9*	14.00	0				
Threapleton, J W	July 20, 1857	July 30, 1918	1881	1881	1	1		8	8*		0				2
Tinsley, H J	Feb 20, 1865	Dec 10, 1938	1890	1891	9	13	0	56	15	4.30	0	57	4	14.25	1
Townsley, R A J	June 24, 1952		1974	1975	2	4	0	22	12	5.50	0	0	0		2/1
Towse, A D	Apr 22, 1968		1988	1988	1	1	0	1	1	1.00	0	50	3	16.66	1
© Trueman, F S	Feb 6, 1931	July 1, 2006	1949	1968	459	533	81	6,852	104	15.15	3	29,890	1,745	17.12	325
© Tunnicliffe, J	Aug 26, 1866	July 11, 1948	1891	1907	472	768	57	19,435	243	27.33	22	388	7	55.42	665
Turner, A	Sept 2, 1885	Aug 29, 1951	1910	1911	9	16	1	163	37	10.86	0				7
Turner, B	July 25, 1938		1960	1961	2	4	2	7	3*	3.50	0	47	4	11.75	
© Turner, C	Jan 11, 1902	Nov 19, 1968	1925	1946	200	266	32	6,132	130	26.20	2	5,320	173	30.75	181

LIST OF PLAYERS AND CAREER AVERAGES IN ALL FIRST-CLASS MATCHES FOR YORKSHIRE (Continued)

Player	Date of Birth	Date of Death (if known)	First Played	Last Played	M	Inns	NO	Runs	HS	Av'ge	100s	Runs	Wkts	Av'ge	Ct/St
Turner, F I	Sept 3, 1894	Oct 18, 1954	1924	1924	5	7	0	33	12	4.71	0	—	—	—	2
Tyson, C T	Jan 24, 1889	Apr 3, 1940	1921	1921	3	5	2	232	100*	77.33	1	—	—	—	1
Ullathorne, C E	Apr 11, 1845	May 3, 1904	1868	1875	27	46	8	283	28	7.44	0	—	—	—	19
Ulyett, G ◎	Oct 21, 1851	June 18, 1898	1873	1893	355	618	31	14,157	199*	24.11	15	8,181	457	17.90	235
§ Usher, J	Feb 26, 1859	Aug 10, 1905	1888	1888	1	2	0	7	7	3.50	0	31	2	15.50	1
van Geloven, J	Jan 4, 1934	Aug 21, 2003	1955	1955	1	2	1	17	16	17.00	0	224	6	37.33	2
§ Vaughan, M P ◎	Oct 29, 1974		1993	2008	146	260	14	9,013	183	36.63	20	4,268	92	46.39	55
§ Verelst, H W *	July 2, 1846	Apr 5, 1918	1868	1869	3	4	1	66	33*	22.00	0	—	—	—	1
Verity, H ◎	May 18, 1905	July 31, 1943	1930	1939	278	294	77	3,898	101	17.96	1	21,353	1,558	13.70	191
Waddington, A ◎	Feb 4, 1893	Oct 28, 1959	1919	1927	255	250	65	2,396	114	12.95	1	16,201	835	19.40	222
Wade, S ◎	Feb 8, 1858	Nov 5, 1931	1886	1890	65	111	20	1,438	74*	15.80	0	2,498	133	18.78	31
Wainwright, D J ◎	Mar 21, 1985		2004	2008	8	11	3	282	104*	35.25	1	489	17	28.76	5
Wainwright, E	Apr 8, 1865	Oct 28, 1919	1888	1902	352	545	30	11,092	228	21.53	18	17,744	998	17.77	327
Wainwright, W	Jan 21, 1882	Dec 31, 1961	1903	1905	24	36	3	648	62	19.63	0	582	19	30.63	21
Wake, W R *	May 21, 1852	Mar 14, 1896	1881	1881	3	3	0	13	11	4.33	0	—	—	—	2
Walker, A *	June 22, 1844	May 26, 1927	1863	1870	9	16	1	138	26	9.20	0	74	1	74.00	3
Walker, C	June 26, 1919	Dec 3, 1992	1947	1948	9	9	2	268	91	38.28	0	71	2	35.50	1
Walker, T	Apr 3, 1854	Aug 28, 1925	1879	1880	14	22	2	179	30	8.95	0	70	4	17.50	3
Waller, G	Dec 3, 1864	Dec 11, 1937	1893	1894	3	4	0	17	13	4.25	0	17	1	17.00	1
Wallgate, L *	Nov 12, 1849	May 9, 1887	1875	1878	3	3	0	9	6	3.00	0	17	0	—	3
Ward, A	Nov 21, 1865	Jan 6, 1939	1886	1886	4	7	1	41	22	6.83	0	16	0	—	—
Ward, A	Aug 31, 1881	Feb 28, 1940	1903	1903	1	1	0	0	0*	0.00	0	—	—	—	1
Ward, H P *	Jan 20, 1899	Dec 16, 1946	1920	1920	1	1	1	10	10*	—	0	—	—	—	—
Wardall, T A ◎	Apr 19, 1862	Dec 20, 1932	1884	1894	43	73	2	1,003	106	14.12	2	489	23	21.26	25
Wardle, J H ◎	Jan 8, 1923	July 23, 1985	1946	1958	330	418	57	5,765	79	15.96	0	27,917	1,539	18.13	210
Waring, J S ◎	Oct 1, 1942		1963	1966	28	27	15	137	26	11.41	0	1,122	53	21.16	17
Waring, S	Nov 4, 1838	Apr 17, 1919	1870	1870	1	1	0	9	9	9.00	0	—	—	—	—
Washington, W A I ◎	Dec 11, 1879	Oct 20, 1927	1900	1902	44	62	6	1,290	100*	23.03	1	—	—	—	18
Watson, H ◎	Sept 26, 1880	Nov 24, 1951	1908	1914	29	35	6	141	41	5.87	0	—	—	—	46/10
Watson, W ◎	Mar 7, 1920	Apr 24, 2004	1939	1957	283	430	65	13,953	214*	38.22	26	75	0	—	170

LIST OF PLAYERS AND CAREER AVERAGES IN ALL FIRST-CLASS MATCHES FOR YORKSHIRE (Continued)

Player	Date of Birth	Date of Death (if known)	First Played	Last Played	M	Inns	NO	Runs	HS	Av'ge	100s	Runs	Wkts	Av'ge	Ct/St
Waud, B W *	June 4, 1837	May 30, 1889	1862	1864	6	10	1	165	42	18.33	0	—	—	—	2
Webster, C	June 9, 1838	Jan 6, 1881	1861	1868	3	5	1	30	10	7.50	0	—	—	—	1
Webster, H H	May 8, 1844	Mar 5, 1915	1868	1868	2	3	0	10	10	3.33	0	—	—	—	—
§ Weekes, L C	July 19, 1971		1994	2000	2	2	0	20	10	10.00	0	—	—	—	1
West, J	Oct 16, 1844	Jan 27, 1890	1868	1876	38	64	13	461	41	9.03	0	191	10	19.10	14
Wharf, A G	June 4, 1975		1994	1997	7	9	1	186	62	23.25	0	853	53	16.09	4
Whatmough, F J	Dec 4, 1856	June 3, 1904	1878	1882	7	11	1	51	20	5.10	0	454	11	41.27	2
Wheater, C H *	Mar 4, 1860	May 11, 1885	1880	1880	2	4	1	45	27	15.00	0	111	5	22.20	4
White, Sir A W * ©	Oct 14, 1877	Dec 16, 1945	1908	1920	97	128	28	1,457	55	14.57	0	7	0	—	3
White, C ...... ©	Dec 16, 1969		1990	2007	221	350	45	10,376	186	34.01	19	7,649	276	27.71	140
Whitehead, J P	Sept 3, 1925	Aug 15, 2000	1946	1951	37	38	17	245	58*	18.42	0	2,610	96	27.47	11
Whitehead, Lees ©	Mar 14, 1864	Nov 22, 1913	1889	1904	119	172	38	2,073	67*	15.47	0	2,408	99	24.32	68
Whitehead, Luther	June 25, 1869	Jan 16, 1931	1893	1893	2	4	0	21	13	5.25	0	—	—	—	—
Whiteley, J P	Feb 28, 1955		1978	1982	45	38	17	231	20	11.00	0	2,410	70	34.42	21
Whiting, C P	Apr 18, 1888	Jan 14, 1959	1914	1920	6	10	2	92	26	11.50	0	416	15	27.73	2
Whitwell, J F *	Feb 22, 1869	Nov 6, 1932	1890	1890	1	2	0	8	4	4.00	0	11	1	11.00	—
§ Whitwell, W F *	Dec 12, 1867	Apr 12, 1942	1890	1890	10	14	2	67	26	5.58	0	518	25	20.72	2
Widdup, S	Nov 10, 1977		2000	2001	11	18	1	245	44	14.41	0	22	1	22.00	5
Wigley, D H	Oct 26, 1981		2002	2002	1	2	1	19	15	19.00	0	116	1	116.00	1
§ Wilkinson, A J A *	May 28, 1835	Dec 11, 1905	1865	1868	5	6	0	57	53	21.50	0	57	—	—	—
Wilkinson, F	May 23, 1914	Mar 26, 1984	1937	1939	14	14	1	129	18*	5.61	0	590	26	22.69	12
Wilkinson, H * ©	Dec 11, 1877	Apr 15, 1967	1903	1905	48	75	3	1,382	113	19.19	0	121	3	40.33	19
Wilkinson, R	Nov 11, 1977		1998	1998	1	1	0	35	35	35.00	0	—	—	—	1
Wilkinson, W H ©	Mar 12, 1881	June 4, 1961	1903	1910	126	192	14	3,812	103	21.41	1	971	31	31.32	93
Williams, A C	Mar 1, 1887	June 1, 1966	1911	1919	12	14	4	95	48*	23.75	0	678	30	22.60	6
Wilson, B B ©	Dec 11, 1879	Sept 14, 1957	1906	1914	185	308	12	8,053	208	27.50	15	278	2	139.00	53
Wilson, C E M * ©	May 15, 1875	Feb 8, 1944	1896	1899	8	13	3	256	91*	25.60	0	257	12	21.41	3
Wilson, D ©	Aug 7, 1937		1957	1974	392	502	85	5,788	83	13.88	0	22,626	1,104	20.49	235
Wilson, E R * ©	Mar 25, 1879	July 21, 1957	1899	1923	66	72	18	902	104*	16.70	0	3,106	197	15.76	30
Wilson, Geoffrey* ©	Aug 21, 1895	Nov 29, 1960	1919	1924	92	94	14	983	70	12.28	0	11	0	—	33

LIST OF PLAYERS AND CAREER AVERAGES IN ALL FIRST-CLASS MATCHES FOR YORKSHIRE (Continued)

Player	Date of Birth	Date of Death (if known)	First Played	Last Played	M	Inns	NO	Runs	HS	Av'ge	100s	Runs	Wkts	Av'ge	Ct/St
Wilson, G A *	Feb 2, 1916	Sept 24, 2002	1936	1939	15	25	5	352	55*	17.60	0	138	1	138.00	7
Wilson, John *	June 30, 1857	Nov 11, 1931	1887	1888	4	5	1	17	13*	4.25	0	165	12	13.75	5
Wilson, J P *	Apr 3, 1889	Oct 3, 1959	1911	1912	9	14	1	81	36	6.23	0	24	1	24.00	2
Wilson, J V	© Jan 17, 1921		1946	1962	477	724	75	20,548	230	31.66	29	313	3	104.33	520
Wood, A	© Aug 25, 1898	Apr 1, 1973	1927	1946	408	481	80	8,579	123*	21.39	1	33	1	33.00	612/243
Wood, B	Dec 26, 1942		1964	1964	5	7	1	63	35	12.60	0				4
Wood, C H	July 26, 1934	June 28, 2006	1959	1959	4	4	1	29	10	7.33	0	319	11	29.00	1
Wood, G W	Nov 18, 1862	Dec 4, 1948	1895	1895	2	2	0	2	2	1.00	0				0/1
Wood, H *	Mar 22, 1855	July 31, 1941	1879	1880	10	16	1	156	36	10.40	0	212	10	21.20	8
Wood, J H *			1881	1881	2	1	0	14	14	14.00	0				—
Wood, M J	© Apr 6, 1977		1997	2007	128	222	20	6,742	207	33.37	16	27	2	13.50	113
Wood, R	June 3, 1929	May 22, 1990	1952	1956	22	18	4	60	17	4.28	0	1,346	51	26.39	5
Woodford, J D	Sept 9, 1943		1968	1972	38	61	2	1,204	101	20.40	1	185	4	46.25	12
Woodhead, F E *	May 29, 1868	Aug 25, 1943	1893	1894	4	8	0	57	18	7.12	0				5
Woodhouse, W H *	Apr 16, 1856	Mar 4, 1938	1884	1885	9	13	0	218	63	16.76	0				6
Wormald, A	May 10, 1855	Feb 6, 1940	1885	1891	11	11	3	161	80	20.12	0				10/2
Worsley, W A *	© Apr 5, 1890	Dec 4, 1973	1928	1929	60	50	4	722	60	15.69	0				32
Wrathmell, L F	Jan 22, 1855	Sept 16, 1928	1886	1886	1	2	0	18	17	9.00	0				—
Wright, R	July 19, 1852	May 25, 1891	1877	1877	2	4	1	28	22	9.33	0				—
Wright, T J *	Mar 5, 1900	Not known	1919	1919	1	1	0	12	12	12.00	0				—
Yardley, N W D *	© Mar 19, 1915	Oct 4, 1989	1936	1955	302	420	56	11,632	183*	31.95	17	5,818	195	29.83	220
Yeadon, W	Dec 10, 1861	May 30, 1914	1888	1888	3	6	2	41	22	10.25	0				5/3
§ Younus Khan	Nov 29, 1977		2007	2007	13	19	2	824	217*	48.47	3	342	8	42.75	11
§ Yuvraj Singh	Dec 12, 1981		2003	2003	7	12	2	145	56	14.50	0	130	3	43.33	12

378

In the career averages it should be noted that the bowling analysis for the second Cambridgeshire innings at Ashton-under-Lyne in 1865 has not been found. G R Atkinson took 3 wickets, W Cuttell 2, G Freeman 4 and R Iddison 1. The respective bowling averages have been calculated excluding these wickets.

MOST APPEARANCES FOR YORKSHIRE

Matches	Player	Matches	Player
883	W Rhodes (1898-1930)	477	J V Wilson (1946-1962)
717	G H Hirst (1891-1929)	472	J Tunnicliffe (1891-1907)
676	D Denton (1894-1920)	459	F S Trueman (1949-1968)
602	H Sutcliffe (1919-1945)	456	J H Hampshire (1961-1981)
548	M Leyland (1920-1947)	445	G G Macaulay (1920-1935)
536	D B Close (1949-1970)	429	D L Bairstow (1970-1990)
517	D Hunter (1888-1909)	427	A Dolphin (1905-1927)
513	S Haigh (1895-1913)	425	P Carrick (1970-1993)
510	Lord Hawke (1881-1911)	414	G Boycott (1962-1986)
496	R Illingworth (1951-1983)	413	E. Robinson (1919-1931)
491	J G Binks (1955-1969) †	411	P J Sharpe (1958-1974)
487	D E V Padgett (1951-1971)	408	A Wood (1927-1946)
485	P Holmes (1913-1933)	401	A Mitchell (1922-1945)

† Kept wicket in 412 consecutive Championship matches 1955-1969

SUMMARY OF RESULTS BY SEASON

Season	Played	Won	Lost	Drawn	Abandoned	Position in Championship
1959	10	4	1	5		7th
1960	10	1	3	6		14th
1961	9	2	2	5	1	11th
1975	14	4	0	10		4th
1976	14	5	5	4		5th
1977	16	9	0	7		1st
1978	15	5	2	8	1	4th
1979	16	5	0	11		3rd
1980	14	5	2	7	1	5th
1981	16	2	3	11		11th
1982	16	2	3	11		14th
1983	11	5	1	5	3	2nd
1984	15	9	3	3		1st
1985	14	3	3	8	1	12th
1986	16	5	1	10		5th
1987	15	5	2	8	1	1st
1988	16	4	1	11		9th
1989	17	2	3	12		9th
1990	16	1	6	9		17th
1991	16	8	1	7		1st
1992	17	5	2	10		5th
1993	17	6	1	10		3rd
1994	17	6	2	9		2nd
1995	17	7	1	9		5th
1996	17	6	3	8		4th
1997	16	8	5	3	1	2nd
1998	15	4	2	9		9th
1999	16	3	8	5	1	14th
2000	14	5	2	7	1	5th
2001	12	8	2	2	1	2nd
2002	12	5	1	6		3rd
2003	10	7	1	2		1st
2004	7	2	0	5	1	8th
2005	12	2	4	6		10th
2006	14	6	4	4		3rd
2007	12	4	5	3		10th
2008	12	4	4	4	2	5th
Totals	523	174	89	260	15	

ANALYSIS OF RESULTS VERSUS EACH COUNTY

County	Played	Won	Lost	Drawn	Abandoned	First Played
Derbyshire	49	11	8	30	2	1959
Durham	23	8	3	12	2	1992
Essex	13	9	2	2		1990
Glamorgan	36	10	3	23	2	1975
Gloucestershire	10	3	3	4		1990
Hampshire	12	4	1	7		1990
Kent	26	5	4	17	1	1981
Lancashire	60	14	15	31	3	1959
Leicestershire	23	9	4	10		1975
MCC Young Cricketers	1	1	0	0		2005
Middlesex	18	7	2	9		1977
Northamptonshire	44	13	5	26	1	1959
Nottinghamshire	51	17	9	25	2	1959
Scotland	2	1	0	1		2007
Somerset	18	9	3	6		1988
Surrey	36	9	9	18	2	1976
Sussex	16	6	5	5		1990
Warwickshire	53	20	10	23		1959
Worcestershire	32	18	3	11		1961
Totals	523	174	89	260	15	

Note: Matches abandoned are not included in the total played.

Highest Total

By Yorkshire: 538 for 9 wkts dec v. Worcestershire at Stamford Bridge, 2007
Against Yorkshire: 567 for 7 wkts dec by Middlesex at RAF Uxbridge, 2000

Lowest Total

By Yorkshire: 69 v. Lancashire at Heywood, 1983
Against Yorkshire: 36 by Lancashire at Elland, 1979

Highest Individual Score

For Yorkshire: 273* by R J Blakey v. Northamptonshire at Northampton, 1986
Against Yorkshire: 235 by O A Shah for Middlesex at Leeds, 1999

Century in Each Innings

For Yorkshire:	C White	209* and 115* v. Worcestershire at Worcester, 1990
	K Sharp	150* and 127 v. Essex at Elland, 1991
	A A Metcalfe	109 and 136* v. Somerset at North Perrott, 1994
	R A Kettleborough	123 and 192* v. Nottinghamshire at Todmorden, 1996
	C R Taylor	201* and 129 v. Sussex at Hove, 2005
	A W Gale	131 and 123 v. Somerset at Taunton, 2006
	J J Sayers	157 and 105 v. Lancashire at Leeds, 2007
Against Yorkshire:	N Nannan	100 and 102* for Nottinghamshire at Harrogate, 1979
	G D Lloyd	134 and 103 for Lancashire at Scarborough, 1989
	A J Swann	131 and 100 for Northamptonshire at York, 1998
	G J Kennis	114 and 114 for Somerset at Taunton, 1999

Best Bowling in an Innings

For Yorkshire: 9 for 27 by G A Cope v. Northamptonshire at Northampton, 1979
Against Yorkshire: 8 for 15 by I Folley for Lancashire at Heywood, 1983

Best Bowling in a Match

For Yorkshire: 13 for 92 (6 for 48 and 7 for 44) by M K Bore v. Lancashire at Harrogate, 1976
Against Yorkshire: 13 for 100 (7 for 45 and 6 for 55) by N J Perry for Glamorgan at Cardiff, 1978

Totals of 450 and over

By Yorkshire (25)

Score	Versus	Ground	Season
538 for 9 wkts dec	Worcestershire	Stamford Bridge	2007
534 for 5 wkts dec	Lancashire	Stamford Bridge	2003
530 for 8 wkts dec	Nottinghamshire	Middlesbrough	2000
514 for 3 wkts dec	Somerset	Taunton	1988
509 for 4 wkts dec	Northamptonshire	Northampton	1986
502	Derbyshire	Chesterfield	2003
497	Derbyshire	Chesterfield	2005
495 for 5 wkts dec	Somerset	Taunton	2006
488 for 8 wkts dec	Warwickshire	Harrogate	1984
486 for 6 wkts dec	Glamorgan	Leeds	1986
476 for 3 wkts dec	Glamorgan	Gorseinon	1984
475 for 9 wkts dec	Nottinghamshire	Nottingham	1995
474 for 3 wkts dec	Glamorgan	Todmorden	2003
470	Lancashire	Leeds	2006
474	Durham	Stamford Bridge	2003
469	Warwickshire	Castleford	1999
462	Scotland	Stamford Bridge	2007
461 for 8 wkts dec	Essex	Stamford Bridge	2006
459 for 3 wkts dec	Leicestershire	Oakham	1997
459 for 6 wkts dec	Glamorgan	Bradford	1992
457 for 9 wkts dec	Kent	Canterbury	1983
456 for 6 wkts dec	Nottinghamshire	York	1986
456 for 5 wkts dec	Gloucestershire	Todmorden	1990
454 for 9 wkts dec	Derbyshire	Chesterfield	1959
452 for 9 wkts dec	Glamorgan	Cardiff	2005

Against Yorkshire (12)

Score	For	Ground	Season
567 for 7 wkts dec	Middlesex	RAF Uxbridge	2000
555 for 7 wkts dec	Derbyshire	Stamford Bridge	2002
525 for 7 wkts dec	Sussex	Hove	2005
498 for 8 wkts dec	Leicestershire	Bingley	1994
493 for 8 wkts dec	Nottinghamshire	Boot's Ground, Nottingham	2002
488 for 8 wkts dec	Warwickshire	Castleford	1999
486	Essex	Chelmsford	2000
485	Gloucestershire	North Park, Cheltenham	2001
477	Lancashire	Leeds	2006
458	Lancashire	Bradford	1997
454 for 7 wkts dec	Lancashire	Todmorden	1993
450 for 7 wkts (inns closed)	Derbyshire	Bradford	1980

Completed Innings under 75

By Yorkshire (3)

Score	Versus	Ground	Season
69	Lancashire	Heywood	1983
74	Derbyshire	Chesterfield	1960
74	Nottinghamshire	Bradford	1998

Against Yorkshire (10)

Score	By	Ground	Season
36	Lancashire	Elland	1979
49	Leicestershire	Leicester	2008
50	Lancashire	Liverpool	1984
60	Derbyshire	Bradford	1977
60	Surrey	Sunbury-on-Thames	1977
62	MCC	High Wycombe	2005
64	Nottinghamshire	Brodsworth	1959
66	Leicestershire	Lutterworth	1977
72	Sussex	Horsham	2003
74	Worcestershire	Barnsley	1978

Individual Scores of 150 and over (54)

Score	Player	Versus	Ground	Season
273*	R J Blakey	Northamptonshire	Northampton	1986
238*	K Sharp	Somerset	Taunton	1988
233	P E Robinson	Kent	Canterbury	1983
221*	K Sharp	Gloucestershire	Todmorden	1990
219	G M Hamilton	Derbyshire	Chesterfield	2003
218*	A McGrath	Surrey	Elland	1994
209*	C White	Worcestershire	Worcester	1990
205	C R Taylor	Glamorgan	Todmorden	2003
204	B Parker	Gloucestershire	Bristol	1993
203	A McGrath	Durham	Leeds	2005
202	M J Wood	Essex	Stamford Bridge	2006
201*	C R Taylor	Sussex	Hove	2005
200*	D Byas	Worcestershire	Worcester	1992
192*	R A Kettleborough	Nottinghamshire	Todmorden	1996
191	P E Robinson	Warwickshire	Harrogate	1984
191	M J Wood	Derbyshire	Rotherham	2000
191	M J Lumb	Nottinghamshire	Middlesbrough	2000
189*	C S Pickles	Gloucestershire	Bristol	1991
184	J D Love	Worcestershire	Leeds	1976
183	A W Gale	Durham	Stamford Bridge	2006
174	G L Brophy	Worcestershire	Stamford Bridge	2007
173	S N Hartley	Warwickshire	Birmingham	1980
173	B Parker	Sussex	Hove	1996
173	A A Metcalfe	Glamorgan	Gorseinon	1984
173	R A Kettleborough	Leicestershire	Oakham	1997
172	A C Morris	Lancashire	York	1995
170*	R A J Townsley	Glamorgan	Harrogate	1975

Individual Scores of 150 and over *(Continued)*

168	M J Wood	Leicestershire	Oakham	1997
166	A A Metcalfe	Lancashire	York	1984
166	C A Chapman	Northamptonshire	York	1998
165*	A Lyth	Durham	Stamford Bridge	2006
165	J J Sayers	Sussex	Hove	2006
164*	A W Gale	Leicestershire	Harrogate	2002
164	J C Balderstone	Nottinghamshire	Harrogate	1960
163	A A Metcalfe	Derbyshire	Chesterfield	1992
162*	D Byas	Surrey	Scarborough	1987
160	A A Metcalfe	Somerset	Bradford	1993
155	S M Guy	Derbyshire	Chesterfield	2005
157	J J Sayers	Lancashire	Leeds	2007
153*	A A Metcalfe	Warwickshire	Bingley	1995
153	C White	Worcestershire	Marske-by-the-Sea	1991
153	R A Stead	Surrey	Todmorden	2002
152	A A Metcalfe	Gloucestershire	Bristol	1993
151*	S J Foster	Kent	Elland	1992
151*	J J Sayers	Durham	Stamford Bridge	2004
151	P J Hartley	Somerset	Clevedon	1989
151	A McGrath	Somerset	Elland	1995
151	V J Craven	Glamorgan	Todmorden	2003
150*	K Sharp	Essex	Elland	1991
150*	G M Fellows	Hampshire	Todmorden	1998
150*	S M Guy	Nottinghamshire	Leeds	2005
150	K Sharp	Glamorgan	Ebbw Vale	1983
150	S N Hartley	Nottinghamshire	Worksop	1988
150	C R Taylor	Derbyshire	Chesterfield	2003

7 Wickets in an Innings (30)

Analysis	Player	Versus	Ground	Season
9 for 27	G A Cope	Northamptonshire	Northampton	1977
9 for 62	M K Bore	Warwicshire	Scarborough	1976
8 for 53	S J Dennis	Nottinghamshire	Nottingham	1983
8 for 57	M K Bore	Lancashire	Manchester	1977
8 for 79	P J Berry	Derbyshire	Harrogate	1991
7 for 13	P Carrick	Northamptonshire	Marske-by-the-Sea	1977
7 for 21	S Silvester	Surrey	Sunbury-on-Thames	1977
7 for 22	J A R Blain	Surrey	Purley	2004
7 for 32	P W Jarvis	Surrey	The Oval	1984
7 for 34	P Carrick	Glamorgan	Leeds	1986
7 for 37	P M Hutchison	Warwickshire	Coventry	2001
7 for 39	G M Hamilton	Sussex	Leeds	1995
7 for 40	M K Bore	Worcestershire	Old Hill	1976
7 for 44	M K Bore	Lancashire	Harrogate	1976
7 for 44	J P Whiteley	Worcestershire	Leeds	1979
7 for 51	J D Middlebrook	Derbyshire	Rotherham	2000
7 for 53	J P Whiteley	Warwickshire	Birmingham	1980
7 for 55	C White	Leicestershire	Bradford	1990

7 Wickets in an Innings *(Continued)*

7 for 58	K Gillhouley	Derbyshire	Chesterfield	1960
7 for 58	P J Hartley	Lancashire	Leeds	1985
7 for 63	M J Hoggard	Worcestershire	Harrogate	1998
7 for 65	M K Bore	Nottinghamshire	Steetley	1976
7 for 70	J D Batty	Leicestershire	Bradford	1992
7 for 71	J D Batty	Hampshire	Harrogate	1994
7 for 81	K Gillhouley	Lancashire	Scarborough	1960
7 for 84	I J Houseman	Kent	Canterbury	1989
7 for 88	I G Swallow	Nottinghamshire	Nottingham	1983
7 for 90	A P Grayson	Kent	Folkestone	1991
7 for 93	D Pickles	Nottinghamshire	Nottingham	1960
7 for 94	K Gillhouley	Northamptonshire	Redcar	1960

12 Wickets in a Match (6)

Analysis	Player	Versus	Ground	Season
13 for 92 (6 for 48 and 7 for 44)	M K Bore	Lancashire	Harrogate	1976
13 for 110 (7 for 70 and 6 for 40)	J D Batty	Leicestershire	Bradford	1992
13 for 111 (4 for 49 and 9 for 62)	M K Bore	Warwickshire	Scarborough	1976
12 for 69 (5 for 32 and 7 for 37)	P M Hutchison	Warwickshire	Coventry	2001
12 for 120 (5 for 39 and 7 for 81)	K Gillhouley	Lancashire	Scarborough	1960
12 for 163 (5 for 78 and 7 for 84)	I J Houseman	Kent	Canterbury	1989

Hat-tricks (4)

Player	Versus	Ground	Season
I G Swallow	Warwickshire	Harrogate	1984
S D Fletcher	Nottinghamshire	Marske-by-the-Sea	1987
I G Swallow	Derbyshire	Chesterfield	1988
M Broadhurst	Essex	Southend-on-Sea	1992

FRIENDS PROVIDENT TROPHY, CHELTENHAM & GLOUCESTER TROPHY, GILLETTE CUP AND NATWEST TROPHY 1963-2008

WINNERS 1965, 1969 AND 2002
SEMI-FINALISTS 1980, 1982, 1995, 1996, 1999, 2004, 2005 AND 2008

Played 129, Won 73 (in Yorkshire 34, Away 39). Lost 50 (in Yorkshire 19, Away 31). No Result 6.

Highest Score:	By Yorkshire:	411:6 v. Devon at Exmouth, 2004
	Against Yorkshire:	339:7 by Northamptonshire at Northampton, 2006
†Lowest Score:	By Yorkshire:	76 v. Surrey at Harrogate, 1970
	Against Yorkshire:	53 by Ireland at Leeds, 1997

| **Highest Individual Score:** | For Yorkshire: | 160 M J Wood v. Devon at Exmouth, 2004 |
| | Against Yorkshire: | 161 D J G Sales for Northamptonshire at Northampton, 2006 |

Highest Partnerships: For Yorkshire:

1st wkt	242*	M D Moxon (107*) and A A Metcalfe (127*) v. Warwickshire at Leeds, 1990
2nd wkt	202	G Boycott (87) and C W J Athey (115) v. Kent at Leeds, 1980
3rd wkt	164	A McGrath (105*) and J A Rudolph (82) v. Scotland at Leeds, 2008
4th wkt	207	S A Kellett (107) and C White (113) v. Ireland at Leeds, 1995
5th wkt	160*	C White (73*) and G M Fellows (80*) v. Surrey at Leeds, 2001
6th wkt	128*	A McGrath (72*) and G M Fellows (68*) v. Essex at Chelmsford, 2002
7th wkt	102	D L Bairstow (92) and C M Old (55*) v. Worcestershire at Leeds, 1982
8th wkt	79	P J Hartley (83) and D Gough (46) v. Ireland at Leeds, 1997
9th wkt	66	T T Bresnan (55) and A Shahzad (33) v. Durham at Chester-le-Street, 2008
10th wkt	29*	R Illingworth (32*) and A G Nicholson (15*) v. Warwickshire at Birmingham, 1968

| **Best Bowling:** | For Yorkshire: | 7 for 27 D Gough v. Ireland at Leeds, 1997 |
| | Against Yorkshire: | 7 for 33 R D Jackman for Surrey at Harrogate, 1970 |

| **Most Economical Bowling:** | For Yorkshire: | 12-9-4-1 D Wilson v. Norfolk at Lakenham, 1969 |
| | Against Yorkshire: | 12-6-10-0 D L Underwood for Kent at Canterbury, 1981 |

| **Most Expensive Bowling:** | For Yorkshire: | 10-0-82-3 T T Bresnan v. Northamptonshire at Northampton, 2006 |
| | Against Yorkshire: | 12-1-96-0 M E Waugh for Essex at Chelmsford, 1995 |

†Lowest score is either the lowest all-out score or the lowest score at completion of 60 overs (65 overs in 1963. 50 overs from 1999)

Centuries (22)

C W J Athey		115 v. Kent at Leeds, 1980
G Boycott		146 v. Surrey at Lord's, 1965
M T G Elliott		128* v. Somerset at Lord's, 2002
J H Hampshire		110 v. Durham at Middlesbrough, 1978
S A Kellett		107 v. Ireland at Leeds, 1995
D S Lehmann (2)		105 v. Glamorgan at Cardiff, 1997
		118* v. Northamptonshire at Northampton, 2006
A McGrath (3)		135* v. Lancashire at Manchester, 2007
		100 v. Durham at Leeds, 2007
		105* v. Scotland at Leeds, 2008
A A Metcalfe		127* v. Warwickshire at Leeds, 1990
M D Moxon (2)		107* v. Warwickshire at Leeds, 1990
		137 v. Nottinghamshire at Leeds, 1996
J A Rudolph		100 v. Leicestershire at Leeds, 2007
M P Vaughan		116* v. Lancashire at Manchester, 2004
C White (4)		113 v. Ireland at Leeds, 1995
		100* v. Surrey at Leeds, 2002
		112 v. Northamptonshire at Northampton, 2006
		101* v. Durham at Chester-le-Street, 2006
M J Wood (2)		118* v. Cambridgeshire at March, 2003
		160 v. Devon at Exmouth, 2004
Younus Khan		100 v. Nottinghamshire at Nottingham, 2007

5 Wickets in an Innings (8)

D Gough (2)	7 for 27 v. Ireland at Leeds, 1997	
	5 for 30 v. Yorkshire CB at Harrogate, 2000	
P J Hartley	5 for 46 v. Hampshire at Southampton, 1990	
M J Hoggard	5 for 65 v. Somerset at Lord's, 2002	
R Illingworth	5 for 29 v. Surrey at Lord's, 1965	
A Sidebottom	5 for 27 v. Glamorgan at Leeds, 1987	
G B Stevenson	5 for 27 v. Berkshire at Reading, 1983	
F S Trueman	6 for 15 v. So.merset at Taunton, 1965	

Man of the Match Awards

M D Moxon	5
J H Hampshire	4
C White	4
M P Vaughan	3
C W J Athey	2
M G Bevan	2
G Boycott	2
D Gough	2
A A Metcalfe	2
P J Sharpe	2
A McGrath	2
C E W Silverwood	2
M J Wood	2

D L Bairstow, T T Bresnan, P Carrick, D B Close, M T G Elliott, G M Fellows, S D Fletcher, P J Hartley, P M Hutchison, R Illingworth, S A Kellett, B Leadbeater, D S Lehmann, M J Lumb, A Sidebottom, G B Stevenson, F S Trueman (1 each). (51 Awards: 30 Players).

versus Derbyshire: Played 5, Won 3 (in Yorkshire 2, at Lord's 1), Lost 1 (in Yorkshire), No result 1

Highest Score:	By Yorkshire	253:4	at Derby, 2007
	By Derbyshire	251:6	at Leeds, 2006
Lowest Score:	By Yorkshire	219:8	at Lord's, 1969
	By Derbyshire	94	at Leeds, 2008
Highest Individual Score:	For Yorkshire	81	J A Rudolph at Derby, 2007
	For Derbyshire	100	C R Taylor at Leeds, 2006
Best Bowling:	For Yorkshire	3 for 16	A McGrath at Leeds, 2008
	For Derbyshire	3 for 31	A Ward at Lord's, 1969

versus Durham: Played 7, Won 3 (in Yorkshire 2, Away 1), Lost 4 (in Yorkshire 2, Away 2)

Highest Score:	By Yorkshire	249:6	at Middlesbrough, 1978
	By Durham	266:8	at Leeds, 2007
Lowest Score:	By Yorkshire	135	at Harrogate, 1973
	By Durham	185	at Leeds, 2008
Highest Individual Score:	For Yorkshire	110	J H Hampshire at Middlesbrough, 1978
	For Durham	124*	J P Maher at Chester-le-Street, 2006
Best Bowling:	For Yorkshire	4 for 9	C M Old at Middlesbrough, 1978
	For Durham	5 for 15	B R Lander at Harrogate, 1973

versus Essex: Played 4, Won 3 (in Yorkshire 1, Away 2), Lost 1 (Away)

Highest Score:	By Yorkshire	307:3	at Chelmsford, 1995
	By Essex	285:8	at Chelmsford, 2008
Lowest Score:	By Yorkshire	198	at Chelmsford, 2008
	By Essex	132	at Leeds, 1982
Highest Individual Score:	For Yorkshire	92	S A Kellett at Chelmsford, 1995
	For Essex	94	A N Cook at Chelmsford, 2008
Best Bowling:	For Yorkshire	3 for 21	A Sidebottom at Leeds, 1982
	For Essex:	3 for 30	R N ten Doeschate at Chelmsford, 2008

versus Glamorgan: Played 2, Won 1 (in Yorkshire), Lost 1 (Away)

Highest Score:	By Yorkshire	236:8	at Cardiff, 1997
	By Glamorgan	237:9	at Cardiff, 1997
Lowest Score:	By Yorkshire	—	
	By Glamorgan	83	at Leeds, 1987

Highest Individual

Score:	For Yorkshire	105	D S Lehmann at Cardiff, 1997
	For Glamorgan	62	M P Maynard at Cardiff, 1997
Best Bowling:	For Yorkshire	5 for 27	A Sidebottom at Leeds, 1987
	For Glamorgan	3 for 26	D A Cosker at Cardiff, 1997

versus Gloucestershire: Played 5, Won 2 (Away 2), Lost 3 (in Yorkshire 1, Away 2)

Highest Score:	By Yorkshire	243:6	at Bristol, 2004
		243:8	at Bristol, 1993
	By Gloucestershire	247:5	at Bristol, 2004
Lowest Score:	By Yorkshire	232:9	at Leeds, 1976
	By Gloucestershire	201	at Bristol, 2008

Highest Individual

Score:	For Yorkshire	90	R B Richardson at Bristol, 1993
	For Gloucestershire	143*	C M Spearman at Bristol, 2004
Best Bowling:	For Yorkshire	4 for 31	T T Bresnan at Bristol, 2008
	For Gloucestershire	4 for 21	M J Procter at Leeds, 1976

versus Hampshire: Played 5, Won 2 (in Yorkshire 1, Away 1), Lost 3 (in Yorkshire 0, Away 3)

Highest Score:	By Yorkshire	233:6	at Bradford, 1974
	By Hampshire	261	at Bournemouth, 1977
Lowest Score:	By Yorkshire	118	at Southampton, 1990
	By Hampshire	192	at Bradford, 1974

Highest Individual

Score:	For Yorkshire	93*	C W J Athey at Southampton, 1980
	For Hampshire	100	S M Ervine at Southampton, 2005
Best Bowling:	For Yorkshire	5 for 46	P J Hartley at Southampton, 1990
	For Hampshire	5 for 35	J M Rice at Bournemouth, 1977

versus Kent: Played 3, Won 1 (in Yorkshire 1, Away 0), Lost 2 (in Yorkshire 0, Away 2)

Highest Score:	By Yorkshire	279:6	at Leeds, 1980
	By Kent	233	at Leeds, 1980
Lowest Score:	By Yorkshire	148	at Canterbury, 1971
	By Kent	233	at Leeds, 1980

Highest Individual

Score:	For Yorkshire	115	C W J Athey at Leeds, 1980
	For Kent	118*	C J Tavaré at Canterbury, 1981
Best Bowling:	For Yorkshire	4 for 35	A Sidebottom at Leeds, 1980
	For Kent	5 for 25	B D Julien at Canterbury, 1971

versus Lancashire: Played 12, Won 5 (in Yorkshire 2, Away 3), Lost 6 (in Yorkshire 1 Away 5), No result 1

Highest Score:	By Yorkshire	292:4	at Leeds, 2006
	By Lancashire	293:9	at Manchester, 1996
Lowest Score:	By Yorkshire	173	at Leeds, 1974
	By Lancashire	169	at Leeds, 1995

Highest Individual

Score:	For Yorkshire	135*	A McGrath at Manchester, 2007
	For Lancashire	141*	B J Hodge at Manchester, 2007
Best Bowling:	For Yorkshire	4 for 18	G S Blewett at Manchester, 1999
	For Lancashire	4 for 17	P Lever at Leeds, 1974

versus Leicestershire: Played 7, Won 3 (in Yorkshire 1, Away 2), Lost 4 (in Yorkshire 3, Away 1)

Highest Score:	By Yorkshire	310:5	at Leicester, 1997
	By Leicestershire	284:4	at Leeds, 2007
Lowest Score:	By Yorkshire	109	at Leeds, 1975
	By Leicestershire	168	at Leicester, 1965
Highest Individual			
Score:	For Yorkshire	100	J A Rudolph at Leeds, 2007
	For Leicestershire	90	I J Sutcliffe at Leicester, 1997
Best Bowling:	For Yorkshire	4 for 18 H P Cooper at Leeds, 1975
	For Leicestershire	5 for 34 P A J DeFreitas at Leeds, 1987

versus Middlesex: Played 5, Won 2 (in Yorkshire 2, Away 0), Lost 3 (in Yorkshire 1, Away 2)

Highest Score:	By Yorkshire	205:9	at Leeds, 1986
	By Middlesex	225:7	at Leeds, 1988
Lowest Score:	By Yorkshire	90	at Lord's, 1964
	By Middlesex	151	at Lord's, 1964
Highest Individual			
Score:	For Yorkshire	73*	D Byas at Leeds, 1996
	For Middlesex	104	P N Weekes at Leeds, 1996
Best Bowling:	For Yorkshire	4 for 29 H P Cooper at Lord's, 1979 and C Shaw at Leeds, 1988
	For Middlesex	4 for 24 N G Cowans at Leeds, 1986

versus Northamptonshire: Played 8, Won 4 (in Yorkshire 2, Away 2), Lost 4 (in Yorkshire 2, Away 2)

Highest Score:	By Yorkshire	341:3	at Northampton, 2006
	By Northamptonshire	339:7	at Northampton, 2006
Lowest Score:	By Yorkshire	165	at Leeds, 1983
	By Northamptonshire	211:7	at Leeds, 1983
Highest Individual			
Score:	For Yorkshire	118*	D S Lehmann at Northampton, 2006
	For Northamptonshire	161	D J G Sales at Northampton, 2006
Best Bowling:	For Yorkshire	4 for 36 D Gough at Northampton, 2000
	For Northamptonshire	5 for 33 B J Griffiths at Leeds, 1983

versus Nottinghamshire: Played 6, Won 5 (in Yorkshire 4, Away 1), Lost 0, No Result 1 (in Yorkshire)

Highest Score:	By Yorkshire	345:5	at Leeds, 1996
	By Nottinghamshire	243	at Nottingham, 2007
Lowest Score:	By Yorkshire	191	at Scarborough, 1969
	By Nottinghamshire	123	at Scarborough, 1969
Highest Individual			
Score:	For Yorkshire	137	M D Moxon at Leeds, 1996
	For Nottinghamshire	100*	J B Bolus at Middlesbrough, 1963
Best Bowling:	For Yorkshire	4 for 30 F S Trueman at Middlesbrough, 1963
	For Nottinghamshire	4 for 33 K Gilhouley at Middlesbrough, 1963

versus Somerset: Played 5, Won 2 (in Yorkshire 0, Away 2), Lost 3 (in Yorkshire 2, Away 1)

Highest Score:	By Yorkshire	260:4	at Lord's, 2002
	By Somerset	256:8	at Lord's, 2002
Lowest Score:	By Yorkshire	150	at Taunton, 1966
	By Somerset	63	at Taunton, 1965
Highest Individual			
Score:	For Yorkshire	128*	M T G Elliott at Lord's, 2002
	For Somerset	87*	I V A Richards at Leeds, 1985
Best Bowling:	For Yorkshire	6 for 15 F S Trueman at Taunton, 1965
	For Somerset	4 for 33 R Palmer at Taunton, 1966

versus Surrey: Played 7, Won 4 (in Yorkshire 2, Away 2), Lost 3 (in Yorkshire 1, Away 2)

Highest Score:	By Yorkshire	317:4	at Lord's, 1965
	By Surrey	256:4	at The Oval, 1989
Lowest Score:	By Yorkshire	76	at Harrogate, 1970
	By Surrey	134	at The Oval, 1969 and 134:8 at Harrogate, 1970

Highest Individual
Score:	For Yorkshire	146	G Boycott at Lord's, 1965
	For Surrey	135*	D J Bicknell at The Oval, 1989
Best Bowling:	For Yorkshire	5 for 29 R Illingworth at Lord's, 1965
	For Surrey	7 for 33 R D Jackman at Harrogate, 1970

versus Sussex: Played 4, Won 1, (in Yorkshire 0, Away 1), Lost 3 (in Yorkshire 2, Away 1)

Highest Score:	By Yorkshire	270	at Hove, 1963
	By Sussex	292	at Hove, 1963
Lowest Score:	By Yorkshire	125	at Leeds, 1986
	By Sussex	212:9	at Hove, 1996

Highest Individual
Score:	For Yorkshire	76	M D Moxon at Hove, 1996
	For Sussex	90	J M Parks at Hove, 1963
Best Bowling:	For Yorkshire	4 for 60 D B Close at Hove, 1963
	For Sussex	4 for 17 G S Le Roux at Leeds, 1986

versus Warwickshire: Played 10, Won 2 (in Yorkshire 1, Away 1), Lost 6 (in Yorkshire 3, Away 3), No Result 2 (in Yorkshire 1, Away 1)

Highest Score:	By Yorkshire	242:0	at Leeds, 1990
	By Warwickshire	245	at Leeds, 1993
Lowest Score:	By Yorkshire	123	at Birmingham, 1991
	By Warwickshire	157	at Birmingham, 1965

Highest Individual
Score:	For Yorkshire	127*	A A Metcalfe at Leeds, 1990
	For Warwickshire	113	K D Smith at Birmingham, 1982
Best Bowling:	For Yorkshire	3 for 26 P Carrick at Leeds, 1990
	For Warwickshire	4 for 16 A A Donald at Birmingham, 1991

versus Worcestershire: Played 4, Won 2 (in Yorkshire), Lost 1 (Away), No Result 1 (in Yorkshire)

Highest Score:	By Yorkshire	290:7	at Leeds, 1982
	By Worcestershire	286:5	at Leeds, 1982
Lowest Score:	By Yorkshire	177	at Worcester, 2003
	By Worcestershire	227:8	at Leeds, 2005

Highest Individual
Score:	For Yorkshire	92	D L Bairstow at Leeds, 1982
	For Worcestershire	105	G M Turner at Leeds, 1982
Best Bowling:	For Yorkshire	3 for 41 I J Harvey at Leeds, 2005
	For Worcestershire	5 for 49 M Hayward at Worcester, 2003

versus Ireland: Played 4, Won 4, Lost 0

Highest Score:	By Yorkshire	299:6	at Leeds, 1995
	By Ireland	228:7	at Leeds, 1995
Lowest Score:	By Yorkshire	249	at Leeds, 1997
	By Ireland	53	at Leeds, 1997

Highest Individual
Score:	For Yorkshire	113	C White at Leeds, 1995
	For Ireland	82	S J S Warke at Leeds, 1995
Best Bowling:	For Yorkshire	7 for 27 D Gough at Leeds, 1997
	For Ireland	3 for 26 P McCrum at Leeds, 1997

versus Scotland: Played 5, Won 5 (in Yorkshire 3, Away 2)

Highest Score:	By Yorkshire	259:8 at Edinburgh, 2007	
	By Scotland	244 at Leeds, 2008	
Lowest Score:	By Yorkshire	—	
	By Scotland	193:8 at Edinburgh, 2008	
Highest Individual			
Score:	For Yorkshire	66 A McGrath at Edinburgh, 2007	
	For Scotland	73 I L Philip at Leeds, 1989	
Best Bowling:	For Yorkshire	3 for 22 T T Bresnan at Edinburgh, 2007	
	For Scotland	3 for 62 J A R Blain at Edinburgh, 2007	

versus Bedfordshire: Played 1, Won 1 (Away)

Highest Score:	By Yorkshire	212:6 at Luton, 2001
	By Bedfordshire	211:9 at Luton, 2001
Highest Individual		
Score:	For Yorkshire	88 D S Lehmann at Luton, 2001
	For Bedfordshire	34 O J Clayton at Luton, 2001
Best Bowling:	For Yorkshire	4 for 39 R J Sidebottom at Luton, 2001
	For Bedfordshire	4 for 54 S Rashid at Luton, 2001

versus Berkshire: Played 2, Won 2 (Away 2)

Highest Score:	By Yorkshire	131:3 at Reading, 1983
	By Berkshire	128:9 at Reading, 1983
Lowest Score:	By Yorkshire	Have not been dismissed, nor batted through entire overs
	By Berkshire	105 at Finchampstead, 1988
Highest Individual		
Score:	For Yorkshire	74* A A Metcalfe at Finchampstead, 1988
	For Berkshire	29 G R J Roope at Reading, 1983
Best Bowling:	For Yorkshire	5 for 27 G B Stevenson at Reading, 1983
	For Berkshire	1 for 15 M Lickley at Reading, 1983

versus Cambridgeshire: Played 3, Won 3 (in Yorkshire 2, Away 1)

Highest Score:	By Yorkshire	299:5 at March, 2003
	By Cambridgeshire	214:8 at March, 2003
Lowest Score:	By Yorkshire	177:3 at Leeds, 1986
	By Cambridgeshire	176:8 at Leeds, 1986
Highest Individual		
Score:	For Yorkshire	118* M J Wood March, 2003
	For Cambridgeshire	85 J D R Benson at Leeds, 1986
Best Bowling:	For Yorkshire	3 for 11 A G Nicholson at Castleford, 1967
	For Cambridgeshire	3 for 53 Ajaz Akhtar at March, 2003

versus Cheshire: Played 1, Won 1 (Away)

Highest Score:	By Yorkshire	160:0 at Oxton, 1985
	By Cheshire	159:7 at Oxton, 1985
Highest Individual		
Score:	For Yorkshire	82* M D Moxon at Oxton, 1985
	For Cheshire	46 K Teesdale at Oxton, 1985
Best Bowling:	For Yorkshire	2 for 17 G B Stevenson at Oxton, 1985
	For Cheshire	No wicket taken

versus Devon: Played 4, Won 4, (Away 4)

Highest Score:	By Yorkshire	411:6 at Exmouth, 2004
	By Devon	279:8 at Exmouth, 2004
Lowest Score:	By Devon	80 at Exmouth, 1998
Highest Individual		
Score:	For Yorkshire	160 M J Wood at Exmouth, 2004
	For Devon	83 P M Roebuck at Exmouth, 1994
Best Bowling:	For Yorkshire	4 for 26 D S Lehmann at Exmouth, 2002
	For Devon	2 for 42 A O F Le Fleming at Exmouth, 1994

versus Dorset: Played 1, Won 1, (Away)

Scores:	By Yorkshire	101:2	at Bournemouth, 2004
	By Dorset	97	at Bournemouth, 2004

Highest Individual

Score:	For Yorkshire	71*	M J Wood at Bournemouth, 2004
	For Dorset	23	C L Park at Bournemouth, 2004
Best Bowling:	For Yorkshire	4 for 18	C E W Silverwood at Bournemouth, 2004
	For Devon	2 for 31	D J L Worrad at Bournemouth, 2004

versus Herefordshire: Played 1, Won 1 (Away)

Highest Score:	By Yorkshire	275:8	at Kington, 1999
	By Herefordshire	124:5	at Kington, 1999

Highest Individual

Score:	For Yorkshire	77	G S Blewett at Kington, 1999
	For Herefordshire	39	R D Hughes at Kington, 1999
Best Bowling:	For Yorkshire	2 for 22	G M Hamilton at Kington, 1999
	For Herefordshire	2 for 41	C W Boroughs at Kington, 1999

versus Norfolk: Played 2, Won 2 (in Yorkshire 1, Away 1)

Highest Score:	By Yorkshire	167	at Lakenham, 1969
	By Norfolk	104	at Leeds, 1990
Lowest Score:	By Yorkshire	167	at Lakenham, 1969
	By Norfolk	78	at Lakenham, 1969

Highest Individual

Score:	For Yorkshire	56*	M D Moxon at Leeds, 1990
	For Norfolk	25	R J Finney at Leeds, 1990
Best Bowling:	For Yorkshire	3 for 8	P Carrick at Leeds, 1990
	For Norfolk	6 for 48	T I Moore at Lakenham, 1969

versus Northumberland: Played 1, Won 1 (Away)

Highest Score:	By Yorkshire	138:2 (51.3 overs)	at Leeds, 1992
	By Northumberland	137	at Leeds, 1992

Highest Individual

Score:	For Yorkshire	38	S A Kellett at Leeds, 1992
	For Northumberland	47	G R Morris at Leeds, 1992
Best Bowling:	For Yorkshire	3 for 18	M A Robinson at Leeds, 1992
	For Northumberland	2 for 22	S Greensword at Leeds, 1992

versus Shropshire: Played 2, Won 1 (Away 1), Lost 1 (Away 1)

Highest Score:	By Yorkshire	192	at Telford, 1984
	By Shropshire	229:5	at Telford, 1984
Lowest Score:	By Yorkshire	192	at Telford, 1984
	By Shropshire	185	at Wellington, 1976

Highest Individual

Score:	For Yorkshire	59	J H Hampshire at Wellington, 1976
	For Shropshire	80	Mushtaq Mohammed at Telford, 1984
Best Bowling:	For Yorkshire	3 for 17	A L Robinson at Wellington, 1976
	For Shropshire	3 for 26	Mushtaq Mohammed at Telford, 1984

versus Wiltshire: Played 1, Won 1 (Away)

Highest Score:	By Yorkshire	304:7	at Trowbridge, 1987
	By Wiltshire	175	at Trowbridge, 1987

Highest Individual

Score:	For Yorkshire	85	A A Metcalfe at Trowbridge, 1987
	For Wiltshire	62	J J Newman at Trowbridge, 1987
Best Bowling:	For Yorkshire	4 for 40	K Sharp at Trowbridge, 1987
	For Wiltshire	2 for 38	R C Cooper at Trowbridge, 1987

FRIENDS PROVIDENT TROPHY, CHELTENHAM & GLOUCESTER TROPHY, GILLETTE CUP AND NATWEST TROPHY 1963-2008

Player	M	Inns	NO	Runs	HS	Av'ge	100s	50s	Runs	Wkts	Av'ge	Ct/St
Athey, C W J ..	15	15	2	485	115	37.30	1	2	41	1	41.00	2
Bairstow, D L ..	34	27	5	492	92	22.36	—	2	—	—	—	38/3
Balderstone, J C	5	3	0	65	34	21.66	—	—	10	1	10.00	1
Batty, J D	3	2	0	7	4	3.50	—	—	97	1	97.00	1
Bevan, M G ...	8	8	2	388	91*	64.66	—	4	89	3	29.66	—
Binks, J G	16	10	1	107	22	11.88	—	—	—	—	—	15/6
Blain, J A R ...	3	2	0	13	7	6.50	—	—	63	3	21.00	—
Blakey, R J	48	35	13	516	75	23.45	—	2	—	—	—	55/3
Blewett, G S ...	3	3	0	83	77	27.66	—	1	57	7	8.14	1
Booth, P A	1	1	1	6	6*	—	—	—	33	0	—	—
Bore, M K	3	2	1	0	0*	0.00	—	—	98	5	19.60	—
Boycott, G	40	39	4	1378	146	39.37	1	9	238	8	29.75	9
Bresnan, T T ..	**34**	**18**	**4**	**307**	**55**	**21.92**	**—**	**1**	**1297**	**40**	**32.42**	**8**
Brophy, G L ...	20	16	5	281	61*	25.54	—	2	—	—	—	22/2
Byas, D	34	32	3	912	73*	31.45	—	8	23	1	23.00	23
Carrick, P	32	23	3	320	54	16.00	—	1	741	24	30.87	6
Chapman, C ...	1	—	—	—	—	—	—	—	—	—	—	1
Claydon, M E ..	7	2	0	15	9	7.50	—	—	293	8	36.62	—
Close, D B	15	15	2	399	96	30.69	—	2	357	22	16.22	6
Cooper, H G ...	11	9	4	49	17	9.80	—	—	347	15	23.13	2
Cope, G A	4	2	2	1	1*	—	—	—	130	5	26.00	3
Craven, V J ...	4	3	1	38	26	19.00	—	—	41	2	20.50	2
Dawson, R K J .	22	7	0	77	24	11.00	—	—	762	15	50.80	9
Dawood, I	4	3	0	26	23	8.66	—	—	—	—	—	1/1
Dennis, S J	5	2	0	14	14	7.00	—	—	202	6	33.66	—
Elliott, M T G ..	1	1	1	128	128*	—	1	—	—	—	—	—
Fellows, G M ..	12	8	3	230	80*	46.00	—	2	55	0	—	3
Fisher, I D	3	1	0	5	5	5.00	—	—	87	3	29.00	2
Fletcher, S D ..	15	7	4	36	16*	12.00	—	—	576	15	38.40	2
Gale, A W ...	**21**	**17**	**4**	**498**	**69***	**38.30**	**—**	**4**	**—**	**—**	**—**	**2**
Gilbert, C R ...	3	2	0	9	6	4.50	—	—	134	6	22.33	—
Gillespie, J N ..	11	2	1	15	15*	15.00	—	—	363	9	40.33	3
Gough, D	**44**	**20**	**3**	**251**	**46**	**14.76**	**—**	**—**	**1596**	**86**	**18.55**	**9**
Gray, A K D ...	3	1	0	0	0	0.00	—	—	152	5	30.40	3
Grayson, A P ..	7	6	0	91	29	15.16	—	—	241	4	60.25	3
Guy, S M	**7**	**3**	**0**	**23**	**13**	**7.66**	**—**	**—**	**—**	**—**	**—**	**8**
Hamilton, G M .	9	8	3	146	39	29.20	—	—	254	15	16.93	2
Hampshire, A W	1	0	0	0	0	0.00	—	—	—	—	—	1
Hampshire, J H .	32	31	5	877	110	33.73	1	6	4	0	—	10
Harden R J	4	4	0	54	37	13.50	—	—	—	—	—	—
Hartley, P J ...	28	17	8	250	83	27.77	—	2	1108	45	24.62	2
Hartley, S N ...	15	12	0	263	69	21.91	—	2	114	1	114.00	5
Harvey, I J	4	4	0	151	74	37.75	—	1	184	6	30.66	1
Hoggard, M J .	**16**	**4**	**4**	**8**	**7***	**—**	**—**	**—**	**555**	**23**	**24.13**	**1**
Hutchison, P M .	3	1	1	4	4*	—	—	—	62	5	12.40	—
Hutton, R A ...	13	10	2	136	61	17.00	—	1	341	13	26.23	4
Illingworth, R ..	15	10	7	150	45	50.00	—	—	260	8	32.50	7
Jaques, P A ...	6	6	1	211	55*	42.20	—	3	—	—	—	—
Jarvis, P W ...	16	9	2	86	16	12.28	—	—	655	19	34.47	3
Johnson, C	4	4	0	62	44	15.50	—	—	—	—	—	—
Katich, S M ...	1	1	1	40	40*	—	—	—	—	—	—	—
Kellett, S A ...	9	7	0	246	107	35.14	1	1	—	—	—	6
Kirby, S P	2	1	0	0	0	0.00	—	—	74	2	37.00	—
Kruis, G J	**17**	**5**	**4**	**23**	**11**	**23.00**	**—**	**—**	**522**	**13**	**40.15**	**2**
Leadbeater, B ..	9	9	0	155	76	17.22	—	—	47	3	15.66	2

Player	M	Inns	NO	Runs	HS	Av'ge	100s	50s	Runs	Wkts	Av'ge	Ct/St
Lehmann, D S ..	23	19	5	853	118*	60.92	2	6	462	20	23.10	4
Lester, E I	1	1	0	0	0	0.00	—	—	—	—	—	—
Love, J D	21	18	3	266	67	17.73	—	3	39	2	19.50	5
Lumb, M J	20	18	3	628	89	41.86	—	4	—	—	—	6
Lumb, R G	12	12	0	222	56	18.50	—	1	—	—	—	—
Lyth, A	**8**	**6**	**1**	**108**	**38***	**21.60**	—	—	—	—	—	**4**
McGrath, A ...	52	46	8	1690	135*	44.47	3	13	688	22	31.27	18
Metcalfe, A A ..	20	20	3	714	127*	42.00	1	5	44	2	22.00	4
Middlebrook, J D	2	1	1	6	6*	—	—	—	38	0	—	3
Morris, A C ...	1	1	1	1	1*	—	—	—	43	1	43.00	—
Moxon, M D ...	34	34	6	1316	137	47.00	2	10	68	4	17.00	12
Nicholson, A G .	17	12	4	42	15*	5.25	—	—	467	21	22.23	6
Old, C M	28	23	3	268	55*	13.40	—	1	799	43	18.58	7
Oldham, S	8	5	3	35	19	17.50	—	—	309	15	20.60	—
Padgett, D E V .	17	15	1	309	46	22.07	—	—	—	—	—	4
Parker, B	6	4	0	87	69	21.75	—	1	—	—	—	—
Patterson, S A .	**4**	**1**	**1**	**3**	**3***	—	—	—	**145**	**3**	**48.33**	—
Pickles, C S ...	3	2	0	15	12	7.50	—	—	111	4	27.75	1
Pyrah, R M ...	**20**	**11**	**2**	**120**	**24**	**13.33**	—	—	**628**	**23**	**27.30**	**10**
Ramage, A	4	1	0	14	14	14.00	—	—	167	4	41.75	1
Rana Naved												
-ul-Hasan	**1**	**1**	**0**	**13**	**13**	**13.00**	—	—	**41**	**2**	**20.50**	—
Rashid, A U ...	11	5	1	42	41*	10.25	—	—	259	7	37.00	3
Richardson, R B	5	5	0	194	90	38.80	—	2	—	—	—	—
Robinson, A L ..	5	2	1	18	18*	18.00	—	—	179	9	19.88	1
Robinson, M A .	11	4	3	1	1*	1.00	—	—	390	12	32.50	—
Robinson, P E ..	8	5	1	113	66	22.60	—	1	—	—	—	3
Rudolph, J A ..	**18**	**17**	**3**	**609**	**100**	**43.50**	**1**	**4**	**8**	**0**	—	**9**
Ryan, M	3	2	1	7	6*	7.00	—	—	149	5	29.80	3
Shahzad, A	**4**	**2**	**1**	**44**	**33**	**44.00**	—	—	**152**	**4**	**38.00**	—
Sharp, K	17	13	2	228	50	20.72	—	1	47	4	11.75	6
Sharpe, P J	22	20	1	331	68	17.42	—	2	—	—	—	18
Shaw, C	6	5	2	10	6*	3.33	—	—	194	11	17.63	—
Sidebottom, A .	25	16	5	192	45	17.45	—	—	700	37	18.91	9
Sidebottom, R J	14	2	1	13	7*	13.00	—	—	432	20	21.60	4
Silverwood,C E W	26	12	3	161	61	17.88	—	1	841	27	31.15	7
Smith, N	1	1	0	5	5	5.00	—	—	—	—	—	—
Squires, P J	2	2	0	46	42	23.00	—	—	—	—	—	1
Stemp, R D	11	3	2	1	1*	1.00	—	—	406	14	29.00	1
Stevenson, G B .	19	13	1	190	34	15.83	—	—	612	30	20.40	5
Stott, W B	2	2	0	30	30	15.00	—	—	—	—	—	—
Stringer, P M ...	2	2	2	7	5*	—	—	—	21	4	5.25	—
Swallow, I G ...	2	1	1	17	17*	—	—	—	16	0	—	—
Taylor, C R	1	—	—	—	—	—	—	—	—	—	—	—
Taylor, K	10	10	0	135	30	13.50	—	—	168	11	15.27	3
Tendulkar, S R .	2	2	1	53	32*	53.00	—	—	—	—	—	1
Thornicroft, N D	2	1	1	10	10*	—	—	—	97	1	97.00	1
Trueman, F S ..	11	9	1	127	28	15.87	—	—	348	21	16.57	5
Vaughan, M P .	**35**	**34**	**3**	**1076**	**116***	**34.70**	**1**	**8**	**267**	**6**	**44.50**	**7**
Wainwright, D J	**3**	**1**	**1**	**7**	**7***	—	—	—	**76**	**1**	**76.00**	—
Waring, J	1	1	1	1	1*	—	—	—	11	0	—	—
White, C	**60**	**55**	**14**	**1809**	**113**	**44.12**	**4**	**10**	**1130**	**40**	**28.25**	**19**
Whiteley, J P ...	1	—	—	—	—	—	—	—	48	0	—	—
Wilson, D	15	13	1	72	16	6.00	—	—	391	21	18.62	10
Wood, M J	28	28	6	908	160	41.27	2	3	45	3	15.00	11
Woodford, J D .	1	1	0	15	15	15.00	—	—	—	—	—	—
Younus Khan ...	7	6	0	234	100	39.00	1	0	124	2	62.00	3
Yuvraj Singh ...	1	1	0	27	27	27.00	—	—	27	0	—	—

WINNERS OF THE GILLETTE CUP
AND NATWEST TROPHY 1963-2000

GILLETTE CUP

1963 **Sussex**, who beat Worcestershire by 14 runs
1964 **Sussex**, who beat Warwickshire by 8 wickets
1965 **Yorkshire**, who beat Surrey by 175 runs
1966 **Warwickshire**, who beat Worcestershire by 5 wickets
1967 **Kent**, who beat Somerset by 32 runs
1968 **Warwickshire**, who beat Sussex by 4 wickets
1969 **Yorkshire**, who beat Derbyshire by 69 runs
1970 **Lancashire**, who beat Sussex by 6 wickets
1971 **Lancashire**, who beat Kent by 24 runs
1972 **Lancashire**, who beat Warwickshire by 4 wickets
1973 **Gloucestershire**, who beat Sussex by 40 runs
1974 **Kent**, who beat Lancashire by 4 wickets
1975 **Lancashire**, who beat Middlesex by 7 wickets
1976 **Northamptonshire**, who beat Lancashire by 4 wickets
1977 **Middlesex**, who beat Glamorgan by 5 wickets
1978 **Sussex**, who beat Somerset by 5 wickets
1979 **Somerset**, who beat Northamptonshire by 45 runs
1980 **Middlesex**, who beat Surrey by 7 wickets

WINNERS OF NATWEST TROPHY:

1981 **Derbyshire**, who beat Northamptonshire by losing fewer wickets
with the scores level.
1982 **Surrey**, who beat Warwickshire by 9 wickets
1983 **Somerset**, who beat Kent by 24 runs
1984 **Middlesex**, who beat Kent by 4 wickets
1985 **Essex**, who beat Nottinghamshire by 1 run
1986 **Sussex**, who beat Lancashire by 7 wickets
1987 **Nottinghamshire**, who beat Northamptonshire by 3 wickets
1988 **Middlesex**, who beat Worcestershire by 3 wickets
1989 **Warwickshire**, who beat Middlesex by 4 wickets
1990 **Lancashire**, who beat Northamptonshire by 7 wickets
1991 **Hampshire**, who beat Surrey by 4 wickets
1992 **Northamptonshire**, who beat Leicestershire by 8 wickets
1993 **Warwickshire**, who beat Sussex by 5 wickets
1994 **Worcestershire**, who beat Warwickshire by 8 wickets
1995 **Warwickshire**, who beat Northamptonshire by 4 wickets
1996 **Lancashire**, who beat Essex by 129 runs
1997 **Essex**, who beat Warwickshire by 9 wickets
1998 **Lancashire**, who beat Derbyshire by 9 wickets
1999 **Gloucestershire**, who beat Somerset by 50 runs
2000 **Gloucestershire**, who beat Warwickshire by 22 runs

BENSON AND HEDGES CUP 1972-2002

WINNERS 1987
LOSING FINALISTS 1972, 1999   SEMI-FINALISTS 1979, 1984, 1991, 1996, 1998, 2001

Played 146, Won 80 (in Yorkshire 40, Away 40), Lost 58 (in Yorkshire 28, Away 30),
No Result 8

Highest Score:	By Yorkshire	317:5 v. Scotland at Leeds, 1986
	Against Yorkshire	276:4 by Warwickshire at Leeds, 1984
†Lowest Score:	By Yorkshire	81 v. Lancashire at Leeds 2002
	Against Yorkshire	50 by Hampshire at Leeds, 1991

Highest Individual
Score:	For Yorkshire	142 G Boycott v. Worcestershire at Worcester, 1980
	Against Yorkshire	136* N Hussain for Essex at Chelmsford, 2002

Highest
Partnerships: For Yorkshire

1st wkt	213	M D Moxon (141*) and A A Metcalfe (84) v. Glamorgan at Cardiff, 1991
2nd wkt	148*	G Boycott (69*) and C W J Athey (74*) v. Combined Universities at Oxford, 1980
3rd wkt	184	M P Vaughan (70) and D S Lehmann (119) v. Durham at Leeds, 1998
4th wkt	118	D S Lehmann (103) and G M Fellows (38) v. Derbyshire at Leeds, 2001
5th wkt	114	B Leadbeater (42*) and C M Old (72) v. Sussex at Hove, 1976
6th wkt	167*	M G Bevan (95*) and R J Blakey (80*) v. Lancashire at Manchester, 1996.
7th wkt	149*	J D Love (118*) and C M Old (78*) v. Scotland at Bradford, 1981
8th wkt	48*	J D Love (40*) and P J Hartley (7*) v. Surrey at Leeds, 1987
9th wkt	41	K Sharp (64*) and P W Jarvis (11) v. Worcestershire at Leeds, 1987
10th wkt	80*	D L Bairstow (103*) and M Johnson (4*) v. Derbyshire at Derby, 1981

Best Bowling:	For Yorkshire	6 for 27 A G Nicholson v. Minor Counties at Middlesbrough, 1972
	Against Yorkshire	7 for 32 R G D Willis for Warwickshire at Birmingham, 1981

Most Economical Bowling:
	For Yorkshire	11-9-3-1 C M Old v. Middlesex at Lord's, 1979
	Against Yorkshire	11-5-7-2 A R Butcher for Surrey at Bradford, 1976

Most Expensive Bowling:
	For Yorkshire	11-2-72-2 PJ Hartley v. Worcestershire at Worcester, 1988
	Against Yorkshire	10-0-80-0 R N Dalton for Minor Counties, Leeds, 1997

†Lowest score is either the lowest all out score or the lowest score at completion of 55 overs.

Centuries (17)

D L Bairstow	103* v. Derbyshire at Derby, 1981
G Boycott (3)	102 v. Northamptonshire at Middlesbrough, 1977
	142 v. Worcestershire at Worcester, 1980
	106 v. Northamptonshire at Bradford, 1984
D Byas (2)	116* v. Surrey at The Oval, 1996
	104* v. Hampshire at Leeds, 1999
D S Lehmann (3)	102* v. Derbyshire at Derby, 1998
	119 v. Durham at Leeds, 1998
	103 v. Derbyshire at Leeds, 2001
J D Love	118* v. Scotland at Bradford, 1981
A McGrath	109* v. Minor Counties at Leeds, 1997
A A Metcalfe	114 v. Lancashire at Manchester, 1991
M D Moxon (2)	106* v. Lancashire at Manchester, 1986
	141* v. Glamorgan at Cardiff, 1991
K Sharp	105* v. Scotland at Leeds, 1986
M P Vaughan	125* v. Somerset at Taunton, 2001
M J Wood	115* v. Derbyshire at Derby, 2002

5 Wickets in an Innings (11)

P J Hartley	5 for 43 v. Scotland at Leeds, 1986
M D Moxon	5 for 31 v. Warwickshire at Leeds, 1991
A G Nicholson (2)	6 for 27 v. Minor Counties at Middlesbrough, 1972
	5 for 24 v. Derbyshire at Bradford, 1975
S Oldham	5 for 32 v. Minor Counties at Scunthorpe, 1975
A Sidebottom	5 for 27 v. Worcestershire at Bradford, 1985
C E W Silverwood	5 for 28 v. Scotland, at Leeds, 1996
G B Stevenson (2)	5 for 28 v. Kent at Canterbury, 1978
	5 for 50 v. Worcestershire at Leeds, 1982
C White	5 for 25 v. Lancashire at Leeds, 2000
D Wilson	5 for 26 v. Lancashire at Bradford, 1972

Gold Awards

G Boycott	9
D L Bairstow	7
M D Moxon	7
D S Lehmann	5
A A Metcalfe	5
C White	4
C W J Athey	3
M G Bevan	3
D Byas	3
J D Love	3
C M Old	3
A Sidebottom	3
R J Blakey	2
J H Hampshire	2
P J Hartley	2
R A Hutton	2
C E W Silverwood	2
M P Vaughan	2

P Carrick, D Gough, G M Hamilton, S N Hartley, C Johnson, A McGrath, A G Nicholson, S Oldham, P E Robinson, R D Stemp, G B Stevenson, D Wilson, M J Wood (1 each). (78 Awards: 31 Players).

ANALYSIS OF RESULTS

Opponents	Played	Won	Tied	Lost	No Result
Derbyshire	14	10	0	1	3
Durham	5	4	0	1	0
Essex	5	2	0	3	0
Glamorgan	1	1	0	0	0
Gloucestershire	3	1	0	2	0
Hampshire	5	4	0	1	0
Kent	4	2	0	2	0
Lancashire	16	6	0	9	1
Leicestershire	7	3	0	4	0
Middlesex	4	1	0	2	1
Northamptonshire	9	3	0	5	1
Nottinghamshire	16	6	0	8	2
Somerset	4	1	0	3	0
Surrey	7	3	0	4	0
Sussex	3	3	0	0	0
Warwickshire	11	7	0	4	0
Worcestershire	11	4	0	7	0
Combined Universities	3	1	0	2	0
Minor Counties	11	11	0	0	0
Scotland	7	7	0	0	0
Totals	146	80	0	58	8

Player	M	Inns	NO	Runs	HS	Av'ge	100s	50s	Runs	Wkts	Av'ge	Ct/St
Athey, C W J ..	29	26	4	608	94*	27.63	—	5	75	4	18.75	13
Bairstow, D L ..	85	59	14	945	103*	21.00	1	1	17	0	—	117/5
Baker, T M	3	1	0	3	3	3.00	—	—	67	3	22.33	2
Batty, J D	4	1	1	2	2*	—	—	—	109	1	109.00	1
Berry, P J	1								28	0	—	
Bevan, M G ...	10	9	4	544	95*	108.80	—	7	25	1	25.00	1
Blakey, R J ...	74	64	18	1308	80*	28.43	—	6	—	—	—	69/7
Blewett, G S ...	3	3	0	84	71	28.00	—	1	23	0	—	
Booth, P A	2	1	0	1	1	1.00	—	—	47	2	23.50	
Bore, M K	6	3	2	13	7*	13.00	—	—	193	8	24.12	1
Boycott, G	57	55	9	2052	142	44.60	3	16	227	2	113.50	14
Bresnan, T T ..	6	4	3	23	16	23.00	—	—	119	3	39.66	1
Byas, D	58	55	5	1427	116*	28.54	2	7	155	5	31.00	17
Carrick, P	60	38	7	340	53	10.96	—	1	1590	42	37.85	9
Cooper, H P ...	28	15	6	76	20*	8.44	—	—	799	42	19.02	4
Cope, G A	4	4	4	34	18*	—	—	—	131	1	131.00	1
Craven, V J ...	1	1	0	1	1	1.00	—	—	—	—	—	1
Dawson, R K J .	3	3	2	16	8	16.00	—	—	35	5	7.00	1
Dennis, S J ...	9	2	0	10	10	5.00	—	—	327	7	46.71	1
Fellows, G M ..	20	18	4	219	38	15.64	—	—	192	9	21.33	3
Fisher, I D	1								26	1	26.00	1
Fletcher, S D ..	27	6	3	20	15*	6.66	—	—	974	35	27.82	6
Gough, D	39	19	6	177	48*	13.62	—	—	1245	45	27.66	11
Gray, A K D ...	3	3	1	17	10*	8.50	—	—	50	1	50.00	—
Grayson, A P ...	9	7	1	117	22*	19.50	—	—	118	3	39.33	2
Hamilton, G M .	17	10	3	170	31	24.29	—	—	474	22	21.55	1
Hampshire, J H .	44	37	4	866	85*	26.24	—	4	—	—	—	12
Harden R J	3	2	0	43	35	21.50	—	—	—	—	—	
Hartley, P J ...	43	26	10	195	29*	12.18	—	—	1539	61	25.22	12
Hartley, S N ...	25	22	6	460	65*	28.75	—	2	421	18	23.38	7
Hoggard, M J ..	11	3	3	10	7*	—	—	—	350	13	26.92	2
Hutchison, P M .	6	2	2	6	4*	—	—	—	112	10	11.20	—
Hutton, R A ...	15	8	3	118	33*	23.60	—	—	434	21	20.66	5
Illingworth, R ..	2	1	1	9	9*	9.00	—	—	51	5	10.20	—
Jarvis, P W	32	14	4	110	42	11.00	—	—	1006	52	19.34	4
Johnson, C	23	16	5	366	73*	33.27	—	1	23	0	—	9
Johnson, M	4	2	2	4	4*	—	—	—	138	7	19.71	
Kellett, S A ...	14	12	1	239	45	21.72	—	—	—	—	—	5
Kirby, S P	1	1	0	0	0	0.00	—	—	43	0	—	
Leadbeater, B ..	21	21	5	601	90	37.56	—	4	10	0	—	5
Lehmann, D S ..	30	30	4	1285	119	49.92	3	8	306	12	25.50	13
Love, J D	42	39	12	1113	118*	41.22	1	5	7	0	—	7
Lumb, M J	11	9	1	126	43	15.75	—	—	—	—	—	3
Lumb, R G	36	34	9	937	90	30.22	—	6	—	—	—	6
McGrath, A	33	31	1	740	109*	24.66	1	1	10	2	5.00	11
Metcalfe, A A ..	31	31	4	1277	114	47.29	1	8	—	—	—	8
Middlebrook, JD	2	1	0	3	3	3.00	—	—	75	0	—	1
Morris, A C	1								4	0	—	1
Moxon, M D ...	50	50	7	1863	141*	43.32	2	14	242	9	26.88	19
Nicholson, A G .	19	5	4	15	8	15.00	—	—	478	35	13.65	2

BENSON & HEDGES CUP 1972-2002

Player	M	Inns	NO	Runs	HS	Av'ge	100s	50s	Runs	Wkts	Av'ge	Ct/St
Old, C M	47	31	7	571	78*	23.79	—	3	1171	71	16.49	11
Oldham, S	26	9	3	13	4*	2.16	—	—	763	44	17.34	7
Parker, B	10	7	2	154	58	30.80	—	1	—	—	—	3
Pickles, C S ...	10	7	2	96	37*	19.20	—	—	348	5	69.60	1
Ramage, A	10	4	3	30	17*	30.00	—	—	353	12	29.41	2
Richardson, R B	2	2	0	59	52	29.50	—	1	—	—	—	—
Robinson, A L ..	18	6	4	16	6*	8.00	—	—	505	15	33.66	2
Robinson, M A .	10	5	2	5	3*	1.66	—	—	305	14	21.78	—
Robinson, P E ..	22	18	3	431	73*	28.73	—	2	—	—	—	7
Sharp, K	45	40	3	1073	105*	29.00	1	6	—	—	—	15
Sharpe, P J	15	14	3	297	89*	27.00	—	2	—	—	—	12
Shaw, C	4	1	1	4	4*	—	—	—	60	2	30.00	—
Sidebottom, A ..	52	27	9	246	32	13.66	—	—	1580	72	21.94	13
Sidebottom, R J	20	7	2	20	8	4.00	—	—	622	12	51.83	8
Silverwood, CEW	32	17	2	150	56	10.00	—	1	1136	50	22.72	7
Squires, P J ...	7	7	1	60	27	10.00	—	—	—	—	—	1
Stemp, R D	17	4	1	3	1*	1.00	—	—	612	19	32.21	—
Stevenson, G B .	44	28	6	234	36	10.63	—	—	1567	74	21.17	8
Stutchbury, S ..	2	1	1	6	6*	—	—	—	89	3	29.66	—
Swallow, I G ...	4	3	2	18	10*	18.00	—	—	151	2	75.50	5
Tendulkar, S R .	2	2	0	23	16	11.50	—	—	65	3	21.66	1
Vaughan, M P ..	40	39	3	1190	125*	33.06	1	7	515	19	27.11	12
Wharf, A G	2	—	—	—	—	—	—	—	89	5	17.80	—
White, C	46	42	7	924	93	26.40	—	5	1479	47	31.47	15
Wilson, D	5	—	—	—	—	—	—	—	153	11	13.90	1
Wood, M J	12	10	2	248	115*	31.00	1	1	—	—	—	4
Woodford, J D .	11	6	2	41	17*	10.25	—	—	226	17	13.29	5

PRO40, NATIONAL AND SUNDAY LEAGUES 1969-2008

JOHN PLAYER SPECIAL LEAGUE WINNERS 1983

Played 627, Won 280 (in Yorkshire 154, Away 126). Lost 288 (in Yorkshire 128, Away 160)
Tie 3   No Result 56

Highest Score:	By Yorkshire	352:6 v. Nottinghamshire at Scarborough, 2001
	Against Yorkshire	375:4 by Surrey at Scarborough, 1994
†Lowest Score:	By Yorkshire	54 v. Essex at Leeds, 2003
	Against Yorkshire	23 by Middlesex at Leeds, 1974
Highest Individual		
Score:	For Yorkshire	191 D S Lehmann v. Nottinghamshire at Scarborough, 2001
	Against Yorkshire	155* B A Richards for Hampshire at Hull, 1970
Most Runs in a Season:		704 M G Bevan in 1995

†Lowest score is the lowest all-out score or the lowest score at completion of allotted overs

Highest
Partnerships: For Yorkshire

1st wkt	201	J H Hampshire (86) and C W J Athey (118) v. Leicestershire at Leicester, 1978
2nd wkt	172	D Byas (86) and D S Lehmann (99) v. Kent at Maidstone, 1998
3rd wkt	176	R J Blakey (86) and S R Tendulkar (107) v. Lancashire at Leeds, 1992
4th wkt	198*	M T G Elliott (115*) and A McGrath (85*) v. Kent at Leeds, 2002
5th wkt	190	R J Blakey (96) and M J Foster (118) v. Leicestershire at Leicester, 1993
6th wkt	110	B Leadbeater (69) and C Johnson (51*) v. Nottinghamshire at Hull, 1972
7th wkt	129*	D Byas (74*) and D Gough (72*) v. Leicestershire at Leicester, 1991
8th wkt	89	R J Blakey (60) and R K J Dawson (41) v. Leicestershire at Scarborough, 2002
9th wkt	88	S N Hartley (67) and A Ramage (32*) v. Middlesex at Lord's, 1982
10th wkt	64*	R J Blakey (47) and R J Sidebottom (30*) v. Glamorgan at Leeds, 2002

| **Best Bowling:** | For Yorkshire | 7 for 15 R A Hutton v. Worcestershire at Leeds, 1969 |
| | Against Yorkshire | 6 for 15 A A Donald for Warwickshire at Birmingham, 1995 |

Most Economical Bowling:		
	For Yorkshire	8-5-3-3 A L Robinson v. Derbyshire at Scarborough, 1973
	Against Yorkshire	9-6-8-2 I D Austin for Lancashire at Leeds, 1999

Most Expensive Bowling:		
	For Yorkshire	9-0-87-1 T T Bresnan v. Somerset at Taunton, 2005
	Against Yorkshire	9-0-78-1 Mohammed Akram for Surrey at The Oval, 2005

| **Most Wickets In A Season:** | | 37 M J Hoggard in 2000 |

Centuries (47)

C W J Athey	118 v. Leicestershire at Leicester, 1978
M G Bevan (2)	103* v. Gloucestershire at Middlesbrough, 1995
	101 v. Worcestershire at Scarborough, 1995
G Boycott (2)	104* v. Glamorgan at Colwyn Bay, 1973
	108* v. Northamptonshire at Huddersfield, 1974
R J Blakey (3)	100* v. Gloucestershire at Cheltenham, 1990
	130* v. Kent at Scarborough, 1991
	105* v. Warwickshire at Scarborough, 1992
D Byas (3)	106* v. Derbyshire at Chesterfield, 1993
	101* v. Nottinghamshire at Leeds, 1994
	111* v. Lancashire at Leeds, 1996

M T G Elliott (2)	109 v. Leicestershire at Leicester, 2002
	115* v. Kent at Leeds, 2002
S P Fleming	139* v. Warwickshire at Leeds, 2003
M J Foster	118 v. Leicestershire at Leicester, 1993
J H Hampshire (6)	108 v. Nottinghamshire at Sheffield, 1970
	119 v. Leicestershire at Hull, 1971
	106* v. Lancashire at Manchester, 1972
	111* v. Sussex at Hastings, 1973
	100* v. Warwickshire at Birmingham, 1975
	114* v. Northamptonshire at Scarborough, 1978
P A Jaques	105 v Sussex at Leeds, 2004
S A Kellett	118* v. Derbyshire at Leeds, 1992
D S Lehmann (3)	103 v. Leicestershire at Scarborough, 2001
	191 v. Nottinghamshire at Scarborough, 2001
	104 v. Somerset at Taunton, 2002
J D Love (3)	100* v. Gloucestershire at Gloucester, 1985
	104* v. Nottinghamshire at Hull, 1986
	118* v. Surrey at Leeds, 1987
R G Lumb	101 v. Nottinghamshire at Scarborough, 1976
A McGrath (2)	102 v. Kent at Canterbury, 2001
	148 v. Somerset at Taunton, 2006
A A Metcalfe (2)	115* v. Gloucestershire at Scarborough, 1984
	116 v. Middlesex at Lord's, 1991
M D Moxon (3)	105 v. Somerset at Scarborough, 1990
	129* v. Surrey at The Oval, 1991
	112 v. Sussex at Middlesbrough, 1991
R B Richardson	103 v. Nottinghamshire at Nottingham, 1993
J A Rudolph (2)	127 v. Somerset at Scarborough, 2007
	120 v. Leicestershire at Leeds, 2008
K Sharp (2)	112* v. Worcestershire at Worcester, 1985
	114 v. Essex at Chelmsford, 1985
S R Tendulkar	107 v. Lancashire at Leeds, 1992
M P Vaughan	116* v. Kent at Leeds, 2005
C White	148 v. Leicestershire at Leicester, 1997
M J Wood (2)	105* v. Somerset at Taunton, 2002
	111 v. Surrey at The Oval, 2005

5 Wickets in an Innings (30)

C W J Athey	5 for 35 v. Derbyshire at Chesterfield, 1981
M G Bevan	5 for 29 v. Sussex at Eastbourne, 1996
P Carrick (2)	5 for 22 v. Glamorgan at Leeds, 1991
	5 for 40 v. Sussex at Middlesbrough, 1991
H P Cooper (2)	6 for 14 v. Worcestershire at Worcester, 1975
	5 for 30 v. Worcestershire at Middlesbrough, 1978
D Gough (2)	5 for 13 v. Sussex at Hove, 1994
	5 for 25 v. Surrey at Leeds, 1998
G M Hamilton (2)	5 for 16 v. Hampshire at Leeds, 1998
	5 for 34 v. Sussex at Scarborough, 2000
P .J. Hartley (2)	5 for 38 v. Worcestershire at Worcester, 1990
	5 for 36 v. Sussex at Scarborough, 1993
M J Hoggard (2)	5 for 28 v. Leicestershire at Leicester, 2000
	5 for 30 v. Northamptonshire at Northampton, 2000
	(consecutive matches)

R A Hutton	7 for 15 v. Worcestershire at Leeds, 1969
P W Jarvis (3)	6 for 27 v. Somerset at Taunton, 1989
	5 for 18 v. Derbyshire at Leeds, 1990
	5 for 29 v. Northamptonshire at Northampton, 1992
A G Nicholson (2)	6 for 36 v. Somerset at Sheffield, 1972
	5 for 17 v. Nottinghamshire at Hull, 1972
	(Consecutive matches).
C M Old (2)	5 for 33 v. Sussex at Hove, 1971
	5 for 38 v. Northamptonshire at Sheffield, 1972
C Shaw	5 for 41 v. Hampshire at Bournemouth, 1984
R J Sidebottom (2)	6 for 40 v. Glamorgan at Cardiff, 1998
	5 for 42 v. Leicestershire at Leicester, 2003
G B Stevenson	5 for 41 v. Leicestershire at Leicester, 1976
S Stuchbury	5 for 16 v. Leicestershire at Leicester, 1982
N D Thornicroft	5 for 42 v. Gloucestershire at Leeds, 2003
C White	5 for 19 v. Somerset at Scarborough, 2002
D Wilson	6 for 18 v. Kent at Canterbury, 1969

versus Derbyshire: Played 37, Won 20 (in Yorkshire 11, Away 9) Lost 13 (in Yorkshire 7, Away 6), Tied 1 (Away), No Result 3

Highest Score:	By Yorkshire	248:5 at Chesterfield, 1979
	By Derbyshire	259:2 at Derby, 1997
Lowest Score:	By Yorkshire	117 at Huddersfield, 1978
	By Derbyshire	87 at Scarborough, 1973
Highest Individual Score:		
	For Yorkshire	118* S A Kellett at Leeds, 1992
	For Derbyshire	109* C J Adams at Derby, 1997
Best Bowling:	For Yorkshire	5 for 18 P W Jarvis at Leeds, 1990
	For Derbyshire	4 for 14 A E Warner at Chesterfield, 1995

versus Durham: Played 14, Won 6 (in Yorkshire 3, Away 3) Lost 6 (in Yorkshire 3, Away 3), No Result 2

Highest Score:	By Yorkshire	269:5 at Chester-le-Street, 2002
	By Durham	256:4 at Chester-le-Street, 2005
Lowest Score:	By Yorkshire	122 at Chester-le-Street, 2007
	By Durham	121 at Scarborough, 1997
Highest Individual Score:		
	For Yorkshire	79* D Byas at Chester-le-Street, 1998
	For Durham	114 W Larkins at Leeds, 1993
Best Bowling:	For Yorkshire	4 for 18 C White at Scarborough, 1997
	For Durham	4 for 20 S J E Brown at Leeds, 1995

versus Essex: Played 35, Won 15 (in Yorkshire 9, Away 6) Lost 17 (in Yorkshire 8, Away 9), No Result 3

Highest Score:	By Yorkshire	264:6 at Ilford, 1997
	By Essex	262:9 at Ilford, 1997
Lowest Score:	By Yorkshire	54 at Leeds, 2003
	By Essex	108 at Leeds, 1996
Highest Individual Score:		
	For Yorkshire	114 K Sharp at Chelmsford, 1985
	For Essex	114 N Hussain at Leeds, 1999
Best Bowling:	For Yorkshire	4 for 21 C White at Leeds, 1996
	For Essex	6 for 18 R E East at Hull, 1969

versus Glamorgan: Played 36, Won 16 (in Yorkshire 7, Away 9),
Lost 18 (in Yorkshire 7, Away 11), No Result 2

Highest Score:	By Yorkshire	253:4 at Leeds, 1991
	By Glamorgan	238:8 at Colwyn Bay, 2003
Lowest Score:	By Yorkshire	139 at Hull, 1981
	By Glamorgan	90 at Neath, 1969
Highest Individual		
Score:	For Yorkshire	104* G Boycott at Colwyn Bay, 1973
	For Glamorgan	97* G P Ellis at Leeds, 1976
Best Bowling:	For Yorkshire	6 for 40 R J Sidebottom at Cardiff, 1998
	For Glamorgan	5 for 16 G C Holmes at Swansea, 1985

versus Gloucestershire: Played 39, Won 15 (in Yorkshire 9, Away 6),
Lost 19 (in Yorkshire 6, Away 13), No Result 5

Highest Score:	By Yorkshire	262:7 at Bristol, 1996
	By Gloucestershire	261:7 at Cheltenham, 1994 (also
		261 at Cheltenham, 1999)
Lowest Score:	By Yorkshire	115 at Leeds, 1973
	By Gloucestershire	90 at Tewkesbury, 1972
Highest Individual		
Score:	For Yorkshire	115* A A Metcalfe at Scarborough, 1984
	For Gloucestershire	146* S Young at Leeds, 1997
Best Bowling:	For Yorkshire	5 for 42 N D Thornicroft at Leeds, 2003
	For Gloucestershire	5 for 33 M C J Ball at Leeds, 2003

versus Hampshire: Played 33, Won 13 (in Yorkshire 7, Away 6),
Lost 18 (in Yorkshire 9, Away 9), No Result 2

Highest Score:	By Yorkshire	264:2 at Southampton, 1995
	By Hampshire	257:6 at Middlesbrough, 1985
Lowest Score:	By Yorkshire	74:9 at Hull, 1970
	By Hampshire	133 at Bournemouth, 1976
Highest Individual		
Score:	For Yorkshire	98* M G Bevan at Leeds, 1996
	For Hampshire	155* B A Richards at Hull, 1970
Best Bowling:	For Yorkshire	5 for 16 G M Hamilton at Leeds, 1998
	For Hampshire	5 for 31 D W White at Southampton, 1969

versus Kent: Played 45, Won 18 (in Yorkshire 11, Away 7),
Lost 24 (in Yorkshire 8, Away 16). No Result 3

Highest Score:	By Yorkshire	299:3 at Leeds, 2002
	By Kent	266:5 at Maidstone, 1998
Lowest Score:	By Yorkshire	75 at Leeds, 1995
	By Kent	105 at Canterbury, 1969
Highest Individual		
Score:	For Yorkshire	130* R J Blakey at Scarborough, 1991
	For Kent	118* M H Denness at Scarborough, 1976
Best Bowling:	For Yorkshire	6 for 18 D Wilson at Canterbury, 1969
	For Kent	4 for 13 M V Fleming at Canterbury, 1996

versus Lancashire: Played 34, Won 10 (in Yorkshire 4, Away 6),
Lost 19 (in Yorkshire 11, Away 8), No Result 5

Highest Score:	By Yorkshire	260:6 at Leeds, 1992
	By Lancashire	264:3 at Leeds, 1992
Lowest Score:	By Yorkshire	81 at Leeds, 1998
	By Lancashire	68 at Leeds, 2000
Highest Individual		
Score:	For Yorkshire	111* D Byas at Leeds, 1996
	For Lancashire	102* N J Speak at Leeds, 1992
Best Bowling:	For Yorkshire	4 for 14 C White at Leeds, 2000
	For Lancashire	6 for 25 G Chapple at Leeds, 1998

versus Leicestershire: Played 47, Won 21 (in Yorkshire 14, Away 7),
Lost 22 (in Yorkshire 11, Away 11), Tie 1, No Result 3

Highest Score:	By Yorkshire	318:7 at Leicester, 1993
	By Leicestershire	302:7 at Leeds, 2008
Lowest Score:	By Yorkshire	89:9 at Leicester, 1989
	By Leicestershire	53 at Leicester, 2000
Highest Individual		
Score:	For Yorkshire	148 C White at Leicester, 1997
	For Leicestershire	108 N E Briers at Bradford, 1984
Best Bowling:	For Yorkshire	5 for 16 S Stuchbury at Leicester, 1982
	For Leicestershire	5 for 31 R Illingworth at Bradford, 1977

versus Middlesex: Played 33, Won 16 (in Yorkshire 10, Away 6),
Lost 13 (in Yorkshire 2, Away 11), No Result 4

Highest Score:	By Yorkshire	271:7 at Scarborough, 1990
	By Middlesex	273:6 at Southgate, 2004
Lowest Score:	By Yorkshire	94 at Lord's, 1969
	By Middlesex	23 at Leeds, 1974
Highest Individual		
Score:	For Yorkshire	116 A A Metcalfe at Lord's, 1991
	For Middlesex	125* O A Shah at Southgate, 2004
Best Bowling:	For Yorkshire	4 for 6 R Illingworth at Hull, 1983
	For Middlesex	4 for 22 K P Dutch at Lord's, 1998

versus Northamptonshire: Played 35, Won 23 (in Yorkshire 11, Away 12),
Lost 9 (in Yorkshire 5, Away 4), No Result 3

Highest Score:	By Yorkshire	251:4 at Tring, 1990
	By Northamptonshire	282:4 at Middlesbrough, 1982
Lowest Score:	By Yorkshire	112 at Northampton, 1975
	By Northamptonshire	109 at Northampton, 2000
Highest Individual		
Score:	For Yorkshire	114* J H Hampshire at Scarborough, 1978
	For Northamptonshire	104* P Willey at Bradford, 1976
Best Bowling:	For Yorkshire	5 for 29 P W Jarvis at Northampton, 1992
	For Northamptonshire	5 for 15 Sarfraz Nawaz at Northampton, 1975

versus Nottinghamshire: Played 36, Won 16 (in Yorkshire 11, Away 5),
Lost 16 (in Yorkshire 6, Away 10), Tie 1, No Result 3

Highest Score:	By Yorkshire	352:6 at Scarborough, 2001
		255:6 at Hull, 1986
	By Nottinghamshire	291:6 at Nottingham, 2004
Lowest Score:	By Yorkshire	147 at Nottingham, 1975
	By Nottinghamshire	66 at Bradford, 1969
Highest Individual		
Score:	For Yorkshire	191 D S Lehmann at Scarborough, 2001
	For Nottinghamshire	123 D W Randall at Nottingham, 1987
Best Bowling:	For Yorkshire	5 for 17 A G Nicholson at Hull, 1972
	For Nottinghamshire	5 for 41 C L Cairns at Leeds, 1996

versus Somerset: Played 42, Won 21 (in Yorkshire 13, Away 8),
Lost 19 (in Yorkshire 8, Away 11), No Result 2

Highest Score:	By Yorkshire	343:9 at Taunton, 2005
	By Somerset	345:4 at Taunton, 2005
Lowest Score:	By Yorkshire	110 at Scarborough, 1977
	By Somerset	139 at Taunton, 2004
Highest Individual		
Score:	For Yorkshire	148 A McGrath at Taunton, 2006
	For Somerset	131 D B Close at Bath, 1974
Best Bowling:	For Yorkshire	6 for 27 P W Jarvis at Taunton, 1989
	For Somerset	5 for 27 J Garner at Bath, 1985

versus Surrey: Played 39, Won 15 (in Yorkshire 9, Away 6),
Lost 22 (in Yorkshire 8, Away 14), No Result 2

Highest Score:	By Yorkshire	334:5 at The Oval, 2005
	By Surrey	375:4 at Scarborough, 1994
Lowest Score:	By Yorkshire	91 at Scarborough, 1970
	By Surrey	90 at Leeds, 1996
Highest Individual		
Score:	For Yorkshire	129* M D Moxon at The Oval, 1991
	For Surrey	136 M A Lynch at Bradford, 1985
Best Bowling:	For Yorkshire	5 for 25 D Gough at Leeds, 1998
	For Surrey	5 for 22 R D Jackman at The Oval, 1978

versus Sussex: Played 38, Won 18 (in Yorkshire 10, Away 8),
Lost 15 (in Yorkshire 7, Away 8), No Result 5

Highest Score:	By Yorkshire	274:8 at Middlesbrough, 1991
	By Sussex	272:6 at Arundel, 2000
Lowest Score:	By Yorkshire	89 at Hove, 1998
	By Sussex	108 at Hove, 1971
Highest Individual		
Score:	For Yorkshire	112 M D Moxon at Middlesbrough, 1991
	For Sussex	129 A W Greig at Scarborough, 1976
Best Bowling:	For Yorkshire	5 for 13 D Gough at Hove, 1994
	For Sussex	4 for 15 Imran Khan at Sheffield, 1985

versus Warwickshire: Played 41, Won 15 (in Yorkshire 8, Away 7),
Lost 19 (in Yorkshire 9, Away 10), Tied 1, No Result 6

Highest Score:	By Yorkshire	274:3 at Leeds, 2003
	By Warwickshire	309:3 at Birmingham, 2005
Lowest Score:	By Yorkshire	56 at Birmingham, 1995
	By Warwickshire	59 at Leeds, 2001
Highest Individual		
Score:	For Yorkshire	139* S P Fleming at Leeds, 2003
	For Warwickshire	137 I R Bell at Birmingham, 2005
Best Bowling:	For Yorkshire	4 for 21 C E W Silverwood at Leeds, 2001
	For Warwickshire	6 for 15 A A Donald at Birmingham, 1995

versus Worcestershire: Played 39, Won 18 (in Yorkshire 5, Away 13),
Lost 19 (in Yorkshire 13, Away 6), No Result 2

Highest Score:	By Yorkshire	223:4 at Huddersfield, 1976
		223:5 at Worcester, 1988
	By Worcestershire	251:4 at Scarborough, 1995
Lowest Score:	By Yorkshire	90 at Worcester, 1987
	By Worcestershire	86 at Leeds, 1969
Highest Individual		
Score:	For Yorkshire	112* K Sharp at Worcester, 1985
	For Worcestershire	113* G A Hick at Scarborough, 1995
Best Bowling:	For Yorkshire	7 for 15 R A Hutton at Leeds, 1969
	For Worcestershire	5 for 30 R J Chapman at Worcester, 1998

versus Scotland: Played 4, Won 4 (in Yorkshire 2, Away 2),

Highest Score:	By Yorkshire	240:5 at Leeds, 2004
	By Scotland	203:9 at Edinburgh, 2005
Lowest Score:	By Yorkshire	199:8 at Edinburgh, 2004
	By Scotland	140 at Edinburgh, 2004
Highest Individual		
Score:	For Yorkshire	88* D S Lehmann at Leeds, 2004
	For Scotland	78 J A Beukes at Edinburgh, 2005
Best Bowling:	For Yorkshire	4 for 20 R K J Dawson at Edinburgh, 2004
	For Scotland	3 for 47 Asim Butt at Edinburgh, 2004

CAREER AVERAGES FOR YORKSHIRE

PRO40, NATIONAL AND SUNDAY LEAGUE RECORDS 1969-2008

Player	M	Inns	NO	Runs	HS	Av'ge	100s	50s	Runs	Wkts	Av'ge	Ct/St
Athey, C W J ..	94	86	8	2560	118	32.82	1	18	315	14	22.50	30
Bairstow, D L ..	279	227	51	3677	83*	20.89	—	16	—	—	—	234/23
Baker, T M	1	—	—	—	—	—	—	—	22	1	22.00	1
Balderstone, J C	8	8	2	108	46	18.00	—	—	28	1	28.00	2
Batty, J D	31	13	6	41	13*	5.86	—	—	1091	40	27.27	16
Bevan, M G ...	29	27	5	1108	103*	50.36	2	7	399	23	17.34	9
Binks, J G	14	11	2	140	34	15.55	—	—	—	—	—	11/2
Blain, J A R ...	11	6	3	21	11*	7.00	—	—	364	11	33.08	3
Blakey, R J	249	218	52	5531	130*	33.32	3	27	—	—	—	244/48
Blewett, G S ...	11	11	0	178	48	16.18	—	—	116	4	29.00	6
Booth, P A	2	—	—	—	—	—	—	—	67	1	67.00	1
Bore, M K	44	18	7	67	15	6.09	—	—	1300	37	35.13	14
Boycott, G ...	163	157	24	5051	108*	37.97	2	37	611	14	43.64	69
Bresnan, T T ..	**76**	**64**	**14**	**672**	**61**	**13.44**	**—**	**1**	**2500**	**72**	**34.72**	**23**
Broadhurst, M ..	1	—	—	—	—	—	—	—	27	0	—	—
Brophy, G L ..	**20**	**18**	**2**	**366**	**66**	**22.87**	**—**	**2**	**—**	**—**	**—**	**17/5**
Byas, D	217	211	27	5352	111*	29.09	3	28	463	19	24.37	88
Carrick, P	210	143	42	1481	48*	14.66	—	—	5030	170	29.58	53
Chapman, C A .	7	6	3	89	36*	29.66	—	—	—	—	—	2
Cleary, M F ...	4	3	1	50	23*	25.00	—	—	159	2	79.50	—
Close, D B	17	16	0	224	50	14.00	—	1	118	1	118.00	8
Cooper, H P ...	103	50	24	358	29*	13.76	—	—	3038	120	25.31	20
Cope, G A	28	14	7	61	16*	8.71	—	—	750	18	41.66	6
Coverdale, S P ..	3	3	2	18	17*	18.00	—	—	—	—	—	3
Craven, V J	36	34	4	540	59	18.00	—	2	297	18	16.50	11
Dalton, A J	17	16	1	280	55	18.66	—	1	—	—	—	7
Dawood, I	20	16	4	212	57	17.66	—	1	—	—	—	17/7
Dawson, R K J .	65	46	9	303	41	8.18	—	—	1914	70	27.34	20
Dennis, S J	41	19	11	87	16*	10.87	—	—	1188	27	44.00	6
Elliott, M T G ..	5	5	2	266	115*	88.66	2	—	—	—	—	—
Elstub, C J	9	3	3	4	4*	—	—	—	259	11	23.55	—
Fellows, G M ..	62	52	8	893	67	20.30	—	4	589	13	45.31	21
Fisher, I D	24	11	3	63	20	7.88	—	—	595	25	23.80	3
Fleming, S P ...	7	7	1	285	139*	47.50	1	1	—	—	—	3
Fletcher, S D ..	86	18	11	49	11*	7.00	—	—	3136	114	27.50	26
Foster, M J	20	14	1	199	118	15.31	1	—	370	6	61.66	6
Gale, A W	**34**	**30**	**3**	**720**	**89**	**26.66**	**—**	**3**	**—**	**—**	**—**	**7**
Gilbert, C R ...	1	1	0	9	9	9.00	—	—	40	2	20.00	—
Gillespie, J N ..	7	2	0	14	11	7.00	—	—	238	9	26.44	3
Gough, D	**129**	**80**	**24**	**845**	**72***	**15.08**	**—**	**1**	**3929**	**159**	**24.71**	**23**
Gray, A K D ...	24	14	6	111	30*	13.88	—	—	612	17	36.00	5
Grayson, A P ...	49	35	6	367	55	12.65	—	1	1051	31	33.90	14
Guy, S M	**17**	**14**	**3**	**188**	**40**	**17.09**	**—**	**—**	**—**	**—**	**—**	**15/7**
Hamilton, G M .	74	52	12	743	57*	18.58	—	2	2033	81	25.10	12
Hampshire, A W	3	2	0	3	3	1.50	—	—	—	—	—	—
Hampshire, J H .	155	152	15	4505	119	32.88	6	26	22	1	22.00	47
Harden, R J	12	10	2	133	42	16.63	—	—	—	—	—	1
Hartley, P J	145	102	31	1164	52	16.39	—	2	4778	174	27.45	26
Hartley, S N ...	130	119	25	2087	83*	22.20	—	9	1587	48	33.06	40
Harvey, I J	24	23	2	486	69	23.14	—	1	766	24	31.91	8
Hoggard, M J .	**53**	**20**	**11**	**23**	**5***	**2.15**	**—**	**—**	**1694**	**80**	**21.17**	**5**

406

Player	M	Inns	NO	Runs	HS	Av'ge	100s	50s	Runs	Wkts	Av'ge	Ct/St
Hutchison, P M .	23	8	5	8	2*	2.66	—	—	670	28	23.93	3
Hutton, R A ...	77	60	19	761	65	18.56	—	3	2215	94	23.56	19
Illingworth, R ...	23	4	3	12	8*	12.00	—	—	453	26	17.42	7
Ingham, P G ...	12	10	4	312	87*	52.00	—	2	—	—	—	2
Inzamam-ul-Haq	3	3	0	69	53	23.00	—	1	—	—	—	—
Jaques, P A	20	19	1	788	105	43.77	1	7	—	—	—	11
Jarvis, P W	94	49	21	316	38*	11.29	—	—	2914	138	21.11	25
Johnson, C	100	81	17	1186	67*	18.53	—	3	5	2	2.50	24
Johnson, M ...	10	4	1	30	15*	10.00	—	—	317	5	63.40	2
Katich, S M ...	2	2	1	39	39*	39.00	—	—	—	—	—	2
Kellett, S A	30	30	2	697	118*	24.89	1	3	16	0	—	6
Kettleborough, RA	10	6	3	71	28	23.66	—	—	72	3	24.00	4
Kirby, S P	25	10	3	38	15	5.43	—	—	919	22	41.77	6
Kruis, G J	26	11	6	92	31*	18.40	—	—	853	32	26.65	5
Lawson, M A K	4	4	0	30	20	7.50	—	—	141	3	47.00	1
Leadbeater, B ..	73	68	14	1423	86*	26.35	—	6	38	2	19.00	18
Lehmann, D S ..	77	77	11	3091	191	46.83	3	24	1222	47	26.00	24
Love, J D	157	146	18	2919	118*	22.80	3	10	83	3	27.66	32
Lucas, D S	5	2	0	40	32	20.00	—	—	187	3	62.33	1
Lumb, M J	71	69	4	1838	92	28.27	—	14	28	0	—	12
Lumb, R G	87	75	10	1588	101	24.43	1	9	—	—	—	21
Lyth, A	9	6	1	78	28	15.60	—	—	3	0	—	3
McGrath, A ...	153	142	22	3823	148	31.85	2	23	1530	47	32.55	49
Metcalfe, A A ..	140	135	7	3529	116	27.57	2	23	—	—	—	32
Middlebrook, J D	14	9	2	52	15*	7.43	—	—	417	13	32.08	1
Milburn, S M ..	4	2	1	14	13*	7.00	—	—	118	2	59.00	1
Morris, A C. ...	23	15	3	208	48*	17.33	—	—	362	15	24.13	6
Moxon, M D ...	151	143	8	4128	129*	30.58	3	24	868	21	41.33	46
Nicholson, A G .	83	28	14	97	13*	6.93	—	—	1998	117	17.07	8
Nicholson, N G .	2	2	1	1	1*	1.00	—	—	—	—	—	2
Old, C M	143	112	27	1711	82*	20.12	—	6	3847	192	20.03	38
Oldham, S	71	26	15	144	38*	13.09	—	—	2064	83	24.86	10
Padgett, D E V .	40	39	2	760	68	20.54	—	2	25	1	25.00	9
Parker, B	56	49	6	723	42	16.81	—	—	18	0	—	8
Patterson, S A .	11	9	8	65	25*	65.00	—	—	422	9	46.88	3
Pickles, C S	56	38	17	259	30*	12.33	—	—	1896	53	35.77	20
Pyrah, R M .	29	22	6	278	42	17.37	—	—	673	27	24.92	9
Ramage, A	20	12	5	90	32*	12.85	—	—	658	14	47.00	—
Ramsden, G	1	—	—	—	—	—	—	—	26	2	13.00	—
Rana Neved												
-ul-Hasan	8	7	0	199	74	28.42	—	2	266	12	22.16	—
Rashid, A U ...	11	7	2	90	33*	18.00	—	—	339	10	33.90	6
Rhodes, S J	2	1	0	6	6	6.00	—	—	—	—	—	3
Richardson, R B	21	21	6	740	103	49.33	1	5	—	—	—	5
Robinson, A L ..	69	28	14	94	14	6.71	—	—	1904	81	23.50	11
Robinson, M A .	65	21	11	35	7	3.50	—	—	2030	63	32.22	7
Robinson, P E ..	104	100	12	2194	78*	24.93	—	11	—	—	—	37
Rudolph, J A ..	15	13	1	653	127	54.41	2	3	15	0	—	8
Sayers, J J	12	12	2	232	62	23.20	—	2	71	1	71.00	—
Scofield, D	3	1	0	0	0	0.00	—	—	111	2	55.50	1
Shahzad, A	4	4	0	8	5	2.00	—	—	131	3	43.66	—
Sharp, K	141	135	13	3392	114	27.80	2	20	1	0	—	45
Sharpe, P J	52	50	0	871	81	17.42	—	4	11	0	—	22

Player	M	Inns	NO	Runs	HS	Av'ge	100s	50s	Runs	Wkts	Av'ge	Ct/St
Shaw, C	38	15	8	117	26	16.71	—	—	1142	45	25.37	8
Sidebottom, A ..	156	86	33	835	52*	15.75	—	—	4561	149	30.61	29
Sidebottom, R J	66	35	18	218	30*	12.82	—	—	2016	72	28.00	9
Silverwood, CEW	106	64	27	555	58	15.00	—	2	3168	146	21.70	11
Smith, N	6	1	1	0	0*	—	—	—	—	—	—	2
Smith, R	3	2	0	17	17	8.50	—	—	—	—	—	1
Squires, P J	47	39	4	602	79*	17.20	—	3	4	0	—	8
Stemp, R D	60	21	7	114	23*	8.14	—	—	1978	67	29.52	13
Stevenson, G B .	153	116	16	1275	81*	12.75	—	2	4641	186	24.95	25
Stringer, P M ...	9	6	4	22	13*	11.00	—	—	235	11	21.36	—
Stuchbury, S ...	20	7	3	15	9*	3.75	—	—	588	26	22.61	2
Swallow, I G ...	2	1	0	2	2	2.00	—	—	31	0	—	—
Swanepoel, P J .	3	2	2	9	8*	—	—	—	100	3	33.33	—
Taylor, C R ...	**5**	**5**	**0**	**102**	**28**	**20.40**	—	—	—	—	—	—
Tendulkar, S R .	13	13	1	464	107	38.66	1	1	102	3	34.00	1
Thornicroft, N D	11	6	3	42	20	14.00	—	—	447	15	29.80	1
Townsley, R A J	5	4	1	81	34	27.00	—	—	62	0	—	1
Vaughan, M P .	**101**	**99**	**7**	**2344**	**116***	**25.47**	**1**	**11**	**988**	**30**	**32.93**	**34**
Wainwright, D J	**15**	**5**	**3**	**55**	**26**	**27.50**	—	—	**338**	**9**	**37.55**	**1**
Warren, A C ...	1	1	0	3	3	3.00	—	—	35	1	35.00	—
Wharf, A G	4	1	1	2	2*	—	—	—	87	3	29.00	1
White, C	**185**	**168**	**18**	**3643**	**148**	**24.28**	**1**	**13**	**3479**	**159**	**21.88**	**50**
Whiteley, J P ...	5	4	0	19	14	4.75	—	—	147	2	73.50	1
Widdup, S	4	4	0	49	38	12.25	—	—	—	—	—	2
Wilson, D	39	32	7	352	46	14.08	—	—	958	42	22.80	11
Wood, M J	103	94	6	2053	111	23.32	2	10	26	0	—	41
Woodford, J D .	60	50	12	834	69*	21.94	—	2	1401	60	23.35	20
Younus Khan ...	4	2	0	14	14	7.00	—	—	20	0	—	2
Yuvraj Singh ...	8	8	0	169	50	21.12	—	1	170	3	56.66	1

ALL LIMITED-OVERS COMPETITIONS OF 40 TO 65 OVERS 1963-2008

Player	M	Inns	NO	Runs	HS	Av'ge	100s	50s	Runs	Wkts	Av'ge	Ct/St
Athey, C W J	138	127	14	3653	118	32.33	2	25	431	19	22.68	45
Bairstow, D L	398	313	70	5114	103*	21.05	1	19	17	0	—	389/31
Baker, T M	4	1	0	3	3	3.00	—	—	89	4	22.25	3
Balderstone, J C	13	11	2	173	46	19.22	—	—	38	2	19.00	3
Batty, J D	38	16	7	50	13*	5.55	—	—	1297	42	30.88	18
Bevan, M G	47	44	11	2040	103*	61.82	2	18	513	27	19.00	10
Binks, J G	30	21	3	247	34	13.72	—	—	—	—	—	26/8
Blain, J A R	14	8	3	34	11*	6.80	—	—	419	12	34.91	3
Blakey, R J	371	317	83	7355	130*	31.43	3	35	—	—	—	366/60
Blewett, G S	17	17	0	560	77	32.94	—	2	196	11	17.82	7
Booth, P A	5	2	1	7	6*	7.00	—	—	147	3	49.00	1
Bore, M K	53	23	10	80	15	6.15	—	—	1591	50	31.82	15
Boycott, G	260	251	37	8481	146	39.63	6	62	1076	24	44.83	92
Bresnan, T T	**116**	**76**	**21**	**1002**	**61**	**18.21**	**—**	**2**	**3916**	**115**	**34.05**	**32**
Broadhurst, M	1	—	—	—	—	—	—	—	27	0	—	—
Brophy, G L	**40**	**33**	**7**	**647**	**66**	**24.88**	**—**	**4**	—	—	—	**39/7**
Byas, D	309	298	35	7691	116*	29.24	5	44	641	25	25.64	127
Carrick, P	302	204	52	2141	54	14.09	—	2	7361	236	31.19	68
Chapman, C A	8	6	3	89	36*	29.66	—	—	—	—	—	3
Claydon, M E	7	2	0	15	9	7.50	—	—	293	8	36.62	—
Cleary, M F	4	3	1	50	23*	25.00	—	—	159	2	79.50	—
Close, D B	32	31	2	623	96	21.48	—	3	475	23	20.65	14
Cooper, H P	142	74	34	483	29*	12.08	—	—	4184	177	23.64	26
Cope, G A	36	20	13	96	18*	13.71	—	—	1011	24	42.13	9
Coverdale, S P	3	3	2	18	17*	18.00	—	—	—	—	—	3
Craven, V J	41	38	5	579	59	17.55	—	2	338	20	16.90	17
Dalton, A J	17	16	1	280	55	18.66	—	1	—	—	—	7
Dawood, I	20	16	7	212	57	23.55	—	1	—	—	—	7/3
Dawson, R K J	90	56	11	396	41	8.80	—	—	2711	90	30.12	30
Dennis, S J	55	23	11	111	16*	9.25	—	—	1717	40	42.93	7
Elliott, M T G	6	6	3	394	128*	131.33	3	—	—	—	—	—
Elstub, C J	9	9	3	4	4*	—	—	—	259	11	23.55	—
Fellows, G M	94	78	15	1342	80*	21.30	—	6	836	22	38.00	27
Fisher, I D	28	12	3	68	20	7.55	—	—	708	29	24.41	6
Fleming, S P	7	7	1	285	139*	47.50	1	1	—	—	—	3
Fletcher, S D	138	33	18	105	16*	7.00	—	—	4686	164	28.57	34
Foster, M J	20	14	1	199	118	15.31	1	—	370	6	61.66	6
Gale, A W	**53**	**47**	**7**	**1218**	**89**	**30.45**	**—**	**7**	—	—	—	**9**
Gilbert, C R	4	3	0	18	9	6.00	—	—	130	6	21.66	—
Gillespie, J N	18	4	1	29	15*	9.66	—	—	601	18	33.38	6
Gough, D	**212**	**119**	**33**	**1273**	**72***	**14.80**	**—**	**1**	**6770**	**290**	**23.34**	**43**
Gray, A K D	30	18	7	128	30*	11.64	—	—	814	23	35.39	8
Grayson, A P	65	48	7	575	55	14.02	—	1	1410	38	37.11	19
Guy, S M	**24**	**17**	**3**	**211**	**40**	**15.07**	**—**	**—**	—	—	—	**23/7**
Hamilton, G M	100	70	18	1059	57*	20.37	—	2	2761	118	23.40	15
Hampshire, A W	4	3	0	3	3	1.00	—	—	—	—	—	1
Hampshire, J H	231	220	24	6248	119	31.88	7	36	26	1	26.00	69
Harden, R J	19	16	2	230	42	16.43	—	—	—	—	—	1
Hartley, P J	216	145	49	1609	83	16.76	—	4	7425	280	26.52	40
Hartley, S N	170	153	31	2810	83*	23.03	—	13	2122	67	31.67	52

Player	M	Inns	NO	Runs	HS	Av'ge	100s	50s	Runs	Wkts	Av'ge	Ct/St
Harvey, I J	28	27	2	637	74	25.48	—	3	950	30	31.66	9
Hoggard, M J	**80**	**27**	**18**	**41**	**7***	**4.55**	**—**	**—**	**2599**	**116**	**22.40**	**8**
Hutchison, P M	32	11	8	18	4*	6.00	—	—	844	43	19.63	3
Hutton, R A	105	78	24	1015	65	17.81	—	4	2990	128	23.36	27
Illingworth, R	40	15	11	171	45	42.75	—	—	764	39	19.59	14
Ingham, P G	12	10	4	312	87*	52.00	—	2	—	—	—	2
Inzamam-ul-Haq ...	3	3	0	69	53	23.00	—	1	—	—	—	—
Jaques, P A	26	24	2	999	105	45.40	1	9	—	—	—	13
Jarvis, P W	142	72	27	512	42	11.38	—	—	4575	209	21.89	32
Johnson, C	127	101	22	1614	73*	20.43	—	4	28	2	14.00	33
Johnson, M	14	6	3	34	15*	11.33	—	—	455	12	37.92	2
Katich, S M	3	3	2	79	40*	79.00	—	—	—	—	—	2
Kellett, S A	53	49	3	1182	118*	25.70	2	4	16	0	—	12
Kettleborough, R A .	10	6	3	71	28	23.66	—	—	72	3	24.00	4
Kirby, S P	28	12	3	38	15	4.22	—	—	1036	24	43.17	6
Kruis, G J	**43**	**16**	**10**	**115**	**31***	**19.16**	**—**	**—**	**1374**	**45**	**30.53**	**7**
Lawson, M A K	4	4	0	30	20	7.50	—	—	141	3	47.00	1
Leadbeater, B	103	98	19	2179	90	27.58	—	11	95	5	19.00	25
Lehmann, D S	130	126	20	5229	191	49.33	8	38	1868	77	24.25	41
Lester, E I	1	1	0	0	0	0.00	—	—	—	—	—	—
Love, J D	220	203	33	4298	118*	25.28	4	18	129	5	25.80	44
Lucas, D S	5	2	0	40	32	20.00	—	—	187	3	62.33	1
Lumb, M J	102	96	8	2592	92	29.45	—	11	28	0	—	31
Lumb, R G	135	121	13	2747	101	25.44	1	16	—	—	—	21
Lyth, A	**17**	**12**	**2**	**186**	**38***	**18.60**	**—**	**—**	**3**	**0**	**—**	**7**
McGrath, A	**238**	**221**	**32**	**6253**	**148**	**33.08**	**6**	**36**	**2228**	**71**	**31.38**	**78**
Metcalfe, A A	191	186	14	5520	127*	32.09	4	36	44	2	22.00	44
Middlebrook, J D ..	18	10	3	61	15*	8.71	—	—	530	13	40.77	5
Milburn, S M	4	2	1	14	13*	7.00	—	—	118	2	59.00	1
Morris, A C	25	16	4	209	48*	17.42	—	—	409	16	25.56	7
Moxon, M D	235	227	21	7307	141*	35.47	7	48	1178	34	43.65	77
Nicholson, A G	119	45	22	154	15*	6.70	—	—	2943	173	17.01	16
Nicholson, N G ...	2	2	1	1	1*	1.00	—	—	—	—	—	2
Old, C M	218	166	37	2550	82*	19.77	—	10	5817	306	19.01	56
Oldham, S	105	40	21	160	38*	8.42	—	—	3136	142	22.08	17
Padgett, D E V ...	57	54	3	1069	68	20.96	—	2	25	1	25.00	13
Parker, B	72	60	8	964	69	18.54	—	2	18	0	—	11
Patterson, S A ...	**15**	**10**	**9**	**68**	**25***	**68.00**	**—**	**—**	**567**	**12**	**47.25**	**3**
Pickles, C S	69	47	19	370	37*	13.21	—	—	2355	62	37.98	22
Pyrah, R M	**49**	**33**	**8**	**398**	**42**	**15.92**	**—**	**—**	**1301**	**50**	**26.02**	**19**
Ramage, A	34	17	8	134	32*	14.88	—	—	1178	30	39.23	3
Rana Naved												
-ul-Hasan	**9**	**8**	**0**	**212**	**74**	**26.50**	**—**	**2**	**307**	**14**	**21.92**	**—**
Rashid, A U	**22**	**12**	**3**	**132**	**41***	**14.66**	**—**	**—**	**598**	**17**	**35.17**	**9**
Rhodes, S J	2	1	0	6	6	6.00	—	—	—	—	—	3
Richardson, R B ...	28	28	6	993	103	45.14	1	8	—	—	—	5
Robinson, A L	92	36	19	128	18*	7.53	—	—	2588	105	24.65	14
Robinson, M A	86	30	16	41	7	2.93	—	—	2725	89	30.62	7
Robinson, P E	134	123	15	2738	78*	25.35	—	14	—	—	—	47
Rudolph, J A	**33**	**30**	**4**	**1262**	**127**	**48.53**	**3**	**7**	**24**	**0**	**—**	**17**
Ryan, M	3	2	1	7	6*	7.00	—	—	149	5	29.80	3
Sayers, J J	**12**	**12**	**2**	**242**	**62**	**24.20**	**—**	**2**	**71**	**1**	**71.00**	**—**

Player	M	Inns	NO	Runs	HS	Av'ge	100s	50s	Runs	Wkts	Av'ge	Ct/St
Scofield, D	3	1	0	0	0	0.00	—	—	111	2	55.50	1
Shahzad, A	**8**	**6**	**1**	**52**	**33**	**10.40**	—	—	**283**	**7**	**40.42**	—
Sharp, K	203	188	18	4693	114	27.61	3	27	48	4	12.00	66
Sharpe, P J	89	84	4	1499	89*	18.74	—	8	11	0	16.50	52
Shaw, C	48	21	11	131	26	13.10	—	—	1396	58	24.07	8
Sidebottom, A	233	129	47	1273	52*	15.52	—	—	6841	258	26.51	34
Sidebottom, R J ..	100	44	21	251	30*	10.91	—	—	3070	104	29.52	34
Silverwood,C E W ..	164	89	32	866	61	15.19	—	4	5145	223	23.07	25
Smith, N	7	2	1	5	5	5.00	—	—	—	—	—	2
Smith, R	3	2	0	17	17	8.50	—	—	—	—	—	1
Squires, P J	56	48	5	708	79*	16.47	—	3	4	0	—	10
Stemp, R D	88	28	10	118	23*	6.55	—	—	2996	100	29.96	14
Stevenson, G B ...	216	157	23	1699	81*	12.68	—	2	6820	290	23.52	38
Stott, W B	2	2	0	30	30	15.00	—	—	—	—	—	—
Stringer, P M	11	8	6	29	13*	14.50	—	—	256	15	17.07	—
Stuchbury, S	22	8	4	21	9*	5.25	—	—	677	29	23.34	2
Swallow, I G	8	5	3	37	17*	18.50	—	—	198	2	99.00	5
Swanepoel, P G	3	2	2	9	8*	—	—	—	100	3	33,33	—
Taylor, C R	**6**	**5**	**0**	**102**	**28**	**20.40**	—	—	—	—	—	—
Taylor, K	10	10	0	135	30	13.50	—	—	168	11	15.27	3
Tendulkar, S R	17	17	2	540	107	36.00	1	1	167	6	27.83	3
Thornicroft, N D ..	13	6	4	52	20	26.00	—	—	544	16	34.00	2
Townsley, R A J ...	5	4	1	81	34	27.00	—	—	62	0	—	1
Trueman, F S	11	9	1	127	28	15.87	—	—	348	21	16.57	5
Vaughan, M P	**176**	**171**	**13**	**4600**	**125***	**29.11**	**3**	**26**	**1770**	**59**	**30.00**	**55**
Wainwright, D J ..	**16**	**6**	**4**	**62**	**26**	**31.00**	—	—	**414**	**10**	**41.40**	**1**
Waring, J	1	1	1	1	1*	—	—	—	11	0	—	—
Warren, A C	1	1	0	3	3	3.00	—	—	35	1	35.00	—
Wharf, A G	6	1	1	2	2*	—	—	—	176	8	22.00	1
White, C	**291**	**265**	**39**	**6376**	**148**	**28.21**	**5**	**28**	**6088**	**246**	**24.74**	**84**
Whiteley, J P	5	4	0	19	14	4.75	—	—	147	2	73.50	1
Widdup, S	4	4	0	49	38	12.25	—	—	—	—	—	2
Wilson, D	59	45	8	424	46	11.46	—	—	1502	74	20.30	22
Wood, M J	143	132	14	3209	160	27.19	5	14	71	3	23.66	56
Woodford, J D	72	57	14	890	69*	20.70	—	2	1627	77	21.13	25
Younus Khan	11	8	0	248	100	31.00	1	—	144	2	72.00	5
Yuvraj Singh	9	9	0	196	50	21.77	—	1	197	3	65.66	1

TWENTY20 CUP 2003-2008

BEST SEASONS — QUARTER-FINALISTS 2006 & 2007

Played 46, Won 21 (in Yorkshire 11, Away 10), Lost 21 (in Yorkshire 8, Away 13),
Tied 1 (in Yorkshire), No Result 3.

Highest Score:	By Yorkshire	211:6 v. Leicestershire at Leeds, 2004
	Against Yorkshire	221:3 by Leicestershire at Leeds, 2004
†Lowest Score:	By Yorkshire	97 v. Lancashire at Manchester, 2005
	Against Yorkshire	98 by Durham at Chester-le-Street, 2006

Highest Individual

Score:	For Yorkshire	109 I J Harvey v. Derbyshire at Leeds, 2005
	Against Yorkshire	111 D L Maddy for Leicestershire at Leeds, 2004

†Lowest score is the lowest all-out score or the lowest score at completion of allotted overs

Highest
Partnerships: For Yorkshire

1st wkt	99	A W Gale (45) and G L Brophy (57*) v. Nottinghamshire at Nottingham, 2008
2nd wkt	124	I J Harvey (109) and P A Jaques (37) v. Derbyshire at Leeds, 2005
3rd wkt	117	J A Rudolph (56) and A McGrath (59) v. Leicestershire at Leicester, 2008
4th wkt	93	P A Jaques (92) and T T Bresnan (42) v. Leicestershire at Leeds, 2004
5th wkt	59	A McGrath (72*) and G L Brophy (13) v. Derbyshire at Derby, 2008
6th wkt	41	M J Lumb (66) and C R Gilbert (26) v. Leicestershire at Leeds, 2006
7th wkt	56	V J Craven (44) and R J Blakey (18) v. Durham at Chester-le-Street, 2004
8th wkt	41*	R M Pyrah (33*) and T T Bresnan (14*) v. Lancashire at Leeds, 2005
9th wkt	33*	A U Rashid (5*) and D Gough (20*) v. Lancashire at Leeds, 2008
10th wkt	22	M A K Lawson (4*) and M J Hoggard (18) v. Lancashire at Manchester, 2005

Best Bowling:	For Yorkshire	4 for 20 R M Pyrah v. Durham at Leeds, 2008
	Against Yorkshire	4 for 9 C K Langerveldt for Derbyshire at Leeds, 2008

Most Economical Bowling (4 overs):

	For Yorkshire	4-0-12-2 T T Bresnan v. Lancashire at Manchester, 2008
	Against Yorkshire	4-0-9-4 C K Langerveldt for Derbyshire at Leeds, 2008

Most Expensive Bowling:

	For Yorkshire	4-0-65-2 M J Hoggard v. Lancashire at Leeds, 2005
	Against Yorkshire	4-0-58-0 G Welch for Derbyshire at Leeds, 2003

versus Derbyshire: Played 7, Won 5 (in Yorkshire 3, Away 2), Lost 1 (in Yorkshire),
No Result 1 (Away).

Highest Score:	By Yorkshire	210:3 at Derby, 2006
	By Derbyshire	195:8 at Leeds, 2005
Lowest Score:	By Yorkshire	108:9 at Derby, 2004
	By Derbyshire	119:7 at Leeds, 2007
Highest Individual Score:		
	For Yorkshire	109 I J Harvey at Leeds, 2005
	For Derbyshire	100* G M Smith at Leeds, 2008
Best Bowling:	For Yorkshire	3 for 23 M J Hoggard at Derby, 2004
	For Derbyshire	4 for 9 C K Langerveldt at Leeds, 2008

versus Durham: Played 10, Won 6 (in Yorkshire 3, Away 3), Lost 3 (in Yorkshire 1, Away 2),
Tied 1 (in Yorkshire)

Highest Score:	By Yorkshire	198:4 at Leeds, 2003
	By Durham	159:7 at Leeds, 2008
Lowest Score:	By Yorkshire	123:7 at Leeds, 2005
	By Durham	98 at Chester-le-Street, 2006
Highest Individual Score:		
	For Yorkshire	65 A McGrath at Leeds, 2008
	For Durham	53 D M Benkenstein at Chester-le-Street, 2005
Best Bowling:	For Yorkshire	4 for 20 R M Pyrah at Leeds, 2008
	For Durham	4 for 38 S J Harmison at Leeds, 2008

versus Essex: Played 1, Lost 1 (Away)

Scores:	By Yorkshire	143:7 at Chelmsford, 2006
	By Essex	149:5 at Chelmsford, 2006
Highest Individual Score:		
	For Yorkshire	43 G L Brophy at Chelmsford, 2006
	For Essex	48* J S Foster at Chelmsford, 2006
Best Bowling:	For Yorkshire	2 for 22 A Shahzad at Chelmsford, 2006
	For Essex	2 for 11 T J Phillips at Chelmsford, 2006

versus Lancashire: Played 10, Won 5 (in Yorkshire 3, Away 2), Lost 4
(in Yorkshire 1, Away 3), No Result 1 (in Yorkshire)

Highest Score:	By Yorkshire	170:2 at Leeds, 2004
	By Lancashire	207 at Manchester, 2005
Lowest Score:	By Yorkshire	97 at Manchester, 2005
	By Lancashire	104:3 at Manchester, 2003
Highest Individual Score:	For Yorkshire	108* I J Harvey at Leeds, 2004
	For Lancashire	101 S G Law at Manchester, 2005
Best Bowling:	For Yorkshire	3 for 18 A K D Gray at Leeds, 2004
	For Lancashire	3 for 10 D G Cork at Manchester, 2005

versus Leicestershire: Played 7, Won 1 (Away), Lost 4 (in Yorkshire 2, Away 3),
No Result 1 (in Yorkshire)

Highest Score:	By Yorkshire	211:6 at Leeds, 2004
	By Leicestershire	221:3 at Leeds, 2004
Lowest Score:	By Yorkshire	134 at Leeds, 2006
	By Leicestershire	154:3 at Leicester, 2008
Highest Individual Score:	For Yorkshire	92 P A Jaques at Leeds, 2004
	For Leicestershire	111 D L Maddy at Leeds, 2004
Best Bowling:	For Yorkshire	2 for 19 G J Kruis at Leeds, 2006
	For Leicestershire	3 for 6 B J Hodge at Leicester, 2003
		3 for 6 J N Snape at Leicester, 2007

versus Nottinghamshire: Played 10, Won 4 (in Yorkshire 2, Away 2)
Lost 6 (in Yorkshire 3, Away 3)

Highest Score:	By Yorkshire	207:7 at Nottingham, 2004
	By Nottinghamshire	210:7 at Nottingham, 2004
Lowest Score:	By Yorkshire	141:8 at Leeds, 2008
	By Nottinghamshire	136:8 at Nottingham, 2008
Highest Individual Score:	For Yorkshire	96* M J Wood at Nottingham, 2004
	For Nottinghamshire	91 M A Ealham at Nottingham, 2004
Best Bowling:	For Yorkshire	4 for 24 A U Rashid at Nottingham, 2008
	For Nottinghamshire	3 for 42 S C G MacGill at Leeds, 2003

versus Sussex: Played 1, Lost 1 (Away)

Scores:	By Yorkshire	155 at Hove, 2007
	By Sussex	193:5 at Hove, 2007
Highest Individual Score:	For Yorkshire	47 C White at Hove, 2007
	For Sussex	57 M W Goodwin at Hove, 2007
Best Bowling:	For Yorkshire	2 for 32 Younus Khan at Hove, 2007
	For Sussex	3 for 26 Naved-ul-Hasan at Hove, 2007

CAREER AVERAGES FOR YORKSHIRE

TWENTY20 CUP 2003-2008

Player	M	Inns	NO	Runs	HS	Av'ge	100s	50s	Runs	Wkts	Av'ge	Ct/St
Azeem Rafiq ..	1	—	—	—	—	—	—	—	18	0	—	—
Blakey, R J	7	5	1	119	32	29.75	—	—	—	—	—	5/1
Bresnan, T T ..	38	28	10	325	42	18.05	—	—	904	39	23.17	14
Brophy, G L ...	26	24	5	480	57*	25.26	—	2	—	—	—	11/3
Claydon, M E ..	7	2	2	14	12*	—	—	—	188	5	37.60	2
Craven, V J	6	6	4	76	44*	38.00	—	—	67	0	—	3
Dawood, I	11	8	3	44	15	8.80	—	—	—	—	—	5/2
Dawson, R K J .	22	8	3	71	22	14.20	—	—	558	24	23.25	7
Fleming, S P ...	4	4	0	62	58	15.50	—	1	—	—	—	1
Gale, A W	28	24	4	365	56	19.92	—	2	—	—	—	13
Gilbert, C R ...	13	9	2	107	36*	15.28	—	—	—	—	—	7
Gillespie, J N ..	17	4	2	14	8*	7.00	—	—	422	17	24.82	5
Gough, D	17	7	3	42	20*	10.50	—	—	416	16	26.00	2
Gray, A K D ...	8	3	0	17	13	5.66	—	—	211	9	23.44	4
Guy, S M	4	2	0	11	7	5.50	—	—	—	—	—	1
Hamilton, G M .	3	3	1	41	41*	20.50	—	—	—	—	—	1
Harvey, I J	10	10	1	438	109	48.66	2	2	258	10	25.80	4
Hoggard, M J .	15	2	1	19	18	19.00	—	—	472	13	36.30	4
Jaques, P A	13	13	1	455	92	37.91	—	3	15	0	—	2
Kirby, S P	3	—	—	—	—	—	—	—	119	4	29.75	1
Kruis, G J	10	2	1	6	5*	6.00	—	—	245	9	27.22	2
Lawson, M A K .	2	1	1	4	4*	—	—	—	87	3	29.00	1
Lehmann, D S ..	9	9	3	252	48	42.00	—	—	180	8	22.50	4
Lumb, M J	26	26	3	442	84*	19.21	—	4	65	3	21.66	8
Lyth, A	1	1	0	0	0	0.00	—	—	—	—	—	—
McGrath, A ...	38	37	7	928	72*	30.93	—	7	494	15	32.93	12
Rudolph, J A ..	17	15	5	317	56	31.70	—	1	110	6	18.33	2
Pyrah, R M ...	25	16	5	126	33*	11.45	—	—	300	20	15.00	11
Rashid, A U ...	8	6	2	18	10	4.50	—	—	162	7	23.14	3
Sayers, J J	3	1	0	12	12	12.00	—	—	—	—	—	2
Shahzad, A	1	1	1	2	2*	—	—	—	22	2	11.00	—
Sidebottom, R J	5	1	0	10	10	10.00	—	—	136	7	19.42	2
Silverwood, C E W	9	5	2	32	13*	10.66	—	—	264	7	37.71	4
Swanepoel, P ..	2	1	1	2	2*	—	—	—	60	3	20.00	1
Taylor, C R ...	2	2	1	10	10*	10.00	—	—	—	—	—	—
Vaughan, M P .	7	7	0	104	34	14.85	—	—	72	1	72.00	1
Wainwright, D J	9	3	1	6	3*	3.00	—	—	173	8	21.62	2
Warren, A C ...	2	—	—	—	—	—	—	—	70	4	17.50	—
White, C	33	31	0	570	55	18.38	—	2	132	2	66.00	8
Wood, M J	15	15	3	328	96*	27.33	—	2	32	2	16.00	11
Younus Khan ...	2	2	0	55	40	27.50	—	—	32	2	16.00	0
Yuvraj Singh ...	5	5	0	154	71	30.80	—	1	51	5	10.20	0

ANNUAL REPORT
and
Statement of Account

for the year ended
December 31, 2008

CHAIRMAN'S REPORT

Although the Club gave a mixed performance on the field in 2008, I am delighted that
this season we will be competing in the top
tier of both the *LV Championship* and the
NatWest Pro40 following our promotion in
the latter competition.

As everyone is aware, the economy has
been in turmoil over the past year or so. **COLIN GRAVES**
However, Yorkshire can look to the future with confidence, as the
Club achieved a profit for the third consecutive year, and the
financial package is now firmly in place for the building of the
iconic Carnegie Pavilion with state-of-the-art players' facilities
and media centre.

Back to the cricket side of our operations. There was a marked
improvement in our one-day form, which resulted in reaching the
semi-finals of the *Friends Provident Trophy* and the clinching of
second place and promotion in the *NatWest Pro40*.

We may well have progressed to Finals Day in the *Twenty20
Cup* but for our failure to register **Azeem Rafiq**, and the Club
apologises for getting it wrong and causing embarrassment. Steps

have been taken to put a process in place to prevent this from ever happening again. We are delighted that Azeem has now acquired British Citizenship, and has this winter been representing England Under-19s in South Africa.

In the *LV Championship* we appeared to struggle on two fronts: we were unable to bowl sides out twice on a regular basis, and we were unable to find a successful opening-batting combination to get our innings off to a healthy start.

But how magnificently the team fought back from potential disaster in the final match of the season, when heroic centuries from **Adil Rashid** and **David Wainwright** pulled the innings round from 80-6 to 400-9 declared. These valiant efforts meant that 12 points could be taken from the drawn match, when none had appeared likely at one stage, and they were sufficient to save us from relegation.

Adil and David also claimed a total of 14 wickets between them in this match, and the two youngsters are a shining example of why the Club has given a commitment to youth in 2009. It did not go unnoticed that the young side which fought so bravely at Hove comprised exactly the same players who had pulled off an outstanding victory against Somerset at Taunton earlier on.

There were several other young players who showed that the investment in them was proving worthwhile. They included fast bowlers **Oliver Hannon-Dalby** and **Ben Sanderson**, who both made their Championship debuts, and batsman and wicket-keeper **Jonathan Bairstow**, who was included in the squad at Hove.

Pacemen **Steven Patterson** and **Ajmal Shahzad** were two others who made the most of their limited opportunities last season, and the challenge now will be in trying to give proof that our youth has got what it takes to succeed at First Class level.

Myself and the Board of Directors could not be more pleased that **Anthony McGrath** has accepted the first-team captaincy from the inspirational **Darren Gough**, who takes into his retirement from First Class cricket our deepest thanks for leading the team with such dedication during his two years in charge.

Goughy has been an outstanding cricketer for both England and Yorkshire, and may I thank him personally for all his efforts over the many years. He has provided us all with a great deal of entertainment.

This year is also Anthony's benefit season, and he has just signed a two-year extension to his contract which will keep him at Headingley Carnegie at least until the end of 2011. Anthony has been a great servant of the Club, and is 100 per cent committed to helping Yorkshire to become a power in the land once again. We wish him every success both on and off the field.

September 4, 2008, was a red-letter day for the Club, because that was the date when planning approval was obtained for the Carnegie Pavilion, subject to a number of small conditions which have now been met. We are grateful to Leeds City Council for their support, and we thank Leeds Metropolitan University for being such a fabulous partner and working so closely with the Club. We are excited at the prospect of moving into the new building in 2010, when we will have one of the finest cricket pavilions in the world.

The Winter Shed has now been demolished to make way for the new development, and it has to be admitted that there was nostalgia in the air when it succumbed to the bulldozers. Great coaches like **George Hirst** and **Maurice Leyland** passed on their expertise there, and it was in that rather gloomy building that players of the calibre of our President, **Brian Close**, and others from that Championship-winning team of 1959 learned their trade.

Since the end of last season an historic piece of work has been going on in installing a new drainage system at Headingley Carnegie and re-laying the outfield, including the removal of the slope. A pop-up sprinkler system has been installed, which can be turned on whenever required and will make preparation work much easier for our conscientious and totally dedicated head groundsman, Andy Fogarty.

Andy has amazed everyone with the speed by which he gets the ground fit for play after heavy rain, and delays should be cut even further with a new drainage system similar to the one which has proved so effective at Lord's in recent times.

At international level the Fourth npower Ashes Test at Headingley Carnegie, starting on August 7, promises to be a thrilling and memorable occasion. I am delighted to report that the first three days were long since sold out and that the fourth day was heading in the same direction at the time of writing.

For the first time, non-refundable tickets will be on sale for the fifth day. If the game looks like running its course with an exciting final day in prospect we do not want thousands queuing outside with no guarantee of getting in.

And so, here we are at the start of one of the most exciting seasons for some time — Yorkshire in the top division of both the *LV County Championship* and the *NatWest Pro40*, the continued growth of the *Twenty20* format of the game, an Ashes Test at our own cricket ground and an investment in our stadium of some £25m plus. Who would have thought it just three years ago when we bought the ground?

I would like to pass on my thanks to the Management Team and staff at Yorkshire CCC for their continued efforts to improve the Club and grow our business for the benefit of us all.

May I wish you all a very enjoyable season in 2009, and thank you for your continued support in developing Yorkshire County Cricket Club into what it is today.

COLIN GRAVES
Chairman

CHIEF EXECUTIVE'S
REPORT

The coming year will be a momentous one for Yorkshire County Cricket Club, what with the staging of the Fourth nPower Ashes Test in front of a guaranteed full house at Headingley Carnegie and the construction work taking place on the new Carnegie Pavilion at the Kirkstall Lane end of the ground.

Our financial projections for 2009 look very positive, given the sales of tickets for the Ashes, **STEWART REGAN** and in 2009 we are very confident of delivering a fourth successive financial surplus for members to follow the encouraging performance we have seen in 2008.

In a year when many companies have struggled we have bucked the trend by delivering a magnificent surplus of £367k and a record turnover of £5.96m. This has been achieved by a superb sales performance of £846k — growth of 21 per cent over 2007. We have also grown our net international match revenue by five per cent to £1.176m, and seen a six per cent increase in the central distribution from the England and Wales Cricket Board to £1.8m.

The absolute number of Yorkshire CCC members fell by 71 over the season to 7,546, but membership subscriptions grew by four per cent to £608k. Ground admissions fell by £80k to £268k, largely due to the abysmal weather which affected our match programme, especially during the *Twenty20* campaign. We now have the second highest commercial income in the country, and I would like to pay tribute to our Sales Director, Richard Kaye, and his team who have done a sterling job in troubled times. A new two-year contract was agreed with our official sponsor, Bradford & Bingley, prior to their own financial difficulties, and our income from this source is protected until the end of the 2010 season.

It has been a difficult second half of the year for the financial markets and banks, and the Club has been under a lot of pressure in securing the finance required for our exciting development. I am delighted to report, however, that the Club has succeeded in raising the necessary finance to

419

complete not only our £7m contribution to the £21m total project cost, but also the £4.85m required to buy out the option payments to LCF&A (agreed in 2005 when we bought the ground) in order to proceed with the work.

The balance of the project cost, some £14m, is being provided by Leeds Metropolitan University, to whom we are eternally grateful. Included in our £7m contribution is £4m from the regional development agency, Yorkshire Forward, who have backed the club to erect a landmark building for the county of Yorkshire.

The Carnegie Pavilion will be the single most viewed building in Yorkshire, watched by over 500m TV viewers when our international matches are broadcast around the world. We are delighted with the support from Yorkshire Forward, and feel sure that they, like us, will be proud of our new Pavilion when it finally opens its doors in 2010. The balance of our £7m contribution will come from Club funds to the tune of £1.5m, with a further £1.5m in rent to be paid over 20 years to Leeds Metropolitan University.

We are also deeply indebted to Leeds City Council, HSBC and to our Chairman, Colin Graves, without whom we would not be able to proceed with our plans for the future. In addition, we would like to thank the England and Wales Cricket Board, who have given the Club a series of grants and loan arrangements in order to carry out essential works at the cricket ground.

It is the chaos surrounding *Twenty20* cricket in India which has led to a number of on-going negotiations with the ECB concerning our overseas player, **Rana Naved-ul-Hasan**, who has been participating in the unauthorized Indian Cricket League. At the time of writing this report and subject to final confirmation from the ECB, it is likely that Rana will be available to play for us in all but *Twenty20* matches in the coming season.

On a more positive and upbeat note, Yorkshire begin their preparations for the new season in earnest when they fly from Birmingham to Dubai to defend the *ProArch Trophy*, which they won so convincingly last year. New captain **Anthony McGrath** and his professional squad will face strong opposition from Surrey, Middlesex and the United Arab Emirates, and we wish them every success in this worthy competition which affords us the ideal opportunity to prepare fully for the battles which lie ahead over the coming months.

As the Chairman mentions in his Report, the Club is placing strong emphasis on youth in 2009, and I am delighted to congratulate the following players who have represented us at various England levels over the past 12 months: **Tim Bresnan**, **Adil Rashid**, **Ben Sanderson** and **Azeem Rafiq**. Azeem in particular deserves a special mention, given the huge media coverage he had to deal with during last summer when the Club failed to register him for his debut at Trent Bridge against Nottinghamshire Outlaws in the *Twenty20 Cup*. The Club were deeply embarrassed by the whole event, and have taken appropriate internal action to deal with the administrative failings. On a positive note, Azeem handled the media extremely professionally, and gained the support of many local dignitaries. His application for British citizenship was accelerated accordingly, and it was great to see him represent England Under-19s in South Africa this year.

Sincere congratulations must also go to Adil Rashid, who becomes the first Yorkshire player of Asian descent to be selected for the full England Test squad. This is a historic moment for the Club, and shows just how far we have come in the past few years in engaging the Asian community and developing such talent as Rashid, **Ajmal Shahzad** and Rafiq to name but three of our up-and-coming young players.

Members will be pleased to learn that the Board has approved the creation of a Museum and Visitors' Centre underneath the Long Room in the East Stand, and this will be developed following the completion of the new pavilion in 2010. The Club's Archive Committee is heavily involved in the planning and design of this most welcome facility, and funding is now in place for this project, thanks to the generosity of one of our members. We are most grateful for this most gracious gesture.

The Club's new cricket structure sees the return to Headingley Carnegie of two much respected former players in **Ashley Metcalfe**, who formed such a formidable opening partnership with Director of Professional Cricket **Martyn Moxon** in their playing days, and **John Blain**, the Scottish international fast bowler. The pair are now in situ: Ashley as the new General Manager of the Bradford and Bingley Indoor Cricket Centre, and John as captain of the Yorkshire Academy team and Assistant Bowling Coach.

Andy Rowsell, who was in charge of the Indoor Cricket Centre, takes up the new post of Head Coach for the Emerging Players' Programme for 11-15-year-olds, an initiative which reinforces the Club's commitment to youth. Andy did a great job in his previous role, and we wish him well going forward. Ashley's experience in both cricket coaching and business — he ran his own PR and marketing consultancy — makes him the ideal candidate for this important post, which involves the development of the Indoor Cricket Centre as a destination for events, conferences and corporate activities as well as the core cricket operation.

In times of economic turmoil, it is important to have strong commercial relationships, and I would like to thank all of our partners for their support. I would like to say a special thank-you to Leeds Metropolitan University for backing the Club in a very difficult financial climate and for their desire to work with us to deliver a world-class cricket ground for our members. In addition, I would like to record my thanks to Bradford & Bingley, who have been our Official Sponsor for the last three seasons. We appreciate the financial difficulties they have had to deal with in recent times, and we wish them and their staff all the very best for the future, and thank them for their loyalty to this Club.

The Members' Liaison Committee, led by Stephen Mann, the Archives Committee, led by David Hall, and the Yearbook Committee, led by David Warner, have continued their fine work during 2008, and it is worth reminding members that all participants in these committees are volunteers who invest a huge amount of time on behalf of the Club. Their efforts are indeed appreciated by us all.

I would like to thank my management team at Headingley Carnegie for another excellent year in what has proved to be very difficult trading conditions. Not only have we had to deal with the economic downturn, but we have had another season of diabolical summer weather which has made it difficult to maximize ticket sales and hospitality. Let us hope that days of sunshine and blue skies lie ahead of us!

Finally, I would just like to say thank you to you, our members. Hopefully you are now starting to see evidence that this club means business and we intend to provide you with one of the finest cricket grounds in the country.

I do hope to see you during the coming season.

With best wishes,

STEWART REGAN
Chief Executive

DIRECTOR OF PROFESSIONAL CRICKET'S REPORT

2009 would best be described as a split season. On the one hand we have been successful in all the one-day competitions, reaching the semi-finals of the *Friends Provident Trophy*, gaining promotion in the *Pro40 League*, and being within one match of *Twenty20* finals day. On the other hand, in a closely contested County Championship, we escaped relegation only in the final match at Hove, despite being in a good position at other times during the season.

We may have been inconsistent, but at times we have played very good cricket, and we gained 95 bonus points during the season. There were occasions when the bowlers put us in a strong position but then failed to bowl a side out, and at other times the batting let us down.

We lost five games, having been in a strong position in three of them, and we should have won or, at any rate, not lost. There were, of course, many good days, too. We remained competitive until the end of the season, and sustained our form better than we had in 2007. The problem was that we missed opportunities to press home the advantage, and this is what we want to rectify this summer.

The match at Hove was one of the most remarkable recoveries in Yorkshire's history, and a great achievement. It was a tough day to bat first, and at the end of the first day we were 84-6. We realised we were in a big hole and needed something special to get out of it. I can't give enough praise to the later batsmen for their skill, concentration and determination, and our brilliant performance in the field was equally credit-worthy — we bowled with great discipline, and **Adil Rashid** was outstanding throughout.

Of the players individually, I must acknowledge **Darren Gough's** work as captain over the last two years. Darren's injuries early in the 2008 season denied him the chance to bowl himself to full fitness, but he made a significant contribution to the team's success. **Anthony McGrath** is looking forward to taking on the role for 2009 and all that goes with being captain of Yorkshire. He is steeped in Yorkshire cricket history, and will maintain our traditions. He will be ably supported by

Jacques Rudolph, who has made a great contribution, both on and off the field, so together they will make a good team.

Matthew Hoggard got better as the season went on, and he will have a big part to play as a senior professional. If **Michael Vaughan** is not selected for England, he will certainly play for us, and we look forward to his input.

Tim Bresnan was selected for the England One-Day International squad last season. He is at his best when used as a strike bowler, rather than a stock bowler, and he could bat as high as No. 6, as he is a very good all-round cricketer.

Adil Rashid continued to progress, and took 62 first-class wickets at the age of 20. At the beginning of the season, I think, he was striving too hard, putting too much pressure on himself. His five wickets at Canterbury settled him down. He is bowling his leg-spin more accurately now, and from this secure base he will be able to introduce more variety as he gains experience. He is a very talented batsman as well, as he showed at Hove. He fully deserved the reward of his 1st XI cap towards the end of the season.

I have been very pleased with **Andrew Gale**, who also was awarded his county cap last year. He batted very well at No. 5 in the Championship, and has acquired the skill and discipline to make hundreds. He has also grown into the difficult role of opening in one-day cricket.

Adam Lyth is an exciting batsman, and his next step is to convert 50s into 100s. He did really well in his first season. I was disappointed that **David Wainwright** did not have more opportunities. He had an excellent match at Hove, and maybe if we get dry weather we can play two spinners more often.

At the time of writing the position of **Rana Naved-ul-Hasan** is not certain because of his involvement with the ICL, but subject to final confirmation from the ECB it is likely that he will be available to play for us in all but *Twenty20* matches in the coming season. The Club has made a commitment to give as many opportunities as possible to players who have been developed by the Club. If they do not have the opportunity to play regularly the Club will never know who of their many talented young cricketers have the ability to make the grade. The teams who did so well at Taunton and Hove were developed predominantly through Yorkshire's own coaching system.

We have a number of promising young fast bowlers, and there should be more opportunities for them now that Darren has retired. **Ajmal Shahzad** and **Steven Patterson** have considerable first-team experience, and **Ben Sanderson**, **James Lee** and **Oliver Hannon-Dalby** will be in contention, as we need to find out about their abilities at top level.

Richard Pyrah had another good year, particularly in the one-day competitions. **Joe Sayers** had a disappointing run, but we have been working on one or two technical problems. and he scored runs in the 2nd XI and the league at the back end of the season. I am confident that he will score runs again in the 1st XI. We hope that **Chris Taylor's** hamstring problems have been sorted out, and he will be another contender.

Gerard Brophy remains our first-choice wicket-keeper. He does not make many mistakes, and scores valuable runs. **Simon Guy** has played well in the 2nd XI, and **Jonathan Bairstow** has made the step up from the Academy, so they will be keeping the pressure on Gerard to perform.

What is most encouraging is that another generation is waiting in the wings. Jonny Bairstow, **Gary Ballance** and Hannon-Dalby are all at Leeds Met University, benefiting from the link with Yorkshire CCC. Other young players like **Azeem Rafiq**, **Joe Root**, **Charlie Roebuck** and many others will be ambitious to do well.

The structure of the coaching and management team has changed for 2009. Anthony McGrath and myself will manage the 1st XI; **Kevin Sharp** with **Craig White** as captain will be the 2nd XI management team, and **Steve Oldham** and **John Blain**, who has been appointed Assistant Bowling Coach, will be responsible for the Academy. There will be flexibility to ensure that we can always respond to every coaching need. Andy Rowsell has been appointed as emerging-players coach, ensuring that each age group has its own management and coaching staff. I hope this structure will enable the Club to identify talent at an early stage, so that the standard of player entering the Academy will be as high as possible.

2009 will certainly be a challenge for us all, but it is one we are looking forward to. I hope you enjoy your cricket, and thank you for your continued support.

MARTYN MOXON
Director of
Professional Cricket

MEMBERS' LIAISON COMMITTEE
CHAIRMAN'S REPORT

The following served on the Members' Committee during the year.

Chairman:	**Mr S J Mann**
Elected Members:	**Mrs C Evers**
	Mr R A Hilliam
	Mr R Levin
	Mr S J Mann
Appointed Members:	**Mrs C Rymer**
	Mr R W Stott
	Mr I Townsend
	Mr J Virr
In Attendance:	**Mr S Regan, Chief Executive**
	Mr R Smith, Director

Committee meetings continued to be held throughout the year, and these were supplemented by discussions of an operational nature with relevant members of the Club's management.

The Committee strove throughout the year to support the management team with the experience held by the various members. While this effort was not always successful, it is pleasing to report that by the end of the year significant foundations had been created which will, hopefully, lead to a more co-operative and productive 2009.

In this report last year I referred to the need to improve the quality and frequency of communications with members. To this end we held a number of member forums in the Long Room prior to the start of play. These proved to be well received, with over 60 members attending one such event. A more extensive programme will be scheduled and published for 2009.

Many members will be aware of my firm belief that a Member' Committee needs to be seen and to be accessible to the membership at large. In 2008 this accessibility improved, and I would submit that the

Committee is now more available to members than previously, but there is still room for improvement.

The Committee were kept fully briefed on progress with the pavilion development, and are working with the Club on operational matters for when the building becomes reality.

Reports on a number of key issues directly affecting members were prepared and presented to the Club during the summer. These included matters of a communication nature such as the website and the *YCM*. Also a detailed list of recommendations on the retail experience offered by the Club was discussed with management. The response to the reports was very positive, and ongoing discussions should lead to a number of enhancements being provided for members in 2009.

There is still an all-too-frequent reference to the membership as being just "supporters". There clearly needs to be a more consistent acknowledgment that this is a members' Club, and until the membership vote otherwise it will remain so. This issue perhaps underlies the difficulties experienced by the Committee during the year. The Committee does not and has not sought decision-making authorities, but does feel that a contribution of substance can be made to the decision process.

It is pleasing to record that overall membership numbers continue to grow, although it is acknowledged that there is some artificiality in this growth due to the attraction of membership when linked to *Ashes* tickets. The challenge for all, including members, will be to hold on to these numbers, and work together to take membership back over 10,000 where, for a Club of this stature, it should be.

It is disappointing to report that Carol Rymer and John Virr decided to step down from the Committee during the year. Carol was one of the founders when she was appointed by the Board to the first Members' Committee in 2003, and her experienced and balanced contribution, together with her passionate commitment to county cricket and the membership, will be greatly missed. John spent a much shorter time on the Committee, but he was no less committed and supportive. My sincere thanks to both.

These resignations leave two vacancies for appointed members of the Committee, and steps will be taken early in 2009 to bring the representation up to strength.

As a Director of the Club Robin Smith attended meetings during the last two years. Robin is a great advocate of YCCC being a Members' Club, and his knowledge and considered views have made a substantial contribution. It is unfortunate that following a Board decision in September he will no longer be attending these meetings. On behalf of all my Committee colleagues we wish to place on record sincere appreciation for his work, advice and support.

I would also like to record my appreciation of my other Committee colleagues for their support and work throughout what was a productive and challenging year. My thanks also go to Vice-Presidents Philip Akroyd and David Drabble for their help in hosting guests from visiting counties.

STEPHEN MANN
Chairman of Yorkshire
County Cricket Club
Members' Liaison Committee

MBE for CM-J

Christopher Martin-Jenkins, one of cricket's most authoritative writers and broadcasters, was appointed MBE in the New Year's Honours List for his services to sport. "CMJ", as he is widely known, has been a familiar voice on BBC Radio's *Test Match Special* for 35 years, and from 1999 until last May he was Chief Cricket Correspondent of *The Times*. He is also a former Cricket Correspondent of the BBC and *The Daily Telegraph*, and once served as editor of *The Cricketer*.

INDEPENDENT AUDITORS' REPORT

TO THE MEMBERS OF THE YORKSHIRE COUNTY CRICKET CLUB

We have audited the financial statements of The Yorkshire County Cricket Club for the year ended 31 December 2008, which comprise the Income and Expenditure Account, the Balance Sheet, the Analysis of Net Debt and the related notes. These financial statements have been prepared under the accounting policies set out therein.

This report is made solely to the Club's members, as a body, in accordance with Section 9 of the Friendly and Industrial and Provident Societies Act 1968. Our audit work has been undertaken so that we might state to the Club's members those matters we are required to state to them in an auditor's report, and for no other purpose. To the fullest extent permitted by law, we do not accept or assume responsibility to anyone other than the Club and the Club's members, as a body, for our audit work, for this report, or for the opinions we have formed.

Respective responsibilities of directors and auditors

As described in the Statement of Directors' Responsibilities on Page 432, the Club's directors are responsible for the preparation of the Annual Report and Accounts and the financial statements in accordance with applicable law and UK Accounting Standards (UK Generally Accepted Accounting Practice).

Our responsibility is to audit the financial statements in accordance with relevant legal and regulatory requirements and International Standards on Auditing (UK and Ireland).

We report to you our opinion as to whether the financial statements give a true and fair view and are properly prepared in accordance with the Industrial and Provident Societies Act 1965 to 2002. We also report to you if, in our opinion, the Directors' Report is not consistent with the financial statements, if the Club has not kept proper accounting records, or if we have not received all the information and explanations we require for our audit.

We read the other information contained in the Annual Report and Accounts, and consider whether it is consistent with the audited financial statements. We consider the implications for our report if we become aware of any apparent mis-statements or material inconsistencies with the financial statements. Our responsibilities do not extend to any other information.

Basis of audit opinion

We conducted our audit in accordance with International Standards on Auditing (UK and Ireland) issued by the Auditing Practices Board. An audit includes examination, on a test basis, of evidence relevant to the amounts and disclosures in the financial statements. It also includes an assessment of the significant estimates and judgments made by the directors in the preparation of the financial statements, and of whether the accounting policies are appropriate to the Club's circumstances, consistently applied and adequately disclosed.

We planned and performed our audit so as to obtain all the information and explanations which we considered necessary in order to provide us with sufficient evidence to give reasonable assurance that the financial statements are free from material mis-statement, whether caused by fraud or other irregularity or error. In forming our opinion, we also evaluated the overall adequacy of the presentation of information in the financial statements.

Opinion

In our opinion the financial statements:

- give a true and fair view, in accordance with UK Generally Accepted Accounting Practice, of the state of affairs of the Club's affairs as at 31 December 2008 and of its profit for the year then ended; and
- have been properly prepared in accordance with the Industrial and Provident Societies Acts 1965 to 2002.

KPMG LLP   FEBRUARY 6, 2009
Chartered Accountants
Registered Auditor
Leeds

CORPORATE GOVERNANCE

The Board is accountable to the Club's members for good corporate governance, and this statement describes how the principles of governance are applied.

THE BOARD

The Board is responsible for approving Club policy and strategy. It meets every other month, or more frequently if business needs require, and has a schedule of matters specifically reserved to it for decision, including all significant commercial issues and all capital expenditure.

Management supply the Board with appropriate and timely information, and the Board Members are free to seek any further information they consider necessary.

NOMINATIONS COMMITTEE

The Nominations Committee is formally constituted with written terms of reference which are defined in the Club Rules and reviewed regularly. It consists of the President, Secretary and two other Board members.

RELATIONS WITH MEMBERS

The Club encourages effective communication with its members, and a specific Committee, as defined in the Club Rules, is appointed for that purpose.

INTERNAL CONTROL

The Board acknowledges its responsibility to maintain a sound system of internal control relating to operational, financial and compliance controls and risk management, to safeguard the members' interests and the Club's assets, and will regularly review its effectiveness. Such a system, however, is designed to manage and meet the Club's particular needs and mitigate the risks to which it is exposed, rather than eliminate the risk of failure to achieve business objectives, and can provide only reasonable and not absolute assurance against material mis-statement or loss.

The Club considers its key components to provide effective internal control and improve business efficiency are:

- Regular meetings with senior management to review and assess progress made against objectives and deal with any problems which arise from such reviews.
- A financial reporting system of annual budgets, periodic forecasts and detailed monthly reporting which includes cash-flow forecasts. Budgets and forecasts are reviewed and approved by the Board.
- A defined management and organisation structure with defined responsibilities and appropriate authorisation limits and short lines of communication to the Chief Executive.

ACCOUNTABILITY AND AUDIT

The Board's responsibilities

The following statement, which should be read in conjunction with the Report of the Independent Auditors, is made with a view to distinguishing for members the respective responsibilities of the Board and of the auditors in relation to the accounts:

"The Board is required by UK law to prepare accounts which give a true and fair view of the state of affairs of the Club at the end of the financial year, and of the surplus or deficiency of the Club for the financial year then ended.

"The Board is also responsible for maintaining adequate accounting records, and for taking reasonable steps to safeguard the assets of the Club and detect irregularities and fraud.

"The Board confirms that in preparing the Club's accounts appropriate policies have been consistently applied, and applicable accounting standards complied with. Further, in all material respects the accounts are supported by prudent judgements and estimates made by reference to information available at the time of their preparation."

All Board members bring independent judgment to bear on their deliberations concerning strategy and performance. The Board is satisfied that it has had access to sufficient information to enable it to make proper decisions in a timely manner, and the Chairman has ensured that Board Members were kept properly briefed.

INCOME AND EXPENDITURE ACCOUNT
for the year ended 31st December, 2008

	Note	2008 £	2007 £
Income			
Subscriptions		607,509	582,456
Ground admissions and match guarantees		307,710	394,480
England and Wales Cricket Board		1,813,591	1,707,270
International matches		1,176,208	1,125,380
Commercial income		1,967,001	1,781,550
Other income		88,528	118,710
		5,960,547	5,709,846
Cricket expenses			
Staff remuneration and employment expenses		1,778,654	1,689,948
Match expenses		402,776	367,904
Development expenses		188,533	147,944
Other cricket expenses		341,686	286,297
Grants received		(169,686)	(190,561)
		2,541,963	2,301,532
Adminstration expenses			
Staff remuneration and employment expenses		379,917	389,604
Printing, postage and advertising		56,865	44,057
Audit fee		20,000	17,500
Other administration expenses		79,035	89,653
		535,817	540,814
Marketing expenses			
Staff remuneration and employment expenses		330,117	228,934
Ticket office expenses		87,404	107,931
Sponsorship expenses		121,839	107,709
Printing, postage and promotional expenses		131,022	177,443
Other marketing expenses		53,326	64,994
		723,708	687,011
Ground expenses			
Staff remuneration and employment expenses		238,669	227,608
Maintenance and utility expenses		318,236	267,869
Lease rentals		928	0
Depreciation		691,082	689,694
Release of capital grants		(156,228)	(156,228)
		1,092,687	1,028,943
Loan interest and similar amounts payable			
Loan interest		376,283	386,104
Bank interest		289,778	384,808
Bank facility fees		25,000	12,000
Lease and finance interest		7,952	2,627
		699,013	785,539
Surplus for the year before taxation		367,359	366,007
Taxation	4	(15,944)	(29,910)
Surplus for the year after taxation	12	£351,415	£336,097

There were no other gains and losses in the current or preceding year other than those stated above. The accompanying notes form an integral part of these accounts.

BALANCE SHEET

as at 31st December, 2008

	Note	2008 £	2008 £	2007 £	2007 £
Assets employed:					
Fixed assets	5		22,093,642		21,210,090
Current assets:					
Stocks		80,000		41,780	
Debtors	6	475,608		248,738	
Cash at bank and in hand		111,895		4,589	
		667,503		295,107	
Creditors: amounts falling due within one year	7	(4,995,467)		(3,909,418)	
Net current liabilities			(4,327,964)		(3,614,311)
Total assets less current liabilities			**£17,765,678**		**£17,595,779**
Funded by:					
Creditors: amounts falling due after more than one year	8		13,450,953		13,492,281
Deferred income — capital grants	9		4,758,854		4,915,082
Provisions for liabilities	10		45,854		29,910
			18,255,661		18,437,273
Capital and Reserves					
Called up share capital	11		374		379
Capital redemption reserve	12		446		345
Income and expenditure account	12		(490,803)		(842,218)
			(489,983)		(841,494)
			£17,765,678		**£17,595,779**

These accounts were approved by the Board on 31st January 2009.

S M REGAN, Chief Executive

C J GRAVES, Chairman

The accompanying notes form an integral part of these accounts.

434

CASH FLOW STATEMENT

for the year ended 31st December, 2008

	Note	2008 £	2007 £
Cash inflow from operating activities	13	1,550,827	1,752,578
Returns on investments and servicing of finance	14	(699,013)	(785,105)
Capital expenditure and financial investment	14	(1,574,634)	(78,433)
Cash inflow before financing		(722,820)	889,040
Financing	14	967,995	269,063
Increase in cash in the period		**£245,175**	**£1,158,103**

	2008 £	2007 £
Reconciliation of net cash flow to movement in net debt		
Increase in cash in period	245,175	1,158,103
Pride Appeal Loan	—	(1,005,000)
HSBC Loan Repayment	456,000	368,000
Leeds City Council Loan Repayment	456,000	368,000
Other loans - ECB	(1,880,000)	—
	£(722,825)	**£889,103**

ANALYSIS OF NET DEBT

	At 1 Jan 2008 £	Cash flow 2008 £	Other changes 2008 £	At 31 Dec 2008 £
Cash at bank and in hand	4,589	107,306	—	111,895
Overdraft - current	(137,869)	137,869	—	—
	(133,280)	245,175	—	111,895
Debt due within one year:				
- HSBC Bank plc loan	(456,000)	456,000	(433,000)	(433,000)
- Leeds City Council loan	(456,000)	456,000	(433,000)	(433,000)
- Other loans ECB	—	(1,050,000)	—	(1,050,000)
Debt due after one year:				
- HSBC Bank plc loan	(4,581,264)	—	433,000	(4,148,264)
- Leeds City Council loan	(7,899,000)	—	433,000	(7,466,000)
- Pride Appeal loan	(1,005,000)	—	—	(1,005,000)
- Other loans ECB	—	(830,000)	—	(830,000)
	(14,397,264)	(968,000)	—	(15,365,264)
Total	**£(14,530,544)**	**£(722,825)**	**£ —**	**£ (15,253,369)**

NOTES TO THE ACCOUNTS

for the year ended 31st December, 2008

1. Accounting policies

The accounts have been prepared in accordance with applicable accounting standards and under the historical cost convention. The principal accounting policies of the Club have remained unchanged from the previous year.

(a) Income

All income is accounted for on an accruals basis, except for donations which are accounted for in the year of receipt.

(b) Fixed assets and depreciation

All expenditure in connection with the development of Headingley Carnegie Cricket Ground and the related facilities has been capitalised. Finance costs relating to and incurred during the period of construction were also capitalised. Depreciation is only charged once a discrete phase of the development is completed.

Depreciation is calculated to write down the cost of fixed assets by equal annual instalments over their expected useful lives.

The periods generally applicable are:

Headingley Carnegie Cricket Ground and Cricket Centre	— buildings	50 years
	— fixtures	4 years
	— plant and equipment	Between 4 and 10 years
Office equipment	— telephone system	4 years
	— computer equipment	2 years

Freehold land is not depreciated.

All other expenditure on repairs to Headingley Carnegie Cricket Ground and other grounds is written off as and when incurred.

(c) Stocks

Stocks are stated at the lower of cost and net realisable value.

(d) Grants

Capital grants relating to the development of Headingley Carnegie Cricket Ground and Cricket Centre are included in the Balance Sheet as deferred income, and are released to the Income and Expenditure account by equal instalments over the expected useful lives of the relevant assets in accordance with accounting policy (b) Fixed assets and depreciation, as set out above.

Grants of a revenue nature are credited to the Income and Expenditure account in the same period as their related expenditure.

(e) Cricket Centre

The Cricket Centre is operated by the Club as a joint venture with Leeds City Council. The Club has a 60 per cent interest in the profits earned by the Centre. Profit is recognised when received by the Club. Full provision is made for any anticipated losses. Losses attributable to Leeds City Council are deducted from the related revenue grant. The assets of the Cricket Centre are all owned and controlled by the Club.

The Cricket Centre bar operation does not form part of the joint venture, and all income and expenditure relating to the bar is solely attributable to the Club.

436

(f) Contribution to pension funds

The pension costs charged in the Income and Expenditure account represent the amount of contributions payable in respect of the accounting period.

(g) Leased assets

Rentals paid under operating leases are charged to the Income and Expenditure account on a straight-line basis over the lease term.

(h) Deferred taxation

Deferred tax is recognised on all timing differences where the transactions or the events that give the Club an obligation to pay more tax in the future, or a right to pay less tax in the future, have occurred by the balance-sheet date. Deferred tax assets are recognised when it is more likely than not that they will be recovered. Deferred tax is measured using rates of tax that have been enacted or substantively enacted by the balance-sheet date.

2. Basis of preparation of the financial statements

Ground Purchase

The Club has an option to make a £3m additional payment to LCF&A within the next 12 years in order to retain the ground. This optional payment escalates during the period until the option is exercised. Should Yorkshire County Cricket Club not make this further payment, then LCF&A hold an option to buy back the land and related assets for £7m at the end of this 12-year period.

Financial Position

The Club is in a net current liability position of £4.2m (2007: £3.6m). This includes deferred income of £2.1m (2007: £1.8m).

Details of the loan and overdraft maturity analysis which impact upon the financial position can be found in Note 8.

Based on approved cash-flow projections, the Club is able to meet the required loan repayments and the related interest amounts as they fall due, as well as having sufficient funds to meet all other liabilities, while remaining within the terms of the current banking facilities.

The Board therefore considers it appropriate to prepare the financial statements on a going-concern basis.

3. Directors' remuneration

	2008	2007
	£	£
Wages and salaries	137,000	164,000
Social security costs	16,847	20,329
Pension costs	19,200	18,562
	£173,047	£202,891

These amounts are included in the Income and Expenditure Account under *Administration Expenses — Staff Remuneration and Employment Expenses*.

4. Taxation

	2008	2007
UK corporation tax		
Current tax on income for the period	—	—
Adjustments in respect of prior periods	—	—
Total current tax	—	—
Income tax	—	—
Deferred tax (See Note 10)	15,944	29,910
Tax on surplus on ordinary activities	£15,944	£29,910

The current tax charge for the period is lower (2007:lower) than the standard rate of corporation tax in the UK of 28.5% (2007:30%). The differences are explained below:

	2008 £	2007 £
Surplus on ordinary activities before taxation	**367,360**	366,006
Current tax at 28.5% (2007:30%)	**104,698**	109,802
Effects of:		
Expenses not deductible for tax purposes	—	2,414
Non taxable income	**(141,661)**	(88,653)
Depreciation for the period in excess of capital allowances	**116,468**	53,371
Losses (utilised) / not utilised	**(79,505)**	(76,934)
Total current tax charge (see above)	**£ —**	**£ —**

The Club has a recognised gross tax liability of £2.1 million (2007: £2.3m) in respect of capital allowances claimed in excess of depreciation, which is partially offset by recognised gross tax trading losses of £1.9 million (2007: £2.2m) to carry forward to future periods.

5. Fixed assets (See opposite page)

	2008 £	2007 £
6. Debtors		
Trade debtors	**324,918**	81,586
Other debtors	**150,690**	167,152
	£475,608	£248,738

7. Creditors: amounts falling due within one year

Leeds City Council loan	**433,000**	456,000
Bank loan	**433,000**	456,000
Bank overdraft (secured)	**—**	137,869
ECB loans	**1,050,000**	—
Trade creditors	**480,690**	431,105
Finance leases	**5,261**	5,260
Social security and other taxes	**200,303**	164,489
Other creditors	**193,411**	256,251
Accruals	**97,394**	161,466
Deferred income	**2,102,408**	1,840,978
	£4,995,467	£3,909,418

8. Creditors: amounts falling due after more than one year

Leeds City Council loan	**7,466,000**	7,899,000
Bank loan	**4,148,264**	4,581,264
ECB loan	**830,000**	—
Pride Appeal loans	**1,005,000**	1,005,000
Finance leases	**1,689**	7,017
	£13,450,953	£13,492,281

| | Cricket Centre | | Headingley Carnegie Cricket Ground | | | | |
	Freehold land and buildings £	Plant & equipment £	Freehold land and buildings £	Plant and equipment £	Assets in the course of construction £	Office equipment £	Total £
Cost							
January 1, 2008	535,837	758,603	19,766,989	3,899,738	—	295,918	25,257,085
Additions	—	—	1,128,099	—	420,203	26,332	1,574,634
December 31, 2008	535,837	758,603	20,895,088	3,899,738	420,203	322,250	26,831,719
Depreciation							
January 1, 2008	52,500	453,248	1,065,272	2,267,027	—	208,948	4,046,995
Provided in the year	9,888	70,308	195,816	367,812	—	47,258	691,082
December 31, 2008	62,388	523,556	1,261,088	2,634,839	—	256,206	4,738,077
Net book amount December 31, 2008	£473,449	£235,047	£19,634,000	£1,264,899	£420,203	£66,044	£22,093,642
Net book amount December 31, 2007	£483,337	£305,355	£18,701,717	£1,632,711	£ —	£86,970	£21,210,090

Included in the above amount are assets with a net book value of £9,750 purchased under finance leases (2007: £14,250).

	2008	2007
	£	£
Loan and overdraft maturity anlysis		
In one year or less or on demand	**1,916,000**	1,049,869
In more than one year but not more than two years	**2,085,000**	1,871,000
In more than two years but not more than five years	**3,544,000**	3,108,000
In more than five years	**7,820,264**	8,506,264
	£15,365,264	£14,535,133

The Leeds City Council loan is repayable by 30 April 2020 at an interest rate of 4.5% per annum. The Club has given a First Legal Charge over the freehold property known as Headingley Carnegie Cricket Ground, St Michael's Lane, Leeds, to Leeds City Council in respect of this loan. Mr C J Graves has provided a shortfall guarantee in respect of this loan.

The Club has also given a First Legal charge to HSBC Bank plc over the Cricket Centre known as 41/43 St Michael's Lane, Headingley, Leeds, and a Second Legal Charge over the freehold property known as Headingley Carnegie Cricket Ground, St Michael's Lane, Leeds, in respect of the bank loan and overdrafts. HSBC Bank plc also has a fixed and floating charge over all the assets of the Club, subject to the Legal Charges referred to above. This loan is repayable by 30 April 2017 at an interest rate of 1.5% over the Bank's base rate. Mr C J Graves has also provided a £6.3m guarantee in respect of the indebtedness to HSBC Bank plc.

The Pride Appeal has received an interest free loan from Mr C J Graves of £1,000,000 which is repayable on demand with 12 months notice. The Pride Appeal has also received a further loan of £5,000 on similar terms.

9. Deferred income - capital grants

	2008	2007
At 1st January 2008	**4,915,082**	5,071,310
Released to Income and Expenditure Account	**(156,228)**	(156,228)
At 31st December 2008	**£4,758,854**	£4,915,082

10. Provisions for liabilities
Deferred taxation

	2008	2007
At 1st January 2008	**29,910**	—
Charge to Income and Expenditure Account for the year	**15,944**	29,910
At 31st December 2008	**£45,854**	£29,910

The elements of deferred taxation are as follows :

	2008	2007
Difference between accumulated depreciation and capital allowances	**590,186**	639,649
Tax losses	**(544,332)**	(609,739)
Deferred tax liability	**£45,854**	£29,910

11. Share capital

	2008	2007
Allotted, called up and fully paid Ordinary shares of 5p each	**£374**	£379

During the year the Club allotted one Ordinary share to each of 1,934 new qualifying members and redeemed 2,027 Ordinary shares in respect of retiring members.
Each member of the Club owns one Ordinary share, and the rights attached thereto are contained within the Club's rules.

	2008 **£**	2007 £

12. Reserves.

	Income and Expenditure Account	Capital Redemption Reserve
At 1st January 2008	**(842,218)**	345
Surplus for the year	**351,415**	—
Shares in respect of retiring members	—	101
At 31st December 2008	**£(490,803)**	£446

13. Reconciliation of operating surplus to operating cash flow

	2008	2007
Operating surplus	**1,066,372**	1,151,111
Depreciation of tangible assets	**691,082**	689,694
Release of capital grants	**(156,228)**	(156,228)
(Increase) in stock	**(38,220)**	(14,680)
(Increase) in debtors	**(226,870)**	(48,854)
Increase in creditors	**214,691**	131,535
Cash inflow from operating activities	**£1,550,827**	£1,752,578

14. Analysis of cash flows

Returns on investment and servicing of finance

	2008	2007
Interest received	—	434
Loan interest and facility fees	**(699,013)**	(785,539)
	£(699,013)	£(785,105)

Capital expenditure and financial investment

	2008	2007
Purchase of tangible fixed assets	**£(1,574,634)**	£(78,433)

Financing

	2008	2007
Other loans received in year	**1,954,000**	—
ECB loan repayment	**(74,000)**	—
Pride Appeal loan	—	1,005,000
HSBC loan repayment	**(456,000)**	(368,000)
Leeds City Council loan repayment	**(456,000)**	(368,000)
Issue of ordinary share capital	**96**	97
Repurchase of ordinary share capital	**(101)**	(34)
	£967,995	£269,063

15. Leasing commitments

Operating lease payments amounting to £26,795 (2007: £26,795) are due within one year. The leases to which these amounts relate expire as follows:

	2008 **Land and** **buildings** **£**	**2008** **Other** **£**	2007 Land and buildings £	2007 Other £
In one year or less	—	—	—	—
Between two and five years	—	**26,795**	—	26,795
In five years or more	—	—	—	—
	£ —	**£26,795**	£ —	£26,795

16. Related party transactions

Mr C J Graves is the Chairman of Costcutter Supermarkets Group.
The Club has purchased printing and software maintenance from Costcutter Supermarkets
Group Limited. The turnover for the year is £6,111 (2007: £4,465) of which £nil remains outstanding at 31 December 2008. Costcutter are also sponsors of the Club and boxholders at
Headingley Carnegie Cricket Ground under the Club's normal commercial terms.
Mr R A Smith is a part-time consultant to DLA Piper Rudnick Gray Cary, who are the Club's
solicitors. The turnover with DLA Piper Rudnick Gray Cary in 2008 amounted to £55,096
(2007: £18,820) of which £nil remained outstanding at 31 December 2008. Mr Smith is also
a non-executive Director of Bartlett Group (Holdings), of which the Club's former insurance
brokers, Bartletts, and current pension advisors, Bartlett Life & Pensions, are subsidiary
companies. The turnover with Bartletts for the year amounted to £1,222 (2007: £137,278) of
which £131 was outstanding at 31 December 2008.
Mr B Bouttell is a Board member of the Leeds Metropolitan University, who are sponsors
of the Club under the Club's normal commercial terms.

17. Pensions

The Club operates defined contribution pension schemes for the benefit of certain employees.
The amounts paid during the year were £157,662 (2007: £147,338). The assets of these
schemes are administered in funds independent from those of the Club.

Adil eclipses Yorkshire's old boys...

Left-arm fast bowler David Lucas, who had a low-key season
with Yorkshire in 2005 after being signed from
Nottinghamshire, came good last summer in his second year on
Northamptonshire's books. He claimed 36 first-class wickets at
42.58 runs apiece. The Yorkshire-born pair of Gary Keedy
(Lancashire) and James Middlebrook (Essex) claimed 28 and 31
first-class wickets respectively, while another former Yorkshire
bowler, Aussie Jason Gillespie, took 24 for Glamorgan. None of
them, however, could get close to Yorkshire's young leg-spin
prodigy, Adil Rashid, who bagged a total of 65 wickets in all
first class cricket.

Notes

Notes

Notes

Notes